"On the broad shoulders of William Perkins, epoch-making pioneer, stood the entire school of seventeenth-century Puritan pastors and divines, yet the Puritan reprint industry has steadily bypassed him. Now, however, he begins to reappear, admirably edited, and at last this yawning gap is being filled. Profound thanks to the publisher and heartfelt praise to God have become due."

—J. I. Packer, Board of Governors' Professor of Theology,
Regent College, Vancouver, British Columbia

"Without a doubt, the Puritans were theological titans. The Puritan theological tradition did not emerge out of a vacuum. It was shaped by leaders and theologians who set the trajectory of the movement and shaped its commitments. William Perkins was one of those men. Perkins's contribution to Puritan theology is inestimable, and this new reprint of his collected works is a much-awaited addition to all who are still shaped and influenced by the Puritans and their commitment to the centrality of the grace of God found only in Jesus Christ. Even now, every true gospel minister stands in debt to Perkins, and in his shadow."

—R. Albert Mohler Jr., president, The Southern
Baptist Theological Seminary

"The list of those influenced by the ministry of William Perkins reads like a veritable Who's Who of the Puritan Brotherhood and far beyond. This reprinting of his works, so long unobtainable except by a few, is therefore a publishing event of the first magnitude."

—Sinclair B. Ferguson, professor of systematic theology,
Redeemer Theological Seminary, Dallas

"The father of Elizabethan Puritanism, Perkins presided over a dynasty of faith. The scope of his work is wide, yet on every topic he treats one discovers erudition and deep reflection. He was the first in an amazing line of ministers at Cambridge University's main church. A pastor to pastors, he wrote a bestseller on counseling, was a formative figure in the development of Reformed orthodoxy, and a judicious reformer within the Church of England. I am delighted to see Perkins's works made available again for a wide audience."

—Michael Horton, J. Gresham Machen Professor of Theology
and Apologetics, Westminster Seminary California

"William Perkins was a most remarkable Christian. In his relatively short life he was a great preacher, pastor, and theologian. His prolific writings were foundational to the whole English Puritan enterprise and a profound influence beyond his own time and borders. His works have become rare, and their republication must be a source of real joy and blessing to all serious Christians. Perkins is the first Puritan we should read."

—W. Robert Godfrey, president, Westminster Seminary California

"This is a welcome collection of the gospel-saturated writings of William Perkins. A faithful pastor, Puritan leader, prolific author, and lecturer, Perkins defended the doctrines of the Protestant Reformation throughout his life. Giving particular emphasis to *solus Christus* and *sola Scriptura*, these Reformed doctrines drove him as a pastor to preach the unsearchable riches of God's truth with confidence and assurance. Sadly, Perkins is unknown to the modern Christian. However, throughout the centuries, the writings, meditations, and treatises of this Puritan luminary have influenced Christians around the world. It is my hope that many will be introduced and reintroduced to the writings of this Reformed stalwart. May his zeal for gospel advance awaken a new generation of biblical preachers and teachers to herald the glory of our sovereign God in this present day."

—Steven J. Lawson, president, OnePassion Ministries, and professor of preaching at The Master's Seminary

"Relatively few in the church's history have left a written legacy of enduring value beyond their own time. Perkins is surely among that select group. Reformation Heritage Books is to be commended for its commitment to making his *Works* available in this projected series, beginning with this volume."

—Richard B. Gaffin Jr., professor of biblical and systematic theology emeritus, Westminster Theological Seminary

"Christians have heard about William Perkins, especially that he was an extraordinary preacher whose sermons made a deep impression on Cambridge and that they were still impacting the town in the decades that followed Perkins's death at a mere forty-four years of age in 1602. He was at the heart of the revival of truth and holy living that made the Reformation a glorious work of God. He was the outstanding Puritan theologian of his time, but most of us have not had the opportunity to study his works because of their rarity. After more than three hundred years, this ignorance is going to be ended with the remarkable appearance during the next decade of the complete works of this man of God. We are looking forward to their appearance very much. There will be sufficient gaps between their publication to ensure a sincere attempt at imbibing the truths of each volume, and then we face the challenge of translating Perkins's teaching into flesh-and-blood living."

—Geoff Thomas, pastor, Alfred Place Baptist Church, Aberystwyth, Wales

The Works of
WILLIAM PERKINS

The Works of
WILLIAM PERKINS

VOLUME 6

A Golden Chain

*A Christian and Plain Treatise of the Manner and
Order of Predestination*

A Treatise on God's Free Grace and Man's Free Will

A Fruitful Dialogue Concerning the End of the World

*The Antidicson of a Certain Man of Cambridge, Along With a Short
Treatise that Fully Explains Dickson's Wicked System of Artificial Memory*

*A Handbook on Memory and the Most Reliable Method
of Accurate Recall*

EDITED BY JOEL R. BEEKE AND GREG A. SALAZAR

General editors:
Joel R. Beeke and Derek W. H. Thomas

REFORMATION HERITAGE BOOKS
Grand Rapids, Michigan

The Works of William Perkins, Volume 6
© 2018 by Reformation Heritage Books

Reformation Heritage Books
2965 Leonard St. NE
Grand Rapids, MI 49525
616-977-0889 / Fax 616-285-3246
orders@heritagebooks.org
www.heritagebooks.org

Printed in the United States of America
18 19 20 21 22 23/10 9 8 7 6 5 4 3 2 1

ISBN 978-1-60178-612-8 (vol. 6)
ISBN 978-1-60178-613-5 (vol. 6) epub

Library of Congress Cataloging-in-Publication Data

Perkins, William, 1558-1602.
  [Works]
  The works of William Perkins / edited by J. Stephen Yuille ; general editors: Joel R. Beeke and Derek W. H. Thomas.
     pages cm
  Includes bibliographical references and index.
  ISBN 978-1-60178-360-8 (v. 1 : alk. paper) 1. Puritans. 2. Theology—Early works to 1800. I. Yuille, J. Stephen, 1968- editor. II. Beeke, Joel R., 1952- editor. III. Thomas, Derek, 1953- editor. IV. Title.
  BX9315.P47 2014
  230—dc23
                                        2014037122

For additional Reformed literature, request a free book list from Reformation Heritage Books at the above regular or e-mail address.

Contents

Table of Contents for Figures and Charts

*Thanks to Rod MacQuarrie who has carefully reworked the charts in this volume to give them a sharper look; Perkins's original punctuation and capitalization have been retained in the charts for historical purposes.

General Preface

William Perkins (1558–1602), often called "the father of Puritanism," was a master preacher and teacher of Reformed, experiential theology. He left an indelible mark upon the English Puritan movement, and his writings were translated into Dutch, German, French, Hungarian, and other European languages. Today he is best known for his writings on predestination, but he also wrote prolifically on many doctrinal and practical subjects, including extended expositions of Scripture. The 1631 edition of his English *Works* filled over two thousand large pages of small print in three folio volumes.

It is puzzling why his full *Works* have not been in print since the early seventeenth century, especially given the flood of Puritan works reprinted in the mid-nineteenth and late twentieth centuries. Ian Breward did much to promote the study of Perkins, but Breward's now rare, single-volume compilation of the *Work of William Perkins* (1970) could only present samplings of Perkins's writings. We are extremely pleased that this lacuna is being filled, as it has been a dream of many years to see the writings of this Reformed theologian made accessible again to the public, including laymen, pastors, and scholars.

Reformation Heritage Books is publishing Perkins's *Works* in a newly typeset format with spelling and capitalization conformed to modern American standards. The old forms ("thou dost") are changed to the modern equivalent ("you do"), except in Scripture quotations and references to deity. Punctuation has also been modernized. However, the original words are left intact, not changed into modern synonyms, and the original word order retained even when it differs from modern syntax. Pronouns are capitalized when referring to God. Some archaic terms and obscure references are explained in the editor's footnotes.

As was common in his day, Perkins did not use quotation marks to distinguish a direct quotation from an indirect quotation, summary, or paraphrase, but simply put all citations in italics (as he also did with proper names). We have removed such italics and followed the general principle of placing citations in quotation marks even if they may not be direct and exact quotations. Perkins generally quoted the Geneva Bible, but rather than conforming his quotations to any particular translation of Scripture, we have left them in his words. Scripture references in the margins are brought into the text and enclosed in square brackets. Parenthetical Scripture references in general are abbreviated and punctuated according to the modern custom (as in Rom. 8:1), sometimes corrected, and sometimes moved to the end of the clause instead of its beginning. Other notes from the margins are placed in footnotes and labeled, "In the margin." Where multiple sets of parentheses were nested within each other, the inward parentheses have been changed to square brackets. Otherwise, square brackets indicate words added by the editor. An introduction to each volume by its editor orients the reader to its contents.

The projected *Works of William Perkins* will include ten volumes, including four volumes of biblical exposition, three volumes of doctrinal and polemical treatises, and three volumes of ethical and practical writings. A breakdown of each volume's contents may be found inside the cover of this book.

If it be asked what the center of Perkins's theology was, then we hesitate to answer, for students of historical theology know that this is a perilous question to ask regarding any person. However, we may do well to end this preface by repeating what Perkins said at the conclusion of his influential manual on preaching, "The sum of the sum: preach one Christ by Christ to the praise of Christ."

—Joel R. Beeke and Derek W. H. Thomas

Preface to Volume 6 of
William Perkins's *Works*

—•••—

William Perkins (1558–1602), often called the "father of Puritanism," laid the foundations of Puritan piety by digging deep into the biblical doctrine of divine predestination. What many have dismissed as an irrelevant or even irreverent doctrine was for him and generations of Puritans after him the bedrock on which they built their faith. This solid foundation was, in Perkins's opinion, none other than Christ Himself.

In this doctrine we draw near to the heart of the Puritan conception of the gospel. Iain Murray says, "The doctrine of election was vital to the Puritans; they believed with Zanchius that it 'is the golden thread that runs through the whole Christian system,' and they asserted that a departure from this truth would bring the visible church under God's judgment and indignation."[1] Predestination was not mere orthodox theology for the Puritans, but was essential to the gospel and to godliness.[2]

Perkins has been evaluated by many scholars.[3] They have offered positive as well as negative commentary about his political, ethical, revivalistic, and

---

1. Iain Murray, "The Puritans and the Doctrine of Election," in *Puritan Papers, Volume One, 1956–1959*, ed. D. Martyn Lloyd-Jones (Phillipsburg, N.J.: P&R, 2000), 5. See Girolamo Zanchi, *The Doctrine of Absolute Predestination* (Conway, Ark.: Free Grace Press, 2012), ch. 5. Parts of this preface have been adapted with permission from Joel R. Beeke, "William Perkins on Predestination, Preaching, and Converion." In *The Practical Calvinist: An Introduction to the Presbyterian and Reformed Heritage, in Honor of D. Clair Davis*, 183–213. Edited by Peter A. Lillback (Fearn, Scotland: Christian Focus, 2002); and Joel R. Beeke, "William Perkins on Predestination," in *A Puritan Theology* by Joel R. Beeke and Mark Jones (Grand Rapids: Reformation Heritage Books, 2014), 117–31.

2. Dewey D. Wallace, Jr., *Puritans and Predestination: Grace in English Protestant Theology, 1525–1695* (Chapel Hill: University of North Carolina Press, 1982), 43–44.

3. Dissertations and theses that contribute to an understanding of Perkins's theology include Ian Breward, "The Life and Theology of William Perkins" (PhD diss., University of Manchester, 1963); William H. Chalker, "Calvin and Some Seventeenth Century English Calvinists" (PhD diss., Duke University, 1961); Lionel Greve, "Freedom and Discipline in the Theology of John Calvin, William Perkins, and John Wesley: An Examination of the Origin and Nature of Pietism" (PhD diss., Hartford Seminary Foundation, 1976); Robert W. A. Letham, "Saving Faith and Assurance in Reformed Theology: Zwingli to the Synod of Dort," 2 vols. (PhD diss., University

ecclesiastical interests. Some have offered contradictory assertions about his theological stand, particularly in the area of predestination.[4] For example,

---

of Aberdeen, 1979); R. David Lightfoot, "William Perkins' View of Sanctification" (ThM thesis, Dallas Theological Seminary, 1984); Donald Keith McKim, *Ramism in William Perkins's Theology* (New York: Peter Lang, 1987); C. C. Markham, "William Perkins' Understanding of the Function of Conscience" (PhD diss., Vanderbilt University, 1967); Richard Alfred Muller, "Predestination and Christology in Sixteenth-Century Reformed Theology" (PhD diss., Duke University, 1976); Charles Robert Munson, "William Perkins: Theologian of Transition" (PhD diss., Case Western Reserve, 1971); Willem Jan op 't Hof, *Engelse piëtistische geschriften in het Nederlands, 1598–1622* (Rotterdam: Lindenberg, 1987); Joseph A. Pipa, Jr., "William Perkins and the Development of Puritan Preaching" (PhD diss., Westminster Theological Seminary, 1985); Victor L. Priebe, "The Covenant Theology of William Perkins" (PhD diss., Drew University, 1967); Paul R. Schaefer, Jr., "The Spiritual Brotherhood on the Habits of the Heart: Cambridge Protestants and the Doctrine of Sanctification from William Perkins to Thomas Shepard" (PhD diss., Keble College, Oxford University, 1994); Mark R. Shaw, "The Marrow of Practical Divinity: A Study in the Theology of William Perkins" (PhD diss., Westminster Theological Seminary, 1981); Rosemary Sisson, "William Perkins" (MA thesis, University of Cambridge, 1952); C. J. Sommerville, "Conversion, Sacrament and Assurance in the Puritan Covenant of Grace to 1650" (MA thesis, University of Kansas, 1963); Young Jae Timothy Song, *Theology and Piety in the Reformed Federal Thought of William Perkins and John Preston* (Lewiston, New York: Edwin Mellin, 1998); Lynn Baird Tipson, Jr., "The Development of a Puritan Understanding of Conversion" (PhD diss., Yale University, 1972); J. R. Tufft, "William Perkins, 1558–1602" (PhD diss., Edinburgh, 1952); Jan Jacobus van Baarsel, *William Perkins: eene bijdrage tot de Kennis der religieuse ontwikkeling in Engeland ten tijde van Koningin Elisabeth* ('s-Gravenhage: H. P. De Swart & Zoon, 1912); William G. Wilcox, "New England Covenant Theology: Its Precursors and Early American Exponents" (PhD diss., Duke University, 1959); James Eugene Williams, Jr., "An Evaluation of William Perkins' Doctrine of Predestination in the Light of John Calvin's Writings" (ThM thesis, Dallas Theological Seminary, 1986); Andrew Alexander Woolsey, "Unity and Continuity in Covenantal Thought: A Study in the Reformed Tradition to the Westminster Assembly" (PhD diss., University of Glasgow, 1988).

4. Perkins's critics—both positive and negative—agree that he provided a major link in Reformed thought between Beza and the Westminster Confession. Those who view that linkage as largely negative include Perry Miller (*Errand into the Wilderness* [Cambridge: Belknap Press, 1956]); Karl Barth (*Church Dogmatics,* III/4 [Edinburgh: T. & T. Clark, 1961], 8); Basil Hall ("Calvin Against the Calvinists," in *John Calvin,* ed. G. E. Duffield [Appleford, England: Sutton Courtney Press, 1966], 19–37); Robert T. Kendall, *Calvin and English Calvinism to 1649* (Oxford: Oxford University Press); "Living the Christian Life in the Teaching of William Perkins and His Followers," in *Living the Christian Life* [London: Westminster Conference, 1974]; "John Cotton—First English Calvinist?," *The Puritan Experiment in the New World* [London: Westminster Conference, 1976]; "The Puritan Modification of Calvin's Theology," in *John Calvin: His Influence in the Western World,* ed. W. Stanford Reid [Grand Rapids: Zondervan, 1982], 199–214); Chalker and Knappen as noted above. Scholars who have reacted positively to Perkins include F. Ernest Stoeffler (*The Rise of Evangelical Pietism* [Leiden: Brill, 1965]); Ian Breward ("William Perkins and the Origins of Puritan Casuistry," *Faith and a Good Conscience* [London: Puritan and Reformed Studies Conference, 1962]; "The Significance of William Perkins," *Journal of Religious History* 4 [1966]: 113–28; "William Perkins and the Origins of Puritan Casuistry," *The Evangelist Quarterly* 40 [1968]: 16–22); Richard Muller ("Perkins' *A Golden Chaine*: Predestinarian System or Schematized *Ordo Salutis?*," *Sixteenth Century Journal* 9, no. 1 [1978]: 69–81; "Covenant and Conscience in English Reformed Theology," *Westminster Theological Journal* 42 [1980]: 308–34; *Christ and the Decree:*

confusion exists on Perkins's Christological emphasis in predestination. Marshall M. Knappen faults Perkins for following Calvin too closely in Christological predestination, while Ian Breward believes Perkins strayed from Calvin at this point. Breward says that the "work of Christ was discussed within the context of predestination rather than providing the key to the decrees of God."[5]

In a recent seminal study on Perkins, W. B. Patterson builds on the work of R. T. Kendall and Breward by demonstrating how Perkins's works on predestination and salvation were staple texts used by English and Continental Churches.[6] Although Patterson's work provides a thorough investigation of Perkins's printed works and consistently links Perkins's life and thought to the broader political and ecclesiastical themes of the Elizabethan period, it is not without problems. For example, Patterson's downplaying of both Perkins's participation in proto-Presbyterian assemblies and Perkins's discontentment with the established church's doctrine and discipline, led him to argue that Perkins's doctrine of predestination was wholly consistent with Article 17 of the Thirtynine Articles (on predestination) and, in our opinion, to erroneously conclude "there is little to link Perkins" to the Elizabethan Puritan movement.[7] In reality, Perkins believed that though the Thirty-nine Articles did not err on the doctrine of predestination, they also did not treat the doctrine with sufficient precision.

Perkins walked the tightrope of Reformed experiential theology, balancing his doctrine so as not to fall into either the abyss of fatalism nor the pit of man-centered religion. While Perkins cannot escape all charges of promoting confusion with his theology, his synthesis of decretal and experimental predestination is Christologically stable and a natural outgrowth of early Calvinism. It is particularly faithful to the theology of Theodore Beza, which promotes a

---

Christology and Predestination in Reformed Theology from Calvin to Perkins [Grand Rapids: Baker, 1988]); Mark R. Shaw ("Drama in the Meeting House: the concept of Conversion in the Theology of William Perkins," *Westminster Theological Journal* 45 (1983): 41–72; "William Perkins and the New Pelagians: Another Look at the Cambridge Predestination Controversy of the 1590s," *Westminster Theological Journal* 58 [1996]: 267–302; Joel R. Beeke (*The Quest for Full Assurance: The Legacy of Calvin and His Successors* [Edinburgh: Banner of Truth, 1999]); Greve, Markham, Munson, op 't Hof, Pipa, Priebe, Schaefer, Sommerville, Song, van Baarsel, and Woolsey, as noted above. See Shaw, "The Marrow of Practical Divinity," 4–29 for a summary of interpretations of Perkins's thought.

5. M. M. Knappen, *Tudor Puritanism: A Chapter in the History of Idealism* (Chicago: University of Chicago Press, 1939), 374–76; Ian Breward, intro. and ed., *The Work of William Perkins,* vol. 3 of The Courtenay Library of Reformation Classics (Abingdon, England: Sutton Courtenay Press, 1970), 86.

6. W. B. Patterson, *William Perkins and the Making of a Protestant England* (Oxford: Oxford University Press, 2014), 64–89.

7. Patterson, *William Perkins,* 49, 86–89. W. B. Patterson, "William Perkins as the Chief Apologist for the Church of England," *Journal of Ecclesiastical History* 57 (2006): 252–69. See also Joel R. Beeke and J. Stephen Yuille, *William Perkins* (Darlington, U.K.: Evangelical Press, 2015).

healthy combination of Reformed theology and piety.[8] William H. Chalker is wrong in his assertion that Perkins kills Calvin's theology as is Kendall's thesis that Beza—and thus Perkins—differ substantially from the Genevan Reformer. Rather, Richard Muller says rightly, "Perkins's thought is not a distortion of earlier Reformed Theology, but a positive outgrowth of the systematic beginnings of Protestant thought."[9]

This essay will introduce readers to Perkins's predestinarian works set forth in this volume in three ways. First, it will provide a brief overview of each work in this volume and the historical contexts in which these works were forged. As we will see, the first three works in this volume—*A Golden Chain, A Christian and Plain Treatise of the Manner and Order of Predestination*, and *A Treatise on God's Free Grace and Man's Free Will*—are Perkins's works on predestination. The second three works—*A Fruitful Dialogue Concerning the End of the World, A Short Treatise that Fully Explains Dickson's Wicked System of Artificial Memory*, and *A Handbook on Memory and the Most Reliable Method of Accurate Recall*—focus on Perkins's defense of Ramistic methodology and the logical framework he used to refute false doctrine. Second, this introduction will explore two features of Perkins's methodology—how he marshalled Scripture, as well as patristic and medieval sources in support of the doctrines he championed and how he sought to demonstrate to his readers the pastoral comforts that predestination affords the believer. Finally, this essay will examine three of Perkins's major contributions in the area of predestination: his Christological, supralapsarian focus; his metaphor of predestination as a golden chain that runs from eternity past to eternity future; and his emphasis on preaching as bringing in the elect.

Content, Context, and Methodology of Perkins's *Works*, Volume Six

In many ways, the Puritan movement was first of all a movement for the reformation of the mind. "The Puritans were educators of the mind," writes J. I. Packer; "the starting point was their certainty that the mind must be instructed and enlightened before faith and obedience become possible."[10] The Puritans' primary method for reforming doctrine was through writing books, as well as the formulation and use of creeds and confessions in catechizing. N. H. Keeble notes how Puritanism "was an intrinsically bookish movement.... Religious works comprised at least half of 100,000 or so titles that represented the total output of the press from the accession of Elizabeth in 1558 to the end of the

---

8. Breward, "Introduction" to *Work of Perkins,* xi.

9. Muller, "Perkins' *A Golden Chaine*," *Sixteenth Century Journal* 9, no. 1 (1978): 69–71, 79–81.

10. J. I. Packer, *A Quest for Godliness: the Puritan Vision of the Christian Life* (Wheaton: Crossway, 1990), 69.

seventeenth century. Of these, a very significant proportion" were written by Puritans.[11] Indeed, the Puritans, beyond nearly any movement in history "revalued not only the book, but the act of reading."[12]

Since Perkins was, according to Philip Benedict, "England's first systematic Reformed theologian to attain international stature," many of the foundational principles of the system of Puritan doctrine can be traced back to him.[13] This is particularly true of Perkins's doctrine of predestination.

Three Works on Predestination: Historical Background

The first three works in this volume are those treatises in which Perkins most fully expounds his doctrine of predestination. Perkins's most famous work and one in which he first articulated his doctrine of predestination was *Armilla Aurea* (1590)—a work which was subsequently translated into English as *A Golden Chain* (1591), by Robert Hill, one of Perkins's students.[14] Perkins's *Golden Chain* was a response to a predestinarian controversy that began in 1570 between the leading Calvinist theologians in Cambridge and two anti-Calvinists—Peter Baro (1534–1599; a French Protestant, who held the Lady Margaret Professorship of Divinity) and William Barrett (*c.* 1561–*c.* 1630; a prominent English divine and Fellow of Caius College), who were opposing Calvinist doctrine.[15] Perkins's work was intended to refute the false doctrinal

---

11. N. H. Keeble, "Puritanism and Literature," in John Coffey and Paul C. H. Lim, eds., *The Cambridge Companion to Puritanism* (Cambridge: Cambridge University Press, 2008), 309.

12. Keeble, "Puritanism and Literature," 311.

13. Philip Benedict, *Christ's Churches Purely Reformed: A Social History of Calvinism* (New Haven: Yale University Press, 2004), 2; Breward, "Introduction" to *Work of Perkins*, xxiv.

14. *Armilla aurea: id est, Miranda series causarum et salutis & damnationis iuxta verbum Dei: Eius synopsin continet annexa tabula* (Cantabrigiae: Iohannis Legatt, 1590); William Perkins, *A Golden Chaine, or the description of theologie, containing the order of the causes of saluation and damnation, according to Gods worde. A viewe of the order wherof, is to be seene in the table annexed. Written in Latin by William Perkins, and translated by another. Hereunto is adioyned the order which M. Theodore Beza used in comforting troubled consciences* (Cambridge: John Legate, 1591). Patterson, *William Perkins*, 69–70. For a list of Perkins's writings, see Munson, "William Perkins: Theologian of Transition" (PhD diss., Case Western Reserve University, 1971), 231–34; McKim, *Ramism in William Perkins's Theology*, 335–37.

15. See Peter Baro, *In Jonam prophetam praelectiones 39. In quibus multa pié doctéque disseruntur & explicantur* (London: John Day, 1579); Andreas Hyperius, *A Speciall Treatise of Gods Providence, and of comforts against all kinde of crosses & calamities to be fetched from the same. With an exposition of the 107. Psalme. Heerunto is added an appendix of certaine sermons & questions, (conteining sweet & comfortable doctrine) as they were uttered and disputed ad clerum in Cambridge, by Peter Baro*, trans. John Ludham (London: Iohn Wolfe, 1588); Patterson, *William Perkins*, 70; Jean-Louis Quantin, *The Church of England and Christian Antiquity: The Construction of Confessional Identity in the 17th Century* (Oxford: Oxford University Press), 171. For manuscript accounts related to the dispute, particularly Laurence Chaderton's interview of William Barrett, see Lambeth Palace Library, MS 2550, 164r–167v. For secondary

positions being put forth by Baro and Barrett and to assist others who were wrestling with these complex doctrinal issues.[16] The conflict escalated in 1595 when Barrett delivered a series of sermons at Great St. Mary's Church that more directly opposed Calvinist doctrine. As a result, Archbishop John Whitgift, William Whitaker (the Regius Professor of Divinity), Laurence Chaderton (Head of Emmanuel College), and others formally opposed Barrett, called on him to recant, and drafted the Lambeth Articles. While Article 17 of the Thirty-nine Articles addressed predestination generally, if rather ambiguously, the Lambeth Articles sought to articulate plainly the particulars of predestinarian doctrine, and especially the doctrine of "double predestination."

While it does not appear that Perkins was ever formally a part of the cohort that opposed the anti-Calvinists in 1595, Perkins's works on predestination both before and after the conflict were intended to refute their theology.[17] It is a testimony to Perkins's resolve to continue defending predestination against false doctrine that three years after the disputes, Perkins published his second treatise on predestination, *De praeedestinationis modo et ordine* (1598).[18] It was also published three times in Basel (1599, 1603, and 1613) and once in Hanae (1603).[19] The work was translated into English and published posthumously by Francis Cacot and Thomas Tuke in 1606 as *A Christian and Plain Treatise of the Manner and Order of Predestination.*

Shortly following its publication the Dutch theologian Jacob Arminius began reading *De praedestinationis.*[20] Arminius had previously studied under

---

accounts of the theological disputes of the 1590s in Cambridge see H. C. Porter, *Reformation and Reaction in Tudor Cambridge* (Cambridge: Cambridge University Press, 1958), 277–413; Peter Lake, *Moderate Puritans and the Elizabethan Church* (Cambridge: Cambridge University Press, 1982), 201–42; David Hoyle, *Reformation and Religious Identity in Cambridge, 1590–1640* (Woodbridge: Boydell Press, 2007), 71–86; Nicholas Tyacke, *Anti-Calvinists: The Rise of English Arminianism* (Oxford: Oxford University Press, 1987), 29–36; Peter White, *Predestination, Policy, and Polemic: Conflict and Consensus in the English Church from the Reformation to the Civil War* (Cambridge: Cambridge University Press, 1992), 101–23. On the use of Pelagianism as a polemical weapon in the 1590s disputes in Cambridge, see Mark R. Shaw, "William Perkins and the New Pelagians: Another Look at the Cambridge Predestination Controversy of the 1590s," *Westminster Theological Journal* 58 (1996): 267–301.

16. Patterson, *William Perkins*, 71.

17. Patterson, *William Perkins*, 79, 82.

18. William Perkins, *De praedestinationis modo et ordine* (Cantabrigiae: Iohannis Legatt, 1598).

19. William Perkins, *A Christian and Plaine Treatise of the Manner and Order of Predestination, and of the largenes of Gods grace* (London: William Welby and Martin Clarke, 1606); Patterson, *William Perkins*, 81.

20. Carl Bangs, *Arminius: A Study in the Dutch* Reformation (Nashville: Abingdon Press, 1971), 83, 115, 186–205; Patterson, *William Perkins*, 84–85.

the Calvinist scholastic Theodore Beza (1519–1605).[21] As such, according to Carl Bangs, he originally "bought the book eagerly, for he was an admirer of Perkins, but read it with dismay."[22] Arminius immediately wrote to Perkins to express his concern and to request a conference in which the two would debate the various issues set forth in his book.[23] Since Perkins died in 1602, Perkins and Arminius never debated each other,[24] but Arminius wrote his own response, *Examination of Perkins's Little Book on the Order and Mode of Predestination* (published posthumously in 1612), which became "in many respects his most important single composition."[25]

Arminius was likewise discontent with Perkins's final work on predestination, *A Treatise of God's Free Grace and Man's Free Will* (1602).[26] Like Perkins's earlier works, *A Treatise of God's Free Grace* was steeped in Perkins's love for Ramistic methodology as it sketched the relationship between God's grace and the state of the human will in the four estates of redemption—"innocency, corruption, regeneration, and glorification."[27] Arminius went on to teach at Leiden University from 1603 to 1609 and to challenge Calvinist views on the doctrine of predestination. Following his death in 1609, Arminius's followers wrote the Five Articles of their famous *Remonstrance* (1610). The work's title gave rise to the name given to Arminius's followers (the "Remonstrants") and the treatise itself outlined a view of predestination that was opposed to the predestinarian doctrine being advanced by most Reformed theologians throughout England and the Continent. A conflict ensued between Arminius's followers

---

21. On Arminius, see Peter Bertius, *The Life and Death of James Arminius, and Simon Episcopius. Professors of divinity in the University of Leyden in Holland. Both of them famous defenders of the doctrine of Gods universal grace, and sufferers for it* (London: Francis Smith, 1673); Bangs, *Arminius*; Keith D. Stanglin and Thomas H. McCall, *Jacob Arminius: Theologian of Grace* (Oxford: Oxford University Press, 2012). Also see James Arminius, *The Works of James Arminius*, trans. James Nichols, 3 vols. (London: Longman and Co., 1825–28).

22. Bangs, *Arminius*, 209.

23. Bangs, *Arminius*, 209; Patterson, *William Perkins*, 85.

24. For a comparison of Perkins's and Arminius's views, see Richard A. Muller, *God, Creation, and Providence in the Thought of Jacob Arminius: Sources and Directions of Scholastic Protestantism in the Era of Early Orthodoxy* (Grand Rapids: Baker, 1991), 22–23, 43, 187–88, 264–66; Keith D. Stanglin, *Arminius on the Assurance of Salvation: The Context, Roots, and Shape of the Leiden Debate, 1603–1609* (Leiden: Brill, 2007), 68, 131–32, 136, 170–71, 179, 182–83, 185, 211–13, 215–17, 223–23, 234; Stanglin and McCall, *Jacob Arminius*, 73, 99, 103, 113, 115–16.

25. Iabobi Arminii, *Examen modestum libelli, quem D. Gulielmus Perkinsius apprime doctus theologus, edidit ante aliquot annos de praedestinationis modo & ordine* (Leiden: Godfrid Basson, 1612); Bangs, *Arminius*, 206.

26. Michael Jinkins, "William Perkins (1558–1602)," *Oxford Dictionary of National Biography*.

27. McKim, *Ramism in William Perkins's Theology*, 96; Leif Dixon, *Practical Predestinarians, c. 1590–1640* (Surrey, U. K.: Ashgate, 2014), 271.

(the "Remonstrants") and Dutch Calvinists (the "Counter-Remonstrants"), and the Synod of Dordrecht (Dort) was called to resolve the divisions within the church.[28]

The impact on the Synod of Dort of Perkins's earlier controversy with Arminius can scarcely be overstated. As Patterson correctly observes, "it is no exaggeration to say that the issues discussed at Dort and ultimately resolved—at least to the satisfaction of the majority of the delegates—were in larger measure those raised by Perkins and Arminius at the turn of the century." Indeed, "the year before the synod met, Arminius's *Examen modestum* was published in a Dutch translation along with a [Dutch] translation of Perkins's *De Predestinationis modo et ordaine*."[29] It is not surprising that Perkins was cited quite regularly at the Synod of Dort. For example, in one session Franciscus Gomarus—"who had been educated for a time at Cambridge University when Whitaker and Perkins were in their pomp"—attempted to demonstrate that the English Church had supported supralapsarianism by arguing "that both Dr Whitaker and Mr Perkins had determined the contrary, whom he took to be such men as would not dissent from the Confession of the Church of England."[30]

Use of Patristic and Medieval Sources

Two facets of Perkins's methodology in his predestinarian works are worth noting. First, in his polemic against anti-Calvinism he paralleled anti-Calvinist claims with Pelagianism and bolstered his arguments by using patristic and medieval sources.[31] Pelagianism was a fifth-century heretical movement arising from the teachings of the British theologian Pelagius, who insisted on man's ability to achieve salvation through human effort, unassisted by divine grace. Pelagius's doctrines were opposed in the early 410s by Augustine of Hippo and were officially denounced in 418 at the Council of Carthage.[32]

In his *Golden Chain*, Perkins avowed that he was contending against both the "old and newe Pelagians; who place the cause of Gods predestination in

---

28. Patterson, *William Perkins*, 86. On the Synod of Dort, see Aza Goudriaan and Fred van Lieburg, eds., *Revisiting the Synod of Dort (1618–1619)* (Leiden: Brill, 2011).

29. Patterson, *William Perkins*, 86; Bangs, *Arminius*, 209.

30. *The British Delegation at the Synod of Dort (1618–1619)*, ed. Anthony Milton (Woodbridge: Boydell Press, 2005), xxxii, 225; John Hales, *Golden Remains of the Ever Memorable Mr. John Hales of Eton College* (London: Robert Pawlet, 1973), Rr1r.

31. Quantin, *Church of England*, 171–72.

32. F. L. Cross and E. A. Livingstone, eds., *The Oxford Dictionary of the Christian Church*, 3rd ed. (Oxford: Oxford University Press, 1997), 130, 1257. For a succinct but fine treatment of these disputes, see Peter Brown, *Augustine of Hippo* (Los Angeles: University of California Press, 2000), 341–53. For an English edition of Augustine's anti-Pelagian writings see Augustine, *Nicene and Post-Nicene Fathers, Volume 5: Augustine: Anti-Pelagian Writings, First Series*, ed. Philip Schaff (Peabody, Mass.: Hendrickson Publishers, 1994).

man," and the "Semipelagian Papists, which ascribe Gods Predestination, partlye to mercye, and partly to mens foreseen preparations and meritorious works."[33] Perkins's use of quotations from patristic and medieval sources is most evident in his *A Christian And Plain Treatise of the Manner and Order of Predestination*. Indeed, the work contains over two hundred citations from Church Fathers such as Augustine, Jerome, Gregory the Great, Cyril of Alexandria, Prosper of Aquitaine, and Fulgenitus; medieval theologians such as Bernard of Clairvaux, Anselm, Thomas Aquinas, Peter Lombard, and Hugh St. Victor; and Reformers such as John Calvin, Theodore Beza, and Peter Martyr Vermigli.

Given that Augustine was Pelagius's chief opponent, it is no surprise that Augustine was Perkins's most frequently cited author.[34] However, Arnoud Visser and Jean Louis Quantin have convincingly argued that in post-Reformation England "'Augustinianism' [was] far from a coherent, unequivocal conception."[35] For example, by examining the marginal notes from Thomas Cranmer's, Peter Martyr Vermigli's, and William Laud's personal editions of Augustine, Visser has demonstrated that ministers from different confessional traditions detached Augustine's anti-Pelagian works from their historical context. Instead, they employed vastly different reading and citation practices that were closely linked with their own personal and polemical agendas. This allowed them to draw opposite conclusions about the same works and thus to exploit Augustine's authority.[36] Indeed, Perkins's own opponent, Peter Baro, likewise claimed he had Augustine's support.[37] This is why Perkins's ultimate aim in his writings was to ground his arguments not on human authorities, but on Scripture alone.[38] As Perkins articulated in his *Godly and Learned Exposition upon the Whole Epistle of Jude*, "traditions can never settle the conscience, for though divers [plausible doctrines] are found in the writings of the Fathers, yet they were the subject of errour, and so might and did erre in them," which he then contrasted with Scripture as the "perfect rule of faith and manners: It is of all things to be beleeued or done to saluation (2 Tim. 3.16)."[39]

---

33. William Perkins, *A Golden Chaine, or the description of Theologie, containing order of the causes of Salvation and Damnation* (London: Iohn Legate, 1591).

34. Cf. Dixon, *Practical Predestinarians*, 72. Also see David M. Barbee, "A Reformed Catholike: William Perkins' use of the church fathers," (PhD diss., The University of Pennsylvania, 2013), 204–259.

35. Arnoud Visser, *Reading Augustine in the Reformation* (Oxford: Oxford University Press, 2011), 7. On the depicting of one's views as Augustinian, rather than Calvinistic, see Quantin, *Church of England*, 176. For later examples, see *British Delegation at the Synod of Dort*, 216.

36. Visser, *Reading Augustine*, 106–13. Also see Quantin, *Church of England*, 18, 173.

37. Patterson, *William Perkins*, 71.

38. Patterson, *William Perkins*, 73.

39. William Perkins, *Godlie and Learned Exposition upon the Whole Epistle of Jude* (London: Thomas Man, 1606), 18. Puritans William Whitaker and John Rainolds also noted the fallacy of

Nevertheless, Perkins's commitment to Scripture as the ultimately authority was supplemented by his extensive knowledge of patristic and medieval sources. He used these citations to substantiate his arguments and to show that his position was a model of apostolic and orthodox faith. In this way, Perkins's use of citations from these sources shielded him from those who would argue that he was merely projecting these terms onto his opponents. By outlining similarities between the views of Pelagius and those of his opponents and appealing to the testimony of divines over the whole of church history, Perkins's aim was to instill confidence in his readers that the Calvinist position would prevail. Moreover, Perkins was not only charging his opponents with error, but with circulating heretical views that had been condemned by the universal church throughout church history.

Perkins's approach was adopted by later English Calvinists in the 1620s as they opposed the English anti-Calvinist Richard Montague.[40] Later anti-

---

grounding one's arguments on human authority. John Rainolds, *The Summe of the Conference betweene Iohn Rainoldes and Iohn Hart: Touching the Head and the Faith of the Church* (London: Iohn Wolfe, 1584), 36, 490, 584; William Whitaker, *An Answere to the Ten Reasons of Edmund Campian the Iesuit* (London: Cuthbert Burby and Edmund Weaver, 1606), Gg2v–3r; also see Joshua Rodda, *Public Religious Disputation in England* (Abingdon: Ashgate), 51–52; Lake, *Moderate Puritans*, 100–1; Quantin, *The Church of England and Christian Antiquity*, 74.

40. For Montague's anti-Calvinist works see Richard Montague, *A Gagg for the New Gospell? No: a New Gagg for an Old Goose* (London: Matthew Lownes and William Barrett, 1624); Richard Montague, *Appello Caesarem: A Iust Appeale from two uniust informers* (London: Matthew Lownes, 1625). For the replies to Montague by Puritans and English Calvinists, see John Yates, *Ibis ad Caesarem* (London: Robert Milbourne, 1626); Samuel Ward, *Gratia discriminans* (Londini: Robert Milbourne, 1626); George Carleton, *An Examination of Those Things wherein the Author of the late Appeale holdeth the doctrines of the Pelagians and Arminians, to be the doctrines of the Church of England* (London: William Turner, 1626). (This work was eventually revised and enlarged in a second edition with a rejoinder: George Carleton, *The Second Edition, Revised and Enlarged by the Author. Whereunto also there is annexed a ioynt attestation* [London: William Turner, 1626]). See also Walter Balcanquhall, *Ioynt Attestation, avowing that the Discipline of the Church of England was not Impeached by the Synode of Dort* (London: Robert Milbourne, 1626). Balcanquhall's work is an appendix to the second edition of Carleton's *Examination*; Anon., *Suffragium collegiale theologorum* (Londini: Robert Milbourne, 1626), which is signed by Thomas Goad, Samuel Ward, Walter Balcanquhall, George Carlton, and John Davenport; Francis Rous, *Testis veritatis: The Doctrine of King Iames our late Saveraigne of famous Memory* (London: W. Jones, 1626); Anthony Wotton, *A Dangerous Plot Discovered* (London: Nicholas Bourne, 1626); Henry Burton, *A Plea to an Appeale: Trauersed Dialogue Wise* (London: W. Jones, 1626); Richard Bernard, *Rhemes against Rome* (London: Robert Milbourne, 1626); Matthew Sutcliffe, *A Briefe Censure upon an Appeale to Caesar* (Oxford: s. n., 1626); Daniel Featley, *Parallelismus nov-antiqui erroris Pelagiarminiani* (Londini: Robert Milbourne, 1626); Daniel Featley, *A Parallel: of New-old Pelagiarminian Error* (London: Robert Milbourne, 1626); Daniel Featley, *A Second Parallel together with a Writ of Error Sued against the Appealer* (London: Robert Milbourne, 1626). Also see British Library, Harleian MS 390, 83r–v. For a helpful summary of these works, see Peter Milward, *Religious Controversies in the Jacobean Age* (London: Scholar Press, 1973), 41–43;

Arminian authors traced the origins of Arminianism in England to the Cambridge debates of the 1590s. And since Arminius had responded to Perkins's arguments originating from these debates, later Calvinists regarded these disputes as a precursor to the Montague debate.[41]

Pastoral Motivations and Practical Applications

A second feature of Perkins's methodology is the pastoral motivation and desire for practical application that underpinned his predestinarian works. Although historians have long acknowledged that there was a strong link for

---

Tyacke, *Anti-Calvinists*, 155–56; Jay T. Collier, *Debating Perseverance: The Augustinian Heritage in Post-Reformation England* (Oxford: Oxford University Press, 2018), ch. 4. Jonathan Adkins has classified the various responses to Montague, placing ministers in one of three categories. See Jonathan Atkins, "Calvinist Bishops, Church Unity and the Rise of Arminianism," *Albion* 18 (1986):423.

41. For the extensive secondary literature related to this dispute and debates between the Calvinists and anti-Calvinists in England see Nicholas Tyacke, "Puritanism, Arminianism and Counter-revolution," in Conrad Russell, ed., *The Origins of the English Civil War* (London: Macmillan, 1973), 119–41; Tyacke, *Anti-Calvinists*; Nicholas Tyacke, "Debate: The Rise of Arminianism Reconsidered," *Past & Present* 115 (1987): 201–16; White, *Predestination*; Peter White, "The Rise of Arminianism Reconsidered," *Past & Present* 101 (1983): 34–54; Peter White, "Debate: The Rise of Arminianism Reconsidered: A Rejoinder," *Past & Present* 115 (1987): 217–29; Peter White, "The *Via Media* in the Early Stuart Church," in Kenneth Fincham, ed., *the Early Stuart Church* (Basingstoke, U.K.: Macmillan, 1993), 211–30; William Lamont, "Comment: The Rise of Arminianism Reconsidered," *Past & Present* 107 (1985): 227–31; Peter Lake, "Calvinism and the English Church 1570–1635," *Past & Present* 114 (1987): 32–76; Peter Lake, "Predestinarian Propositions," *Journal of Ecclesiastical History* 46 (1995): 112–13; Kenneth Fincham, *Prelate as Pastor: The Episcopate of James I* (Oxford: Oxford University Press, 1990); Conrad Russell, *The Causes of the English Civil War* (Oxford: Oxford University Press, 1990); Anthony Milton, *Catholic and Reformed: The Roman and Protestant Churches in English Protestant Thought, 1600–1640* (Cambridge: Cambridge University Press, 1995); David Como, "Puritans, Predestination and the Construction of Orthodoxy in Early Seventeenth-Century England," in Peter Lake and Michael Questier, eds., *Conformity and Orthodoxy in the English Church, c.1560–1660* (Woodbridge: Boydell Press, 2000), 64–87; David Como, "Predestination and Political Conflict in Laud's London," *Historical Journal* 46 (2003): 263–94; Charles Prior, *Defining the Jacobean Church: The Politics of Religious Controversy, 1603–1625* (Cambridge: Cambridge University Press, 2005); Judith Maltby, *Prayer Book and People in Elizabethan and Early Stuart England* (Cambridge: Cambridge University Press, 1998); Kevin Sharpe, *The Personal Rule of Charles I* (New Haven: Yale University Press, 1992); Kevin Sharpe, "The Personal Rule of Charles I," in Howard Tomlinson, ed., *Before the English Civil War: Essays on Early Stuart Politics and Government* (New York: Macmillan, 1984), 53–78; Kevin Sharpe, "Archbishop Laud," *History Today* 33 (1983): 26–30; Mark Kishlansky, "Charles I: A Case of Mistaken Identity," *Past & Present* 189 (2005): 48–49; Sheila Lambert, "Richard Montagu, Arminianism and Censorship," *Past & Present* 124 (1989): 36–68; Hillel Schwartz, "Arminianism and the English Parliament, 1624–1629," *Journal of British Studies* 12 (1973): 41–68; David Hoyle, "A Commons Investigation of Arminianism and Popery in Cambridge on the Eve of the Civil War," *Historical Journal* 29 (1986): 419–25; Atkins, "Calvinist Bishops, Church Unity, and the Rise of Arminianism," 411–27.

Perkins and other Puritan ministers between predestination and pastoral issues such as assurance of salvation, recent studies have clarified our understanding of these issues. Leif Dixon modified Kendall's famous distinction between experimental and credal predestinarians.[42] Dixon redefined "experimental predestinarians" as "practical predestinarians," arguing that Perkins and other ministers challenged believers to find personal assurance primarily in order that they might please God rather than simply achieve inward confirmation of salvation. Dixon challenged the assumption that issues of predestination were inextricably tied to spiritual angst by demonstrating that Perkins and other Puritan divines (such as Richard Greenham and Richard Rogers) stressed pursuing outward expressions of good works rather than inward navel gazing. In a chaotic and uncertain culture, the doctrine of predestination provided a stabilizing source of comfort and assurance.[43]

For Perkins, the differences over predestination between him and his opponents were not merely doctrinal, but also deeply pastoral. Patterson highlights that whereas *A Golden Chain* is "in part about predestination it is more fundamentally about what it means to experience salvation," it "is pastorally oriented, in the sense of being directed to the practical needs of the parishioners seeking help in their spiritual journey."[44] In Perkins's mind, a salvation that was in any way dependent on man's volition was extremely precarious. By contrast, by maintaining that salvation was ultimately dependent on the will of God, predestination provided ultimate comfort and security for the believer. In this way, as Arnold Hunt has convincingly shown, the doctrine of predestination was

---

42. According to Kendall, "experimental predestinarians were mainly pastors who not only believed but vigorously stressed that one's election *may* be known by experimental knowledge; indeed it *must* be known lest one deceive himself and, in the end, be damned." By contrast, "credal predestinarians" is a "term used to designate the position of the majority of bishops… who, though not generally known for their stress upon experimental divinity, were none the less predestinarian in their theology as a whole." Kendall, *Calvin and English Calvinism*, 79–80; also see 8–9. Richard Muller has been arguably the strongest critic of Kendall's argument. See Richard Muller, *The Unaccommodated Calvin: Studies in the Foundation of a Theological Tradition* (Oxford: Oxford University Press, 2000), 17, 159, 172; Richard Muller, *After Calvin: Studies in the Development of a Theological Tradition* (Oxford: Oxford University Press, 2003), 83; Richard Muller, *Calvin and the Reformed Tradition: On the Work of Christ and the Order of Salvation* (Grand Rapids: Baker, 2012), *passim*.

43. Dixon, *Practical Predestinarians*, 7, 11–12, 15. On similar ideas, see Leif Dixon, "William Perkins, 'Atheism,' and the Crises of England's Long Reformation," *Journal of British Studies* 50 (2011): 790–812. Also see, Michael Winship, "Weaker Christians, Backsliders, and Carnal Gospelers: Assurance of Salvation and the Pastoral Origins of Puritan Practical Divinity in the 1590s," *Church History* 70 (2001):462–81; Lake, "Calvinism and the English Church 1570–1635," 39; Joel R. Beeke, *The Quest for Full Assurance of Faith: The Legacy of Calvin and His Successors* (Edinburgh: Banner of Truth, 1999), 31–33, 83–86.

44. Patterson, *William Perkins*, 75.

not confined to the debates of elite academicians, but was a matter of critical importance for ministers who wanted the laity to benefit spiritually from the comfort and assurance to be found in predestination.[45]

Ramistic Methodology

The latter three works of this volume focus on Perkins's defense of Ramistic methodology and the biblical framework for logic he used to refute false doctrine. In 1584, Perkins became entangled in what would be identified later by historians as one of the most heated controversies during this time, over the relationship between the use of various systems of memory and false doctrine. Perkins's opponent was the philosophical writer and political agent, Alexander Dickson (*bap.* 1558, *d.* 1603/4). Although Dickson was born in Scotland and educated at St. Andrews, at some point between 1577 and 1583 he spent several years studying on the Continent, probably in Paris. During this time, he was heavily influenced by the Italian cosmologist and hermetic philosopher, Giordano Bruno (*c.* 1548–1600), and his philosophies on the art of memory. As a result, in 1584 Dickson published an influential philosophical treatise shadowing Bruno's mnemonic theories entitled, *De umbra rationis & judicii, sive* (The Shadow of Reason and Judgment), based on Bruno's own *De umbris idearum* (On the Shadows of Ideas).[46]

In 1584, Perkins wrote two works refuting Dickson—*Antidicsonus* (The Antidickson) and *Libellus de memoria, verissimaque bene recordandi scientia* (A Handbook on Memory and the Most Reliable Method of Accurate Recall).[47]

---

45. Hunt, *The Art of Hearing*, 342–89.

46. Alexander Dickson, *Alexandri Dicsoni arelii de vmbra rationis & iudicij, siue de memoriæ virtute Prosopopœia* (Londini: Thomas Vautrollerius, 1683 [*sic*] 1584).

47. G. [William] P. [Perkins], *Antidicsonus. Accessit libellus, in quo dilucidè explicatur impia Dicsoni artificiosa memoria* (Londini: Henricus Midletonus, 1584). G. [William] P. [Perkins], *Libellus de memoria, verissimaque bene recordandi scientia. Huc accessit eiusdem admonitiuncula ad A. Disconum [sic], de artificiosæ memoriæ, quam publicè profitetur, vanitate* (Londini: Robert Waldengrave, 1984). There are some since at least the 19th century, who have falsely attributed Perkins's work to the English divine Gerard Peeters. David Crankshaw, "Gerard Peeters (*bap.* 1562?, *d.* 1598)," *Oxford Dictionary of National Biography*; Peter Beal, "Alexander Dicsone [Dickson] (*bap.* 1558, *d.* 1603/4)," *Oxford Dictionary of National Biography*. One possible reason that readers (especially those familiar with Perkins's writings) might doubt Perkins's authorship is Perkins's use of strong language throughout his refutations of Dickson. However, we should bear in mind that Perkins's polemicism was motivated by a strong pastoral concern to protect the English Church from harmful ideologies that threatened the spiritual well-being of the sheep. On the dynamics of polemicism in this period, see Joshua Rodda, Public Religious Disputation in England, 1558–1626 (Farnham: Ashgate, 2014). Perkins's writings against Dickson are translated in this volume for the first time into English, for which we express gratitude to the quality work of David Noe.

According to Francis Yates, in Perkins's dedication of *Antidicsonus* to Thomas Moufet, he articulated the difference between himself and Dickson, namely that "there are two kinds of arts of memory, one using places and 'umbrae,' [Dickson's] the other by 'logical disposition as taught' by Peter Ramus [Perkins's]." According to Perkins, "the former is utterly vain; [and] the latter is the only true method."[48] However, the main reason why Perkins chose to oppose strenuously Dickson was his conviction that his system of memory was not only erroneous, but spiritually harmful. Perkins's concerns were ultimately rooted in his conviction that Dickson's approach was connected with "a hermetic religious cult" (i.e., relating to the occult or pseudo-science of alchemy), Roman Catholic uses of images, and idolatry.[49] Indeed, Dickson even mockingly flaunted Perkins's labelling him a "Scepsian" (one who employs "the zodiac in his impious artificial memory") by including it in the title of his reply to Perkins, *Heii Scepsii defensio*.[50] James Worthen and Reed Hunt's summary of the dispute is worth quoting at length:

> Perkins was a theologian and Puritan leader who advocated for Peter Ramus's organizational mnemonic techniques. Thus, the dispute between Dickson and Perkins was just as much about religion as it was about mnemonic techniques. Specifically, as led by Perkins, the Puritans associated imagery-based mnemonic techniques with the occult as well as with the Catholic Church. Making an argument similar to that which they directed at the Catholic Church for the veneration of saints, the Puritans maintained that the use of mental imagery amounted to heresy as it reflected a form of idol worship. Moreover, the Puritans were especially opposed to the use of the zodiac symbols in Bruno's mnemonic system.[51]

As noted previously, Ramistic methodology was a key component of Perkins's doctrinal and homiletical approach.[52] However, Perkins's defense of Ramistic methodology in his dispute with Dickson demonstrates the ways in

---

48. Francis A. Yates, *The Art of Memory* (London: Pimlico, 1992), 265.

49. Beal, "Alexander Dickson."

50. Alexander Dickson, *Heii Scepsii Defensio pro Alexandro Dicsono Arelio aduersus quendam G.P. Cantabrigien* (Londini: Thomas Vautroullerius, 1584); Beal, "Alexander Dickson."

51. James B. Worthen and R. Reed Hunt, *Mnemonology: Mnemonics for the 21st Century* (New York: Psychology Press, 2011), 6. Also see Yates, *The Art of Memory*, 261, 266–67; Also see Marsha Keith Schuchard, *Restoring the Temple of Vision: Cabalistic Freemasonry and Stuart Culture* (Leiden: Brill, 2002), 204–5. For other literature on this dispute see Walter J. Ong, *Rhetoric, Romance, and Technology: Studies in the Interaction of Expression* (Ithaca: Cornell University Press, 1971), 112; Paolo Rossi, *Logic and the Art of Memory: The Quest for a Universal Language* (London: Continuum, 2000), 280.

52. For the best study on Perkins's Ramistic methodology see Donald K. McKim, *Ramism in William Perkins's Theology* (New York: Peter Lang, 1987).

which Perkins and the Puritans sought to reform the mind not merely through formulating biblical doctrine, but by restoring the connection between the very purpose of man's God-given intellect and the appropriate use of logic and reason.

Likewise, Perkins's *A Fruitful Dialogue Concerning the End of the World* (1587), was concerned with the folly of pagan approaches to knowledge, particularly astrological predictions about the end of the world. The work itself is a dialogue between two characters—"Christian" and "Worldling," the latter who was vexed with the conviction that the world would end the following year. Perkins had "'Christian' point to all the times in the past when prognosticators were wrong in predicting the world's end."[53] Thus, although the genre of the work was different from the others in this volume, his single-minded conviction concerning the folly of worldly means of knowledge remained the same.

Christ-centered Supralapsarian Predestination

Primarily concerned with the conversion of souls and subsequent growth in godliness, Perkins believed that a biblical experience of God's sovereign grace in predestination was vital for spiritual comfort and assurance. He believed that salvation worked out experimentally in the souls of believers was inseparable from sovereign predestination in Christ. Far from being harsh and cold, sovereign predestination was the foundation upon which experimental faith could be built.[54] It offered solid ground for hope to the true believer.

In the introduction to his *A Golden Chain*, Perkins identified four viewpoints on this matter:

- The old and new Pelagians, who place the cause of predestination in man, in that God ordained men to life or death according to His foreknowledge of their free-will rejection or receiving of offered grace.

---

53. McKim, *Ramism in William Perkins's Theology*, 58.

54. Experimental or experiential preaching addresses how a Christian experiences the truth of scriptural doctrine in his life. The term *experimental* comes from *experimentum,* meaning trial, and is derived from the verb *experior,* to know by experience, which in turn leads to "experiential," meaning knowledge gained by experiment. Calvin used experimental and experiential interchangeably, since both words indicate the need for measuring experienced knowledge against the touchstone of Scripture. Experimental preaching seeks to explain in terms of biblical truth how matters ought to go, how they do go, and what the goal of the Christian life is. It aims to apply divine truth to the whole range of the believer's personal experience as well as in his relationships with family, the church, and the world around him. Cf. Kendall, *Calvin and English Calvinism*, 8–9; Joel R. Beeke, "The Lasting Power of Reformed Experiential Preaching," in *Feed My Sheep: A Passionate Plea for Preaching,* ed. Don Kistler (Morgan, Pa.: Soli Deo Gloria, 2002), 94–128; Joel R. Beeke, *Reformed Preaching: Preaching the Word from the Heart of the Preacher to the Heart of His People* (Wheaton, Ill. Crossway, 2018).

- The Lutherans, who teach that God chose some to salvation by His mere mercy but rejected the rest because He foresaw they would reject His grace.
- The semi-Pelagian Roman Catholics, who ascribe God's predestination partly to mercy and partly to foreseen human preparations and meritorious works.
- Finally, those who teach that God saves some merely of His mercy and damns others entirely because of man's sin, but that the divine predestination concerning both has no other cause than His will.

Perkins concluded, "Of these four opinions, the three former I labour to oppugn [oppose] as erroneous, and to maintain the last, as being truth which will bear weight in the balance of the sanctuary."[55] The latter expression refers to a scale, figuratively applied to assigning each truth its proper weight according to Holy Scripture. Perkins thereby declared his intention of presenting a biblical and balanced theology of predestination. Decretal theology exalts God and abases man. Experimental theology identifies the saved by the fruition of election in a life of faith and increasing holiness, "a life consonant with God's choice," as Irvonwy Morgan said.[56] In Perkins's theology, the decree in Christ and the experience in Christ are conceptually and realistically linked together.

Predestination for the Glory of God Alone

The terms supralapsarian and infralapsarian concern the logical order of God's decree related to man's eternal state. Sometimes supralapsarianism is called "high Calvinism." Supralapsarian literally means "above or before the fall" and infralapsarian means "below or after the fall" (Latin *supra* = above; *infra* = below; *lapsus* = fall). Supralapsarians believe that the decree of divine predestination must logically precede the decree concerning mankind's creation and fall in order to preserve the absolute sovereignty of God. Infralapsarians maintain that the decree of predestination must logically follow the decree of creation and the fall, believing it to be inconsistent with the nature of God for Him to reprobate any man without first contemplating him as created, fallen, and sinful.[57]

---

55. Breward, ed., *Work of Perkins*, 175–76. Cf. Michael T. Malone, "The Doctrine of Predestination in the Thought of William Perkins and Richard Hooker," *Anglican Theological Review* 52 (1970): 103–17.

56. Edmund Morgan, *Puritan Spirituality: Illustrated from the Life and Times of the Rev. Dr. John Preston* (London: Epworth Press, 1973), 25.

57. See Joel R. Beeke, "Did Beza's Supralapsarianism Spoil Calvin's Theology?," *Reformed Theological Journal* 13 (Nov. 1997): 58–60; William Hastie, *The Theology of the Reformed Church*

Perkins was a supralapsarian more for practical than metaphysical reasons. Adhering to high Calvinism for the framework of his predestination and practical theology, Perkins believed that accenting the sovereignty of God and His decree gave God the most glory and the Christian the most comfort. This emphasis also served as the best polemic against Lutherans and semi-Pelagian Roman Catholics such as Robert Bellarmine (1542–1621), and anti-predestinarians in England such as Peter Baro and William Barrett. Though greatly indebted to Calvin, Perkins also relied upon such theologians as Theodore Beza, Girolamo Zanchi (1516–1590), Zacharias Ursinus (1534–1583), and Caspar Olevianus (1536–1587).[58] Freely admitting that he had consulted these writers (he even appended a work of Beza to his *Golden Chain*), Perkins nonetheless used his gifts to add to the treasury of high Calvinism.

It is impossible to understand predestination without realizing that God's decrees flow from the inner life of the triune God. Perkins defined God's glory as "the infinite excellency of his most simple and most holy divine nature."[59] Proceeding from this internal glory, God's decree, as well as its execution, aims at "the manifestation of the glory of God."[60] Perkins wrote, "The decree of God, is that by which God in himself, hath necessarily, and yet freely, from all eternity determined all things (Eph. 1:11; Matt. 10:29; Rom. 9:21)."[61] Predestination, which is only God's decree insofar as it concerns man, is that "by which he hath ordained all men to a certaine and everlasting estate: that is, either to salvation or condemnation, for his own glory."[62]

Predestination is the means by which God manifests His glory to the human race. Election is God's decree "whereby on his own free will, he hath ordained certain men to salvation, to the praise of the glory of his grace."[63] Reprobation is "that part of predestination, whereby God, according to the most free and just

---

(Edinburgh: T. & T. Clark, 1904); Klaas Dijk, *De Strijd over Infra- en Supralapsarisme in de Gereformeerde Kerken van Nederland* (Kampen: Kok, 1912).

58. W. Stanford Reid, *John Calvin: His Influence in the Western World* (Grand Rapids: Zondervan, 1982), 206–7; Kendall, *Calvin and English Calvinism*, 30–31, 76; Otto Grundler, "Thomism and Calvinism in the Theology of Girolamo Zanchi" (PhD diss., Princeton Theological Seminary, 1960), 123; Wallace, *Puritans and Predestination*, 59; Lyle D. Bierma, *German Calvinism in the Confessional Age: The Covenant Theology of Caspar Olevianus* (Grand Rapids: Baker, 1996), 176–81. Cf. C. M. Dent, *Protestant Reformers in Elizabethan Oxford* (Oxford: University Press, 1983), 98–102.

59. *Works*, 1:13.

60. *Works*, 1:15.

61. *Works*, 1:15.

62. *Works*, 1:16.

63. *Works*, 1:24.

purpose of his will, hath determined to reject certain men unto eternal destruction, and misery, and that to the praise of his justice."[64]

Like Beza, Perkins held a supralapsarian position of denying that God, in reprobating, considered man as fallen. Perkins supported this belief with Beza's argument (drawing on Aristotle) that the end is first in the intention of an agent. Thus God first decided the end—the manifestation of His glory in saving and damning—before He considered the means, such as creation and the fall. Ultimately, predestination must not be understood in terms of what it does for man, but in terms of its highest goal—the glory of God. Absolute sovereignty in double predestination for the pure glory of God: this is the heartbeat of Perkins's theology.

Answering Objections: The Predestining God is Righteous

As a theological tightrope walker, Perkins knew that his view prompted two objections: (1) it makes God the author of sin; (2) it diminishes the role of Christ.[65]

In addressing the first objection, Perkins adamantly rejected the idea that God is the author of sin. God decreed the fall of man, but He did not cause man to sin. Perkins insisted that the Scriptures teach that God ordains all that shall come to pass.[66] We must not think that man's fall was by chance, or by God's failure to foreknow it, or by barely winking at it, or by allowing it against His will. Rather, man fell away from God, "not without the will of God, yet without all approbation of it."[67] In other words, God had a good purpose for the fall, although He did not see the fall as good.

God's decree did not cause Adam's sin. The decree of God "planted nothing in Adam, whereby he should fall into sin, but left him to his own liberty, not hindering his fall when it might."[68] If it is objected that man cannot have liberty not to sin if God decreed the fall, Perkins distinguished the necessity of infallibility and the necessity of compulsion. As a consequence of God's decree, what He decreed will infallibly come to pass. But the voluntary acts of the creature are in no way coerced or compelled by God's secret decree. God works through means as secondary causes. He does not handle men as if they were mindless

---

64. *Works*, 1:106.

65. Twentieth-century theologians also made the accusation that supralapsarian predestination subordinates Christ to the decree, diminishing Him to a mere "carrier of salvation"—that He plays no active role since the decree of predestination is made prior to grace (e.g., J. K. S. Reid, "The Office of Christ in Predestination," *Scottish Journal of Theology* 1 [1948]:5–19, 166–83; James Daane, *The Freedom of God* [Grand Rapids: Eerdmans, 1973], ch. 7).

66. *Works*, 1:15.

67. Breward, ed., *Work of Perkins*, 197–98.

68. *Works*, 2:619.

stones, but moves their wills by working through their understanding.[69] The devil and Adam—not God—are responsible for sin. The proper cause of the fall, according to Perkins, was "the devil attempting our overthrow, and Adam's will, which when it began to be prooved by temptations, did not desire God's assistance, but voluntarily bent itself to fall away."[70]

This raises the question of how God executed His decree that man would fall without God compelling man to sin. Perkins's answer is that God withheld from Adam the grace of perseverance. God gave Adam a righteous human will, a revelation of God's commandment, and the inward ability to will and do what is good. But God did not give Adam the grace to persevere in willing and doing good under temptation. Nor can He be blamed for withholding this grace because God owes no man any grace, and God had good purposes for withholding it.[71] Perkins used the illustration of an unpropped house in a windstorm. As an unsupported house would fall with the blowing of the wind, so man without the help of God falls. Thus, the cause of the fall is not the owner but the wind.[72]

Here then, said Perkins, is the biblical balance. Though the decree of God "doth altogether order every event, partly by inclining and gently bending the will in all things that are good, and partly by forsaking it in things that are evil: yet the will of the creature left unto itself, is carried headlong of [its] own accord, not of necessity in itself, but contingently that way which the decree of God determined from eternity."[73]

Answering Objections: Christ is the Heart of Predestination

As for the charge that supralapsarianism subordinates Christ, Perkins firmly maintains that not election considered absolutely, but election *in Christ* draws the line of separation between the elect and reprobate. Contrary to accusations, Perkins emphasizes Christ-centered predestination. For Perkins, salvation is never focused on a bare decree, but always upon the decreed and decreeing Christ. The election and work of Christ is not commanded by God's decree; rather, it is voluntarily chosen by the Son. Franciscus Gomarus (1563–1641) would state at the Synod of Dort, "Christ in accordance with his divine nature also participated in the work of election," but he may not be called "the

---

69. *Works*, 2:619.

70. *Works*, 2:607.

71. *Works*, 1:160; cf. 1:16; 2:611.

72. Munson, "William Perkins: Theologian of Transition," 79.

73. *Works*, 2:621.

foundation" of election.[74] Perkins went even further; he showed no qualms stating that Christ is the foundation, means, and end of election:

> Election is God's decree whereby of his own free will he hath ordained certain men to salvation, to the praise of the glory of his grace…. There appertain three things to the execution of this decree: first the foundation, secondly the means, thirdly the degrees. The foundation is Christ Jesus, called of his Father from all eternity to perform the office of the Mediator, that in him all those which should be saved might be chosen.
>
> Q. How can Christ be subordinate unto God's election seeing he together with the Father decreed all things?
>
> A. Christ as he is Mediator is not subordinate to the very decree itself of election, but to the execution thereof only.[75]

Elsewhere Perkins wrote of "the actual or real foundation of God's election, and that is Christ: and therefore we are said to be chosen 'in Christ.' He must be considered two ways: as he is God, we are predestinated *of him*, even as we are predestinated of the Father and the holy Ghost. As he is our Mediator, we are predestinated *in him*."[76]

Perkins went on to say that this act of predestination has "no inward impulsive cause over and beside the good pleasure of God: and it is with regard to Christ the Mediator, in whom all are elected to grace and salvation; and to dream of any election out of him, is against all sense: because he is the foundation of election to be executed, in regard of the beginning, the means, and the end."[77]

Perkins wrote, "The ordaining of a Mediator is that, whereby the second person being the Son of God, is appointed from all eternity to be a Mediator between God himself and men. And hence it is that Peter saith, that Christ was foreknown before the foundation of the world. And well saith Augustine, that Christ was predestinated to be our head. For howsoever as he is the substantial word (*logos*) of the Father, or the Son, he doth predestinate with the Father, and the Holy Ghost; yet as he is the Mediator, he is predestinated himself."[78]

With approval, Perkins quoted Cyril of Alexandria (*c.* 376–444), who wrote, "Christ knoweth his sheep, electing and foreseeing them unto everlasting life." He also cited Augustine of Hippo (354–430), who wrote, "Christ by his secret dispensation hath out of an unfaithful people predestinated some to everlasting

---

74. G. C. Berkouwer, *Divine Election*, trans. Hugo Bekker (Grand Rapids: Eerdmans, 1960), 143.
75. Breward, ed., *Work of Perkins,* 197–98.
76. *Works*, 1:282.
77. *Works*, 1:283.
78. *Works,* 2:608.

liberty, quickening them of his free mercy: and damned others in everlasting death, in leaving them by his hidden judgement in their wickedness."[79]

Perkins was more Christ-centered in his predestinarianism than most scholars realize. Breward is correct in saying that Perkins's "definition of theology was a combination of Peter Ramus and John Calvin, and the arrangement of the whole work [*A Golden Chain*], prefaced as it was by a formidable looking diagram, owed a good deal to Ramistic categories of arrangement and Aristotelian logic."[80] But Breward errs in failing to recognize how Perkins centered predestination on Christ. Muller more accurately observes that prior to Perkins's time, no one had so meticulously placed the Mediator in such a central relation to the decree and its execution. The *ordo salutis* originates and is effected in Christ.[81]

A Golden Chain from Sovereign Pleasure to Sovereign Glory
In *A Golden Chain*, Perkins stressed that the will of God in Christ is immovable, not only in its sovereign decree, but also in the execution of that sovereign decree. The title page expresses this conviction by describing *A Golden Chain* as: "The Description of Theology, Containing the order of the causes of Salvation and Damnation, according to God's word."[82] The "Table" shows that Perkins taught that God not only decreed man's destiny but also the means through which the elect might attain eternal life, and without which the reprobate could not be saved. At the top of the chart is the triune God as the source of the decree. At the bottom is God's glory as the goal of the decree. On the left is a line or chain of the steps by which God saves His elect. On the right is a line or chain by which the reprobate descend into damnation for their sins. In the center is a line representing the work of Christ the Mediator in His humiliation and exaltation. Perkins drew lines connecting the work of Christ to every step of the order of salvation to show that all of salvation is in Him.[83]

The Foundation of Decretal Execution: Jesus Christ
Predestination does not affect anyone apart from the work of Jesus Christ. Without Christ, man is totally hopeless. Christ is the foundation of election,

---

79. *Works*, 2:607.

80. Breward, introduction to *Work of Perkins*, 85–86.

81. Muller, "Perkins's *A Golden Chaine*," 76.

82. *Works,* 1:9.

83. See Perkins's chart in *Works*, 1:11. For an exposition of Perkins's chart, see Cornelis Graafland, *Van Calvijn tot Barth: Oorsprong en ontwikkeling van de leer der verkiezing in het Gereformeerd Protestantisme* ('s-Gravenhage: Boekencentrum, 1987), 72–84. Both Beza's chart and Perkins's chart were recently reproduced in Lillback, ed., *The Practical Calvinist*, 580–83. Perkins's chart may also be found in Breward, ed., *Work of Perkins*, 169.

as the center of Perkins's chart shows. He is predestined to be Mediator. He is promised to the elect. He is offered by grace to the elect. And, finally, He is personally applied to their souls in all His benefits, natures, offices, and states.[84]

This Christ-centeredness is what sets Perkins's theological chart apart from Beza's *Tabula*. Perkins's chart is similar to Beza's in showing the following contrasts:

- God's love for His elect versus His hatred for the reprobate
- Effectual calling versus ineffectual calling
- The softening of the heart versus the hardening of the heart
- Faith versus ignorance
- Justification and sanctification versus unrighteousness and pollution
- The glorification of the elect versus the damnation of the reprobate

Kendall errs in stating that "Perkins's contribution to Beza's chart was merely making it more attractive and more understandable."[85] The greatest contrast between Beza's and Perkins's tables is the center of the diagram. The central column of Beza's table is empty between the fall and the Final Judgment. By contrast, the center of Perkins's table is filled with the work of Christ as "mediator of the elect." Christ is thus central to predestination and its outworking in the calling, justification, sanctification, and glorification of the elect.[86]

The Means of Decretal Execution: The Covenants

After introducing Christ as the foundation of election, Perkins explains how predestination is carried out through the covenants. Although his chart does not show this connection, a major part of his discussion falls under covenantal headings.[87] Perkins taught that God established a covenant of works with Adam in Paradise, thus setting a covenantal context for the fall.[88] Similarly He made the covenant of grace as the context for the salvation of the elect. In a dipleuric (two-sided) view of the covenant of grace, the pact between God and man implies mutual, voluntary interaction between God and man. This view is consistent with Perkins's emphasis on apprehending Christ to open the door for the application of His benefits. To this Perkins added a monopleuric

---

84. Cf. *Works,* 2:608.

85. Reid, *John Calvin,* 204–5.

86. Muller, "Perkins's *A Golden Chaine*," 76–77.

87. Shaw, "The Marrow of Practical Divinity," 124. Shaw concludes that "the background of Perkins's covenant of grace was election in Christ as its formal cause and the work of Christ as its material cause."

88. *Works,* 1:32.

(one-sided) view of the covenant as a testament in which sinners are made heirs through God's gracious and unmerited gift of salvation in Christ.

Perkins offered this view of the covenant as a way to relieve the tension between God's sovereignty and man's responsibility. Without the covenant of grace, man cannot fulfill God's demands, whereas with it, man finds his will renewed through the Holy Spirit to the point that he is capable of choosing repentance. In Perkins's diagram, man becomes active in "mortification and vivification" which lead to "repentance and new obedience." According to Richard Muller, for Perkins, conversion is "the point of reconciliation" at which the monopleuric and dipleuric aspects of covenant theology can unite. This "allowed the Christian life" to be "systematized" and "stated as a vast series of cases of conscience." It also allowed "the covenant to be presented in the form of" a voluntary act "by the regenerate in their search for personal assurance." The greatest case of conscience would naturally be whether a man be a child of God or no, that is, "whether a man" is savingly brought into "the covenant of grace and converted."[89]

Consequently, Perkins could say that though faith and repentance are the conditions of the covenant of grace, man is totally incapable of initiating or meriting the covenant relation through any goodness or obedience in himself. Ultimately, the decree of election and the covenant of grace stand upon the good pleasure of God. God chose to be in covenant with man; God initiates the covenant relation; God freely, out of His sovereign will alone, brings man into the covenant of grace by granting him the conditions of faith and repentance. The decreeing, establishing, and maintaining of the covenant are all dependent on the free grace of God. Man does not bind or tame God by the covenant, as Perry Miller implied.[90] Rather, God binds Himself to man in covenant.

For Perkins the covenant of grace from a divine perspective is one-sided and initiated by grace. God's dealings with Abel and Cain, Isaac and Ishmael, and Jacob and Esau are examples of His role as the divine Initiator of the covenant. From them we learn that "when God receives any man into covenant of eternal life, it proceeds not of any dignity in the man whom God calleth, but from his mercy and alone good pleasure.... As for the opinion of them that say, that foreseen faith and good works are the cause that moved God to choose men to salvation, it is frivolous. For faith and good works are the fruits and effects of God's election."[91]

---

89. Muller, "Covenant and Conscience," 310–11.
90. Perry Miller, *Errand in the Wilderness* (Cambridge: Harvard University Press, 1978), 48–98.
91. *Works*, 1:279, 281.

Since God's covenant is made with man, apart from any effort put forth by him, "in this covenant we do not so much offer, or promise any great matter to God, as in a manner only receive." In its fullest manifestation, the covenant is the gospel itself as well as "the instrument, and, as it were, the conduit pipe of the holy Ghost, to fashion and derive faith unto the soul: by which faith, they which believe, do, as with an hand, apprehend Christ's righteousness."[92] Far from being capricious, God's covenant assures man that God can be counted on graciously to fulfill the golden chain of salvation in the hearts of the elect (Rom. 8:29–30). Thus the covenant of grace forms the heart of salvation itself. Perkins wrote, "We are to know God, not as he is in himself, but as he hath revealed himself unto us in the covenant of grace; and therefore we must acknowledge the Father to be our Father, the Son to be our Redeemer, the holy Ghost to be our comforter, and seek to grow in the knowledge and experience of this."[93]

Without abandoning the Calvinist view of God's eternal decrees, Perkins's covenant emphasis helps us to focus on God's relationship with man. By focusing on the covenant, Perkins and other Puritans reduced the inscrutable mystery of God's dealings to laws that are somewhat understandable to us. They saw, though through a glass darkly, the movement of God's secret counsels in the revealed covenants, and His concern for man particularly in the covenant of grace. While retaining Calvin's concern for the glory of God, Perkins offered more emphasis on the conversion of man. As F. Ernest Stoeffler says, "Hand in hand with this reorientation goes his…concern for the practical aspects of Christianity which is typical of all Pietistic Puritanism."[94] This is particularly evident in Perkins's *Golden Chain*, of which the vast majority is devoted to practical concerns rather than theoretical aspects of theology.

The Degrees of Decretal Execution: Calling, Justification, Sanctification, Glorification

According to Perkins, God shows "degrees of love" in carrying out election in Jesus Christ by means of covenant, that is, steps by which He puts into action His eternal love. By "degree" Perkins did not mean that God loves one Christian more than another, but that He works their salvation in various steps from sin to glory.

Effectual calling, the first part of the process, represents the saving grace "whereby a sinner being severed from the world, is entertained into God's family."[95] The first part of effectual calling is a right hearing of the Word by

---

92. *Works*, 1:70.
93. *Works*, 2:258.
94. Stoeffler, *The Rise of Evangelical Pietism*, 55.
95. *Works*, 1:77.

those who were dead in sin; their minds are illuminated by the Spirit with irresistible truth. The preaching of the Word accomplishes two things: "the Law shewing a man his sin and the punishment thereof, which is eternal death" and "the Gospel, shewing salvation by Christ Jesus, to such as believe." Both become so real that "the eyes of the mind are enlightened, the heart and ears opened, that he [the elect sinner] may see, hear, and understand the preaching of the word of God."[96]

The second part of this process is the breaking of the sinner's heart. Under the preaching of the Word, it is "bruised in pieces, that it may be fit to receive God's saving grace offered unto it." To accomplish this, God uses four "principal hammers":

- The knowledge of the law of God,
- The knowledge of sin, both original and actual, and its due punishment,
- Pricking the heart with a sense of the wrath of God, and
- Despairing of human ability to gain eternal life.[97]

The product of effectual calling is saving faith, which Perkins defines as "a miraculous and supernatural faculty of the heart, apprehending Christ Iesus being applied by the operation of the holy Ghost, and receiving him to itself."[98] The act of receiving Christ is not something that man does in his own strength; rather, by Spirit-wrought faith the elect receives the grace that Christ brings, thereby bringing the believer into union with every aspect of Christ's saving work through faith. As Munson says, "Faith then saves the elect, not because it is a perfect virtue, but because it apprehends a perfect object, which is the obedience of Christ. Whether faith is weak or strong does not matter for salvation rests on God's mercy and promises."[99]

According to Perkins, God "accepts the very seeds and rudiments of faith and repentance at the first, though they be but in measure, as a grain of mustard seed."[100] Once a sinner has been effectually called, he is justified. Justification, as the "declaration of God's love," is the process "whereby such as believe, are accounted just before God, through the obedience of Christ Iesus." The foundation of justification is the obedience of Christ, expressed in "his Passion in life and death, and his fulfilling of the Law joined therewith." Christ frees the elect from the twofold debt of fulfilling the law "every moment, from our first beginning, both in regard of purity of nature and purity of action," and of making

---

96. *Works,* 1:78.
97. *Works,* 1:79.
98. *Works,* 1:79.
99. Munson, "William Perkins: Theologian of Transition," 100.
100. *Works,* 1:79–80.

"satisfaction for the breach of the law." Christ is our surety for this debt, and God accepts His obedience for us, "it being full satisfaction." Justification thus consists of "remission of sins, and imputation of Christ's righteousnesse."[101] It is experienced subjectively when a sinner is brought in his conscience before God's judgment seat, pleads guilty, and flees to Christ as his only refuge for acquittal.[102] Justification is clearly a judicial, sovereign act of God's eternal good pleasure.

Justification includes other benefits as well. Outwardly it offers reconciliation, afflictions that serve as chastisements rather than punishments, and eternal life. Inwardly, it offers peace, quietness of conscience, entrance into God's favor, boldness at the throne of grace, an abiding sense of spiritual joy, and intimate awareness of the love of God.[103]

Sanctification, the third part of this process, received more attention from Perkins than any other part. He defined sanctification as that work, "By which a Christian in his mind, in his will and in his affections is freed from the bondage and tyranny of sin and Satan and is little by little enabled through the Spirit of Christ to desire and approve that which is good and walk in it."[104] Sanctification has two parts. "The first is mortification, when the power of sin is continually weakened, consumed, and diminished. The second is vivification, by which inherent righteousness is really put into them and afterward is continually increased."[105] Sanctification includes a changed life, repentance, and new obedience—in short, the entire field of "Christian warfare."[106] All the benefits of salvation that begin with regeneration are tied to a living relationship with Jesus Christ, to whom the believer is bound by the Holy Spirit.[107]

Perkins taught that just as a fire without fuel will soon go out, so God's children will grow cold and fall away unless God warms them with new and daily supplies of His grace.[108] Victor Priebe says, "Sanctification, then, is dependent upon a moment by moment renewal as the believer looks away from himself and his deeds to the person and work of Christ. Mortification and vivification are evidence of that most vital and definitive reality—union with Christ upon

---

101. *Works*, 1:81–82.
102. *Works*, 2:204.
103. *Works*, 1:368.
104. *Works*, 1:370.
105. *Works*, 1:370.
106. *Works*, 1:85.
107. *Works*, 1:83, 370.
108. Thomas F. Merrill, ed., *William Perkins, 1558–1602, English Puritanist—His Pioneer Works on Casuistry: "A Discourse of Conscience" and "the Whole Treatise of Cases of Conscience"* (Nieuwkoop, The Netherlands: B. DeGraaf, 1966), 103.

which all reception of grace depends…. It is unquestionably clear that sanctification is the result of the activity of divine grace in man."[109]

After sanctification comes the final step: glorification. This part of God's love is "the perfect transforming of the saints into the image of the Son of God," Perkins said. Glorification awaits the fulfillment of the Last Judgment, when the elect shall enjoy "blessedness…whereby God himself is all in all to his elect." By sovereign grace the elect will be ushered into perfect glory, a "wonderful excellency" that includes beholding the glory and majesty of God, fully conforming to Christ, and inheriting "the new heavens and the new earth."[110]

The Descent of the Reprobate towards Hell

Perkins's chart reveals that he developed reprobation nearly as carefully and meticulously as he did election. Indeed, the dark chain of reprobation from man's perspective is really a golden chain from God's perspective, for it, too, issues in the glory of God at the last.

Reprobation involves two acts. The first act is God's decision to glorify His justice by leaving certain men to themselves. This act is absolute, based on nothing in man but only the will of God. The second act is God's decision to damn these men to hell. This second act is not absolute, but based on their sins. It is the act of God's righteous hatred against sinners. Therefore, Perkins did not teach that God damns men arbitrarily; no one will go to hell except those who deserve it for their sins.[111]

Perkins saw reprobation as a logical concomitant of election. He wrote, "If there be an eternal decree of God, whereby he chooseth some men, then there must needs be another whereby he doth pass by others and refuse them."[112]

Two differences of emphasis exist between reprobation and election, however. First, God willed the sin and damnation of men but not with the will of approval or action. God's will to elect sinners consisted of His delight in showing grace and His intent to work grace in them. But God's will to reprobate sinners did not include any delight in their sin, nor any intent to work sin in them. Rather, He willed not to prevent their sinning because He delighted in the glorification of His justice.[113] Second, in executing reprobation, God primarily passes over the reprobate by withholding from them His special, supernatural grace of election. Perkins even speaks of God permitting the reprobate to fall into sin. By using infralapsarian language such as "passing over" and "permitting,"

---

109. Priebe, "Covenant Theology of Perkins," 141.
110. *Works,* 1:92, 94.
111. *Works,* 1:105; 2:612.
112. *Works,* 1:287.
113. *Works,* 2:613–14.

Perkins again shows his tendency to move from a supralapsarian view of God's decree to an infralapsarian conception of its execution.[114]

According to Perkins, there are two types of reprobates: those who are not called, and those who are called, but not effectually. Those with no calling proceed from "ignorance and vanity of mind" to "heart hardening" to "a reprobate sense" to "greediness in sin" to "fullness of sin."[115] Those who are called may go as far as "yielding to God's calling"—which may include "a general illumination, penitence, temporary faith, a taste, [and] zeal"—before they "relapse" into sin by means of "the deceit of sin, the hardening of the heart, an evil heart, an unbelieving heart, [and] apostasy." Ultimately, also the ineffectually called are led to "fullness of sin," so that the two streams of reprobates become one prior to death. For the reprobate, all calls remain ineffectual because all fail to bring them to Christ. Taken captive by their own sins, of which the greatest sin is "an unbelieving heart," the reprobate make themselves ripe for divine judgment and damnation.[116]

However, no one should conclude that his present sins and unbelief prove him to be reprobate of God. Rather, he should seek God's grace and place himself under the means of grace, especially the preaching of the Scriptures.

Understanding the covenantal grace in Christ and God's inescapable wrath outside of this grace inevitably prompts questions, such as, "Am I one of God's favored elect? How can I avail myself of the salvation wrought in Christ? How can I be sure that I have true faith? If reprobates can also behave in ways that seem motivated by grace, how can I know whether I am a child of God?"[117] These questions lead to the crucial task of preaching.

Preaching: Bringing in the Elect

No Puritan was more concerned about preaching than William Perkins.[118] Preaching was uniquely honored by God "in that it serveth to collect the church and to accomplish the number of the elect" and also "it driveth away the wolves from the folds of the Lord."[119] In essence, Perkins's goal was to help preachers realize their responsibility as God's instruments to reveal and realize election and the covenant. Biblically balanced preaching was paramount, for the Word preached is the power of God unto salvation, without which there would be no

---

114. *Works*, 2:611–618; Graafland, *Van Calvijn tot Barth*, 80.
115. *Works*, 1:107.
116. See chart on *Works*, 1:11.
117. Chalker, "Calvin and Some Seventeenth Century Calvinists," 91.
118. See his preaching manual, *The Arte of Prophesying*.
119. *Works*, 2:645.

salvation.[120] Perkins taught that preaching is "the mighty arm" by which God "draws his elect into his kingdom and fashions them to all holy obedience."[121] The Word evidences its divine power in that "it converteth men, and, though it be flatly contrary to the reason and affections of men, yet it winneth them unto itself."[122] With such a high view of preaching, Perkins did not hesitate to assert that the sermon was the climax of public worship.

Munson writes, "Perkins' golden chain of the causes of salvation...is linked to the elect through the instrument of preaching."[123] As we observed earlier, the covenant is the means by which God executes His decree.[124] Perkins wrote, "The covenant of grace, is that whereby God freely promising Christ, and his benefits, exacts again of man, that he would by faith receive Christ, and repent of his sins."[125] It promises "that now for all such as repent and believe in Christ Jesus, there is prepared a full remission for all their sins, together with salvation and life everlasting."[126] This gospel must be preached (Rom. 10:14). It is the "allurer of the soul, whereby men's froward minds are mitigated and moved from an ungodly and barbarous life unto Christian faith and repentance."[127] Therefore, Perkins said, "The gospel preached is...that ordinary means to beget faith."[128] So we see that for Perkins the gospel is preached to all men without distinction. It views all men as possibly elect and demands a response. This accounts for the detailed exposition of the way of salvation and for the almost tangential treatment of reprobation in Perkins's work. *A Golden Chain* asks all men to inquire within themselves for signs of election as they encounter the means of grace.

Since the elect are only known to God, Perkins assumed that everyone who listened to a sermon could potentially be gathered into gospel grace. He thus pressed every sinner to accept God's offer of salvation in Christ. The gospel promise must be offered freely to every hearer as a "precious jewel," Perkins said.[129]

---

120. *Works,* 1:83.
121. Quoted in Munson, "William Perkins: Theologian of Transition," 197.
122. *Works*, 2:650.
123. Munson, "William Perkins: Theologian of Transition," 183.
124. *Works*, 1:31.
125. *Works*, 1:70.
126. *Works*, 1:70.
127. *Works*, 2:645.
128. *Works*, 1:71.
129. Breward, ed., *Work of Perkins*, 300.

Plain and powerful preaching of Scripture was not merely the work of a man, but a heavenly intrusion where the Spirit of the electing God speaks.[130] Perkins said, "And every prophet is…the voice of God…in preaching…. Preaching of the word is prophecying in the name and room of Christ, whereby men are called into the state of grace, and conserved in it (2 Cor. 5:19–20)."[131]

Conclusion: Reformed Scholastic Piety

Perkins earned the titles of both "scholastic, high Calvinist" and "father of pietism."[132] His theology affirms divine sovereignty in the predestination decree of the Father, the satisfaction made by Christ for the elect, and the saving work of the Spirit. Yet, Perkins never allows sovereignty to prevent a practical, evangelical emphasis on the individual believer working out his own salvation as hearer of the Word, follower of Christ, and warrior of the conscience. Divine sovereignty, individual piety, and the gospel offer of salvation are always in view.

Perkins's emphasis on sound doctrine and the reform of souls influenced Puritanism for years to come.[133] J. I. Packer writes, "Puritanism, with its complex of biblical, devotional, ecclesiastical, reformational, polemical and cultural concerns, came of age, we might say, with Perkins, and began to display characteristically a wholeness of spiritual vision and a maturity of Christian patience that had not been seen in it before."[134] Contemporary scholars have called Perkins "the principal architect of Elizabethan Puritanism," "the Puritan theologian of Tudor times," "the most important Puritan writer," "the prince of Puritan theologians," "the ideal Puritan clergyman of the quietist years," "the most famous of all Puritan divines," and have classed him with Calvin and Beza as third in "the trinity of the orthodox."[135] He was the first theologian to be more widely published in England than Calvin and the first English Protestant theologian to have a major impact in the British isles, on the continent, and in

---

130. *Works*, 2:670; William Haller, *The Rise of Puritanism* (New York: Columbia University Press, 1938), 130–31.

131. *Works*, 2:646.

132. Heinrich Heppe, *Geschichte des Pietismus und der Mystik in der reformierten Kirche namentlich in der Niederlande* (Leiden: Brill, 1879), 24–26.

133. Richard Muller, "William Perkins and the Protestant Exegetical Tradition: Interpretation, Style, and Method," in William Perkins, *A Commentary on Hebrews 11,* ed. John H. Augustine (New York: Pilgrim Press, 1991), 72.

134. Packer, "An Anglican to Remember," 4.

135. John Eusden, *Puritans, Lawyers, and Politics* (New Haven: Yale University Press, 1958), 11; Knappen, *Tudor Puritanism,* 375; Haller, *Rise of Puritanism,* 91; Collinson, *Elizabethan Puritan Movement,* 125; Paul Seaver, *The Puritan Lectureships: The Politics of Religious Dissent, 1560–1662* (Palo Alto, Calif.: Stanford University Press, 1970), 114; Christopher Hill, *God's Englishman: Oliver Cromwell and the English Revolution* (New York: Harper & Row, 1970), 38; Packer, "An Anglican to Remember," 1.

North America. Little wonder that Puritan scholars marvel that Perkins's rare works remain largely unavailable until now.[136]

Though Reformed theologians continued to debate supralapsarianism versus infralapsarianism, they remained unified in the basic lines of predestinarian doctrine. Richard Sibbes (1577–1635) wrote that regardless of where they fell on the lapsarian question, all his fellow Reformed divines agreed,

> first, that there was an eternal separation of men in God's purpose; secondly, that this first decree of severing man to his ends, is an act of sovereignty over his creature, and altogether independent of anything in the creature as a cause of it, especially in comparative reprobation, as why he rejected Judas and not Peter. Sin foreseen cannot be the cause, because that was common to both, and therefore could be no cause of severing. Thirdly, all agree in this, that damnation is an act of divine justice, which supposeth demerit; and therefore the execution of God's decree is founded on sin, either of nature or life, or both.[137]

One might object, as did Erasmus centuries ago, that predestination should not be preached because it will discourage saints from assurance of their salvation and encourage the wicked to sin. Zanchius replied to such objections with the insights of Luther and Bucer:

- God teaches us predestination in His Word, and we must not be ashamed of His doctrine but proclaim it with reverence and trust in His wisdom.

- This doctrine humbles our pride and magnifies God's grace for it shows us that we can do nothing to save ourselves—God alone saves sinners.

- Faith by nature receives doctrines of God which it cannot see and fully comprehend by human reasoning.

- Election comforts and sustains the saints with God's unchangeable love for them when Satan attacks with doubts and accusations.

- Predestination reveals the infinite glory and sovereignty of the eternal and unchangeable God so that we know Him and worship Him.

- Predestination guards the gospel of salvation *by grace alone.*

- This doctrine brings us a vibrant vision of God's special love for His people in Christ Jesus which is the joy of His people and fuel of their love to Him.

---

136. Louis Wright, "William Perkins: Elizabethan Apostle of 'Practical Divinitie,'" *Huntington Library Quarterly* 3 (1940): 171; Mosse, *The Holy Pretense,* 48.

137. Richard Sibbes, preface to Paul Bayne[s], *An Entire Commentary upon the Whole Epistle of St Paul to the Ephesians* (Edinburgh: James Nichol, 1866), 2.

• Predestination moves God's people to diligent holiness of life.[138]

Perkins's predestinarian theology did not make him cold and heartless when dealing with sinners and saints in need of a Savior. Rather, his warm, biblical theology and scholastic piety set the tone for Puritan "practical divinity" literature that would pour forth from the presses in the seventeenth century. It inspired generations of preachers to call men to turn from sin to a loving Savior, and to follow Him through trials to glory.

—Joel R. Beeke and Greg A. Salazar

---

138. Jerome Zanchius, *The Doctrine of Absolute Predestination* (Perth, Scotland: R. Morison Jr., 1793), 97–107.

A Golden Chain

Or,

The Description of
Theology:

Containing the order of the causes of Salvation and Damnation,
According to God's Word. A view whereof is to be seen in the Table annexed.

Written in Latin by William Perkins, and translated by another

Hereto is adjoined the order which M. Theodore Beza used
in comforting afflicted consciences.

Cambridge
Printed by John Legate,
Printer to the University of Cambridge
And are to be sold at the sign of the Sunne in Paules Churchyard in London

1591

Contents

To the Christian Reader

Christian reader,

There are at this day four several opinions of the order of God's predestination. The first is of the old and new Pelagians, who place the causes of God's predestination in man in that they hold that God did ordain men either to life or death according as He did foresee that they would by their natural free will either reject or receive grace offered. The second of them, who (of some) are termed Lutherans, which teach that God, foreseeing how all mankind being shut up under unbelief would therefore reject grace offered, did hereupon purpose to choose some to salvation of His mere mercy without any respect of their faith or good works and the rest to reject, being moved to do this because He did eternally foresee that they would reject His grace offered them in the gospel. The third, Semi-Pelagian papists, which ascribe God's predestination partly to mercy and partly to men's foreseen preparations and meritorious works. The fourth, of such as teach that the cause of the execution of God's predestination is His mercy in Christ in them which are saved, and in them which perish, the fall and corruption of man—yet so as that the decree and eternal counsel of God concerning them both has not any cause besides His will and pleasure. Of these four opinions, the three former I labor to oppugn[1] as erroneous and to maintain the last as being truth, which will bear weight in the balance of the sanctuary.

A further discourse whereof here I make bold to offer to your godly consideration. In reading whereof, regard not so much the thing itself penned very slenderly as my intent and affection who desire among the rest to cast my mite into the treasury of the Church of England and for want of gold, pearl, and precious stone to bring a ram's skin or two and a little goat's hair to the building of the Lord's tabernacle (Ex. 35:23).

The Father of our Lord Jesus Christ grant that according to the riches of His glory you may be strengthened by His Spirit in the inner man, that Christ may dwell in your heart by faith, to the end that you, being rooted and grounded in love, may be able to comprehend with all saints what is the breadth and length

---

1. *Oppugn*: to oppose a statement or argument. All word definitions are taken from *The Oxford English Dictionary* (Online edn.; Oxford, 2010–2017).

and height thereof, and to know the love of Christ which passes knowledge, that you may be filled with all fullness of God [Eph. 3:16–19]. Amen.

Farewell, July 23, the year of the last patience of saints, 1592.
Yours in Christ Jesus,
William Perkins

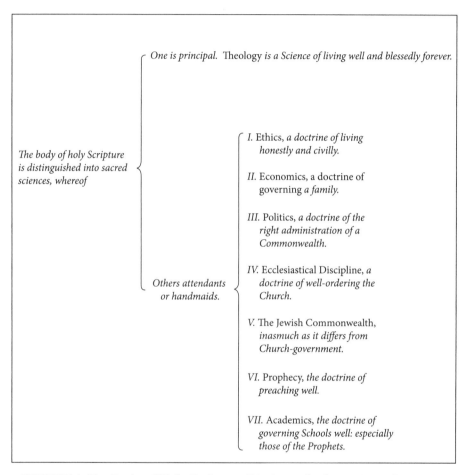

FIGURE 1: The Body of Holy Scripture Distinguished Into Sacred Sciences

Chapter 1

Of the Body of Scripture and Theology

The body of Scripture is a doctrine sufficient to live well.

It comprehends many holy sciences, whereof one is principal; others are handmaids or retainers.

The principal science is theology.

Theology is the science of living blessedly forever. Blessed life arises from the knowledge of God: "This is life eternal, that they know thee to be the only very God, and whom thou hast sent, Christ Jesus" (John 17:3). "By his knowledge shall my righteous servant"—viz., Christ—"justify many" (Isa. 53:11). And therefore it arises likewise from the knowledge of ourselves, because we know God by looking into ourselves.

Theology has two parts: the first, of God; the second, of His works.

Chapter 2

Of God and the Nature of God

That there is a God, it is evident (1) by the course of nature; (2) by the nature of the soul of man; (3) by the distinction of things honest and dishonest; (4) by the terror of conscience; (5) by the regiment of civil societies; (6) the order of all causes having ever recourse to some former beginning; (7) the determination of all things to their several ends; (8) the consent of all men well in their wits.[1]

God is Jehovah Elohim. "And Elohim spake to Moses, and said unto him, I am Jehovah: and I appeared unto Abraham, to Isaac, and to Jacob, by the name of God Almighty, but by my name Jehovah was I not known unto them" (Ex. 6:2–3). "If they say unto me, what is his name? What shall I say unto them? And God answered Moses, I am that I am. Also he said, Thus shalt thou say unto the children of Israel, I am hath sent me unto you. And God spake further to Moses, Thus shalt thou say unto the children of Israel, Jehovah Elohim, etc., hath sent me unto you" (3:13–15). In these words, the first title of God declares His nature; the second, His persons.

The nature of God is His most lively and most perfect essence.

The perfection of the nature of God is the absolute constitution thereof whereby it is wholly complete within itself. "I am that I am" (Ex. 3:14). "God that made the world, and all things that are therein, seeing that he is the Lord of heaven and earth, dwelleth not in temples made with hands, neither is worshiped with men's hands as though He needed anything, seeing he giveth to all life and breath, and all things" (Acts 17:24–25).

The perfection of His nature is either simpleness or the infiniteness thereof.

The simpleness of His nature is that by which He is void of all logical relation in arguments. He has not in Him subject or adjunct. "As the Father hath life in himself, so hath he given to the Son to have life in himself" (John 5:26); conferred with, "I am the way, the truth, and the life" (John 14:6). "But if we walk in his light, as he is light" (1 John 1:7); conferred with verse 5, "God is light, and in him is no darkness." Hence it is manifest that to have life and to be life, to be in light and to be light in God are all one. Neither is God subject to generality

---

or specialty, whole or parts, matter or that which is made of matter. For so there should be in God divers things and one more perfect than another. Therefore, whatever is in God is His essence; and all that He is, He is by essence. The saying of Augustine is fit to prove this: "In God," says he, "to be and to be just or mighty are all one; but in the mind of man, it is not all one to be and to be mighty or just. For the mind may be destitute of these virtues and yet [be] a mind."[2]

Hence it is manifest that the nature of God is immutable and spiritual.

God's immutability of nature is that by which He is void of all composition, division, and change. "With God there is no variableness nor shadow of changing" (James 1:17). "I am the Lord, and am not changed" (Mal. 3:6). Where it is said that God "repenteth," etc. (Gen. 6:6), the meaning is that God changes the action as men do that repent. Therefore, "repentance" signifies not any mutation in God, but in His actions and such things as are made and changed by Him.

God's nature is spiritual in that it is incorporeal and therefore invisible. "God is a spirit" (John 4:24). "The Lord is the Spirit" (2 Cor. 3:17). "To the King eternal, immortal, invisible, only wise God, be glory and honor for ever and ever" (1 Tim. 1:17). "Who is the image of the invisible God" (Col. 1:15).

The infiniteness of God is twofold: His eternity and exceeding greatness.

God's eternity is that by which He is without beginning and ending. "Before the mountains were made, and before thou hadst formed the earth and the round world, even from everlasting to everlasting, thou art our God" (Ps. 90:2). "I am Alpha and Omega, that is, the beginning and ending, saith the Lord: which is, which was, and which is to come" (Rev. 1:8).

God's exceeding greatness is that by which His incomprehensible nature is everywhere present both within and without the world. "Great is the Lord, and worthy to be praised, and his greatness is incomprehensible" (Ps. 145:3). "Is it true indeed that God will dwell on the earth? Behold the heavens, and the heavens of heavens are not able to contain thee: how much less is this house that I have built?" (1 Kings 8:27). "Do not I fill the heaven and earth, saith the Lord?" (Jer. 23:24). Hence it is plain:

First, that He is only one, and that indivisible, not many. "One Lord, one faith, one baptism, one God and Father of all" (Eph. 4:5–6). "Unto thee it was showed, that thou mightest know that the Lord, he is God, and that there is none but he alone" (Deut. 4:35). "We know that an idol is nothing in the world,

---

2. In-text citation: in his sixth book and fourth chapter of the Trinity [Augustine (354–430 A.D.), *On the Trinity*, bk. 6, ch. 4. Augustine was a Christian theologian, philosopher, and the most important of the Church Fathers. In most cases, biographical information of authors cited by Perkins is taken from either F. L. Cross and E. A. Livingstone, eds., *The Oxford Dictionary of the Christian Church* (3rd edition, Oxford, 1997) or *Oxford Dictionary of National Biography* (Online edition; Oxford, 2004–2016).

and that there is none other God but one" (1 Cor. 8:4). And there can be but one thing infinite in nature.

Secondly, that God is the knower of the heart. For nothing is hidden from that nature which is within all things and without all things, which is included in nothing nor excluded from anything, because "the Lord searcheth all hearts, and understandeth every work of the mind" (1 Chron. 28:9); "Thou knowest my sitting down, and my rising up, thou understandest my cogitation afar off" (Ps. 139:1–2).

Chapter 3

Of the Life of God

Hitherto we have spoken of the perfection of God's nature. Now follows the life of God by which the divine nature is in perpetual action, living and moving in itself. "My soul thirsteth for God, even for the living God, when shall I come and appear before the presence of God?" (Ps. 42:2). "See there be not at any time in any of you an evil heart to depart from the living God" (Heb. 3:12).

The divine nature is especially in perpetual operation by three attributes, the which do manifest the operation of God toward His creatures. These are His wisdom, will, and omnipotence.

The wisdom or knowledge of God is that by the which God does not by certain notions abstracted from the things themselves, but by His own essence, nor successively and by discourse of reason, but by one eternal and immutable act of understanding distinctly and perfectly know Himself and all other things though infinite, whether they have being or not. "No man knoweth the Son but the Father, nor the Father but the Son, and he to whom the Son will reveal him" (Matt. 11:27). "There is nothing created, which is not manifest in his sight: but all things are naked and open to his eyes, with whom we have to do" (Heb. 4:13). "His wisdom is infinite" (Ps. 147:5).

God's wisdom has these parts: His foreknowledge and His counsel.

The foreknowledge of God is that by which He most assuredly foresees all things that are to come. "Him have ye taken by the hands of the wicked, being delivered by the determinate counsel and foreknowledge of God, and have crucified and slain" (Acts 2:23). "Those which he knew before, he also predestinated to be made like to the image of his Son" (Rom. 8:29). This is not properly spoken of God, but by reason of men to whom things are past or to come.

The counsel of God is that by the which He does most rightly perceive the best reason of all things that are done. "I have counsel and wisdom, I am understanding, and I have strength" (Prov. 8:14).

The will of God is that by the which He both most freely and justly with one act wills all things. "He hath mercy on whom he will, and whom he will he hardeneth" (Rom. 9:18). "Who hath predestinated us to be adopted through Jesus Christ unto himself, according to the good pleasure of his will" (Eph. 1:5).

"For that which you should say, If the Lord will, and we live, we will do this or that" (James 4:15).

God wills that which is good by approving it; that which is evil, inasmuch as it is evil, by disallowing and forsaking it. And yet He voluntarily does permit evil because it is good that there should be evil. "Who in time past suffered all the Gentiles to walk in their own ways" (Acts 14:16). "So I gave them up to the hardness of their heart, and they have walked in their own counsels" (Ps. 81:12).

The will of God by reason of divers objects has divers names and is either called love and hatred, or grace and justice.

The love of God is that by the which God approves first Himself and then all His creatures as they are good without their desert and in them does take delight. "God is love, and who so remaineth in love, remaineth in God, and God in him" (1 John 4:16). "So God loved the world, that he gave his only begotten Son," etc. (John 3:16). "God setteth out his love toward us, seeing that while we were yet sinners, Christ died for us" (Rom. 5:8).

The hatred of God is that by the which He dislikes and detests His creature offending for his fault. "But many of them the Lord misliked, for they perished in the wilderness" (1 Cor. 10:5). "Thou hatest all the workers of iniquity" (Ps. 5:5). "Thou hast loved justice and hated iniquity" (45:7).

The grace of God is that by which He freely declares His favor to His creatures. "If it be of grace, it is no more of works: otherwise grace is not grace, but if it be of works, it is no more grace" (Rom. 11:6). "The saving grace of God shined to all men, teaching us to deny impiety," etc. (Titus 2:11–12).

The grace of God is either His goodness or His mercy.

The goodness of God is that by which He, being in Himself absolutely good, does freely exercise His liberality upon His creatures. "Why callest thou me good? There is none good but one, even God" (Matt. 19:17). "He maketh the sun to shine upon the good and bad, and he raineth upon the just and unjust" (5:45).

God's mercy is that by which He freely assists all His creatures in their miseries. "Yet will the Lord wait, that he may have mercy upon you" (Isa. 30:18). "It is the Lord's mercy that we are not consumed, because his compassions fail not" (Lam. 3:22). "I take pity on whom I take pity, and am merciful to whom I am merciful" (Ex. 33:19).

God's justice is that by which He in all things wills that which is just. "The just Lord loveth justice" (Ps. 11:7). "For thou art not a God that loveth wickedness" (5:4).

God's justice is in word or deed.

Justice in word is that truth by which He constantly and indeed wills that which He has said. "Let God be true, and every man a liar" (Rom. 3:4). "Heaven and earth shall pass away, but my word shall not pass away" (Matt. 24:35). Hence it is that there is a certain justice of God in keeping His promise. "If we confess our sins, God is faithful and just to forgive our sins" (1 John 1:9). "Henceforth is laid up for me the crown of righteousness, which the Lord the righteous Judge shall give me at that day" (2 Tim. 4:8).

Justice in deed is that by which He either disposes or rewards.

God's disposing justice is that by which He as a most free lord orders rightly all things in His actions. "The Lord is righteous in all his ways" (Ps. 145:17).

God's rewarding justice is that by which He renders to His creature according to his work. "It is justice with God, to render affliction to such as afflict you, but to you which are afflicted, releasing with us" (2 Thess. 1:6). "Therefore, if you call Him Father, which without respect of person judgeth according to every man's work, pass the time of your dwelling here in fear" (1 Peter 1:17). "The Lord that recompenseth shall surely recompense" (Jer. 51:56).

The justice of God is either His gentleness or anger.

God's gentleness is that by which He freely rewards the righteousness of His creature. "Which is a token of the righteous judgment of God, that ye may be counted worthy the kingdom of God, for the which ye also suffer" (2 Thess. 1:5). "He that receiveth a prophet, in the name of a prophet, shall have a prophet's reward: and he that receiveth a righteous man, in the name of a righteous man, shall have the reward of a righteous man. And whosoever shall give unto one of these little ones to drink a cup of cold water only in the name of a disciple, verily I say unto you, he shall not lose his reward" (Matt. 10:41–42).

God's anger is that by which He wills the punishment of the creature offending. "For the wrath of God is revealed from heaven against all ungodliness, and unrighteousness of men, which withhold the truth in unrighteousness" (Rom. 1:18). "He that obeyeth not the Son, shall not see life, but the wrath of God abideth on him" (John 3:36).

Thus much concerning the will of God; now follows His omnipotence.

God's omnipotence is that by which He is most able to perform every work. "With men this is impossible, but with God all things are possible" (Matt. 19:26).

Some things notwithstanding are here to be excepted. First, those things whose action argues an impotency, as to lie, to deny His word. "Which God, that cannot lie, has promised" (Titus 1:2). "He cannot deny himself" (2 Tim. 2:13). Secondly, such things as are contrary to the nature of God, as to destroy Himself and not to beget His Son from eternity. Thirdly, such things as imply contradiction. For God cannot make a truth false, or that which is when it is not to be.

God's power may be distinguished into an absolute and actual power.

God's absolute power is that by which He can do more than He either does or will do. "I say to you, God is able of these stones to raise up children to Abraham" (Matt. 3:9). "According to the working, whereby he is able to subdue even all things to himself" (Phil. 3:21).

God's actual power is that by which He causes all things to be which He freely wills. "All things which God will, those he doth in heaven, and in earth, and in all depths" (Ps. 135:6).

Chapter 4

Of God's Glory and Blessedness

Out of the former attributes by which the true Jehovah is distinguished from a feigned god and from idols arise the glory of God and His blessedness.

God's glory or majesty is the infinite excellency of His most simple and most holy divine nature. "Who being the brightness of his glory, and the engraved form of his person," etc. (Heb. 1:3). "Let them praise thy glorious name, O God, which excellest above all thanksgiving and praise" (Neh. 9:5).

By this we see that God only can know Himself perfectly. "Not that any man hath seen the Father, save he which is of God, he hath seen the Father" (John 6:46). "Who only hath immortality, and dwelleth in the light that none can attain unto, whom never man saw, neither can see" (1 Tim. 6:16). "Thou canst not see my face" (Ex. 33:20).

Notwithstanding, there is a certain manifestation of God's glory—partly more obscure, partly more apparent.

The more obscure manifestation is the vision of God's majesty in this life by the eyes of the mind through the help of things perceived by outward senses. "I saw the Lord sitting upon a high throne, and lifted up, and the lower parts thereof filled the temple" (Isa. 6:1). "And while my glory passeth by, I will put thee in a cleft of the rock, and will cover thee with my hand while I pass by: after I will take away mine hand, and thou shalt see my back parts, but my face shall not be seen" (Ex. 33:22–23). "Now we see as through a glass darkly" (1 Cor. 13:12).

The more apparent manifestation of God is the contemplation of Him in heaven face to face. "But then shall we see face to face" (v. 12). "I beheld till the thrones were set up, and the Ancient of Days did sit, whose garment was white as snow," etc. (Dan. 7:9–10).

God's blessedness is that by which God is in Himself and of Himself all-sufficient. "I am God all-sufficient, walk before me, and be thou upright" (Gen. 17:1). "For in him dwelleth all the fullness of the Godhead bodily" (Col. 2:9). "Which in due time he shall show, that is the blessed and only prince" (1 Tim. 6:15).

Chapter 5

Concerning the Persons of the Godhead

The persons are they which subsisting in one Godhead are distinguished by incommunicable properties. "There are three that bear record in heaven, the Father, the Word, and the Holy Ghost, and these three are one" (1 John 5:7). "Then Jehovah rained upon Sodom and upon Gomorrah, brimstone, and fire from Jehovah in heaven" (Gen. 19:24). "In the beginning was the Word, and the Word was with God, and that Word was God" (John 1:1).

They therefore are coequal and are distinguished not by degree but by order.

The constitution of a person is when as a personal propriety or the proper manner of subsisting is adjoined to the deity or the one divine nature.

Distinction of persons is that by which albeit every person is one and the same perfect God, yet the Father is not the Son or the Holy Ghost, but the Father alone; and the Son is not the Father or the Holy Ghost, but the Son alone; and the Holy Ghost is not the Father or the Son, but the Holy Ghost alone. Neither can they be divided by reason of the infinite greatness of that most simple essence, which one and the same is wholly in the Father, wholly in the Son, and wholly in the Holy Ghost. So that in these there is diversity of persons, but unity in essence.

The communion of the persons, or rather union, is that by which each one is in the rest and with the rest by reason of the unity of the Godhead. And therefore, every each one does possess love and glorify another and work the same thing. "Believest thou not that I am in the Father, and the Father is in me? The word that I speak unto you, I speak not of myself, but the Father that dwelleth in me, he doth the works" (John 14:10). "The Lord hath possessed me in the beginning of his way: I was before the works of old" (Prov. 8:22). And, "Then was I with him as a nourisher, and I was daily his delight, rejoicing always before him" (v. 30). "In the beginning was the Word, and the Word was with God, and that Word was God" (John 1:1). And, "The Son can do nothing of himself, save that he seeth the Father do: for whatsoever things he doth, the same doth the Son also" (5:19).

There be three persons: the Father, the Son, and the Holy Ghost. "And Jesus, when he was baptized, came straight out of the water, and lo, the heavens were opened unto him, and John saw the Spirit of God descending like a dove and lighting upon him: and lo, a voice came from heaven, saying, 'This is my beloved Son, in whom I am well pleased'" (Matt. 3:16–17).

The Father is a person without beginning, from all eternity begetting the Son. "Who being the brightness of the glory, and the engraved form of his person" (Heb. 1:3). "Thou art my Son, this day have I begotten thee" (Ps. 2:7).

In the generation of the Son, these properties must be noted: (1) He that begets and He that is begotten are together and not one before another in time; (2) He that begets does communicate with Him that is begotten not some one part but His whole essence; (3) the Father begot the Son not out of Himself, but within Himself.

The incommunicable property of the Father is to be unbegotten, to be a father, and to beget. He is the beginning of actions because He begins every action of Himself, effecting it by the Son and the Holy Ghost. "Yet unto us, there is but one God, which is the Father, of whom are all things, and we in him, and one Lord Jesus Christ, by whom are all things, and we by him" (1 Cor. 8:6). "For of him, and through him, and for him, are all things" (Rom. 11:36).

The other two persons have the Godhead or the whole divine essence of the Father by communication—namely, the Son and the Holy Ghost.

The Son is the second person, begotten of the Father from all eternity. "For unto which of the angels said he at any time, Thou art my Son, this day begat I thee?" (Heb. 1:5). "Who is the image of the invisible God, the firstborn of every creature" (Col. 1:15). "And we saw the glory thereof, as the glory of the only begotten Son of the Father" (John 1:14). "He who spared not his own Son" (Rom. 8:32).

Although the Son be begotten of His Father, yet nevertheless He is of and by Himself very God. For He must be considered either according to His essence or according to His filiation or sonship. In regard of His essence, He is αυτοθεος—that is, of and by Himself very God. For the deity, which is common to all the three persons, is not begotten. But as He is a person and the Son of the Father, He is not of Himself, but from another. For He is the eternal Son of His Father. And thus He is truly said to be "very God of very God."[1]

For this cause He is said to be sent from the Father. "I proceeded forth and came from God, neither came I of myself, but he sent me" (John 8:42). This sending takes not away the equality of essence and power, but declares the order of the persons. "Therefore the Jews sought the more to kill him, not only because he had broken the Sabbath: but said also that God was his Father, and

---

1. See The Nicene Creed.

made himself equal with God" (5:18). "Who being in the form of God, thought it no robbery to be equal with God" (Phil. 2:6).

For this cause also He is "the Word of the Father," not a vanishing but essential word—because as a word is, as it were, begotten of the mind, so is the Son begotten of the Father; and also because He brings glad tidings from the bosom of His Father.[2]

The property of the Son is to be begotten.

His proper manner of working is to execute actions from the Father by the Holy Ghost. "Our Lord Jesus Christ, by whom are all things, and we by him" (1 Cor. 8:6). "Whatsoever things he doth, the same doth the Son also" (John 5:19).

The Holy Ghost is the third person, proceeding from the Father and the Son. "But when the Comforter shall come, whom I will send unto you from the Father, even the Spirit of truth, which proceedeth of the Father, he shall testify of me" (15:26). "But ye are not in the flesh, but in the spirit, seeing the Spirit of God dwelleth in you. But if there be any that hath not the Spirit of Christ, he is not his" (Rom. 8:9). "But when the Spirit of truth shall come: he shall conduct you into all truth: for he shall not speak of himself, but whatsoever he heareth, he shall speak, and shall declare unto you such things as are to come. He shall glorify me, for he shall receive of mine, and show it to you" (John 16:13–14).

And albeit the Father and the Son are two distinct persons, yet are they both but one beginning of the Holy Ghost.

What may be the essential difference between proceeding and begetting, neither the Scriptures determine nor the church knows.

The incommunicable property of the Holy Ghost is to proceed.

His proper manner of working is to finish an action, effecting it as from the Father and the Son.

---

2. In-text citation: Nazianzus in his oration of the Son [A reference to Gregory of Nazianzus (*c.* 329–390 A.D.), and one of his theological orations]; Basil in his preface before John's Gospel. [Probably a reference to Basil of Caesarea, sometime known as Basil the Great (*c.* 329/330–379 A.D.) and the preface to his commentary on John's Gospel].

Chapter 6

Of God's Works and His Decree

Thus far concerning the first part of theology; the second follows of the works of God.

The works of God are all those which He does out of Himself—that is, out of His divine essence.

These are common to the Trinity, the peculiar manner of working always referred to every person.

The end of all these is the manifestation of the glory of God. "For him are all things, to him be glory forever" (Rom. 11:36).

The work or action of God is either His decree or the execution of His decree.

The decree of God is that by which God in Himself has necessarily and yet freely from all eternity determined all things. "In whom also we are chosen when we were predestinate, according to the purpose of him, which worketh all things after the counsel of his own will" (Eph. 1:11); and verse 4, "As he hath chosen us in him before the foundation of the world." "Are not two sparrows sold for a farthing, and not one of them falleth on the ground without your Father?" (Matt. 10:29). "Has not the potter power on the clay, to make of the same lump one vessel to dishonor, and another to honor?" (Rom. 9:21).

Therefore, the Lord according to His good pleasure has most certainly decreed every thing and action, whether past, present, or to come, together with their circumstances of place, time, means, and end.

Yes, He has most justly decreed the wicked works of the wicked. For if He had nilled them, they should never have been at all. And albeit they of their own nature are and remain wicked, yet in respect of God's decree they are some ways good. For there is not anything absolutely evil. "For it is better (if the will of God be so) that ye suffer for well doing, than for evil doing" (1 Peter 3:17).

The thing which in its own nature is evil in God's eternal counsel is respectively good in that it is some occasion and way to manifest the glory of God in His justice and His mercy.

God's foreknowledge is conjoined with His decree and indeed is in nature before it—yet not in regard of God, but us, because knowledge goes before the will and the effecting of a work. For we do nothing but those things that we have before willed, neither do we will anything which we know not before.

God's foreknowledge in itself is not a cause why things are, but as it is conjoined with His decree. For things do not therefore come to pass because that God did foreknow them; but because He decreed and willed them, therefore they come to pass.

The execution of God's decree is that by which all things in their time are accomplished which were foreknown or decreed, and that even as they were foreknown and decreed.

The same decree of God is the first and principal working cause of all things, which also is in order and time before all other causes. For with God's decree is always His will annexed, by the which He can will that which He has decreed. And it were a sign of impotency to decree anything which He could not will. And with God's will is conjoined an effectual power by which the Lord can bring to pass whatever He has freely decreed.

The first and principal cause, howbeit in itself it be necessary, yet it does not take away freedom of will in election or the nature and property of second causes, but only brings them into a certain order. That is, it directs them to the determinate end, whereupon the effects and events of things are contingent or necessary, as the nature of the second cause is. So Christ according to His Father's decree died necessarily (Acts 17:3), but yet willingly (Matt. 26:53; John 10:18). And if we respect the temperature[1] of Christ's body, He might have prolonged His life. And therefore in this respect [He] may be said to have died contingently.

The execution of God's decree has two branches: His operation and His operative permission.

God's operation is His effectual producing of all good things which either have being or moving or which are done.

God's operative permission is that by which He only permits one and the same work to be done of others as it is evil. But as it is good, He effectually works the same. "You indeed had purposed evil against me, but God decreed that for good that he might, as he hath done this day, preserve his people alive" (Gen. 50:20). And, "God hath sent me before you to preserve your posterity in this land" (45:7). "Woe unto Ashur, the rod of my wrath, and the staff in their hands in mine indignation, I will give him a charge against the people of my wrath to take the spoil, and to take the prey, and to tread them under feet like the mire in the street. But he thinketh not so, neither doth his heart esteem it so: but he imagineth to destroy, and to cut off not a few nations" (Isa. 10:5–7).

---

1. *Temperature*: the state or constitution of a body.

God permits evil by a certain voluntary permission, in that He forsakes the second cause in working evil. And He forsakes His creature either by detracting the grace it had or not bestowing that which it wants. "For this cause God gave them up unto vile affections" (Rom. 1:26). "Instructing them with meekness that are contrary minded, proving if God at any time will give repentance, that they may know the truth. And that they may come to amendment out of the snare of the devil, which are taken of him at his will" (2 Tim. 2:25–26).

Neither must we think God herein unjust, who is indebted to none. "I will have mercy on him to whom I will show mercy" (Rom. 9:15). Yes, it is in God's pleasure to bestow how much grace and upon whom He will. "Is it not lawful for me to do as I will with mine own?" (Matt. 20:15).

That which is evil has some respect of goodness with God. First, in that it is the punishment of sin, and punishment is accounted a moral good in that it is the part of a just judge to punish sin. Secondly, as it is a mere action or act. Thirdly, as it is a chastisement, a trial of one's faith, martyrdom, propitiation for sin, as the death and passion of Christ (Acts 2:23; 4:24). And if we observe these caveats, God is not only a bare permissive agent in an evil work, but a powerful effector of the same—yet so as He neither instills an aberration in the action nor yet supports or intends the same, but that He most freely suffers[2] evil and best disposes of it to His own glory. The like we may see in this similitude: let a man spur forward a lame horse. In that he moves forward, the rider is the cause; but that he halts, he himself is the cause. And again, we see the sunbeams shining through a glass, where the light is from the sun, [while] the color not from the sun but from the glass.

---

2. *Suffers*: allows.

Chapter 7

Of Predestination and Creation

God's decree, inasmuch as it concerns man, is called predestination, which is the decree of God by the which He has ordained all men to a certain and everlasting estate—that is, either to salvation or condemnation, for His own glory. "For God hath not appointed us to wrath, but to obtain salvation by the means of our Lord Jesus Christ" (1 Thess. 5:9). "As it is written, I have loved Jacob, and hated Esau" (Rom. 9:13). And, "What and if God would, to show his wrath, and to make his power known, suffer with long patience the vessels of wrath prepared to destruction: and that he might declare the riches of his glory upon the vessels of mercy, which he hath prepared unto glory?" (v. 22).

The means of accomplishing God's predestination are twofold: the creation and the fall.

The creation is that by which God made all things very good of nothing—that is, of no matter which was before the creation. "In the beginning God created the heaven," etc. (Gen. 1:1, and to the end of the chapter).

God's manner of creating, as also of governing, is such as that by His word alone He without any instruments, means, assistance, or motion produced all sorts of things. For to will anything with God is both to be able and to perform it. "By faith we understand, that the world was ordained by the word of God, so that the things which we see, are not made of things which did appear" (Heb. 11:3). "Let them praise the name of the Lord, for he commanded, and they were created" (Ps. 148:5).

The goodness of the creature is a kind of excellency by which it was void of all defect, whether punishment or fault.

The creation is of the world or inhabitants in the world.

The world is a most beautiful palace, framed out of a deformed substance and fit to be inhabited.

The parts of the world are the heavens and earth.

The heavens are threefold: the first is the air; the second, the sky; the third, an invisible and incorporeal essence, created to be the seat of all the blessed, both men and angels. This third heaven is called "paradise" (2 Cor. 12:4).

The inhabitors of the world are reasonable creatures made according to God's own image. They are either angels or men. "Furthermore, God said, Let us make man in our own image, according to our likeness" (Gen. 1:16). "When the children of God came and stood before the Lord, Satan came also among them" (Job 1:6).

The image of God is the goodness of the reasonable creature, resembling God in holiness. "And put on the new man, which after God is created in righteousness and true holiness" (Eph. 4:24).

Chapter 8

Of Angels

The angels, each of them being created in the beginning, were settled in an upright estate, in whom these things are to be noted. First, their nature. Angels are spiritual and incorporeal essences. "For he in no sort took the angels, but he took the seed of Abraham" (Heb. 2:16). "And of the angels, he saith, He maketh the spirits his messengers, and his ministers a flame of fire" (1:7).

Secondly, their qualities. First, they are wise. "My lord the king is even as an angel of God, in hearing good and bad" (2 Sam. 14:17). (2) They are of great might. "When the Lord Jesus shall show himself from heaven with his mighty angels" (2 Thess. 1:7). "David saw the angel that smote the people" (2 Sam. 24:17). "The same night the angel of the Lord went out and smote in the camp of Ashur, an hundred, fourscore, and five thousand" (2 Kings 19:35). (3) They are swift and of great agility. "Then flew one of the seraphim unto me with a hot coal in his hands" (Isa. 6:6). "The man Gabriel whom I had seen before in a vision came flying and touched me" (Dan. 9:21). This is the reason why the cherubim in the tabernacle were painted with wings.

Thirdly, they are innumerable. "Now Jacob went forth on his journey, and the angels of God met him" (Gen. 32:1). "Thousand thousands ministered to him, and ten thousand thousands stood before him" (Dan. 7:10). "Thinkest thou I cannot pray to my Father, and he will give me more than twelve legions of angels?" (Matt. 26:53). "To the company of innumerable angels" (Heb. 12:22).

Fourthly, they are in the highest heaven, where they ever attend upon God and have society with Him. "In heaven their angels always behold the face of my Father which is in heaven" (Matt. 18:10). "The chariots of God are twenty thousand thousand angels, and the Lord is among them" (Ps. 68:17). "But are as angels in heaven" (Mark 12:25).

Fifthly, their degree. That there are degrees of angels, it is most plain. "By him were all things created, which are in heaven, and in earth, things visible and invisible: whether they be thrones, or dominions, or principalities, or powers" (Col. 1:16). "Neither angels, nor principalities, nor powers," etc. (Rom. 8:38). "The Lord shall descend with the voice of the archangel, and with the trumpet of God" (1 Thess. 4:16). But it is not for us to search who or how many be of each order; neither ought we curiously to inquire how they are distinguished, whether in essence, gifts, or offices. "Let no man at his pleasure bear rule over you by humbleness of mind, and worshiping of angels, advancing himself in those things which he never saw" (Col. 2:18).

Sixthly, their office. Their office is partly to magnify God and partly to perform His commandments. "Praise the Lord, ye his angels that excel in strength, that do his commandment in obeying the voice of his word. Praise the Lord, all ye his hosts, ye his servants that do his pleasure" (Ps. 103:20–21).

Seventhly, the establishing of some angels in that integrity in which they were created.

Chapter 9

Of Man and the Estate of Innocency

Man, after he was created of God, was set in an excellent estate of innocency. In this estate, seven things are chiefly to be regarded.

(1) The place. The Garden of Eden, that most pleasant garden. "Then the Lord took the man and put him into the Garden of Eden" (Gen. 2:15).

(2) The integrity of man's nature, which was "created in righteousness and true holiness" (Eph. 4:24). This integrity has two parts.

The first is wisdom, which is a true and perfect knowledge of God and of His will, inasmuch as it is to be performed of man. Yes, and of the counsel of God in all His creatures. "And have put on the new man, which is renewed in knowledge, after the image of him that created him" (Col. 3:10). "When the Lord God had formed on the earth every beast of the field, and every fowl of the heaven, he brought them unto the man, to see how he would call them: for howsoever the man called the living creature, so was the name thereof" (Gen. 2:19).

The second is justice, which is a conformity of the will, affections, and powers of the body to do the will of God.

(3) Man's dignity, consisting of four parts. First, his communion with God by which, as God rejoiced in His own image, so likewise man did fervently love God. This is apparent by God's familiar conference with Adam. "And God said, Behold, I have given unto you every herb bearing seed, etc., that shall be to you for meat" (1:29). Secondly, his dominion over all the creatures of the earth. "Thou hast made him lord over the works of thine hands, and hast set all things under his feet," etc. (2:19; Ps. 8:6). Thirdly, the decency and dignity of the body, in which, though naked, as nothing was unseemly, so was there in it imprinted a princely majesty. "Thou hast made him little lower than God, and crowned him with glory and worship" (Psalm 8). "They were both naked, and neither ashamed" (Gen. 2:25). "Upon those members of the body, which we think most unhonest, put we more honesty on: and our uncomely parts have more comeliness on" (1 Cor. 12:23). Fourthly, labor of the body without pain or grief. "Because thou hast obeyed the voice of thy wife, etc., cursed is the earth for thy sake, in sorrow shalt thou eat of it all the days of thy life," etc. (Gen. 3:17, 19).

(4) Subjection to God, whereby man was bound to perform obedience to the commandments of God, which are two. The one was concerning the two trees; the other, the observation of the Sabbath.

God's commandment concerning the trees was ordained to be a proof and trial of man's obedience. It consists of two parts. The first is the giving of the Tree of Life, that as a sign it might confirm to man his perpetual abode in the Garden of Eden, if still he persisted in his obedience. "To him that overcometh, will I give to eat of the tree of life, which is in the midst of the paradise of God" (Rev. 2:7). "She is a tree of life to them which lay hold on her: and blessed is he that retaineth her" (Prov. 3:18).

The second is the prohibition to eat of the Tree of the Knowledge of Good and Evil, together with a commination[1] of temporal and eternal death, if he transgressed this commandment. "Of the tree of the knowledge of good and evil, thou shalt not eat of it: for in the day that thou eatest thereof, thou shalt die the death" (Gen. 2:17). This was a sign of death and had his name of the event because the observation thereof would have brought perpetual happiness, as the violation gave experience of evil—that is, of all misery, namely of punishment and of guiltiness of sin.

God's commandment concerning the observation of the Sabbath is that by which God ordained the sanctification of the Sabbath. "God blessed the seventh day, and sanctified it" (v. 3).

(5) His calling, which is the service of God, in the observation of His commandments and the dressing of the Garden of Eden. "God made all things for himself" (Prov. 16:4). "He placed him in the Garden of Eden, to dress and keep it" (Gen. 2:15).

(6) His diet was the herbs of the earth and fruit of every tree except the Tree of the Knowledge of Good and Evil. "And God said, behold, I have given unto you every herb bearing seed, which is upon all the earth, and every tree, wherein is the fruit of a tree bearing seed, that shall be to you for meat" (1:29). And, "But of the tree of knowledge of good and evil, thou shalt not eat" (2:17).

(7) His free choice both to will and perform the commandment concerning the two trees and also to neglect and violate the same, whereby we see that our first parents were indeed created perfect, but mutable. For so it pleased God to prepare a way to the execution of His decree.

---

1. *Commination*: threat of divine punishment.

Chapter 10

Of Sin and the Fall of Angels

The fall is a revolting of the reasonable creature from obedience to sin.

Sin is the corruption or rather deprivation of the first integrity. More plainly, it is a falling or turning from God, binding the offender by the course of God's justice to undergo the punishment.

Here a doubt may be moved, whether sin be a thing existing or not. The answer is this: of things which are, some are positive, others privative. Things positive are all substances together with those their properties, powers, inclinations, and affections, which the Lord has created and imprinted in their natures. The thing is called privative which grants or presupposes the absence of some such thing as ought to be in a thing. Such a thing is sin, which properly and of itself is not anything created and existing, but rather the absence of that good which ought to be in the creature. And though it be inherent in things positive as a privation, yet it is always to be distinguished from them.

Sin has two parts: a defect or impotency and disorder.

Impotency is nothing else but the very want or loss of that good which God has engrafted in the nature of His creature.

Disorder is the confusion or disturbance of all the powers and actions of the creature.

The fall was effected on this manner. First, God created His reasonable creatures good indeed, but withal changeable, as we have showed before. For to be unchangeably good is proper to God alone. Secondly, God tried their obedience in those things about which they were conversant. "Thou shalt not hearken to the words of the prophet, or unto that dreamer of dreams: for the Lord your God proveth you, to know whether you love the Lord our God, with all your heart, and with all your soul" (Deut. 13:3). Thirdly, in this trial God does not assist them with new grace to stand, but for just causes forsakes them. Lastly, after God has forsaken them and left them to themselves, they fall quite from God—no otherwise than when a man staying up a staff on the ground, it stands upright; but if he never so little withdraw his hand, it falls of itself.

The fall is of men and angels.

The fall of angels is that by which the understanding pointing out a more excellent estate and of its own according approving thereof, and the will choosing the same as pleasing to it (their nature in the meanwhile remaining fit to make choice either of the contrary or of a divers object), they are the sole authors of their fall from God. "If God spared not the angels which sinned, but cast them down into hell, and delivered them into chains of darkness, to be kept to damnation," etc. (2 Peter 2:4). "The angels which kept not their first estate, but left their own habitation, he hath reserved in everlasting chains" (Jude 6). "He was a murderer from the beginning, and continued not in the truth: for there is no truth in him" (John 8:44).

In the fall of angels, consider first their corruption arising from the fall, which is the deprivation of their nature and is either that fearful malice and hatred by which they set themselves against God, or their insatiable desire to destroy mankind. To the effecting whereof, they neglect neither force nor fraud. "He that commiteth sin is of the devil, because the devil sinned from the beginning. For this cause was the Son of God revealed, to dissolve the works of the devil" (1 John 3:8). "Your adversary the devil goeth about like a roaring lion, seeking whom he may devour" (1 Peter 5:8). "You strive not against flesh and blood but against principalities and powers, and worldly governors; the princes of darkness of this world, against spiritual wickedness, which are in supercelestial things" (Eph. 6:12).

(2) Their degree and diversity. For of these angels, one is chief, and the rest attendants. The chief is Beelzebub, prince of the rest of the devils and the world, far above them all in malice. "Away from me ye cursed, into everlasting fire, prepared for the devil and his angels" (Matt. 25:41). "Whose minds the god of this world has blinded" (2 Cor. 4:4). "And there was war in heaven, Michael, and his angels, fought with the dragon, and the dragon and his angels fought" (Rev. 12:7).

Ministering angels are such as wait upon the devil in accomplishing his wickedness.

(3) Their punishment. God after their fall gave them over to perpetual torments, without any hope of pardon. "God spared not the angels that had sinned, but cast them down into hell, and delivered them into chains of darkness, to be kept unto damnation" (Jude 6; 2 Peter 2:4). This He did, first, to admonish men what great punishment they deserved; secondly, to show that grievous sins must more grievously be punished.

The fall of angels was the more grievous because both their nature was more able to resist and the devil was the first founder of sin.

Their punishment is easier or more grievous.

Their easier punishment is double. The first is their delection[1] from heaven. "God cast the angels that sinned into hell" (2 Peter 2:4). The second is the abridging and limitation of their power. "The Lord said unto Satan, Behold, all that he has is in thine hand, only upon him lay not thine hand" (Job 1:12).

The more grievous pain is that torment in the deep, which is endless and infinite in time and measure. "And they besought him that he would not command them to go down into the deep" (Luke 8:31).

––––––––––––

1. *Delection:* meaning uncertain, probably to cast out or away.

Chapter 11

Of Man's Fall and Disobedience

Adam's fall was his willing revolting to disobedience by eating the forbidden fruit. In Adam's fall, we may note the manner, greatness, and fruit of it.

(1) The manner of Adam's fall was on this sort. First, the devil, having immediately before fallen himself, insinuates to our first parents that both the punishment for eating the forbidden fruit was uncertain, and that God was not true in His word to them. Secondly, by this legerdemain,[1] he blinded the eyes of their understanding. Thirdly, being thus blinded, they began to distrust God and to doubt of God's favor. Fourthly, they thus doubting are moved to behold the forbidden fruit. Fifthly, they no sooner see the beauty thereof but they desire it. Sixthly, that they may satisfy their desire, they eat of the fruit which by the hands of the woman was taken from the tree, by which act they become utterly disloyal to God (Gen. 3:1–8).

Thus, without constraint they willingly fall from their integrity, God upon just causes leaving them to themselves and freely suffering them to fall. For we must not think that man's fall was either by chance or God not knowing of it or barely winking at it or by His bare permission or against His will—but rather miraculously, not without the will of God, and yet without all approbation of it.

(2) The greatness of this transgression must be esteemed not by the external object or the baseness of an apple, but by the offence it contains against God's majesty. This offence appears by many trespasses committed in that action. The (1) is doubting of God's word. (2) Want of faith, for they believe not God's threatening: "In that day ye eat thereof you shall die the death." But being bewitched with the devil's promise, "ye shall be like gods," they cease to fear God's punishment and are inflamed with a desire of greater dignity. (3) Their curiosity in forsaking God's word and seeking other wisdom. (4) Their pride in seeking to magnify themselves and to become like God. (5) Contempt of God in transgressing His commandments against their own conscience. (6) In that they prefer the devil before God. (7) Ingratitude, that inasmuch as in them lies

---

1. *Legerdemain:* an act of skillful deception, sleight-of-hand, or trickery.

they expel God's Spirit dwelling in them and despise that everlasting, blessed union. (8) They murder both themselves and their progeny.

(3) The fruit or effects. Out of this corrupt estate of our first parents arose the estate of infidelity or unbelief whereby God has included all men under sin, that He might manifest His mercy in the salvation of some and His justice in the condemnation of others. "God hath shut up all men in unbelief, that he might have mercy on all" (Rom. 11:32). "The Scripture hath concluded all under sin, that the promise by the faith of Jesus Christ should be given to them that believe" (Gal. 3:22).

In this estate, we must consider sin and the punishment of sin. Sin is threefold.

The first is the participation of Adam's both transgression and guiltiness, whereby in his sin all his posterity sinned. "As by one man sin entered into the world, and by sin death: so death entered upon all men, in that all men have sinned" (Rom. 5:12). The reason of this is ready. Adam was not then a private man, but represented all mankind; and therefore, look what good he received from God, or evil elsewhere, both were common to others with him. "As in Adam all men die, so in Christ all men rise again" (1 Cor. 15:22).

Again, when Adam offended, his posterity was in his loins, from whom they should by the course of nature issue and therefore take part of the guiltiness with him. "And to say as the thing is, Levi, etc., paid tithes to Melchizedek: for he was yet in the loins of his father Abraham, when Melchizedek met him" (Heb. 7:9–10).

Chapter 12

Of Original Sin

Out of the former transgression arises another—namely, original sin, which is corruption engendered in our first conception whereby every faculty of soul and body is prone and disposed to evil. "I was born in iniquity, and in sin hath my mother conceived me" (Ps. 51:5). "We ourselves were in times past unwise, disobedient, deceived; serving the lusts and divers pleasures, living in maliciousness and envy, hateful, and hating one another" (Gen. 6:5; Titus 3:3). "Let us cast away every thing that presseth down, and the sin that hangeth so fast on" (Heb. 12:1).

By this we see that sin is not a corruption of man's substance, but only of faculties; otherwise neither could men's souls be immortal nor Christ take upon Him man's nature.

All Adam's posterity is equally partaker of this corruption. The reason why it shows not itself equally in all is because some have the spirit of sanctification; some, the spirit only to bridle corruption; some, neither.

The propagation of sin from the parents to the children is either because the soul is infected by the contagion of the body, as a good ointment by a fusty[1] vessel, or because God in the very moment of creation and infusion of souls into infants does utterly forsake them. For as Adam received the image of God both for himself and others, so did he lose it for himself and others.

But whereas the propagation of sin is as a common fire in a town, men are not so much to search how it came as to be careful how to extinguish it.

That we may the better know original sin in the several faculties of man's nature, three circumstances must be considered: (1) how much of God's image we yet retain; (2) how much sin man received from Adam; (3) the increase thereof afterward.

(1) In the mind. The remnant of God's image is certain notions concerning good and evil—as, that there is a God and that the same God punishes transgressions; that there is an everlasting life; that we must reverence our superiors and not harm our neighbors. But even these notions, they are both general and

---

1. *Fusty*: possessing the quality of being stale-smelling, musty; having lost its freshness.

corrupt and have none other use but to bereave man of all excuse before God's judgment seat. "That which may be known concerning God, is manifest in them: for God hath showed it to them. For the invisible things of him, that is, his eternal power and Godhead, are seen by the creation of the world, being considered in his works, to the intent they should be without excuse" (Rom. 1:19–20).

Men's minds received from Adam (1) ignorance—namely, a want or rather a deprivation of knowledge in the things of God, whether they concern His sincere worship or eternal happiness. "The natural man perceiveth not the things of the Spirit of God, for they are foolishness unto him, neither can he know them, because they are spiritually discerned" (1 Cor. 2:14). "The wisdom of the flesh is enmity to God, for it is not subject to the law of God, neither indeed can be" (Rom. 8:7).

(2) Impotency, whereby the mind of itself is unable to understand spiritual things, though they be taught. "Then opened he their understanding, that they might understand the Scripture" (Luke 24:45). "Not that we are sufficient of ourselves, to think anything as of our selves: but our sufficiency is of God" (2 Cor. 3:5).

(3) Vanity, in that the mind thinks falsehood truth, and truth falsehood. "Walk no more as other Gentiles, in the vanity of your understanding" (Eph. 4:17). "It pleased God by the foolishness of preaching, to save those which believe. We preach Christ crucified, to the Jews a stumbling block, but to the Grecians foolishness" (1 Cor. 1:21, 23). "There is a way which seemeth good in the eyes of men, but the end thereof is death" (Prov. 14:12).

(4) A natural inclination only to conceive and devise the thing which is evil. "The Lord saw that the wickedness of men was great upon earth, and all the imaginations of the thoughts of the heart were only evil continually" (Gen. 6:5). "They are wise to do evil, but to do well they have no knowledge" (Jer. 4:22).

Hence it is apparent that the original and, as I may say, the matter of all heresies is naturally engrafted in man's nature. This is worthy the observation of students in divinity.

The increase of sin in the understanding is (1) a reprobate sense, when God withdraws the light of nature. "He hath blinded their eyes, and hardened their hearts, lest they should see with their eyes, and understand with their hearts, and I should heal them, and they be converted" (John 12:40). "As they regarded not to know God, so God delivered them up unto a reprobate mind, to do those things which are not convenient" (Rom. 1:28). (2) The spirit of slumber. "God hath given them the spirit of slumber," etc. (11:8). (3) A spiritual drunkenness. "They are drunken, but not with wine, they stagger, but not with strong drink" (Isa. 29:9). (4) Strong illusions. "God shall send them strong illusions, and they shall believe lies" (2 Thess. 2:11).

The remnant of God's image in the conscience is an observing and watchful power, like the eye of a keeper, reserved in man partly to reprove, partly to repress the unbridled course of his affections. "Which show the effect of the law written in their hearts, their conscience also bearing witness, and their thoughts accusing one another or excusing" (Rom. 2:15).

That which the conscience has received of Adam is the impureness thereof. "To them, that are defiled and unbelieving nothing is pure, but even their minds and consciences are defiled" (Titus 1:15). This impurity has three effects. The first is to excuse sin, as, if a man serve God outwardly, he will excuse and cloak his inward impiety. "Thou knowest the commandments, Thou shalt not, etc., Then he answered, and said, Master, all these things have I observed from my youth" (Mark 10:19–20). Again, it excuses intents not warranted in God's word. "When they came to the threshing floor of Chidon, Uzza put forth his hand to hold the ark, for the oxen did shake it" (1 Chron. 13:9).

The second is to accuse and terrify for doing good. This we may see in superstitious idolaters, who are grieved when they omit to perform counterfeit and idolatrous worship to their gods. "Touch not, taste not, handle not, which all perish with using, and are after the commandments and doctrines of men" (Col. 2:21–22). "And their fear toward me was taught them by the precepts of men" (Isa. 29:13).

The third is to accuse and terrify for sin. "When Joseph's brethren saw that their father was dead, they said, It may be that Joseph will hate us, and will pay us again all the evil which we did unto him" (Gen. 50:15). "And when they heard it, being accused by their own consciences, they went out one by one" (John 8:9). "If our heart condemn us, God is greater than our heart" (1 John 3:20). Though the conscience shall accuse a man truly, yet that will not argue any holiness in it, which appears in that Adam in his innocency had a good, yet no accusing conscience.

Impureness increased in the conscience is first such a senseless numbness as that it can hardly accuse a man of sin. "Who being past feeling, have given themselves to wantonness, to work all uncleanness, even with greediness" (Eph. 4:19). "Having their consciences burned with a hot iron" (1 Tim. 4:2). This senselessness springs from a custom in sinning. "Then in the morning when the wine was gone out of Nabal, his wife told him those words, and his heart died within him, and he was like a stone" (1 Sam. 25:37).

(2) Some grievous horror and terror of the conscience. "Behold thou hast cast me this day from the earth, and from thy face I shall be hid" (Gen. 4:14); and verse 13, "My punishment is greater than I can bear." The symptoms of this disease are blasphemies, trembling of body, fearful dreams. "And as he disputed of righteousness, and temperance, and the judgment to come, Felix trembled,"

etc. (Acts 24:25). "Then the king's countenance was changed, and his thoughts troubled him, so that the joints of his loins were loosed, and his knees smote one against the other" (Dan. 5:6).

In the will, the remnant of God's image is a free choice. First, in every natural action belonging to each living creature, as to nourish, to engender, to move, to perceive. Secondly, in every human action—that is, such as belong to all men. And therefore man has free will in outward actions, whether they concern manners, a family, or the commonwealth, albeit both in the choice and refusal of them it be very weak. "The Gentiles which have not the law, by nature do those things which are of the law" (Rom. 2:14).

The will received (1) an impotency whereby it cannot will or so much as lust after that which is indeed good—that is, which may please and be acceptable to God. "The natural man perceiveth not the things of the Spirit of God, for they are foolishness unto him; neither can he know them, because they are spiritually discerned" (1 Cor. 2:14). "Christ, when we were yet of no strength, at his time died for the ungodly" (Rom. 5:6). "It is God which worketh in you both the will and the deed, even of his good pleasure" (Phil. 2:13; 2 Tim. 2:26).

(2) An inward rebellion, whereby it utterly abhors that which is good, desiring and willing that alone which is evil.

By this it appears that the will is no agent, but a mere patient[2] in the first act of conversion to God, and that by itself it can neither begin that conversion or any other inward and sound obedience due to God's law.

That which the affections receive is a disorder by which they therefore are not well affected because they eschew that which is good and pursue that which is evil. "They that are Christ's, have crucified the flesh with the affections and lusts thereof" (Gal. 5:24). "Therefore God gave them over to filthy lusts" (Rom. 1:26). "The king of Israel said unto Jehoshaphat, Yet is there one of whom thou mayest take counsel, but him I hate," etc. (1 Kings 22:8). And, "Therefore Ahab came home to his house discontented and angry for the word which Nabal spake unto him, and he laid himself on his bed, turning away his face lest he should eat meat" (21:4).

That which the body has received is (1) fitness to begin sin. This does the body in transporting all objects and occasions of sin to the soul. "The woman seeing that the tree was good for meat, and pleasant to the eyes, etc., took of the fruit thereof, and did eat" (Gen. 3:6). (2) A fitness to execute sin, so soon as the heart has begun it. "Neither give your members as weapons of injustice to sin" (Rom. 6:13); and verse 19, "As you have given your members as servants to uncleanness and iniquity, to commit iniquity," etc.

---

2. *Patient:* a passive recipient.

Chapter 13

Of Actual Sin

After original sin in Adam's posterity, actual transgression takes place. It is either inward or outward. Inward is of the mind, will, and affections.

The actual sin of the mind is the evil thought or intent thereof contrary to God's law. Examples of evil thoughts God (the only knower of the heart) has in divers places set down in His Word. (1) That there is no God. "The wicked is so proud, that he seeketh not for God, he thinketh always there is no God" (Ps. 10:4). "The fool saith in his heart, there is no God" (14:1). (2) That there is neither providence nor presence of God in this world. "He saith in his heart, God has forgotten: he hideth away his face and will never see" (10:11); "Wherefore doth the wicked contemn God? He saith in his heart, Thou wilt not regard" (v. 13). (3) It imagines safeguard to itself from all perils. "He saith in his heart, I shall never be moved nor be in danger" (10:6). "She saith in her heart, I sit being a queen, and am no widow, and shall see no mourning" (Rev. 18:7). (4) It esteems itself more excellent than others. "I sit as a queen" (18:7). "The Pharisee standing thus prayed to himself, I thank thee, O God, that I am not as other men, extortioners, unjust, adulterers, nor yet as this publican. I fast twice in the week, and give tithe of all my possessions" (Luke 18:11–12). (5) That the gospel of God's kingdom is mere foolishness. "The natural man perceiveth not the things of the Spirit of God, for they are foolishness unto him" (1 Cor. 2:14). (6) To think uncharitably and maliciously of such as serve God sincerely. "When the Pharisees heard that, they said, He casteth not out devils, but by the prince of devils" (Matt. 12:24). "They said in their hearts, Let us destroy them altogether" (Ps. 74:8). (7) To think the day of death far off. "Ye have said, we have made a covenant with death, and with hell we are at agreement, though a scourge run over us, and pass through, it shall not come at us" (Isa. 28:15). (8) That the pains of hell may be eschewed. In the place before mentioned, they say, "With hell have we made agreement." (9) That God will defer His both particular and last general coming to judgment. "I will say unto my soul, Soul, thou hast much goods laid up for many years" (Luke 12:19); and verse 45, "If that servant say in his heart, My master will defer his coming," etc.

Many carnal men pretend their good meaning. But when God opens their eyes, they shall see these rebellious thoughts rising in their minds as sparkles out of a chimney.

The actual sin of both will and affection is every wicked motion, inclination, and desire. "The flesh lusteth against the Spirit" (Gal. 5:17).

An actual outward sin is that to the committing whereof the members of the body do together with the faculties of the soul concur. Such sins as these are infinite. "Innumerable troubles have compassed me; my sins have taken such hold on me, that I am not able to look up: yea, they are more in number than the hairs of my head" (Ps. 40:12).

Actual sin is of omission or commission. Again, both these are in words or deeds.

In the sin of commission, observe these two points. The degrees in committing a sin and the difference of sins committed.

The degrees are in number four. "Every man is tempted, when he is drawn away by his own concupiscence, and is enticed: then when lust hath conceived, it bringeth forth death" (James 1:14–15).

The first degree is temptation, whereby man is allured to sin. This does Satan by offering to the mind that which is evil. "The devil had now put into the heart of Judas Iscariot, Simon's son, to betray him" (John 13:2). "Peter said to Ananias, Why has Satan filled thine heart that thou shouldest lie?," etc. (Acts 5:3). "And Satan stood up against Israel, and provoked David to number Israel" (1 Chron. 21:1). This is also effected upon occasion of some external object which the senses perceive. "I have made a covenant with mine eyes, why then should I look upon a maid?" (Job 31:1).

Temptation has two parts: abstraction and inescation.[1]

Abstraction is the first cogitation of committing sin, whereby the mind is withdrawn from God's service to the which it should be always ready-prest.[2] "Thou shalt love the Lord thy God, with all thy heart, and all thy soul, with all thy thought" (Matthew 22:37).

Inescation is that whereby an evil thought conceived and for a time retained in the mind by delighting the will and affections does, as it were, lay a bait for them to draw them to consent.

The second degree is conception, which is nothing else but a consent and resolution to commit sin. "He shall travel with wickedness, he has conceived mischief, but he shall bring forth a lie" (Ps. 7:14).

---

1. *Inescation*: the action of attracting with a bait; alluring; an enticement or allurement.
2. *Ready-prest*: to make oneself to be ready to engage in; to hasten.

The third degree is the birth of sin—namely, the committing of sin by the assistance both of the faculties of the soul and the powers of the body.

The fourth degree is perfection, when sin being by custom perfect and as it were ripe, the sinner reaps death—that is, damnation.

This appears in the example of Pharaoh; wherefore, custom in any sin is fearful.

Sin actually committed has five differences.

First, to consent with an offender and not actually to commit sin. "Have no fellowship with the unfruitful works of darkness, but reprove them rather" (Eph. 5:11). This is done three manner of ways.

(1) When a man in judgment somewhat allows the sin of another. "Moses and Aaron gathered the congregation together before the rock, and Moses said to them, Hear now ye rebels: shall we bring you water out of the rock? The Lord spake to Moses and Aaron, because ye believed me not, to sanctify me in the presence of the children of Israel, therefore ye shall not bring the congregation into the land which I have given them" (Num. 20:10, 12).

(2) When the heart approves in affection and consent. Hither may we refer both the ministers and the magistrates concealing and winking at offences. "Eli said, Why do ye such things? for of all this people I hear evil of you. Do no more my sons," etc. (1 Sam. 2:23). Now that Eli will agree with his sons' sins it is manifest: "Thou honorest thy children above me" (v. 29).

(3) In deed, by counsel, presence, enticement. "They do not only do the same, but also favor them that do them" (Rom. 1:32). "She said unto her mother, What shall I ask: and she said, John Baptist's head," etc. (Mark 6:25). "When the blood of thy martyr Steven was shed, I also stood by, and consented to his death, and kept the clothes of them that slew him" (Acts 22:20).

The second difference is to sin ignorantly, as when a man does not expressly and distinctly know whether that which he does be a sin or not, or if he knows it does not acknowledge and mark it. "I was before a blasphemer, and a persecutor, and an oppressor; but I was received to mercy, for I did it ignorantly through unbelief" (1 Tim. 1:13). "If he punished him unadvisedly and not of hatred, or cast upon him any thing without laying of wait, or any stone (whereby he might be slain) and saw him not, or caused it to fall upon him, and he die, and was not his enemy, neither sought him any harm: then the congregation shall judge between the slayer, and the avenger of blood, according to these laws" (Num. 35:22–24). "I know nothing by my self, yet am I not thereby justified" (1 Cor. 4:4). "Cleanse me from my secret sins" (Ps. 19:13).

The third difference is to sin upon knowledge, but yet of infirmity, as when a man, fearing some imminent danger or amazed at the horror of death, does against his knowledge deny that truth which otherwise he would acknowledge and embrace. Such was Peter's fall, arising from the over-much rashness of the mind, mingled with some fear.

Thus men offend when the flesh and inordinate desires so overrule the will and every good endeavor that they provoke man to that which he from his heart detests. "I do not the good thing which I would, but the evil which I would not, that do I" (Rom. 7:19).

The fourth difference is presumptuous sinning upon knowledge. "Keep thy servant from presumptuous sins: let them not reign over me" (Ps. 19:13). Hitherto belongs (1) every sin committed with a high hand that is in some contempt of God. "The person that does presumptuously, etc., shall be cut off from among his people: because he hath despised the word of the Lord, and hath broken his commandment" (Num. 15:30). (2) Presumption of God's mercy in doing evil. "Because sentence against an evil work is not executed speedily, therefore the heart of the children of men is fully set in them to do evil" (Eccl. 8:11). "Despisest thou the riches of his bountifulness, etc., not knowing that the bountifulness of God leadeth thee to repentance" (Rom. 2:4).

The fifth difference is to sin upon knowledge and set malice against God, and to this is the sin against the Holy Ghost referred.

Chapter 14
Of the Common Punishment of Sin

Hitherto we have entreated of sin wherewith all mankind is infected. In the next place succeeds the punishment of sin, which is threefold. (1) The first is in this life, and that divers ways. The first concerns the body, either in the provision with trouble for the things of this life (Gen. 3:17) or a proneness to diseases. "Son, be of good comfort, thy sins be forgiven thee" (Matt 9:2). "Behold, thou art made whole, sin no more, lest a worse thing fall upon thee" (John 5:14). "The Lord shall make the pestilence clean unto thee, until he has consumed thee from the land," etc. (Deut. 28:21–22). Or shame of nakedness (Gen. 3:7). Or in women's pains in childbirth. "Unto the woman be said, I will greatly increase thy sorrows, and conceptions: in sorrow shalt thou bring forth children" (v. 16).

(2) The soul is punished with trembling of conscience, care, trouble, hardness of heart, and madness. "The Lord shall smite thee with madness, and with blindness, and with astonishment of heart" (Deut. 28:28).

(3) The whole man is punished (1) with fearful subjection to the regiment of Satan. "Which freed us from the power of darkness, and translated us into the kingdom of his beloved Son" (Col. 1:13). "He also himself took part with them, that he might destroy through death, him that had power of death, that is the devil" (Heb. 2:14). (2) A separation from the fellowship of God and trembling at His presence. "Having their cogitation darkened, and being strangers from the life of God" (Eph. 4:18). "I heard thy voice in the garden, and was afraid, because I was naked, therefore I hid myself" (Gen. 3:10).

(4) Upon a man's goods, divers calamities and damages. "Thou shalt ever be oppressed with wrong, and be spoiled, and no man shall succor thee" (Deut. 28:29, to the end of the chapter). To this place may be referred distinction of lordships, and of this comes a care to enlarge them and bargaining with all manner of civil servitudes.

(5) The loss of that lordly authority which man had over all creatures; also their vanity, which is not only a weakening but also a corrupting of that excellency of the virtues and powers which God at the first put into them. "The creature is subject to vanity, not of its own will, but by reason of him, which has subdued it under hope," etc. (Rom. 8:20–21).

(6) In a man's name, infamy and ignominy sometimes after his death (Jer. 24:9).

The second is at the last gasp—namely, death or a change like to death. "The wages of sin is death" (Rom. 6:23).

The third is after this life even eternal destruction from God's presence and His exceeding glory. "Who shall be punished with everlasting perdition from the presence of God, and the glory of his power" (2 Thess. 1:9).

Chapter 15

Of Election and of Jesus Christ the Foundation Thereof

Predestination has two parts: election and reprobation. "God hath not appointed us to wrath, but to obtain salvation by the means of our Lord Jesus Christ" (1 Thess. 5:9).

Election is God's decree whereby on His own free will He has ordained certain men to salvation to the praise of the glory of His grace. "He hath chosen us in him, before the foundation of the world, according to the good pleasure of his will, to the praise of the glory of his grace" (Eph. 1:4–6).

This decree is that book of life wherein are written the names of the elect. "Another book was opened, which is the book of life, and the dead were judged of those things, that were written in the books according to their works" (Rev. 20:12). "The foundation of God remaineth sure, and hath this seal, The Lord knoweth who are his" (2 Tim. 2:19).

The execution of this decree is an action by which God, even as He purposed with Himself, works all those things effectually which He decreed for the salvation of the elect. For they whom God elected to this end that they should inherit eternal life were also elected to those subordinate means whereby, as by steps, they might attain this end, and without which it were impossible to obtain it. "Those which he knew before, he also did predestinate to be made like to the image of his Son, that he might be the firstborn among many brethren: moreover, whom he did predestinate, them he called, whom he called, them he justified, and whom he justified, them also he glorified" (Rom. 8:29–30).

There appertain three things to the execution of this decree: first, the foundation; secondly, the means; thirdly, the degrees.

The foundation is Christ Jesus, called of His Father from all eternity to perform the office of the Mediator, that in Him all those which should be saved might be chosen. "Christ took not to himself this honor, to be made the high priest, but he that said unto him, Thou art my Son, this day begat I thee, gave it him," etc. (Heb. 5:5). "Behold my Servant: I have put my Spirit upon him; he shall bring forth judgment to the Gentiles" (Isa. 42:1). "He hath chosen us in him" (Eph. 1:4)—meaning, Christ.

Question. How can Christ be subordinate to God's election, seeing He together with the Father decreed all things?

Answer. Christ, as He is a mediator, is not subordinate to the very decree itself of election, but to the execution thereof only. "Christ was ordained before the foundation of the world" (1 Peter 1:20). "Christ was predestinate that He might be our head."[1]

In Christ, we must especially observe two things: His incarnation and His office.

To the working of His incarnation concur three things: first, both His natures; secondly, their union; thirdly, their distinction.

Christ's first nature is the Godhead inasmuch as it belongs to the Son, whereby He is God. "Who being in the form of God, thought it no robbery to be equal with God" (Phil. 2:6). "In the beginning was the Word, and the Word was with God, and that Word was God" (John 1:1).

It was requisite for the Mediator to be God:

(1) That He might the better sustain that great misery wherewith mankind was overwhelmed—the greatness whereof these four things declare: (1) the grievousness of sin, wherewith God's majesty was infinitely offended; (2) God's infinite anger against this sin; (3) the fearful power of death; (4) the devil's tyranny, who is prince of this world.

(2) That He might make His human nature both of plentiful merit and also of sufficient efficacy for the work of man's redemption.

(3) That He might instill into all the elect eternal life and holiness. "I am the Lord, and there is none besides me a savior; I have declared, and I have saved, and I have showed, when there was no strange god among you; therefore ye are my witnesses, saith the Lord, that I am God" (Isa. 43:12).

I say, the Godhead, as it is the Godhead of the Son, is Christ's divine nature—not as it is the Godhead of the Father or of the Holy Ghost. For it is the office of the Son to have the administration of every outward action of the Trinity from the Father by the Holy Ghost. "And he being by nature the Son of the Father, bestoweth this privilege on those that believe, that they are the sons of God by adoption" (2 Cor. 6:18). "As many as received him, to them he gave power to be the sons of God" (John 1:12).

If either the Father or the Holy Ghost should have been incarnate, the title of Son should have been given to one of them who was not the Son by eternal generation; and so there should be more sons than one.

---

1. In-text citation: Augustine, in his book of the *Predestination of the Saints*, chapter 15 [Augustine, *Predestination of the Saints*, ch. 15].

Christ's other nature is His humanity whereby He, the Mediator, is very man. "One God, and one Mediator between God and man, the man Christ Jesus" (1 Tim. 2:5).

It was necessary that Christ should be man, first, that God might be pacified in that nature wherein He was offended; secondly, that He might undergo punishment due to sin, the which the Godhead could not, being void and free from all passion.

Furthermore, Christ, as He is man, is like to us in all things, sin only excepted. "In all things it became him to be made like unto his brethren" (Heb. 2:17; 2 Cor. 13:4).

Christ therefore is a perfect man, consisting of an essential and true soul and body, whereto are joined such faculties and properties as are essential to both. In His soul is understanding, memory, will, and such like; in His body, length, breadth, and thickness. Yea, it is comprehended in one only place, visible, subject to feeling, neither is there anything wanting in Him which may either adorn or make for the being of man's nature.

Again, Christ in His humanity was subject to the infirmities of man's nature, which are these: (1) to be tempted. "Jesus was carried by the Spirit to the desert, to be tempted of the devil" (Matt. 4:1). (2) To fear. "Who in the days of his flesh, did offer up prayers and supplications with strong crying and tears, unto him that was able to save him from death, and was also heard in that which he feared" (Heb. 5:7). (3) To be angry. "Then he looked round about on them angrily, mourning also for the harness of their hearts, and said unto the man, Stretch forth thine hand" (Mark 3:5). (4) Forgetfulness of His office imposed to Him by reason of the agony astonishing His senses. "He went a little further, and fell on his face, and prayed, saying, O Father, if it be possible, let this cup pass from me: nevertheless, not as I will but as thou wilt" (Matt. 26:39).

We must hold these things concerning Christ's infirmities: (1) they were such qualities as did only affect His human nature and not at all constitute the same, and therefore might be left of Christ. (2) They were such as were common to all men, as to thirst, to be weary, and subject to die, and not personal, as are agues,[2] consumptions, the leprosy, blindness, etc. (3) He was subject to these infirmities not by necessity of His human nature, but by His free will and pleasure, pitying mankind. Therefore, in Him such infirmities were not the punishment of His own sin as they are in us, but rather part of that His humiliation which He did willingly undergo for our sakes.

---

2. *Agues*: a disease accompanied by a high fever, especially when recurring periodically.

Chapter 16

Of the Union of the Two Natures in Christ

Now follows the union of the two natures in Christ, which especially concerns His mediation. For by this union it comes to pass that His humanity did suffer death upon the cross in such sort as He could neither be overcome nor perpetually overwhelmed by it. Three things belong to this uniting of natures.

(1) Conception, by which His human nature was by the wonderful power and operation of God both immediately—that is, without man's help—and miraculously framed of the substance of the Virgin Mary. "The Holy Ghost shall come upon thee, and the power of the Most High shall overshadow thee" (Luke 1:35).

The Holy Ghost cannot be said to be the Father of Christ, because He did minister no matter to the making of the humanity but did only fashion and frame it of the substance of the Virgin Mary.

(2) Sanctification, whereby the same human nature was purified—that is, altogether severed by the power of the Holy Ghost—from the least stain of sin, to the end that it might be holy and He made fit to die for others. "That holy thing which shall be born of thee shall be called the Son of God" (v. 35). "Christ hath once suffered for sins, the just for the unjust" (1 Peter 3:18). "Who did not sin, neither was there guile found in his mouth" (2:22).

(3) Assumption, whereby the Word—that is, the second person in Trinity—took upon Him flesh and the seed of Abraham, namely, that His human nature, to the end that it being destitute of a proper and personal subsistence might in the person of the Word obtain it, subsisting and as it were being supported of the Word forever. "That word was made flesh" (John 1:14). "He took not upon him the nature of angels, but the seed of Abraham" (Heb. 3:16).

In the assumption, we have three things to consider. (1) The difference of the two natures in Christ. For the divine nature, as it is limited to the person of the Son, is perfect and actually subsisting in itself; the human nature, which consists in whole of body and soul, does neither subsist in itself nor by itself. (2) The manner of union. The person of the Son did by assuming the human nature create it, and by creating, assume it, communicating His subsistence to it—the like example of union is nowhere to be found. (3) The product of the union. Whole Christ, God and man, was not made a new person of the two natures, as of parts compounding a new thing, but remained still the same person. Now whereas the ancient fathers termed Christ a compound person, we must understand them not properly, but by proportion. For as the parts are united in the whole, so these two natures do concur together in one person, which is the Son of God.

By this we may see that Christ is one only Son of God, not two; yet in two respects He is the Son of God. As He is the eternal Word, He is by nature the Son of the Father. As He is man, the same Son also, yet not by nature or by adoption, but only by personal union. "This is my beloved Son," etc. (Matt. 3:17; Luke 1:35).

The phrase in Scripture agreeing to this union is the communion of properties, which is a true and real predication, even as it arises of the true and real union of natures, concerning which observe two rules.

(1) Of those things which are spoken or attributed to Christ, some are only understood of His divine nature. As that, "Before Abraham was, I am" (John 8:58). And that, "Who is the image of the invisible God, the firstborn of every creature" (Col. 1:15). Some again agree only to His humanity, as born, suffered, dead, buried, etc. "And Jesus increased in wisdom, and stature, and in favor with God and man" (Luke 2:52). Lastly, other things are understood only of both natures united together, as, "This is my beloved Son, in whom only I am well pleased, hear him" (Matt. 17:5). "He has made subject all things under his feet, and has appointed him over all things to be the head to the church" (Eph. 1:22).

(2) Some things are spoken of Christ as He is God which must be interpreted according to His human nature. "To feed the church of God"—that is, Christ—"which he"—according to His manhood—"has purchased with his own blood" (Acts 20:28). "If they had known this, they would never have crucified the Lord of glory" (1 Cor. 2:8). Contrarily, some things are mentioned of Christ as He is man which only are understood of His divine nature. "No man ascended up to heaven, but he that hath descended from heaven, the Son of Man which is in heaven" (John 3:13). This is spoken of His manhood, whereas we must understand that only His deity came down from heaven. "What if ye should see the Son of Man"—viz., Christ's human nature—"ascend up, where he"—viz., His deity—"was before" (6:62).

Lastly, by reason of this union Christ, as He is man, is exalted above every name. Yea, He is adored and has such a great (though not infinite) measure of gifts as far surpass the gifts of all saints and angels. "And set him at his right hand in heavenly places, far above all principality, and power, and might, and domination, and every name that is named, not in this world only, but in that also that is to come" (Eph. 1:21). "When he bringeth his first begotten Son into the world, he saith, And let all the angels of God worship him" (Heb. 1:6). "In whom all the treasures of wisdom and knowledge are hidden" (Col. 2:3). "Therefore God exalted him on high, and gave him a name above all names, that at the name of Jesus every knee should bow"—namely, worship and be subject to Him—"both of things in heaven, and things in earth, and things under the earth" (Phil. 2:9–10).

Chapter 17
Of the Distinction of Both Natures

The distinction of both natures is that whereby they with their properties and operations remain distinct without composition, mingling, or conversion. "Therefore doth my Father love me, because I lay down my life, that I may take it again. No man taketh it from me, but I lay it down of my self. I have power to lay it down, and have power to take it again" (John 10:17–18). "Now is the Son of Man glorified, and God is glorified in him. If God be glorified in him, God shall also glorify him in himself" (13:31–32). Here we may observe that there is one will in Christ as God; another, as man. "Not as I will, but as thou wilt" (Matt. 26:39). This also approves the sentence of the Chalcedon Creed: "We confess, that one and the same Christ Jesus, both Son, Lord, only begotten, is known and preached to be in two natures without confusion, mutation, distinction, or separation."[1]

Lastly, hereby it is manifest that Christ, when He became that which He was not—namely, man—continued still that which He was (very God).

---

1. The Chalcedonian Creed.

Chapter 18

Of Christ's Nativity and Office

Thus much concerning Christ's incarnation; the clear declaration there was by His nativity.

The nature of Christ is that whereby Mary, a virgin, did after the course of nature and the custom of women bring forth Christ, that Word of the Father and the son of David, so that those are much deceived which are of opinion that Christ after a miraculous manner came into the world, the womb of the Virgin being shut. "Every man child which first openeth the womb, shall be called holy to the Lord" (Luke 2:23), the which place of Scripture is applied to Mary and our Savior Christ. Hence is it that the Virgin Mary is said θεοτοκος, to bring forth God, albeit she is not any way mother of the Godhead. For Christ, as He is God, is without mother, and as man, without father.

It is convenient to be thought that Mary continued a virgin until her dying day, albeit we make not this opinion any article of our belief.[1] (1) Christ, being now to depart the world, committed His mother to the tuition and custody of His disciple John, which it is like He would not have done if she had any children, by whom as custom was she might have been provided for (John 19:26). (2) It is likely that she who was with child by the Holy Ghost would not after know any man. (3) It is agreed of by the church in all ages.

Christ being now born was circumcised the eighth day, that He might fulfill all the righteousness of the law. And being thirty years of age, He was baptized, that He being publicly and solemnly invested into the office of His mediatorship might take upon Him the guilt of our sins. He was both circumcised and baptized that we might learn (1) that the whole efficacy of the sacraments depends alone and wholly upon Him; (2) that He was Mediator of mankind

---

1. In this paragraph, Perkins is saying that he believes that the doctrine of Mary's perpetual virginity is not an essential doctrine of the faith (as it is in Roman Catholicism); nevertheless, he rather surprisingly views this doctrine to be a probability despite the clear references in the gospels to Jesus having siblings and the author of James most likely being his half-brother. Even more surprising, however, is Perkins's assertion that Mary's perpetual virginity is agreed upon "by the church in all ages," when, though that may be true of many in the ancient and medieval church, many of the Reformers and Puritans disagreed with it.

both before and under the law, as also under grace; (3) that He is the knot and bond of both covenants.

His office follows, to the perfect accomplishing whereof He was anointed of His Father—that is, He was sufficiently furnished with both gifts and authority. "Therefore God, even thy God hath anointed thee with the oil of gladness above thy fellows" (Heb. 1:9). "The Spirit of the Lord was upon me, therefore he anointed me" (Isa. 61:1). "God giveth him not the Spirit of measure" (John 3:34).

If any man enforce this as a reason that Christ could not perform the office of a mediator, being not the mean or middle between God and man, but the party offended, and so one of the extremes—we must know that Christ is two ways said to be the middle or mean: (1) between God and all men, for being both God and man, He does participate with both extremes; (2) between God and the faithful only. First, according to His humanity, whereby He received the Spirit without measure. Secondly, according to His divine nature—namely, as He is the Word. Now the Word is middle between the Father and the faithful (1) in regard of order, because the Word was begotten of the Father and by it we have access to the Father. This subordination which is of the Son to the Father is not in the divine essence severally and distinctly considered, but in the relation or manner of having the essence. And those things which are subordinate after this manner cannot be unequal if they have one and the same singular essence. (2) In regard of His office, the which being imposed on Him by His Father, He did willingly undergo and of His own accord.

Christ does exercise this office according to both natures united in one person and according to each nature distinct one from the other. For in reconciling God and man together, the flesh performs some things distinctly, and the Word other things distinctly. Again, some other things are done not by the Word or flesh alone, but by both together.

This office is so appropriate to Christ that neither in whole or in part can it be translated to any other. "This man because he endureth forever, hath an everlasting priesthood, or a priesthood that cannot pass from one man to another" (Heb. 7:24).

Therefore, Christ, as He is God, has under Him emperors, kings, princes to be His vice-regents, who therefore are called gods (Ps. 82:1). But as He is Mediator—that is, a priest, a prophet, and king of the church of God—He has no vice-regent, vicar, or lieutenant who is His kingly, priestly, or prophetical office, in two of these or in one can be in His stead.

Christ's office is threefold: priestly, prophetical, regal (Ps. 110:1–4; Isa. 42:1).

Christ's priesthood is an office of His wherein He performed all those things to God whereby is obtained eternal life. "And being consecrate, was made the author of eternal salvation, unto all them that obey him; and is called of God an high priest forever after the order of Melchisedec" (Heb. 5:9–10). "This man because he endureth forever, hath an everlasting priesthood; wherefore he is able also perfectly to save all them that come unto God by him" (7:24–25).

His priesthood consists of two parts: satisfaction and intercession.

Satisfaction is that whereby Christ is a full propitiation to His Father for the elect. "If there be a messenger with him or an interpreter, one of a thousand, to declare unto man his righteousness, then will he have mercy upon him, and will say, Deliver him that he go not down into the pit, for I have found a reconciliation" (Job 33:23–24). "And are justified freely by his grace, through the redemption that is in Christ Jesus, whom God hath set forth to be a reconciliation through faith in his blood" (Rom. 3:24–25). "He is a propitiation for our sins" (1 John 2:2).

Christ satisfied God's anger for man's offence according to His humanity by performing perfect obedience to the will of God; according to His deity by ministering to the same perfect obedience, especial dignity—to wit, merit before God—and efficacy. "For their sakes sanctify I myself, that they also may be sanctified through the truth" (John 17:19). "To feed the flock of God, which he has purchased with his own blood" (Acts 20:28). "God was in Christ, and reconciled the world to himself, not imputing their sins unto them" (2 Cor. 5:19).

Satisfaction comprehends His passion and fulfilling the law.

His passion is the first part of satisfaction by which He, having undergone the punishment of sin, satisfied God's justice and appeased His anger for the sins of the faithful. His passion was on this manner.

Somewhat before His death (Matt. 26:38; Mark 4:32), partly fear arising from the sense of God's wrath imminent upon Him, partly grief possessing, as it were, each part of Him, so disturbed His sacred mind that inwardly (14:35; John 12:27) for awhile it stroke into Him a strange kind of astonishment or rather oblivion of His duty imposed upon Him, and outwardly made Him pray (Matt. 26:37, 41; John 12:29; Heb. 5:7) to His Father (if He would) to remove that cup from Him, the which He did express with no small cry, many tears, and a bloody sweat (Luke 12:44), trickling from His body to the ground. But when He came again to Himself (Isa. 53:10–11; 1 Cor. 5:7; Heb. 9:5), He freely yielded Himself to His Father to satisfy upon the cross for the transgression of man. After this His agony was overpassed (Matt. 26:47) by Judas's treachery, Christ is apprehended (John 18:13–14) and first He is brought to Annas, after to Caiaphas, where Peter denied Him (v. 29). From Caiaphas, He is led bound to Pilate (Luke 23:7–8). Pilate posts[2] Him over to Herod (Luke 23:15); he transposts Him back again to Pilate (Matt. 27:24, 26), who acknowledges

---

2. *Posts*: sends.

His innocency and yet condemns Him as an offender. This innocent thus condemned (v. 16) is pitifully scourged, crowned with thorns, scoffed, spitted at, spitefully adjudged to the death of the cross (John 19:18) on which His hands and feet are fastened with nails. Here stayed not His passions, but after all these (Gal. 3:13) He became as accursed to God the Father. That is, God poured out upon Him, being thus innocent, such a sea of His wrath as was equivalent to the sins of the whole world. He now being under this curse through the sense and a feeling of this strange terror (Matt. 27:35, 46) complains to His Father that He is forsaken, who notwithstanding encountering then with Satan and his angels did utterly vanquish (Col. 1:14–15) and overcome them. When this was ended, His heart (John 19:34) was pierced with a spear, till the blood gushed out from His sides; and He gave up the ghost (Heb. 9:15–16) and commended His spirit (Luke 23:43, 46) to His Father's protection, the which immediately went into paradise. His body (John 19:33, 42), whereof not one bone was broken, was buried and three days was ignominiously (Acts 1:13) captivated of death.

In this description of Christ's passion, we may note five circumstances especially.

(1) His agony—namely, a vehement anguish arising upon the conflict of two contrary desires in Him. The first was to be obedient to His Father; the second, to avoid the horror of death. "Being in agony, He prayed more earnestly, and His sweat was like drops of blood, trickling down to the ground" (Luke 22:44). "In the days of his flesh did offer up prayers and supplications with strong crying and tears to him, that was able to save him from death, and was also heard in that which he feared" (Heb. 5:7).

(2) His sacrifice, which is an action of Christ's offering Himself to God the Father as a ransom for the sins of the elect. "Now in the end of the world has he appeared once to put away sin, by the sacrifice of himself" (9:26).

In this sacrifice, the oblation was Christ as He was man. "By the which will we are sanctified, even by the offering of Jesus Christ once made" (10:10).

The altar also was Christ as He was God. "We have an altar, whereof they have no authority to eat which serve in the tabernacle" (13:10). "How much more shall the blood of Christ, which through the eternal Spirit offered himself without spot to God, purge your conscience from dead works to serve the living God?" (9:14). Hence it is that Christ is said to sanctify Himself as He is man—"For their sakes, sanctify I myself" (John 17:19)—as the altar, the gift; and the temple, the gold (Matt. 23:17, 19).

Christ is the priest as He is God and man. "Thou art a priest forever after the order of Melchisedec" (Heb. 5:6). "One Mediator between God and man, the man Christ Jesus, who gave himself a ransom for all men, to be a testimony in due time" (1 Tim. 2:5–6).

(3) God the Father's acceptation of that His sacrifice, in which He was well pleased. For had it been that God had not allowed of it, Christ's suffering had been in vain. "This is my beloved Son, in whom I am well pleased" (Matt. 3:17). "Even as Christ loved us, and gave himself for us, to be an offering and a sacrifice of a sweet smelling savor to God" (Eph. 5:2).

(4) Imputation of man's sin to Christ, whereby His Father accounted Him as a transgressor, having translated the burden of man's sins to His shoulders. "He has borne our infirmities, and carried our sorrows: yet we did judge him as plagued and smitten of God, and humbled: but he was wounded for our transgressions, he was broken for our iniquities," etc. (Isa. 53:4–5). "He was counted with the transgressors, and he bare the sins of many" (v. 12). "He has made him to be sin for us, which knew no sin, that we should be made the righteousness of God in him" (2 Cor. 5:21).

(5) His wonderful humiliation, consisting of two parts. (1) In that He made Himself of small or no reputation in respect of His deity. "He made himself of no reputation, and he humbled himself, and became obedient to the death, even the death of the cross" (Phil. 2:7–8).

We may not think that this debasing of Christ came because His divine nature was either wasted or weakened, but because His deity did, as it were, lay aside and conceal His power and majesty for a season. And as Irenaeus says, "The Word rested that the human nature might be crucified and dead."

(2) In that He became execrable, which is, by the law accursed for us. "Cursed is everyone that remaineth not in all things written in the book of the law to do them" (Gal. 3:10).

This accursedness is either inward or outward.

Inward is the sense of God's fearful anger upon the cross. "He it is that treadeth the winepress of the fierceness and wrath of almighty God" (Rev. 19:15). "He is grieved for our transgressions, the chastisement of our peace was upon him and with his stripes we were healed" (Isa. 53:5). This appeared by those drops of blood which issued from Him, by His cryings to His Father upon the cross, and by lending of an angel to comfort Him. Hence was it that He so much feared death, which many martyrs entertained most willingly.

His outward accursedness stands in three degrees. (1) Death upon the cross, which was not imaginary but true, because blood and water issued from His heart. For seeing that water and blood gushed forth together, it is very like the casket or coat which invests the heart, called "pericardium," was pierced (John 19:34).[3]

---

3. In-text citation: As Columbus observes in his *Anatomy*, book 7. [Probably a reference to the Italian professor of anatomy, Realdo Colombo (*c.* 1515–59) and his *De Re Anatomica*].

His death was necessary that He might confirm to us the testament or covenant of grace promised for our sakes. "For this cause he is the mediator of the New Testament, that through death…and they which were called, might receive the promise of eternal inheritance: for where a testament is, there must be the death of him that made the testament," etc. (Heb. 9:15–17).

(2) Burial, to ratify the certainty of His death.

(3) Descending into hell, which we must not understand that He went locally into the place of the damned, but that for the time of His abode in the grave He was under the ignominious dominion of death. "Whom God hath raised up, and loosed the sorrows of death, because it was impossible that he should be holden of it" (Acts 2:24). "In that he ascended, what was it but that he also descended first into the lowest part of the earth?" (Eph. 4:9).

It was necessary that Christ should be captivated of death that He might abolish the sting—that is, the power thereof. "O death where is thy sting? O hell where is thy victory?" (1 Cor. 15:55).

Thus, we have heard of Christ's marvelous passion, whereby He has abolished both the first and second death due to us for our sins, the which (as we may further observe) is a perfect ransom for the sins of all and every one of the elect. "Who gave himself a ransom for all men" (1 Tim. 2:6). For it was more that Christ, the only begotten Son of God, yea, God Himself, for a small while should bear the curse of the law than if the whole world should have suffered eternal punishment.

This also is worthy our meditation, that then a man is well grounded in the doctrine of Christ's passion when his heart ceases to sin and is pricked with the grief of those sins whereby as with spears he pierced the side of the immaculate Lamb of God. "Who so sinneth, neither hath seen him, nor known him" (1 John 3:6). "And they shall look upon him, whom they have pierced, and they shall lament for him, as one lamenteth for his only son, and be sorry for him, as one is sorry for his first born" (Zech. 12:10).

After Christ's passion follows the fulfilling of the law by which He satisfied God's justice in fulfilling the whole law. "God sent his own Son, that the righteousness of the law might be fulfilled by us" (Rom. 8:3–4).

He fulfilled the law partly by the holiness of His human nature and partly by obedience in the works of the law. "The law of the spirit of life, which is in Christ Jesus, hath freed me from the law of sin, and of death" (Rom. 8:2). "It becometh us to fulfill all righteousness," etc. (Matt 3:15; John 17:19).

Now succeeds the second part of Christ's priesthood—namely, intercession, whereby Christ is an advocate and entreater of God the Father for the faithful. "Christ is at the right hand of God, and maketh request for us" (Rom. 8:34). Christ's intercession is directed immediately to God the Father. "If any man sin, we have an advocate with the Father, even Jesus Christ the just" (1 John 2:1). Now as the Father is first of the Trinity in order, so if He be appeased, the Son and the Holy Ghost are appeased also. For there is one and the same agreement and will of all the persons of the Trinity.

Christ makes intercession according to both natures. First, according to His humanity, partly by appearing before His Father in heaven, partly by desiring the salvation of the elect. "Christ is entered into very heaven to appear now in the sight of God for us" (Heb. 9:24). And, "He is able perfectly to save them that come to God by him, seeing he ever liveth to make intercession for them" (7:25). Secondly, according to His deity, partly by applying the merit of His death, partly by making request by His Holy Spirit in the hearts of the elect with sighs unspeakable. "Elect according to the foreknowledge of the Father to the sanctification of the Spirit" (1 Peter 1:2). "The Spirit helpeth our infirmities: for we know not what to pray as we ought, but the Spirit itself maketh request for us with sighs which cannot be expressed" (Rom. 8:26).

We are not therefore to imagine or surmise that Christ prostrates Himself upon His knees before His Father's throne for us. Neither is it necessary, seeing His very presence before His Father has in it the force of a humble petition.

The end of Christ's intercession is that such as are justified by His merits should by this means continue in the state of grace. Now Christ's intercession preserves the elect in covering their continual slips, infirmities, and imperfect actions by an especial and continual application of His merits, that by this means man's person may remain just, and man's works acceptable to God. "He is a reconciliation for our sins, and not for ours only, but for the sins of the whole world" (1 John 2:2). "Yea as lively stones, be made a spiritual house and holy priesthood, to offer up spiritual sacrifices acceptable to God by Jesus Christ" (1 Peter 2:5). "And another angel came and stood before the altar, having a golden censer, and much odors was given to him that he should offer with the prayers of all saints upon the golden altar, which is before the throne, and the smoke of the odors with the prayers of the saints, went up before God out of the angel's hand" (Rev. 8:3–4).

Thus far concerning Christ's priesthood; now follow His prophetical and regal offices.

His prophetical office is that whereby He immediately from His Father reveals His word and all the means of salvation comprised in the same. "The Son, which is in the bosom of his Father, he hath declared to you" (John 1:18). "Those things which I hear of my Father, I speak to the world" (8:26). "I will raise them up a prophet," etc. (Deut. 18:18).

The word was first revealed partly by visions, by dreams, by speech; partly by the instinct and motion of the Holy Ghost. "At sundry times, and in divers manners, God spake in old time to our fathers the prophets: in these last days he hath spoken to us by his Son" (Heb. 1:1). "Prophecy came not in old time by the will of man, but holy men of God spake as they were moved by the Holy Ghost" (2 Peter 1:21).

The like is done ordinarily only by the preaching of the word, where the Holy Ghost does inwardly illuminate the understanding. "Then opened he their understanding that they might understand the Scriptures" (Luke 24:45). "I will give you a mouth and wisdom, where against all your adversaries shall not be able to speak, nor resist" (21:15). "Whose heart the Lord opened that she attended on the things that Paul spake" (Acts 16:14). For this cause, Christ is called the doctor, lawgiver, and counselor of His church. "Be not called doctors, for one is our doctor, Jesus Christ" (Matt. 23:10). "There is one lawgiver which is able to save and to destroy" (James 4:12). "He shall call his name Counselor," etc. (Isa. 9:6). Yea, He is the apostle of our profession (Heb. 3:1), the Angel of the Covenant (Mal. 3:1), and the Mediator of the new covenant (Heb. 9:15). Therefore, the sovereign authority of expounding the Scripture only belongs to Christ. And the church has only the ministry of judgment and interpretation committed to her.

Christ's regal office is that whereby He distributes His gifts and disposes all things for the benefit of the elect. "The Lord said unto my Lord, sit thou on my right hand till I make thine enemies thy footstool" (Psalm 2; 110:1–2).

The execution of Christ's regal office comprehends His exaltation.

Christ's exaltation is that by which He after His lowest humiliation was by little and little exalted to glory, and that in sundry respects according to both His natures.

The exaltation of His divine nature is an apparent declaration of His divine properties in His human nature without the least alteration thereof. "Declared mightily to be the Son of God, touching the spirit of sanctification by the resurrection from the dead" (Rom. 1:4). "God hath made him both Lord and Christ, whom ye have crucified" (Acts 2:36).

The exaltation of His humanity is the putting off from Him His servile condition and all infirmities and the putting on of such habitual gifts, which, albeit they are created and finite, yet they have so great and so marvelous perfection as possibly can befall any creature. The gifts of His mind are wisdom, knowledge, joy, and other unspeakable virtues; of His body, immortality, strength, agility, brightness. "Who shall change our vile body, that it may be fashioned like unto his glorious body" (Phil. 3:21). "He was transfigured before them, and his face did shine as the sun, and his clothes were as white as the light" (Matt. 17:2). "God even thy God hath anointed thee with the oil of gladness above thy fellows" (Heb. 1:9; Eph. 1:20, 22).

Christ's body, although it be thus glorified, yet is it still of a solid substance, compassed about, visible, palpable, and shall perpetually remain in some certain place. "Behold my hands, and my feet, it is even I; touch me, and see; a spirit hath no flesh and bones, as ye see me have" (Luke 24:39).

There be three degrees of Christ's exaltation.

(1) His resurrection, wherein by His divine power He subdued death and raised up Himself to eternal life. "Though he was crucified concerning his infirmity, yet liveth he through the power of God" (2 Cor. 13:4). "He is not here, for he is risen, as he said: Come, see the place where the Lord was laid" (Matt. 28:6).

The end of Christ's resurrection was to show that His sanctification by His passion and death was fully absolute. For one only sin would have detained the Mediator under the dominion of death, though He had fully satisfied for all the rest. "If Christ be not raised, your faith is in vain: ye are yet in your sins" (1 Cor. 15:17). "Who was delivered to death for our sins, and is risen again for our justification" (Rom. 4:25).

(2) His ascension into heaven, which is a true, local, and visible translation of Christ's human nature from earth into the highest heaven of the blessed by the virtue and power of His deity. "When he had spoken these things, while they beheld, he was taken up: for a cloud took him out of their sight: and while they looked steadfastly toward heaven, as he went, behold two men stood by them in white apparel, which also said, Ye men of Galilee, why stand ye gazing into heaven? This Jesus which is taken up from you into heaven, shall come as ye have seen him go into heaven" (Acts 1:9–11). "He ascended far above all the heavens" (Eph. 4:10).

The end of Christ's ascension was that He might prepare a place for the faithful, give them the Holy Ghost, and then enjoy eternal glory. "In my Father's house are many mansions; if it were not so, I would have told you: I go to prepare a place for you" (John 14:2). "If I go not away, the Comforter will not come unto you: but if I depart, I will send him to you" (16:7).

(3) His sitting at the right hand of God the Father, which metaphorically signifies that Christ has in the highest heavens actually all glory, power, and dominion. "By himself he hath purged our sins, and sitteth at the right hand of the majesty in the highest places" (Heb. 1:3). "The Lord said to my Lord, sit thou at my right hand, till I make thine enemies thy footstool" (Ps. 110:1). "He must reign till he hath put all his enemies under his feet" (1 Cor. 15:25). "He being full of the Holy Ghost, looked steadfastly into heaven, and saw the glory of God, and Jesus standing at the right hand of God" (Acts 7:55; Matt. 20:21).

His regal office has two parts. The first is His regiment of the kingdom of heaven, part whereof is in heaven, part upon earth—namely, the congregation of the faithful.

In the government of His church, He exercises two prerogatives royal. The first is to make laws. "There is one lawgiver which is able to save and to destroy" (James 4:12). The second is to ordain His ministers. "He gave some to be apostles, others prophets, others evangelists, some pastors and teachers," etc. (Eph. 4:11). "God hath ordained some in the church; as first, apostles; secondly, prophets; thirdly teachers, then them that do miracles, after that, the gifts of healing, helpers, governors, diversity of tongues" (1 Cor. 12:28).

Christ's government of the church is either by collection of it out of the world or conservation being collected (Psalm 110; Eph. 4:12).

The second part of this regal office is the destruction of the kingdom of darkness. "Who hath delivered us from the kingdom of darkness" (Col. 1:13). "Thou shalt crush them with a scepter of iron, and break them in pieces like a potter's vessel" (Ps. 2:9). "Those mine enemies, that would not that I should reign over them, bring hither, and slay them before me" (Luke 19:27).

The kingdom of darkness is the whole company of Christ's enemies.

The prince of this kingdom and of all the members thereof is the devil. "Ye walked once according to the course of the world, and after the prince that ruleth in the air, even the prince that now worketh in the children of disobedience" (Eph. 2:2). "The god of this world hath blinded the eyes of the infidels" (2 Cor. 4:4). "What concord hath Christ with Belial, or what part has the believer with the infidel?" (6:15).

The members of this kingdom and subjects to Satan are his angels; and unbelievers, among whom the principal members are atheists, who say in their heart there is no God (Ps. 14:1); and magicians, who bargain with the devil to accomplish their desires (1 Sam. 28:7; Ps. 58:5); idolaters, who either adore false gods or the true God in an idol (1 Cor. 10:7, 20). Turks[4] and Jews are of this bunch; so are heretics, who are such as err with pertinacy in the foundation of religion (2 Tim. 2:18); apostates or revolters from faith in Christ Jesus (Heb. 6:6); false christs, who bear men in hand they are true christs (Matt. 24:26). There were many such about the time of our Savior Christ's first coming, as Josephus witnesses.[5] Lastly, that antichrist, who as it is now apparent can be none other but the pope of Rome. "Let no man deceive you by any means, for that day shall not come, except there come a departing first, and that man of sin be disclosed, even the son of perdition, which is an adversary, and exalteth himself against all that is called God, or that is worshiped so that he doth sit as God in the temple of God, showing himself that he is God" (2 Thess. 2:3–4).

---

4. *Turks*: Muslims.

5. In-text citation: Book 20, of *Jewish antiquities*, the 11th, 12, and 14th chapters [Flavius Josephus (37–*c*.100 A.D.), *Jewish antiquities*, bk. 20, chs. 11–14. Josephus was a Jewish historian, whose works serve as important sources for the study of early Christianity].

"And I beheld another beast coming out of the earth, which had two horns like the Lamb, but he spake like the dragon: and he did all that the first beast could do before him, and he caused the earth, and them that dwell therein, to worship the beast, whose deadly wound was healed" (Rev. 13:11–12).

There were then first antichrists at Rome when the bishops thereof would be entitled universal, or bishops over the whole church through the world. But then were they complete, when they together with ecclesiastical censure usurped civil authority.

After that Christ has subdued all His enemies, these two things shall ensue: (1) the surrendering over of His kingdom to God the Father, as concerning the manner of regiment and spiritual policy, consisting in word and Spirit together; (2) the subjection of Christ only in regard of His humanity. The which then is when the Son of God shall most fully manifest His majesty, which before was obscured by the flesh as a veil, so that the same flesh remaining both glorious and united to the Son of God may by infinite degrees appear inferior.

We may not therefore imagine that the subjection of Christ consists in diminishing the glory of the humanity, but in manifesting most fully the majesty of the Word.

Chapter 19

Concerning the Outward Means of Executing the Decree of Election and of the Decalogue

After the foundation of election which has hitherto been delivered, it follows that we should entreat of the outward means of the same.

The means are God's covenant and the seal thereof.

God's covenant is His contract with man concerning the obtaining of life eternal upon a certain condition.

This covenant consists of two parts: God's promise to man; man's promise to God.

God's promise to man is that whereby He binds Himself to man to be his God, if he perform the condition.

Man's promise to God is that whereby he vows his allegiance to his Lord and to perform the condition between them.

Again, there are two kinds of this covenant: the covenant of works and the covenant of grace. "Behold the days come, saith the Lord, that I will make a new covenant with the house of Israel, and with the house of Judah, not according to the covenant I made with their fathers, when I took them by the hand to bring them out of the land of Egypt; the which my covenant they brake, although I was a husband to them, saith the Lord. But this shall be the covenant, that I will make with the house of Israel: after those days, saith the Lord, I will put my law in their inward parts, and write it in their hearts, and will be their God, and they shall be my people" (Jer. 31:31–33).

The covenant of works is God's covenant made with condition of perfect obedience and is expressed in the moral law.

The moral law is that part of God's Word which commands perfect obedience to man as well in his nature as in his actions, and forbids the contrary. "Moses thus describeth the righteousness which is of the law, that the man, which doeth these things, shall live thereby" (Rom. 10:5). "The end of the commandment, is love out of a pure heart, and of a good conscience, and faith unfeigned" (1 Tim. 1:5). "Thou shalt love the Lord thy God, with all thine heart, with all thy soul, and with all thy strength" (Luke 10:27). "We know that the law is spiritual" (Rom. 7:14).

The law has two parts. The edict commanding obedience and the condition binding to obedience. The condition is eternal life to such as fulfill the law, but to transgressors, everlasting death.

The Decalogue or Ten Commandments is an abridgement of the whole law and the covenant of works. "And the Lord said unto Moses, Write thou these words, for after the tenor of these words, I have made a covenant with thee, and with Israel. And he was there with the Lord forty days and forty nights, and did neither eat bread, nor drink water, and he wrote in the tables the words of the covenant, even the Ten Commandments" (Ex. 34:27–8). "Nothing was in the ark, save the two tables of stone, which Moses had put there at Horeb, where the Lord made a covenant with the children of Israel, when he brought them out of the land of Egypt" (1 Kings 8:9). "On these two commandments hangeth the whole law and the prophets" (Matt. 22:40).

The true interpretation of the Decalogue must be according to these rules.

(1) In the negative, the affirmative must be understood; and in the affirmative, the negative.

(2) The negative binds at all times and to all time; and the affirmative binds at all times, but not to all times. And therefore negatives are of more force.

(3) Under one vice expressly forbidden are comprehended all of that kind. Yea, the least cause, occasion, or enticement thereto is forbidden—as, "Whosoever hateth his brother is a manslayer" (1 John 3:15; Matt. 5:21, to the end), evil thoughts are condemned as well as evil actions.

(4) The smallest sins are entitled with the same names that that sin is which is expressly forbidden in that commandment to which they appertain. As in the former places, hatred is named murder, and to look after a woman with a lusting eye is adultery.

(5) We must understand every commandment of the law so as that we annex this condition: unless God command the contrary. For God, being an absolute lord and so above the law, may command that which His law forbids. So He commanded Isaac to be offered, the Egyptians to be spoiled, the brazen serpent to be erected, which was a figure of Christ, etc.

The Decalogue is described in two tables.

The sum of the first table is that we love God with our mind, memory, affections, and all our strength. "This is the first"—to wit, in nature and order—"and great commandment"—namely, in excellency and dignity (Matt. 22:38).

Chapter 20

Of the First Commandment

The first table has four commandments.

The first teaches us to have and choose the true God for our God. The words are these: "I am Jehovah thy God, which brought thee out of the land of Egypt, and out of the house of bondage. Thou shalt have none other gods before my face" [Ex. 20:2].

The Resolution

"I am." If any man rather judge that these words are a preface to all the commandments than a part of the first, I hinder him not. Nevertheless, it is like that they are a persuasion to the keeping of the first commandment; and that they are set before it to make way to it, as being more hard to be received than the rest. And this may appear in that the three commandments next following, which are less than this, have their several reasons.

"Jehovah." This word signifies three things: (1) Him who of Himself and in Himself was from all eternity. "Who is, who was, and who is to come" (Rev. 1:8). (2) Him which gives being to all things when they were not, partly by creating, partly by preserving them. (3) Him which mightily causes that those things which He has promised should both be made and continued (Ex. 6:1; Rom. 4:17).

Here begins the first reason of the first commandment, taken from the name of God. It is thus framed:

He that is Jehovah must alone be your God.

But I am Jehovah.

Therefore, I alone must be your God.

This [major] proposition is wanting; the assumption is in these words, "I am Jehovah"; the conclusion is the commandment.

"Your God." These are the words of the covenant of grace (Jer. 31:33), wherein the Lord covenants with His people concerning remission of sins and eternal life. Yea, these words are as a second reason of the commandments drawn from the equality of that relation which is between God and His people.

If I be your God, you again must be My people and take Me alone for your God.

But I am your God.

Therefore, you must be My people and take Me alone for your God.

"Which brought." The assumption or second part of this reason is confirmed by an argument taken from God's effects, when He delivered His people out of Egypt, as it were, from the servitude of a most tyrannous master. This delivery was not appropriate only to the Israelites but in some sort belongs to the church of God in all ages, in that it was a type of a most surpassing delivery from the fearful kingdom of darkness. "I would not have you ignorant, brethren, that all our fathers were under the cloud, and all passed through the Red Sea, and were all baptized to Moses in the cloud, and in the sea" (1 Cor. 10:1–2). "Who hath delivered us from the power of darkness, and translated us into the kingdom of his dear Son" (Col. 1:13).

"Other gods," or, "strange gods." They are so called not that they by nature are such or can be, but because the corrupt and more-than-devilish heart of carnal man esteems so of them. "Whose god is their belly" (Phil. 3:19). "Whose minds the god of this world hath bewitched" (2 Cor. 4:4).

"Before my face." That is (figuratively), "in my sight or presence," to whom the secret imaginations of the heart are known. And this is the third reason of the first commandment, as if He should say, "If you in My presence reject Me, it is a heinous offence. See therefore you do it not." After the same manner reasons the Lord: "I am God almighty, therefore walk before me, and be thou upright" (Gen. 17:1).

The Affirmative Part: Make Choice of Jehovah to Be Your God

The duties here commanded are these:

(1) To acknowledge God—that is, to know and confess Him to be such a God as He has revealed Himself to be in His Word and creatures. "Increasing in the knowledge of God" (Col. 1:10). "And I will give them a heart to know me, that I am the Lord, and they shall be my people, and I will be their God: for they shall return unto me with their whole heart" (Jer. 24:7). In this knowledge of God must we glory. "Let him that glorieth, glory in this, that he understandeth and knoweth me: for I am the Lord which showeth mercy, judgment and righteousness in the earth" (Jer. 9:24).

(2) A union with God, whereby man is knit in heart with God. "Stick fast unto the Lord your God, as ye have done to this day" (Josh. 23:8). "He exhorted all, that with purpose of heart, they would cleave to the Lord" (Acts 11:23). Man cleaves to God three manners of ways: in affiance, in love, and fear of God.

Affiance is that whereby a man acknowledging the power and mercy of God does steadfastly rest himself in Him against all assaults whatever. "Put your trust in the Lord your God, and ye shall be assured; believe his prophets and ye shall prosper" (2 Chron. 20:20). "God is my light, and my salvation, whom shall I fear? God is the strength of my life, of whom should I be afraid?" (Ps. 27:1). "Though a host be pitched against me, mine heart shall not be afraid: though war be raised against me, I will be secure" (v. 3).

Hence arises patience and alacrity in present perils. "I should have been dumb, and not opened my mouth, because thou didst it" (Ps. 39:9). "The king said, What have I to do with you, ye sons of Zeruiah? If he cursed, because the Lord said, Curse David, what is he that dare say, why doest thou so?" (2 Sam. 16:10). "Be not sad, neither grieved with yourselves, that ye sold me hither: for God did send me before you for your preservation" (Gen. 45:5). "Now then, you sent me not, but God himself" (v. 8). "Fear not, for they that be with us, are more than they that be with them" (2 Kings 6:16).

This affiance engenders hope, which is a patient expectation of God's presence and assistance in all things that are to come. "Commit thy way unto the Lord, and trust in him, and he shall bring it to pass" (Ps. 37:5). "Wait patiently upon the Lord, and hope in him" (v. 7). "Commit thy works unto the Lord, and thy thoughts shall be directed" (Prov. 16:3).

The love of God is that whereby man acknowledging God's goodness and favor toward him does again love Him above all things. "Thou shalt love the Lord thy God with all thine heart, with all thy soul, and with all thy strength" (Deut. 6:5).

The marks of the true love of God are these: (1) to hear willingly His word; (2) to speak often of Him; (3) to think often of Him; (4) to do His will without irksomness;[1] (5) to give body and all for His cause; (6) to desire His presence above all and to bewail His absence; (7) to embrace all such things as appertain to Him; (8) to love and hate that which He loves and hates; (9) in all things to seek to please Him; (10) to draw others to the love of Him; (11) to esteem highly of such gifts and graces as He bestows; (12) to stay ourselves upon His counsels revealed in His Word; [13] lastly, to call upon His name with affiance.

The fear of God is that whereby man acknowledging both God's mercy and justice does as the greatest evil fear to displease God. "With thee is mercy, that thou mayest be feared" (Ps. 130:4). "When I heard it, my belly trembled, my lips shook at the voice: rottenness entered into my bones, and I trembled in myself, that I might rest in the day of trouble, when he cometh up against the people to destroy them" (Hab. 3:16). "Tremble, and sin not" (Ps. 4:4).

---

1. *Irksomness*: the state of being tired, disgusted, or wearied.

Hence arises the godly man's desire to approve himself in all things to his God. "And Enoch walked with God, after that," etc. (Gen. 5:22). "God said to him, I am all-sufficient, walk before me, and be thou perfect" (17:1).

Out of these three former virtues proceeds humility, whereby a man acknowledging God's free bounty and prostrating himself before Him does ascribe to Him all praise and glory. "Let him that glorieth glory in the Lord" (1 Cor. 1:31). "Deck yourselves inwardly with lowliness of mind: for God resisteth the proud, and giveth grace to the humble. Humble yourselves therefore under the mighty hand of God, that he may exalt you in due time" (1 Peter 5:5–6). "And David said, Blessed be thou O Lord God of Israel our Father forever, and thine, O Lord, is greatness and power, and glory, and victory, and praise, for all that is in heaven, and in earth is thine," etc. (1 Chron. 29:10–11). "But who am I, and what is my people, that we should be able to offer willingly on this sort: for all things come of thee, and of thine own hand we have given thee," etc. (v. 14).

The Negative Part: Account not That as God Which Is by Nature no God

In this place are these sins forbidden:

(1) Ignorance of the true God and His will, which is not only not to know but also to doubt of such things as God has revealed in His Word. "My people is foolish, they have not known me: they are foolish children, and have not understanding: they are wise to do evil, but to do well they have no knowledge" (Jer. 4:22). "They proceed from evil to worse, and have not known me, saith the Lord" (9:3).

(2) Atheism, when the heart denies either God or His attributes, as His justice, wisdom, providence, presence. "The fool has said in his heart there is no God" (Ps. 14:1). "Ye had no hope, and were without God in the world" (Eph. 2:12). "I love you, saith the Lord, yet ye say, wherein have we spoken against thee?" (Mal. 1:2). "Ye have said, it is in vain to serve God: and what profit is it, that we have kept his commandments, and that we walked humbly before the Lord of Hosts?" (3:14).

(3) Errors concerning God, the persons of the deity, or the attributes. Here is to be reproved Hellenism,[2] which is the acknowledging and adoring of a multiplicity of gods.[3]

Again, Judaism is here condemned, which worships one God without Christ.

---

2. *Hellenism*: polytheism, especially as associated with the ancient Greeks.

3. In-text citation: Augustine, in his sixth book of the *City of God*, chapter 7 [Augustine, *City of God*, bk. 6, ch. 7].

The like may be said of the heresies of the Manichaeans[4] and Marcian,[5] who denied God to be the Creator of the world; of Sabellius,[6] denying the distinction of three persons; and Arius,[7] who says that Christ, the Son of God, is not very God.

(4) To withdraw and remove the affections of the heart from the Lord and set them upon other things. "The Lord said, this people draweth near me with their mouth, and honoreth me with their lips, but their heart is far from me" (Isa. 29:13). "Thou art more in their mouth, and far from their reins" (Jer. 12:2). The heart is many ways withdrawn from God.

(1) By distrust in God. "The just shall live by faith, but if any withdraw himself, my soul shall have no pleasure in him" (Heb. 10:38). From this diffidence arise (1) impatience in suffering afflictions. "Cursed be the day wherein I was born, and let not the day wherein my mother bare me, be blessed" (Jer. 20:14). "Cursed be the man, that showed my father, saying, a man child is born unto thee, and comforted him" (v. 13). "How is it that I came forth of the womb, to see labor and sorrow, that my days should be consumed with shame?" (v. 18). (2) Tempting of God, when such as distrust or rather contemn Him seek experiment of God's truth and power. "Thou shalt not tempt the Lord thy God" (Matt. 4:7). "Neither let us tempt God, as they tempted him, and were destroyed by serpents. Neither murmur ye, as some of them murmured, and were destroyed of the destroyer" (1 Cor. 10:9–10). (3) Desperation. "Mine iniquity is greater than can be pardoned" (Gen. 4:13). "Sorrow ye not as they which have no hope" (1 Thess. 4:13). (4) Doubtfulness concerning the truth of God or of His benefits present or to come. "I said in my haste all men are liars" (Ps. 116:11).

---

4. *Manichaeans*: followers of Manichaeism—a heretical movement and radical sect of Gnosticism based on the teachings of its founder Mani (also called Manes or Manichaeus, *c.* 216–276), who taught a dualistic view of the world as chiefly a cosmic battle between light and darkness.

5. *Marcian* (traditionally spelled Marcion, *d.* 160) was a heretical teacher who gathered a significant following during the late second and early third centuries. He taught that the Creator God of the Old Testament (the Demiurge) was a God of Law and completely opposed to the Supreme God of Love put forward in the New Testament—chiefly in the person of Jesus Christ, who came to overthrow the Demiurge. His teachings were opposed by many of the Church Fathers and the movement was eventually absorbed into Manichaeism.

6. *Sabellius* (*fl. c.* 215) was an early third-century heretical Roman theologian who founded Sabellianism, a Modalist form of Monarchianism that taught that the only differentiation in the Godhead was the mere succession of modes or operations. His teaching was repudiated by the Church Fathers.

7. *Arius* (*d.* 336) was a fourth-century heretical theologian and founder of Arianism, a movement that was condemned at the Council of Nicaea in 325 A.D. for its denial of the full divinity of Jesus and positing that Jesus was created from nothing by the Father in the ages before the world was created.

(2) Confidence in creatures, whether it be in their strength, as, "Cursed is the man that has his confidence in man, and maketh flesh his arm, but his heart slideth from the Lord" (Jer. 17:5). Or riches: "Ye cannot serve God and riches" (Matt. 6:24). "No covetous person, which is an idolater, hath inheritance in the kingdom of Christ and of God" (Eph. 5:5). Or defensed places: "Thy fear, and the pride of thine heart hath deceived thee, that thou dwellest in the cleft of the rock, and keepest the height of the hill: though thou shouldest make thy nest as high as the eagle, I will bring thee down from thence, saith the Lord" (Jer. 49:16). Or pleasure and dainties: "To such their belly is their God" (Phil. 3:19). Or in physicians: "And Asa in the nine and thirtieth year of his reign, was diseased in his feet, and his disease was extreme, yet he sought not the Lord in his disease, but to physicians" (2 Chron. 16:12). Briefly, to this place principally may be adjoined that devilish confidence which magicians and all such as take advice at them do put in the devil and his works. "If any turn after such as work with spirits, and after soothsayers, to go a whoring after them, then will I set my face against that person, and will cut him off, from among his people" (Lev. 20:6).

(3) The love of the creature above the love of God. "He that loveth father or mother more than me, is not worthy of me, and he that loveth son or daughter more than me, is not worthy of me" (Matt. 10:37). "They loved the praise of man, more than the praise of God" (John 12:43). To this belongs self-love (2 Tim. 3:2).

(4) Hatred and contempt of God, when man by reason of his declining nature from God does flee from Him and is angry toward God when He punishes sin. "The wisdom of the flesh, is enmity with God" (Rom. 8:7). "Haters of God, doers of wrong" (1:30).

(5) Want of the fear of God. "Wickedness saith to the wicked man, even in mine heart, that there is no fear of God before their eyes" (Ps. 36:1).

(6) Fear of the creature more than the Creator. "The fearful, and unbelieving, shall have their part in the lake which burns with fire and brimstone" (Rev. 21:8). "Fear not them which kill the body, but fear him that can cast both body and soul into hell fire" (Matt 10:28). "Be not afraid of the signs of heaven, though the heathen be afraid of such" (Jer. 10:2).

(7) Hardness of heart or carnal security, when a man neither acknowledging God's judgments nor his own sins dreams he is safe from God's vengeance and such perils as arise from sin. "Thou after thine hardness, and heart that cannot repent, heapest to thyself wrath against the day of wrath" (Rom. 2:5). "Take heed to yourselves, lest at any time your hearts be oppressed with surfeiting, and drunkenness, and cares of this life, and lest that day come on you at unawares" (Luke 21:34).

(8) These all do jointly engender pride, whereby man ascribes all he has that is good not to God, but to his own merit and industry, referring and disposing them wholly to his own proper credit. "That ye might learn by us, that no man presume above that which is written, that one swell not against another, for any man's cause. For who separateth thee? Or what hast thou, that thou hast not received? If thou hast received it, why rejoices thou, as though thou hadst not received it?" (1 Cor. 4:6–7). "God doth know, that when ye shall eat thereof, your eyes shall be opened, and ye shall be as gods, knowing good and evil" (Gen. 3:5). The highest stair of pride's ladder is that fearful presumption by which many climb rashly into God's seat of majesty, as if they were gods. "The people gave a shout, saying, The voice of God, and not of man: but immediately the Angel of the Lord smote him, because he gave not glory unto God, so that he was eaten up of worms, and gave up the ghost" (Acts 12:22–23). "Which is an adversary, and exalteth himself against all that is called God, or that is worshipped, so that he doth sit as God in the temple of God, showing himself that he is God" (2 Thess. 2:4).

Chapter 21

Of the Second Commandment

Hitherto have we entreated of the first commandment, teaching us to entertain in our hearts and to make choice of one only God. The other three of the first table concern that holy profession which we must make toward the same God. For first, it is necessary to make choice of the true God; secondly, to make profession of the same God.

In the profession of God, we are to consider the parts thereof and the time appointed for this profession.

The parts are two: the solemn worship of God and the glorifying of Him.

The second commandment then concerns the manner of performing holy and solemn worship to God. The words of the commandment are these:

"Thou shalt make thee no graven image, neither any similitude of things which are in heaven above, neither that are in the earth beneath, nor that are in the waters under the earth: thou shalt not bow down to them, neither serve them, for I am the Lord thy God, a jealous God, visiting the iniquity of the fathers upon the children, upon the third generation, and upon the fourth of them that hate me, and show mercy unto thousands upon them that love me and keep my commandments" [Ex. 20:4–6].

The Resolution

"Thou shalt not make." This is the first part of the commandment, forbidding to make an idol. Now an idol is not only a certain representation and image of some feigned god, but also of the true Jehovah. The which may be proved against the papists by these arguments. The first is, "Take therefore good heed unto yourselves: for ye saw no image in the day that the Lord spake to you in Horeb, out of the midst of the fire, that ye corrupt not yourselves, and make you a graven image or representation of any figure: whether it be the likeness of male or female" (Deut. 4:15–16). Out of the words uttered by Moses, a reason may be framed thus:

If you saw no image—namely, of God—you shall make none.
But you saw no image, only heard a voice.
Therefore, you shall make no image of God.

The second reason: that idolatry which the Israelites committed, the very same is prohibited in this commandment.

But the Israelites' idolatry was the worship of God in an image. "At that day, saith the Lord, thou shalt call me no more Baali, but shalt call me Ishi" (Hos. 2:16).

The golden calf was an image of God; for when it was finished, Aaron proclaimed that "tomorrow should be a feast to Jehovah" (Ex. 32:5). And the same calf is termed an idol (Acts 7:41).

Therefore, the worshipping of God in an image is here prohibited.

"Any graven image." Here the more special is put for the more general—namely, a graven image for all counterfeit means of God's worship.

The first part of the commandment is here illustrated by a double distribution. The first is drawn from the causes: "Thou shalt not make thee an idol, whether it be engraven in wood, or stone or whether it be painted in a table." The second is taken from the place: "Thou shalt not make thee an idol of things in heaven, as stars and birds: or in the earth, as of man, woman, beast: or under the earth, as fishes."

This place is so expounded by Moses (Deut. 4:14–20).

"Thou shalt not bow down to them." This is the second part of the commandment, forbidding all men to fall down before an idol. In this word "bow down" is again the special put for the general; for in it is inhibited all feigned worship of God.

"For I." These words are a confirmation of this commandment, persuading to obedience by four reasons.

"The Lord" (which is strong). The first reason, God is strong and so able to revenge idolatry (Heb. 10:31).

"A jealous God." This speech is taken from the estate of wedlock; for God is called the husband of His church (Isa. 5:4–5; Eph. 5:26–27). And our spiritual worship is as it were a certain marriage of our souls consecrated to the Lord. "I remember thee with the kindness of thy youth, and the love of the marriage, when thou wentest after me in the wilderness, in a land that was not sown" (Jer. 2:2). Whence also idols are rightly called God's co-rivals. Here is another argument drawn from a comparison of things that be like. God's people must alone worship Him because they are linked to Him as a wife to her husband, to whom alone she is bound. Therefore, if His people forsake Him and betroth themselves to idols, He will undoubtedly give them a bill of divorcement, and they shall be no more espoused to Him.

"Visiting." To visit is not only to punish the children for the fathers' offences, but to take notice and apprehend them in the same faults; by reason they are given over to commit their fathers' transgressions, that for them they may be punished. And this is the third reason drawn from the effects of God's anger.

"Hate me." It may be this is a secret answer, the objection whereof is not here in express words set down, but may be thus framed: "What if we use idols to enflame and excite in us a love and remembrance of Thee?" The answer is this by the contrary: "You may think that your use of idols kindles in you a love of Me, but it is so far from that that all such as use them cannot choose but hate Me."

"Show mercy." The fourth reason derived from the effects of God's mercy to such as observe this commandment. Here may we first observe that God is more ready to show mercy than to punish. "The Lord is full of compassion and mercy, slow to anger, and of great kindness" (Ps. 103:8). "The loving kindness of the Lord, endureth forever" (v. 17). "He will not always chide, neither keep His anger forever" (v. 9). Secondly, we may not surmise that this excellent promise is made to everyone particularly who is born of faithful parents. For godly Isaac had godless Esau to his son, and godless Saul had godly Jonathan.

The Negative Part: You shall neither Worship False Gods, nor the True God with False Worship

Many things are here forbidden.

(1) The representation of God by an image. For it is a lie. "What profiteth the image? For the maker thereof hath made it an image and a teacher of lies" (Hab. 2:18). "The idols have spoken vanity" (Zech. 10:2). "The stock is a doctrine of vanity" (Jer. 10:8). The Elib. Council in the thirty-ninth canon[1] has this edict: "We thought it not meet to have images in churches, lest that which is worshipped and adored, should be painted upon walls."[2] "That serpent by others is wont to speak these words: We in honor of the invisible God, are accustomed to adore visible images, the which out of all controversy is very false."[3]

The images also of the cross and of Christ crucified and of the saints ought to be abolished out of churches, as the brazen serpent was (2 Kings 18:4). Hezekiah is commended for breaking in pieces the brazen serpent to which the children of Israel did then burn incense. This did Hezekiah, albeit at the first this serpent was made by the Lord's appointment (Num. 21:8) and was a type of Christ's passion (John 3:14). Origen in his Seventh Book against Celsus: "We

---

1. *Council of Elivira*: a Spanish Council held at Granada, dated to 305–306 A.D. that passed 81 canons dealing with apostasy and adultery. Perkins actually references canon 36.

2. In-text citation: Clem. Book 5.ad Iocob. Dom [Clement of Alexandria (*c.*150–215), *Stromata*, bk. 5. Clement of Alexandria was an important Christian theologian and Church Father].

3. In-text citation: Augustine, in his treatise upon the 112th Psalm [Augustine, *Exposition upon the Psalms*, Psalm 112].

permit not any to adore Jesus upon the altars in images, or upon church walls, because it is written, 'Thou shalt have none other gods but Me.'"[4]

Epiphanius in that epistle which he wrote to John, bishop of Jerusalem, says, "It is against the custom of the church, to see any image hanging in the church, whether it be of Christ, or any other saint, and therefore even with His own hands rent He asunder the veil, wherein such an image was painted."

Some object the figure or sign which appeared to Constantine,[5] wherein he should overcome; but it was not the sign of the cross (as the papists do triflingly imagine), but of Christ's name. For the thing was made of these two Greek letters, Χρ, conjoined together.[6]

Neither serve the cherubim which Solomon placed in the temple for the defense of images; for they were only in the Holy of Holiest, where the people could not see them. And they were types of the glory of the Messiah, to whom the very angels were subject, the which we have now verified in Christ.

If any man reply that they worship not the image, but God in the image, let him know that the creature cannot comprehend the image of the Creator; and if it could, yet God would not be worshiped in it, because it is a dead thing— yea, the work of man's hands, not of God—and therefore is more base than the smallest living creature, of the which we may lawfully say it is the work of God. This evinces that no kind of divine worship belongs to an image, either simply or by relation, whatever the sophistical schoolmen jangle to the contrary.

If any man be yet desirous of images, he may have at hand the preaching of the gospel a lively image of Christ crucified. "O foolish Galatians, who hath bewitched you, that ye should not obey the truth, to whom Jesus Christ before was described in your sight, and among you crucified?" (Gal. 3:1). The like may be said of the two sacraments. And that saying of Clement is true in his fifth book of Recognut: "If you will truly adore the image of God, do good to man, and you shall worship His true image; for man is the image of God."[7]

(2) The least approbation of idolatry. "They say one to another whilst they sacrifice a man, let them kiss the calves" (Hos. 13:2). Now a kiss is an external sign of some allowance of a thing (Gen. 48:10).

---

4. In-text citation: Origen in his Seventh Book against Celsus [Origen of Alexandria (*c.* 184– *c.* 253), *Contra Celsum*, bk. 7. Origen was a Hellenistic scholar and early Christian theologian].

5. *Constantine*: that is, Constantine I, or Constantine the Great (*d.* 337 A.D.), the Roman emperor from 306–337 A.D., who was the first emperor to legalize Christianity.

6. In-text citation: Eusebius (260/265–339/340 A.D.), *Life of Constantine*, book 1, chapter 22 and 25 [Eusebius, *The Life of Constantine*, bk. 1, ch. 22 and 25. Eusebius was an important historian of the early church].

7. This is a reference to *The Recognitions of Clement of Alexandria*, a work that was part of the body of Clementine Literature—apocryphal writings written under the name St. Clement of Rome which circulated in the early church.

Therefore, it is unlawful to be present at mass or any idolatrous service, though our minds be absent. "Ye are bought with a price, therefore glorify God in your body, and in your spirits, which are God's" (1 Cor. 6:20). "What saith the Scripture? I have reserved unto myself seven thousand men, which have not bowed their knee to Baal" (Rom. 11:4). "The martyrs, when they were hauled to the temple of idols, cried out, and with a loud voice in the midst of their tortures testified, that they were not idolatrous sacrificers, but professed and constant Christians, rejoicing greatly that they might make such a confession."[8]

That which may be objected of Naaman the Syrian, who worshiped in the temple of Rimmon, is thus answered, that he did it not with purpose to commit idolatry but to perform that civil obeisance which he was wont to exhibit to the king's majesty (2 Kings 5:17–18).

And for this cause are utterly forbidden all such dancing professions, plays, and such feasts as are consecrated to the memorial and honor of idols. "They rose up the next day in the morning, and offered burnt offerings, and brought peace offerings: also the people sat them down to eat and drink, and rose up to play" (Ex. 32:6). "Neither be ye idolaters as some of them were, as it is written," etc. (1 Cor. 10:7). And Paul in 1 Corinthians 8:4 to the end, earnestly dehorts[9] the Corinthians from sitting at table in the idols' temple, albeit they "knew that an idol is nothing in the world." [The] *Tripartite History* [notes], "Certain soldiers of Justan refused to adore, as the custom was, the emperor's banner, in which were painted the images of Jupiter, Mercury, and Mars; others bring again the rewards, which they, after they had burned incense on an altar in the emperor's presence, had received, crying that they were Christians and would live and die in that profession. And as for their former fact, it was of ignorance—yea, though they had polluted hands with idolatry of the Painyms, yet they kept their conscience clean."[10]

(3) All relics and monuments of idols; for these, after the idols themselves are once abolished, must be erased out of all memory. "Ye shall make no mention of the name of other gods, neither shall it be heard out of thy mouth" (Ex. 23:13). "And ye shall pollute the covering of the images of silver, and the rich ornament of the images of gold, and cast them away as a menstruous cloth, and thou shalt say unto it, Get thee hence" (Isa. 30:22).

---

8. In-text citation: Eusebius. 8. Book. C.3 [Eusebius, *Ecclesiastical History*, bk. 8, ch. 3].

9. *Dehorts*: To use exhortation to dissuade a person from a course or purpose; to advise or counsel against an action.

10. In-text citation: Tripartite History, bk. 6, ch. 30. [*Historiae Ecclesiasticae Tripartitae Epitome*, the abridged history (in twelve books) of the early Christian church known as the *Tripartite History*, was the standard manual of church history in Medieval Europe].

(4) Society with infidels is here unlawful, which serves not only to maintain concord but also to join men in brotherly love. Of this society there are many branches.

The first is marriage with infidels. "The sons of God saw the daughters of men that they were fair, and they took them wives of all that they liked" (Gen. 6:2). "Judah hath transgressed, and an abomination is committed on Israel, and in Jerusalem: for Judah hath defiled the holiness of the Lord, which he loved, and hath married the daughters of a strange God" (Mal. 2:11). "Should we return to break thy commandments, and join in affinity with the people of such abomination?" (Ezra 9:14). "He walked in the ways of the kings of Israel, as did the house of Ahab: for the daughter of Ahab was his wife; and he did evil in the sight of the Lord" (2 Kings 8:18).

The second is the league in war—namely, a mutual confederacy to assist one another in the same war and to have one and the same enemies. This is sundry ways impious. (1) If it be unlawful to crave assistance of God's enemies, it is likewise unlawful to indent with them that we will assist them. (2) It obscures God's glory as though He Himself either would not or could not aid His church. (3) It is a thousand to one lest we be infected with their idolatry and other impieties. (4) It endangers us to be made partakers of their punishments. "And Jehu the son of Hanani, the seer, went out to meet him, and said to King Jehoshaphat, Wouldest thou help the wicked, and love them that hate the Lord? Therefore for this thing is the wrath of the Lord upon thee" (2 Chron. 19:2).

The third is traffic,[11] as when a man wittingly and willingly does in hope to enrich himself make sale of such things as he knows must serve to an idolatrous use. This condemns all those merchants which transport wares to idolaters and sell them frankincense, wax, cloth, or other such things as help them in the service of their idols.

The fourth is trial or suits in law before judges which are infidels, when Christian courts may be frequented; but if they cannot, and we have to deal with infidels, we may appeal to infidels. "Brother goeth to law with brother, and that under infidels" (1 Cor. 6:6). "Paul appealeth to Caesar" (Acts 25:11).

The fifth is the worshiping of the beast and receiving his mark. "If any man worship the beast, and his image, and receive the mark in his forehead or in his hand, the same shall drink of the wine of the wrath of God" (Rev. 14:9–10). This beast is the Church of Rome—I mean not that old, but this new Rome, now no better than a heretical and apostatical synagogue.

(5) Will-worship, when God is worshiped with a naked and bare good intention not warranted by the Word of God. "Which things indeed have a

---

11. *Traffic*: trade.

show of wisdom in voluntary religion, and humbleness of mind, and in not sparing the body: neither have they it in estimation to satisfy the flesh" (Col. 2:23). "And Saul said, Bring a burnt offering to me, and peace offerings: and he offered a burnt offering. And as soon as he had made an end of offering the burnt offering, behold, Samuel came, and said to Saul, Thou hast done foolishly, thou hast not kept the commandment of the Lord thy God, which he commanded thee" (1 Sam. 13:9–10, 13). Hitherto may we add popish superstitions in sacrifices, meats, holidays, apparel, temporary and bead-ridden prayers,[12] indulgences, austere life, whipping, ceremonies, gestures, gait, conversation, pilgrimage, building of altars, pictures, churches, and all other of that rabble.

To these may be added consort in music in divine service, feeding the ears, not edifying the mind. "What is it then? I will pray with the spirit, but I will pray with the understanding also. I will sing with the spirit, but I will sing with the understanding also" (1 Cor. 14:15). Justin Martyr[13] said, "It is not the custom of the churches to sing their meters with any such kind of instruments, etc., but their manner is only to use plain song."[14]

Lastly, monastical vows, which (1) repugn the law of God, as that unchaste vow of single life and proud promise of poverty do plainly evince: "for he that laboreth not, must not eat" (2 Thess. 3:10). "And it is better to marry, than to burn in lust" (1 Cor. 7:9). (2) They are greater than men's nature can perform, as in a single life to live perpetually chaste. (3) They disannul Christian liberty and make such things necessary as are indifferent. (4) They renew Judaism. (5) They are idolatrous, because they make them parts of God's worship and esteem them as meritorious. (6) Hypocrisy, which gives to God painted worship—that is, if you regard outward behavior, great sincerity; if the inward and hearty affections, none at all. "Hypocrites, well hath Isaiah prophesied of you, saying, This people cometh near me with their mouth, and honoreth me with their lips, but their heart is far from me" (Matt. 15:7). "The wicked man is so proud, that he seeketh not for God" (Ps. 10:4).

The effects of hypocrisy are these: (1) To seek the pomp and glory of the world and by all means to enrich itself, notwithstanding it make a glorious show of the service of God. (2) It is sharp-sighted and has eagle's eyes to observe other men's behavior, when in the regarding its own it is as blind as a beetle. (3) To be more curious in the observation of ancient traditions than the statutes and

---

12. *Bead-ridden*: a reference to the rosary.

13. *Justin Martyr* (c. 100–c. 165) is generally regarded as the most exceptional of the second-century "Apologists," who wrote defenses of Christianity while facing Roman persecution.

14. In-text citation: in his book of Christian questions and answers 107 [Probably a reference to the apocryphal writing spuriously attributed to Justin Martyr entitled, *A Christian's Questions to the Greeks*].

commandments of almighty God. (4) To stumble at a straw and skip over a block—that is, to omit serious affairs and hunt after trifles (Matt. 23:4–5). To do all things that they may be seen of men (6:5).

Popish fasting is mere hypocrisy, because it stands in the distinction of meats, and it is used with an opinion of merit.

External abstinence from meats without internal and spiritual fasting from sin and unlawful desires. "Is this such a fast as I have chosen, that a man should afflict his soul for a day, and bow down his head as a bulrush, and lie down in sackcloth and ashes? Wilt thou call this as fasting, or an acceptable day to the Lord? Is not this the fasting that I have chosen, to loose the bands of wickedness, to take off the heavy burdens, and to let the oppressed go free, and that ye break every yoke?" (Isa. 58:5–6).

(7) Contempt, neglect, and intermission of God's service. "I know thy works, that thou art neither cold, nor hot: I would thou wert cold or hot. Therefore, because thou art lukewarm, and neither cold nor hot, it will come to pass, that I shall spew thee out of my mouth" (Rev. 3:15–16).

(8) Corrupting of God's worship and that order of government which He has ordained for His church, the which is done when anything is added, detracted, or any way against His prescript mangled. "Everything which I command you, that do: neither add to it, nor detract from it" (Deut. 12:32). This condemns that popish elevation of bread in the Lord's Supper and the administration of it alone to the people without wine, together with that fearful abomination of the mass.

By this we may learn to reject all popish traditions. "In vain do they worship me, teaching for doctrines, men's precepts" (Matt. 15:9). Now it is manifest that all popish traditions, they either on their own nature or others abusing of them, serve as well to superstition and false worship as to enrich that covetous and proud hierarchy, whereas the Scriptures, contained in the Old and New Testament, are all-sufficient not only to confirm doctrines but also to reform manners. "The whole Scripture is given by inspiration of God, and is profitable to teach, to improve, and to correct, and to instruct in righteousness: that the man of God may be absolute, being made perfect to all good works" (2 Tim. 3:16).

The Romish hierarchy is here also condemned from the parratour[15] to the pope, the government whereof is an express image of the old Roman empire, whether we consider the regiment itself or the place of the empire or the large circuit of that government. "And it was permitted to him, to give a spirit to the image of the beast, so that the image of the beast should speak, and should

---

15. *Parratour:* an apparitor or summoning officer of an ecclesiastical court.

cause that as many as would not worship the image of the beast, should be killed" (Rev. 13:15).

(9) A religious reverence of the creature, when we attribute more to it than we ought. "When I had heard and seen, I fell down to worship before the feet of the angel, which showed me these things. But he said to me, See thou do it not: for I am thy fellow servant" (Rev. 22:8). "As Peter came in, Cornelius met him, and fell down at his feet, and worshiped him. But Peter took him up saying, Stand up, for even I myself am a man" (Acts 10:25).

If then it be so heinous a thing to reverence the creature, much more to pray to it, whether it be saint or angel. "How shall they call upon him in whom they have not believed" (Rom. 10:14). "Thou shalt worship the Lord thy God, and him only shalt thou serve" (Matt. 4:10).

Neither might we pray to Christ, unless as He is man so He were also God; for we direct not our worship to the humanity considered by itself, but to the deity to which the humanity is knit by an hypostatical union.

This teaches us plainly that invocation of any creature is unlawful, for we must pray to them that are able to know the secrets of the heart and discern the wisdom of the Spirit. Now none is able to do that, but such a nature as is omnipotent. "He that searcheth the hearts, knoweth what is the meaning of the spirit: for he maketh request for the saints, according to the will of God" (Rom 8:27).

Nevertheless, such as are saints indeed are to be honored by an approbation of God's gifts in them and by an honorable mention of them and also by imitation of their manners and lives, being as patterns for us to walk after.

(10) Worship of devils. (1) Magic, which is a mischievous art, accomplishing wonders by Satan's assistance. For it is appropriate to God to do miracles, for He alone both beyond and against the course of nature does wonderful things. Now the instruments which God uses in producing miracles are only they who do in the true church of God make profession of the faith. "These signs shall follow them that believe" (Mark 16:17).

Albeit the devils cannot work miracles, yet may they effect marvels or wonders, and that not by making a new thing which before was not at all, but rather by moving, transporting, and applying natural things diversely, by causing a thin body (as the air) to be thick and foggy, and also by bewitching the senses of men.

The foundation of magic is a covenant with Satan.

A covenant with Satan is such a contract by which magicians have mutually to do with the devil. In this observe:

The original of this mutual contract. (1) Satan makes choice of such men to be his servants as are by nature either notoriously bad persons or very silly souls. (2) He offers to them diverse means either by other magicians or by some books written by such. Satanical means I call those which are used in the producing of such an effect to the which they neither by any express rule out of God's Word nor of their own nature were ever ordained. Such are obscure words, words of the Scripture wrested and abused to the great contumely and disgrace of the Lord God; holy, or rather unholy water, signs, seals, glasses, images, bowings of the knee, and such like divers gestures. (3) When the wicked see these means offered to them, they presently are not a little glad and assuredly believe that in those things there is virtue to work wonders by. (4) They declare this their satanical confidence by their earnest endeavor, practicing, and abusing the means. Then the devil is at their elbows, being thus affected that he may both assist them and show them divers tricks of his legerdemain, because he alone does by means void of all such virtue effect that which his wicked instrument intended.

Again, observe Satan's counterfeiting of God. He is God's ape and takes upon him as though he were God. (1) As God has His Word, His sacraments, and faith due to Him, so the devil has certain words of his own. And to seal them to the wicked, he annexes certain signs—namely, characters, gestures, sacrifices, etc.—as it were sacraments, that both he may signify his devilish pleasure to his magicians, and they again testify both their satanical obedience and confidence to him. (2) As God hears such as call upon, trust in, and obey Him, so the devil is greatly delighted with magical ceremonies and invocations, because by them God is dishonored and he magnified. Therefore, if God cut him not short, he is ready pressed to assist such as shall use such ceremonies or invocations.

The covenant is either secret or express.

Secret or implicit, when one does not expressly compact with Satan, yet in his heart allows of his means, assuredly and upon knowledge believing that if such means were used, there might indeed that great wonder be wrought which he desired.

Express, when one does not only put his confidence in Satan, but covenants with him upon this condition: that he giving himself wholly over to the devil may again by observing certain ceremonies accomplish his desire.

Magic is either divining or working.

Divining, whereby things to come are foretold by the help of the devil. Now of predictions, some are done with means; others without.

Predictions done with means are these:

(1) Soothsaying, which is divination by the flying of birds (Deut. 8:10).

(2) The kind of divination, which is by looking into beasts' entrails. "The king of Babylon, etc., consulted with idols, and looked in the liver" (Ezek. 21:21).

(3) Necromancy or conjuring, by which the devil in the form of some dead man is sought to for counsel. "Then said the woman, Whom wilt thou I call up unto thee? And he said, Call up Samuel unto me. Then said he unto her, Fear not, but what sawest thou? And the woman said unto Saul, I saw gods ascending out of the earth. Then said he unto her, What fashion is he of? And she answered, An old man cometh up lapped in a mantle. And Saul knew that it was Samuel, and he inclined his face to the ground, and bowed himself. And Samuel said unto Saul, Why hast thou disquieted me, to bring me up? Then Saul answered, I am in great distress: for the Philistines make war against me," etc. (1 Sam. 28:11, 13–14). This Samuel was not that true prophet of God, who anointed Saul king over Israel, for (1) the souls of the saints departed are far from the devil's claws and dominion. (2) That good Samuel, if it had been he indeed, would never have permitted Saul to worship him. (3) He says to wicked Saul, "Tomorrow shalt thou be with me" (v. 14). Neither could this be a bare illusion and, as I may say, legerdemain of the witch; for he plainly foretold Saul's destruction, which an ignorant woman could not know, much less durst she constantly avouch any such matter to the king. It remains then that this Samuel was a mere illusion of Satan.

Divining without means is called pythonism, when such as are possessed with an unclean spirit use immediately the help of the same spirit to reveal secrets. "A certain maid having a spirit of divination, met us, which got her master much vantage with divining" (Acts 16:16). "Thy voice shall be out of the ground, like him that has a spirit of divination, and thy talking shall whisper out of the dust" (Isa. 29:4).

Magic operative or working has two parts: juggling and enchantments.

Juggling, whereby through the devil's conveyance many great and very hard matters are in show effected. "Aaron cast forth his rod before Pharaoh, and before his servants, and it was turned into a serpent: then Pharaoh called also for the wisemen, and sorcerers, and those charmers also of Egypt did in like manner with their enchantments: for they cast down every man his rod, and they were turned into serpents: but Aaron's rod devoured their rods" (Ex. 7:10–12).

Enchantment or charming is that whereby beasts, but especially young children and men of riper years are by God's permission infected, poisoned, hurt, bounden,[16] killed, and otherwise molested; or contrarily, sometimes cured of Satan by mumbling up some few words, making certain characters and figures, framing circles, hanging amulets about the neck or other parts, by herbs, medicines, and such like trumpery, that thereby the punishment of the faithless may be augmented in reposing their strength upon such rotten staves,

---

16. *Bounden*: bound or tied.

and the faithful may be tried, whether they will commit the like abomination. "Their poison is even like the poison of a serpent: like the deaf adder that stoppeth his ears, which heareth not the voice of the enchanter, though he be most expert in charming" (Ps. 58:4). "If the serpent bite when he is charmed," etc. (Eccl. 10:11).

Thus have we heard magic described out of God's Word, the which, how common it is as yet in those especially which are without God in the world and whom Satan by all means strongly deludes, the lamentable experience which many men and most places have thereof, can sufficiently prove to us. And surely if a man will but take a view of all popery, he shall easily see that a great part of it is mere magic.

They which spread abroad by their writing or otherwise that witches are nothing else but melancholic, doting women, who through the devil's delusion suppose that they themselves do that which indeed the devil does alone, albeit they endeavor cunningly to cloak this sin, yet by the same means they may defend murder, adultery, and whatever other sin.

(2) Those which do consult with magicians do also worship the devil; for they revolt from God to the devil, however they plaster up their impiety with untempered mortar, that they seek God's help, though by the means of magicians. "The woman said to Saul, I saw gods ascending from the earth" (1 Sam. 28:13). "If any turn after such as work with spirits, and after soothsayers, to go a-whoring after them, then will I set my face against that person, and will cut him off from among his people" (Lev. 20:6) "When they shall say to you, enquire at them which have a spirit of divination, and at the soothsayers, which whisper and murmur. Should not a people enquire at their God? From the living to the dead? To the law, and to the testimony?" (Isa. 8:19–20).

The Affirmative Part: You Shall Worship God in Spirit and Truth

"God is a Spirit, and they that worship Him, must worship Him in spirit and truth" (John 4:24). For so soon as any man begins to worship God after an overthwart and unlawful manner, he then adores an idol, however he seems to color his impiety. Paul therefore says that "such as worshiped the creature, and turned the glory of the incorruptible God, to the similitude of a corruptible man, did forsake the Creator" (Rom. 1:23, 25). And, "Those things which the Gentiles sacrifice, they sacrifice to devils, and not unto God" (1 Cor. 10:20).

To this part therefore appertain such things as respect the holy and solemn service of God.

(1) The true and ordinary means of God's worship, as calling upon the name of the Lord by humble supplication and hearty thanksgiving and the ministry of the word and sacraments. "They that gladly received his word, were

baptized: and the same day there were added to the church about three thousand souls. And they continued in the apostles' doctrine, and fellowship, and breaking of bread, and of prayers" (Acts 2:41–42). "I exhort you especially, that prayers and supplications be made for all men, for kings, and all in authority" (1 Tim. 2:1). "The first day of the week, the disciples being come together to break bread, Paul preached unto them, ready to depart on the morrow, and continued the preaching to midnight" (Acts 20:7). "We come into the assembly and congregation, that with our prayers, as with an army, we might compass God. This kind of violence offered to God, is acceptable to Him. If any men so offend, that he must be suspended from the public place of prayer, and holy meetings, all approved elders sit in judgment, being advanced to this honor, and not by bribes, but by their good report," etc. Read the rest.[17] The like has Justin Martyr in his oration to the Emperor Antoninus Pius.[18]

(2) A holy use of the means, first, in the ministers, who ought to administer all things belonging to God's worship according to His Word. "Teaching them to observe all things, which I have commanded" (Matt. 28:20). "I have received of the Lord that, which also I have delivered" (1 Cor. 11:23). Secondly, in the rest of the assembly, whose duty is in praying to God, in hearing the word preached and read, and in receiving the sacraments to behave themselves outwardly in modesty and without offence. "Let all things be done honestly, and by order" (14:40). Inwardly, they must take heed that their hearts be well prepared to serve God. "Take heed to both thy feet, when thou enterest into the house of God" (Eccl. 4:17). "Be not rash with thy mouth, nor let thine heart be hasty to utter a thing before God" (5:1). Having confidence of His mercy, together with a contrite and repentant heart for all their sins. "The word that they heard profited not, because it was not mixed with faith in those that heard it" (Heb. 4:2). "I will wash mine hands in innocency, O Lord, and so compass thine altar" (Ps. 26:6).

(3) The helps and furtherances of the true worship are two: vows and fasting. And they are not to be taken as the worship of God itself. For we may not obtrude anything to God as good service and as though it did bind the conscience, except He have ordained it for that end and purpose.

A vow in the New Testament is a promise to God with a full intent to observe some corporal and external duties which a Christian has on his own accord without injunction imposed upon himself, that he may thereby the better be excited to repentance, meditation, sobriety, abstinence, patience, and

---

17. In-text citation. Tertullian.Apolog.chap. 39 [Tertullian (c. 155–240), *Apology*, ch. 39. Tertullian was one of the most prolific and important Church Fathers].

18. A reference to Justin Martyr, *First Apology*, that was addressed to the Emperor of Rome Antoninus Pius (r. 138–161) and his adopted sons (Marcus Aurelius and Lucius).

thankfulness toward God. "Then Jacob vowed a vow, saying, If God will be with me, and will keep me in this journey, which I go, and will give me bread to eat, and clothes to put on, so that I come again to my father's house in safety: then shall the Lord be my God, and this stone which I have set up as a pillar, shall be God's house, and of all that thou shalt give me, I will give the tenth to Thee" (Gen. 28:20).

In vowing, we have these things to observe. (1) We must not vow that which is unlawful. (2) We ought not to vow the performance of that which is contrary to our vocation. (3) Vows must be of that which we can do. (4) They must be far from so much as a conceit of merit or worship of God. (5) We must so perform our vows, as that they encroach not upon the liberty of conscience which Christ has given us, and therefore look how the probable causes thereof do remain or are taken away, so accordingly stands our liberty in keeping a vow. "Thou shalt neither bring the hire of a whore, nor the price of a dog, into the house of the Lord thy God, for any vow" (Deut. 23:18). "When thou shalt vow a vow unto the Lord thy God, thou shalt not be slack to pay it: for the Lord thy God will surely require it of thee; but when thou abstainest from vowing, it shall be no sin unto thee," etc. (vv. 21, 23). "I will pay my vows which my lips have promised" (Ps. 66:14).

Fasting is when a man perceiving the want of some blessing or suspecting and seeing some imminent calamity upon himself or other abstains not only from flesh for a season, but also from all delights and sustenance, that he thereby may make a more diligent search in his own sins and offer most humble prayers to God that He would withhold that which His anger threatened or bestow upon us some such good thing as we want. "Can the children of the marriage chamber mourn, so long as the bridegroom is with them?" (Matt. 9:15). "Defraud not one another, except for a time, that ye may the better fast and pray" (1 Cor. 7:5). "Wherefore even now, saith the Lord, be ye turned to me, with all your heart, with fasting and prayer. Rend your hearts, and not your garments, and turn unto the Lord your God: for he is gracious and merciful, long suffering, and of great kindness, that he might repent him of this evil. Blow the trumpet in Sion, sanctify a fast, call a solemn assembly. Gather the people, sanctify the congregation, gather the elders, assemble the children, and those that suck the breasts. Let the bridegroom go forth of his chamber, and the bride out of her bride chamber. Let the priests the ministers of the Lord weep between the porch and the altar, and let them say, Spare thy people, O God" (Joel 2:12–13, 15–17).

A fast is sometime private, sometimes public. "Jehoshaphat feared, and set himself to seek the Lord, and proclaimed a fast throughout all Judah" (2 Chron.

20:3). "Fast ye for me, and neither eat nor drink for the space of three days and nights, I also and my maids will fast" (Esth. 4:16).

A fast is either for one day alone or for many days together. Each of them is as occasion serves an abstinence from meat at dinner alone or supper alone or both dinner and supper. "The children of Israel had gone up and wept before the Lord unto the evening," etc. (Judg. 20:23). "I Daniel was in heaviness for three weeks of days, I ate no pleasant bread, neither came flesh nor wine in my mouth" (Dan. 10:3).

(4) Leagues of amity among such as truly fear God according to His Word are lawful, as contracts in matrimony, league in war, especially if the war be lawful and without confidence in the power of man (2 Chron. 19:2; Mal. 2:11).

To these may be added that covenant which the magistrate and people make among themselves and with God for the preservation of Christian religion. "And they made a covenant to seek the Lord God of their fathers with all their heart, and with all their soul, etc. And they sware to the Lord with a loud voice, and with shouting, and with trumpets, and with cornets" (2 Chron. 15:12, 14).

Chapter 22

Of the Third Commandment

The third commandment concerns the glorifying of God in the affairs of our life out of the solemn service of God.

"Thou shalt not take the name of the Lord thy God in vain; for the Lord will not hold him guiltless that taketh his name in vain."

The Resolution

"Name." This word properly signifies God's title. Here, figuratively it is used for anything whereby God may be known as men are by their names—so it is used for His Word, works, judgments. "He is an elect vessel, to convey my name among the Gentiles" (Acts 9:15). "O Lord our God, how great is thy name through all the world, which setteth thy glory above the heavens" (Ps. 8:1).

"Take." That is, "usurp." This word is translated from precious things which may not be touched without license. And in truth, men, which are no better than worms creeping on the earth, are utterly unworthy to take, or as I may say, touch the sacred name of God with mind or mouth. Nevertheless, God of His infinite kindness permits us so to do.

"In vain." Namely, for no cause, no matter, and upon each light and fond occasion.

"For." The reason of this commandment is taken from the penalty annexed. He that abuses God's name is guilty of sin before God's judgment seat and therefore is most miserable. "Blessed is the man whose iniquity is forgiven, and whose sin is covered: blessed is the man to whom God imputeth not sin" (Ps. 32:1–2).

"Guiltless." That is, he shall not be unpunished.

The Negative Part: You Shall not Bereave God of That Honor That Is Due to Him

Here is included each several abuse of anything that is used in the course of our lives out of the solemn service of God.

(1) Perjury, when a man performs not that which as he meant in his heart he sware to do. "Thou shalt not forswear thyself, but perform thine oath to the Lord" (Matt. 5:33).

Perjury contains in it four capital sins: (1) lying; (2) false invocation on God's name, because a forswearer calls on God to confirm a lie; (3) contempt of God's threatenings that He will most grievously punish perjury; (4) a lie in his covenant with God, for the forswearer binds himself to God and lies to God.

(2) To swear that which is false. This is to make God like to the devil. "Ye are of your father the devil, and when he speaketh a lie, he speaketh of himself, because he is a liar, and the father of lies" (John 8:44). "It shall enter into the house of him that sweareth falsely by my name" (Zech. 5:4).

(3) To swear in common talk. "Let your communication be yea, yea, and nay, nay: for whatsoever is more than these, cometh of evil" (Matt. 5:37).

(4) To swear by that which is no God. "But I say unto you, swear not at all, neither by heaven, for it is God's throne: neither by the earth, for it is his footstool: neither by Jerusalem, for it is the city of the great king" (Matt. 5:34–35). "Jezebel sent a messenger to Elias, saying, Thus do the gods, and so let them deal with me, if I by tomorrow this time, make not thy life, as is the life of every one of them" (1 Kings 19:2). "They taught my people to swear by Baal" (Jer. 12:16). "Thy sons forsake me, and swear by them which are no gods" (5:7).

This place condemns that usual swearing by the mass, faith, and such like. "He that sweareth by heaven, sweareth by God's throne, and him that sitteth thereon" (Matt. 23:22).

But for a man to swear by Christ's death, wounds, blood, and other parts of His is most horrible and is as much as to crucify Christ again with the Jews or account Christ's members as God Himself.

(5) Blasphemy, which is a reproach against God; and the least speech that favors of contempt to His majesty. "Whosoever curseth his God, shall bear his sins. And he that blasphemeth the name of the Lord, shall be put to death" (Lev. 24:15–16). "So shall ye say to the king of Judah: let not thy God deceive thee, in whom thou trustest, saying, Jerusalem shall not be given into the hand of the king of Ashur" (2 Kings 19:10). Ajax, in the *Tragedy*, has this blasphemous speech that every coward may overcome, if he have God on his side; as for him, he can get the victory without God's assistance.[1] That sly taunt of the pope is likewise blasphemous wherein he calls himself "the servant of all God's servants," when as in truth he makes himself Lord of Lords and God subject to his vain fantasy.

(6) Cursing our enemies, as, "Go with a vengeance," or, "The devil go with you." Or, ourselves, as, "I would I might never stir," or, "As God shall judge my soul," etc. To this place we may refer the execrations of Job 3 and Jeremiah 15.

---

1. A reference to the play *The Ajax,* a Greek tragedy written in the fifth century B.C. by Sophocles.

(7) To use the name of God carelessly in our common talk, as when we say, "Good God, how slow you are!"; "Good Lord, where have you been!"; "O Jesus!"; or, "Jesus God!," etc. "At the name of Jesus, shall every knee bow: of things in heaven, things in earth, and things under the earth" (Phil. 2:10). "Every knee shall bow to me, and every tongue shall swear by me" (Isa. 45:23).

(8) Abusing God's creatures, as when we either deride the workmanship of God or the manner of working; again, when we debase the excellence of the work, obscure God's good gifts in our brother, or discommend such meats as God has sent us to eat; finally, when as we in the use and contemplation of any of God's creatures give not Him the due praise and glory. "Whether ye eat or drink, or whatsoever ye do else, see that ye do all to the glory of God" (1 Cor. 10:31). "The heavens declare the glory of God, and the firmament showeth his handiwork" (Ps. 19:1).

(9) Lots, as when we search what must be (as they say) our fortune by dice, bones, books, or such like. For we are not to use lots, but with great reverence, in that the disposition of them immediately comes from the Lord, and their proper use is to decide great controversies. "The lot is cast into the lap, but the whole disposition thereof is in the Lord" (Prov. 16:33). "The lot causeth contentions to cease and maketh a partition among the mighty" (18:18). For this cause the land of Canaan was divided by lots (Joshua 14–15). By which also both the high priests and the kings were elected, as Saul (1 Samuel 10), and Matthias into the place of Judas Iscariot (Acts 1:26).

(10) Superstition, which is an opinion conceived of the works of God's providence, the reason whereof can neither be drawn out of the Word of God nor the whole course of nature. As for example, that it is unlucky for one in the morning to put on his shoe awry, or to put the left shoe on the right foot; to sneeze in drawing on his shoes; to have salt fall toward him; to have a hare cross him; to bleed some few drops of blood; to burn on the right ear. Again, that it is contrarily good luck to find old iron, to have drink spilled on him, for the left ear to burn, to pare our nails on some day of the week, to dream of some certain things. The like superstition is to surmise that beasts may be tamed by verses, prayers, or the like; that the repetition of the [Apostles'] Creed or the Lord's Prayer can infuse into herbs a faculty of healing diseases (Deut. 18:11). Here also is palmistry condemned, when by the inspection of the hand our fortune is foretold.

These and such like, albeit they have true events, yet are we not to give credence to them; for God permits them to have such success, that they which see and hear such things may be tried, and it may appear what confidence they have in God (Deuteronomy 13).

(11) Astrology, whether it be in casting of nativities[2] or making prognostications. This counterfeit art is nothing else but a mere abuse of the heavens and of the stars. (1) The twelve houses, which are the ground of all figures, are made of the feigned signs of a supposed zodiac in the highest sphere commonly called "the first moveable"; and therefore to these houses a man cannot truly ascribe any influence or virtue. (2) This art arises not from experience, because the same position of all stars never happens twice; and if it did, yet could there not be any observation made from thence, because the efficacy and influence of the stars is confusedly mixed both in the air and in the earth, as if all herbs were mingled together in one vessel. (3) This art withdraws men's minds from the contemplation of God's providence, when as they hear that all things fall out by the motion and position of the stars. (4) Stars were not ordained to foretell things to come, but to distinguish days, months, and years. "Let there be lights in the firmament of the heaven, to separate the day from the night: and let them be for signs, and for seasons, and for days, and for years" (Gen. 1:14). "Thou art wearied in the multitude of thy counsels: let now the astrologers, the star gazers, and prognosticators stand up and save thee from these things that shall come upon thee. Behold, they shall be as stubble: the fire shall burn them," etc. (Isa. 47:13–14). "The king commanded to call the enchanters, astrologers, sorcerers, and Chaldeans, to show the king his dreams" (Dan. 2:2). "Many of them which used curious arts, brought their books and burned them before all men" (Acts 19:10). (6) Astrological predictions are conversant about such things which either simply depend on the mere will and dispensation of God and not on the heavens, or else such as depending upon man's free will are altogether contingent and therefore can neither be foreseen nor foretold. (7) It is impossible by the bare knowledge of such a cause, as is both common to many and far distant from such things as it works in, precisely to set down particular effects. But the stars are common causes of those which are done upon earth and also far remote; and therefore a man can no more surely foretell what shall ensue by the contemplation of the stars, than he which sees a hen sitting can tell what kind of chicken shall be in every egg.

Question. Have then the stars no force in inferior things?

Answer. Yes, undoubtedly the stars have a very great force, yet such as manifests itself only in that operation which it has in the four principal qualities of natural things—namely, in heat, cold, moisture, and dryness. And therefore in altering the state and disposition of the air and in diversely affecting compound bodies, the stars have no small effect. But they are so far from enforcing the will to do anything that they cannot so much as give to it the least inclination. Now

---

2. *Nativities*: an astrological determination of birth or origin.

to define how great force the stars have, it is beyond any man's reach. For albeit the effects of the sun in the constitution of the four parts of the year are apparent to all, and the operation of the moon not very obscure, yet the force and nature both of planets and fixed stars, which are to us innumerable, are not so manifest. Therefore, seeing man knows only some stars and their only operation and not all with their forces, it cannot be that he should certainly foretell future things, although they did depend on the stars. For what if the position of such and such certain stars do demonstrate such an effect to ensue? May not the aspects of such as you yet know not hinder that and produce the contrary?

Question. Is then the use of astrology utterly impious?

Answer. That part of astrology which concerns the alteration of the air is almost all both false and frivolous, and therefore in a manner all predictions grounded upon that doctrine are mere toys by which the silly and ignorant people are notably deluded. As for that other part of astrology concerning nativities, revolutions, progressions, and directions of nativities, as also that which concerns election of times and the finding again of things lost—it is very wicked; and it is probable that it is of the same brood with implicit and close magic. My reasons are these. (1) The Word of God reckoning astrologers among magicians adjudges them both to one and the same punishment. (2) But the astrologer says he foretells many things which as he said come to pass. Be it so; but how, I demand? And by what means? He says by art, but that I deny. For the precepts of his art will appear to such as read them not with a prejudiced affection very ridiculous. Whence then, I pray you, does this curious diviner foreshow the truth but by an inward and secret instinct from the devil? This is Augustine's opinion. "If we weigh all those things," says he, "we will not without cause believe that astrologers, when they do wonderfully declare many truths, work by some secret instinct of evil spirits which desire to fill men's brains with erroneous and dangerous opinions of starry destinies and not by any art derived from the inspection and consideration of the horoscope, which indeed is none."[3]

(12) Popish consecration of water and salt to restore the mind to health and to chase away devils.[4]

(13) To make jests of the Scripture phrase, "I will look, even to him that is poor, and of a contrite spirit, and which trembleth at my words" (Isa. 66:2). We have an example of such scoffing, "The heathen did grievously oppress the Christians and inflicted sometimes upon their bodies corporal punishments.

---

3. In-text citation: In his 5th Book and 7th chapter of the City of God [Augustine, *The City of God*, bk. 5, ch. 7]

4. In-text citation: The reformed Missal. Pg. 96 [This may be a reference to the Reformed Chaldean Liturgy].

The which when the Christians signified to the emperor, he disdained to assist them and sent them away with this scoff: 'You are to suffer injuries patiently, for so ye are commanded of your God.'"[5]

(14) Lightly to pass over God's indictments, which are seen in the world. "Verily, verily, I say unto thee, this night before the cock crow, thou shalt deny me thrice. Peter said unto him, Though I should die with thee, I will not deny thee" (Matt. 26:34–35). "There was a certain man present at the same season, that showed him of the Galileans, whose blood Pilate had mingled with their own sacrifices. And Jesus answered and said unto them, Suppose ye that these Galileans were greater sinners than all the other Galileans, because they have suffered such things? I tell you nay, but except ye amend your lives, ye shall likewise perish" (Luke 13:1–3).

(15) A dissolute conversation. "Let your light so shine before men, that they seeing your good works, may glorify your Father which is in heaven" (Matt. 5:16). "Because that by this deed, thou hast made the enemies of the Lord to blaspheme, the child that is born unto thee shall surely die" (2 Sam. 12:14).

The Affirmative Part: In All Things Give God His Due Glory (1 Cor. 10:31)
To this appertain:

(1) Zeal of God's glory above all things in the world besides. "When Phineas the son of Eleazer saw it, he followed the man of Israel into his tent, and thrust them both through: to wit, both the man of Israel, and the woman through her belly" (Num. 25:8). "The zeal of thine house hath eaten me up, and the reproaches of the scornful have fallen upon me" (Ps. 69:9).

(2) To use God's titles only in serious affairs, and that with all reverence. "If thou wilt not keep and do all the words of this law (that are written in this book) and fear this the glorious and fearful name, THE LORD THY GOD" (Deut. 28:58). "Of whom are the fathers, and of whom, concerning the flesh, Christ came, who is God over all, blessed forever, Amen" (Rom. 9:5).

(3) A holy commemoration of the creature whereby we in the contemplation and admiration of the dignity and excellency thereof yield an approbation when we name it and celebrate the praise of God brightly shining in the same. "And all men shall see it, and declare the work of God, and they shall understand what he hath wrought: but the righteous shall be glad in the Lord, and trust in him: and all that are upright of heart shall rejoice" (Ps. 64:9–10). "And all they that heard it, wondered at the things that were told them of the shepherds, but

---

5. In-text citation: in the Tripart.hist. chap.39. book 6 [*Historiae Ecclesiastica Tripartita*, ch. 39, bk. 6. The *Historiae Ecclesiastica Tripartita* (sometimes called the Tripartite history) is a brief historical account of the early Christian Church compiled by the Roman statesman, author, and monastic founder Cassiodorus (485/90–*c.* 580) and his assistant Epiphanius Scholasticus].

Mary kept all these things, and pondered them in her heart" (Luke 2:18–19). "Fear ye not me, saith the Lord? Or will ye not be afraid at my presence, which have placed the sands for the bounds of the sea, by the perpetual decree, that it cannot pass it, and though the waves thereof rage, yet can they not prevail, though they roar, yet can they not pass over it?" (Jer. 5:22).

(4) An oath, in which we must regard (1) how an oath is to be taken; (2) how it is to be performed. In taking an oath, four circumstances must be observed.

(1) The matter or parts of an oath. The parts are in number four: (1) confirmation of a truth; (2) invocation of God alone as a witness of the truth and a revenger of a lie; (3) confession that God is a revenger of perjury when He is brought in as a false witness; (4) a binding over to punishment if we use deceit.

(2) The form. We must swear (1) truly, lest we forswear; (2) justly, lest we swear to that which is wicked; (3) in judgment, lest we swear rashly or for a trifle. "Thou shalt swear the Lord liveth, in truth, in judgment, and righteousness" (4:2). "Which swear by the name of the Lord, and make mention of the God of Israel, but not in truth nor in righteousness," etc. (Isa. 48:1). Therefore, the oath of drunken, furious, and frantic men, also oaths of children, they do not impose an observation of them, but by law are no oaths.

(3) The end—namely, to confirm some necessary truth in question. "Men swear by him that is greater than themselves: and an oath for confirmation, is among them an end of all strife" (Heb. 6:16). I call that a necessary truth when some doubt which must necessarily be decided can none other way be determined than by an oath, as when God's glory, our neighbors' safety and credit, a man's own necessity and faithfulness is in question. "God is my witness (whom I serve in my spirit in the gospel of his Son) that without ceasing I make mention of you" (Rom. 1:9). "I call God for a record to my soul, that to spare you I came not as yet unto Corinth" (2 Cor. 1:23).

(4) The divers kinds or sorts of others. An oath is public or private.

Public, when the magistrate without any peril to him that swears does upon just cause exact a testimony under the reverence of an oath.

A private oath is which two or more take privately. This, so that it be sparingly and warily used, is lawful. For if in serious affairs and matter of great importance it be lawful in private to admit God as a judge, why should He not as well be called to witness? Again, the examples of holy men show the practice of private oaths as not unlawful. Jacob and Laban confirmed their covenant one with another by oath; the like did Boaz in his contract with Ruth.

To this place may be added an asseveration, the which albeit it be like an oath, yet indeed is none and is nothing else but an earnest assertion of our meaning, the name of a creature being sometime used. Such was Christ's assertion, "Verily, verily, I say unto you"; and Paul's, "I call God to record in my spirit." Where is both an oath and asseveration: "By our rejoicing which I have in Jesus Christ, I die daily" (1 Cor. 15:31). "Indeed, as the Lord liveth, and as thy soul liveth, there is but a step between me and death" (1 Sam. 20:3). And surely in such a kind of asseveration there is great equity; for albeit it be unlawful to swear by creatures lest God's honor and power should be attributed to them, yet thus far may we use them in an oath as to make them pledges and as it were cognizances of God's glory.

The performance of an oath is on this manner. If the oath made be of a lawful thing, it must be performed, be it of much difficulty, great damage, or extorted by force of him that made it. "He that sweareth to his hindrance and changeth not, he shall dwell in God's tabernacle" (Ps. 15:4). Yet may the magistrate as it shall seem right and convenient either annihilate or moderate such oaths.

Contrarily, if a man swear to perform things unlawful and that by ignorance, error, or infirmity, or any other way, his oath is to be recalled. For we may not add sin to sin. "And David said, Indeed I have kept all in vain that this fellow had in the wilderness.... So and more also do God to the enemies of David: for surely I will not leave of all that he hath, by the dawning of the day, any that pisseth against the wall. David said, Blessed be thy cornfield, and blessed be thou, which hast kept me this day from coming to shed blood, and that mine hand hath not saved me" (1 Sam. 25:21–23; 2 Sam. 19:23). David promises that Shimei should not die; but David says to Solomon, "Though I sware so, yet thou shalt not count him innocent, but cause his hoar head to go down to the grave with blood" (1 Kings 2:8–9).

(5) Sanctification of God's creatures and ordinances, the which is a separation of them to a holy use. Thus ought we to sanctify our meats and drinks, the works of our calling, and marriage bed.

The means of this sanctification are two: God's Word and prayer. "All which God hath created is good, and nothing must be rejected, if it be received with thanksgiving: for it is sanctified by the word and prayer" (1 Tim. 4:4).

By the Word we are instructed, first, whether God allows the use of such things or not. Secondly, we learn after what holy manner, in what place, at what time, with what affection, and to what end we must use them. "Without faith it is impossible to please God" (Heb. 11:6). "Thy testimonies are my delight, they are my counselors" (Ps. 116:24; Josh. 22:19–20; 1 Sam. 15:23).

Prayer, which sanctifies, is petition and thanksgiving.

By petition, we obtain of God's majesty assistance by His grace to make a holy use of His creatures and ordinances. "Whatsoever ye shall do in word or deed, do all in the name of the Lord Jesus, giving thanks to God even the Father by him" (Col. 3:17). "Then said David to the Philistine, Thou comest to me with a sword, and with a spear, and with a shield: but I come to thee in the name of the Lord of Hosts, the God of the host of Israel, whom thou hast railed upon" (1 Sam. 17:45). "We must walk in the name of the Lord our God forever and ever" (Mic. 4:5). Here may we observe prayer made upon a particular occasion. (1) For a prosperous journey. "When the days were ended, we departed, and went our way, and they all accompanied us with their wives and children, even out of the city: and we kneeling down on the shore prayed," etc. (Acts 21:5). (2) For a blessing upon meats at the table. "Then Jesus took the bread, and when he had given thanks, he gave it to his disciples, and his disciples to them that were set down: and likewise of the fishes as much as they would" (John 6:11). "He took bread and gave thanks to God, in presence of them all, and brake it, and began to eat" (Acts 27:35). (3) For issue in childbirth. This did Anna (1 Sam. 1:12) and Zacharias (Luke 1:13). (4) For good success in business. Abraham's servant prayed (Gen. 24:12).

Thanksgiving is the magnifying of God's name, even the Father through Christ, for His grace, aid, and blessing in the lawful use of the creatures. "In all things let your requests be showed unto God in prayer, and supplication, and giving of thanks" (Phil. 4:6). "In all things give thanks: for this is the will of God in Christ toward you" (1 Thess. 5:18). This we may ready use (1) after meat. "When thou hast eaten and filled thyself, thou shalt bless the Lord thy God, for the good land which he hath given thee" (Deut. 8:10). (2) After the loss of outward wealth. "And Job said, Naked came I out of my mother's womb; and naked shall I return again: the Lord hath given, and the Lord hath taken away, blessed be the name of the Lord forevermore" (Job 1:21). (3) For deliverance out of servitude. "Jethro said, Blessed be the Lord, who hath delivered you out of the hands of the Egyptians, and out of the hand of Pharaoh, who also hath delivered the people from under the hand of the Egyptians" (Ex. 18:10). (4) For children. "She conceived again and bare a son, saying, now I will praise the Lord, therefore she called his name Judah" (Gen. 29:35). (5) For victory. "And David spake the words of this song unto the Lord, what time the Lord had delivered him out of the hands of all his enemies, and out of the hand of Saul, and said, The Lord is my rock, and my fortress," etc. (2 Sam. 22:1). (6) For good success in domestic affairs. Abraham's servant "blessed the Lord of his master Abraham" (Gen. 24:48).

Chapter 23

Of the Fourth Commandment

The fourth commandment concerns the Sabbath—namely, that holy time consecrated to the worship and glorifying of God. The words are these:

"Remember the Sabbath day to keep it holy: six days shalt thou labor, and do all thy work: but the seventh day is the Sabbath of the Lord thy God; in it thou shalt do no manner of work; thou, nor thy son, nor thy daughter, thy man servant, nor thy maid, nor thy beast, nor thy stranger that is within thy gates. For in six days the Lord made the heaven and the earth, the sea, and all that in them is, and rested the seventh day: therefore the Lord blessed the seventh day, and hallowed it" [Ex. 20:8–11].

The Resolution

"Remember." This cause does insinuate that in times past there was great neglect in the observation of the Sabbath, and would that all degrees and conditions of men should prepare themselves to sanctify the same—especially those that be governors of families, incorporations, and cities, to whom this commandment is directed.

"To keep it holy," or, "to sanctify it." To sanctify is to sever a thing from common use and to consecrate the same to the service of God. Here are described the two parts of this commandment: the first whereof is rest from labor; the second, sanctification of that rest.

"Six days." These words contain a close answer to this objection: "It is much to cease from our callings one whole day." The answer (together with a first reason to enforce the sanctification of the Sabbath) is in these words, which is taken from the greater to the less. "If I permit you to follow your calling six whole days, you may well and must leave one only to serve Me."

But the first is true. Therefore, the second.

The first proposition is wanting; the second or assumption of these words, "six days," etc. The conclusion is the commandment itself.

Here we may see that God has given us free liberty to work all the six days, the which freedom no man can annihilate. Nevertheless, upon extraordinary occasions, the church of God is permitted to separate one day or more of the six as need is, either to fasting or for a solemn day of rejoicing for some benefit received (Joel 2:15).

"The seventh day." The second reason of this commandment is taken from the end thereof.

If the Sabbath were consecrated to God and His service, we must that day abstain from our labors.

But it was consecrated to God and His service.

The assumption is in these words, "the seventh day," etc., where we must note that God alone has this privilege to have a Sabbath consecrated to Him. And therefore, all holy days dedicated to whatever either angel or saint are unlawful, however the Church of Rome have imposed the observation of them upon many people.

"In it thou shalt do." This is the conclusion of the second reason, illustrated by a distribution from the causes. "You, your son, your daughter, your servant, your cattle, your stranger shall cease that day from your labors."

"Any work." That is, any ordinary work of your callings and such as may be done the day before or left well undone till the day after. Yet for all this, we are not forbidden to perform such works even on this day as are both holy and of present necessity.

Such are those works which do upon that day preserve and maintain the service and glory of God, as (1) a Sabbath day's journey. "Which is near to Jerusalem, containing a Sabbath day's journey" (Acts 1:13). (2) The killing and dressing of sacrificed beasts in the time of the laws. "Have ye not read in the law, how that on the Sabbath days the priests in the temple break the Sabbath, and are blameless?" (Matt. 12:5). (3) Journeys to the prophets and places appointed to the worship of God. "He said, Why wilt thou go unto him this day? It is neither new moon nor Sabbath day" (2 Kings 4:23). "They go from strength to strength, till everyone appear before God in Zion" (Ps. 84:7).

Such also are the works of mercy, whereby the safety of life or goods is procured, as that which Paul did. "As Paul was long preaching, Eutychus overcome with sleep, fell down from the third loft and was taken up dead: but Paul went down and laid himself upon him and embraced him, saying, Trouble not yourselves; for his life is in him. And they brought the boy alive, and they were not a little comforted" (Acts 20:9, 12). (2) To help a beast out of a pit. "Which of you shall have an ox, or an ass fallen into a pit, and will not straightway pull him out on the Sabbath day?" (Luke 14:5). (3) Provision of meat and drink. "Jesus went through the corn on the Sabbath day, and his disciples were anhungered, and began to pluck the ears of corn, and to eat" (Matt. 12:1). In provision, we must take heed that our cooks and household servants break not the Sabbath. The reason of this is framed from the less to the greater out of that place, "David longed and said, Oh that one would give me to drink of the water of the well of Bethlehem, which is by the gate. Then the three mighties brake into the host of the Philistines, and drew water out of the well of Bethlehem that was by the gate, and took and brought it to David, who would not drink thereof, but poured it for an offering to the Lord. And said, O Lord, be it far from me that I should do this: is not this the blood of the men that went in jeopardy of their lives? Therefore would he not drink" (2 Sam. 23:15–17). The reason stands thus: If David would not have his servants adventure their corporal lives for his provision nor drink the water when they had provided it, much less ought we for our meats to adventure the souls of our servants. (4) Watering of cattle. "The Lord answered and said, thou hypocrite, will not any of you on the Sabbath days, loose his ox or ass out of the stable, and bring him to the water?" (Luke 13:15). Upon the like present and holy necessity, physicians upon the Sabbath day may take a journey to visit the diseased, mariners their voyage, shepherds may tend their flock, and midwives may help women with child. "The Sabbath was made for man, and not man for the Sabbath" (Mark 2:27).

"Within thy gates." This word "gate" signifies by a figure jurisdiction and authority. "The gates of hell shall not overcome it" (Matt. 16:18). Let this be a looking glass wherein all enholders and entertainers of strangers may look into themselves and behold what is their duty.

"For in six days." The third reason of this commandment from the like example.

That which I did, you also must do.

But I rested the seventh day and hallowed it.

Therefore, you must do the like.

God sanctified the Sabbath when He did consecrate it to His service. Men sanctify it when they do worship God in it. In this place, we are to consider the Sabbath, how far forth it is ceremonial and how far forth moral.

The Sabbath is ceremonial in respect of the strict observation thereof, which was a type of the internal sanctification of the people of God, and that is, as it were, a continual resting from the work of sin. "Speak thou also unto the children of Israel, and say; notwithstanding keep ye my Sabbath: for it is a sign between me and you in your generation, that ye may know that I, the Lord do sanctify you" (Ex. 31:13) The same is recorded [in] Ezekiel 20:12.

It signified also that blessed rest of the faithful in the kingdom of heaven. "From month to month, and from Sabbath to Sabbath, shall all flesh come to worship before Me, saith the Lord" (Isa. 66:23), "If Jesus had given them a rest," etc. (Heb. 4:8–10).

The Sabbath is likewise ceremonial in that it was observed the seventh day after the creation of the world and was then solemnized with such ceremonies.

"But on the Sabbath day; ye shall offer two lambs of a year old without spot, and two tenth deals of fine flour for a meat offering, mingled with oil, and the drink offering thereof. This is the burnt offering of every Sabbath, beside the continual burnt offering and drink offering thereof" (Num. 28:9–10).

But now in the light of the gospel and the churches professing the same, the ceremony of the Sabbath is ceased. "Let no man condemn you in meat and drink, or in respect of an holy day, or of the new moon, or of the Sabbath: which are but shadows of things to come, but the body is Christ" (Col. 2:16–17). The observation of the Sabbath was translated by the apostles from the seventh day to the day following. "The first day of the week, the disciples being come together to break bread, Paul preached to them" (Acts 20:7). "Concerning the gathering for the saints, as I have ordained in the churches of Galatia, so do ye also every first day of the week, let every one of you put aside by himself, and lay up as God hath prospered him, that then there be no gatherings when I come" (1 Cor. 16:1–2). This day by reason that our Savior did upon it rise again is called the Lord's Day. "I was ravished in the Spirit on the Lord's day" (Rev. 1:10).

The observation of the Sabbath thus constituted by the apostles was nevertheless neglected of those churches which succeeded them, but after was revived and established by Christian emperors as a day most apt to celebrate the memory of the creation of the world and to the serious meditation of the redemption of mankind.[1]

The observation of the Sabbath is moral inasmuch as it is a certain seventh day which preserves and conserves the ministry of the word and the solemn worship of God, especially in the assemblies of the church. And in this respect we are upon this day as well enjoined a rest from our vocations as the Jews were. "If thou turn away thy foot from the Sabbath, from doing thy will on mine holy day: and call my Sabbath a delight, to consecrate it, as glorious to the Lord, and shalt honor him, not doing thine own ways," etc. (Isa. 58:13).

Finally, it is moral in that it frees servants and cattle from their labors which on other days do service to their owners.

The Affirmative Part: Keep Holy the Sabbath Day

This we do if we cease from the works of sin and of our ordinary calling, performing those spiritual works which we are commanded in the second and third commandments.

(1) To arise early in the morning that so we may prepare ourselves to the better sanctifying of the Sabbath ensuing. This preparation consists in private prayers and taking account of our several sins. "In the morning very early before

---

1. Leo and Anton, *Edict. Of Holy Days.*

day, Jesus arose and went into a solitary place, and there prayed. The day following was the Sabbath, when he preached in the synagogues" (Matt. 1:35, 39). "Aaron proclaimed, saying, Tomorrow shall be the holy day of the Lord: so they rose up the next day early in the morning" (Ex. 32:5–6). "Take heed to thy feet when thou enterest into the house of God" (Eccl. 4, last verse).

(2) To be present at public assemblies at ordinary hours, there to hear reverently and attentively the word preached and read, to receive the sacraments, and publicly with the congregation call upon and celebrate the name of the Lord. "When they departed from Perga, they came to Antiochia, a city of Pisidia, and went into the synagogue on the Sabbath day and sat down. And after the lecture of the law and prophets, the rulers of the synagogue sent to them, saying, ye men and brethren, if ye have any word of exhortation for the people, say on" (1 Tim, 2:1–3; Acts 20:7; 2 Kings 4:22–23; Acts 13:14–15).

(3) When public meetings are dissolved, to spend the rest of the Sabbath in the meditation of God's Word and His creatures (Psalm 92, from the beginning to the ending). "These were also more able men, than they which were at Thessalonica, which received the Word with all readiness, and searched the Scriptures daily, whether those things were so" (Acts 17:11). We must also exercise then the works of charity, as to visit the sick, give alms to the needy, admonish such as fall, reconcile such as are at jar and discord among themselves, etc. "Then all the people went to eat and to drink, and to send away part, and to make great joy" (Neh. 8:12).

The Negative Part: Pollute not the Sabbath of the Lord

This is a grievous sin. "Pray that your flight be not in winter, nor on the Sabbath day" (Matt. 24:20). "The adversaries saw her, and did mock at her Sabbaths" (Lam. 1:7). "Ye shall keep my Sabbaths, and reverence my sanctuary, I am the Lord" (Lev. 19:30). In this part are these things forbidden.

(1) The works of our calling, wherein if we do ought it must be altogether in regard of charity and not in regard of our own private commodity.

(2) Unnecessary journeys. "Tarry every man in his place, let no man go out of his place the seventh day" (Ex. 16:29). By this reason, the master of the family must that day remain at home to sanctify the Sabbath with his household.

(3) Fairs upon the Sabbath day. "When the gates of Jerusalem began to be dark before the Sabbath, I commanded to shut the gates, and charged that they should not be opened till after the Sabbath, and some of my servants set I at the gate, that there should no burden then be brought in on the Sabbath day" (Neh. 13:19; read vv. 15–19).

(4) All kind of husbandry, as plowing, sowing, reaping, mowing, bringing home harvest, and other the like. "In the seventh day shalt thou rest, both in earing time, and in harvest shalt thou rest" (Ex. 34:21).

(5) To use jests, sports, banqueting, or any other thing whatever, which is a means to hinder or withdraw the mind from that serious attention which ought to be in God's service. For if the works of our calling must not be exercised, much less these whereby the mind is as well distracted from God's service, as by the greatest labor.

(6) An external observation of the Sabbath without the inward power of godliness. "My soul hateth your new moons, and your appointed feasts, they are a burden unto me, I am weary to bear them: and when you shall stretch forth your hands, I will hide mine eyes from you, and though you make many prayers, I will not hear: for your hands are full of blood" (Isa. 1:14–15). "Which have a show of godliness, but deny the force thereof: such therefore avoid" (2 Tim. 3:5).

(7) The manifest profanation of the Sabbath in pampering the belly, surfeiting, adultery, and other like profaneness, which is nothing else but to celebrate a Sabbath to the devil and not to God.

Chapter 24

Of the Fifth Commandment

Hitherto we have spoken of the commandments of the first table; now follows the second table, which concerns the love of our neighbor. "Thou shalt not commit adultery, thou shalt not kill, thou shalt not steal, thou shalt not bear false witness, thou shalt not covet: and if there be any other commandment, it is briefly comprehended in this saying, namely, thou shalt love thy neighbor as thyself" (Rom. 13:9).

Our neighbor is everyone which is of our own flesh. "When thou seest the naked, cover him, and hide not thyself from thine own flesh" (Isa. 58:7).

The manner of loving is so to love our neighbor as ourselves—to wit, truly and sincerely—when as contrarily, the true manner of loving God is to love God without measure.

The second table contains six commandments, whereof the first, and in the order of the Ten Commandments the fifth, concerns the preservation of the dignity and excellency of our neighbor.

The words are these:

"Honor thy father and thy mother, that they may prolong thy days in the land, which the Lord thy God giveth thee" [Ex. 20:12].

The Resolution

"Honor." This word by a figure signifies all that duty whereby our neighbor's dignity is preserved, but especially our superior's. This dignity proceeds of this, that every man bears in him some part of the image of God, if we respect the outward order and decency which is observed in the church and commonwealth. In the magistrate, there is a certain image of the power and glory of God. "O King, thou art a king of kings, for the God of heaven hath given thee a kingdom, power, and strength, and glory" (Dan. 2:37). Hence it is that magistrates are called "gods" (Ps. 82:1). In an old man is the similitude of the eternity of God; in a father, the likeness of His fatherhood. "And call no man your father upon the earth: for there is but one, your Father which is in heaven" (Matt. 23:9). In the man is the image of God's providence and authority. "For a man ought not to cover his head, because he is the image of the glory of God: but the woman is the glory of her husband" (1 Cor. 11:7). Finally, in a learned man is the likeness of the knowledge and wisdom of God. Now therefore that person in whom even the least title of the image of God appears is to be honored and reverenced.

"Thy father." By a figure we must here understand all those that are our superiors, as parents and such like of our kindred or alliance which are to us instead of parents, magistrates, ministers, our elders, and those that do excel us in any gifts whatever. The kings of Gerar called Abimelech "my father the king." "God hath made me a father unto Pharaoh, and lord over all his house" (Gen. 20:2; 45:8). "For though ye have ten thousand instructors in Christ, yet have ye not many fathers: for in Christ Jesus I have begotten you" (1 Cor. 4:15). "But his servants came and spake unto him, and said, Father, if the prophet had commanded thee a great thing, Wouldest thou not have done it?" (2 Kings 5:13). "And Elisha saw it, and he cried, My father, my father, the chariot of Israel, and the horsemen thereof" (2:12).

"And thy mother." This is added, lest we should despise our mothers because of their infirmities. "Obey thy father which hath begotten thee, and despise not thy mother when she is old" (Prov. 23:22).

Here we are put in mind to perform due honor to our stepmothers and fathers-in-law, as if they were our proper and natural parents. "Afterward Naomi her mother-in-law said unto her, My daughter, shall not I seek rest for thee, that thou mayest prosper? And she answered her, All that thou biddest me, I will do" (Ruth 3:1, 5). "But Moses' father-in-law said unto him, The thing which thou doest is not well. Hear now my voice, I will give thee counsel, and God shall be with thee. So Moses obeyed the voice of his father-in-law, and did all that he had said" (Ex. 18:17, 19, 24). "For the son revileth the father, the daughter riseth up against her mother, the daughter-in-law, against her mother-in-law" (Micah 7:6).

"That they may prolong." Parents are said to prolong the lives of their children because they are God's instruments whereby their children's lives are prolonged; for oftentimes the name of the action is attributed to the instrument wherewith the action is wrought. "Make you friends with the riches of iniquity, that when ye shall want, they may receive you into everlasting habitations" (Luke 16:9). "For in doing so, thou shalt both save thy self and them that hear thee" (1 Tim. 4:16).

But parents do prolong the lives of their children in commanding them to walk in the ways of the Lord by exercising justice and judgment (Gen. 18:19). For being become godly, they have the promise both of this life and the life to come (1 Tim. 4:8).

Further, they effect the same thing by their prayers made in the behalf of their children. Hereby it plainly appears that the usual custom of children saluting their parents to ask them their blessings is no light or vain thing.

Moreover, in these words the reason to move us to the obedience of this commandment is drawn from the end, which reason is also a promise, yet[1] a special promise. "Honor thy father and thy mother, which is the first commandment with promise" (Eph. 6:2). I say special, because the promise of the second commandment is general and belongs to all the rest of the commandments.

And God promises long life not absolutely, but so far as it is a blessing, "That it may be well with thee, and that thou mayest live long on earth" (Eph. 6:3). For we must think that long life is not always a blessing, but that sometime it is better to die than to live. "The righteous perisheth, and no man considereth it in heart: and merciful men are taken away, and no man understandeth that the righteous is taken away from the evil to come" (Isa. 57:1).

But if at any time the Lord gives a short life to obedient children, He rewards them again with eternal life in heaven; and so the promise fails not, but changes for the better.

The Affirmative Part: Preserve the Dignity of Your Neighbor

Under this part is commanded:

First, reverence toward all our superiors, the actions whereof are: reverently to rise up before them when they pass by us. "Rise up before the hoary head, and honor the person of the old man, and dread thy God: I am the Lord" (Lev. 19:32). To meet them when they come toward us. "And he lifted up his eyes and looked: and lo, three men stood by him, and when he saw them, he ran to meet them from the tent door" (Gen. 18:2). "When Bathsheba came to speak to King Solomon, the king rose to meet her, and bowed himself unto her" (1 Kings 2:19). "And when he was gone out of the way, there came one running and kneeled to him" (Mark 10:17). "He ran to meet them, and bowed himself to the ground" (Gen. 18:2). To stand by them when they sit down. "And he took butter, and milk, and the calf that he had prepared, and set before them, and stood himself by them under the tree, and they did eat" (v. 18). "Now on the morrow, when Moses sat to judge the people, the people stood about Moses from morning unto even" (Ex. 18:13). To give them the chief seat, "And he sat down on his throne, and he caused a seat to be set for the king's mother, and she sat down at his right hand" (1 Kings 2:19). "He spake also a parable unto the guests, when he marked how they chose out the chief rooms, and said to them, When thou shalt be bidden of any man to a wedding, set not thyself down in

---

1. This is "yet" in the original, but was likely intended to be "yea."

the chiefest place, lest a more honorable man than thou be bidden of him, and he that bade both him and thee, come and say to thee, Give this man room, and thou then begin with shame to take the lowest room" (Luke 14:7–9). "So they sat before him, the eldest according to his age, and the youngest according to his youth, and the men marveled among themselves" (Gen. 43:33). To let our superiors speak before us (Job 32:6–7, 17). To keep silence in courts and judgment places until we be bidden to speak. "Then Paul after that the governor had beckoned unto him that he should speak, answered" (Acts 24:10). To give them such their right and just titles as declare our reverence when we speak to them. "As Sarah obeyed Abraham, and called him lord: whose daughters ye are, while ye do well" (1 Peter 3:6). "Good master, what shall I do, that I may possess eternal life? Then he answered, and said to him, Master, all these things have I observed from my youth" (Mark 10:17, 20). "And Eli said unto her, How long wilt thou be drunk? Put away thy drunkenness from thee: then Hannah answered and said, Nay my Lord, but I am a woman troubled in spirit: I have drunk neither wine nor strong drink" (1 Sam. 1:14–15).

Secondly, toward those that are our superiors in authority; and first, obedience to their commandments. "Let every soul be subject to the higher power" (Rom. 13:1).

We are to be admonished to obedience because every higher power is the ordinance of God, and the obedience which we perform thereto God accepts it as though it were done to Himself and to Christ. "Whosoever therefore, resisteth the power, resisteth the ordinance of God, and they that resist, shall receive to themselves judgment" (v. 2). "And whatsoever ye do, do it heartily, as unto the Lord, and not to men. Knowing that of the Lord ye shall receive the reward of the inheritance: for ye serve the Lord Christ" (Col. 3:23–24). Obedience is to be performed to our superiors with diligence and faithfulness. "Abraham said unto his eldest servant of his house, which had the rule over all that he had: put now thy hand under my thigh, and I will make thee swear by the Lord God of heaven, and God of the earth, that thou shalt not take a wife unto my son of the daughters of the Canaanites, among whom I dwell" (Gen. 24:2). "So the servant took ten camels of his master's, and departed. And he said, O Lord God of my master Abraham, I beseech Thee send me good speed this day, and show mercy unto my master Abraham" (v. 12). "Afterward the meat was set before him, but he said, I will not eat, until I have said my message: And Laban said, Speak on" (v. 33). "But he said, Hinder me not, seeing the Lord has prospered my journey: send me away that I may go to my master (v. 56). "This twenty years have I been with thee, thine ewes and thy goats have not cast their young, and the rams of thy flock have I not eaten. Whatsoever was torn of beasts, I brought it not unto thee, but made it good myself: of mine hand didst thou require it, were it stolen by day, or stolen by night. I was in the day consumed with heat, and with frost in the night, and my sleep departed from mine eyes" (31:38–40).

Furthermore, we must yield obedience to our superiors, yea, although they be cruel and wicked, but not in wickedness. "Servants be subject to your masters with all fear, not only to the good and courteous, but also to the froward" (1 Peter 2:18). "Whether it be right in the sight of God, to obey you rather than God, judge ye" (Acts 4:19).

Subjection in suffering the punishments inflicted by our superiors. "Then Abraham said to Sarai, Behold thy maid is in thine hand, do with her as pleaseth thee: then Sarai dealt roughly with her: wherefore she fled from her, Then the angel of the Lord said unto her, Return to thy dame, and humble thyself under her hands" (Gen. 16:6, 9).

And although the punishment should be unjust, yet must we suffer it until we can get some lawful remedy for the same. "For it is thankworthy, if a man for conscience toward God endure grief, suffering wrongfully. For what praise is it, if when ye be buffeted for your faults, ye take it patiently? But and if, when ye do well, ye suffer wrong, and take it patiently, this is acceptable to God" (1 Peter 2:19–20).

(3) Thankfulness, (1) in our prayers, "I exhort you therefore, that first of all, supplications, prayers, intercessions, and giving of thanks be made for all men, for kings, and for all that be in authority, that we may lead a quiet and peaceable life, in all godliness and honesty" (1 Tim. 2:1–2). (2) In outward maintenance. "Elders that rule well, are worthy of double honor" (5:17). "Haste you and go to my father, and tell him, Thus saith thy son Joseph, God hath made me lord over all Egypt, come down to me, tarry not. And thou shalt dwell in the land of Goshen. Also I will nourish thee there, for yet remain five years of famine, lest thou perish through poverty, thou and thy household, and all that thou hast" (Gen. 45:9–11).

Thirdly, toward those that excel us in gifts, our duty is to acknowledge the same gifts and speak of them to their praise (2 Cor. 8:22–23).

Fourthly, toward all our equals, to think reverently of them. "Let nothing be done through contention or vain glory, but in meekness of mind, let every man esteem other better than himself" (Phil. 2:3).

In giving honor, to go one before another, and not in receiving it. "Submit yourselves one to another in the fear of God" (Rom. 12:10). To salute one another with holy signs, whereby may appear the love which we have one to another in Christ. "Greet one another with the kiss of love" (1 Peter 5:14). "Salute one another with an holy kiss" (Rom. 16:16). "And Moses went out to meet his father-in-law, and did obeisance and kissed him" (Ex. 18:7). "And behold, Boaz came from Bethlehem, and said unto the reapers, The Lord be with you. And they answered, The Lord bless thee" (Ruth 2:4).

Fifthly, the duties of all superiors toward their inferiors, (1) saving their place and dignity, to carry themselves as brethren. "That his heart be not lifted up above his brethren, and he turn not from the commandment, to the right hand or to the left" (Deut. 17:20). "If I did contemn the judgment of my servant, and of my maid" (Job 31:13). "And his servant came and spake unto him, and said" (2 Kings 5:13). "Then he went down, and washed himself seven times in Jordan," etc. (v. 14). (2) To shine before their inferiors by an example of a blameless life. "That the elder men be sober, honest, discrete, sound in faith, in love, and in patience. The elder women likewise, that they be in such behavior as becometh holiness, not false accusers, not given to much wine, but teachers of honest things" (Titus 2:2–3). "Not as though ye were lords over God's heritage, but that ye may be ensamples to the flock" (1 Peter 5:3; Phil. 4:9). (3) To show forth gravity joined with dignity by their countenance, gesture, deeds, and words; for hereby they must grace the image of God which they bear before their inferiors (Titus 2:3–7). "The young men saw me, and hid themselves, the aged arose and stood up" (Job 29:8).

Sixthly, toward inferiors in obedience—that is, toward their subjects. (1) To rule them in the Lord, that they do not offend. "Submit yourselves unto all manner ordinance of man, for the Lord's sake, whether it be to kings as unto superiors, or unto governors, as unto them that are sent of the king, for the punishment of evil doers, and for the praise of them that do well" (1 Peter 2:13–14). "And it shall be with him (namely the book of the law) and he shall read therein all the days of his life, that he may learn to fear the Lord his God, and to keep all the words of this law, and these ordinances to do them" (Deut. 17:19) "Ye masters do unto your servants, that which is just and equal: knowing that ye also have a master in heaven" (Col. 4:1). (2) To provide such things as shall be to the good of their subjects, whether they belong to the body or to the soul. "For he is the minister of God for thy wealth" (Rom. 13:4). "And kings shall be thy nursing fathers, and queens shall be thy nurses" (Isa. 49:23). "Lord remember David with all his troubles. Who sware unto the Lord, and vowed to the mighty God of Jacob, saying, I will not enter into the tabernacle of mine house, nor come upon my pallet or bed, nor suffer mine eyes to sleep, nor mine eyelids to slumber, until I find out a place for the Lord, an habitation for the mighty God of Jacob" (Ps. 132:1–5). (3) To punish their faults, the lighter by rebuking, the greater by correction—that is, by inflicting real or bodily punishment.

There is a holy manner of punishing the guilty, whereto is required (1) after diligent and wise examination is had, to be assured of the crime committed. (2) To show forth of God's Word the offence of the sin, that the conscience of the offender may be touched. (3) It is convenient to defer or omit the punishment, if thereby any hope of amendment may appear. "Give not thy heart also to all the words that men speak, lest thou do hear thy servant cursing thee. For oftentimes also thine heart knoweth, that thou likewise hast cursed others" (Eccl. 7:23–24). "But the wicked men said, How shall he save us? So they despised him, and brought him no presents; but he held his tongue" (1 Sam. 10:27). (4) To inflict deserved punishment, not in his own name, but in God's name, adding the same holily and reverently. "Then Joshua said to Achan, My son, I beseech thee, give glory to the Lord God of Israel, and make confession unto Him, and show me now what thou hast done, hide it not from me. And Achan answered unto Joshua, and said, Indeed I have sinned against the Lord God of Israel, and thus have I done. And Joshua said, Inasmuch as thou hast troubled us, the Lord shall trouble thee this day: and all Israel threw stones at him, and burned them with fire, and stoned them with stones" (Josh. 7:19–20, 25). (5) And lastly, when you punish, aim at this one only thing, that the evil may be purged and amended, and that the offender by sorrowing for his sin may unfeignedly repent for the same. "The blueness of the wound serveth to purge evil, and the stripes within the bowels of the belly" (Prov. 20:30).

Seventhly and lastly, there is a certain duty of a man to be performed toward himself, which is that a man should preserve and maintain with modesty the dignity and worthiness which is inherent in his own person. "Furthermore, brethren, whatsoever things are true, whatsoever things are honest, whatsoever things are just, whatsoever things are pure, whatsoever things pertain to love, whatsoever things are of good report, if there be any virtue, or if there be any praise, think on these things" (Phil. 4:8).

The Negative Part: Diminish not the Excellency or Dignity Which Is in the Person of Your Neighbor

Hither are referred these sins:

First, against our superiors. (1) Unreverent behavior and contempt of them. The sins hereof are, deriding our superiors. "And when Ham the father of Canaan saw the nakedness of his father, he told his two brethren without" (Gen. 9:22). "The eye that mocketh his father, and despiseth the instruction of his mother, let the ravens of the valley pick it out, and the young eagles eat it" (Prov. 30:17). To speak evil of or revile our superiors. "And he that curseth his father or his mother, shall die the death" (Ex. 21:17).

(2) Disobedience, whereby we contemn their just commandments. "Disobedient to parents" (Rom. 1:30; 2 Tim. 3:2). The sins hereof are: to make contracts of marriage without the counsel and consent of the parents. "Then the sons of God saw the daughters of men that they were fair, and they took

them wives of all that they liked" (Gen. 6:2). "And Esau seeing that the daughters of Canaan displeased Isaac his father, then went Esau to Ishmael, and took unto the wives which he had, Mahalath the daughter of Ishmael, Abraham's son, the sister of Nabajoth, to be his wife" (28:8–9). The eye-service of servants. "Servants be obedient to them that are your masters according to the flesh, in all things, not with eye service as men pleasers, but in singleness of heart, fearing God" (Col. 3:22). "Not with service to the eye, as men pleasers" (Eph. 6:6). Answering again when they are reprehended. "Let servants be subject to their masters; and please them in all things, not answering again" (Titus 2:9). Deceitfulness and wasting their master's goods. "Neither pickers, but that they show all good faithfulness" (v. 10). To flee from the power of their superior. "Then Sarai dealt roughly with her wherefore she fled from her" (Gen. 16:6) To resist the lawful authority of their superiors (1 Peter 2:20). To obey them in things unlawful (Acts 4:19). To extol themselves above their betters—this is the sin of antichrist. "Which (man of sin) exalteth himself against all that is called God" (2 Thess. 2:3–4). Lastly, the freedom of the papists, whereby they free children from the government of their parents and subjects from the authority of their princes, so as they make it lawful for them to plot and procure their death. "Then said Abishai to David, God hath closed thine enemy into thine hand this day: now therefore I pray thee, let me smite him once with a spear to the earth, and I will not smite him again: and David said to Abishai, Destroy him not: for who can lay his hand on the Lord's anointed and be guiltless?" (1 Sam. 26:8–9).

(3) Ingratitude and want of a loving affection toward parents. "But ye say, whosoever shall say to father or mother, By the gift that is offered by me, thou mayest have profit, though he honor not his father or mother, shall be free" (Matt. 15:5–6; 1 Tim. 5:4).

Secondly, we offend against our equals in preferring ourselves before them in talking or in sitting down. "Then came unto him the mother of Zebedee's children, with her sons, worshiping him, and desiring a certain thing of him. And he said, What wouldest thou? And she said to him, Grant, that these my two sons may sit, the one at thy right hand, and the other at thy left hand, in thy kingdom. And when the other ten heard this, they disdained at the two brethren" (Matt. 20:20–21, 24).

Thirdly, toward our inferiors (1) through negligence in governing them and providing for their good estate. "Is it time for yourselves to dwell in your ceiled houses, and this house to lie waste?" (Hag. 1:4; Dan. 3:28). This condemns those mothers which put forth their children to be nursed, having both sufficient strength and store of milk themselves to nurse them. "If she have nourished her children" (1 Tim. 5:10). (2) By too much gentleness and lenity in correcting them. "Then Adonijah the son of Haggith exalted himself, saying, I will be king.

And his father would not displease him from his childhood, to say, why hast thou done so?" (1 Kings 1:5–6). "So Eli was very old, and heard all that his sons did unto all Israel, and how they lay with the women that assembled at the door of the tabernacle of the congregation. And he said unto them: Why do ye such things? For of all this people I hear evil reports of you. Do no more, my sons, for it is no good report that I hear, namely, that ye make the Lord's people to trespass. Notwithstanding they obeyed not the voice of their father, because the Lord would slay them" (1 Sam. 2:22–25). (3) By overmuch cruelty and threatenings. "And ye fathers, provoke not your children to wrath. And ye masters do the same things unto them, putting away threatenings" (Eph. 6:4, 9).

Fourthly and lastly, a man offends against himself when through his naughty behavior he does obscure and almost extinguish those gifts which God has given him (Matt. 25:26). Or contrarily, when he is proud and too wise in his own conceit. "For I say, through the grace that is given unto me, to everyone that is among you, that no man presume to understand, above that which is meet to understand" (Rom. 12:3).

Chapter 25

Concerning the Sixth Commandment

The sixth commandment concerns the preservation of our neighbor's life. The words are these:

"Thou shalt not kill" [Ex. 20:13].

The Resolution

"Kill." The part is here set for the whole by a synecdoche, for killing signifies any kind of endamaging the person of our neighbor.

The equity of this commandment appears by this, that man is created after the likeness of God. "He that sheddeth man's blood, by man shall his blood be shed: for in the image of God hath he made man" (Gen. 9:6). Again, all men are the same flesh. "When thou seest the naked cover him, and hide not thy face from thine own flesh" (Isa. 58:7).

Neither ought we to be ignorant of this also, that it is unlawful for any private person not called to that duty to kill another; but a public officer may—that is, if he be warranted by a calling. So did Moses: "And he looked round about, and when he saw no man, he slew the Egyptian, and hid him in the sand" (Ex. 2:12). "For he supposed his brethren would have understood, that God by his hand should give them deliverance" (Acts 7:25). And Phinehas: "And he followed the man of Israel into the tent, and thrust them both through (to wit, the man of Israel and the woman) through her belly: so that the plague ceased from the children of Israel. Phinehas the son of Eleazar, hath turned mine anger away from the children of Israel, while he was zealous for my sake among them: therefore I have not consumed the children of Israel in my jealousy" (Num. 25:8, 11). And Elijah: "And Elijah said to them, take the prophets of Baal, let not a man of them escape: and they took them, and Elijah brought them to the brook Kidron, and slew them there" (1 Kings 18:40). And soldiers in battles waged upon just causes. "Fear ye not, neither be afraid of this great multitude: for the battle is not yours, but God's" (2 Chron. 20:15).

**The Negative Part: You Shall neither Hurt nor Hinder
either Your Own or Your Neighbor's Life**

The sins then that are referred to this part are such as are committed against our neighbor or ourselves.

Against our neighbor are these following: (1) in heart, as (1) hatred against him. "Whoso hateth his brother, is a manslayer" (1 John 3:15). (2) Unadvised anger. "I say unto you, whosoever is angry with his brother unadvisedly, is in danger of judgment" (Matt. 5:22). (3) Envy. "Full of envy, murder, contention" (Rom. 1:29). (4) Grudges. "If ye have bitter envying and strife in your hearts, rejoice not" (James 3:14). (5) Want of compassion and sorrow at our neighbor's calamities. "They sing to the sound of the viol, etc., but no man is sorry for the affliction of Joseph" (Amos 6:5–6). (6) Frowardness, when we will not be reconciled to our neighbor. "Such as can never be appeased, unmerciful" (Rom. 1:30). (7) Desire of revenge. "The Lord will abhor the bloody men and deceitful" (Ps. 5:6).

(2) In words. (1) Bitterness in speaking. "There is that speaketh words, like the prickings of a sword: but the tongue of wise men is health" (Prov. 12:18). (2) Reproaches and railing, which is a casting of a man's sins in his teeth which he has committed, or an objecting to him some inherent infirmities. "Whosoever saith unto his brother, raca, shall be worthy to be punished by the council. And whosoever shall say, fool, shall be worthy to be punished with hell fire" (Matt. 5:22). "As the Ark of the Lord came into the city of David, Michal, Saul's daughter, looked through a window, and saw King David leap and dance before the Lord, and she despised him in her heart. And Michal the daughter of Saul came out to meet David, and said, O how glorious was the king of Israel this day, which was uncovered today in the eyes of the maidens of his servants, as a fool uncovereth himself" (2 Sam. 6:16, 20). (3) Contentions, when two or more strive in speech one with another for any kind of superiority. (4) Brawlings in any conference. (5) Crying, which is an unseemly elevation of the voice against one's adversary. "The works of the flesh are manifest, which are; emulations, contentions, seditions" (Gal. 5:19–20). "Let all bitterness, and anger and wrath, crying, and evil speaking be put away from you, with all maliciousness. Be courteous one to another" (Eph. 4:31–32). "He"—viz., Ishmael—"shall be a wild man, his hand shall be against every man, and every man's hand against him" (Gen. 16:12). (6) Complaints to everyone of such as offer us injuries. "Grudge not against one another, brethren, lest ye be condemned" (James 5:9).

(3) In countenance and gesture, all such signs as evidently decipher the malicious affections lurking in the heart. "His countenance fell down: and the Lord said unto Cain, Why art thou so wroth?" (Gen. 4:5–6). "They that passed by railed on him, nodding their heads" (Matt. 27:39).

Hence is it that derision is termed persecution. "Sarah saw the son of Hagar the Egyptian mocking," etc. (Gen. 31:9). "He that was born after the flesh, persecuted him that was born after the spirit" (Gal. 4:29).

(4) In deeds. (1) To fight with or to beat our neighbor and to maim his body. "If any man cause any blemish in his neighbor: as he hath done, so shall it be done to him, breach for breach, eye for eye, tooth for tooth" (Lev. 24:19–20). (2) To procure any way the death of our neighbor, whether it be by the sword, famine, or poison. "Cain rose up against his brother, and slew him" (Gen. 4:8). (3) To exercise tyrannous cruelty in inflicting punishments. "Forty stripes shall he cause him to have, and not past, lest if he should exceed, and beat him above that with many stripes, thy brother should appear despised in thy sight" (Deut. 25:3). "Of the Jews I received five times forty stripes save one" (2 Cor. 11:24). (4) To use any of God's creatures hardly. "A righteous man regardeth the life of his beast, but the mercies of the wicked are cruel" (Prov. 12:10). "If thou find a bird's nest in the way, in any tree, or on the ground, whether they be young, or eggs, and the dam sitting upon the young, or upon the eggs, thou shalt not take the dam with the young, but shalt in any wise let the dam go, and take the young to thee, that thou mayest prosper and prolong thy days" (Deut. 22:6). (5) To take occasion by our neighbor's infirmities to use him discourteously and to make him our laughing stock or taunting recreation. "Thou shalt not curse the deaf, nor put a stumbling block before the blind" (Lev. 19:14). "Little children came out of the city, and mocked him, and said unto him, Come up thou baldhead, come up thou baldhead" (2 Kings 2:23). (6) To injure the impotent, feeble, poor, strangers, fatherless, or widows. "Thou shalt not do injury to a stranger, neither oppress him: for ye were strangers in the land of Egypt. Ye shall not trouble any widow, or fatherless child. Thou shalt not be a usurer to the poor" (Ex. 22:21–22, 25). We then injure these (1) if we pay not the laborer his hire. "Thou shalt not oppress a hired servant that is needy and poor, neither of thy brethren, nor of the stranger that is within thy gates. Thou shalt give him his hire for his day: neither shall the sun go down upon it: for he is poor, and therewith sustaineth his life: lest he cry against thee to the Lord, and it be sin unto thee" (Deut. 24:14–15). (2) If you restore not the pledge of the poor. "If thou take thy neighbor's raiment to pledge, thou shalt restore it to him before the sun goes down: for that is his garment only, and his covering for his skin" (Ex. 22:26–27). (3) If we withdraw corn from the poor. "He that withdraweth the corn, the people will curse him: but blessing shall be upon the head of him that selleth corn" (Prov. 11:26).

Again, this law is as well transgressed by not killing when the law charges to kill and by pardoning the punishment due to murder, as by killing when we should not. "If one smite another with an instrument of iron, that he die, he is a murderer, and the murderer shall die the death. The land cannot be cleansed of the blood that is shed therein, but by the blood of him that shed it" (Num. 35:16, 33).

By this place also are combats of two men hand-to-hand for deciding of controversies utterly unlawful (1) because they are not equal means ordained of God to determine controversies; (2) in that it falls out in such combats that he is conqueror before man who indeed is guilty before God.

This also condemns popish sanctuaries and places of privilege, as churches and the like, wherein murderers shelter and shroud themselves from the danger of the law. For God expressly commands, "that such a one shall be taken from his altar, that he may die" (Ex. 21:14). And Joab (1 Kings 2:34), touching the horns of the altar, was slain in the temple.

Hitherto in like sort belong such things as concern the soul of our neighbor. (1) To be a scandal or offence to the soul of our neighbor either in life or doctrine. "Woe be to the world because of offences: it is necessary that offences should come: but woe be to them by whom they do come" (Matt. 18:7).

(2) To minister occasions of strife and discord, the which we then do (1) when we cannot be brought to remit somewhat of our own right. (2) When we return snappish and crooked answers. (3) When we interpret everything amiss and take them in the worst part. "Nabal is his name, and folly is with him" (1 Sam. 25:25). "And the princes of the children of Ammon said unto Hanun their lord: Thinkest thou that David doth honor thy father, that he hath sent comforters to thee? Has not David rather sent his servants unto thee, to search the city, to spy it out, and to overthrow it? Wherefore Hanun took David's servants, and shaved off the half of their beards, and cut off their garments in the middle, even to their buttocks, and sent them away" (2 Sam. 10:3).

(3) The ministers' sin against their neighbors is this: not to preach the word of God to their charge, that they thereby might be instructed in the ways of life. "Where there is no vision the people decay, but he that keepeth the law is blessed" (Prov. 29:18). "Their watchmen are all blind, they have no knowledge, they are all dumb dogs, they cannot bark: they lie and sleep, and delight in sleeping. And these greedy dogs can never have enough, and these shepherds they cannot understand: for they all look to their own way, every one for his advantage, and for his own purpose" (Isa. 56:10–11). "When I shall say to the wicked, Thou shalt surely die, and thou givest him not warning, the same wicked man shall die in his iniquity, but his blood will I require at thy hands" (Ezek. 3:18).

And not only not to preach at all, but to preach negligently is utterly condemned. "Cursed be he that doth the work of the Lord negligently" (Jer. 48:10). "Because thou art lukewarm, and neither hot nor cold: it will come to pass that

I spew thee out of my mouth" (Rev. 3:16). This reproveth non-residency of ministers, which is an ordinary absence of the minister from his charge—namely, from that particular congregation committed to him. "I have set watchmen upon thy walls, O Jerusalem, which all the day and all the night continually shall not cease: ye that are mindful of the Lord keep not silence, and give him no rest, till he repair and till he set up Jerusalem the praise of the world" (Isa. 62:6). "Take heed therefore to yourselves, and to all the flock whereof the Holy Ghost has made you overseers, to feed the church of God, which he has purchase with his own blood. For I know this, that after my departing, shall grievous wolves enter in among you, not sparing the flock. Moreover, of yourselves shall men arise, speaking perverse things to draw disciples after them. Therefore, watch and remember, that by the space of three years, I ceased not to warn every one night and day with tears" (Acts 20:28–31). "Feed the flock of God, which dependent upon you, caring for it, not by constraint, but willingly: not for filthy lucre, but of a ready mind, not as though ye were lords over God's heritage, but that ye may be ensamples to the flock" (1 Peter 5:2–3; Ezek. 34:4, 33). "If any bishop by imposition of hands inducted into a charge and appointed to govern a people do neglect to take upon him that office and delays to go to the congregation allotted to him, such a one shall be prohibited from the Lord's Table, till he be enforced to attend upon that charge or at the least somewhat be determined by a complete assembly of the ministers of that province."[1] "We remember that our brethren in a former assembly decreed that if any layman remaining three Sabbaths or Lord's Days, that is, three weeks in a city, did not in the same city frequent the church assemblies, he should be excommunicated; if then such things are not allowable in laymen, much less in ministers. For whom it is neither lawful nor convenient, without urgent necessity, to be absent from his parish church longer than the time above mentioned. To this decree there was not one *non placet*,[2] but everyone said, it likes us well."[3] The 8th Council held at Constantinople in the 24th Canon decreed that "Ministers ought not to have their substitutes, or vicars, but in their own persons, with fear and cheerfulness, perform all such duties, as are required of them in the service of God."[4] The Canon law does conclude the same things.[5] "The Bishops," says the Canon, "ought to be continually resident in God's tabernacle, that they may learn somewhat of God and the people of them whilst they read often and meditate upon God's Word." Again, in the Canons "The Bishops which take upon

---

1. In-text citation: The Council of Antioch, the 17. Can. [The Council of Antioch, canon 17].
2. *Non placet*: there was none who was displeased.
3. In-text citation: The Council of Sardice, the 14. Can [The Council of Sardice, canon 14].
4. Probably a reference to the Fourth Council of Constantinople, canon 24.
5. In-text citation: Can. *Si quis vult*. Distinct. 36. Debent indesinenter, etc.

them to feed God's flock, ought not to depart from their duty, lest they lose that excellent talent which God has bestowed upon them, but rather strive with that one talent to get three more talents."[6] And there is [also the] express[ed] mandate that "such, whether Bishop or Senior, who attends not upon their office in the church shall forthwith be removed from that place."[7] "Let no man be ordained minister of two churches, in two several cities, but let him remain in that to which he was first called. And if for vainglory he shall afterward go to a greater congregation, let him immediately be recalled to his first charge, and in that only exercise his ministry. But if one be called to another charge, let him simply give over the former, and have no interest in the same" etc.[8]

There are, notwithstanding the former testimonies, some cases wherein it is permitted to the minister that he may be absent, if by his absence the congregation be not endamaged. (1) Sickness. "If a Bishop be not at home, or be sick, or upon some exigent cannot be present at his parish, let him procure one who upon Sabbaths and festival days will preach to his charge."[9] And Augustine testifies that he was absent on the like occasion.[10]

(2) Allowance of the church to be absent for a time upon some necessary and public commodity for the same. "Epaphras is their minister" (Col. 1:7); but in chapter 4:12 he being absent "saluteth them." And Ambrose, though he were bishop of Milan, yet went he twice as ambassador into France to make agreement between Maximus and Valentinian.[11]

(3) If by reason of persecution he be enforced to flee and see no hope to procure the safety of his people. This made Cyprian to be absent from Carthage, as he testifies in his epistles.

Thus much concerning sins against our neighbor. Now follow such sins as a man commits against his own person, as when a man does hurt, kill, and endanger himself. "If any man will follow me, let him deny himself, take up his cross, and follow me" (Matt. 16:24). "He said unto him, If thou be the Son of God, cast thyself down headlong: for it is written, He shall give his angels charge over thee, and with their hands they shall lift thee up lest at, etc. Jesus said to him: It is written again, Thou shalt not tempt the Lord thy God" (4:6–7).

---

6. In-text citation: Pontiffs and *Si quis in clero Episcopes, qui dominici gregis suscipiunt curam, etc.*

7. In-text citation: Canons of the Apostles, canon 80.

8. In-text citation: The Chalcedon Council, Canon 10. In the margin: For this thing look [at] the decrees of Damas[c]us and the Council of Trent, Section. 9. Canon 8.

9. In-text citation: The Council of Mentz, Canon 25.

10. In-text citation: Letter 138.

11. In the margin: Ambrose li.5.& 27 [Letter from Ambrose to Valentinian II (*r.* 371–392), the Roman emperor, Ambrose was the Bishop of Milan and a Church Father who had a significant influence on Augustine].

Therefore, for a man to be his own executioner, though to escape a most shameful evil, is utterly unlawful and ungodly.

The Affirmative Part: You Shall Preserve the Life of Your Neighbor
Hitherto may we refer these duties:

(1) Such as appertain to the person of our neighbor and concern, first his welfare both of body and mind, as to rejoice with them that rejoice (Rom. 12:15). "Then he answered and said to him, all these things I have observed from my youth. And Jesus beheld him, and loved him" (Matt. 19:21). (2) His miseries, to be grieved with him for them. "Mourn with those that mourn" (Rom. 12:15). "And I said, My leanness, my leanness, woe is me, the transgressors have offended; yea the transgressors have grievously offended" (Isa. 24:16). "Mine eyes gush out with water, because men observe not thy law" (Ps. 119:136). Again, we must help him as much as in us lies. "I was as an eye to the blind, and a foot to the lame" (Job 29:15). "To their power, yea, beyond their power, they were willing" (2 Cor. 8:3). And that we do, we must do speedily. "Say not to thy neighbor, Go and come again tomorrow, and I will give thee, if thou now have it" (Prov. 3:28). "Thou shalt plainly rebuke thy neighbor," etc. (Lev. 19:17). (3) Concerning such injuries as he offers to you, (1) you shall not be angry against him upon a small occasion. "Moses was a meek man above all that lived upon the earth" (Num. 12:3). "The discretion of a man defers his anger, and his glory is to pass by an offence" (Prov. 19:11). (2) You must be slow to wrath and never angry but for a most just cause. "Then he looked round about on them angrily, mourning also for the hardness of their hearts" (Mark 3:5). "He that is slow to wrath, is of great wisdom: but he that is of a hasty mind exalteth folly" (Prov. 14:29). (3) Your anger must be but for awhile. "Be angry and sin not, let not the sun go down upon thy wrath" (Eph. 4:26). (4) Forgive freely an injury and revenge it not. "Be ye courteous one to another, and tender-hearted, forgiving one another, even as God for Christ's sake forgave you" (v. 32).

(4) His wants and infirmities. (1) Avoid occasions whereby they may be stirred and laid open. "Then said Abraham to Lot, Let there be no strife I pray thee, between thee and me, neither between thy herdsmen and mine: for we are brethren. Is not the whole land before thee? Depart, I pray thee, from me: if thou wilt take the left hand, I will take the right: or if thou go to the right hand, I will take the left" (Gen. 13:8–9). "And tarry with him a while until thy brother's fierceness be assuaged. And till thy brother's wrath turn away from thee, and he forget the things which thou hast done to him" (27:44–45). (2) Depart sometimes from your own right. "What thinkest thou Simon? Of whom do the kings of the earth take tribute, or poll money? Of their children, or of strangers? Peter said to him, Of strangers. Then said Jesus to him, Then are the children free.

Nevertheless, lest we should offend them, go to the sea, and cast in an angle, and take the first fish that cometh up, and when thou hast opened his mouth, thou shalt find a piece of twenty pence: that take and give it to them for me and thee" (Matt. 17:25–27). (3) To appease anger kindled, which is done (1) by overcoming evil with goodness. "Be not overcome of evil, but overcome evil with goodness" (Rom. 12:21). (2) By following after peace. "Decline from evil, and do good, seek peace, and follow after it" (1 Peter 3:11). (3) By courteous answers. "A soft answer putteth away wrath: but grievous words stir up anger" (Prov. 15:1). "Eli said unto her, How long wilt thou be drunken? Put away thy drunkenness from thee. Then Hannah answered, and said, Nay my Lord, but I am a woman troubled in spirit: I have drunk neither wine nor strong drink, but have poured out my soul before the Lord" (1 Sam. 1:14–15). "It may be that he therefore departed for a season, that thou shouldest receive him forever" (Philemon 15). (4) By overpassing some wants and infirmities in men's words and deeds. "It is a man's honor to pass by infirmities" (Prov. 19:11). (5) By covering them with silence. "Above all things have fervent love among you, for love covereth a multitude of sins" (2 Peter 4:8). "He that covereth transgressions seeketh love: but he that repeateth a matter separates friends" (Prov. 17:9). (6) By taking everything (if it be possible) in the best part. "Love thinketh none evil" (1 Cor. 13:5).

This shows the lawfulness of truces, covenants, and other agreements concerning peace, being made to avoid injuries, maintain ancient bounds, procure security in traffic, possessions, and journeys, set pensions, commons for cattle, liberties of hunting, fishing, or fowling, and getting fuel or other necessities for public commodities, if there be no unlawful conditions annexed to the same. And we may make this covenant not only with Christians, but for the maintenance of peace with infidels also. For that which is godly to be performed is no less godly to be promised. But it is a note of true godliness to be as much as may be at peace with all men. Therefore, to promise peace by covenant is very godly. We may see the experience of this in the lives of holy men. "At that same time Abimelech and Phichol his chief captain, spake unto Abraham, saying, God is with thee in all that thou doest. Now therefore swear to me here by God, that thou wilt not hurt me, nor my children, nor my children's children, etc. Then Abraham said, I will swear. Then Abraham took sheep and oxen, and gave them to Abimelech: and they two made a covenant" (Gen. 21:22–24, 27). "Now therefore come and let us make a covenant, I and thou, which may be a witness between me and thee. Then Laban said to Jacob, Behold this heap, and behold this pillar, which I have set up between me and thee. The God of Abraham, and the God of Nahor, and the God of their father be judge between us. But Jacob sware by the fear of his father Isaac" (31:44–45, 53).

(2) Concerning his body, we are to regard it alive and dead. Being alive, we ought if need be (1) to minister to it food and raiment. "Depart from me ye cursed into everlasting fire, which is prepared for the devil and his angels. For I was an hungered, and ye gave me no meat, I thirsted, and ye gave me no drink, etc. Inasmuch ye did it not to one of the least of these, ye did it not to me" (Matt. 25:41–42, 45). (2) To lend our helping hand when our neighbor's body is in any danger. "Hereby we perceived love; that he laid down his life for us, therefore also ought we to lay down our lives for the brethren" (1 John 3:16).

When a man is dead, we ought to commit the dead corpse to the grave, as may appear by these arguments. (1) The instinct of nature itself. (2) The examples of the patriarchs and other holy personages. "Abraham buried Sarah" (Gen. 23:19). "Jacob is buried by his sons" (50:12). "Steven by religious, and devout men" (Acts 8:2). (3) The Lord's own approbation of burial in that He numbers it among His benefits. For the want thereof is a curse. "He"—viz., Jehoiakim—"shall be buried as an ass is buried, even drawn and cast forth without the gates of Jerusalem" (Jer. 22:19). Therefore, rather than Moses should be unburied, the Lord Himself did bury him. "Moses the servant of the Lord died in the land of Moab, according to the Word of the Lord. And he buried him in a valley, in the land of Moab, over against Beth-peor, but no man knoweth of his sepulcher unto this day" (Deut. 34:5–6). (4) There is no dead carcass so loathsome as man's, the which both argues the necessity of burial and how ugly we are in the sight of God by reason of sin. (5) The body must rise again out of the earth, that it may be made a perpetual mansion house for the soul to dwell in. (6) The bodies of the faithful are the temples of the Holy Ghost and therefore must rise again to glory. (7) Burial is a testimony of the love and reverence we bear to the deceased.

A funeral ought to be solemnized after an honest and civil manner— namely, agreeable to the nature and credit as well of those which remain alive as them which are dead. Concerning the living, they must see that (1) their mourning be moderate and such as may well express their affection and love to the party departed. "He said, Where have ye laid him? They answered, Lord, come and see. Then Jesus wept. And the Jews said, Behold how he loved him" (John 11:34–36). (2) They must avoid superstition and not surmise that funeral ceremonies are available to the dead. Such are the rites of the Church of Rome, as to be buried in a church, especially under the altar and in a friar's cowl. (3) They ought to take heed of superfluous pomp and solemnities. For of all ostentations of pride, that is most foolish to be boasting of a loathsome and deformed corpse. "Thus saith the Lord God of Hosts, Go get thee to that treasurer, to Shebnah the steward of the house, and say, What hast thou to do here? And whom hast thou here? That thou shouldest here hew thee out a sepulcher;

as he that heweth out his sepulcher in a high place, or that graveth a habitation for himself in a rock" (Isa. 22:15–16).

To this commandment belong these duties. (1) Before the vintage or harvest, we ought to permit any man for the repressing of hunger to gather grapes or pluck off the ears of corn in the field. "When thou comest into thy neighbor's vineyard, then thou mayest eat grapes at thy pleasure, as much as thou wilt: but thou shalt put none in thy vessel. When thou comest into thy neighbor's corn, thou mayest pluck the ears with thine hand, but thou shalt not move a sickle to thy neighbor's corn" (Deut. 23:24–25). "Jesus went on the Sabbath day through the corn, and his disciples were an hungered, and began to pluck the ears of the corn, and to eat," etc. (Matt. 12:1). (2) In the vintage and time of harvest, we ought neither to leave the trees naked of grapes nor rake up after the reaping ears of corn, but to leave the after-gatherings for the poor. "When you reap the harvest of your land, thou shalt not rid clean the corners of thy field when thou reapest: neither shalt thou make after-gathering of thy harvest; but shalt leave them to the poor, and to the stranger: I am the Lord your God" (Lev. 23:22). "Go to none other field to gather, neither go from hence, but abide here by my maidens. So she gleaned in the field until evening" (Ruth 2:8–9).

(3) Concerning the soul of our neighbor, (1) we must seek all means to win him to the profession of Christian religion. "I please all men in all things, not seeking mine own profit, but the profit of many, that they might be saved" (1 Cor. 10:33). "Let us consider one another, to provoke unto love and to good works" (Heb. 10:24). (2) We must live among men without offence. "Give no offence, neither to the Jews, nor to the Grecians, nor to the church of God" (1 Cor. 10:32). "If meat offend my brother, I will east no flesh while the world standeth, that I may not offend my brother" (8:13). (3) The light of our good life must be as a lantern to direct the ways of our neighbors. "This I confess unto thee, that after the way (which they call heresy) so worship I the God of my fathers, believing all things which are written in the law and the prophets. And have hope toward God, that the resurrection of the dead, which they themselves look for also, shall be both of just and unjust. And herein I endeavor myself to have always a clear conscience toward God, and toward men" (Acts 24:14–16). (4) If our neighbor offend, we are to admonish him. "We desire you, brethren, admonish them that are unruly: comfort the feeble minded: bear with the weak: be patient toward all men" (1 Thess. 5:14). (5) If our neighbor run the ways of God's commandment (as David speaks), we ought to encourage him in the same.

(4) We may refer such things to this commandment as appertain to the peculiar preservation of every several man's life. (1) Recreation, which is an exercise joined with the fear of God conversant in things indifferent for the

preservation of bodily strength and confirmation of the mind in holiness. "I said of laughter, thou art mad; and of joy, what is this that thou doest?" (Eccl. 2:2). "The harp, viol, tabret, and pipe, and wine, are in their feasts, but they regard not the work of the Lord, neither consider the works of his hands" (Isa. 5:12). "Neither be ye idolaters, as were some of them, as it is written: The people sat down to eat and drank, and rose up to play" (1 Cor. 10:7). "Woe be to you that laugh: for ye shall wail and weep" (Luke 6:25). "There ye shall eat before the Lord your God, and ye shall rejoice in all that you put your hands unto, both ye and your households, because the Lord thy God has blessed thee" (Deut. 12:7). To this end has the Word of God permitted shooting. "He bad them teach the children of Judah to shoot, as it is written in the book of Jashur" (2 Sam. 1:18). And musical consort. "Besides their servants and maids which were seven thousand, three hundred, and seven and thirty: they had two hundred and five and forty singing men, and singing women" (Neh. 7:67). And putting forth of riddles. "Samson said unto them, I will now put forth a riddle to you, and if you can declare it me within seven days of the feast, and find it out, I will give you thirty sheets, and thirty change of garments. And they answered him, Put forth thy riddle, that we may hear it. And he said unto them, Out of the eater came meat, and out of the strong came sweetness: and they could not in three days expound the riddle" (Judg. 14:12–14). And hunting of wild beasts. "Take us the foxes, the little foxes which destroy the vines: for our vines have small grapes" (Song 2:15). Lastly, the searching out or the contemplation of the works of God. "And he spake of trees, from the cedar tree that is in Lebanon, even unto the hyssop that springeth out of the wall: he spake also of beasts, and of fowls, and of creeping things, and of fishes" (1 Kings 4:33). (2) Physic,[12] the use whereof is holy, if before the receipt of it a man crave remission of his sins and repose his confidence only upon God, not upon the means. "And lo, they brought to him a man sick of the palsy, lying on a bed. And Jesus seeing their faith, said to the sick of the palsy, Son be of good comfort, thy sins are forgiven thee. Then he said to the sick of the palsy, Arise, take up thy bed and walk to thine house" (Matt. 9:2, 6). "A certain man was there which had been diseased eight and thirty years. Jesus said to him, Take up thy bed and walk. After that Jesus found him in the temple; and said to him, Behold, thou art made whole: sin no more, lest a worse thing come to thee" (John 5:5, 8, 14). "And Asa in the nine and thirtieth year of his reign, was diseased in his feet, and his disease was extreme: yet he sought not to the Lord in his disease, but to the physicians" (2 Chron. 16:12). (3) Avoiding of an injury offered by some private person. This, if it be against an unruly and unstayed adversary and the defense be faultless,

---

12. *Physic*: medicine.

is very lawful and is so far from private revenge that it is to be accounted a just defense. The defense is then faultless when a man does so assault his adversary as that he neither purposes his own revenge or his enemy's hurt, but only his alone safety from that imminent danger.

A Doubt. Whether may a man flee in the plague time? *Answer.* Such as be hindered by their calling may not, as magistrates and pastors, having charge of souls. Yet free men, not bound by calling, may. *Reasons.* (1) A man may provide for his own safety if it be not to the hindrance of another. (2) A man may flee wars, famine, floods, fire, and other such dangers; therefore, the plague. (3) There is less danger of sickness the more the multitude or people is diminished. *Objection.* (1) To flee is a token of distrust. *Answer.* This diffidence is no fault of the fact but of the person. (2) It is offensive. *Answer.* The offence is taken, not given. (3) To flee is to forsake our neighbor against the rule of charity. *Answer.* It is not, if kinsfolk and magistrates be present. (4) Men are to visit the sick by God's appointment. *Answer.* Lepers were excepted among the Jews; and so likewise they in these days which are infected with a disease answerable to the leprosy—namely, if it be dangerously contagious.

Chapter 26

Of the Seventh Commandment

The seventh commandment shows how that we should preserve the chastity of ourselves and of our neighbor.

The words are these: "Thou shalt not commit adultery" [Ex. 20:14].

The Resolution

"Adultery." To commit adultery signifies as much as to do anything whatever way whereby the chastity of ourselves or our neighbors may be stained (Matt. 5:28).

The Negative Part: You Shall No Way either Hurt or Hinder Your Neighbor's Chastity

In this place are prohibited:

(1) The lust of the heart or the evil concupiscence of the flesh. "I say unto you, whosoever looketh on a woman to lust after her, he has already committed adultery with her in his heart" (5:28). "Mortify your members which are on earth: fornication, uncleanness, the inordinate affection, evil concupiscence" (Col. 3:5).

(2) Burning in the flesh, which is an inward fervency of lust whereby the godly motions of the heart are hindered, overwhelmed, and as it were with contrary fire burned up. "If they cannot abstain, let them marry, for it is better to marry than to burn" (1 Cor. 7:9).

(3) Strange pleasures about generation[1] prohibited in the Word of God, the which are many.

(1) With beasts. "Thou shalt not lie with any beast to be defiled therewith; neither shall any woman stand before a beast to lie down thereto: for it is an abomination" (Lev. 18:23).

(2) With the devil, as witches do by their own confession. For why should not a spirit as well have society with a witch, as to eat meat?

(3) With one of the same sex. "Thou shalt not lie with the male as one lieth with a woman: for it is abomination" (v. 22). This is a sin which they commit

---

1. *Generation*: a loose term encompassing various forms of sexual intercourse.

whom God has given over into a reprobate sense. "For this cause God gave them up to vile affections: for even their women did change their natural use, into that which is against nature. And the men left the natural use of the woman, and burned in their lusts one toward another, and man with man wrought filthiness" (Rom. 1:26–27). It was the sin of Sodom (Genesis 19), where it was so common that to this day it is termed sodomy.

(4) With such as be within the degrees of consanguinity or affinity,[2] prohibited in the Word of God. "None shall come near to any of the kindred of his flesh, to uncover her shame, I am the Lord" (Lev. 18:5).

(5) With unmarried persons. This sin is termed fornication. "If any man find a maid that is not betrothed, and take her and lie with her, and they be found, then the man that lay with her, shall give unto the maid's father fifty shekels of silver, and she shall be his wife, because he has humbled her: he cannot put her away all his life" (Deut. 22:28–29). "Neither let us commit fornication, as some of them committed fornication, and fell in one day three and twenty thousand" (1 Cor. 10:8).

(6) With those whereof one is married or at the least betrothed. This sin is called adultery; and God has inflicted by His Word the same punishment upon them which commit this sin after they be betrothed as He does upon such as are already married. "If a man be found lying with a woman married to a man, then they shall die even both twain: to wit, the man that lay with the wife, and the wife: so thou shalt put away evil from Israel. If a maid be betrothed to a husband, and a man find her in the town and lie with her, then shall ye bring them both out unto the gates of the same city, and shall stone them to death with stones" (Deut. 21:22–24). This is a marvelous great sin, as may appear in that it is the punishment of idolatry. "They turned the glory of the incorruptible God, to the similitude of the image of a corruptible man, etc. Wherefore God gave them up unto their heart's lusts, to uncleanness" (Rom. 1:23–24). Yea, this sin is more heinous than theft. "Men do not despise a thief, when he stealeth to satisfy his soul, when he is hungry. But he that committeth adultery with a woman, is destitute of understanding, he that does it, destroyeth his own soul" (Prov. 6:30, 32). Again, the adulterer breaks the covenant of marriage, which is God's covenant. "Which forsaketh the guide of her youth, and forgetteth the covenant of her God" (2:17). Adulterers dishonor their own bodies. "Flee fornication, every sin that a man doth, is without the body: but he that committeth fornication sinneth against his own body" (1 Cor. 6:18). And bereave their neighbors of a great and unrecoverable benefit—namely, of chastity. As for the children which are begotten in this sort, they are shut out from that preeminence which

---

2. *Consanguinity or affinity*: close relatives by blood or marriage.

they otherwise might obtain in the congregation. "A bastard shall not enter into the congregation of the Lord: even to his tenth generation shall he not enter into the congregation of the Lord" (Deut. 23:2). He makes his family astew, as appears in David, whose adultery was punished by Absalom's lying with his father's concubines. "Ahithophel said to Absalom, Go to thy father's concubines, which he has left to keep the house" (2 Sam. 16:21). "If mine heart have been deceived by a woman, or if I have laid wait at the door of my neighbor: let my wife grind unto another man: and let other men bow down upon her" (Job 31:9–10). Man's posterity feels the smart of this sin. "This"—adultery—"is a fire that shall devour to destruction, and which shall root out all mine increase" (v. 12). To conclude, though this sin be committed never so closely, yet God will reveal it (Num. 5:12–23). And it usually has one of these two as companions— namely, dullness of heart or a marvelous horror of conscience. "Whoredom, and wine, take away their heart" (Hos. 4:11).

As for the patriarchs' polygamy or marrying of many wives, albeit it cannot be defended, yet it may be excused, either because it served to the enlarging of the number of mankind when there were but few, or at the least to the propagation of the church of God.

(7) With man and wife. They abuse their liberty if they know each other so long as the woman is in her flowers.[3] "In thee have they discovered their fathers' shame: in thee have they vexed her that was polluted in her flowers" (Ezek. 22:10). "Thou shalt not go to a woman to uncover her shame, as long as she is put apart for her disease" (Lev. 18:10). "If a man has not lain with a menstrous woman" (Ezek. 18:6). Or using marriage bed intemperately. Ambrose says that he commits adultery with his wife who in the use of wedlock has neither regard of seemliness nor honesty.[4] Jerome in his first book against Jovinianus says, "A wise man ought to love his wife in judgment, not in affection. He will not give the bridle to headstrong pleasure, nor headily company with his wife. Nothing," says he, "is more shameless, than to love a wife as though she were a strumpet."

(8) Nocturnal pollutions,[5] which arise of immoderate diet or unchaste cogitations going before in the day (Deut. 23:10). Onan's sin (Gen. 38:8) was not much unlike these.

(9) Effeminate wantonness, whereby occasions are sought to stir up lust. "The works of the flesh are manifest, which are adultery, fornication, uncleanness, wantonness" (Gal. 5:19). Occasions of lust are (1) eyes full of adultery. "Having eyes full of adultery, and that cannot cease to sin" (2 Peter 2:14).

---

3. *In her flowers*: menstruating.
4. In-text citation: Lib. De Philof. Which Augustine citeth, lib. 2. Contra Julian [Ambrose, *Book of Philosophy*, which Augustine cites in *Contra Julian*, bk. 2].
5. *Nocturnal pollutions*: nocturnal emissions.

(2) Idleness. "When it was evening tide, David arose out of his bed, and walked upon the roof of the king's palace: and from the roof he saw a woman washing herself: and the woman was very beautiful to look upon. And David sent, and inquired what woman it was: and one said, Is not this Bathsheba the daughter of Elia, wife to Uriah the Hittite? Then David sent messengers, and took her away: and she came unto him, and he lay with her" (2 Sam. 11:2–3). (3) Riotous and lascivious attire. "The women shall array themselves in comely apparel, with shamefastness and modesty, not with braided hair, or gold or pearls, or costly apparel, but (as becometh women that profess the fear of God) with good works" (1 Tim. 2:9). "Because the daughters of Zion are haughty, and walk with stretched out necks, and with wandering eyes, walking and mincing as they go, and making a tinkling with their feet. Therefore, shall the Lord make the heads of the daughters of Zion bald, and the Lord shall discover their secret parts. In that day shall the Lord take away the ornament of the slippers, and the cauls, and the round tires. The sweet balls, and the bracelets, and the bonnets, the tiers of the head, and the stops, and headbands, and the tables, and the earrings, the rings and the mufflers, the costly apparel and the veils, and the wimples, and the crisping pins, and the glasses, and the fine linen, and the hoods, and the veils" (Isa. 3:16–23). And no marvel if the prophet be so sharp against excessive and wanton apparel; for this is (1) a lavish and prodigal wasting of the benefits of God, which might well be employed upon better uses. (2) It is a testimony and as it were the cognizance or ensign of pride whereby a man would have himself in greater reputation than another. (3) It is a note of great idleness and slothfulness. For commonly such as bestow much time in tricking and trimming themselves up do quite neglect other business and of all things cannot [do] away with pains. (4) It argues levity in devising every day some new fashion or imitating that which others devise. (5) It makes a confusion of such degrees and callings as God has ordained, when as men of inferior degree and calling cannot be by their attire discerned from men of higher estate. (4) Fullness of bread and meat, which provoke lust. "This was the iniquity of thy sister Sodom, pride, fullness of bread, and idleness was in her, and in her daughters" (Ezek. 16:49). "There was a certain rich man, which was clothed in purple and fine linen, and fared well and delicately every day" (Luke 16:19). "Walk honestly, as in the daytime, not in gluttony and drunkenness, neither in chambering and wantonness" (Rom. 13:13). (5) Corrupt, dishonest, and unseemly talk. "Err not, evil talk corrupteth good manners" (1 Cor. 15:33). Such are vain love songs, ballads, interludes, and amorous books. This is the thing we are carefully to shun in the readings of poets, yet so as mariners do in navigation, who forsake not the sea, but decline and flee from the rocks. (6) Lascivious representations of love matters in plays and comedies.

"Fornication and all uncleanness, let it not once be named among you, as it becometh saints, neither filthiness, nor foolish talking, neither jesting, which are things not comely" (Eph. 5:3, 4). (7) Indecent and unseemly pictures. "Abstain from all appearance of evil" (1 Thess. 5:22). (8) Lascivious dancing of man and woman together. "The daughter of the same Herodias came in and danced, and pleased Herod," etc. (Mark 6:22). (9) Company with effeminate persons. "Let not thine heart decline to her ways: wander thou not in her paths" (Prov. 7:25).

(5) To appoint some light or sheete[6] punishment for adultery, such as that Romish synagogue does. For it is nothing else but to open a gap for other lewd persons to run headlong into the like impiety.

The Affirmative Part: You Shall Preserve the Chastity of Your Neighbor
Chastity is the purity of soul and body, as much as belongs to generation. The mind is chaste when it is free or at the least freed from fleshly concupiscence. The body is chaste when it puts not in execution the concupiscences of the flesh. "This is the will of God, even your sanctification, and that ye should abstain from fornication. That every one of you should know have to possess his vessel in holiness and honor. And not in the lust of concupiscence, even as the Gentiles, which know not God" (1 Thess. 4:3–5), "The unmarried woman careth for the things of the Lord, that she may be holy both in body and spirit" (1 Cor. 7:34).

There are two especial virtues which preserve chastity: modesty and sobriety. Modesty is a virtue which keeps in each work a holy decorum or comeliness. And it is seen (1) in the countenance and eyes—namely, when they neither express nor excite the concupiscence of the heart. "I made a covenant with mine eye, why then should I think on a maid?" (Job 31:1). "Rebekah lift up her eyes, and when she saw Isaac, she lighted down from the camel. So she took a veil, and covered her face" (Gen. 24:64–65). "She caught him, and kissed him, and with an impudent face said unto him," etc. (Prov. 7:13). "Then Adam knew Eve his wife: who," etc. (Gen. 4:1). "A Psalm of David, when the prophet Nathan came to him, after he had gone into Bathsheba" (Ps. 51:1). "In that day shall the Lord shave with a razor that is hired, even by them beyond the river, by the king of Ashur, the head and the hair of the feet, and it shall consume the beard" (Isa. 7:20). "When he was gone out, his servants came: who seeing that the doors of the parlor were shut, they said, Surely he covereth his feet"—that is, he does his easement[7]—"in his summer chamber" (Judg. 3:24). Again, a man's talk must be

---

6. *Sheete*: referring to performing penance in a sheet (originally for fornication).
7. *Easement*: relieving the body by urinating or defecating.

little and submiss. "Behold my servant whom I have chosen; he shall not strive, nor cry, neither shall any man hear his voice in the streets" (Matt. 12:19). "In many words there cannot want iniquity: but he that refraineth his lips, is wise" (Prov. 10:19). And it is a note of a strumpet to be a giglot[8] and loud-tongued. "She is babbling, and loud" (7:11). (3) In apparel, we must observe a holy comeliness. "The elder women must be of such behavior, as becometh holiness" (Titus 2:3). Holy comeliness is that which expresses to the eye the sincerity—that is, the godliness, temperance, and gravity—either of man or woman. This decency will more plainly appear if we consider the ends of apparel, which are in number five. (1) Necessity, to the end that our bodies may be defended against the extremity of parching heat and pinching cold. (2) Honesty, that the deformity of our naked bodies might be covered, which immediately followed the transgression of our parents. (3) Commodity, whereby men, as their calling, work, and trade of life is different, so do they apparel themselves. And hence it is, that some apparel is more decent for certain estates of men, than other. (4) Frugality, when a man's attire is proportional to his ability and calling. (5) Distinction of persons, as of sex, ages, offices, times, and actions. For a man has his set attire, a woman hers. A young man is appareled on this fashion, an old man on that. And therefore it is unseemly for a man to put on a woman's apparel or a woman the man's. "The woman shall not wear that which pertaineth to the man, neither shall a man put on woman's raiment: for all that do so, are an abomination to the Lord thy God" (Deut. 22:5).

To set down precisely out of God's Word what apparel is decent is very hard. Wherefore, in this cause the judgment and practice of modest, grave, and sincere men in every particular estate is most to be followed; and men must rather keep too much within the bounds of measure than to step one foot without the precincts. (4) In purging the excrements of nature, care must be had that they must be cast forth into some separate and close place, and there also covered. "Thou shalt have a place without the host, whither thou shalt resort, and thou shalt have a paddle among thy weapons, and when thou wouldest sit down without, thou shalt dig therewith, and returning, thou shalt cover thine excrement. For the Lord thy God walketh in the midst of the camp to deliver thee; therefore thine host shall be holy, that He see no filthy thing in thee, and turn away from thee" (Deut. 23:12–14). "And he came to the sheepcotes by the way, where there was a cave, and Saul went in to cover his feet" (1 Sam. 24:4).

Sobriety is a virtue which concerns the usage of our diet in holiness. For the better observation thereof, these rules may serve. (1) The chiefest at the banquet, let him consecrate the meats to God by saying grace. "The people will

---

8. *Giglot*: a giddy, laughing, romping girl or one excessively given to merriment.

not eat, till he"—that is, Samuel—"come, because he will bless the sacrifice: and then eat they, that be bidden to the feast" (1 Sam. 9:13). "He commanded them to make them all sit down by companies upon the grass, etc. And he took the five loaves and two fishes, and looked up to heaven, and gave thanks" (Mark 6:39, 41). "When he had thus said, he"—that is, Paul—"gave thanks in the presence of them all, and when he had broken bread, he began to eat" (Acts 27:35). (2) It is lawful to furnish a table with store of dishes not only for necessity, but also for the good entertainment of a friend and for delight. "Levi made him"— that is, Jesus—"a great feast in his own house, where there was a great company of publicans, and of other that sat at table with him" (Luke 5:29). "He giveth wine that maketh glad the heart of man, and oil to make the face shine, and bread that strengtheneth man's heart" (Ps. 104:15). "There they made him a supper, and Martha served, but Lazarus was one of them that sat at table with him. Then took Mary a pound of ointment of spikenard very costly, and anointed Jesus' feet" (John 12:2–3). (3) Choose the lower room at a banquet and rather than be troublesome sit as the master of the feast assigns you. "He spake a parable to the guests, when he marked how they chose one of the chief rooms, and said, When thou shalt be bidden of any man to a wedding, set not thyself down in the chiefest place, lest a more honorable man than thou be bidden of him. And he that bade both him and thee, come and say, Give this man room. But go and sit down in the lowest room, that when he that bade thee, cometh, he may say to thee, Friend, sit up higher" (Luke 14:7–10). "Stand not in the place of great men," etc. (Prov. 25:6). (4) Man must eat at due times, not at unseasonable hours. "Woe be to thee, O land, when thy princes eat in the morning. Blessed art thou, O land, when thy princes eat in time" (Eccl. 10:16–17). (5) Man must eat and drink moderately, so that the body may receive strength thereby, and the soul be more fresh and lively to perform the actions of godliness. "Take heed to yourselves, lest at any time your hearts be oppressed with surfeiting and drunkenness" (Luke 21:34). "To whom is woe? Etc. Even to them that tarry long at wine, to them that go and seek mixed wine. Look not thou upon the wine when it is red, and when it showeth his color in the cup, and goeth down pleasantly," etc. (Prov. 23:29–30). "If thou hast found honey, eat that is sufficient for thee, lest thou be overfull and vomit" (25:16). "It is not for kings to drink wine, nor for princes strong drink, lest he drink and forget the decree, and change the judgment of all the children of affliction" (31:4). (6) We must then especially regard these things when we eat at great men's tables. "When thou sittest to eat with a ruler, consider diligently what is before thee. Put the knife to thy throat, if thou be a man given to thine appetite. Be not desirous of his dainty meats for it is a deceivable meat" (23:1–3). (7) Godly mirth at meat is tolerable. "They did eat their meat together with gladness and singleness of heart" (Acts 2:46).

(8) Table talk (according as occasion of talk is offered) must be such as may edify. Such was Christ's talk at the Pharisee's table (Luke 14:1–16). (9) See that after the banquet ended the broken meat be not lost, but reserved. "When they were satisfied, he said to his disciples, Gather up the broken meat which remaineth, that nothing be lost" (John 6:12). (1) At a feast leave somewhat. "She did eat, and was sufficed, and left thereof" (Ruth 2:14).

Chastity is double: one of single life; another in wedlock. They that are single must (1) with great care keep their affections and bodies in holiness. "How shall a young man purge his ways? By directing the same after thy Word" (Ps. 119:9). "I write unto you fathers, because ye have known Him, that is from the beginning. I write unto you young men, because ye have overcome that wicked one. I write unto you babes, because ye have known the Father" (1 John 23:13–14). "Remember thy Creator in the days of thy youth, while the evil days come not, nor the years approach, wherein thou shalt say, I have no pleasure in them" (Eccl. 12:1). (2) They must fast often. "I beat down my body, and bring it into subjection, lest by any means, after I have preached to others, I myself should be reproved" (1 Cor. 9:27). (3) They must take heed they burn not in lust; for "it is better to marry, than to burn" (7:9).

Chastity in wedlock is when the holy and pure use of wedlock is observed. "Marriage is honorable among all, and the bed undefiled, but whoremongers and adulterers God will judge" (Heb. 12:4). To preserve purity in wedlock, these cautions are profitable. (1) Contracts must be in the Lord and with the faithful only. "Judah has transgressed, and an abomination is committed in Israel, and in Jerusalem: for Judah has defiled the holiness of the Lord, which he loved, and has married the daughter of a strange god" (Mal. 2:11). "If her husband be dead, she is at liberty to marry with whom she will, only in the Lord" (1 Cor. 7:39). (2) Both parties must separate themselves in the time of a woman's disease[9] and at appointed fasts (Ezek. 18:6). "Defraud not one another, except it be with consent for a time, that ye may give yourselves to fasting and prayer, and again come together, that Satan tempt you not for your incontinency" (1 Cor. 7:5). (3) Wedlock must be used rather to suppress than to satisfy that corrupt concupiscence of the flesh and especially to enlarge the church of God, which is done by a holy seed. "Put on the Lord Jesus Christ, and take not care of the flesh to satisfy the lusts thereof" (Rom. 13:14). (4) It must be used with prayer and thanksgiving (1 Tim. 4:3–4).

---

9. *Woman's disease*: during menstruation.

Chapter 27

Of the Eighth Commandment

This commandment concerns the preservation of our neighbor's goods. The words are these:

"Thou shalt not steal" [Ex. 20:15].

The Resolution

"Steal." To steal is properly to convey anything closely from another. "Jacob stole away the heart of Laban the Aramite" (Gen. 31:20). In this place is signified generally to wish that which is another man's, to get it by fraud, and any way to impair his wealth.

The Negative Part: You Shall neither Be Wanting to Preserve nor a Means to Hinder or Hurt Your Neighbor's Goods

In this place, these sins are forbidden. (1) Inordinate living, whether it be in no set calling or idly, wherein by neglecting their duties such persons misspend their time, goods, and revenues. "We hear that there are some among you which walk inordinately, and work not at all, but are busybodies" (2 Thess. 3:11). "In the sweat of thy brows shalt thou eat thy bread, till thou return to the earth" (Gen. 3:19). "If there be any that provideth not for his own, especially for them of his household, he denieth the faith, and is worse than an infidel" (1 Tim. 5:8).

(2) Unjust dealings, which is either in heart or deed. Unjust dealing in heart is named covetousness. "Out of the heart come evil thoughts, murders, adulteries, fornications, thefts," etc. (Matt. 15:19). Covetousness is idolatry. "We know that no covetous person, which is an idolater, shall enter into the kingdom of Christ and of God" (Eph. 5:5). Yea, it is the very root of all evil, not begetting but nourishing all kind of sin. "The love of money is the root of all evil, which while some lusted after, they erred from the faith, and pierced themselves through with many sorrows" (1 Tim. 6:10).

Unjust dealing in deed is in bargaining or out of bargaining. Unjust dealing in bargaining has many branches. "Let no man oppress, or deceive his neighbor in a bargain: for God is the avenger of such things" (1 Thess. 4:6).

(1) To sell or bargain for that which is not saleable. Of this kind (1) is the gift of the Holy Ghost, which cannot be bought with money. "When Simon saw, that through laying on of the apostles' hands, the Holy Ghost was given, he offered them money, saying, give me also this power, that on whom soever I lay the hands, he may receive the Holy Ghost. Then Peter said unto him, Thy money perish with thee, because thou thinkest that the gift of God may be obtained with money" (Acts 8:13, 16, 20). (2) Church goods are not saleable. Therefore, it is not to be allowed for men to sell or alienate them from the church. "It is destruction for a man to devour that which is sanctified, and after the vows to enquire" (Prov. 20:25; Mal. 3:8). Church goods are the possession of the Lord. (3) Whatever is unprofitable either to the Church or commonwealth must not be sold.

(2) All colored forgery and deceit in bargaining, as (1) using forged cavilation.[1] "Zacchaeus stood forth, and said unto the Lord, Behold, Lord, the half of my goods I give to the poor: and if I have taken ought from any man by forged cavilation, I restore it four fold" (Luke 19:8). (2) When men sell that which is counterfeit for good, as copper for gold, and mingle any ways bad with good, making show only of the good. "Hear this ye that swallow up the poor, saying, when will the new month be gone, etc. that we may sell the refuse of the wheat" (Amos 8:4–6). (3) When men falsify their measures and weights. "Thou shalt not have in thy bag two manner of weights, a great and a small. But thou shalt have a right and a just weight; a perfect and a just measure shalt thou have" (Deut. 25:13–14). "Ye shall not do unjustly in judgment, in line, in weight, or in measure. Ye shall have just balances, true weights, a true ephah, and a true hin" (Lev. 19:35–36). "Hear this, ye that say, When will the Sabbath be gone, that we may sell corn, and make the ephah small, and the shekel great, and falsify the weights by deceit?" (Amos 8:4).

(3) When the buyer conceals the goodness of the thing or the seller the faults of it and blindfolds the truth with counterfeit speeches. "Whatsoever ye would that men should do to you, even so do to them: for this is the law and the prophets" (Matt. 7:12). "It is naught, it is naught, saith the buyer, but when he is gone apart, he boasteth" (Prov. 20:14).

(4) When in buying and selling the people are oppressed. And this is done (1) when the just price of things is raised. For in bargaining, it is not lawful to purse one penny without the giving of a pennyworth. (2) Sale upon a set day, which is when day is given that the price may be enhanced. For what is this, I pray you, but to sell time and to take more of our neighbor than right?

---

1. *Cavilation*: the making of frivolous, quibbling, or unfair objections, arguments, or charges, in legal proceedings; the use of legal quibbles, or taking advantage of technical flaws, so as to overreach or defraud.

(3) To engross, which is to buy up all of one commodity into your own hands, that when no other has any of the same, you may sell it at your own price. (4) To become bankrupt, that you may be enriched by the damages and goods of other men. (5) Not to restore that which was lent to one, pledged to one, or found by him. "Neither has oppressed any, but hath restored the pledge to his debtor: he that hath spoiled none by violence," etc. (Ezek. 18:7). (6) To delay any kind of restitution from one day to another. "Say not to thy neighbor, Depart, and come again, tomorrow I will pay you, when thou mayest do it then" (Prov. 3:28). "The wicked man borroweth, and payeth not again, but the righteous is merciful and lendeth" (Ps. 37:21). (7) To practice usury. "Which hath not put his money to usury" (15:5). "If thou lendest money to my people, to the poor man which dwelleth with thee, be not to him as a usurer, lay not usury upon him" (Ex. 22:25).

Usury is a gain exacted by covenant above the principal only in lieu and recompense of the lending of it. Usury being considered as it is thus described is quite contrary to God's Word and may very fitly be termed "biting lucre." "If any man hath borrowed anything of another, whatsoever is hurt or dieth, if the owner of the thing be not present, let him be recompensed. If he be present, recompense him not if he be hired for a price, it is sold for the same price" (Ex. 22:14–15). "He hath not given to usury, neither has taken increase" (Ezek. 18:8). "Neither is it that other men should be eased and you grieved. But upon like condition at this time, your abundance supplieth their lack, that also their abundance may be for your lack: that there may be equality" (2 Cor. 8:13–14).

And this usury positive laws do not only restrain, but not allow.

Answer. Yes surely, with these conditions. (1) If a man take heed that he exact nothing but that which his debtor can get by good and lawful means.

(2) He may not take more than the gain, nay not all the gain, not that part of the gain which drinks up the living of him that uses the money.

(3) He must sometimes be so far from taking gain that he must not require the principal if his debtor be by inevitable and just casualties brought behind, and it be also plain that he could not make, no not by great diligence, any commodity of the money borrowed.

The reasons why a man may take sometimes above the principal are (1) that which the debtor may give, having himself an honest gain besides, and no man any ways endamaged that the creditor may safely receive.

(2) It is convenient that he which has money lent him and gains by it should show all possible gratitude to him by whose goods he is enriched.

(3) It is often for the benefit of the creditor to have the goods in his own hands which he lent.

Objection. Money is not fruitful; therefore, it is unlawful to receive more than we lent out.

Answer. Albeit money in itself be not fruitful, yet it is made very fruitful by the borrower's good use, as ground is which is not fruitful except it be tilled.

Last of all, when a man detains the laborer's wages. "Behold, the hire of the laborers (which have reaped your fields, which is of you kept back by fraud) crieth, and the cries of them which have reaped, are entered into the ears of the Lord of Hosts" (James 5:4).

Unjust dealing out of bargaining is likewise manifold. (1) To pronounce false sentence or judgment for a reward, either proffered or promised. "Thy princes are rebellious, and companions of thieves: every one loaneth gifts, and followeth after rewards: they judge not the fatherless, neither doth the widows' cause come before them" (Isa. 1:23). This is the lawyers' and judges' sin. (2) To feed or clothe stout and lusty rogues or beggars. "When we were with you, we enjoined you this, that if any would not labor, the same should not eat" (2 Thess. 3:10). What then think you, must those licensed rogues and beggars by authority, I mean, all idle monks and abby-lubbers[2] have? Socrates in the Tripartite history says plainly that "that monk which laboreth not with his hands, is no better than a thief."[3] (3) Gaming for money and gain. For you maye not enrich yourself by impoverishing your brother. This gaming is worse fare than usury and in a short while will more enrich a man. (4) To get money by unlawful arts. Such are magic, judicial astrology, stage plays, and such like. "Let him that hath stolen, steal no more, but rather let him labor, working with his own hands the thing that is good, that he may give to him that hath need" (Eph. 4:28; Deut. 18:11; Eph. 5:3). "Abstain from all appearance of evil" (1 Thess. 5:22). (5) To filch or pilfer the least pin or point from another, though it were for the greatest good. "Thou shalt not steal, thou shalt not hurt any man" (Mark. 10:19). "And (as we are blamed, and as some affirm that we say) why do we not evil that good may come thereof? Whose damnation is just" (Rom. 3:8). (6) To remove ancient bounds. "Thou shalt not remove the ancient bounds which thy fathers have made" (Prov. 22:28). "The princes of Judah are like them which remove the bounds" (Hos. 5:10). (7) To steal other men's servants or children to commit sacrilege or robbery. "To whoremongers, buggerers,[4] and men-stealers" (1 Tim. 1:10). "Achan's theft" (Josh. 7:19). "Neither thieves, nor covetous persons nor robbers, etc., shall inherit the kingdom of God" (1 Cor. 6:10). For robberies

---

2. *Abby-lubber:* during the English Reformation, this was a derogatory term for a monk living in idleness and self-indulgence.

3. This may be a reference to the *Historiae Ecclesiastica Tripartita* referenced above; however, this work was compiled by Cassiodorus and Epiphanius Scholasticus.

4. *Buggerers:* those who commit unnatural forms of intercourse.

these sorts of men especially are famous: thieves by the highways, pirates upon the seas, soldiers not content with their pay, and whoever they be that by main force take that which is none of their own. "The soldiers asked him saying, What shall we do? He said, Do violence to no man, neither accuse any man falsely, and be content with your wages" (Luke 3:14). (8) To conspire with a thief, whether by giving advice how he may compass his enterprise or by concealing his fact that he be not punished. "He that is partaker with a thief, hateth himself, and he that heareth cursing, and discovereth it not" (Prov. 29:24).

The punishment of theft may at the discretion of the judge be sometimes aggravated, as he sees the quality of the offence to be. Therefore, thieves sometimes are punished with death.

Now if any man object that the judicial law of God does only require the restitution thereof fourfold for such an offence, I answer that the civil magistrate, when he sees some one or many offences to increase, he may by his authority increase the civil punishment due to that sin. Now it is manifest that the sin of the theft is far more grievous in our commonwealth than it was among the Jews. For first, the inhabitants of this commonwealth are generally by many degrees poorer than the Jews were. Therefore, to steal a thing, but of some small value, from one in this country does more endamage[5] him than a thing of great value would have done the Jews.

Again, the people of this country are of a more stirring and fierce disposition, the which makes thieves to be more outrageous, with their robberies joining violence and the disturbance of the public tranquility of the country, whereof more regard ought to be had than of one private man's life.

The Affirmative Part: You Shall Preserve and Increase Your Neighbor's Goods

To this are required these that follow:

(1) A certain calling, wherein every man according to that gift which God has given him must bestow himself honestly to his own and his neighbor's good. "Let every man wherein he was called therein abide with God" (1 Cor. 7:24; Eph. 4:28). "According as every man hath received a gift, so let him administer to another, that ye may be good dispensers of the manifold graces of God" (1 Peter 4:10). "In love serve one another" (Gal. 5:13).

(2) The true use of riches and all the goods a man has, to which belong two virtues: contentation and thriftiness.

Contentation is a virtue whereby a man is well pleased with that estate wherein he is placed. "Godliness is great gain with a contented mind." "For

---

5. *Endamage*: to cause loss or damage to.

we brought nothing into the world, neither shall we carry anything out of the world. But having food and raiment let us be content" (1 Tim. 6:6–7). "I have learned in whatsoever state I am, therewith to be content. I can be abased, and I can abound, everywhere in all things I am instructed, both to be full, and to be hungry, and to be abased, and to have want" (Phil. 4:11–12). "Give us this day our daily bread" (Matt. 6:11). "Let your conversation be without covetousness, and be content with the things which you have, for he saith, I will not forsake thee, nor leave thee" (Heb. 13:5).

Thriftiness or frugality is a virtue whereby a man carefully keeps his goods which he has gotten and employs them to such uses as are both necessary and profitable. "Drink the water of thy cistern, and of the rivers out of the midst of thine own well. Let thy fountains flow forth, and the rivers of waters in the streets. Let them be thine on me, yea, thine only, and not the strangers with thee" (Prov. 5:15–17). "The thoughts of the diligent do surely bring abundance. He that loveth pastime, shall be a poor man, and he that loveth wine and oil shall not be rich" (21:5, 17) "The deceitful man roasteth not that which he has taken in hunting: but the riches of the diligent are precious" (12:27; John 6:12).

(3) To speak the truth from the heart and to use a harmless simplicity in all affairs. "He that walketh uprightly, and worketh righteousness, he that speaketh the truth in his heart" (Ps. 15:2). "Ephron said to Abraham, The land is worth four hundred shekels of silver, what is that between me and thee? Bury therefore thy dead. So Abraham harkened to Ephron, and Abraham weighed to Ephron the silver, which he had named in the audience of the Hittites, even four hundred shekels of current money among merchants," etc. (Gen. 23:15, 18).

(4) Just dealing (1 Thess. 4:6). Of this there are many kinds:

(1) In buying and selling; in letting and hiring of farms, tenements, lands; in merchandise and all manner of commodities, men must rack nothing but keep a just price. A just price is then observed when as the things prized[6] and the price given for them are made equal, as near as may be. For the observation of this equality, these four rules are to be considered, for by them all bargains must be ordered. (1) There must be a proportion and equality in all contracts, the which will then be when as the seller does not value the thing only according to his own pains and cost bestowed upon it, but also sees what profit it may be to the buyer and in what need he stands of it. "When thou sellest ought to thy neighbor, or buyest ought at his hands, ye shall not oppress one another. But according to the number of the years after the jubilee, thou shalt buy of thy neighbor. Also according to the number of years of thy revenues, he shall sell to thee. According to the number of years thou shalt increase the price thereof:

---

6. This is "prized" in the original, but was likely intended to be "priced."

and according to the fewness of years, thou shalt abate the price of it: for the number of fruits does he sell to thee" (Lev. 25:14–16). (2) They must be squared according to the law of nature, the sum whereof Christ propounds in these words: "Whatsoever ye would that men should do to you, do the same to them" (Matt. 7:12). (3) The bond of nature must be kept which binds him that receives a benefit and makes a lawful gain of another man's goods, that he being once enriched shall make proportionable and natural recompense, even above the principal. (4) Men must communicate and make use of their goods with that caveat which Paul gives—not so to bestow them "as that others may be eased, and they grieved" (2 Cor. 8:13), or contrariwise.

(2) Men must make sale of such things as are in their kind substantial and fit for use.

(3) They must use just weights and measures. "Thou shalt not have in thy bag two manner of weights, a great and a small: but thou shalt have a right and just weight, a perfect and just measure shalt thou have" (Deut. 25:13). "Ye shall have just balances, a true ephah, and a true bath" (Ezek. 45:10). "Shall I justify the wicked balances, and the bag of deceitful weights?" (Mic. 6:11).

(4) He that hires anything must not only pay the appointed hire, but make that which he hired good, if ought but good come to it by his default. "If a man borrow anything of his neighbor, and it be hurt, he shall surely make it good," etc. (Ex. 22:14–15).

(5) The pledge or pawn ought to be redeemed; and if it be of important necessity, as that which preserves the life of our neighbor, it must be restored to him incontinently. "If thou take thy neighbor's raiment to pledge, thou shalt restore it again before the sun go down: for that is his covering only" (Ex. 22:26). "No man shall take the nether or upper millstone to pledge, for this gage is his living" (Deut. 24:6). Neither may a man in a pledge be his own carver,[7] but he must take such a one as is offered. "When thou shalt ask a game of thy neighbor any thing lent, thou shalt not go into his house to fetch his pledge. But thou shalt stand without, and the man that borrowed of thee, shall bring the pledge out of the doors to thee. Furthermore, if it be a poor body, thou shalt not sleep with his pledge, but shalt restore him the pledge," etc. (Deut. 24:10–14).

(6) To become surety only for men that are honest and very well known, and that warily, with much deliberation. "He shall be sore vexed that is surety for a stranger. And he that hateth suretyship is sure" (Prov. 11:15). "A man destitute of understanding toucheth the hand, and becometh surety for his neighbor" (17:18; 22:26). But if it be so that a man has entangled himself by suretyship, the best way is to crave his creditor's favor by his own humble suit and the instant

---

7. *Be his own carver*: to take or choose for oneself at one's own discretion.

request of his friends. "My son if thou be surety for thy neighbor, and hast stricken hands with the strangers, thou art snared with the words of thine own mouth. Do this now, my son, and deliver thyself, seeing thou art come into the hand of thy neighbor, go, and humble thyself, and solicit thy friends. Give no sleep to thine eyes, nor slumber to thine eye lids. Deliver thyself, as a doe from the hand of the hunter, and as a bird from the hand of the fowler" (Prov. 6:1–5).

(7) All just covenants and promises, though they be to our hindrance, must be performed. For a promise does bind if it be lawful, so far forth as he will to whom we make the promise. "Which sweareth to his hurt, and changeth not" (Ps. 15:4). "A man that boasteth and keepeth not promise, is like clouds and wind without rain" (Prov. 25:14). "The spies saw a man come out of the city, and they said unto him, Show us we pray thee, the way into the city, and we will show thee mercy. And when he had showed them the way into the city, they smote the city with the edge of the sword, but they let the man and all his household depart" (Judg. 1:24–25). Therefore, if after promise made he either see that he shall be endamaged thereby or hindered in the performance of his promise, he may crave release, and if it be granted accept of it.

(8) To lend that we do freely. "Lend, looking for nothing again, and your reward shall be great" (Luke 6:35). And when we borrow, we must be careful to make restitution, even if need be, with the sale of our own goods. "Here the wife of the sons of the prophets selleth her oil which God sent by the hand of Elisha, to pay her creditor" (2 Kings 4:2–7).

(9) To restore that which is committed to our custody without delay. "He will destroy the evil husbandmen, and let out his vineyard to others, which shall deliver him the fruits in their season" (Matt. 21:41; Prov. 3:28). But if such a thing be lost not by our default, we are not urged to repay it. "If a man deliver his neighbor money, or stuff to keep, and it be stolen out of his house, if the thief be found, he shall pay the double. If the thief be not found, then the master of the house shall be brought before the judges to swear, whether he have put his hand to his neighbor's goods or no" (Ex. 22:7).

(10) That which a man finds is to be kept in his own hand if the true owner cannot be heard of; but if he be, he must restore it. "Thou shalt not see thy brother's ox, nor his sheep go astray, and withdraw thyself from them; but shall bring them again to thy brother. If he be not near to thee, or thou know him not, thou shalt bring it to thine house, and it shall remain with thee until thy brother seek after it, then shalt thou deliver it to him again. So shalt thou do withal lost things" (Deut. 22:1–3).

(11) To get our own, we may if we cannot do otherwise sue our neighbor in law. But we must follow our suits in all holy manner and with these caveats. (1) In all suits, we must not do anything that may prejudice the profession of

Christian religion. Therefore, all suitors in law offend when they trust more in man than in God and make their religion a jest to worldlings partly by striving about things of small importance and partly by not admitting any conditions of reconciliation. "Dare any of you, having business against another, be adjudged under the unjust, and not under the saints?" (1 Cor. 6:1). (2) Law must be the last remedy, as a desperate medicine is the last remedy the physician uses. We must assay all means possible before we use this, especially to a brother. "There is utterly a fault among you, because ye go to law one with another: why rather suffer ye not wrong? Why rather sustain ye not harm?" (v. 7). (3) In all suits of law, we must be mindful of the law of charity and not so much endeavor to maintain our own right as to recall our brother which errs into the right way.

Chapter 28

Concerning the Ninth Commandment

The ninth commandment concerns the preservation of our neighbor's good name. The words are these:

"Thou shalt not bear false witness against thy neighbor" [Ex. 20:16].

The Resolution

"Thou shalt not bear." That is, answer when you are asked before a judge. "Then both the men which strive together, shall stand before the Lord, even before the priests and judges which shall be in those days. And the judges shall make diligent inquisition, and if the witness be found false, and hath given false witness against his brother" (Deut. 19:17–18).

"Witness" by a figure signifies every word whereby the credit and estimation of our neighbor is either impaired or diminished.

The Negative Part: You Shall not Diminish or Hurt the Good Name and Estimation of Your Neighbor

Here is forbidden:

(1) Envy, disdain of others, desire of a man's own glory. "He is puffed up, and knoweth nothing, but doteth about questions, and strife of words, whereof cometh envy, strife, railings" (1 Tim. 6:4). "Wherefore, laying aside all maliciousness, and envy, and all guile, and evil speaking" (1 Peter 2:1). "But when the chief priests and scribes saw the marvels that he did, and the children crying in the temple, and saying, Hosanna the Son of David; they disdained" (Matt. 21:15).

(2) Evil suspicions. "And Eliab his eldest brother heard when he spake to the men, and Eliab was angry with David, and said, Why camest thou down hither? And with whom hast thou left those few sheep in the wilderness? I know thy pride and the malice of thine heart" (1 Sam. 17:28; 1 Tim. 6:4). "Now when the barbarians saw the worm hang on his hand, they said among themselves, This man surely is a murderer, whom though he has escaped the sea, yet vengeance has not suffered him to live" (Acts 28:4). Here are condemned hard censures and sinister judgments against our neighbor. "Judge not, that ye be not judged.

For with what judgment ye judge, ye shall be judged: and with what measure ye mete, it shall be measured to you again" (Matt. 7:1–2). These judgments which Christ forbids are private and reproachful or slanderous judgments—namely, when either a good or an indifferent action is interpreted to the worse part; or when a light offence is made heinous through evil will without all desire either to amend or to cover the same. "And others mocked and said, they are full of new wine. But Peter standing with the eleven, lift up his voice, and said to them, Ye men of Judea, and all ye that inhabit Jerusalem, be this known to you, and hearken to my words: for these are not drunken, as ye suppose, since it is but the third hour of the day" (Acts 2:13–15). "For Hannah spake in her heart, her lips did move only, but her voice was not heard, therefore Eli thought she had been drunken" (1 Sam. 1:13). But we must know that there are three kinds of judgments which are not forbidden by this commandment of Christ. The first is the ministry of the gospel, which judges and reproves sin. The second is the judgment of the magistrate. The third is the judgment of a friend admonishing us, as when he says, "Abstain from the company of such a man, for I know him to be a drunkard," etc.

(3) A relation of the bare words only and not of the sense and meaning of our neighbor. "Now the chief of the priests, and the elders, and all the whole council, sought false witnesses against Jesus, to put him to death. But they found none, and though many false witnesses came, yet found they none: but at the last came two false witnesses. And said, This man said, I can destroy the temple of God, and build it in three days" (Matt. 26:59–61). Indeed, Christ said some such thing in words, as appears: "Jesus answered and said to them, Destroy this temple, and in three days I will raise it up again" (John 2:19).

(4) A lie, whereby every falsehood with purpose to deceive is signified, whether in words or in deeds, or concealing the truth or any other way whatever—be it for never so great a good to our neighbor.

(5) To pronounce unjust sentence in judgment; to rest in one witness; to accuse another wrongfully; to betray a man's cause by collusion. "They proclaimed a fast, and set Naboth among the chief of the people. And there came two wicked men, and sat before him, and the wicked men witnessed against Naboth in the presence of people, saying, Naboth did blaspheme God and the king: then they carried him away out of the city, and stoned him with stones that he died" (1 Kings 21:12–13). "At the mouth of two or three witnesses shall he that is worthy of death, die: but at the mouth of one witness he shall not die" (Deut. 17:6).

(6) Openly to raise forged and hurtful tales and reports of our neighbor or privily to devise the same. "Whisperers, backbiters, haters of God, proud, boasters, inventers of evil things" (Rom. 1:29–30). "Thou shalt not walk about

with tales among thy people; thou shalt not stand against the blood of thy neighbor: I am the Lord" (Lev. 19:16). "And likewise also being idle, they learn to go about from house to house: yea they are not only idle, but also prattlers and busy bodies, speaking things which are not comely" (1 Tim. 5:13). To spread abroad flying tales or to feign and add anything to them. "Without wood the fire is quenched, and without a tale-bearer strife ceaseth. As a coal maketh burning coals, and wood a fire, so the contentious man is apt to kindle strife. The words of a tale-bearer are as flatterings, and they go down into the bowels of the belly" (Prov. 26:20–22). "For I fear lest when I come, I shall not find you such as I would, and lest there be strife, envying, wrath, contentions, backbitings, whisperings, swellings, and discord among you" (2 Cor. 12:20). To receive or believe those tales which we hear of others. "Thou shalt not receive a false tale, neither shalt thou put thine hand with the wicked, to be a false witness" (Ex. 23:1). "And David said to Saul, Wherefore givest thou an ear to men's words, that say, behold David seeketh evil against thee?" (1 Sam. 24:10).

(7) To accuse our neighbor for that which is certain and true through hatred and with intent to hurt him. "Then answered Doeg the Edomite (who was appointed over the servants of Saul) and said, I saw the son of Jesse when he came to Nob, to Ahimelech the son of Ahitub, who asked counsel of the Lord for him, and gave him victuals, and he gave him also the sword of Goliath the Philistine" (1 Sam. 22:9–10). Of this deed David thus speaks: "Why boastest thou thyself in thy wickedness, O man of power? The loving kindness of the Lord endureth forever. Thy tongue imagineth mischief, and is like a sharp razor, that cutteth deceitfully; thou dost love evil more than good; and lies, more than to speak the truth. Thou lovest all words that may destroy, O deceitful tongue" (Ps. 52:1–4).

(8) To open or declare our neighbor's secrets to any man, especially if he did it of infirmity. "Moreover, if thy brother trespass against thee, go and tell him his fault between thee and him alone: if he hear thee, thou hast won thy brother" (Matt. 18:15). "He that goeth about as a slanderer, discovereth a secret: but he that is of a faithful heart, concealeth a matter" (Prov. 11:13).

(9) All babbling talk and bitter words. "But fornication and all uncleanness, let it not be once named among you. Neither filthiness, neither foolish talking, neither jesting, which are not comely, but rather giving of thanks" (Eph. 5:3–4). "They answered and said to him, Thou art altogether born in sins, and dost thou teach us? So they cast him out" (John 9:34). This jesting or as it is now termed wit, which Aristotle the philosopher makes a virtue, is by Paul the apostle accounted a vice—and that not without cause. (1) Such quips as sting others, though they be a great pleasure for some to hear, yet are they very

offensive to such as are so girded. (2) It is very hard to make Christian godliness and gravity to agree with such behavior.

Objection. But salty and tart speeches are usual in the Scriptures (1 Kings 18:27). Elijah mocked the priests of Baal (Isa. 14:9).

Answer. Such speeches are not spoken to please others but are sharply denounced against God's enemies to His glory.

(10) Flattery, whereby we praise our neighbor above that we know in him. "The wounds of a lover are faithful, but the kisses of an enemy are to be shunned. He that praiseth his friend with a loud voice, rising early in the morning; it shall be counted to him as a curse" (Prov. 27:6, 14). "And the people gave a shout, saying, The voice of God, and not of man" (Acts 12:22). This is a grievous sin in the ministers of the word. "Neither did we ever use flattering word, as ye know, nor colored covetousness, God is record" (1 Thess. 2:5). "For from the least of them, even to the greatest of them, everyone is given to covetousness, and from the prophet, even to the priest, they all deal falsely. They have healed also the hurt of the daughter of my people with sweet words, saying, Peace, peace, when there is no peace" (Jer. 6:13–14). "For they that are such, serve not the Lord Jesus Christ, but their own bellies, and with fair speech and flattering, deceive the hearts of the simple" (Rom. 16:18).

(11) Foolish and over-confident boasting. "Boast not thyself of tomorrow, for thou knowest not what a day may bring forth. Let another praise thee, and not thine own mouth, a stranger, and not thine own lips" (Prov. 27:1).

(12) To accuse or witness against one falsely. "Naboth blasphemed God and the king" (1 Kings 21:13).

The Affirmative Part: Preserve the Good Name of Your Neighbor

"A good name is better than a good ointment" (Eccl. 7:3).

Here is commanded:

(1) A rejoicing for the credit and good estimation of your neighbor. "But the fruit of the Spirit, is love, joy, peace, gentleness" (Gal. 5:22). "First I thank my God through Jesus Christ, for you all, because your faith is published throughout the whole world" (Rom. 1:8).

(2) Willingly to acknowledge that goodness we see in any man whatever and only to speak of the same. "That they speak evil of no man, that they be no fighters, but soft, showing all meekness to all men" (Titus 3:2). Moreover, we must with all desire receive and believe reports of our neighbors' good. "Then came he to Derbe and Lystra, and behold, a certain disciple was there, named Timotheus, a woman's son which was a Jewess, and believed, but his father was a Grecian. Of whom the brethren which were at Lystra and Iconium, reported well. Therefore, Paul would that he should go forth with him, and took and

circumcised him" (Acts 16:1–3). Notwithstanding, this must so be performed of us that in no wise we prove and allow of the vices and faults of men. "And he did uprightly in the eyes of the Lord, but not with a perfect heart" (2 Chron. 25:2); "And he did uprightly in the sight of the Lord, according to all that his father Uzziah did, save that he entered not into the temple of the Lord, and the people did yet corrupt their ways" (27:2).

(3) To interpret a doubtful evil to the better part. "Love thinketh not evil. It believeth all things, it hopeth all things" (1 Cor. 13:5, 7). "And they took Joseph's coat and killed a kid of the goats, and dipped the coat in the blood. So they sent that parti-colored coat, and they brought it to their father, and said, This have we found, see now, whether it be thy son's coat or no. Then he knew it, and said, It is my son's coat, a wicked beast has devoured him, Joseph is surely torn in pieces" (Gen. 37:31–33).

And here observe the religion of that Joseph which was betrothed to Mary, who when he saw that Mary was with child was readier to conclude that before her betrothing she was with child by committing fornication than after by committing adultery (Matt. 1:19). But for all this, men must not be too credulous or light of belief. "But Jesus did not commit himself to them because he knew them all" (John 2:24).

(4) Not to believe an evil report running abroad among the common people by the whisperings of talebearers, as it were by conduit pipes. "He that slandereth not with his tongue, nor doeth evil to his neighbor, nor receiveth a false report against his neighbor" (Ps. 15:3). "And they said to him, Knowest thou not, that Baalis the king of the Ammonites, has sent Ishmael, the son of Nethaniah, to slay thee? But Gedaliah the son of Ahikam, believed him not. But Gedaliah the son of Ahikam, said to Johanan the son of Kareah, thou shalt not do this thing, for thou speakest false of Ishmael" (Jer. 40:14, 16). But we ought also to be angry at such whisperings. "As the north wind driveth away the rain, so does an angry countenance the slandering tongue" (Prov. 25:23).

(5) To keep secret the offence of our neighbor, except it must of necessity be revealed. "Hatred stirreth up contention: but love covereth all trespasses" (Prov. 10:12). "Then Joseph her husband, being a just man, and not willing to make her a public example, was minded to put her away secretly" (Matt. 1:19).

A man would suppose that by this means we should be partakers of other men's sins. But we must know that we ought to conceal our neighbor's imperfections, lest he should be provoked to offence; yet in the mean season he must be admonished that he may amend (Gal. 6:1). "Brethren, if any of you have erred from the truth, and some man has converted him, let him know that he which has converted the sinner from going astray out of his way, shall save a soul from death, and shall hide a multitude of sins" (James 5:19–20).

But if the sin which is concealed cannot thereby be taken away, then must we in love and charity declare the same to those which may remove and amend the same. "When Joseph was seventeen years old, he kept sheep with his brethren, and the child was with the sons of Bilhah, and with the sons of Zilpah, his father's wives: and Joseph told to their father, their evil sayings" (Gen. 37:2). "For it has been declared to me, my brethren, of you, by them that are of the house of Chloe, that there are contentions among you" (1 Cor. 1:11). "But if he hear thee not, take with thee one or two, that by the mouth of two or three witnesses every word may be confirmed" (Matt. 18:16).

(6) To get a good name and estimation among men and to keep the same when we have gotten it. "Furthermore brethren, whatsoever things are true, whatsoever things are honest, whatsoever things are just, whatsoever things are pure, whatsoever things are of good report, if there be any virtue, if there be any praise, think on these things" (Phil. 4:8). A good name is gotten (1) if we, seeking the kingdom of God before all things, do repent us of all our sins and with an earnest desire embrace and follow after righteousness. "The memorial of the just shall be blessed, but the name of the wicked shall rot" (Prov. 10:7). "Verily I say to you, wheresoever this gospel shall be preached throughout the whole world, this also, that she has done, shall be spoken of in remembrance of her" (Mark 14:9). (2) We must have a care both to judge and speak well of others. "With what judgment ye judge, ye shall be judged" (Matt. 7:2). "Give not thine heart also to all the words that men speak, lest thou do hear thy servant cursing thee. For oftentimes also thine heart knoweth, that thou likewise hast cursed others" (Eccl. 7:23–24). (3) We must abstain from all kind of wickedness, for one only vice or sin does obscure and darken a man's good name. "Dead flies cause to stink, and putrefy the ointment of the apothecary: so does a little folly him that is in estimation for wisdom, and for glory" (Eccl. 10:1). (4) We must in all things earnestly seek for the glory of God only, and not our own. "And when thou prayest, be not as the hypocrites for they love to stand and pray in the synagogues, and in the corners of the streets, because they would be seen of men: verily, I say to you, they have their reward. But when thou prayest, enter into thy chamber, and when thou hast shut thy door, pray to thy Father which is in secret, and thy Father which seeth in secret shall reward thee openly" (Matt. 6:5–6).

But if when we seek the glory of God honest and godly men do pray and testify well of us, we must not despise this their testimony and commendation; and although they never praise us nor testify of us at all, yet must we take it in good part. "For our rejoicing is this, the testimony of our conscience, that in simplicity and godly pureness, and not in fleshly wisdom, but by the grace of God, we have had our conversation in the world, and most of all to youwards"

(2 Cor. 1:12). "But we will not rejoice of things which are not within our measure, but according to the measure of the line, whereof God has distributed to us a measure, to attain even to you" (10:13). "The Lord is the portion of mine inheritance, and of my cup: thou shalt maintain my lot. The lines are fallen to me in pleasant places: yea, I have a fair heritage" (Ps. 16:5). "He that rejoiceth, let him rejoice in the Lord" (1 Cor. 1:31).

Chapter 29

Of the Tenth Commandment

The tenth commandment concerns concupiscences against our neighbor. The words are these:

"Thou shalt not covet thy neighbor's house, thou shalt not covet thy neighbor's wife, nor his servant, nor his maid, nor his ox, nor his ass, nor anything that thy neighbor has" [Ex. 20:17].

The Resolution

"Covet." The cogitation or motion of the heart is of three sorts. The first is some glancing or sudden thought suggested to the mind by Satan which suddenly vanishes away and is not received of the mind. This is no sin. For it was in Christ when He was tempted by the devil (Matt. 4:1, 3). The second is a more permanent thought or motion, the which as it were tickles and inveighs the mind with some inward joy. The third is a cogitation drawing from the will and affection full assent to sin. We are to understand this commandment of the second sort of motions only; for the third kind, which have consent of will, belong to the five former commandments.

Now then to covet is to think inwardly and also to desire anything whereby our neighbor may be hindered, albeit there ensue no assent of the will to commit that evil. For the very philosophers condemn covetousness of the heart, and civilians disallow a purpose only to do evil if it be conjoined with a manifest deliberation. And as for the concupiscence in this place forbidden, we may well think it is more close and secret because St. Paul, a doctor of the law, was altogether ignorant of it. "I had not known lust, except the law had said, Thou shalt not lust" (Rom. 7:7). Again, if that concupiscence immediately going before the consent were not prohibited in this place, there must be a great confusion in the Decalogue. For the seventh commandment forbids some kind of coveting of our neighbor's wife.

"House." The commandment is illustrated by an argument drawn from the distribution of the objects of concupiscence, whence it is apparent that only evil concupiscence is condemned in this place (Col. 3:5). For there is a good concupiscence or desire, as of meat and drink, and that of the Spirit. "The Spirit lusteth against the flesh" (Gal. 5:17).

The Negative Part: You Shall not Covet That Which Is Your Neighbor's

Here are prohibited:

(1) Concupiscence itself—namely, original corruption, inasmuch as it is hurtful to our neighbor (James 1:14).

(2) Each corrupt and sudden cogitation and passion of the heart springing out of the bitter root of concupiscence. "The flesh lusteth against the spirit" (Gal. 5:17). "Thou shalt love the Lord, with all thy soul" (Luke 10:27). To this place appertains Satan's suggestion, if after the first offer it be entertained and received in the closet of the heart.

(3) The least cogitation and motion, the which though it procure not consent delights and tickles the heart. Of this kind are these foolish wishes: "I would such a house were mine, such a living, such a thing," etc. And hitherto may we refer all unchaste dreams arising from the force of concupiscence.

The Affirmative Part: Covet That Only Which Is Available to Your Neighbor's Good

Here are commanded:

(1) A pure heart toward our neighbor. "The end of the commandment is love, out of a pure heart, a good conscience, and faith unfeigned" (1 Tim. 1:5).

(2) Holy cogitations and motions of the spirit. Paul prays that "the Thessalonians may be holy, not only in body and soul, but also in spirit" (1 Thess. 5:23; Eph. 4:23).

(3) A conflict against the evil affections and lusts of the flesh. "I rejoice in the law of God, in regard of the inward man. But I see another law of my members, rebelling against the law of my mind, and making me captive to the law of sin, which is in my members. Miserable man that I am, who shall deliver me from this body of death?" (Rom. 7:22–24; 2 Cor. 12:7–9).

Chapter 30

Of the Use of the Law

The use of the law in unregenerate persons is threefold.

The first is to lay open sin and make it known. "By the works of the law shall no flesh be justified in his sight: for by the law cometh the knowledge of sin" (Rom. 3:20).

The second use is accidently[1] to effect and augment sin by reason of the flesh, the which causes man to decline from that which is commanded and ever to incline to that which is prohibited. "Sin took occasion by the commandment, and wrought in me all manner of concupiscence; for without the law sin is dead. For I once was alive without the law, but when the commandment came, sin revived. But I died, and that commandment, which was ordained to life, was found to be to me to death" (Rom. 7:8–10).

The third use is to denounce eternal damnation for the least disobedience without offering any hope of pardon. This sentence the law pronounces against offenders; and by it, partly by threatening, partly by terrifying, it reigns and rules over man. "We know that whatsoever the law saith, it saith to them which are under the law, that every mouth may be stopped, and all the world be culpable before God" (3:19). "As many as are of the works of the law are under the curse for it is written, Cursed is everyone that continueth not in all that is written in the book of the law to do them" (Gal. 3:10). "If the ministration of death written with letters, and engraven in stones, was glorious, how shall not the ministration of the spirit be more glorious? For if the ministration of condemnation were glorious," etc. (2 Cor. 3:7–8).

The end why sin reigns in man is to urge sinners to flee to Christ. "The Scripture has concluded all under sin, that the promise by the faith of Jesus Christ should be given to them that believe. Wherefore the law was our schoolmaster to Christ" (Gal. 3:22, 24; Heb. 12:18–20).

The continuance of this power of the law is perpetual, unless a sinner repent, and the very first act of repentance so frees him that he shall no more be under the law, but under grace. "Then said David to Nathan, I have sinned

---

1. *Accidently*: non-essentially, incidentally, as a subsidiary or secondary effect.

against the Lord: wherefore Nathan said to David, The Lord also has forgiven thy sin, and thou shalt not die" (2 Sam. 12:13). "Sin shall not have dominion over you: for ye are not under the law, but under grace" (Rom. 6:14).

If therefore you desire seriously eternal life, first, take a narrow examination of yourself and the course of your life by the square of God's law. Then, set before your eyes the curse that is due to sin, that thus bewailing your misery and despairing utterly of your own power to attain everlasting happiness, you may renounce yourself and be provoked to seek and sue to Christ Jesus.

The use of the law in such as are regenerate is far otherwise; for it guides them to new obedience in the whole course of their life, which obedience is acceptable to God by Christ. "Do we therefore through faith make the law of none effect? God forbid: nay we rather establish the law" (Rom. 3:31). "Thy testimonies are my delight; they are my counselors. Thy word is a lanthorn to my feet, and a light to my path" (Ps. 119:24, 105).

Chapter 31

Of the Covenant of Grace

Hitherto concerning the covenant of works and of the law; now follows the covenant of grace.

The covenant of grace is that whereby God freely promising Christ and His benefits exacts again of man that he would by faith receive Christ and repent of his sins. "In that day will I make a covenant for them, etc. And I will marry thee to me forever: yea, I will marry thee to me in righteousness, and in judgment, and in mercy, and in compassion. I will marry thee to me in faithfulness, and thou shalt know the Lord" (Hos. 2:18–20). "I will pour clean water upon you, and ye shall be clean: yea, from all your filthiness, and from all your idols will I cleanse you. And I will give you a new heart, and a new spirit will I put within you. And cause you to walk in my statutes" (Ezek. 36:25–27). "The Lord, whom ye seek, shall speedily come to his temple: even the messenger of the covenant whom ye desire: behold, he shall come, saith the Lord of Hosts" (Mal. 3:1).

This covenant is also named a testament; for it has partly the nature and properties of a testament or will. For it is confirmed by the death of the testator. "Where a testament is, there must be the death of him that made the testament. For the testament is confirmed when men are dead; for it is yet of no force, so long as he that made it is alive" (Heb. 9:16–17). Secondly, in this covenant we do not so much offer or promise any great matter to God, as in a manner only receive; even as the last will and testament of a man is not for the testator's but for the heirs' commodity.

This covenant, albeit it be one in substance, yet is it distinguished into the Old and New Testament.

The Old Testament or covenant is that which in types and shadows prefigured Christ to come and to be exhibited.

The New Testament declares Christ already come in the flesh and is apparently shown in the gospel.

The gospel is that part of God's Word which contains a most worthy and welcome message—namely, that mankind is fully redeemed by the blood of Jesus Christ, the only begotten Son of God, manifested in flesh, so that now for all such as repent and believe in Christ Jesus there is prepared a full remission of all their sins, together with salvation and life everlasting. "As Moses lifted up the serpent in the wilderness: so must the Son of Man be lifted up. That whoso believeth in him, should not perish but have everlasting life" (John 3:14–15). "To Him also gave all the prophets witness, that through his name, all that believe in him, shall receive remission of sins" (Acts 10:43).

The end and use of the gospel is first to manifest that righteousness in Christ whereby the whole law is fully satisfied and salvation attained. Secondly, it is the instrument and as it were the conduit pipe of the Holy Ghost to fashion and derive faith into the soul, by which faith they which believe do as with a hand apprehend Christ's righteousness. "I am not ashamed of the gospel of Christ, for it is the power of God to salvation to as many as believe, to the Jew first, and then to the Grecian. For the justice of God is revealed by it, from faith to faith" (Rom. 1:16–17). "It is the Spirit which quickeneth, the flesh profiteth nothing: the words which I speak are spirit and life" (John 6:63). "It pleased God by the foolishness of preaching, to save such as believe" (1 Cor. 1:21).

The gospel preached is in the flourishing estate of Christ's church that ordinary means to beget faith; but in the ruinous estate of the same, when as by apostate the foundations thereof are shaken and the clear light of the word is darkened, then this word read or repeated, yea, the very sound thereof being but once heard is by the assistance of God's Spirit extraordinarily effectual to them whom God will have called out of that great darkness into His exceeding light. "How shall they call on him, in whom they have not believed? And how shall they believe in him, of whom they have not heard? and how shall they hear without a preacher?" (Rom. 10:14). "And they which were scattered abroad because of the affliction that arose about Steven, walked throughout till they came to Phenice, and Cyprus, and Antiochia, preaching the word to no man, but to the Jews only. Now some of them were men of Cyprus and Cyrene, which when they were come into Antiochia, spake to the Grecians and preached the Lord Jesus. And the hand of the Lord was with them, so that a great number believed, and turned to the Lord" (Acts 11:19–21). "The woman then left her water-pot, and went her way into the city, and said to the men, Come, and see a man which has told me all things that ever I did: Is not he the Christ? Then they went out of the city, and came to him. Now many of the Samaritans believed in him, for the saying of the woman which testified, He has told me all things that ever I did. And many more believed, because of his own word. And they said to the woman, now we believe not because of thy saying: for we have heard him ourselves, and know that this is indeed the Christ, the Savior of the world" (John 4:18, 29, 39, 41–42). "I demand, have they not heard? No doubt their sound went out through all the earth, and their words into the ends of the world" (Rom. 10:18). Thus, we may see how many of our forefathers and ancestors in the midst of popery obtained eternal life. "The dragon was wroth with the woman, and went and made war with the remnant of her seed, which kept the commandments of God, and have the testimony of Jesus Christ" (Rev. 12:17). "What saith the divine oracle? I have reserved to me seven thousand men, which never bowed knee to Baal" (Rom. 11:4).

Chapter 32

Of the Sacraments

Thus much of the preaching of the word; now follow the appendants to the same—namely, the sacraments.

A sacrament is that whereby Christ and His saving graces are by certain external rites signified, exhibited, and sealed to a Christian man. "He received the sign of circumcision, as the seal of the righteousness of the faith which he had, when he was uncircumcised" (Rom. 4:11). "Ye shall circumcise the foreskin of your flesh, and it shall be a sign of the covenant between me and you" (Gen. 17:11).

God alone is the author of a sacrament, for the sign cannot confirm anything at all but by the consent and promise of him at whose hands the benefit promised must be received. Therefore, God it is alone which appoints signs of grace, in whose alone power it is to bestow grace.

And God did make a sacrament by the sacramental word, as Augustine witnesses, saying: "Let the word come to the element, and there is made a sacrament." The sacramental word is the word of institution, the which God after a several manner has set down in each sacrament. Of this word, there are two parts: the commandment and the promise. The commandment is by which Christ appoints the administrations of the sacraments and the receiving of the same. As in baptism, "Go into the whole world, baptizing them in the name," etc. (Matt. 28:19). In the Lord's Supper: "Take, eat, drink, do ye this" (26:26). The promise is the other part of the institution, whereby God ordained elements that they might be instruments and seals of His grace. As in baptism, "I baptize thee in the name of the Father, of the Son, and of the Holy Ghost." In the Supper, "This is my body given for you," and, "This is my blood of the New Testament." Therefore, this word in the administration of the sacrament ought to be pronounced distinctly and aloud, yea, and as occasion serves explained also, to the end that all they to whom the commandment and promise appertains may know and understand the same. And hence it is very plain that the minister's impiety does not make a nullity of the sacrament, neither does it any whit hinder a worthy receiver—no more than the piety of a good minister can profit an unworthy receiver—because all the efficacy and worthiness thereof depends only upon God's institution, so be it that be observed.

The parts of a sacrament are the sign and the thing of the sacrament.

The sign is either the matter sensible or the action conversant about the same.

The matter sensible is usually called the sign.

The mutation of the sign is not natural by changing the substance of the thing, but respective—that is, only in regard of the use. For it is severed from a common to a holy use. Therefore, there is not any such either force or efficacy of making us holy inherent or tied to the external signs, as there is naturally baths to purify corrupt diseases. But all such efficacy is wholly appropriate to the Holy Spirit, yet so as it is an inseparable companion of true faith and repentance and to such as name to the Lord is together with the sign exhibited. Whence it comes to pass that by God's ordinance a certain signification of grace and feeling thereof agrees to the sign.

The thing of the sacrament is either Christ and His graces which concern our salvation or the action conversant about Christ.

I say first "Christ," and then "His grace," because no man receives grace from Christ unless he be made truly partaker of His very body and blood—even as no man can by right reap any fruit of the ground whereof first he has no just title and interest.

The action about Christ is spiritual and is either the action of God or of faith.

The action of God is either the offering or the application of Christ and His graces to the faithful.

The action of faith is the consideration, desire, apprehension, and receiving of Christ in the lawful use of the sacrament.

Thus much of the parts of a sacrament; now follows the union of the parts.

This sacramental union (1) is not natural according to place, for there is no mutation of the sign into the thing signed; neither is the thing signed either included in or fastened upon the sign. But (2) it is respective, because there is a certain agreement and proportion of the external things with the internal and of the actions of one with the actions of the other, whereby it comes to pass that the signs, as it were certain visible words, incurring into the external senses do by a certain proportionable resemblance draw a Christian mind to the consideration of the things signified and to be applied.

This mutual and, as I may say, sacramental relation is the cause of so many figurative speeches and metonymies which are used, as when one thing in the sacrament is put for another, as:

(1) The sign is used for the thing signified. "I am the living bread, which came down from heaven: if any eat of this bread, he shall live forever, and the

bread which I will give is my flesh, which I will give for the life of the world" (John 6:51). "Christ our passover is sacrificed for us" (1 Cor. 5:7). "We that are many, are one bread, and one body, because we are all partakers of one bread" (10:17).

(2) The name of the thing signified is given to the sign, as, "The bread is Christ's body, the cup is Christ's blood" (1 Cor. 11:24; Matt. 26:28). "Ye shall eat it"—namely, the lamb—"in haste, for it is the Lord's Passover" (Ex. 12:11).

(3) The effect of the thing signified is given to the sign, as circumcision is a covenant (Gen. 17:10; Acts 7:8). "The cup is the New Testament in Christ's blood" (Luke 22:20). "Baptism is the washing of the new birth" (Titus 3:5).

(4) That which properly belongs to the sign is attributed to the thing signified. "Circumcise the foreskin of your hearts" (Deut. 10:16). "Unless ye eat the flesh of the Son of Man, and drink his blood, ye shall have no life in you" (John 6:53).

The end why a sacrament was ordained is (1) for the better confirmation of our faith, for by it as by certain pledges given God of His great mercy does as it were bind Himself to us. Now a sacrament does confirm our faith not by any inherent or proper power it has in itself, as has a sovereign medicine received by a patient, the which, whether a man sleep or wake, confirms his strength; but rather by reasoning and using the signs when the Holy Ghost shall frame in our hearts such a conclusion, as this:

All such as are converted, rightly using the sacraments, shall receive Christ and His graces.

But I am converted and either now do or before have rightly used the sacraments.

Therefore, I shall receive Christ and His graces.

(2) That it may be a badge and note of that profession by which the true church of God is distinguished from other congregations.

(3) That it might be a means to preserve and spread abroad the doctrine of the gospel.

(4) It serves to bind the faithful that they do continue both loyal and grateful to their Lord God.

(5) It is the bond of mutual amity between the faithful.

How a sacrament is necessary to salvation. The covenant of grace is absolutely necessary to salvation; for of necessity a man must be within the covenant and receive Christ Jesus, the very substance thereof, or perish eternally. But a sacrament is not absolutely necessary, but only as it is a prop and stay for faith to lean upon. For it cannot entitle us into the inheritance of the sons of God, as the covenant does, but only by reason of faith going before it does seal that which before was bestowed upon us—as we see in human contracts the bond arises from the mutual consent of the parties, but the instrument or bill and the setting to of the seal they do not make but rather confirm the bond mutually before made, the which mutual consent remaining firm, the contract stands still in force, though the instrument or seal be wanting.

Therefore, the want of a sacrament does not condemn, but the contempt is that which will condemn a man. The want of a sacrament is when we are justly hindered from the receiving of the same, as when one is prevented by death or lives in such a place where he cannot receive the sacrament. And as for the neglect of a sacrament, albeit it be a very grievous sin, yet it is such a one as for which he that is heartily penitent for the same may well hope for pardon.

The holy use of a sacrament is when such as are truly converted do use those rites which God has prescribed to the true ends of the sacrament. Therefore, (1) the reprobate, though God offer the whole sacrament to them, yet they receive the signs alone without the things signified by the signs, because the sign without the right use thereof is not a sacrament to the receiver of it. So Paul says, "Circumcision verily is profitable if thou keep the law: but if thou be a transgressor of the law, thy circumcision is made uncircumcision" (Rom. 2:25). And Augustine has this saying, "If you receive it carnally, yet ceases it not to be spiritual, though to you it be not so." (2) The elect as yet not converted to the Lord do receive in like manner the bare signs without the thing signified, yet so as that sacrament shall in them afterward have its good effect. For the Sacrament received before a man's conversion is afterward to the penitent both ratified and becomes profitable; and that use of the sacrament which before was utterly unlawful does then become very lawful. (3) The elect already converted do to their salvation receive both the sign and the thing signified together, yet so as that for their unworthy receiving thereof, the which comes to pass by reason of their manifold infirmities and relapse into sin, they are subject to temporal punishments.

The difference between a sacrament and a sacrifice is in a sacrament God bestows His graces upon us; but in a sacrifice we return to God faith and obedience.

There are many differences between the sacraments of the Old Testament and these of the New. (1) They were many; these but few. (2) They pointed at Christ to come; these show that He is come. (3) They were appropriate to the posterity of Abraham, but these are common to the whole church called out of the Jews and Gentiles.

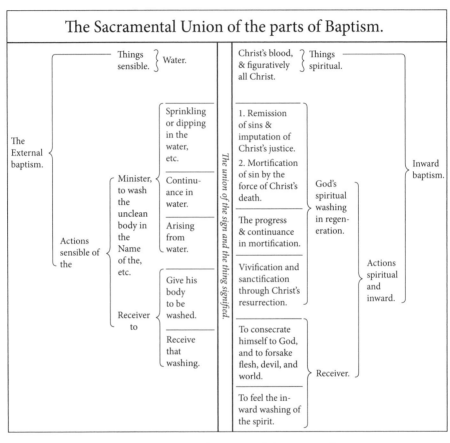

FIGURE 3: Sacramental Union of the Parts of Baptism

Chapter 33

Of Baptism

There are two sacraments. "I would not have you ignorant, that all our fathers were under the cloud, and all passed through the sea. And were all baptized to Moses in the cloud, and in the sea. And did all eat the same spiritual meat, and drank all the same spiritual drink: (for they drank of the spiritual rock that followed them, which rock was Christ)" (1 Cor. 10:1–4).[1]

The first sacrament is that whereby Christians are initiated and admitted into the church of God, and this is baptism.

The second sacrament, whereby they are perpetually preserved and nourished in the same church, is the Lord's Supper.

Baptism is a sacrament by which such as are within the covenant are washed with water in the name of the Father, the Son, and the Holy Ghost, that being thus engrafted into Christ they may have perpetual fellowship with Him. "Go, teach all nations, baptizing them in the name of the Father, the Son, and the Holy Ghost" (Matt. 28:19). "He that believeth and is baptized, shall be saved: he that believeth not, shall be condemned" (Mark 16:16). "Is Christ divided? Was Paul crucified for you? Or were ye baptized into the name of Paul? I thank God, I baptized none of you but Crispus and Gaius. Lest any should say, I had baptized into mine own name" (1 Cor. 1:14–15).

Within the covenant are all the seeds of Abraham or the seed of the faithful. These are either of riper years or infants.

Those of riper years are all such as adjoining themselves to the visible church do both testify their repentance of their sins and hold the foundations of religion taught in the same church. "And they were baptized of him in Jordan, confessing their sins" (Matt. 3:6). "As they went they came to a water, then the eunuch said, See, here is water, what hindereth me to be baptized? Then Philip said, If thou believe with all thine heart, thou mayest: he said, I believe that Jesus Christ is the Son of God. And they went down into the water, both Philip and the eunuch, and he baptized him" (Acts 8:36–38). "If a stranger dwell

---

1. In-text citation: Tertul. 4. Book contra Marcion. August. De Symbol., ad Catechum. 4. Book. 6. Chap. [Tertullian, *Contra Marcion*, bk. 4; Augustine, *De Symbol ad Catechum*, bk. 4, ch. 6].

with thee, and will observe the passover of the Lord, let him circumcise all the males that belong to him, and then let him come and observe it, and then he shall be as one that is born in the land: for none uncircumcised person shall eat thereof" (Ex. 12:48).

Infants within the covenant are such as have one at the least of their parents faithful. "The unbelieving husband is sanctified by the wife, and the unbelieving wife is sanctified by the husband, else were your children unclean, but now they are holy" (1 Cor. 6:14). "If the first fruits be holy, so is the whole lump: and if the root be holy, so are the branches" (Rom. 11:16). "I will establish my covenant between me and thee, and thy seed after thee, in their generation for an everlasting covenant, to be God to thee, and thy seed after thee. He that is born in thine house, and he that is bought with money, must needs be circumcised: so my covenant shall be in your flesh, for an everlasting covenant" (Gen. 17:7, 13). "They said, believe in the Lord Jesus, and thou shalt be saved, and thy whole household" (Acts 16:31).

Question. How are the children of faithful parents in the covenant?

Answer. Holy parents are two ways to be considered. First, as they were the sons of the first Adam, and so are as yet partly carnal. In this estate, they in like sort do beget their sons the children of wrath. For the father begets a son not as he is a good man, but simply as a man. And therefore being impure, he must needs beget that which is impure. Secondly, we must consider the parents as they are the sons of God, engrafted into the second Adam. In this estate, though they cannot derive faith to their posterity (for the sons of God are not made such by natural generation, but by the adoption of God the Father), yet may they believe both for themselves and others according to the tenor of the covenant of grace—as Adam did sin both for himself and others, and as parents in bargains do covenant both for themselves and their heirs after them. Hence it is that Paul says (1 Cor. 7:14) that the parents are like "to the first fruits which sanctify the whole lump." So then, the faith of the parents makes those their children to be accounted in the covenant, which by reason of their age do not yet actually believe.

To be baptized into the name of the Father, etc., is by the receipt of the outward sign of washing to be made one of God's family, which is His church, and to be partaker of the privileges thereof. "The angel which has delivered me from all evil, bless the children, and let my name be named upon them, and the name of my father, Abraham and Isaac, that they may grow as fish into multitude, in the midst of the earth" (Gen. 48:16). "In that day shall seven women take hold of one man, saying, We will eat our own bread, and we will wear our own garments: only let us be called by thy name, and take away our reproach" (Isa. 4:1).

By this it is manifest that in this washing of baptism there is propounded and sealed a marvelous solemn covenant and contract first of God with the baptized, that God the Father vouchsafes to receive him into favor, the Son to redeem him, the Holy Ghost to purify and regenerate him; secondly, of the baptized with God, who promises to acknowledge, invocate, and worship none other God but the true Jehovah, which is the Father, Son, and Holy Ghost.

The external and visible matter of baptism is water, for the minister may not baptize with any other liquor,[2] but only with natural water.

This was the judgment of the primitive church. For when as a "certain minister, for want of water, took sand, and baptized one with that: the party thus besanded, was further baptized, the former being esteemed of none effect."[3]

The external form of baptism is the minister's washing of the baptized according to the prescript rule of God's Word.

The ancient custom of baptizing was to dip and, as it were, to dive all the body of the baptized in the water, as may appear in Paul (Romans 6) and the councils of Laodicea and Neocaesarea.[4] But now especially in cold countries, the church uses only to sprinkle the baptized by reason of children's weakness; for very few of ripe years are nowadays baptized. We need not much to marvel at this alteration, seeing charity and necessity may dispense with ceremonies and mitigate in equity the sharpness of them.

The sacramental union of the parts of baptism is on this sort.

The element of water whereby the uncleanness of the body is purified by a most convenient proportion shadows out the blood of Christ and by the figure synecdoche, taking the part for the whole Christ. "And the blood of Jesus Christ cleanseth us from all sin" (1 John 1:7).

The action of the minister is his washing of the party baptized with the element of water. This seals and confirms a double action of God. (1) The engrafting or incorporating of the party baptized into Christ. "As many as are baptized into Christ, have put on Christ" (Gal. 3:27). "By one Spirit we are all baptized into one body" (1 Cor. 12:13). (2) Our spiritual regeneration. "Not by the works of righteousness which we had done, but according to His mercy

---

2. *Liquor*: liquid.

3. In-text reference: Niceph.histor.3.book,33.chapter [Possibly a reference to bk. 3, ch. 33 of Nicephorus Callistus's (*c.* 1256–*c.* 1335) massive twenty-three volume (eighteen of which have survived to the present) work *Ecclesiasticae Historiae*. Little is known about this author].

4. The Council of Laodicea was a fourth-century Church Council that passed fifty-nine canons of ecclesiastical law. The Council of Neocaesara was a Capadocian Council of an uncertain date (probably early fourth century, before 325 A.D.) that passed fifteen canons largely concerning disciplinary and marriage questions.

He saved us, by the washing of the new birth, and the renewing of the Holy Ghost" (Titus 3:5).

Of washing, there be three parts: the putting into the water, the continuance in the water, and the coming out of the water.

The putting into or the sprinkling of water does ratify (1) the shedding of the blood of Christ for the remission of all our sins and the imputation of His righteousness. "Arise and be baptized, and wash away thy sins in calling on the name of the Lord" (Acts 22:16). "And such were some of you, but ye are washed, but ye are sanctified, but ye are justified, in the name of the Lord Jesus, and by the Spirit of our God" (1 Cor. 6:11). (2) The mortification of sin by the power of Christ's death. "Know ye not, that all we which have been baptized into Jesus Christ, have been baptized into His death? Know this, that our old man is crucified with Him, that the body of sin might be destroyed, that henceforth we should not serve sin: for he that is dead is freed from sin" (Rom. 6:3, 6–7).

The continuance in the water notes the burial of sin—namely, a continual increase of mortification by the power both of Christ's death and burial. "We are buried then with Him by baptism into His death" (Rom. 6:4).

The coming out of the water does confirm our spiritual vivification to newness of life in all holiness and justice, the which we attain to by the power of Christ's resurrection. "Like as Christ was raised up from the dead by the glory of the Father: so we also should walk in the newness of life. For if we be grafted with him to the similitude of His death, even so shall we be to the similitude of his resurrection" (Rom. 6:4–5).

The action of the party to be baptized is twofold.

The first is to offer himself to be baptized before the minister, and that in the presence of the congregation. This signifies that he does consecrate himself to the Lord, and that he utterly renounces the flesh, the world, and the devil. "To the which also the figure which now saveth us, even baptism agreeth, (not the putting away of the filth of the flesh, but in that a good conscience maketh request to God) by the resurrection of Jesus Christ" (1 Peter 3:21).

The second is to receive the external washing by water. This signifies that the party baptized does receive the internal washing which is by the blood of Christ, or at the least that it is offered to him.

Rebaptizing is at no hand to be admitted; for as in natural generation man is once only born, so it is in spiritual regeneration. Therefore, they that are baptized of a minister which is a heretic not yet degraded from that calling (if the external form of administration be observed) must not be baptized again of the church of God, especially if after baptism they have been made partakers of the Lord's Supper. Only, they ought to be instructed in the true faith.

Eusebius says,[5] "There was with us an ancient professor of the faith, yea, before I was crated Bishop, nay, before my predecessor Heraclas: who when he was present at the baptism of some, and heard what questions they were asked, and what answers they returned, forthwith came weeping to me, and humbling himself before me, confessed that he was baptized by an heretic: yet in regard of that administration which he saw in our church, he accounted that no baptism, in that the confession there used, was fraught with blasphemies. This also he added, that he was for this offence so sore grieved, that he durst not so much as lift up his eyes to heaven: wherefore he most earnestly besought me, that he might be cleansed and purified with the baptism of our church, and so receive the grace of the Holy Ghost. The which notwithstanding, I durst not presume to administer, but said, it was sufficient for him that he had been so long a professor among us, and that at the receipt of the Lord's Supper, he answered, Amen. These things I told him were of force enough to purge him. And therefore I advised him, to rest himself in his former faith and conscience already sufficiently purified, especially in that he so long was partaker with us in the Sacraments."[6]

The right use of baptism is this. When inwardly in your heart you sensibly feel that through the heat of concupiscence you are moved to commit some sin, then begin to have some holy meditation of that solemn vow which you did make to God in baptism.

Again, if through infirmity you fall once or often into some sin, still have recourse to baptism, that there you may receive courage to your soul. For although baptism be but once only administered, yet that once testifies that all man's sins past, present, and to come are washed away (Eph. 5:25–27; 1 Peter 3:21). Therefore, baptism may be truly termed the "sacrament of repentance" and as it were a board to swim upon, when a man shall fear the shipwreck of his soul (Mark 1:4; Rom. 6:4, 6; 1 Tim. 1:19).

Last of all, see you never rest till such time as you have a feeling of that renewing power signified in baptism—namely, the power of Christ's death mortifying sin and the virtue of His resurrection in the renovation of the spirit.

---

5. In-text citation: Eccles.hist.lib.7.cap [Eusebius, *Ecclesiastical History*, bk. 7, ch. 8].

6. In-text citation: August.lib.3.c.2.contra Petil.literas [Augustine, *Answer to the Letters of Petilianus*, bk. 3, ch. 2].

The Sacramental relation, which is in the Lord's Supper, is on this manner.				
	Things sensible.	1. Bread. 2. Wine.	1. The body 2. The blood } of Christ.	Things spiritual.
The sensible and external actions of the	Minister to	Take bread and wine in his hands.	To seal Christ, to bear the office of a Mediator, *John 6:27.*	The spiritual and internal actions.
		Consecrate the bread & wine by repeating the promise, and prayers made for that end.	To send Christ to be Mediator, for which he was sealed from all eternity.	
		Break bread and pour out wine.	The execrable passion of Christ, and effusion of his blood.	
		Give the bread and wine into the receivers hands.	To offer Christ to all, even to the hypocrites, but to give him only to the true Christians.	
	Christian receivers to	Take the bread and cup in his hand.	To apprehend Christ by faith.	
		Eat the bread and drink the wine, for the nourishment of his body.	To apply Christ unto him, that the true union and communion with Christ may be increased.	

The union of the sign and the thing signified.

God. — The Christian receiver.

FIGURE 4: Sacramental Relation which is in the Lord's Supper

Chapter 34

Of the Lord's Supper

The Lord's Supper is a sacrament wherewith in the signs of bread and wine such as are engrafted into Christ are in Him daily in a spiritual manner nourished to eternal life (Rom. 6:5; 1 Cor. 11:23–25).

The proportion of the parts of the Lord's Supper is on this wise:

The elements of bread and wine are signs and seals of the body and blood of Christ.

The action of the minister is a note of God's action.

The minister's action is fourfold.

The first is his taking the bread and wine in his own hands. This does seal the action of God the Father by which He from all eternity did separate and elect His Son to perform the duty of a mediator between God and man. "For Him has the Father sealed" (John 6:27).

The second is his blessing of it whereby he by the recital of the promises and prayers conceived to that end does actually separate the bread and wine received from their common to a holy use. This does seal that action of God by which He did in the fullness of time send Christ to perform the office of a mediator, to the which He was foreordained.

The third is the breaking of the bread and pouring out of the wine. This does seal the passion of Christ by which He verily upon the cross was both in soul and body bruised for our transgressions.

The fourth is his distributing of the bread and wine into the hands of the communicants. This seals the action of God, offering Christ to all, yea, to the hypocrites, but giving Him indeed to the faithful for the daily increase of their faith and repentance.

The action of the receiver is double.

The first is his taking the bread and wine in his hand. This seals a spiritual action of the receiver—namely, his apprehension of Christ by the hand of faith (John 1:12).

The second is his eating of the bread and drinking of the wine to the nourishment of his body. This seals the application of Christ by faith, that the feeling of his true union and communion with Christ may daily be increased. "The cup of blessing which we bless, is it not the communion of the blood of Christ? The bread which we break, is it not the communion of the body of Christ?" (1 Cor. 10:16).

The doctrine of transubstantiation, which teaches that the bread is turned into the very body of Christ and the wine into His blood, is a very fable. The reasons why are these: (1) in the first institution of the Supper, which was before Christ's passion, the body of Christ was then eaten as already crucified. Now, how the body of Christ crucified should after a corporal manner be eaten, He Himself being not as yet crucified, it is impossible to imagine. (2) The bread after the consecration is distributed into parts, but the whole body of Christ is received of every singular communicant. (3) The bread is the communion of Christ's body; therefore, not His very body. (4) By this means the body of Christ should not only be made of the substance of the Virgin Mary, but also of the baker's bread. (5) Let the bread and wine be kept for a time, and the bread will mold, and the wine turn to vinegar after the consecration—by which we may conclude that there did remain the substance of bread and wine. (6) This opinion quite overthrows the sacramental union—namely, the proportion which is between the sign and the thing signified.

The like may be said of the Lutherans' consubstantiation, whereby they bear men in hand that there is a coexistence by which the body of Christ is either in or with or under the bread. Against this, these reasons may suffice: (1) the whole action of the Supper is done in remembrance of Christ. Now what need that, if the body of Christ were really present? (2) "Whom the heavens must contain, until the time that all things must be restored" (Acts 3:21). (3) This is an essential property of every magnitude, and therefore of the body of Christ, to be in one place and circumscribed or compassed of one place. (4) If that Christ's body were eaten corporally, then should the wicked as well as the faithful be partakers of the flesh of Christ; but to eat His flesh is to believe in Him and to have eternal life. (5) It were very absurd to think that Christ, sitting among His disciples, did with His own hands take His own body and give it wholly to each of His disciples.

Such as will in a holy sort prepare themselves to celebrate the Lord's Supper must have:

First, a knowledge of God and of man's fall and of the promised restoration into the covenant by Christ. "So often as ye shall eat this bread, and drink of this cup, ye show the death of the Lord till He come. And discern His body" (1 Cor. 11:26, 29).

Secondly, true faith in Christ for every man receives so much as he believes he receives. "For to us was the Gospel preached, as also to them: but the word that they heard, profited not them, because it was not mixed with faith in those that heard it" (Heb. 4:2). Furthermore, true repentance of their sins. "He that killeth a bullock, is as if he slew a man: he that sacrificeth a sheep, as if he cut off a dog's neck: he that offereth an oblation, as if he offered swine's blood: he that remembereth incense, as if he blessed an idol: yea, they have chosen their own ways, and their soul delighteth in their abominations" (Isa. 66:3). "I wash mine hands in innocency, O Lord, and so come before Thine altar" (Ps. 26:6).

Thirdly, renewed faith and repentance for daily and new sins committed upon infirmity, because every new sin requires a new act both of repentance and faith. And this renovation must be seen by our reconciliation of ourselves to our neighbors for injuries and wrongs. "If thou bring thy gift to the altar, and there rememberest thy brother has ought against thee, leave thy gift before the altar, and go, first be reconciled to thy brother, then come and offer thy gift" (Matt. 5:22, 24). If you can come furnished with these things, abstain not from the Lord's Table by reason of your many infirmities.

If being thus prepared you feel that you have a corrupt and rebellious heart, know this: that then you are well disposed to the Lord's Table when you are lively touched with a sense of your crooked disposition. "The Spirit of the Lord is upon me, because He has anointed me, that I should preach the Gospel to the poor: He has sent me, that I should heal the broken hearted, that I should preach deliverance to the captives, and recovering of sight to the blind, that I should set at liberty them that are bruised" (Luke 4:18). "He answered, and said, I am not sent, but to the lost sheep of the house of Israel" (Matt. 15:24). The Lord's Supper is a medicine to the diseased and languishing soul; and therefore men must as well seek to purify and heal their hearts in it as to bring pure and sound hearts to it.

If you feel in yourself some great defect and want of faith, pray to God earnestly that He will vouchsafe to increase it. "The father of the child crying with tears, said, Lord, I believe, help mine unbelief" (Mark 9:24).

If you cannot do this yourself, use the aid of the faithful, which may by their faith carry you as men did the sick of the palsy upon their shoulders and laid him before Christ (Mark 2:3).

If you come not furnished on this manner to the Lord's Table, you shall be adjudged guilty of the body and blood of Christ, as he is guilty of high treason who does counterfeit or clip the prince's coin. "He that eateth this bread, and drinketh this cup unworthily, shall be guilty of the body and blood of Christ" (1 Cor. 11:27).

But such as feel not themselves penitent, they neither can come to the Lord's Table without repentance, lest they eat and drink their own damnation, neither must they defer repentance by which they may come, lest they procure to themselves final destruction.

Chapter 35
Of the Degrees of Executing God's Decree of Election

We have hitherto declared the outward means whereby God's decree of election is executed. Now follow the degrees of executing the same.

The degrees are in number two: the love of God and the declaration of His love. "To the praise of the glory of his grace, wherewith he has made us accepted in his blood. And has opened to us the mystery of his will, according to his good pleasure, which he has purposed in him" (Eph. 1:6, 9).

God's love is that whereby God does freely love all such as are chosen in Christ Jesus, though in themselves altogether corrupt. "We loved him because he loved us first" (1 John 4:19). "God setteth out his love toward us, seeing that, while we were yet sinners, Christ died for us. For if when we were enemies, we were reconciled to God by the death of his Son, much more we being reconciled, shall be saved by his life" (Rom. 5:8, 10).

The declaration of God's love is twofold: the first, toward infants elected to salvation; the second, toward men of riper years.

The declaration of God's love toward infants is on this manner.

Infants already elected, albeit they in the womb of their mother before they were born or presently after depart this life—they, I say, being after a secret and unspeakable manner by God's Spirit engrafted into Christ obtain eternal salvation. "By one Spirit we are all baptized into one body, whether Jews, or Grecians, bond, or free, and have been all made to drink into one spirit" (1 Cor. 12:13). "The angel answered, and said to her, The Holy Ghost shall come upon thee, and the power of the Most High shall overshadow thee: therefore also that holy thing which shall be born of thee, shall be called the Son of God. And it came to pass, as Elisabeth heard the salutation of Mary, the babe sprang in her belly and Elisabeth was filled with the Holy Ghost. And his mouth was opened immediately, and his tongue loosed, and he spake and praised God. And the child grew, and waxed strong in spirit" (Luke 1:35, 41, 64, 80). "Before I formed thee in the womb, I knew thee, and before thou camest out of the womb, I sanctified thee" (Jer. 1:5).

I call the manner of infants' salvation secret and unspeakable, because (1) they want actual faith to receive Christ; for actual faith necessarily presupposes a knowledge of God's free promise, the which he that believes does apply to himself. But this infants cannot any ways possibly perform. And surely if infants should have faith actually, they generally either lose it when they come to men's estate or at least show no signs thereof—neither of which could be true if before they had received actual faith. Nay, we see that in those of riper years there are not so much as the shadows or sparks of faith to be seen before they be called by the preaching of the gospel. (2) Infants are said to be regenerated only in regard of their internal qualities and inclinations, not in regard of any motions or actions of the mind, will, or affections. And therefore they want those terrors of conscience which come before repentance as occasions thereof in such as are of riper years of discretion. Again, they are not troubled with that conflict and combat between the flesh and the spirit, wherewith those faithful ones that are of more years are marvelously exercised.

Chapter 36

Concerning the First Degree of the Declaration of God's Love

The declaration of God's love in those of years of discretion has especially four degrees (Rom. 8:30; 1 Cor. 1:30).

The first degree is an effectual calling whereby a sinner being severed from the world is entertained into God's family. "And came, and preached peace to you, which were afar off, and to them that were near. Now therefore you are no more strangers and foreigners, but citizens with the saints, and of the household of God" (Eph. 2:17, 19).

Of this, there be two parts. The first is election, which is a separation of a sinner from the cursed estate of all mankind. "If ye were of the world, the world would love his own; but because ye are not of the world, but I have chosen you out of the world, therefore the world hateth you" (John 15:19).

The second is the reciprocal donation or free gift of God the Father whereby He bestows the sinful man to be saved upon Christ, and Christ again actually and most effectually upon that sinful man, so that he may boldly say, "This thing"—namely, Christ, both God and man—"is mine, and I for my benefit and use enjoy the same." The like we see in wedlock; the husband says, "This woman is my wife, whom her parents have given to me, so that she being fully mine, I may both have her and govern her." Again, the woman may say, "This man is mine husband, who has bestowed himself upon me and does cherish me as his wife." "He spared not his own Son, but gave him for us" (Rom. 8:32). "To us a child is born, and to us a Son is given" (Isa. 9:6). "Thou hast given him power upon all flesh, that he should give eternal life to all them whom thou hast given him. I have declared thy name to the men which thou gavest me out of the world: thine they were, and thou gavest them me, and they kept thy word. Now they know that all things whatsoever thou hast given me, are of thee" (John 17:2, 6–7). "My Father, which gave them me, is greater than all, and none is able to take them out of my Father's hands" (10:29).

Hence comes that admirable union or conjunction which is the engrafting of such as are to be saved into Christ and their growing up together with Him, so that after a peculiar manner Christ is made the head and every repentant sinner a member of His mystical body. "I pray not for these alone, but for them also which shall believe in me, through their word. That they all may be one, as thou, O Father, art in me, and I in thee: even that they may be also one in us" (John 17:20–21). "We are members of his body, of his flesh, and of his bones" (Eph. 5:30). "I am that true vine, and my father is the husbandman. Every branch that beareth not fruit in me, he taketh away: and every one that beareth fruit, he purgeth it, that it may bring forth more fruit" (John 15:1–2). "Built upon the foundation of the prophets and apostles, whose cornerstone is Jesus Christ. In whom all the building coupled together, groweth to a holy temple in the Lord. In whom you are also built together, to be the habitation of God by the Spirit" (Eph. 2:20–22).

This, albeit it be a most near and real union, yet we must not think that it is by touching, mixture, or, as it were, by soldering of one soul with another, neither by a bare agreement of the souls among themselves, but by the communion and operation of the same Spirit, which being by nature infinite is of sufficient ability to conjoin those things together which are of themselves far distant from each other—the like we see in the soul of man, which conjoins the head with the foot (Eph. 3:22). "Whereby most great and precious promises are given to us, that by them you should be partakers of the Godly nature, in that ye flee the corruption, which is in the world through lust" (2 Peter 1:4). "If there be any consolation in Christ, if any comfort of love, if any fellowship of the Spirit," etc. (Phil. 2:1).

The things united. In this union not our soul alone is united with Christ's soul or our flesh with His flesh, but the whole person of every faithful man is verily conjoined with the whole person of our Savior Christ, God and man.

The manner of their union is this. A faithful man first of all and immediately is united to the flesh or human nature of Christ, and afterward by reason of the humanity to the Word itself or divine nature. For salvation and life depends on that fullness of the Godhead which is in Christ, yet it is not communicated to us but in the flesh and by the flesh of Christ. "Except ye eat the flesh, and drink the blood of the Son of Man, ye have no life in you. He that eateth my flesh, and drinketh my blood, dwelleth in me, and I in him" (John 6:53).

The bond of this union. This union is made by the Spirit of God applying Christ to us, and on our parts by faith receiving Christ Jesus offered to us. And for this cause it is termed a spiritual union.

Christ, because He is the head of the faithful, is to be considered as a public man sustaining the person of all the elect. Hence is it that the faithful are said to be crucified with Christ and with Him to die and to be buried (Rom. 6:4–6), to be quickened (Eph. 2:5), to be raised up and placed in heaven (v. 6; Col. 3:1). The which is not only in regard of the hope of the faithful, but because they are accepted of God certainly to have done all these things in Christ, even as in Adam's first sin all his posterity afterward was tainted of sin.

A member of Christ is diversely distinguished, and it is so either before men or God.

Before men, they are the members of Christ who outwardly professing the faith are charitably reputed by the church as true members. But such deceiving at length both themselves and the church may be reprobates, and therefore in God's presence they are no more true members than are the noxious humors in man's body or a wooden leg or other joint cunningly fastened to another part of the body.

Again, members before God are such as either are decreed to be so or actually are so already.

Such as are decreed to be so are they who being elect from all eternity are either as yet not born or not called. "Other sheep have I, which are not of this fold: them also must I bring" (John 10:16).

Actual members of Christ are either living or dying members.

An actual living member of Christ is everyone elected which being engrafted by faith and the Spirit into Christ does feel and show forth the power of Christ in him.

An actual dying or decaying member is everyone truly engrafted into Christ who has no feeling of the power and efficacy of the quickening Spirit in him. He is like to a benumbed leg without sense, which indeed is a part of man's body and yet receives no nourishment. Such are those faithless ones who for a time do faint and are overcome under the heavy burden of temptations and their sins; such are also those excommunicate persons who in regard of their engrafting are true members, however in regard of the external communion with the church and efficacy of the Spirit they are not members till such time as they being touched with repentance do begin as it were to live again.

God executes this effectual calling by certain means.

The first is the saving hearing of the word of God, which is when the said word outwardly is preached to such a one as is both dead in his sins and does not so much as dream of his salvation. And first of all, the law, showing a man his sin and the punishment thereof, which is eternal death; afterward the gospel, showing salvation by Christ Jesus to such as believe. And inwardly the eyes of the mind are enlightened, the heart and ears opened that he may see, hear, and understand the preaching of the word of God. "When I passed by thee, I saw thee polluted in thine own blood, and said to thee, when thou wast in thy blood, thou shalt live" (Ezek. 16:6). "Ho, everyone that thirsteth, come ye to the waters, and ye that have no silver, come buy, and eat: come, I say, and buy wine and milk without silver, and without money" (Isa. 55:1). "As many as received him to them he gave this privilege, that they should become the sons of God namely, to them which believed in his name" (John 1:12). "I knew not sin, but by the law: for I had not known lust, except the law had said, Thou shalt not lust" (Rom. 7:7). "But the anointing which ye received of him, dwelleth in you: and ye need not that any man teach you: but as the same anointing teacheth you of all things, and is true, and is not lying, and as it taught you, ye shall abide in him" (1 John 2:27). "A certain woman named Lydia, a seller of purple, of the city of the Thyatira, a worshiper of God, heard us, whose heart God opened, that she attended to the things that Paul spake" (Acts 16:14). "Thou art not delighted with sacrifice and burnt offerings, but mine ears hast thou opened" (Ps. 40:6). "No man can come to me, except the Father which has sent me, draw him: and I will raise him up at the last day" (John 6:44). "The Lord has called thee, being as a woman forsaken, and as a young wife, when thou wast refused, saith the Lord" (Isa. 54:6).

The second is the mollifying of the heart, the which must be bruised in pieces that it may be fit to receive God's saving grace offered to it. "I will give them one heart, and I will put a new Spirit within their bowels: and I will take the stony heart out of their bodies, and I will give them a heart of flesh" (Ezek. 11:19).

There are for the bruising of this stony heart four principal hammers. The first is the knowledge of the law of God. The second is the knowledge of sin both original and actual and what punishment is due to them. The third is compunction or pricking of the heart—namely, a sense and feeling of the wrath of God for the same sins. The fourth is a holy desperation of a man's own power in the obtaining of eternal life. "When they heard these things, they were pricked in heart, and said to Peter, and the rest of the apostles, Men and brethren, what shall we do? Peter said to them, Repent and be baptized every one of you in the name of Jesus for the remission of sins, and ye shall receive the gift of the Holy Ghost" (Acts 2:37–38). "Then he came to himself, and said, How many hired servants at my father's have bread enough, and I die for hunger: I will rise and go to my father, and say to him, Father, I have sinned against heaven, and before thee, and am no more worthy to be called thy son: make me as one of thy hired servants," etc. (Luke 15:17–19). "He answered, and said, I am not sent, but to the lost sheep of Israel" (Matt. 15:24).

The third is faith, which is a miraculous and supernatural faculty of the heart apprehending Christ Jesus being applied by the operation of the Holy Ghost and receiving Him to itself (John 1:12). "Jesus said to them, I am the bread of life, he that cometh to me, shall never hunger, and he that believeth in me, shall never thirst" (6:35). "What shall we say then? The Gentiles which follow not righteousness, have attained to righteousness, even the righteousness which is of faith" (Rom. 9:30).

Christ is received when every several person does particularly apply to himself Christ with His merits by an inward persuasion of the heart, which comes none other way but by the effectual certificate of the Holy Ghost concerning the mercy of God in Christ Jesus. "We have received, not the spirit of the world, but the Spirit which is of God, that we might know the things that are given to us of God" (1 Cor. 2:12). "I will pour the spirit of grace and of compassion upon the house of David, and upon the inhabitants of Jerusalem, and they shall look to Me, whom they have wounded" (Zech. 12:10). "His Spirit beareth witness to our spirit, that we are the sons of God" (Rom. 8:16). "In whom also ye have trust, after that ye heard the word of truth, even the Gospel of your salvation, wherein also after that ye believed, ye were sealed with the Holy Spirit of promise" (Eph. 1:13; 2 Cor. 1:22).

In the work of faith, there are five degrees or motions of the heart linked and united together, and are worthy the consideration of every Christian.

The first is knowledge of the gospel by the illumination of God's Spirit. "By his knowledge shall my Servant justify many" (Isa. 53:11). "This is life eternal, that they know Thee to be the only very God, and whom Thou hast sent, Jesus Christ" (John 17:3).

To this in such as are truly humbled is annexed a serious meditation of the promises in the gospel stirred up by the sensible feeling of their own beggary.

And after the foresaid knowledge in all such as are enlightened comes a general faith, whereby they subscribe to the truth of the gospel. "To us was the Gospel preached, as also to them: but the word that they heard profited not them, because it was not mixed with faith in those that heard it" (Heb. 4:2). "Having faith and a good conscience, which some have put away, and as concerning the faith, have made shipwreck" (1 Tim. 1:19). "Who will that all men should be saved, and come to the knowledge of the truth" (2:4).

This knowledge, if it be more full and perfect, is called (1) in Greek πληροφορία τῆς συνέσεως—that is, the full assurance of understanding. "That their hearts might be comforted, and they knit together in love, and in all riches, of the full assurance of understanding, to know the mystery of God, even the Father, and of Christ" (Col. 2:2). "I know, and am persuaded through the Lord Jesus, that there is nothing unclean of itself" (Rom. 14:14). "For as much as many have taken in hand, to set forth the story of those things, whereof we are fully persuaded" (Luke 1:1). "Our Gospel was to you, not in word only, but also in power, and to the Holy Ghost, and in much assurance" (1 Thess. 1:5).

The second is hope of pardon, whereby a sinner, albeit he yet feels not that his sins are certainly pardoned, yet he believes that they are pardonable. "I will go to my father, and say, Father, I have sinned against heaven and against thee, and am no more worthy to be called thy son; make me as one of thy hired servants" (Luke 15:18).

The third is a hungering and thirsting after that grace which is offered to him in Christ Jesus, as a man hungers and thirsts after meat and drink (John 6:35; 7:37). "And He said to me, It is done. I am Alpha and Omega, the beginning and the end, I will give to him that is athirst of the well of the water of life freely" (Rev. 21:6). "Blessed are they which hunger and thirst after righteousness, for they shall be satisfied" (Matt. 5:6).

The fourth is the approaching to the throne of grace, that there, flying from the terror of the law, he may take hold of Christ and find favor with God. "Let us therefore go boldly to the throne of grace, that we may receive mercy, and find grace to help in time of need" (Heb. 4:16).

This approaching has two parts. The first is a humble confession of our sins before God particularly, if they be known sins; and generally, if unknown. This done, the Lord forthwith remits all our sins. "I thought, I will confess against myself my wickedness to the Lord, and thou forgavest the punishment of my sin. Selah" (Ps. 32:5). "David said to Nathan, I have sinned against the Lord: wherefore Nathan said to David, The Lord has taken away thy sin, thou shalt not die" (2 Sam. 12:13; Luke 15:19).

The second is the craving pardon of some sins with unspeakable sighs and in perseverance (v. 21). "Repent of this wickedness, and pray God, that if it be possible, the thought of thine heart may be forgiven thee" (Acts 8:22). "The Spirit helpeth our infirmities: for we know not what to pray as we ought: but the Spirit itself maketh request for us, with sighs which cannot be expressed" (Rom. 8:26). "O Israel, return to the Lord thy God, for thou hast fallen by thine iniquity. Take to you words, and turn to the Lord, and say to him, Take away all iniquity, and receive us graciously" (Hos. 14:2–3).

The fifth arising of the former is an especial persuasion imprinted in the heart by the Holy Ghost whereby every faithful man does particularly apply to himself those promises which are made in the gospel. "They brought to him a man sick of the palsy lying on a bed and when Jesus saw their faith, he said to the sick of the palsy, Son, be of good comfort, thy sins are forgiven thee" (Matt. 9:2). "O woman, great is thy faith, be it to thee as thou desirest" (15:28). "I live, yet not I now, but Christ liveth in me; and in that I now live in the flesh, I live by the faith of the Son of God, who has loved me, and given himself for me" (Gal. 2:20).

This persuasion is and ought to be in every one, even before he have any experience of God's mercies. "A woman, a Canaanite, came out of the same coast, and cried, saying to Him, Have mercy on me, O Lord, the Son of David, my daughter is miserably vexed with a devil," etc. (Matt. 15:22–27). "Jesus said to him, Thomas, because thou hast seen me, thou believest: blessed are they which have not seen and have believed" (John 20:29). "Faith is the ground of things hoped for, and the evidence of things which are not seen" (Heb. 11:1). In philosophy, we first see a thing true by experience and afterward give our assent to it—as in natural philosophy, I am persuaded that such a water is hot because when I put mine hand into it, I perceive by experience a hot quality. But in the practice of faith, it is quite contrary. For first, we must consent to the word of God, resisting all doubt and diffidence, and afterward will an experience and feeling of comfort follow. "Put your trust in the Lord your God, and ye shall be assured: believe His prophets, and ye shall prosper" (2 Chron. 20:20). They therefore do very ill who are still in a doubt of their salvation, because as yet they feel not in themselves especial motions of God's Spirit.

Thus much concerning the way which God uses in the begetting of faith. There are beside this two notable degrees of faith. The one is the lowest, and as I may speak, the positive degree; the other is the highest or superlative.

The lowest degree of faith is called ὀλιγοπιζία, a little or weak faith, like a grain of mustard seed or smoking flax, which can neither give out heat nor flame but only smoke. "His disciples awaked him, saying, Save us, Master, we perish. And he said to them, Why are ye fearful, O ye of little faith? (Matt. 8:25–26). "If ye have faith as much as a grain of mustard seed, ye shall say to this mountain, Remove hence to yonder place; and it shall remove" (Matt. 17:20). "The smoking flax shall he not quench" (Isa. 42:3).

Faith is then said to be weak and feeble when as of those five degrees above mentioned either the first, which is knowledge, or the fifth, which is application of the promises, is very feeble, the rest remaining strong. "One believeth that he may eat all things, and another which is weak, eateth herbs. Let not him that eateth, despise him that eateth not: and let not him which eateth not, judge him which eateth: for God has received him" (Rom. 14:2). The apostles, although they believed that Christ was the Son of the living God, yet they were ignorant of His death and resurrection (Matt. 16:16; 17:22; John 6:69). "They understood not that word: for it was hid from them so that they could not perceive it" (Luke 9:45). "They asked him, saying, Lord, wilt thou restore at this time the kingdom to Israel?" (Acts 1:6).

For the better knowledge of this kind of faith, we must observe these two rules.

(1) A serious desire to believe and an endeavor to obtain God's favor is the seed of faith. "Blessed are they which hunger and thirst after righteousness; for they shall be satisfied" (Matt. 5:6). "I will give to him that is athirst, of the well of the water of life freely" (Rev. 21:6). "He will fulfill the desire of them that fear him; also he will hear their cry, and will save them" (Ps. 145:19). For in such as begin to believe and to be renewed, the mind will not lie idle but being moved

by the Holy Ghost strive with doubtfulness and distrust and endeavor to put their assent to the sweet promises made in the gospel and firmly to apply the same to themselves and in the sense of their weakness desire assistance from above; and thus faith is bestowed.

(2) God does not despise the least spark of faith, if so be it by little and little do increase, and men use the means to increase the same. "The apostles said to the Lord, Increase our faith. And the Lord said, If ye had faith as much as a grain of mustard seed, and should say to this mulberry tree, Pluck thyself up by the roots, and plant thyself in the sea, it should even obey you" (Luke 17:5). Man must therefore stir up his faith by meditation of God's word, serious prayers, and other exercises belonging to faith.

The highest degree of faith is πληροφορία, a full assurance, which is not only a certain and true but also a full persuasion of the heart whereby a Christian much more firmly taking hold on Christ Jesus makes full and resolute account that God loves him and that He will give to him by name Christ and all His graces pertaining to eternal life. "Neither did he doubt of the promise of God through unbelief, but was strengthened in the faith, and gave glory to God. Being fully assured, that he which had promised, was able also to do it" (Rom. 4:20–21). "I am persuaded, that neither life, nor death, etc., can separate us from the love of God which is in Christ Jesus" (8:38). "Thy servant slew both the lion and the bear: therefore this uncircumcised Philistine shall be as one of them, seeing he has railed on the host of the living God" (1 Sam. 17:36). "Doubtless, kindness and mercy shall follow me all the days of my life" (Ps. 23:6; cf. vv. 1–4).

Man comes to this high degree after the sense, observation, and long experience of God's favor and love.

Question. Whether is justifying faith commanded in the law?

Answer. It is commanded in the law of faith—namely, the gospel—but not in the law of works, that is, in the moral law (Rom. 3:27). The reasons are these: (1) that which the law reveals not, that it commands not; but the law is so far from revealing justifying faith that it never knew it. (2) Adam had fully before his fall written in his heart the moral law, yet had he not justifying faith, which apprenhended Christ.

Objection 1. Incredulity is condemned by the law.

Answer. That incredulity which is toward God is condemned in the law; but that incredulity which is against the Messiah, Christ Jesus, is condemned by the gospel. For as by the gospel, not by the law, incredulity in the Son as Mediator appears to be a sin, so likewise not by the law is incredulity in the Messiah condemned, but by the gospel, which commands us to hear Him and to believe in Him (Matt. 17:5; 1 John 3:23). Thus, it is plain that this sin not to believe in

Christ is expressly and distinctly made manifest and condemned by the gospel. And albeit the knowledge of sin be by the law, yet not everything which does reprove and declare some sin is the law of works or belongs thereto.

Objection 2. But ceremonies belong to the Decalogue.

Answer: Ceremonies may be as examples referred to the Decalogue, but indeed they are appendants to the gospel.

Chapter 37

Concerning the Second Degree of the Declaration of God's Love

The second degree is justification, whereby such as believe are accounted just before God through the obedience of Christ Jesus. "He has made Him to be sin for us, which knew no sin: that we should be made the righteousness of God in Him" (2 Cor. 5:21; 1 Cor. 1:30). "As by one man's disobedience many were made sinners, so by the obedience of one (that is, Jesus Christ), shall many also be made righteous" (Rom. 5:19).

Question. Whether did Christ perform full obedience to the law for us men alone or for Himself also?

Answer. (1) Not for Himself, as some not rightly would have Him; for the flesh of Christ being hypostatically united to the Word and so in itself fully sanctified was even from the first moment of conception most worthy to be blessed with eternal life. Therefore, by all that obedience which He performed after His conception, Christ merited nothing for Himself. (2) For us—namely, for the faithful—He fulfilled all the righteousness of the law, and hence it is that He is called "the end of the law to righteousness, to everyone that believeth" (Rom. 10:4).

Here may be objected (1) Christ as He is man is bound to perform obedience to the law for Himself.

Answer. He is not bound by nature, but of His own accord. For He was not a mere man, but God and man. And albeit Christ did never suffer nor fulfill the law but in that flesh which He took upon Him, yet by reason of the hypostatical union this His passion and obedience has respect to the whole person, considered as God and man; and therefore His obedience was not due on His part and so was without merit to Himself. Yea, in that the flesh of Christ is united to the person of the Word and so exalted in dignity and sanctity above all angels, it may seem to be exempted from this natural obligation of performing the law.

Objection 2. If then Christ performed the law for us, we are no more bound to the observance of the same, as we do not undergo eternal punishments for our sins, the which Christ in His person did bear upon the cross.

Answer. If we keep the same respect of performing obedience to the law, the consequence is very true; otherwise it is not so. For Christ performed obedience to the law for us as it is the satisfaction of the law; but the faithful, they are bound to obedience not as it is satisfactory, but as it is a document of faith and a testimony of their gratitude toward God or a means to edify their neighbors. Even as Christ suffering eternal punishments for our sins, we also suffer punishments as they are either trials or chastisements to us.

Objection 3. The law and justice of God does not together exact both — namely obedience and punishment.

Answer. In man's perfect estate, the justice of God requires only obedience; but in his state corrupted, He requires both obedience and punishment. Punishment, as the law is violated; obedience, that legal justice may be performed (Gal. 3:10). It is therefore plain that not only Christ's passion but also His legal obedience is our righteousness before God.

Justification has two parts: remission of sins and imputation of Christ's righteousness.

Remission of sins is that part of justification whereby he that believes is freed from the guilt and punishment of sin by the passion of Christ. "You has he now reconciled in the body of his flesh through death, to make you holy and unblameable, and without fault in his sight" (Col. 1:21–22). "Who, in his own flesh, bare our sins in his body, on the tree, that we being delivered from sin, should live in righteousness, by whose stripes ye are healed" (1 Peter 2:24).

Imputation of righteousness is the other part of justification, whereby such as believe, having the guilt of their sins covered, are accounted just in the sight of God through Christ's righteousness (2 Cor. 5:21). "Blessed is he, whose wickedness is forgiven, and whose sin is covered" (Ps. 32:1). Romans 4, the whole chapter, where the apostle repeats imputation eleven times. "I have counted all things loss, and do judge them to be dung, that I might win Christ, and might be found in him, that is, not having mine own righteousness which is by the law, but that which is through the faith of Christ, even the righteousness which is of God through faith" (Phil. 3:8–9).

The form of justification is as it were a kind of translation of the believer's sins to Christ and again Christ's righteousness to the believer by a reciprocal or mutual imputation. As is apparent in this picture following.

This obedience of Christ is called the righteousness of God and of Christ. Of God, (1) not because it is in God, but of God; for it takes all the power and merit it has from the deity of the Son. Whence it is that Jeremiah says, "Jehovah our Righteousness." (2) God does only accept of it for us because that alone makes us boldly to approach to God's throne of grace, that we may have pardon for our sins and be received to eternal life. It is also called the "righteousness of Christ," because being out of us it is in the humanity of Christ as in a subject.

Objection 1. No man is made just by any other man's justice.

Answer. This justice is both another's and ours also. Another's, because it is in Christ as in a subject; ours, because by means of the forenamed union Christ with all His benefits is made ours.

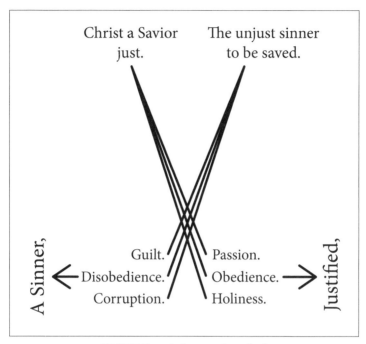

FIGURE 5: A Sinner Justified

Objection 2. The ancient fathers never dreamed of this imputative justice, and it may seem to be of no greater continuance than fifty years.

Answer. This is both false and impious to affirm. Augustine says, "All such as are justified by Christ are just not in themselves, but in Him."[1] Bernard in his sermon says, "*Mors in Christi morte fugatur, and Christi justitia nobis iimputatur*"—that is, "Death in Christ's death is put to flight, and the justice of Christ is imputed to us."[2] And "Where is there any rest but in the wounds of our Savior? I will forever sing, but what? Mine own justice? Nay, O Lord, I will remember Thy justice alone; for that is also my justice. For Thou wast made of God to me justice. But should I fear whether that one justice would suffice two? Nay it is not a short cloak that is not able to cover a couple. Thy justice is justice

---

1. In-text citation: 3. Tract upon Joh [Augustine, *Tractates on the Gospel of John*, tractate 3].

2. In-text citation: *ad milites temple, cap.* II [Bernard of Clairvaux (1090–1154), *Liber ad milites templi de laude novae militia*, ch. 2. Bernard was a French abbot and significant monastic figure].

for evermore, and will both cover Thee and me: it is largely large and eternal justice: and in me it covereth the multitude of my sins," etc.[3] Augustine says "We must understand this saying so: the doers of the law shall be justified, that we may know that there are no doers of the law but such as are justified, so that they are not first doers of the law and then justified, but first justified and then doers of the law."[4] So it is said, "They shall be justified," as if it should be said, "They shall be reputed just and accounted just."

Justification has annexed to it adoption, whereby all such as are predestinate to be adopted receive power to be actually accounted the sons of God by Christ. "Who has predestinated us to be adopted through Jesus Christ, to himself, according to the good pleasure of his will" (Eph. 1:5).

By means of adoption God has bestowed many notable privileges upon His children. (1) They are the Lord's heir apparent. "If we be children, we be also heirs, even the heirs of God" (Rom. 8:17).

(2) They are fellow heirs with Christ, yea kings. "And made us kings and priests, even to God his Father" (Rev. 1:6).

(3) All their afflictions, yea even their wants and offences are turned to trials or fatherly chastisements, inflicted upon them for their good. "We know that all things work together for the best, to them that love God. It is written, for thy sake are we killed all the day long: we are counted as sheep for the slaughter. Nevertheless, in all these things, we are more than conquerors through him that loved us" (Rom. 8:28, 36–37). "I will visit their transgression with the rod, and their iniquity with strokes. Yet My loving kindness will I not take from him" (Ps. 89:32–33). "There was given to me a prick in the flesh, the messenger of Satan to buffet me, because I should not be exalted out of measure" (2 Cor. 12:7). "I will be to him a Father, and he shall be to me a son: and if he sin, I will chasten him with the rod of men, and with the plagues of the children of men" (2 Sam. 7:14).

(4) They have dominion over all creatures, yet so as that in this life they have only right to the thing, but after this life they shall have right in the same. "Whether it be Paul, or Apollos, or Cephas, or the world, or life, or death, whether they be things present, or things to come, even all are yours" (1 Cor. 3:22–23). "Thou madest him little inferior to the angels; thou crownedst him with glory and honor, and hast set him above the works of thine hands. Thou hast put all things in subjection under his feet" (Heb. 2:7–8).

---

3. In-text citation: in his 62 sermon upon the Canticles [Bernard of Clairvaux, *Sermons on the Canticle of Canticles*, sermon 62]

4. In-text citation: *lib. Despiritu and litera, cap. 9 and 26* [Augustine, *On the Spirit and the Letter*, chs. 9 and 26].

Last of all, they have angels as ministering spirits attending upon them for their good. "Are they not all ministering spirits, sent forth to minister for their sakes which shall be heirs of salvation? (Heb. 1:14). "The Angel of the Lord pitcheth round about them that fear him, and delivereth them" (Ps. 34:7).

Whence it is apparent that the faithful alone have the true use of the Lord's goods (1) because their persons are in Christ acceptable to Him, in whom also they have restitution made to them of those goods which they lost in Adam, that they may with a good conscience use them. (2) They use them with thanksgiving to their end appointed by God.

Chapter 38

Concerning the Third Degree of the Declaration of God's Love

The third degree is sanctification, whereby such as believe, being delivered from the tyranny of sin, are by little and little renewed in holiness and righteousness. "Whosoever is born of God, sinneth not: for his seed remaineth in him; neither can he sin, because he is born of God" (1 John 3:9). "There is no condemnation to those which are in Christ Jesus, which walk not after the flesh but after the spirit" (Rom. 8:1).

Sanctification has two parts: mortification and vivification.

The mortification of sin is the first part of sanctification, whereby the power of sin is abated and crucified in the faithful. "How shall we that are dead to sin, live yet therein: know ye not, that all we which have been baptized into Jesus Christ, have been baptized into his death? We are buried then with him by baptism into His death, that like as Christ was raised up from the dead, by the glory of the Father, so we also should walk in newness of life" (Rom. 6:2–4; Eccl. 5:6–7, 11–13). "They which are Christ's have crucified the flesh, with the affections and lusts thereof" (Gal. 5:24).

The means of mortification is the death and burial of Christ, from which proceeds such virtue as at the first giving sin his deadly wound does bereave it of power to rage and reign in man and causes it to die and consume as it were in a grave.

The virtue of Christ's death is a certain power issuing from His deity into His humanity when He died. Whereby He did in the same humanity vanquish our sin imputed unto Him, being our surety, as well in regard of the punishment as of the guilt thereof, that in like sort by the same power He might abolish the corruption of sin in us His members.

Vivification is the second part of sanctification, whereby inherent holiness being begun is still augmented and enlarged. First, we receive the first fruits of the Spirit; then, a continual increase of them. "Be renewed in the spirit of your mind. And put on the new man, which after God is created in righteousness, and true holiness" (Eph. 4:23–24). "And you has he quickened that were dead in trespasses and sins" (2:1). "Thus I live, yet not I now, but Christ in me: and in that I now live in the flesh, I live by the faith of the Son of God, who has loved me, and given Himself for me" (Gal. 2:20). "We which have the first fruits of the Spirit, even we do sigh in ourselves, waiting for the adoption, even the redemption of our bodies" (Rom. 8:23). "The first man Adam was made a living soul, and the second Adam was made a quickening spirit" (1 Cor. 15:45).

The means of vivification is a virtue derived from Christ's resurrection to those that are quickened, which makes them to rise up to newness of life. "That I may know him, and the virtue of His resurrection" (Phil. 3:10).

The power of Christ's resurrection is that whereby He first did in His own flesh as conqueror over death and sin begin to live with God and to be exalted above every name, and then in His members, sin being dead and buried, He causes in them an endeavor and purpose to live according to the will of God.

The efficient cause of them both is the Holy Ghost, who does by His divine power convey Himself into the believers' hearts and in them by applying the power of Christ's death and resurrection creates holiness (Job 33:24–25). "Now ye are not in the flesh, but in the spirit, because the Spirit of God dwelleth in you: but if any man have not the Spirit of Christ, the same is not his. But if the Spirit of him that raised up Jesus from the dead dwell in you, he that raised up Christ from the dead, shall also quicken your mortal bodies, because that his Spirit dwelleth in you" (Rom. 8:9, 11).

Furthermore, this inherent holiness is to be distinguished into parts according to the several faculties of the body and soul of man. "The very God of peace sanctify you throughout: and I pray God, that your whole spirit, soul, and body may be kept blameless, to the coming of our Lord Jesus Christ" (1 Thess. 5:23).

(1) The holiness or renewing of the mind, which is the illumination thereof to the knowledge of the will of God. "We cease not to pray for you, and to desire that ye might be fully filled with knowledge of his will, in all wisdom and spiritual understanding" (Col. 1:9). "To one is given by the spirit the speech of wisdom, to another the speech of knowledge, by the same spirit" (1 Cor. 12:8).

Illumination is either spiritual understanding or spiritual wisdom.

Spiritual understanding is an illumination of the mind whereby it acknowledges the known truth of the Word of God.

Spiritual wisdom is an illumination of the mind whereby the same truth is applied to the good ordering of particular both things and actions, as person, place, and time require.

These two have the effects which follow:

[First,] to discern between good and evil. "Strong meat belongeth to them that are of age, which through long customs have their wits exercised to discern both good and evil" (Heb. 5:14). "That we may discern things that differ one from another" (Phil. 1:10).

[Second,] to discern of spirits. "Dearly beloved, believe not every spirit, but try the spirits whether they be of God" (1 John 4:1). "Try all things, and keep that which is good" (1 Thess. 5:21). "These were more noble men, than they which were at Thessalonica, which received the Word with all readiness, and searched the Scriptures daily, whether these things were so" (Acts 17:11).

[Third,] to meditate upon the words and works of God. "But his delight is in the law of God, and in that law does he exercise himself day and night" (Ps. 1:2). "I will meditate on thy precepts, and consider thy ways" (119:15; Psalm 107).

[Fourth,] to discern and acknowledge man's own inward blindness. "Teach me, O Lord, the way of thy statutes, and I will keep it to the end" (119:33). "Open mine eyes that I may see the wonders of thy law" (v. 18).

(2) The sanctity of the memory is an ability to keep a good thing when it is offered to the mind and as need serves to remember it. "I have hid thy promise in mine heart, that I might not sin against thee" (v. 11). "I will praise the Lord who has given me counsel: my reins also teach me in the night" (16:7). "His mother kept all these things in her heart" (Luke 2:51).

(3) The sanctity of conscience is a grace of God whereby a man's conscience excuses him for all sins after they are forgiven him in Christ, as also of his upright walking in the whole course of his life. "Having faith and a good conscience, which some having put away," etc. (1 Tim. 1:19). "I know nothing by myself: yet am I not thereby justified" (1 Cor. 4:4). "Paul said, I have in all good conscience, served God until this day" (Acts 23:1). "I endeavor myself to have always a clear conscience toward God and toward man" (24:16). "Judge me, O Lord, for I have walked in mine innocency, my trust has been also in the Lord therefore shall I not slide. Prove me, O Lord, and try me, examine my reins and mine heart. For thy loving kindness is before mine eyes, therefore have I walked in thy truth" (Ps. 26:1–3).

Hence, in all godly men arises the inward peace of God and the outward alacrity in the countenance. "The peace of God which passeth all understanding, shall preserve your hearts and minds in Jesus Christ" (Phil. 4:7). "The wicked flee, when none pursueth: but the righteous are bold as a lion" (Prov. 28:1).

(4) Sanctity of will, whereby man begins to will that which is good and to refuse the contrary. Therefore, in this estate, the will is partly freed from bondage, partly in bondage to sin. "It is God which worketh in you, both the will and the deed, even of his own pleasure" (Phil. 2:13). "I know that in me, that is, in my flesh, dwelleth no good thing: for to will is present with me, but I find no means to perform that which is good," etc. (Rom. 7:18–22).

(5) Sanctity of affections is the right moving of them (Rom. 7:24; 1 Thess. 5:23).

Affections of most especial note are these:

(1) Hope, whereby men with sighing look for the accomplishing of their redemption (Rom. 8:23).

This hope, when it is once strong and lively, has also her πληροφορία—that is, full assurance—as faith has. "And we desire that every one of you show the same diligence, to the full assurance of hope to the end" (Heb. 6:11). "Blessed be God, even the Father of our Lord Jesus Christ, which, according to his abundant mercy, has begotten us again to a lively hope, by the resurrection of Jesus Christ from the dead" (1 Peter 1:3).

(2) Fear of offending God, because of His mercy. "If ye call him Father, which without respect of person, judgeth according to every man's work, pass the time of your dwellings here in fear" (v. 17). "There is mercy with thee, that thou mayest be feared" (Ps. 130:4).

(3) A base account of all worldly things in respect of Christ Jesus. "But the things that were advantage to me, I accounted loss for Christ's sake. Yea doubtless, I think all things but loss, for the excellent knowledge sake of Christ Jesus my Lord, for whom I have counted all things, and do judge them to be dung, that I might win Christ" (Phil. 3:7–8).

(4) The love of God in Christ, which is like to death and as a fire that cannot be quenched. "Love is strong as death, jealousy is cruel as the grave, the coals thereof are fiery coals, and a vehement flame" (Song 8:6).

(5) A fervent zeal to God's glory. "I would with myself to be separate from Christ, for my brethren, that are my kinsmen, according to the flesh" (Rom. 9:3).

(6) Anguish of mind for our own sins and others' also. "Mine eyes gush out with tears, because men keep not thy law" (Ps. 119:136). "And delivered just Lot, being vexed with the uncleanly conversation of the wicked. For he being righteous, and dwelling among them, in seeing, and hearing, vexed his righteous soul from day to day, with their unlawful deeds" (2 Peter 2:7).

(7) Exceeding great joy in the Holy Ghost. "The kingdom of God is not meat and drink, but righteousness, and peace, and joy in the Holy Ghost" (Rom. 14:17).

(8) Sanctity of body, whereby it is a fit instrument for the soul to accomplish that which is good. "As ye have given your members servants to uncleanness, and to iniquity, to commit iniquity: so now give your members servants to righteousness in holiness" (6:19).

Chapter 39

Of Repentance and the Fruits Thereof

From sanctification, repentance is derived, because no man can earnestly repent except he, denying himself, do hate sin even from his heart and embrace righteousness. This no man either will or can perform, but such a one as is in the sight of God regenerated and justified and endued with true faith. Therefore, albeit in such as are converted repentance does first manifest itself, yet regarding the order of nature, it follows both faith and sanctification. Hence also is it evident that this repentance (legal contrition being some occasion and as it were a preparation to true conversion) is wholly begotten by the preaching of the gospel.

Repentance is when a sinner turns to the Lord. "He showed first to them of Damascus, and at Jerusalem, and through all the coasts of Judea, and then to the Gentiles, that they should repent and turn to God, and do works worthy amendment of life" (Acts 26:20). "Every man that has this hope in him, purgeth himself, as he is pure" (1 John 3:3).

This is performed when as anyone by the instinct of the Holy Ghost does purpose, will, desire, and endeavor to relinquish his former sins and to become a new man. "I have applied my heart to fulfill thy statutes always, even to the end" (Ps. 119:112; 1 John 3:3). "Who when he was come, and had seen the grace of God, was glad, and exhorted all, that with purpose of heart they would cleave to the Lord" (Acts 11:23).

The fruit of repentance is a Christian conversation wherein are brought forth fruits worthy amendment of life. "Bring ye therefore forth fruits worthy of repentance" (Matt. 3:8).

A Christian conversation is such a course of life whereby we following Christ's example do by Him perform new obedience to God. "Take my yoke upon you, and learn of me, that I am meek and lowly in heart: and ye shall find rest to your souls" (11:29). "For as much as Christ has suffered for us in the flesh, arm yourselves likewise with the same mind, which is, that he which has suffered in the flesh, has ceased from sin" (1 Peter 4:1). "For hereto are ye called, for Christ also suffered for us, leaving us an example that we should follow his steps" (2:21). "If any man long after life, and to see good days, let him refrain his tongue from evil, and his lips that they speak no guile. Let him eschew evil, and do good: let him seek peace, and follow after it" (3:10–11).

There are two parts of new obedience: the denial of ourselves and the profession of Christ. "If any man will follow me, let him forsake himself, take up his cross, and follow me" (Matt. 16:24).

The denial of ourselves consists partly in Christian warfare, partly in the patient bearing of the cross.

Chapter 40

Of Christian Warfare

Christian warfare is concerning the right way of fighting in the spiritual battle. The parts thereof are the preparation to battle and the combat itself.

To the preparation, we must use the complete armor of God. "For this cause, take to you the whole armor of God, that ye may be able to resist in the evil day, and having finished all things, stand fast" (Eph. 6:13).

The parts hereof are especially six: (1) truth; (2) justice; (3) evangelical obedience; (4) faith; (5) the Word of God; (6) continual and fervent prayer with watching. "Stand therefore, and your loins girded about with verity, and having on the breastplate of righteousness, and your feet shod with the preparation of the gospel of peace. Above all, take the shield of faith, wherewith ye may quench all the fiery darts of the wicked. And take the helmet of salvation, and the sword of the Spirit, which is the word of God. And pray always with all manner prayer and supplication in the spirit, and watch thereto with all perseverance and supplication for all saints" (Eph. 6:14–18). "Be sober, and watch: for your adversary the devil, as a roaring lion, walketh about seeking whom he may devour" (1 Peter 5:8).

The combat is a mutual conflict of them that fight spiritually.

The warriors are the tempter and the Christian soldier. "For we wrestle not against flesh and blood, but against principalities, against powers, and against the worldly governors, the princes of the darkness of this world, against spiritual wickednesses, which are in high places" (Eph. 6:12).

The tempter is the prince or his helpers. The prince is Satan and his angels, which are spiritual wickednesses in high things. His helpers are the flesh and the world.

The conflict of all these is temptation, whereby man is provoked to commit such wickedness as is hurtful to the salvation of his soul. "Dearly beloved, I beseech you as strangers and pilgrims, abstain from fleshly lusts, which fight against the soul" (2 Peter 2:11).

In the soldier, two things are to be considered: his resisting and his fall.

Resistance is an action whereby the soldier does withstand temptation through grace working inwardly in him. "I write to you babes, because ye have known the Father; I have written to you fathers, because ye have known him that is from the beginning: I have written to you young men, because ye are strong and the word of God abideth in you, and ye have overcome the wicked" (1 John 2:14; 1 Peter 5:8; Eph. 6:16). "Thou shalt walk upon the lion and asp, the young lion and the dragon shalt thou tread under feet" (Ps. 19:13).

To confirm this, these preservatives which follow are very necessary.

(1) When you are tempted to sin, do not only [be] abasing[1] from it, but earnestly love and follow after the contrary (John 8:44).

(2) Never yield or consent to Satan's words, whether he speak the truth, accuse falsely, or flatter dissemblingly. "Ye are of your father the devil, and the lusts of your father ye will do: he has been a murderer from the beginning, and abode not in the truth, because there is no truth in him: when he speaketh a lie, then speaketh he of his own: for he is a liar, and the father thereof" (John 8:44). "And cried with a loud voice, and said, What have I to do with Thee, Jesus, the Son of the most high God? And Jesus said, Hold thy peace and come out of him" (Mark 1:24). "She followed Paul and us, and cried, saying, These men are the servants of the most high God, which show to us the way of salvation," etc. (Acts 16:17).[2]

(3) One temptation is to be looked for after another, and then especially when our enemy, as though he had made truce with us, is at rest—for the devil never makes an end of his malice (1 Peter 5:8).

The fall is whereby the soldier through infirmity faints, being subdued by the power of the enemy. "Brethren, if a man be fallen by occasion into any fault, ye which are spiritual, restore such a one with the spirit of meekness, considering thyself, lest thou also be tempted" (Gal. 6:1).

To this appertains the spiritual remedy. A remedy is a thing having aptness to restore him which is fallen to his former estate (v. 1).

And here two things must always be thought on.

(1) If there be a willing mind, everyone is accepted for that grace which he has, not for that which he has not. "For if there be first a willing mind, it is accepted according to that a man has, and not according to that he has not" (2 Cor. 8:12).

(2) In all these things, whoever will lead a godly life in Christ, the power of God is to be made perfect through their infirmity. "And he said to me, My grace is sufficient for thee, for my power is made perfect through weakness. Very gladly therefore will I rejoice rather in mine infirmities, that the power of God may dwell in me. Therefore, I take pleasure in infirmities, in reproaches, in necessities, in persecutions, in anguish for Christ's sake, for when I am weak, then am I strong" (12:9–10).

---

1. *Abasing*: be humbled.
2. In-text citation: Aug. serm. 241 [Augustine, *Sermons*, sermon 241].

Chapter 41

Of the First Assault

Assaults are threefold.

The first is about the Christian man's effectual calling. The temptation is the enterprise of the devil to blindfold man's mind and to harden his heart, lest the word of God should work in him to salvation. "And as he sowed some fell by the wayside, and the fowls came and devoured them up. And some fell upon stony ground, where they had not so much earth, and anon they sprang up, because they had no depth of earth. And when the sun rose up, they were parched, and for lack of rooting withered away. And some fell among thorns, and the thorns sprung up and choked them. Whensoever a man heareth the Word of the kingdom, and understandeth it not, the evil one cometh, and catcheth away that which was sown in his heart: and this is he which has received the seed by the wayside" (Matt. 13:4–7, 19).

A resistance in those that are to be called is wrought by the Spirit of God, that causes man to lend their ears to hear and does engraft the word in their hearts, that the immortal seed of regeneration may spring in them (Ps. 40:6; John 6:44; Acts 16:14). "Wherefore lay apart all filthiness, and superfluity of maliciousness, and receive with meekness, the word that is grafted in you, which is able to save your souls" (James 1:21). "Seeing your souls are purified in obeying the truth through the spirit, to love brotherly, without feigning, love one another with a pure heart fervently" (1 Peter 1:22). "Whosoever is born of God sinneth not: for his seed remaineth in him, neither can he sin, because he is born of God" (1 John 3:9). A resistance in those that are called is when in a sincere heart they do join the word which they have heard with faith. "But that which fell in good ground, are they which with an honest and good heart, hear the Word, and keep it, and bring forth fruit with patience" (Luke 8:15; Heb. 4:2).

Here are certain preservatives to be noted.

(1) Premeditation of the power and use of the word. "Take heed to thy feet, when thou enterest into the house of the Lord, and be more near to hear, than to give the sacrifice of fools, for they know not that they do evil" (Eccl. 4:17). "Be not rash with thy mouth, nor let thine heart be hasty to utter a thing before

God: for God is in the heaven, and thou art on the earth, therefore let thy words be few" (5:1).

(2) Diligent attention of the mind (Acts 16:14).

(3) A hungering desire of the heart. "Now in the last and great day of the feast, Jesus stood and cried, saying, If any man thirst let him come to me, and drink" (John 7:37).

(4) Integrity of life (Ps. 26:6).

(5) The casting away of evil affections. "And be ye doers of the Word, and not hearers only, deceiving your own souls" (James 1:22).

(6) The inward consent and agreement of the heart with the word preached (Acts 2:37).

(7) A hiding of the word in the heart, lest we should sin. "I have hidden thy Word in mine heart, that I might not sin against thee" (Ps. 119:11).

(8) A trembling at the presence of God in the assembly of the church. "For all these things has mine hand made, and all these things have been, saith the Lord, and to him will I look, even to him that is poor and of a contrite spirit, and trembleth at my words" (Isa. 66:2). "Then sent I for thee immediately, and thou hast well done to come. Now therefore are we all here present before God, to hear all things that are commanded thee of God" (Acts 10:33).

The fall is either a coldness in receiving the word and a neglect thereof, or else a falling into errors.

The remedy for this is subjection, which must be made to the judgment and censure of the brethren and ministers. "I know thy works, that thou art neither cold nor hot" (Rev. 3:15; Gal. 6:2). "Of whom is Hymeneus and Alexander, whom I have delivered to Satan, that they might learn not to blaspheme" (1 Tim. 1:20).

Chapter 42

Of the Second Assault

The second assault is concerning faith.

The temptation is an illusion which the devil casts into the hearts of godly men, as when he says, "You are not of the elect; you are not justified; you have no faith; you must certainly be condemned for your sins." "Then came to him the tempter, and said, If thou be the Son of God: command that these stones be made bread" (Matt. 4:3).

The occasions which he takes of these illusions are:

(1) Adversity, as dangers, losses, persecutions, grievous offences, etc. "Lo these are the wicked, yet prosper they always, and increase in riches. Certainly, I have cleansed mine heart in vain, and washed mine hands in innocency" (Ps. 73:12–13). "How many are mine iniquities and sins? Show me my rebellion and my sin. Wherefore hidest thou thy face, and takest me for Thine enemy? Wilt thou break a leaf driven to and fro, and wilt thou pursue the dry stubble?" (Job 13:23–25).

(2) The remembrance of sins past. "For thou writest bitter things against me, and makest me to possess the iniquity of my youth" (v. 2).

(3) A feeling of death even already at hand.

The resistance is made by a true faith applying Christ with all His merits particularly, after this manner: "I assuredly believe that I shall not be condemned, but that I am elected and justified in Christ, and am out of all doubt that all my sins are pardoned." "He shall see the travail of his soul, and shall be satisfied: by his knowledge shall my righteous servant justify many: for he shall bear their iniquities" (Isa. 53:11). "For I am persuaded, that neither death, nor life, nor angels, nor principalities, nor powers, nor things present, nor things to come, nor height, nor depth, nor any other creature shall be able to separate us from the love of God, which is in Christ Jesus our Lord" (Rom. 8:38–39).

The preservative is in temptation not to behold faith but the object of faith, which is Christ. "Not as though I had already attained to it, either were already perfect: but I follow, if that I may comprehend that, for whose sake also I am comprehended of Christ Jesus. One thing I do, I forget that which is behind, and endeavor myself to that which is before. And follow hard toward the mark, for the price of the high calling of God in Christ Jesus" (Phil. 3:12–14). "And as Moses lift up the serpent in the wilderness, so must the Son of Man be lift up, that he that believeth in him," etc. (John 3:14).

The falling is doubtfulness and distrust of our election and of God's mercy. "I called to remembrance my song in the night: I communed with my own heart, and my spirit searched diligently. Will the Lord absent himself forever? And will he show no more favor? Is his mercy clean gone forever? Does his promise fail forevermore?" (Ps. 77:6–8). So David of himself says, "My God, my God, why hast thou forsaken me, and art so far from my health, and from the words of my roaring?" (22:1).

The remedy is double.

First, the operation of the Holy Spirit stirring up faith and increasing the same. "I am persuaded of this same thing, that he that has begun this good work in you, will perform it to the day of Jesus Christ" (Phil. 1:6). "And the apostle said to the Lord, Increase our faith" (Luke 17:5).

The second is a holy meditation, which is manifold.

(1) That it is the commandment of God that we should believe in Christ. "This is then his commandment, that we believe in the name of his Son Jesus Christ, and love one another; as he gave commandment" (1 John 3:23).

(2) That the evangelical promises are indefinite and do exclude no man, unless peradventure any man do exclude himself. "Ho, every one that thirsteth, come ye to the waters, and ye that have no silver, come, buy, and eat: come, I say, buy wine and milk without silver and without money" (Isa. 55:1). "Come to me, all ye that are weary and laden, and I will ease you" (Matt. 11:28). "That whosoever believeth in him should not perish but have eternal life" (John 3:15). Also the sacraments of baptism and the Lord's Supper do to every one severally apply indefinite promises and therefore are very effectual to enforce particular assurance or plerophory[1] of forgiveness of sins.

(3) That doubtfulness and despair are most grievous sins.

(4) That contrary to hope men must under hope believe with Abraham. "Which Abraham above hope, believed under hope, that he should be the father of many nations: according to that which was spoken to him, so shall thy seed be" (Rom. 4:18).

(5) That the mercy of God and the merit of Christ's obedience, being both God and man, are infinite. "For the mountains shall remove, and the hills shall fall down: but my mercy shall not depart from thee, neither shall my covenant

---

1. *Plerophory*: full assurance or certainty.

of peace fall away, saith the Lord, that has compassion on thee" (Isa. 54:10). "For as high as the heaven is above the earth, so great is his mercy toward them that fear him" (Ps. 103:11). "My babes, these things write I to you, that ye sin not: and if any man sin, we have an advocate with the Father, Jesus Christ, the just. And he is the reconciliation for our sins: and not for ours only, but also for the sins of the whole world" (1 John 2:1–2). "Let Israel wait on the Lord, for with the Lord is mercy, and with him is great redemption" (Ps. 130:7).

(6) That God measures the obedience due to Him rather by the affection and desire to obey than by the act and performance of it. "For they that are after the flesh, savor the things of the flesh, but they that are after the spirit, the things of the spirit. Because the wisdom of the flesh, is enmity against God: for it is not subject to the law of God, neither indeed can be" (Rom. 8:5). "Now if I do that I would not, it is no more I that do it, but the sin that dwelleth in me. I find then by the law, that when I would do good, evil is present with me. For I delight in the law of God, concerning the inner man" (7:20–22). "I will spare them, as a man spareth his son that reverenceth him" (Mal. 3:17).

(7) When one sin is forgiven, all the rest are remitted also; for remission being given once without any prescription of time is given forever. "For the gifts and calling of God, are without repentance" (Rom. 11:29). "To him also give all the prophets witness, that through his name, all that believe in him, shall receive remission of sins" (Acts 10:43).

(8) That grace and faith are not taken by falls of infirmity but thereby are declared and made manifest. "Moreover, the law entered thereupon, that the offence should abound: nevertheless, where sin abounded, there grace abounded much more" (Rom. 5:20). "And lest I should be exalted out of measure, etc., there was given to me a prick in the flesh, the messenger of Satan to buffet me. For this thing I besought the Lord thrice, that it might depart from me. He said, My grace is sufficient for thee" (2 Cor. 12:7–8).

(9) That all the works of God are by contrary means. "My power is made perfect through weakness" (2 Cor. 12:9).

Chapter 43

Of the Third Assault

The third assault is concerning sanctification.

The temptation is a provoking to sin according to the disposition of every man and as occasion shall offer itself. "And Satan stood up against Israel, and provoked David to number Israel" (1 Chron. 21:1). "And when supper was done, and the devil had now put into the heart of Judas Iscariot, Simon's son, to betray him" (John 13:2).

In this temptation, the devil does wonderfully diminish and extenuate those sins which men are about to commit, partly by objecting closely the mercy of God and partly by covering or hiding the punishment which is due for the sin.

Then there are helps to further the devil in this his temptation.

First, the flesh, which lusts against the spirit, sometimes by begetting evil motions and affections, and sometimes by overwhelming and oppressing the good intents and motions. "For the flesh lusteth against the spirit, and the spirit against the flesh: and these are contrary one to another, so that ye cannot do the same things that ye would. Moreover the works of the flesh are manifest, which are adultery, fornication, uncleanness, wantonness, idolatry, witchcraft, hatred, debate, emulations, wrath, contentions, seditions, heresies, envy, murders, drunkenness, gluttony, and such like, whereof I tell you before, as I also have told you before, that they which do such things shall not inherit the kingdom of God" (Gal. 5:17–21). "But every man is tempted, when he is drawn away by his own concupiscence, and is enticed" (James 1:14).

Secondly, the world, which brings men to disobedience through pleasure, profit, honor, and evil examples. "Among whom we also had our conversation in time past, in the lust of our flesh, in fulfilling the will of the flesh, and of the mind, and were by nature the children of wrath, as well as others" (Eph. 2:3). "For all that is in the world, as the lust of the flesh, and the lust of the eyes, and pride of life, is not of the Father, but is of this world" (1 John 2:16).

Resistance is made by the desire of the spirit, which works good motions and affections in the faithful and drives forth the evil. "But the fruit of the spirit is love, joy, peace, long suffering, gentleness, goodness, faith, meekness, temperancy: against such there is no law. For they that are Christ's, have crucified the flesh, with the affections and the lusts thereof. Let us not be desirous of vainglory, provoking one another, envying one another" (Gal. 5:22–24, 26).

The preservatives are these, whereby men are strengthened in resisting.

(1) To account no sin light or small. "A little leaven does leaven the whole lump" (Gal. 5:9). "For the wages of sin is death, but the gift of God is eternal life, through Jesus Christ our Lord" (Rom. 6:23).

(2) To avoid all occasions of sin. To these rather agreeth the proverb used of the plague: *longe, tarde, cito*—that is, "aloof, slowly, quickly." "Abstain from all appearance of evil" (1 Thess. 5:22). "And others save with fear, pulling them out of the fire, and hate even the garment spotted by the flesh" (Jude 23).

(3) To accustom yourself to subdue the lesser sins, that at the last you may overcome the greater (Rom. 13:4).

(4) To apply yourself to your appointed calling and always to be busily occupied about something in the same.

(5) To oppose the law, the judgments of God, the last judgment, the glorious presence of God, and such like against the rebellion and looseness of the flesh. "Blessed is the man that feareth always: but he that hardeneth his heart shall fall into evil" (Prov. 28:14). "There is no man greater in his house than I: neither has he kept anything from me, but only thee, because thou art his wife: how then can I do this great wickedness, and so sin against God?" (Gen. 39:9).

Here certain preservatives take place.

Against unjust anger or private desire of revenge, here meditate (1) that injuries happen to us by the Lord's appointment for our good (2 Sam. 16:10). (2) God of His great goodness forgives us far more sins than it is possible for us to forgive men. (3) It is the duty of Christian love to forgive others. (4) We must not desire to destroy them whom Christ has redeemed with His precious blood. (5) We ourselves are in danger of the wrath of God if we suffer our wrath to burn against our brother. "Forgive," says He, "and it shall be forgiven" (Matt. 6:14). (6) We know not the circumstances of the facts, what the mind was, and purposes of them against whom we swell.

Bridles or external remedies are these. (1) In this we shall imitate the clemency of the Lord, who for a very great season does often tolerate the wicked. "Learn of me, for I am humble and meek" (Matt. 11:29). (2) There must be a pausing and time of delay between our anger and the execution of the same. Athenodorus counseled Augustus, that he being angry should repeat all the letters of the alphabet, or A, B, C, before he did either speak or do anything against another. (3) To depart out of those places where those are with whom we are angry. (4) To avoid contention both in word and deed. "Do nothing through contention" (Phil. 2:3).

Remedies against those bad desires of riches and honor, (1) God does even in famine quicken and revive them which fear Him. "The eye of the Lord is upon them that fear Him, to deliver their souls from death, and to preserve them from famine" (Ps. 33:18–19). (2) Godliness is great gain if the mind of man can be therewith content (1 Tim. 6:6). (3) We do wait and look for the resurrection of the body and eternal life; therefore, we should not take such carking[1] care for this present mortal life. (4) We are servants in our Father's house, therefore look what is convenient for us, that will He lovingly bestow upon us. (5) The palpable blindness of an ambitious mind desires to be set aloft, that he may have the greater downfall; and he feared to be humbled, lest he should not be exalted. (6) Adam, when he would needs be checkmate[2] with God, did bring both himself and his posterity headlong to destruction. (7) He is a very ambitious rob-God[3] which desires to take that commendation to himself which is appropriate only to the Lord.

Preservatives against the desires of the flesh, (1) he that will be Christ's disciple must every day take up his cross (Luke 9:23). (2) They which are according to the Spirit savor of such things as are according to the Spirit (Rom. 8:5). (3) They that walk after the flesh shall die (v. 13). (5) We ought to behave ourselves as citizens of the kingdom of heaven (Phil. 3:20). (5) We are the temple of God (1 Cor. 3:16). Our members, they are the members of Christ (6:15). And we have dwelling within us the Spirit of Christ, which we should not grieve (Eph. 4:30). Concerning this, look more in the explication of the seventh commandment.

In this temptation, the fall is when a man being overtaken falls into some offence (Gal. 6:1).

Here Satan does wonderfully aggravate the offence committed and does accuse and terrify the offender with the judgments of God. "Then when Judas which betrayed him, saw that he was condemned, he repented himself, and brought again the thirty pieces of silver to the chief priests and elders, saying, I have sinned, betraying the innocent blood: but they said, What is that to us? See thou to it. And when he had cast down the silver pieces in the temple, he departed and went and hanged himself" (Matt. 27:3–5).

The remedy is a renewed repentance, the beginning whereof is sorrow in regard of God for the same sin, the fruits whereof are especially seven. "Now I rejoice not that ye were sorry, but that ye sorrowed to repentance: for ye

---

1. *Carking*: anxious, fretting, distressing, burdening, and grieving.
2. *Checkmate*: the act of threatening or attacking the King.
3. *Rob-God*: someone who steals from God.

sorrowed godly, so that in nothing ye were hurt by us. For godly sorrow causeth repentance to salvation, not to be repented of: but worldly sorrow causeth death. For behold, this thing that ye have been godly sorry, what great care has it wrought in you: yea, what clearing of yourselves: yea, what indignation: yea, what fear: yea, how great desire: yea, what zeal: yea, what punishment: in all things ye have showed yourselves, that ye are pure in this matter" (2 Cor. 7:9–11).

(1) An endeavor and purpose to do well according to the rule of God's Word.

(2) An apology, that is a confession of the sin before God with an earnest entreaty of pardon for the offence. "Then I acknowledged my sin to thee, neither hid I mine iniquity: for I thought, I will confess against myself, my wickedness to the Lord, and thou forgavest the punishment of my sin" (Ps. 32:5). "Then David said to Nathan, I have sinned against the Lord: and Nathan said to David, The Lord also has put away thy sin, thou shalt not die" (2 Sam. 12:13).

(3) Indignation against a man's self for his offence.

(4) A fear not so much for the punishment as for offending the Lord. "If thou straitly markest iniquities, O Lord, who shall stand? (Ps. 130:3).

(5) A desire to be fully renewed and to be delivered from sin.

(6) A fervent zeal to love God and to embrace and keep all His commandments.

(7) Revenge whereby the flesh may be tamed and subdued, lest at any time afterward, such offence be committed.

Chapter 44

Of the Patient Bearing of the Cross

The patient bearing of the cross teaches how Christians should undergo the burden.

The cross is a certain measure of afflictions appointed by God to every one of the faithful. "If any man will follow me, let him forsake himself, take up his cross, and follow me" (Matt. 16:24). "Now rejoice I in my sufferings for you, and fulfill the rest of the afflictions of Christ in my flesh, for his body's sake, which is the church" (Col. 1:24).

We ought to take up His cross willingly, even with both hands, when it shall please God to lay it upon us. And after we have taken it up, we must bear it with patience and perseverance: "Strengthened with all might, through his glorious power, to all patience and longsuffering with joyfulness" (Col. 1:11). "Possess your souls with patience" (Luke 21:19).

The preservatives of patience are (1) strength by the Holy Ghost. "I am able to do all things through the help of Christ, which strengtheneth me" (Phil. 4:13). "It is given to you for Christ, that not only ye should believe in him, but also suffer for his sake" (1:29). (2) A holy meditation, which is manifold.

(1) That the afflictions of the faithful come not by chance, but by the counsel and providence of God, which disposes all things in a most excellent sort. It was God that sent Joseph into Egypt (Gen. 45:4–5). "The Lord biddeth Shemei curse David" (2 Sam. 16:10). "It was good for me, that I was afflicted, that I might learn thy statutes" (Ps. 119:71). Hence it is evident that afflictions to the godly are inevitable. "By many afflictions you must enter into the kingdom of God" (Acts 14:22). "The gate is strait, and the way narrow that leadeth to life, and few there be that find it" (Matt. 7:14). "In the world ye shall have troubles" (John 16:33).

(2) That albeit afflictions are grievous, yet are they good and profitable; for they are helps whereby men being humbled for their sins before God obtain peace and holiness of life. "We received sentence of death in ourselves, because we should not trust in ourselves, but in God, which raiseth the dead" (2 Cor. 1:9). "Lord, in trouble have they visited thee, they poured out a prayer, when thy chastening was upon them" (Isa. 26:16). "I will go, and return to my place,

till they acknowledge their fault, and seek me: in their affliction they will seek me diligently" (Hos. 5:15). "When he slew them, they sought him, and they returned, and they sought God early" (Ps. 78:34). "I have heard Ephraim lamenting thus, Thou hast corrected me, and I was chastised as an untamed calf: convert me, and I shall be converted" (Jer. 31:18). "No chastisement for the present seemeth joyous, but grievous: but afterward it bringeth the quiet fruit of righteousness to them, which are thereby exercised" (Heb. 12:11). "Weeping may abide at evening; but joy cometh in the morning" (Ps. 30:5). "Every branch that beareth fruit, he purgeth it, that it may bring forth more fruit" (John 15:2). "Wherein ye rejoice, though now for a season (if need require) ye are in heaviness through many temptations" (1 Peter 1:6). "The God of all comfort, which comforteth us in all our tribulations, that we may be able to comfort them which are in any affliction, by the comfort wherewith we ourselves are comforted of God" (2 Cor. 1:4). "We glory in afflictions, knowing that affliction bringeth patience" (Rom. 5:3). "He did consecrate the Prince of their salvation through afflictions" (Heb. 2:10). We permit surgeons that they should both bind us lying diseased in our beds and sear us with hot irons, yea, lance and search our members with razors; and lastly, we send them away usually with friendly and kind speeches and often with a golden fee for their thus handling us. Shall we then suffer so many things of a surgeon to cure a bodily disease, and will we not give God leave to cure by afflictions the most festered diseases of our souls?

By this also may we gather that the afflictions of the godly are signs of their adoption. "Whom the Lord loveth he chasteneth, and he scourgeth every son that he receiveth. If ye endure chastisement God offereth himself to you, as to sons" (Heb. 12:6). And that they are to them the king's highway to heaven. "Blessed is the man that endureth temptation: for when he is tried, he shall receive the crown of life, which the Lord has promised to them that love him" (James 1:12). "For our light afflation which is but for a moment, causeth to us a far more excellent and an eternal weight of glory" (2 Cor. 4:17).

(3) That God has promised favor, mitigation of punishment, His presence, and deliverance (Phil. 1:29). "God is faithful, who will not suffer you to be tempted above measure, but with temptation will give deliverance" (1 Cor. 10:13; 2 Sam. 7:14). "Call upon me in the day of trouble, and I will deliver thee, and thou shalt glorify me" (Ps. 50:15). "He that keepeth Israel will neither slumber nor sleep" (121:4). "When thou passest through the waters, I will be with thee, and through the floods that they do not overflow thee: when thou walkest through the very fire, thou shalt not be burnt, neither shall the flame kindle upon thee. For I am the Lord thy God, the holy one of Israel, thy Savior" (Isa. 43:2–3).

(4) That in all troubles of the faithful, Christ is a companion. "Rejoice, that ye are partakers of the afflictions of Christ" (1 Peter 4:13). "Everywhere we bear about in our body the dying of Christ, that the life of Jesus might also be made manifest in our bodies" (2 Cor. 4:10; Col. 1:24).

(5) That the angels are ready to defend such as fear God (Ps. 34:7). "Fear not, there are more with us than against us" (2 Kings 6:16).

Chapter 45

Of the Calling upon God

Thus much concerning the denial of ourselves; now follows the profession of Christ, which respects either Christ Himself or His members—namely, the faithful. "Verily I say to you, inasmuch as ye did it to one of the least of my brethren, ye did it to me" (Matt. 25:40).

That profession which directly concerns Christ is either continual or only in the time of danger.

Continual is the calling upon the name of God and ought ever to be performed of us in the name of Christ Jesus our Mediator. "To the church of God which is at Corinth, to them that are sanctified in Christ Jesus, saints by calling, with all that call on the name of our Lord Jesus Christ in every place, both their Lord and ours" (1 Cor. 1:2). "He has authority from the high priest, to bind all that call upon thy name" (Acts 9:14). "Whatsoever ye shall do in word or in deed, do it in the name of the Lord Jesus, giving thanks to God, and the Father by him" (Col. 3:17).

The calling upon God's name is by prayer or thanksgiving. "In all things let your requests be shown to God, in prayer and supplication, with giving of thanks" (Phil. 4:6).

Prayer has two parts: petition and assent. "I say to you, whatsoever ye desire when ye pray, believe that ye shall have it, and it shall be done to you" (Mark 11:24).

Petition is the first part of prayer, whereby we according to the rule of God's Word ask His help for the obtaining of such necessaries as we want. "This is the assurance that we have in him, that if we ask anything according to his will, he heareth us" (1 John 5:14).

In every petition, we must express two things: (1) a sense of our wants; (2) a desire of the grace of God to supply those wants. "She was troubled in her mind, and prayed to the Lord, and wept sore" (1 Sam. 1:10). "And I prayed to the Lord my God, and made my confession saying, We have sinned and have committed iniquity, etc. O Lord, according to thy righteousness, I beseech thee, let thine anger and thy wrath be turned from the city Jerusalem," etc. (Dan. 9:4–5, 16–20). "Out of the deep I called to thee, O Lord" (Ps. 130:1). "Then

Hannah answered and said, Nay my Lord, but I am a woman troubled in spirit: I have drunken neither wine nor strong drink, but have poured out my soul before the Lord," etc. (1 Sam. 1:15–17). "I stretch forth mine hands to thee, my soul desireth after thee, as the thirsty land" (Ps. 143:6).

Assent is the second part of prayer, whereby we believe and profess it before God that He in His due time will grant to us those our requests which before we have made to His majesty. "This is the assurance that we have in him, that if we ask anything according to his will, he heareth us. And if we know that he heareth us, whatsoever we ask, we know that we have the petitions that we have desired of him" (1 John 5:14–15). "Lead us not into temptation, but deliver us from evil. For thine is the kingdom, thine is the power, and thine is the glory, forever and ever, Amen" (Matt. 6:13).

As for the faithful, however they in their prayers betray many infirmities, yet no doubt they have a notable sense of God's favor, especially when they pray zealously and often to the Lord. "Pray one for another, that ye may be healed: for the prayer of a righteous man availeth much if it be fervent" (James 5:16). "The angel said to him, Fear not Zacharias: for thy prayer is heard" (Luke 1:13). "It displeased Jonah exceedingly, and he was angry. And Jonah prayed to the Lord, and said, I pray thee, O Lord, was not this my saying, when I was yet in my country? Therefore I prevented it to flee to Tarshish: for I knew that thou art a gracious God, and merciful, slow to anger, and of great kindness, and repentest thee of the evil" (Jonah 4:1–2; Rom. 8:26). "Lot said to them, Do not so, I pray you my lords," etc. (Gen. 19:28). "O Lord, rebuke me not in thine anger, neither chastise me in thy wrath," etc. (Ps. 6:1–5; 8:9; 16:7; 20:5; 35:9, 18, 28).

Thanksgiving is a calling upon God's name, whereby we with joy and gladness of heart do praise God for His benefits either received or promised. "Mine heart will utter forth a good matter, I will entreat in my words of the king: my tongue is as the pen of a swift writer" (Ps. 45:1). "Giving thanks always for all things to God even the Father, in the name of our Lord Jesus Christ" (Eph. 5:20). "How excellent is thy mercy, O God! Therefore the children of men trust under the shadow of thy wings. They shall be satisfied with the fatness of thine house, and thou shalt give them drink out of the rivers of thy pleasures" (Ps. 36:8–9; Col. 3:16–17).

Chapter 46

Of Christian Apology and Martyrdom

The profession of Christ in dangers is either in word or deed.

Profession in word is Christian apology or the confession of Christ. "With the heart, man believeth to righteousness; and with the mouth man confesseth to salvation" (Rom. 10:10). "I will declare thy name to my brethren: in the midst of the congregation will I praise thee" (Ps. 22:22).

Christian apology is the profession of Christ in word, when as we are ready with fear and meekness to confess the truth of Christian religion so often as need requires and the glory of God is endangered, even before unbelievers, especially if they be not past all hope of repentance. "Sanctify the Lord God in your hearts: and be ready always to give an answer to every man that asketh you a reason of the hope that is in you. Add that with meekness and reverence, having a good conscience, that when they speak evil of you as of evil doers, they may be ashamed, which blame your good conversation in Christ" (1 Peter 3:15–16). Acts 7, the whole chapter, Steven there makes an apology for himself. "Give not that which is holy to dogs, nor cast your pearls before swine, lest they tread them under their feet, and turning again all to rend you" (Matt. 7:6).

Profession which is in deed is called martyrdom. Martyrdom is a part of Christian profession, when as a Christian man does for the doctrine of faith, for justice, and for the salvation of his brethren undergo the punishment of death imposed upon him by the adversaries of Christ Jesus. "John told Herod, It is not lawful for thee to have thy brother's wife. And immediately the king sent the hangman in, and gave him charge that his head should be brought: so he went and beheaded him in the prison" (Mark 6:18, 27–28). "I will most gladly bestow, and be bestowed for your souls, though the more I love you, the less am I loved" (2 Cor. 12:15).

Notwithstanding, it is lawful for Christians to fly in persecution if they find themselves not sufficiently resolved and strengthened by God's Spirit to stand. "When they persecute you in one city, flee into another. Verily I say to you, ye shall not have finished all the cities of Israel, till the Son of Man come" (Matt. 10:23). "Again they studied to apprehend him, but he escaped out of their hands" (John 10:39). "When the brethren knew it, they brought him to Caesarea, and sent him forth to Tarsus" (Acts 9:30). "Was it not told my Lord what I did, when Jezebel slew the prophets of the Lord, how I hid a hundred men of the Lord's prophets by fifties in a cave, and fed them with bread and water?" (1 Kings 18:13). "Now behold, I go bound in the spirit to Jerusalem, and know not what things shall come to me there" (Act 20:22).

Chapter 47

Of Edification and Alms among the Faithful

That profession of Christ which concerns His members—namely, the saints and faithful ones—is either edification or alms.

Edification is every particular duty toward our brethren whereby they are furthered either to grow up in Christ or else are more surely united to Him. "Let us follow those things which concern peace, and wherewith one may edify another" (Rom. 14:19).

To edification, these things which follow appertain.

(1) To give good example. "Let your light so shine before men, that they may see your good works, and glorify your Father which is in heaven" (Matt. 5:16). "Have your conversation honest among the Gentiles, that they which speak evil of you as of evil doers, may by your good works which they shall see, glorify God in the day of visitation" (1 Peter 2:12).

(2) To exhort. "Exhort one another daily, while it is called today, lest any of you be hardened through the deceitfulness of sin" (Heb. 3:13). "That I might be stirred up together with you, through our mutual faith, both yours and mine" (Rom. 1:12).

(3) To comfort. "Comfort the feeble minded, bear with the weak, be patient toward all men" (1 Thess. 5:14). "Acknowledge your faults one to another, and pray one for another, that ye may be healed. He that converteth a sinner from going astray out of his way, shall save a soul from death, and shall hide a multitude of sins" (James 5:16, 20). "Comfort yourselves one another with these words" (1 Thess. 4:18).

(4) To admonish. "I myself am persuaded of you, brethren, that ye also are full of goodness, and filled with all knowledge: and are able to admonish one another" (Rom. 15:14). "We desire you, brethren, admonish them that are unruly" (1 Thess. 5:14).

They shall observe a holy manner of admonition who in the spirit of meekness and as it were guilty of the like infirmity themselves do admonish forthwith all their brethren of such faults as they certainly know by them, and that out of God's Word. "Brethren, if any man by occasion be fallen into any faults, ye which are spiritual, restore such a one in the spirit of meekness, considering thyself, lest thou also be tempted" (Gal. 6:1). "Thou hypocrite, cast out first the beam out of thine own eye, and then shalt thou see to take the mote out of thy brother's eye" (Matt. 7:5). "Preach the Word: be instant in season and out of season: reprove,[1] rebuke, exhort, with all longsuffering and doctrine" (2 Tim. 4:2). "If thy brother trespass against thee, go and tell him his fault between thee and him alone: if he hear thee, thou hast won thy brother" (Matt. 18:15; Rom. 15:24; 2 Tim. 4:2). "Thou shalt not hate thy brother in thine heart, but thou shalt plainly rebuke thy neighbor, and suffer him not to sin" (Lev. 19:17).

Relief peculiar to the godly among themselves is a duty whereby the rich do out of their plenty supply the wants of the poor both according to their ability and sometimes beyond their ability. "To their power (I bear record) yea, beyond their power they were willing" (2 Cor. 8:3). "All that believed were in one place, and had all things common: and they sold their possessions and goods, and parted them to all men, as everyone had need" (Act 2:44–45).

---

1. The original says "improve" but should read "reprove."

Chapter 48

Of the Fourth Degree of the Declaration of God's Love and of the Estate of the Elect after This Life

The fourth degree of the declaration of God's love is glorification (Rom. 8:30).

Glorification is the perfect transforming of the saints into the image of the Son of God. "Who shall change our vile body, that it may be fashioned like to his glorious body, according to the working whereby he is able even to subdue all things to himself" (Phil. 3:21). "It is sown a natural body, and it is raised a spiritual body: there is a natural body, and there is a spiritual body. As it is also written, the first man Adam was made a living soul: the last Adam was made a quickening spirit. And as we have borne the image of the earthy, so shall we bear the image of the heavenly" (1 Cor. 15:44–45, 49). "I will behold thy face in righteousness, and when I awake, I shall be satisfied with thine image" (Ps. 17:15).

The beginning of glorification is in death, but it is not accomplished and made perfect before the last day of judgment.

The death of the elect is but a sleep in Christ whereby the body and soul are severed: the body, that after corruption it may rise to greater glory; the soul, that it being fully sanctified may immediately after departure from the body be transported into the kingdom of heaven. "If Christ be not raised, they which are asleep in Christ, are perished" (1 Cor. 15:17). "When he had thus spoken he slept" (Acts 7:60). "O soul, that which thou sowest is not quickened, except it die" (1 Cor. 15:36). "There shall enter into it none unclean thing, neither whatsoever worketh abomination or lies: but they which are written in the Lamb's book of life" (Rev. 21:27). "I myself in my mind serve the law of God, but in my flesh the law of sin" (Rom. 7:25). "He said to Jesus, Lord, remember me when thou comest into thy kingdom. Then Jesus said to him, This day shalt thou be with me in paradise" (Luke 13:42–43). "Then I heard a voice from heaven, saying to me, Write, Blessed are the dead, which hereafter die in the Lord. Even so saith the spirit: for they rest from their labors, and their works follow them" (Rev. 14:13).

Against the fear of death, note these preservatives.

(1) Death, it frees the godly from the tyranny of Satan, sin, the world, the flesh, and eternal damnation, yea, from both infinite perils and losses, and does place us both safe and happy under the shadow, as it were, of Christ's wings.

(2) Christ by His death has sanctified to us both death and the grave.

(3) Christ is both in life and death gain to the godly (Phil. 1:21).

(4) Those consolations which the Spirit of Christ does suggest to the souls of the faithful do by many degrees surmount the dolors of death.

(5) The desire of that most bright and glorious beholding of God and the presence of those saints which are departed before us.

(6) Instead of our bodies, we shall be clothed with glory (2 Cor. 5:1).

(7) The sting of death—namely, sin—is then so taken away as that the serpent can no more hurt us. "O death, where is thy sting! O grave, where is thy victory!" (1 Cor. 15:55). "That he might deliver all them, which for fear of death, were all their lifetime subject to bondage" (Heb. 2:15).

(8) We should not so much think of our death as to take an exact account of our life. For that man cannot die ill who has lived well, and he seldom dies well that has lived badly.

(9) The angels, they stand at our elbows, that so soon as a saint departs they may with all speed immediately transport his soul into heaven.

Souls being once in heaven remain there till the last day of judgment. Here, they partly magnify the name of God and partly do wait and pray for the consummation of the kingdom of glory and full felicity in body and soul. "And when he had taken the book, the four beasts, and the four and twenty elders fell down before the Lamb, having every one harps, and golden vials full of odors, which are the prayers of the saints. And they sang a new song, saying, Thou art worthy to take the book, and to open the seals thereof, because thou wast killed, and hast redeemed us to God by thy blood, out of every kindred, and tongue, and people, and nation" (Rev. 5:8–9). "I heard the voice of harpers harping with their harps. And they sang as it were, a new song before the throne" (14:2–3). "And they cried with a loud voice, saying, How long, Lord, holy and true; dost not thou judge, and avenge our blood on them that dwell on the earth?" (6:10).

Chapter 49

Of the Estate of the Elect at the Last Day of Judgment

The last day of judgment shall be on this manner:

(1) Immediately before the coming of Christ, the powers of heaven shall be shaken; the sun and moon shall be darkened; and the stars shall seem to fall from heaven, at which sight the elect then living shall rejoice, but the reprobate shall shake every joint of them. "Immediately after the tribulation of those days, shall the sun be darkened, and the moon shall not give her light, the stars shall fall from heaven, and the powers of heaven shall be shaken. And then shall appear the sign of the Son of Man in heaven: and then shall all the kindreds of the earth mourn, and they shall see the Son of Man come in the clouds of heaven, with power and great glory" (Matt. 24:29–30). "Men's hearts shall fail them for fear, and for looking after those things, which shall come on the world. And when these things begin to come to pass, then look up, and lift up your heads, for your redemption draweth near" (Luke 21:26, 28). "Henceforth is laid up for me the crown of righteousness, which the Lord, the righteous judge, shall give me at that day; and not to me only, but to them also that love his appearing" (2 Tim. 4:8).

(2) Then the heavens, being all set on fire, shall with a noise like to that of chariot wheels suddenly pass away, and the elements with the earth and all therein shall be dissolved with fire. "Looking for, and hasting to the coming of the day of God, by which the heavens being set on fire, shall be dissolved, and the elements shall melt with heat. But we look for new heavens, and a new earth, according to his promise, wherein dwelleth all righteousness" (2 Peter 3:12–13).

At the same time, when as all these things shall come to pass, the sound of the last trumpet shall be heard, sounded by the archangel. And Christ shall come suddenly in the clouds with power and glory and a great train of angels. "And he shall send his angels with a great sound of a trumpet" (Matt. 24:31). "The Lord himself shall descend from heaven with a shout, even with the voice of the archangel, and with the trumpet of God: and the dead in Christ shall rise first" (1 Thess. 4:16; Matt. 24:30). "Then shall we which live and remain, be caught up with them also in the clouds to meet the Lord in the air and so shall we ever be with the Lord" (1 Thess. 4:17).

(3) Now at the sound of the trumpet, the elect which were dead shall rise with those very bodies which were turned to dust, and one part rent from another shall by the omnipotent power of God be restored, and the souls of them shall descend from heaven and be brought again into those bodies. As for them which then shall be alive, they shall be changed in the twinkling of an eye, and this mutation shall be instead of death. And at that time, the bodies shall receive their full redemption; and all the bodies of the elect shall be made like the glorious body of Christ Jesus and therefore shall be spiritual, immortal, glorious, and free from all infirmity. "We shall not all sleep; but we shall be changed, in a moment, in the twinkling of an eye, at the last trumpet. It is sown in dishonor, it is raised in honor: it is sown in weakness, it is raised in power. It is sown a natural body, it is raised a spiritual body" (1 Cor. 15:51–52, 43–44).

(4) Last of all, when they are all convened before the tribunal seat of Christ, He will forthwith place the elect, severed from the reprobate and taken up into the air, at His right hand, and to them being written in the book of life will He pronounce this sentence: "Come ye blessed of my Father, possess the kingdom prepared for you from the foundations of the world" (Matt. 25:33). "He shall set the sheep on his right hand, and the goats on the left" (v. 33; 1 Thess. 4:17). "Whosoever was not found written in the book of life, was cast into the lake of fire" (Rev. 20:15).

Chapter 50

Of the Estate of the Elect after Judgment

The last judgment being once finished, the elect shall enjoy immediately blessedness in the kingdom of heaven.

Blessedness is that whereby God Himself is all in all [to] His elect. "When all things shall be subdued to him, then shall the Son also himself be subject to him, that did subdue all things under him, that God may be all in all" (1 Cor. 15:28). And it is the reward of good works, not because works can merit, but by reason of God's favor, who thus accepts works, and that in respect of the merit of Christ's righteousness imputed to the elect. "The wages of sin is death, but eternal life is the gift of God through Jesus Christ our Lord" (Rom. 6:23; 2 Tim. 4:8). "Behold, I come shortly, and my reward is with me, to give every man according as his works shall be" (Rev. 22:12).

Blessedness has two parts: eternal life and perfect glory.

Eternal life is that fellowship with God whereby God Himself is through the Lamb Christ life to the elect. For in the kingdom of heaven, the elect shall not need meat, drink, sleep, air, heat, cold, physic, apparel, or the light of the sun and moon, but in place of all these shall they have in them God's Spirit, by which immediately they shall be quickened forever. "If any man love me, he will keep my Word, and my father will love him, and we will come to him, and dwell with him" (John 14:23). "Whosoever confesseth that Jesus Christ is the Son of God, God dwelleth in him, and he in God" (1 John 4:15). "And I heard a voice, saying, Behold the tabernacle of God is with men, and he will dwell with them: and they shall be his people, and God himself shall be their God with them. And that city has no need of sun or moon to shine in it: for the glory of God did light it, and the Lamb is the light of it" (Rev. 21:3, 23). "In the midst of the street of it, and on either side of the river, was there the tree of life, which bare twelve manner of fruits, and gave fruit every month: and the leaves of the tree served to heal the nations with. And there shall be no night there, and they need no candle, nor light of the sun, for the Lord giveth them light, and they shall reign forevermore" (Rev. 22:2, 5; 1 Cor. 15:45). "If the Spirit of him that raised up Jesus from the dead, dwell in you, he that raised up Christ from the dead, shall also quicken your mortal bodies, because that his Spirit dwelleth in you" (Rom. 8:11).

Perfect glory is that wonderful excellency of the elect whereby they shall be in a far better estate than any heart can wish. This glory consists in three points. (1) In that they shall still behold the face of God, which is His glory and majesty. "And they shall see his face, and his name shall be in their foreheads" (Rev. 22:4). "I will behold thy face in righteousness, and when I awake I shall be satisfied with thine image" (Ps. 17:15). (2) In that they shall be most like to Christ—namely, just, holy, incorruptible, glorious, honorable, excellent, beautiful, strong, mighty, and nimble. "Dearly beloved, now are we the sons of God, but yet it does not appear what we shall be: and we know that when he shall appear, we shall be like him: for we shall see him as he is" (1 John 3:2). "We shall change our vile body, that it may be fashioned like to his glorious body, according to the working whereby he is able even to subdue all things to himself" (Phil. 3:21). (3) They shall inherit the kingdom of heaven; yea, the new heavens and the new earth shall be their inheritance. "God has begotten you to an inheritance immortal and undefiled, and that fadeth not away, reserved in heaven for you" (1 Peter 1:4). "Then shall the king say to them on his right hand, Come ye blessed of my Father, possess the kingdom prepared for you before the foundations of the world were laid" (Matt. 25:34). "Thou hast made us to our God kings and priests, and we shall reign on the earth" (Rev. 5:10). "He that overcometh shall inherit all things, and I will be his God, and he shall be my son" (21:7).

The fruit that comes from both these parts of blessedness is of two sorts: eternal joy and the perfect service of God. "Thou wilt show me the path of life; in thy presence is the fullness of joy: and at thy right hand there are pleasures forevermore" (Ps. 16:11). "They shall be satisfied with the fatness of thine house, and thou shalt give them drink out of the river of thy pleasures. For with thee is the well of life, and in thy light shall we see light" (36:8–9).

The parts of God's service are praise and thanksgiving. "And I heard a great voice out of heaven, saying, Behold, the tabernacle of God is with men, and He will dwell with them: and they shall be his people, and God Himself shall be their God with them" (Rev. 21:3). "Saying with a loud voice, Worthy is the Lamb that was killed, to receive power, and riches, and wisdom, and strength, and honor, and glory, and praise," etc. (5:12–13). "The four and twenty elders which sat before God on their seats, fell upon their faces and worshiped God, saying, We give thee thanks, Lord God almighty, which art, and which was, and which art to come: for thou hast received thy great might, and hast obtained thy kingdom" (11:17).

The manner of performing this service is to worship God by God Himself immediately. In heaven, there shall neither be temple, ceremony, nor sacrament, but all these wants shall God Himself supply together with the Lamb—that is, Christ. "I saw no temple therein, for the Lord God Almighty, and the Lamb, are the temple of it" (21:22).

This service shall be daily and without intermission. "They are in the presence of the throne of God, and serve him day and night in his temple" (Rev. 7:15).

A Corollary or the Last Conclusion
Thus, God in saving the elect does clearly set forth His justice and mercy: His justice, in that He punished the sins of the elect in His Son's own person; His mercy, in that He pardoned their sin for the merits of His Son. "That the eyes of your understanding may be lightened, that ye may know what the hope is of his calling, and what the riches of his glorious inheritance is in his saints. And what is the exceeding greatness of his power toward us which believe, according to the working of his mighty power, which he wrought in Christ" (Eph. 1:18–20). "That ye may be able to comprehend with all saints, what is the breadth, and length, and depth, and height: and to know the love of Christ" (3:18–19).

All these things the Lord Himself has thus decreed and in His good time will accomplish them to the glorious praise of His name. "The Lord has made all things for his own sake: yea, even the wicked for the day of evil" (Prov. 16:4).

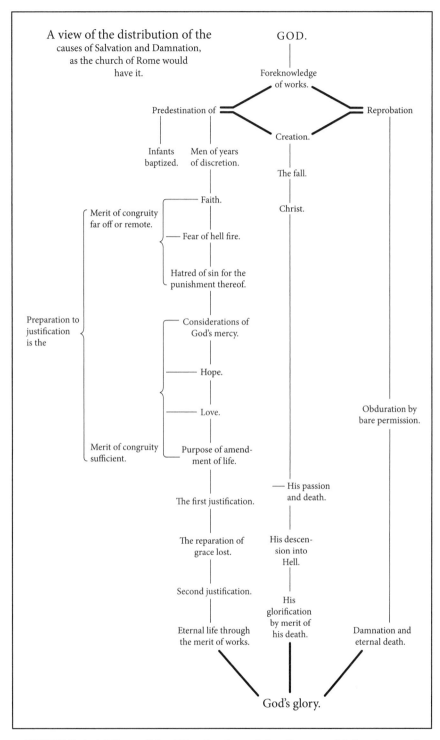

FIGURE 6: A View of the Distribution of the Causes of Salvation and Damnation, as the Church of Rome would have it

Concerning the Order of the Causes of Salvation according to the Doctrine of the Church of Rome

There are two things requisite to obtain salvation: predestination and the execution thereof.

Predestination is a foreordaining of the reasonable creature to grace in this life and glory in the life to come.[1]

This in regard of the first effects thereof, which are vocation, election, and ordination to eternal life, has the cause of it in God—namely, His will. But in regard of the last effect, which is the execution of such an ordinance and the obtaining of eternal life, it has the cause of it in man, because according to the common opinion God's predestination is by reason of works foreseen in men—that is, God does therefore predestinate or reject some man because He foresees that he will well or badly use His grace. But for the more evident declaration of this, these seven conclusions must be set down.

(1) The predestination and reprobation of God do not constrain or enforce any necessity upon the will of man.

(2) God has predestinated all men—that is, He has appointed and disposed all men so as they might obtain eternal salvation.

(3) Man is neither by necessity nor chance saved or condemned, but voluntarily.

(4) God has predestinated some; others has He rejected.

(5) Those whom God has predestinated by His absolute predestination, which cannot be lost, shall infallibly die in grace; but they which are predestinate by that predestination which being according to present justice may be lost by some mortal sin which follows are not infallibly saved, but oftentimes such are condemned and lose their crown and glory. Hence arises that position

---

1. In-text citation: Sebastian.Cattaneus. Enchir.tract.1.cap.last [Perkins's reference to Sebastian Cattaneo's (1545–1609) *Enchiridion*, tractate 1, final chapter could be either to his *Enchiridion, Eorvm Qvae In Controversiam Vocantvr: Omnibvs Verae Pietatis Cvltoribvs Perutile ac necessarium* (1589) or his *Enchiridion de Sacramentis novae Legis* (1584). Little is known about this figure].

of theirs that he which is justified may be a reprobate and perish eternally.[2] Therefore, predestination is not certain, seeing it may be lost.

(6) God alone does know the certain and set number of them which are predestinate.

(7) There is one set number of them which are predestinate or rejected, and that can neither be increased nor diminished.

The execution of predestination is either in infants or those of years of discretion.

Concerning infants, the merit of Christ is applied to them by baptism rightly administered, so that whatsoever in original corruption may truly and properly be accounted for sin is not only, as I may say, not pared away or not imputed, but utterly taken away. For there is nothing that God can hate in such as are renewed.[3]

Nevertheless, we must confess that there remains yet in such as are baptized concupiscence or the relics of sin. The which, seeing it is left in men for them to wrestle withal, it has no power to hurt such as yield to it.

The execution of predestination in such as are of riper years has six degrees.

The first is vocation, whereby men not for their own merits but by God's preventing grace through Christ are called to turn themselves to God.

The second is a preparation to righteousness, whereby men through the inherent power of free will do apply themselves to justification, after that the same power is stirred up by the Holy Ghost. For free will is only somewhat diminished and not extinguished; and therefore so soon as the Holy Ghost touches and enlightens the heart, it works together with the same Spirit, freely assenting to the same. This preparation has seven degrees.[4]

The first is faith, which is a knowledge and an assent whereby men agree that those things are true which are delivered concerning God and His will, revealed in the Word of God.

This is the foundation of justification and prepares the heart, because it stirs up free will that it may affect the heart with those motions by which it is prepared to justification.

(1) The act of faith is to apprehend the ugliness of sin and the wages thereof.

(2) After this follows a fear of God's anger and of hellfire.

(3) Then, begin men to dislike and in some sort to detest sin.

---

2. In-text citation: Torrensis Aug.Confess. 2.book, 4.chap.20.Sect [Augustine, *Confessions*, bk. 2, ch. 4, sect. 20].

3. In-text citation: Concil.Trid.5. sect.5.Can [Council of Trent, sect. 5, canon 5].

4. In-text citation: Biel.4.book 14.dist.2.quest [This is probably a reference to Gabriel Biel (*c.* 1420–1495) and bk. 4, disputation 14, q. 2 of Biel's most important work, his commentary on Peter Lombard's *Sentences*. Biel was a German scholastic philosopher].

And herein stands the disposition of congruity, not immediately, nor sufficient, but far removed.

(4) At the length, faith turns itself to the contemplation of God's mercies and believes that God is ready to forgive sins by the infusion of charity into those which are before sufficiently prepared and disposed.

(5) Out of this contemplation proceeds the act of hope whereby they begin to desire God as the chiefest good.

(6) Out of this act of hope arises love, whereby God is loved above all things by the strength of nature.

(7) After this love follows a new dislike and detestation of sin, not so much in regard of fear of the punishment in hellfire as in regard of the offence to God, who is finally loved more than all other things.

(8) After all these follows a purpose of amendment of life, and here comes in the measure of congruity—that is, sufficient, or else the immediate, sufficient, and last disposition before the infusion of grace.

The third degree of predestination is the first justification, whereby men of unjust are made just not only through the remission of their sins but also by a sanctification of the inward man by his voluntary receiving of grace and gifts.

The efficient cause of this justification is the mercy of God and the meritorious passion of our Savior Christ, whereby He purchased justification for men. The instrumental cause is baptism. The formal cause is not that justice which was inherent in Christ, but which He infuses into man—and that is especially hope and charity.

The fourth degree is the second justification, whereby men are of just made more just. The cause hereof is faith joined with good works.

It is possible for such as are renewed to keep the commandments; and therefore it is false that a just man commits so much as a venial sin in his best actions, much less that he deserves eternal death for the same.

The fifth degree is the reparation of a sinner by the sacrament of penance—the which is, as it were, the second board after a shipwreck. The cause why this reparation is necessary is because men lose the grace of justification by every mortal sin.

The last degree is the fruit of justification—namely, the glory of eternal life, the which works done in grace do *ex condigno*, condignly merit, or sufficient worthiness.

Condign merit is when as the reward is after such sort due as that if it be not given injustice will be committed. This by the rigor of justice is due.

Two conditions are requisite to make a merit. (1) That a reward should by some compact or bargain be due. And this condition is in works in regard of God. For God in the Scriptures has promised a reward to such as work well.

(2) That besides this compact whereby the debtor is bound, there should be also some worthiness in the work or some proportion of the work to the reward.

The worthiness or dignity of the work depends (1) on Christ, because Christ did not only merit that His own proper actions should be meritorious, but the actions also of His members; (2) on the Holy Ghost, for the Holy Ghost does conspire, excite, and move men to do; (3) on a habitual grace, which is a certain participation of the divine essence.

Thus much concerning the degrees of executing predestination. Now follows the applying of predestination particularly to the persons of men.

No man so long as he lives in this mortal life ought so much to presume on the secret mystery of God's predestination as to determine undoubtedly that he is in the number of them whom God has ordained to eternal happiness. For no man without especial revelation can know whom God has chosen to be His heirs.[5]

The sum of all these is this: God by a certain grace given freely, or rather a grace preventing or coming before, the which is termed an effectual aid, does move a man that he may dispose himself to his justifying grace—namely, that he may believe, fear, repent, love, and propound to himself newness of life, etc.

Furthermore, if a sinner do by his free will yield his assent to this divine motion and does consequently and accordingly rightly dispose himself, God does incontinently forgive him his sin and withal does infuse into him justifying grace, by which he may do good works and so by them merit eternal life.[6]

Errors of the Papists in Their Distributing of the Causes of Salvation
And this is the doctrine of the Church of Rome—surely a very blasphemous doctrine, and no better to be accounted of than as a gallows set up for the torture and massacre of men's consciences. And that this may the more manifestly appear to be so, I will set down the most principal errors of popish doctrine in this case.

The First Error
Predestination is only of the elect; the reprobate, they are only foreknown.

The confutation. The name of predestination by a figure called synecdoche, the whole for the part, is taken indeed sometimes in the good part and spoken of the elect and faithful called—as, "Whom he predestinated, them also he called, and whom he called, them also he justified, and whom he justified, them

---

5. In-text citation: Sesl.6.c.12.
6. In-text citation: Ballarm [A reference to the Roman Catholic Cardinal Robert Bellarmine (1542–1621), though the work is not specified. Robert Bellarmine was an influential Roman Catholic cardinal and opponent of Protestantism during the Reformation].

also he glorified" (Rom. 8:30). So are the Ephesians said to be "predestinate into the adoption of the sons of God" (Eph. 1:5). Yet may this word "predestination" nevertheless generally be extended to the decree of God, whether it be that of predestination to eternal life or the other to eternal death. The reasons: (1) "They gathered themselves together against thine holy Son Jesus: to do whatsoever thine hand and thy counsel had determined" (or foreordained, or predestinated, προώρισεν "before to be done") (Acts 4:27–28). (2) Augustine calls "predestination" the "disposition of future works."[7] And in his *City of God*, he divides "all mankind into two cities: whereof one is predestinate to reign with God eternally, the other predestinate to undergo eternal punishment with the devil."[8] And he says, "That God has justly predestinated wicked men to punishment, and mercifully predestinated the good to grace."[9] Thomas Aquinas says, "It matters not in regard of the name of predestination, whether a man be said to be predestinate to life eternal or not."[10]

Furthermore, for a man to say that the reprobates are foreknown and not predestinate is very injurious, because God's foreknowledge may in nothing which is to be be severed from His will and eternal decree. For that which being hereafter to be is foreknown of God, that assuredly will come to pass and shall be, and that either by the will of God or without His will. If with His will, then no doubt He both decreed and preordained the same; if without or against His will, how is God then omnipotent? And surely evil itself, albeit God will it not in His approving or allowing will, yet wills He the free and willing permission thereof. Augustine has an excellent saying to this purpose: "Although," says he, "that those things which are evil, in that they are evil, cannot be good, yet that there are not only good, but also evil things, it is very good: to the intent that after a marvelous and unspeakable manner, that thing may not be besides, or without His will, which also is done against His will, because it should not be done, unless He suffered it, neither does He suffer it, against His will, but willingly."[11]

---

7. In-text citation: August.de Bono persev.Chap.17. [Augustine, *A Treatise on the Gift of Perseverance*, ch. 17. In some editions, the title is, *On the Benefit (de Bono) of Perseverance*].

8. In-text citation: 15. Book of the *City of God*, chapter 1 [Augustine, *City of God*, bk. 15, ch. 1].

9. In-text citation: in his *Manuel to Laurentius* chapter 100 [This is a reference to Augustine, *Enchiridion*, ch. 100].

10. In text citation: I. part. Quest. 23. artic. 4 [Thomas Aquinas (1225–1274), *Summa Theologicae*, part 1, q. 23, art. 4. Thomas Aquinas was the most important Christian theologian and philosopher of the medieval period. This is a reference to his most important work, which was intended to be a "sum of all theology"].

11. In-text citation: in his *Manuel or Enchiridion to Laurentius* chapter 100 [This is a reference to Augustine, *Enchiridion*, ch. 100].

The Second Error

That predestination is mutable. For (according to the common opinion of the papists) whoever is predestinate, he is contingently predestinated as well on God's part as on man's. Whence it follows that he which is predestinated—that is, appointed to salvation—may be condemned. And he which is foreknown—that is, appointed to damnation—may be saved.

The Confutation. The contrary to this their doctrine is most true. Namely, that the decree of God concerning both every man's eternal salvation and damnation is from all eternity set down and immutable. The reasons: (1) testimonies of Scripture. "The gifts and calling of God they are such as are without repentance" (Rom. 11:26).[12] "There shall arise false Christs, and false prophets: and shall do great signs and miracles, so that (if it were possible) they should deceive even the elect" (Matt. 24:24). "Who shall lay anything to the charge of God's chosen? It is God that justifieth; who shall condemn? (Rom. 8:33). "The foundation of God standeth sure, and has this seal, The Lord knoweth who are his" (2 Tim. 2:19). (2) Election and reprobation are in God, not in men. Now there can be nothing in God which is not immutable. "I Jehovah am not changed" (Mal. 3:6). "My counsel shall stand, and I will do whatsoever I will" (Isa. 64:10). (3) If this popish conclusion should be granted, then would it follow of necessity that the foreknowledge of God must be made void, His power weakened, and His will changed, each of which is impious once to dream of. For he which changes his counsel or his will does therefore change it either because he at the length sees that he might have taken better advice, or else in that he sees that he could not bring his former purpose about as he would—either of which are far from our Lord God. (4) If we resolve that the counsel of God is any ways mutable, it will by this come to pass that every man must be uncertain whether he be predestinate to life or not—whereby that notable stay and only ground of our full assurance to be saved is utterly shaken and overturned. Wherefore, let this truth be maintained of us—namely, that both the election and reprobation of God stand immutable, so that neither the elect can become reprobates, nor the reprobates elect; and consequently neither these be saved, nor they condemned.

Against this doctrine the popish sort except. If you speak in a compound sense or meaning (*in sensu composito*[13]), it is very true that the predestinate cannot be damned, nor such as are foreknown be saved; but if in a sense divided (*in sensu diviso*[14]), it is not so.[15] This distinction is plain by this example. White

---

12. The Greek here is illegible.
13. *In sensu composito*: in the composite sense.
14. *In sensu diviso*: in the divided sense.
15. For a helpful discussion of *sensus compositus* and *sensus divisus* see Richard A. Muller,

color in a compound meaning cannot be black, because blackness is repugnant and contrary to whiteness. But in a divided sense, white color now may afterward be made black. In like sort, one predestinated to salvation may by reason of the free will he has sin and so be damned. *Answer.* These are silly shifts and mere sophisms, because such as are predestinated to the end—namely, salvation—are necessarily predestinate to the means of salvation, the which they cannot but use and by them come to the end itself.

The Third Error

All men are predestinate that be disposed and ordained of God, so as they might attain eternal life.[16]

The Confutation. This is manifestly false. For (1) infants, who so soon as they are born depart this life, seeing for want of time they cannot in this life use the means of salvation, albeit they may have life eternal, yet obtain they it not by using the means to the same. (2) That which the Lord indeed actually does, the very same has He determined to do. For He does nothing neither unadvisedly or unwillingly; but He actually forsakes a very great part of mankind, the which being shut up under contumacy He does leave to itself. "Who in times past suffered all the Gentiles to walk in their own ways" (Acts 14:16). Hence also it is that Ephesians 2:12, all the Gentiles are said to be ἄθεοι, "without God in the world." Therefore, God decreed to forsake some men in this life, and consequently He ordained not all men to the obtaining of eternal life. Nay, if God once but would in His secret will that all men should be saved, it were impossible for any to perish, because God's willing is His doing of it. And if He that was ordained to salvation perish, then must God now needs have left off to will that which He would from all eternity, or else begin to will that which before He would not, the which cannot be said of God without blasphemy. (3) Paul says in 2 Thessalonians 2:10 that there be certain men ἀπολλύμενοι "which perish"; and them he distinguishes from the elect (v. 13): "Has not the potter power," etc. (Rom. 9:21–22). Where there is not only mention made of vessels of glory and mercy, but also of certain made and fashioned in God's eternal counsel as vessels of wrath. Now look whom God has made to wrath and destruction, them He never disposed to obtain eternal life.

The Fourth Error

Predestination in regard of the last effects thereof has his cause in man—that is, in man's free will and works. For they whom God had foreseen that they would

---

Divine Will and Human Choice: Freedom, Contingency, and Necessity in Early Modern Reformed Thought (Grand Rapids: Baker, 2017), 36.

16. In-text citation, Sebast.Catteneus in his Enchirid. chap. of Predest [Sebastian Cattaneo, *Enchiridion*, chapter on predestination].

receive grace offered in Christ and lead their life according to the law, them He predestinated not of works, but of His mercy; yet so as that He had respect to works or to deal with them according to their works, or (as others say) to ordain them by their works foreseen. As for example, God did from all eternity foresee and foreknow that Peter should be saved and Judas condemned, because He from the same eternity did both foresee and foreknow that Peter would accept of the grace offered to him and after use the same aright, and He did also foresee that Judas should receive the grace offered, yet notwithstanding by reason of his perverse will use the same perversely.

The Confutation. This forged device of foreseen works (1) Paul does show to be plainly counterfeit, when as he says that the Ephesians were "elected in Christ before the foundations of the world were laid" (Eph. 1:4), and that not because He did foresee that they would be holy, but "that they might be holy and unblameable before God with love." And in chapter 2, verse 10, he says they were "created to good works in Christ, that they might walk therein." In which places, good works, they are made effects of predestination; but the effect foreseen cannot be the cause of his cause, for that every cause in the order both of nature and knowledge does go before his effect. (2) "Not of works which we have done, but according to His mercy did God elect and save us" (Titus 3:5). (3) God in electing us did not regard anything out of Himself, but in Himself did He elect us (Eph. 1:4, 9). Therefore, did He not regard future works. (4) Some of the popish schoolmen confess that predestination does put nothing in the party predestinated in respect of him, for which God did predestinate him.[17] (5) Election is only on God's mercy (Rom. 9:16). (6) God saw no grace in man but that which He Himself must bestow upon him; whence it is apparent that in election the beginning thereof procedeth from grace. (7) Seeing there is nothing either above God or greater than God, it must needs be impious to assign any cause of His will either out of or above His majesty; and therefore that His foreknowledge of faith and works should be accounted the impulsive cause of His decree concerning man's salvation, we do rightly deny.

The Fifth Error
By baptism rightly administered, not only the guiltiness but also the corruption of original sin is so washed away as that it is not afterward properly accounted a sin.

The Confutation. We contrarily do thus distinguish of sin. Sin in regard of the guiltiness of God's wrath and also in regard of the punishment together by

---

17. In-text citation: Thom. 1. Primae.quaest.23.art.2 [Thomas Aquinas, *Summa Theologicae*, Part 1, q. 23, art. 2].

one act is taken away in baptisms. But in regard of that error and corruption of nature, it is not at the first quite taken away, but successively and by little and little it is extinguished even as our renovation wrought by the Holy Ghost is by little and little begun and increased in us. Reasons. (1) Paul would not so greatly bewail his original sin if after baptism it ceased any more to be sin. "I see," says he, "another law in my members, rebelling against the law of my mind and leading me captive to the law of sin which is in my members. O miserable man! Who shall deliver me from this body of death?" (Rom. 7:23–24). (2) Original sin is called a "sin out of measure sinful" (v. 13), and "a sin that hangeth fast on" or "easily compasseth us about" (Heb. 12:1). (3) Concupiscence is the root of actual sin; and therefore even after baptism, it must properly be a sin. (4) Unless that concupiscence were a sin, where would or could be that vehement and hot combat between the flesh and the spirit (Gal. 5:17)?

The Sixth Error
Baptism is absolutely necessary to salvation, especially for children.

The Confutation. We deny that baptism is of absolute necessity to salvation. Reasons. (1) Sacraments do not confer grace, but rather confirm grace when God has conferred the same. The children of faithful parents are born holy not by natural generation, but by the grace of God, and are not first made holy by baptism. And as for such as are of years of discretion before they be baptized, they cannot be baptized unless they believe. Now all such as believe are both justified and reconciled to God; and therefore albeit they without their own default are deprived of the sacraments, it is impossible for them to perish. (2) God did precisely appoint circumcision to be on the eighth day, not on the first or the second. Now there is no doubt but that many infants before their eighth day were prevented of circumcision by death, all which for a man peremptorily to set down as condemned were very absurd. (3) If circumcision were of such absolute great necessity, why was it for the space of forty years in the desert intermitted? And that only because the Israelites being often in journey, such as were circumcised were by it in jeopardy of death. No doubt Moses and Aaron would never have omitted this sacrament so long, if it had been absolutely necessary to salvation. (4) This doctrine of the absolute necessity of baptism was unknown to the ancient fathers. For the primitive church did tolerate very godly men (though we allow not their fact) that they should defer their baptism many years, yea often to the time of their death. Hence was it that Constantine the Great was not baptized till a little before his death; and Valentinian by reason of his delay was not at all baptized, whom notwithstanding

Ambrose pronounces to be in heaven. And Bernard disputes that not every deprivation of baptism, but the contempt of palpable negligence, is damnable.[18]

The Seventh Error

Man after the fall of Adam has free will as well to do that which is good as that which is evil, although it be in a divers manner—that is, he has free will to do evil simply and without any external aid; but to do well, none at all, but by the grace of God preventing or guiding us, the which grace notwithstanding every man has, and to the which grace it is in our free will either to consent and together work with the same, or not. And therefore the power of free will to do that which is good and acceptable to God is only attenuated and weakened before conversion, not quite taken away; and therefore man can of himself work a preparation to justification.

The Confutation. Man not regenerated has free will to do only that which is evil, none to do good. He being not already converted cannot so much as will to have faith and be converted. Reasons. (1) Man is not said to be weak or sick, but "dead in sins" (Eph. 2:1; Col. 1:13). As he therefore that is corporally dead cannot stir up himself that he may perform the works of the living, no, not then when others help him, so he that is spiritually dead cannot move himself to live to God. (2) "He is the servant of Satan, and bondslave of sin" (Eph. 2:2; Rom. 6:13). Now we know that a servant stands at the beck and pleasure of another, and can do nothing else. (3) That which no man can by himself know and believe, the same he cannot will; but no man can know and believe those things that appertain to the kingdom of God. "The natural man perceiveth not the things of the spirit of God" (1 Cor. 2:14). "We are not sufficient of ourselves, to think anything as of ourselves" (1 Cor. 2:14). Therefore, no man can will by himself those things that appertain to God's kingdom. (4) That which is a deadly enemy to goodness and is directly repugnant thereto, the same desires not that which is good; but the will is an enemy and directly repugnant to goodness. "The wisdom of the flesh is barred against God for it is not subject to the law of God, neither indeed can be" (Rom. 8:7).

Objection 1. God gives many precepts by which we are commanded to repent, believe, obey God, etc. Therefore, to do these we have free will. *Answer.* Such places do admonish us not of our strength but of our duty and infirmity; neither do they show what men can do, but what men should do.

Objection 2. They are instruments of the Holy Ghost whereby He does renew and convert such as shall be saved. *They object again.* God in commanding these does not require things impossible. *Answer.* He does not indeed to men in their

---

18. In-text citation: in his 77.epist [Bernard of Clairvaux, *Letters*, letter 77].

innocency; but now to all such as fell in Adam He does, and that by their own default, not God's.

Objection 3. "Work your salvation with fear and trembling" (Phil. 2:12). *Answer.* Paul speaks of such as are already converted, which have their will in part freed.

Objection 4. If the will be a mere patient, it is constrained to do that which is good. *Answer.* The will both in itself and of itself is a mere patient in her first conversion to God; but if it be considered as it is moved by the Spirit of God, it is an agent. For, being moved, it moves. It is not therefore compelled, but of a nilling[19] will, is made a willing will.

The Eighth Error

The Holy Ghost does not give grace to will, but only does unloose the will which before was chained and also does excite the same, so that the will by her own power does dispose herself to justification.

The Confutation. It is apparently false. To will those things which concern the kingdom of God, as faith, conversion, and new obedience, is the mere gift of God's Spirit. "No man knoweth the Father but the Son, and he to whom the Son will reveal him" (Matt. 11:27). "To you it is given to know the mysteries of the kingdom of God" (Luke 8:20). "It is God which worketh in you to will and to do" (Phil. 2:12). "No man can say that Jesus is the Lord, but by the Holy Ghost" (1 Cor. 12:3). Briefly, he who according to God is to be "created in righteousness and holiness" (Eph. 4:24) cannot any ways dispose himself to justification or new creation. For it is impossible that a thing not created should dispose itself to his creation.

The Ninth Error

That preparation to grace, which is caused by the power of free will, may by the merit of congruity deserve justification.

The Confutation. These things smell of more than satanical arrogancy. For what man but such a one as were not in his right mind would believe that he to whom so many millions of condemnations are due could once merit the least dram of grace? The prodigal son was not received into favor by reason of his deserts, but by favor. "His son said to him, I have sinned against heaven, and against thee, and am no more worthy to be called thy son" (Luke 15:21).

---

19. *Nilling*: literally, "to not will."

The Tenth Error

The faith of the godly or that which justifies, is that whereby a man does in general believe the promised blessedness of God, and by which also he gives his assent to other mysteries revealed of God concerning the same.

The Confutation. Faith is not only a general knowledge and assent to the history of the gospel, but further also a certain power both apprehending and severally applying the promises of God in Christ, whereby a man does assuredly set down that his sins are forgiven him and that he is reconciled to God. Reasons. (1) A particular assurance of the favor of God is of the nature of faith. "By whom we have boldness, and entrance with confidence, by faith in Him" (Eph. 3:10). "Neither did he doubt of the promise of God through unbelief, but was strengthened in the faith, and gave glory to God, being fully assured that He which had promised, was also able to do it" (Rom. 4:20). "Let us draw near with a true heart in assurance of faith" (Heb. 10:22). (2) Particular doubting is reprehended. "O thou of little faith, why didst thou doubt?" (Matt. 14:21). "Hang ye not in suspense" (Luke 12:29). (3) That which a man prays for to God, that must he assuredly believe to receive (Mark 11:24). But the faithful in their prayers make request for adoption, justification, and life eternal; and therefore they must certainly believe that they shall receive these benefits. (4) "We being therefore justified, have peace with God" (Rom. 5:1). But there can be no peace where there is not a particular assurance of God's favor. (5) That which the Spirit of God does testify particularly, that must also be believed particularly. But the Spirit of God does give a particular testimony of the adoption of the faithful (Rom. 8:16; Gal. 4:6). This therefore is [of] like sort to be believed.

Whereas they say that no man has a particular assurance but by especial revelation, as was that which Abraham and Paul had, is false. For the faith of these two is set down in Scripture as an example which we should all follow. For this cause Abraham is called the "father of the faithful" (Rom. 4:11), and Paul testifies the very same of himself. "For this cause," says he, "was I received to mercy, that Jesus Christ should first show on me all long suffering, to the example of them, which shall in time to come believe in Him to eternal life" (1 Tim. 1:16). Again, whereas they say that we have a mortal assurance, but not the assurance of faith, it is a popish device. For "the Spirit of adoption (συμμαρτυνρεῖ) together beareth witness to our spirits" (Rom. 8:16). Here we see two witnesses of our adoption: our own spirit and the Spirit of God. Our spirit does testify morally of our adoption by sanctification and the fruits thereof; and therefore also the Spirit of God witnesses after another manner—namely, by the certainty of faith, declaring and applying the promises of God.

Objection 1. We are commanded to work out salvation with fear and trembling. *Answer.* This fear is not in regard of God's mercy forgiving our sins, but in respect of us and our nature, which is ever prone to slide away and starting from God.

Objection 2. In respect of God's mercy, we must hope for salvation; but in respect of our unworthiness, we must doubt. *Answer.* (1) We may not all lawfully doubt of God's mercy, because doubtfulness is not of the nature of faith, but rather a natural corruption. (2) If we consider our own unworthiness, it is out of all doubt; we must be out of all hope and despair of our salvation.

Objection 3. There be many sins unknown to us, and so also uncertain whether they be pardoned to us. *Answer.* He that certainly and truly knows that but one sin is pardoned him, he has before God all his sins remitted, whether they be known or unknown.

Objection 4. No man dare swear or die in the defense of this proposition: "I am the child of God, or in God's favor, and justified." *Answer.* They which have an unfeigned faith will, if they be lawfully called, not only testify their adoption by an oath, but seal it also by their blood.

Objection 5. A man may have this faith which the Protestants talk of and lie in a mortal sin and have also a purpose to persevere in a mortal sin. *Answer.* It is far otherwise; for "true faith purifieth the heart" (Acts 15:9).

These sophisters do further affirm that this faith, which to them is nothing but a knowledge and illumination of the mind concerning the truth of God's word, is the root and foundation of justification. The which, if it be true, why should not the devil be just? For he has both a knowledge of God's word and thereto by believing does give his assent—who notwithstanding he have such a faith, yet can he not be called one of the faithful [James 2:19].

Here they except, and say, the devil's faith is void of charity, which is the form of faith. But this is a doting surmise of their own brain. For charity is the effect of faith (1 Tim. 1:5). But the effect cannot inform the cause.

The Eleventh Error
Man's love of God does in order and time go before his justification and reconciliation with God.

The Confutation. Nay, contrarily, unless we be first persuaded of God's love toward us, we never love Him. "For we love him, because he loved us first" (1 John 4:19). Again, it is impossible that God's enemy should love Him; but he which is not as yet justified or reconciled to God, he is God's enemy (Rom. 5:9–10). Neither is any man before the act of justification made of God's enemy His friend.

The Twelfth Error
Infused or inherent justice is the formal cause of justification, whereby men are justified in the sight of God formally.

The Confutation. We do contrarily hold that the material cause of man's justification is the obedience of Christ in suffering and fulfilling the law for us; but as for the formal cause, that must needs be imputation, the which is an action of God the Father, accepting the obedience of Christ for us as if it were our own. *Reasons.* (1) Look by what we are absolved from all our sins and by which we are accepted to eternal life, by that alone are we justified. But by Christ's perfect obedience imputed to us we are absolved from all our sins, and through it we are accepted of God to eternal life—the which we cannot attain to by inherent holiness. Therefore, by Christ's perfect obedience imputed to us are we alone justified. This will appear to be true in the exercises of invocation on God's name and also of repentance. For in temptation and conflicts with sin and Satan, faith does not reason thus: "Now I have charity and inherent grace, and for these God will accept of me." But faith does more rightly behold the Son of God as He was made a sacrifice for us and sits at the right hand of His Father, there making intercession for us. To Him, I say, does faith flee and is assured that for this His Son God will forgive us all our sins and will also be reconciled to us, yea, and account us just in His sight, not by any quality inherent in us, but rather by the merit of Jesus Christ (Rom. 5:19). (2) As Christ is made a sinner, so by proportion such as believe are made just. But Christ was by imputation only made and accounted a sinner for us (2 Cor. 5:21). For He became a surety for us and a sacrifice for our sins, upon which all both the guiltiness of God's wrath and punishment for us was to be laid. Hence it is that He is said to become κατάρα "a curse" for us. Therefore, we again are made just only by imputation. (3) The contrary to condemnation is remission of sins, and justification is the opposite of condemnation. "It is God that justifieth, who shall condemn?" (Rom. 8:33). Therefore, justification is the remission of sins. Now remission of sins depends only upon this imputation of Christ's merits. (4) Albeit infused and inherent justice may have his due place, his praise, and also deserts, yet as it is a work of the Holy Ghost. It is not in this life complete, and by reason of the flesh whereto it is united it is both imperfect and infected with the dregs of sin (Isa. 64:6). Therefore, before God's judgment seat it cannot claim this prerogative to absolve any from the sentence of condemnation.

Objection 1. This imputation is nothing else but a vain conceit. *Answer.* (1) Yes, it is a relation or divine ordinance whereby one relative is applied to his correlative, or as the logicians say, is as the foundation to the terminus. (2) As the imputation of our sins to Christ was indeed something, so the imputation of Christ's justice to us must not be thought a bare conceit. (3) Again, the

Church of Rome does herself maintain imputative justice—namely, when as by ecclesiastical authority she does apply the merits and satisfactions of certain persons to other members of that church. Whence it is apparent that even the popes' indulgences, they are imputative.

Objection 2. Imputative justice is not everlasting. But that justice which the Messiah brings is everlasting. *Answer.* Although after this life there is no pardon of sins to be looked for, yet that which is given us in this life shall to our salvation continue in the life to come.

Objection 3. If justification be by imputation, he may before God be just who indeed is a very wicked man. *Answer.* Not so any ways; for he that is once by imputation justified, he is also at that same instant sanctified.

The Thirteenth Error
There is also a second justification, and that is obtained by works.

The Confutation. That popish device of a second justification is a satanical delusion For (1) the Word of God does acknowledge no more but one justification at all, and that absolute and complete of itself. There is but one justice, but one satisfaction of God being offended. Therefore, there cannot be a manifold justification. (2) If by reason of the increase of inherent justice justification should be distinguished into several kinds or parts, we might as well make an hundred kinds or parts of justification as two. (3) That which by order of nature does follow after full justification before God cannot be said to justify. But good works do by order of nature follow man's justification and his absolution from sins, because no work can please God except the person itself that works the same do before please Him. But no man's person can please God but such a one as being reconciled to God by the merits of Christ has peace with Him. (4) Such works as are not agreeable to the rule of legal justice, they before the tribunal seat of God cannot justify, but rather both in and of themselves are subject to God's eternal curse. For this is the sentence of the law: "Cursed is every one that continueth not in all things written in the book of the law to do them" (Deut. 27:26). Now the works even of the regenerate are not squared according to the rule of legal justice. Wherefore, David being as it were stricken with the consideration of this durst not once oppose, no not his best works to the judgment of God, that by them he might plead pardon of his sins—whence it is that he cries out and says, "Enter not into judgment with Thy servant, O Lord, for then no flesh living shall be justified in Thy sight" (Ps. 143:2). The like does Job 9:3: "If he"—namely, such a one as says he is just—"contend with God, he cannot answer him one of a thousand." And, "We do not present our supplications before thee for our own righteousness, but for thy great tender mercies" (Dan. 9:18). (5) Justification by works, let them be whatever they can be, does quite overturn the foundation of our faith. "If ye be circumcised, Christ will profit you nothing. Ye are abolished from Christ, whosoever are justified by the law: ye are fallen from grace" (Gal. 5:2, 4). In this place the apostle speaks of them not which did openly resist Christ and the gospel, but of such as did with the merit of Christ mingle together the works of the law, as though some part of our salvation consisted in them. *Exception.* This place does only exclude such moral works of the flesh as do go before faith or the works of the law of Moses. *Answer.* This is virtue. For even of Abraham being already regenerated and of those his works which were done when he was justified, Paul speaks thus: "To him, not which worketh, but which believeth, is faith imputed" (Rom. 4:5). Those works which God has prepared that the regenerate should walk in them are moral works and works of grace; but these are excluded from justification and working man's salvation (Eph. 2:10). And Paul being regenerate says thus of himself, "I am not guilty to myself of anything, yet am I not thereby justified" (1 Cor. 4:4). (6) The cause of the cause is the cause of the thing caused; but grace without works is the cause of man's predestination, the which is the cause of his justification. And therefore grace without works shall much more be said to be the cause of justification.

Objection 1. "He that keepeth my statutes shall live in them" (Lev. 18:5). *Answer.* This saying is a legal sentence and therefore shows not what men can do, but what they should do.

Objection 2. "Blessed are those that walk in the law of the Lord" (Ps. 119:1). *Answer.* Man is not here said to be blessed because he walks uprightly, but because the person of such a walk is by the merits of Christ justified before God.

Objection 3. "Judge me according to my righteousness" (Ps. 7:8). And the act of Phineas was imputed to him for righteousness. *Answer.* These places are not meant of that righteousness of the person by which it is righteous before God, but of the righteousness of some particular cause or work. For whereas David was accused of this crime that he did affect Saul's kingdom, he in this point does in the words above mentioned testify his innocency before God.

Objection 4. "We are judged according to our works; therefore also by them justified" (Matt. 25:34–35, etc.) *Answer.* The reason is not like, because the last judgment is not the justifying of a man, but a declaration of that justification which he had before obtained. Therefore, the last judgment must be pronounced and taken not from the cause of justification but from the effects and signs thereof.

Objection 5. "Make you friends of unrighteous mammon, etc., that they may receive you into eternal habitations" (Luke 16:9). *Answer.* This they do not as authors of salvation, but as witnesses of the same.

Objection 6. "Redeem thy sins by righteousness, and thine iniquity by mercy toward the poor" (Dan. 4:14). *Answer.* It is rather, "break off thy sins" than redeem, for so is the original. Now men break off their sins by ceasing from them, not satisfying for them.

Objection 7. Evil works condemn; therefore, good works justify. *Answer.* It follows not, because good works are not perfectly good, as evil works are perfectly evil.

Objection 8. We are saved by hope (Rom. 8:24). *Answer.* We must distinguish between justification and salvation. Salvation is the end; justification is one degree to come to the end. But there is more required to the end than to a degree subordinate to the end. Therefore, we are saved by hope and faith, but justified by faith alone.

Objection 9. Affliction causeth eternal glory (2 Cor. 4:17). *Answer.* This it does not as by its own merit effecting the same, but rather as a path and way manifesting and declaring the same.

Objection 10. "Abraham was justified by works" (James 2:21). *Answer.* Not as any cause of justification, but as a manifestation thereof.

Objection 11. "He that is just, let him be more just" (Rev. 22:11). *Answer.* This place must be understood of justification before men—namely, of sanctification or a holy life—not of justification in the sight of God.

Objection 12. We are justified by faith; therefore, by a work. *Answer.* We are justified by faith not as it is a virtue and a work, but as it is an instrument apprehending the justice of Christ, whereby we are justified. And in this respect faith is said by the figure called metonymia,[20] to be imputed to us to righteousness.

Objection 13. The works of grace are dyed in the blood of Christ. *Answer.* They are indeed dyed therein, but to the end they might the better please God, not justify man. And whereas they are so stained as that they need dyeing in the blood of Christ, therefore can they not any ways justify sinful man. And the person of the worker is as well dyed in Christ's blood as is his work, yet he cannot say that his person does therefore justify him.

And as I have now proved that this doctrine of the papists is very erroneous, so I also avouch that it is most ridiculous. Because for a man to say that inherent righteousness is augmented by good works—namely, the fruits of righteousness—is as if a man should say that the vine is made more fruitful by bearing grapes, or that the internal light of the sun is augmented by the external emission of the beams. Luther's saying is far more true, "Good works do not make a good man, but a good man does make works good."

---

20. *Metonymia*: a thing used or regarded as a substitute for or symbol of something else.

The Fourteenth Error
Grace is quite extinguished, or rather utterly lost by any mortal sin.

The Confutation. (1) The Word of God does manifestly declare that it is far otherwise. "All that the Father giveth me, shall come to me; and him that cometh to me, I cast not away" (John 6:37). "Thou art Peter, and upon this rock will I build my church; so that the gates of hell shall not prevail against it" (Matt. 16:18). "They went out from us, but they were not of us; for if they had been of us, they would have continued with us" (1 John 2:19). "Being therefore justified, we have peace with God" (Rom. 5:1). Now how could this be true, if he that was before justified could any way quite fall from grace and so perish? (2) The elect after their very grievous fallings from God forthwith repented them of their sins, as we may see in the example of David, Peter, etc.—the which argues that they had not quite fallen from grace and lost the Spirit of God. (3) If grace be once utterly lost, then the engrafting of that party into Christ is quite abolished. Therefore, for such as repent, there must needs succeed a second new engrafting into Christ; and then it will also follow that they must of necessity be baptized anew, which is absurd to think.

But for all this we deny not but grace may in part and for a time be lost, to the end that the faithful may thereby acknowledge and know their weakness and for it be humbled. But that there is any total or final falling from grace, we utterly deny.

The Fifteenth Error
It is possible to fulfill the law in this life.

The Confutation. The law is evangelically fulfilled by believing in Christ; but not legally by doing the works thereof. Reason. They which are carnal cannot possibly fulfill the law of God; but the most regenerate, so long as they live in this life, are carnal in part. "I am," says Paul of himself, "canal, and sold under sin" (Rom. 7:14). "Who can say, Mine heart is pure, I am pure from sin?" (Prov. 20:9). "There is none so just upon earth, which doeth good, and sinneth not" (Eccl. 7:22). "If thou Lord, observe what is done amiss, Lord who shall abide it?" (Ps. 130:3). We are daily taught to pray to God, "Forgive us our sins" (Matt. 6:12). *Exception.* Indeed if the justice of the faithful be absolutely considered, it is imperfect; but as God does exact it of our frailty, it is perfect. *Answer.* This is but the fancy of some doting Jesuit. For this sentence of the law is simple, eternal, and immoveable. "Cursed is everyone that continueth not in all things, which are written in this book, to do them" (Gal. 3:10). Neither may we imagine that God will not therefore exact the full accomplishing of the law because we are frail. For we are creatures and debtors. Now we know that the debt does not decrease by reason of the debtors' poverty.

Objection. The faithful are said to be perfect in this life. *Answer.* There is a twofold perfection: the one incomplete, the which is an endeavor or care to obey God in the observation of all His precepts; the other is termed complete. This is that justice which the law requires—namely, a perfect and absolute justice according to that measure which man performed to God in his innocency. In the first sense, the faithful are said to be perfect—not in this latter.

The Sixteenth Error
Works done in grace, do (*ex condigno*[21]) condignly merit eternal life.

The Confutation. (1) Eternal life is the free gift of God. "The wages of sin is death, but the gift of God is eternal life through Christ Jesus" (Rom. 6:23). Therefore, it is not obtained by the merit of works. (2) The merit of condignity is an action belonging to such a nature as is both God and man, not to a bare creature. For the angels themselves cannot merit anything at God's hands; yea, and Adam also, if he had stood in his first innocency, could have deserved nothing of God, because it is the bounded duty of the creature to perform obedience to his Creator. The merit therefore of condignity does only agree to Christ, God and man, in whom each nature does to the effecting of this merit perform that which belongs to it. For the humanity does minister matter to the meritorious work by suffering and performing obedience; but the deity of Christ, whereto the humanity is hypostatically united, does confer full and sufficient worthiness to the work. Hence is it that the Father does speak thus of His Son: "This is my beloved Son, in whom I am well pleased"[22] (Matt. 3:17). (3) In the second commandment, God does promise eternal life to the keepers of His commandments; yet He says not that they shall obtain it by desert, but that He will show mercy to thousands of them that love Him and keep His commandments. (4) That a work may be meritorious, first, it must have an equal proportion with legal justice and eternal life; secondly, merit does presuppose this also, that in God there must be a due debt toward man, for God then ought on duty not by favor to accept of the person of man. But all our works, yea, our most holy works cannot come near to legal righteousness. For seeing all the regenerate are partly carnal and partly spiritual, all their good works in like sort are imperfectly good. For look what the causes are, such must the effect needs be. Again, good works do presuppose a due debt in man, none in God. (5) The ancient fathers do not acknowledge this merit of condignity as current. Augustine in his manual: "My merit is God's mercy."[23] Gregory the Great: "Grace

---

21. *Ex condigno*: of condignity, or merit, that worthiness of eternal life in Roman Catholic theology which a man may possess through good works performed while in a state of grace.
22. The Greek here is illegible.
23. In-text citation: in his manual chapter 22 [Augustine, *Enchiridion*, ch. 22].

found me void of merit at my first conversion, and the same grace has kept me void of merit ever since."[24] Bernard [wrote], "It is sufficient to know this, that merits are not sufficient."[25] And "Man's justice is God's goodness."[26] And, "That the satisfaction of one may be imputed to all, as the sins of all were borne by one."[27] And as for ancient doctors, merit was nothing else to them but a good work acceptable to God. Augustine: "If it be grace, then it is not bestowed by reason of any merit, but upon free mercy. What merit of his own can he that is set at liberty brag of, who if he had his merits should have been condemned? Good works are wrought by man, but faith is wrought in man, without which no man could work good works."[28] So the word "merit" does signify to do well, to be acceptable, to please—as the old interpreter has: for εὐδόκησα, signifying to please God, used this Latin word *promereri*, to merit.

Objection 1. Works have attributed to them reward. *Answer.* Reward is not so much attributed to the work as to the worker, and to him not for himself, but for Christ's merits apprehended by faith. Therefore, not our merit or personal merit, but Christ's merit and our reward are correlatives.

Objection 2. "It is a righteous thing with God to recompense tribulations," etc. (2 Thess. 1:6). It is righteous not because God ought so to do of duty, but because He promised. Now for God to stand to His word is a part of justice.

Objection 3. Christ has merited that works might merit. *Answer.* (1) This takes quite away the intercession of Christ. (2) It is against the nature of a legal work to merit (*ex condigno)* condignly, because both the law of nature and creation do bind man to perform legal works to God. And further, all works are very imperfect and mixed with sin. (3) This doctrine concerning works does obscure and darken the merit of Christ, because that the obtaining of eternal life is withdrawn from His death and obedience and attributed to works. For they say this, that Christ by His passion did merit indeed for the sinner justification, but a sinner once justified does for himself by his own merits even condignly merit eternal life.

Objection 4. The works of the regenerate are the works of the Holy Ghost; therefore, perfect and pure. *Answer.* (1) The works of God are all perfect, but yet in their time and by degrees. Therefore, sanctification, which is a work of

---

24. In-text citation: Greg.mor.2.book.chap.4 [Probably a reference to Gregory I (Gregory the Great, *c.* 540–604), *Morals on the Book of Job*, bk. 2, ch. 4. Gregory was a significant figure in the early church].

25. In-text citation: Bernard, serm.68 upon the Cant. [Bernard of Clairvaux, *Sermons on the Canticle of Canticles*, sermon 68].

26. In-text citation: sermon 61.Cant [Bernard of Clairvaux, *Sermons on the Canticle of Canticles*, sermon 61].

27. In-text citation: And epistle. 190 [Bernard of Clairvaux, *Letters*, letter 190].

28. In-text citation: Augustine.epist.105. to Sixtus [Augustine, *Letters*, letter 105 to Sixtus].

God, must in this life remain incomplete and is made perfect in the world to come. (2) The works of God are pure, as they are the works of God alone, not of God and impure man. But now good works, they do come immediately from the natural faculties of the soul—namely, from the understanding and the will (in which they being as yet but partly regenerated, some corrupt qualities of sin do yet remain) and are not immediately and simply or wholly derived from God's Spirit. And hence it is that they are all stained with sin.

The Seventeenth Error
Man knows not but by special revelation whether he be predestinated or not.

The Confutation. The contrary to this is a plain truth. Reason. (1) That which a man must certainly believe, that may be also certainly known without an especial revelation. But every faithful man must believe that he is elected. It is God's commandment that we should believe in Christ (1 John 3:23). Now to believe in Christ is not only to believe that we are adopted, justified, and redeemed by Him, but also in Him elected from eternity, whereby it is apparent that he which believes not this does not believe the whole gospel. (2) That which is sealed to us by the Spirit of God, of that we are very sure without special revelation. But our adoption and so consequently our election is sealed to us by the Spirit of God. "We have not received the spirit of the world, but the spirit which is of God: that we might know the things that are given to us of God" (1 Cor. 2:12). Therefore is our election certainly known to us. "In whom also ye have trusted after that ye heard the word of truth, even the Gospel of your salvation, wherein also after that ye believed, ye were sealed with the Holy Spirit of promise" (Eph. 1:13).

Exception. The Holy Ghost does seal to us our adoption morally by works, and therefore the knowledge of our adoption is but only probable. *Answer.* It seals to us our adoption by begetting a special trust and confidence. For when as we hear God's promises and withal think upon them, then does the Holy Ghost by the same promises move our understandings and wills to embrace them and in moving them does make us both to give our assent to them and in them to rest ourselves, whence arises a special assurance that we are adopted and in the favor of God. "Rejoice rather that your names are written in heaven" (Luke 10:20). But no man can be glad for that good which he is in doubt whether he have received it or not. (4) "Study to make your vocation and election sure βεβαὶανποιεῖσθαι" (2 Peter 1:10). But this is not in respect of God, but ourselves.

Objection. No man must by the catholic faith believe anything which God has not revealed either in the written or unwritten word—namely, tradition. But there is no such either writing or tradition as this—namely, that such a particular man, suppose Peter or Henry is predestinated of God. Therefore, no man must particularly believe that he is saved. *Answer.* Albeit this particular proposition, "I am elected," is not expressly set down in the Scriptures, yet is it inclusively comprehended in them as the species in his genus, as the logicians speak, so that it may by just consequent be gathered out of God's Word, if we reason thus: "They which truly believe are elected (John 6:35). I truly believe; for he which believes does know himself to believe. Therefore, I am elected." The first proposition is taken from the Scriptures; the second, from the believers' conscience; and from them both, the conclusion is easily derived.

Chapter 52

Concerning the Decree of Reprobation

Thus much shall suffice for the decree of election; now follows the decree of reprobation.

The decree of reprobation is that part of predestination whereby God according to the most free and just purpose of His will has determined to reject certain men to eternal destruction and misery, and that to the praise of His justice. "Has not the potter power over the clay, to make of the same lump one vessel to honor and another to dishonor?" (Rom. 9:21). "To them which stumble at the word, being disobedient, to which thing they were even ordained" (1 Peter 2:8). "There are certain men crept in, which were before of old ordained to this condemnation" (Jude 4). "God has not appointed us to wrath, but to salvation" (1 Thess. 5:9). In the Scriptures, Cain and Abel, Ishmael and Isaac, Esau and Jacob are propounded to us as types of mankind, partly elected and partly rejected.

Neither do we here set down any absolute decree of damnation, as though we should think that any were condemned by the mere and alone will of God without any causes inherent in such as are to be condemned. For to the decree of God itself there are certain means for the execution thereof annexed and subordinate. And therefore though we never do or can separate God's decree and the means to execute the same, yet do we distinguish them and do consider the purpose of God sometimes by itself alone, and sometimes again not by itself, but with middle causes subordinate thereto. And in this second respect, Christ is said to be predestinate; but in the former—namely, as the decree is considered by itself—He is not predestinated, but together with God the Father is a predestinator.

Again, the decree of God is secret (1) because it arises only from the good pleasure of God, unsearchable, and adored of the very angels themselves; (2) because it is not known but by that which is after it—namely, by the effects thereof.

Chapter 53
Concerning the Execution of the Decree of Reprobation

In the executing of this decree, there is to be considered the foundation or beginning and the degrees or proceeding thereof.

The foundation of executing the decree of reprobation is the fall of Adam, by which fall he was subject both to sin and damnation. "For God has shut up all in unbelief, that He might have mercy on all" (Rom. 11:32; 1 Peter 2:8). Here we must note that God has so decreed to condemn some as that notwithstanding all the fault and desert of condemnation remains in the men only.

Further, whom God rejects to condemnation, those He hates. This hatred of God is whereby He detests and abhors the reprobate when he is fallen into sin for the same sin. And this hatred which God has to man comes by the fall of Adam. And it is neither an antecedent nor a cause of God's decree, but only a consequent and follows the decree.

Reprobates are either infants or men of riper age.

In reprobate infants, the execution of God's decree is this: as soon as they are born, for the guilt of original and natural sin, being left in God's secret judgment to themselves, they dying are rejected of God forever. "But death reigned from Adam to Moses, even over them also that sinned not after the like manner of the transgression of Adam, which was the figure of Him that was to come" (Rom. 5:14). "For ere the children were born, and when they had neither done good nor evil, that the purpose of God might remain according to election, not by works, but by Him that calleth" (9:11).

Reprobates of riper age are of two sorts. They that are called (namely, by an ineffectual calling), and they that are not called.

In the reprobates which are called, the execution of the decree of reprobation has three degrees—to wit, an acknowledgement of God's calling, a falling away again, and condemnation.

The acknowledgement of God's calling is whereby the reprobates for a time do subject themselves to the calling of God, which calling is wrought by the preaching of the word. "For many are called but few are chosen" (Matt. 22:14). And of this calling there are five other degrees.

The first is an enlightening of their minds whereby they are instructed of the Holy Ghost to the understanding and knowledge of the Word. "For it is impossible that they which were once lightened," etc. (Heb. 6:4). "For if they, after they have escaped from the filthiness of the world, through the knowledge of the Lord, and of the Savior Jesus Christ, are yet tangled again therein, and overcome, the latter end is worse with them than the beginning" (2 Peter 2:20).

The second is a certain penitence whereby the reprobate (1) does acknowledge this sin; (2) is pricked with the feeling of God's wrath for sin; (3) is grieved for the punishment of sin; (4) does confess his sin; (5) acknowledges God to be just in punishing sin; (6) desires to be saved; (7) promises repentance in his misery or affliction in these words, "I will sin no more." "Then when Judas which betrayed Him, saw that He was condemned, he repented himself, and brought again the thirty pieces of silver, to the chief priest and elders" (Matt. 27:3). "For ye know, how that afterward also when he would have inherited the blessing, he was rejected: for he found no place of repentance, though he sought the blessing with tears" (Heb. 12:17). "Now when Ahab heard those words, he rent his clothes, and put sackcloth upon him, and fasted, and lay in sackcloth, and went softly" (1 Kings 21:27). "Let me die the death of the righteous, and let my last end be like his" (Num. 23:10). "For all this, they sinned still, and believed not His wondrous works. Therefore, their days did He consume in vanity, and their years hastily. And when He slew them, they sought Him, and they returned, and sought God early. They remembered that God was their strength, and the most high God their Redeemer" (Ps. 8:32–35).

The third degree is a temporary faith whereby the reprobate does confusedly believe the promises of God made in Christ. I say confusedly, because he believes that some shall be saved, but he believes not that he himself particularly shall be saved, because he being content with a general faith does never apply the promises of God to himself, neither does he so much as conceive any purpose, desire, or endeavor to apply the same or any wrestling or striving against security or carelessness and distrust. "Thou believest that there is one God, thou doest well: the devils also believe it, and tremble" (James 2:19). "And he that received seed in the stony ground, is he which heareth the word, and incontinently with joy receiveth it. Yet has he no root in himself, and endureth but a season" (Matt. 13:20–21). "Now when he was at Jerusalem at the Passover in the feast, many believed in His Name when they saw His miracles which He did. But Jesus did not commit Himself to them, because He knew them all" (John 2:23–24).

The fourth is a tasting of heavenly gifts, as of justification and of sanctification and of the virtues of the world to come. This tasting is verily a sense in the hearts of the reprobates whereby they do perceive and feel the excellency of

God's benefits, notwithstanding they do not enjoy the same. For it is one thing to taste of dainties and a banquet, and another thing to feed and to be nourished thereby. "For it is impossible, that they which were once lightened, and have tasted of the heavenly gifts, and were made partakers of the Holy Ghost, and have tasted," etc. (Heb. 6:4–5).

The fifth degree is the outward holiness of life for a time, under which is comprehended a zeal in the profession of religion, a reverence and fear toward God's ministers, and amendment of life in many things. "For Herod feared John knowing that he was a just man, and a holy, and reverenced him, and when he heard him, he did many things, and heard him gladly" (Mark 6:20). "Then Simon himself believed also, and was baptized, and continued with Philip, and wondered when he saw the signs and great miracles which were done" (Acts 8:13). "O Ephraim, what shall I do to thee? O Judah, how shall I entreat thee? For your goodness is as a morning cloud, and as the morning dew it goeth away" (Hos. 6:4).

The second degree of the execution of God's counsel of reprobation in men of ripe age which are called is a falling away again, which for the most part is effected and wrought after this manner. First, the reprobate is deceived by some sin. Secondly, his heart is hardened by the same sin. Thirdly, his heart being hardened becomes wicked and perverse. Fourthly, then follows his incredulity and unbelief, whereby he consents not to God's Word when he has heard and known it. Fifthly, an apostasy or falling away from faith in Christ does immediately follow this unbelief. "Take heed, brethren, lest at any time there be in any of you an evil heart, and unfaithful, to depart away from the living God" (Heb. 3:12–13; 1 Tim. 1:19).

This apostasy is sometimes sin against the Holy Ghost. In the sin against the Holy Ghost, we have these several points to be considered. (1) The name. It is called a sin against the Holy Ghost not because it is done against the person or deity of the Holy Ghost (for in this respect he that sins against the Holy Ghost sins in like sort against both the Father, and the Son), but it is so called because it is done contrary to the immediate action—namely, the illumination of the Holy Ghost. For albeit this be an action common to the whole Trinity, yet the Father and the Son do effect the same by the Holy Ghost. (2) The efficient cause of it, which is a set and obstinate malice against God and against His Christ. Therefore, when a man does in the time of persecution either for fear or rashly deny Christ, he does not commit this sin against the Holy Ghost, as may appear by the example of Peter, who denied Christ (Matt. 26:73–75). Neither does he which persecutes Christ and His church upon ignorance fall into this sin. Paul persecuted the church of Christ, and yet God had mercy on him because he did it ignorantly (1 Tim. 1:13). Many of the Jews crucified our Savior Christ who afterward, because they committed that grievous fact upon ignorance, repenting at Peter's sermon, they did obtain remission of their sins (Acts 3:17; 2:37). (3) The object—namely, God Himself and the Mediator, Christ Jesus. For the malice of this sin is directed against the very majesty of God Himself and against Christ. "Of how much sorer punishment suppose ye shall he be worthy, which treadeth underfoot the Son of God, and counteth the blood of the testament as an unholy thing, wherewith he was sanctified, and does despite the spirit of grace?" (Heb. 10:29). Therefore, this sin does directly respect the first table of the moral law and is not some particular slipping aside from the observation of those commandments which are contained in this first table, such as are some doubtings concerning God or of the truth of the Scriptures or of Christ, etc., but it is a general defection and apostasy from God, and that totally. (4) The subject in which it is. This sin is found in none at all but such as have been enlightened by the Holy Ghost and have tasted of the good gifts of God (Heb. 6:4, 6). Neither is it in him a bare cogitation alone, but an external action, or rather such a blasphemy against God as proceeds from a malicious and obstinate heart (Matt. 12:31). (5) The elect cannot commit this sin; and therefore, they who feel in themselves a sure testimony of their election need never to despair. Nay, this sin is not in every reprobate; for many of them die before they have this illumination by God's Spirit. (6) This sin cannot be forgiven, not because it is greater than that Christ's merit can satisfy for it, but because after a man has once committed this sin it is impossible for him to repent. For the gift of repentance proceeds from the Holy Ghost, and the Holy Ghost remains in us through Christ apprehended by faith. Now no man does apprehend Christ that does maliciously despise and contemn Him.

(7) It is very hard to know when a man commits this sin, because the root thereof—namely, set malice—lurks inwardly in the heart and is not so easily discerned.

Out of all this which has been spoken, we may thus define this sin. The sin against the Holy Ghost is a voluntary and obstinate denial of and blasphemy against the Son of God or that truth which was before acknowledged concerning Him, and so consequently a universal defection from God and His true church. We have an example of this sin partly in the devil, who albeit he knew well enough that Jesus was that Christ yet he never ceased both wittingly and willingly with all his power to oppugn the sacred majesty of God, together with the kingdom of Jesus Christ and, as far forth as he could, utterly to supplant the same; [and] partly in the Pharisees (Matt. 12:32; John 3:2).

After apostasy follows pollution, which is the very fullness of all iniquity, altogether contrary to sanctification. "And in the fourth generation they shall come hither again, for the wickedness of the Amorites is not yet full" (Gen. 15:16).

The third degree is damnation, whereby the reprobates are delivered up to eternal punishment. The execution of damnation begins in death and is finished in the last judgment. "And it was so that the beggar died, and was carried by the angels into Abraham's bosom: the rich man also died and was buried. And being in hell torments, he lift up his eyes and saw Abraham afar off, and Lazarus in his bosom" (Luke 16:22–23).

The execution of the decree of reprobation in infidels which are not called is this. First, they have by nature ignorance and vanity of mind. After that follows hardness of heart, whereby they become void of all sorrow for their sins. Then comes a reprobate sense, which is when the natural light of reason and of the judgment of good and evil is extinguished. Afterward when the heart ceases to sorrow, then arises a committing of sin with greediness. Then comes pollution, which is the fullness of sin. Lastly, a just reward is given to all these— to wit, fearful condemnation. "Having their cogitation darkened, and being strangers from the life of God through the ignorance that is in them, because of the hardness of their hearts" (Eph. 4:18). "For as they regarded not to know God, even so God delivered them up to a reprobate mind, to do those things which are not convenient" (Rom. 1:28).

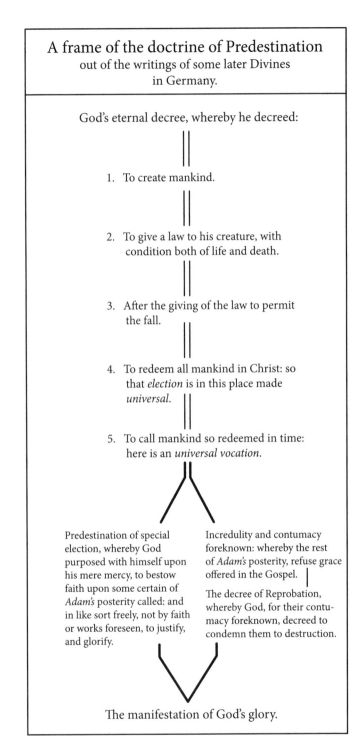

A frame of the doctrine of Predestination
out of the writings of some later Divines
in Germany.

God's eternal decree, whereby he decreed:

1. To create mankind.

2. To give a law to his creature, with condition both of life and death.

3. After the giving of the law to permit the fall.

4. To redeem all mankind in Christ: so that *election* is in this place made *universal.*

5. To call mankind so redeemed in time: here is an *universal vocation.*

Predestination of special election, whereby God purposed with himself upon his mere mercy, to bestow faith upon some certain of *Adam's* posterity called: and in like sort freely, not by faith or works foreseen, to justify, and glorify.

Incredulity and contumacy foreknown: whereby the rest of *Adam's* posterity, refuse grace offered in the Gospel.

The decree of Reprobation, whereby God, for their contumacy foreknown, decreed to condemn them to destruction.

The manifestation of God's glory.

FIGURE 7: A Frame of the Doctrine of Predestination out of the Writings of Some Later Divines in Germany

Concerning a New Devised Doctrine of Predestination Taught by Some New and Late Divines

Certain new doctrines of our age, have of late erected up a new doctrine of predestination, in which, fearing belike lest they should make God both unjust and unmerciful, they do in the distribution of the causes of salvation and damnation turn them upside down, as may appear by their description in this table.

But this their doctrine has some foul errors and defects, the which I according as I shall be able will briefly touch.

The First Error
There is a certain universal or general election whereby God without any either restraint or exception of persons has decreed to redeem by Christ and to reconcile to Himself all mankind wholly, fallen in Adam, yea every singular person, as well the reprobate as the elect.

The Confutation. The very name of election does fully confute this; for none can be said to be elected if so be that God would have all men elected in Christ. For he that elects or makes choice cannot be said to take all; neither can he that accepts of all be said to make choice only of some.

Objection. Election is nothing else but dilection or love. But this we know, that God loves all His creatures. Therefore, He elects all His creatures.

Answer. (1) I deny that to elect is to love, but to ordain and appoint to love (Rom. 9:13). (2) God does love all His creatures, yet not all equally, but every one in their place.

Furthermore, this position does flatly repugn the most plain places of holy Scripture. "Who gave Himself for us, that He might redeem us from all iniquity, and purge us to be a peculiar people to Himself" (Titus 2:14). "I give My life for My sheep" (John 10:15). *Answer.* John adds, "And My sheep hear My voice, and I know them, and they follow Me, and I give to them eternal life, neither shall they perish" (John 10:27–28). Christ is "the head of the church," and the same is the Savior of His body. "Christ loved the church and gave Himself for it" (Eph. 5:23, 25). Redemption and remission of sins is the inheritance of the saints and of such as are made heirs of the kingdom of Christ (Col. 1:12–14).

Again, look for whom Christ is an advocate, to them only is He a redeemer; for redemption and intercession, which are parts of Christ's priesthood, the one is as general and large as the other and are so surely united and fastened together as that one cannot be without the other. But Christ is only an advocate of the faithful (John 17:9). In that His solemn prayer, He first prays for His own—namely, His disciples, elected not only to the apostleship but also to eternal life. And then verse 20, He prays likewise for them that should believe in Him by their word. Now against these, He opposes "the world," for which He prays not that it may attain eternal life. And, "Who shall accuse God's elect? Christ sitteth at the right hand of the Father, and maketh His intercession for us" (Rom. 8:34). Furthermore, the members of Christ's church are called the "redeemed of the Lord" (Ps. 107:2). Therefore, this privilege is not given to all alike.

Exception. This universal reconciliation is not in respect of man, but of God Himself, who both made it for all and offers it to all. *Answer.* If Christ became once before God a reconciliation for all men's sins, yea and also satisfied for them all, it must needs follow that before God all those sins must be quite blotted out of His remembrance. For the actual blotting out of sins does inseparably depend upon satisfaction for sins; and satisfaction with God does necessarily imply the very real and general abolishment of the guilt and punishment of sin.

Objection 1. Christ took upon Him man's nature. Therefore, He redeemed man's nature generally. *Answer.* (1) It follows not, except we would say that Christ redeemed His own humanity, which cannot be any ways possible. (2) Every woman does partake the human nature of every man, yet is not every man each woman's husband, but hers alone with whom by the covenant in matrimony he is made one flesh. And in like sort Christ did by His incarnation (συα σαρκώσοι) take also upon Him man's nature, and that common to all Adam's progeny; yet is He the husband of His church alone by another more peculiar conjunction—namely, the bond of the Spirit and of faith. And by it the church is become flesh of His flesh, and bone of His bone (Eph. 5:30). And therefore she alone may justly claim title to the death of Christ and all His merits.

Objection 2. Christ's redemption is as general as Adam's fall was; and therefore it appertains to all Adam's posterity. *Answer.* Adam was a type of Christ, and Christ a counter-type correspondent to Adam. Adam was the root of all his successors, or all that should come of him, from the which first Adam was sin and death derived. Again, Christ is also a root, but of the elect only, and such as believe, to whom from Him proceed righteousness and life eternal. He cannot be said to be the root of all and every singular man, because that all do not drink and receive this His righteousness and life, neither are they actually by Him made righteous (Rom. 11:17, 19). *Objection.* The benefit of Christ's death redounded to all. *Answer.* It did, to all that believe. For as Adam destroyed all those that were born of him, so Christ does justify and save all those that are born anew by Him, and none other. *Objection.* If that Adam's sin destroyed all, and Christ's merit does not save all, then is Adam's sin more forcible to condemn than Christ's mercy is to save. *Answer.* We must not esteem of the mercy of Christ by the number of men which receive mercy (for so indeed, I grant, that as Adam's fall made all unjust, so the mercy of Christ and His redemption should actually justify all), but we must rather measure it by the efficacy and dignity thereof than by the number on whom it is bestowed. For it was a more easy thing to destroy all sin than by grace to save but one. Man, being but mere man, could destroy all; but to save even one, none could do it, but such a one as was both God and man.

Objection 3. Many places of Scripture there are which affirm this, that the benefit of Christ's death does appertain to all. "God has shut up all under sin, that He might have mercy upon all" (Rom. 11:32). "God would have all men to be saved" (1 Tim. 2:4). "God would not have any to perish, but all come to repentance" (2 Peter 3:9). *Answer.* (1) You must understand "all that believe" as it is in Matthew 11:28: "All that are weary, and heavy laden" (Matt. 11:28); "All that believe" (John 3:16); "The Scripture has concluded all under sin, that the promise by the faith of Jesus Christ, should be given to them which believe" (Gal. 3:22); "All which believe" (Acts 10:43). And surely there is as well a generality of them that believe, as of the whole world. (2) We may understand by "all" of all sorts, some, not every singular person of all sorts. So in Revelation 5:9, Christ is said to have redeemed some "out of every kindred, and tongue, and people, and nation." And, "There is neither Jew nor Grecian, neither bond nor free, there is neither male nor female, for ye are all one in Christ Jesus" (Gal. 3:28). In Matthew 4:23, Christ is said to have healed "every disease"—that is, every kind of disease. And Augustine to this purpose has a fit rule: all "is often used for many," as Romans 5:18–19. "It is thus said," says Augustine, "God would have all to be saved, not because there was no man which He would have damned, who therefore would not do miracles among them, which would, as He saith, have repented, if He had done miracles, but that by all men, we should understand all sorts of men, howsoever distinguished, whether kings, private persons," etc.[1] And "It is said 'he would have all to be saved' so as we must understand all such as are predestinate to be saved, because among them there are of all sorts' of men, as He said to the Pharisees, 'You tithe every herb.'"[2]

---

1. In-text citation: Augustine in his manual to Laur. Chap. 103. [Augustine, *Enchiridion*, ch. 103].

2. In-text citation: Augustine, Corrept. & Gratia, chap. 14. [Augustine, *On Rebuke and Grace*, ch. 14].

(3) These two—to be willing to save a man, and that he should come to the saving knowledge of the truth—are inseparably united together (1 Tim. 2:4). But the second we see does not agree to all and every singular person; therefore, the first cannot.

Objection 4. In many places of Scripture Christ is said to redeem the world, as, "He is a propitiation for the sins of the whole world" (1 John 2:2). *Answer.* This word "world" signifies (1) the frame of heaven and earth; (2) all men both good and bad together; (3) the company of unbelievers and malignant haters of Christ; (4) the congregation of the elect dispersed over the face of the whole earth and to be gathered out of the same. In this fourth signification we must understand such places as are above mentioned. Abraham is called "the heir of the world" (Rom. 4:13)—that is, of many nations (Gen. 17:4–5).

Objection 5. God would not the death of a sinner, but rather that he may repent and live (Ezek. 18:23). *Answer.* Augustine answers this objection: "You must," says he, "distinguish between man, as he is man, and man as he is a sinner. For God is not delighted with the destruction of man, as he is man, but as he is a sinner: neither wills He simply the death of any as he is a sinner, or as it is the ruin and destruction of His creature; but in that, by the detestation and revenge of sin with eternal death, His glory is exceedingly advanced."[3] God therefore wills the death of a sinner, but as it is a punishment—that is, as it is a means to declare and set out His divine justice. And therefore it is an untruth for a man to say that God would have none condemned. For whereas men are once condemned, it must be either with God's will or without it. If without it, then the will of God must needs suffer violence, the which to affirm is great impiety. If with His will, God must needs change His sentence before set down, but we must not presume to say so.

Objection 6. God is the Father of all (Mal. 2:10). *Answer.* This place is meant of God's church, out of which all men standing in that corrupt estate by Adam are the children of wrath and of the devil (John 8:44; Eph. 2:2).

Objection 7. If God did elect some and reject others, He must needs be προσωπολήπτης, a respecter of persons. *Answer.* (1) One is said then to accept or have respect of persons when as he by some circumstances inherent in the person is moved to do this or that. Now as for God, He did upon His mere pleasure elect some and reject others eternally, not moved or urged thereto by anything whatsoever out of Himself. (2) He is debtor to none, but may by good right do with His creatures what seems good to Him in His own eyes. (3) It is one thing with God to accept of persons, and another to make choice of men.

---

3. In-text citation: first book to Simplicius, 2.quest. [Augustine, *De Diversis Quaestionibus ad Simplicianum*, bk. 1, q. 2].

This if we should not grant, it would follow that God must be deemed blameworthy because He made not all His creatures most glorious angels.

Objection 8. If God decreed to reject certain men, then did He hate His creature. *Answer.* God decreed to reject His creature and workmanship not because He hated it, but because He appointed it to hatred. And it is one thing to hate, and another to appoint to hatred. And indeed God does not actually hate anything, but for sin. That saying of Augustine to Simplicius is fit for this purpose: "When God maketh the wicked, whom He does not justify, vessels of wrath, He doeth it not to hate that which He made: for in that He made them vessels, they have their use, namely, that by their pains to which they were ordained, the vessels of honor might reap profit. God therefore does not hate them, in that they are men, or vessels, neither anything that He made in them by creation, or ordination. For God hateth nothing which He has made. But in as much as He made them vessels of destruction, He did it to instruct others. As for their impiety, which He never made, that He hateth utterly. As therefore a judge hateth theft in a man, but he does not hate his punishment that he is sent to work in the mines; for the thief does the first, the judge the latter; so God, whereas of the company of them that perish, He maketh vessels of perdition, He does not therefore hate that which He maketh, that is, the condemnation of those which perish in their due punishment for sin."

Objection 9. The reprobates are said in many places of Scripture to be redeemed by Christ, as 2 Peter 2:1. *Answer.* First, we must not understand such places meant of all reprobates, but of such as are for a time in the church. (2) They are said to be redeemed, justified, and sanctified both in their own judgments and the church's also, inasmuch as they make an external profession of the faith. But this is a judgment of charity, not of certainty.

Objection 10. God might be thought evil, if that He had ordained the greatest part of the world to destruction. *Answer.* God could well enough have decreed that even all men should utterly have been rejected, and yet He should have been never a whit either cruel or unjust. Reasons. (1) He adjudged all and every one of those foul and wicked spirits which fell from Him to eternal torments. (2) He decreed also, as is apparent by the event, that men should live by the slaughter of beasts; and yet God is not therefore cruel against them, and surely God is no more bounden to man than to the very brute beasts.

Exception. God appointed all to be saved, with this caveat and condition: if they believe. *Answer.* This is absurd to affirm, for (1) by this means the decree of God should depend upon the will of man, when as contrarily God's decree does limit and order all inferior causes. (2) It quite takes away the certainty of God's decree, because a conditional proposition does set down nothing as being—or, it does not certainly affirm anything.

Objection. If the merit of Christ did not extend itself as far as the fall of Adam, then is not the head of the serpent broken, nor Satan's kingdom abolished by Christ. *Answer.* This bruising of the serpent's head is seen in them only which are at enmity with the serpent—namely, in such as truly believe (Gen. 3:15; compared with Rom. 16:20).

To conclude, that is not true which they say—namely, that this opinion of a universal and effectual redemption of every singular man is a notable remedy to comfort afflicted consciences. For I appeal to the judgments of all men whether there is in this manner of consolation, any great comfort to the conscience afflicted: Christ died for all men; you are a man; therefore, Christ died for you.

The Second Error

God did foreknow the fall of Adam, but He did not by His eternal decree foreordain the same, and therefore that his fall was without the agent permission of God.

The Confutation. It is false. For (1) there is not the least thing in nature but it comes to pass by the decree and will of God (Matt. 10:30). Wherefore, such as affirm that God did only foreknow this or that, they do either quite overturn the providence of God, or at the least, imagine that it is a very idle providence. (2) The fact of Herod and Pilate in delivering Christ against their own consciences to be crucified may seem to be as heinous as was Adam's fall, and yet they are said to have done that which "the hand of the Lord had foreordained to be done" (Acts 4:28). Again, the fall of Adam was two manner of ways by God's active or rather operative permission. (1) Inasmuch as the fall was an action; for in God alone we live, we move, and have our being. (2) Inasmuch as that his fall was but a bare trial of his loyalty to God, whereby God would try both the power and will of His creature.

The Third Error

God by reason that He did foresee the disobedience of some, or, that they would contemn the Gospel, did decree their destruction and condemnation.

The Confutation. We utterly deny that the foreseeing of the contempt of grace in any was the first and principal cause of the decree of reprobation. Reasons. (1) Paul, Romans 1:18, does derive the common condemnation of the Gentiles from hence—namely, that they "withheld the truth in unrighteousness," that is, because they did wittingly extinguish that light of nature by their wicked doings, which they had of the knowledge of God, and would not obey their consciences inwardly checking them for the same. (2) If that faith foreseen be not the cause of the decree of election, it cannot be that the want of faith foreseen should be the cause of the decree of reprobation. But rather, as faith does in order of causes follow after election, so must incredulity, reprobation. For there is the like reason or proportion of contraries. (3) Many infants depart this life both being out of the true church and before they have any use of reason; and again, many there are which albeit they live long, yet being either idiots and fools or born deaf, they cannot come to the true use of reason—in all which it is not credible that there should be suspected any contempt of the gospel, which they could not learn. (4) Esau was hated of God for none other cause but for that it so pleased Him (Rom. 9:18). (5) If this opinion should be true, then would it follow that men should be condemned for nothing else but incredulity, the which is not so (John 3:36). Christ speaking of unbelief says not that for it the wrath of God came upon man, but "remaineth upon him." And why should we daily ask pardon for our sins, if nothing but incredulity or unbelief condemned us? Nay, although that there were never any contempt of the gospel, yet that corruption of original sin were sufficient enough to condemn men. (6) Also that admiration which Paul has, "O man, who art thou, which disputeth with God!" (Rom. 9:20), does plainly show that the cause of the decree of God in rejecting some is unsearchable, and that it does not at all depend upon any foreseen contumacy toward the grace of God offered in the gospel. For if it were otherwise, we might easily give a reason of God's decree. Augustine says very well: "Who," says he, "created the reprobates, but God? and why, but because it pleased Him? But why pleased it Him? O man, who art thou that disputest with God?"[4]

Some divines perceiving that this is a hard sentence, they go about to mitigate it in this sort: "The matter," say they, "or object of predestination, is a reasonable creature, and that not simply or absolutely considered, but partly as it fell, partly as of itself it was subject to fall: and thereupon God preordaining men from everlasting, considered them, not simply as He was to make them men, but as they were such men as might fall into sin, and again be redeemed by Christ, and after called to the light of the Gospel. The efficient or first motive cause, was not any foreknown cause, either this or that, but the mere will of God. For He disposeth all things not of, and by His foreknowledge, but rather according to the same." But these things, albeit they may seem to be subtle devices, yet are they not altogether true. Reasons. (1) The potter, when he purposes to make some vessel, does not consider the clay and regard in it some inherent quality to make such a vessel; but he makes it of such and such a form, to this or that use, even of his alone free will and pleasure. (2) "Has not the potter power to make of the same lump one vessel to honor, and another to dishonor?" (Rom. 9:21). In which place we may not understand by the name

---

4. In-text citation: epist. 105. [Augustine, *Letters*, letter 105].

"lump" all mankind corrupted and fallen, and so to be redeemed in Christ; for then Paul would not have said that God made vessels of wrath, but rather that He did forsake them after they were made. (3) This seems preposterous that God did first foreknow mankind created, fallen, and redeemed in Christ; and that afterward He ordained them so foreknown to life or to death. For the end is the first thing in the intention of the agent; neither will a very unskillful workman first prepare means by which he may be helped to do a thing before he has set down in his mind all the ends, both such as are most near, and them that are very far off. Now we know this, that man's creation and his fall in Adam are but means to execute God's predestination and therefore are subordinate to it; but the end of God's decree is the manifestation of His glory in saving some and condemning others. Therefore, we may not once imagine that God did first consult of the means whereby He determined to execute His decree before He deliberated of the election and reprobation of man.

The Fourth Error
God's calling to the knowledge of the gospel is universal, yea, of all men and every singular person without exception.

The Confutation. This is a very unreasonable position. Reasons. (1) God would not have all men called to Christ. "Many are called, but few are chosen" (Matt. 20:16). He says not that all, but many are called. Christ in His disciples' first embassy charges them that they should not preach to the Gentiles of His coming; and to the Canaanitish woman He says, "It is not mete to give the children's bread to dogs" (Matt. 15:26). "It is not given to everyone to know the mysteries of the kingdom of God" (13:11). "The mysteries of the Gospel"— whether it be meant of Christ or the calling of the Gentiles—"was kept secret from the beginning of the world" (Rom. 16:25). (2) There be many millions of men which have not so much as heard of Christ. "God in times past suffered all the Gentiles to walk in their own ways" (Acts 14:16). (3) The greatest part of the world has ever been out of the covenant of grace. "Ye were, I say, at that time without Christ, and were aliens from the commonwealth of Israel, and strangers from the covenants of promise, and had no hope, and were without God in the world but now ye are no more strangers and foreigners, but citizens with the saints," etc. (Eph. 2:12, 19).

Objection. They are said to be ἀπηλλοτριώμεν, not simply alienated, but abalienated[5] from God. Now how could they be abalienated, except either they or [their] predecessors had been in the covenant? *Answer.* The Gentiles are not said to be abalienated from the covenant, but from the commonwealth of

---

5. *Abalienated*: to estrange or alienate in feeling or to cause to feel removed or distant.

Israel, because that God has then by certain laws, rites, and ceremonies utterly severed and distinguished the people of the Jews from all other nations.

Objection. This general calling is not to be understood simply of the ministry of the word, but of the will of God delivered presently after the fall in His unwritten word and afterward in His written word; and this all men ought to know, although many through their own default know it not. *Answer.* But the Scriptures were committed to the custody of the church of God, and every one was not credited with them. "To the Jews were of credit committed the oracles of God" (Rom. 3:2). "The church is the pillar and the ground of truth" (1 Tim. 3:15). "He showed His words to Jacob, and His statutes and laws to the house of Israel. He has not dealt so with every nation: therefore they have not known His laws" (Ps. 147:19). "The Lord is famous in Judea, and in Israel is His name great" (76:1).

Objection. The covenant of grace was made with Adam and Eve, and in them all mankind was received both into the church and covenant and also called to the knowledge of God. *Answer.* (1) This reason wants even common reason and sense to say that God giving His promise in the days of Adam and Noah did in them call all mankind that should come after. (2) Adam before his fall did indeed receive the grace both for himself and for others also, and in the fall, he lost it both for himself and for all others. But after the fall, he received the promise for himself alone and not for the whole world, otherwise the first Adam should not only have been a living creature but a quickening spirit, the which is proper to the second Adam (1 Cor. 15:45).

The Conclusion

If we should grant this doctrine to be true, then must we needs allow of these absurdities in divinity which follow. (1) That God would have all and each singular man to be saved, and with all He would have some ordained to hatred and perdition; or, that in regard of God all men are elected and redeemed, but in regard of the event many perish. (2) The guilt of Adam's sin must not be imputed to any one of his posterity, because that God, having mercy on all generally in Christ, did take into the covenant of reconciliation all mankind. Now if but the guiltiness of Adam's fall be taken away, the punishment forthwith ceases to be a punishment, and corruption itself is by little and little abolished in all men.

Chapter 55

Of the State and Condition of the Reprobates When They Are Dead

The death of the reprobates is a separation of the body and the soul: of the body, that for a time it may lie dead in the earth; of the soul, that it may feel the torments of hell, even until the time of the last judgment, at which time the whole man shall be cast into the most terrible and fearful fire of hell. "By the which He also went and preached to the spirits that are in prison" (1 Peter 3:19; cf. Luke 8). "For if God spared not the angels that sinned, but cast them down into hell, and delivered them into chains of darkness to be kept to damnation," etc. (2 Peter 2:4).

The reprobate when they die do become without sense and astonished like to a stone, or else they are overwhelmed with a terrible horror of conscience and despairing of their salvation, as it were with a gulf of the sea overturning them. "Then in the morning when the wine was gone out of Nabal, his wife told him those words, and his heart died within him, and he was like a stone. And about ten days after the Lord smote Nabal that he died" (1 Sam. 25:37–38). "And when he had cast down the silver pieces in the temple, he departed, and went and hanged himself" (Matt. 27:5).

Chapter 56

Of the Condemnation of the Reprobates at the Last Judgment

In the last judgment, at the sound of the trumpet, the living, being stricken with horror and fear, shall be changed in a moment. The dead shall rise again to condemnation. Both the living and the dead shall then have immortal bodies, but without glory; and they standing upon the earth at the left hand of Christ, the Judge, shall hear the sentence of condemnation: "Depart from Me ye cursed into everlasting fire, which is prepared for the devil and his angels" (Matt. 25:41). "And they shall come forth that have done good, to the resurrection of life: but they that have done evil, to the resurrection of condemnation" (John 5:29). "For the Lord Himself shall descend from heaven with a shout, and with the voice of the Archangel, and with the trumpet of God, and the dead in Christ shall rise first. Then shall we, which live and remain, be caught up with them also in the clouds, to meet the Lord in the air: and so shall we be ever with the Lord" (1 Thess. 4:16–17).

Chapter 57

Of the Estate of the Reprobates in Hell

After that the sentence of condemnation is pronounced, then follows everlasting death, whereof this is the estate:

(1) The reprobates are separated from the presence and glory of God.

(2) They are punished with eternal confusion and most bitter reproaches, because all their secret wickedness and sins are revealed. "Which shall be punished with everlasting perdition, from the presence of the Lord, and from the glory of His power" (2 Thess. 1:9). "Blessed are the pure in heart, for they shall see God" (Matt. 5:8). "And now little children, abide in Him, that when He shall appear, we may be bold, and not be ashamed before Him at His coming" (1 John 2:28).

(3) They have fellowship with the devil and his angels (Matt. 25:41).

(4) They are wholly in body and soul tormented with an incredible horror and exceeding great anguish through the sense and feeling of God's wrath poured out upon them forever. "And they shall go forth, and look upon the carcasses of men, that have transgressed against Me; for their worm shall not die, neither shall their fire be quenched, and they shall be an abhorring to all flesh" (Isa. 66:24).

Hereupon is the punishment of those that are condemned called hellfire, a worm, weeping, and gnashing of teeth, utter darkness, etc. "But the fearful, and unbelieving, and the abominable, and murderers, and whoremongers, and sorcerers, and idolaters, and all liars, shall have their part in the lake which burneth with fire and brimstone, which is the second death" (Rev. 21:8). "And shall cast them into a furnace of fire, there shall be weeping and gnashing of teeth" (Matt. 13:42; Isa. 66:24).

A Corollary

And this is the full execution of God's decree of reprobation, whereby appears the great justice of God in punishing sin; from whence also comes God's glory, which He propounds to Himself as the last and chiefest end in all these things. Therefore, let every Christian propound the same end to himself. "What shall we say then? Is there unrighteousness with God? God forbid. For He said to

Moses, I will have mercy on him, to whom I will show mercy; and will have compassion on him, on whom I will have compassion. So then, it is not in him that willeth; or in him that runneth, but in God that showeth mercy. For the Scripture saith to Pharaoh, For this same purpose have I stirred thee up, that I might show My power in thee, and that My name might be declared throughout all the earth" (Rom. 9:14–17). "Whether therefore ye eat, or drink, or whatever ye do, do all to the glory of God" (1 Cor. 10:31).

Chapter 58

Of the Application of Predestination

The right applying of predestination to the persons of men is very necessary, and it has two parts. The first is the judgment of particular predestination, and the second is the use of it.

The judgment and discerning of a man's own predestination is to be performed by means of these rules which follow.

(1) The elect alone and all they that are elect not only may be but also in God's good time are sure of election in Christ to eternal life (1 Cor. 2:12; 2 Cor. 13:5).

(2) They have not this knowledge from the first causes of election, but rather from the last effects thereof; and they are especially two: the testimony of God's Spirit and the works of sanctification (Rom. 8:16; 2 Peter 1:10).

(3) If any doubt of this testimony, it will appear to them whether it come from the Spirit of God or their own carnal presumption. First, by a full persuasion which they shall have; for the Holy Ghost will not barely say it, but persuades such that they are the children of God, the which the flesh cannot in any wise do. Secondly, by the manner of persuasion; for the Holy Ghost draws not reasons from the works or worthiness of man, but from God's favor and love. And this kind of persuasion is far different from that which Satan uses. Thirdly, by the effects of that testimony. For if the persuasion arise from presumption, it is a dead persuasion; but contrarily, it is most lively and stirring if it come from the Holy Ghost. For such as are persuaded that they are elected and adopted children of God, they will love God, they will trust in Him, and they will call upon Him with their whole heart.

(4) If the testimony of God's Spirit be not so powerful in the elect, then may they judge of their election by that other effect of the Holy Ghost—namely, sanctification—like as we use to judge by heat that there is fire, when we cannot see the flame itself.

(5) And of all the effects of sanctification, these are most notable. (1) To feel our wants and in the bitterness of heart to bewail the offence of God in every sin. (2) To strive against the flesh—that is, to resist and to hate the ungodly

motions thereof and with grief to think them burdenous and troublesome. (3) To desire earnestly and vehemently the grace of God and merit of Christ to obtain eternal life. (4) When it is obtained, to account it a most precious jewel (Phil. 3:8). (5) To love the minister of God's word, in that he is a minister; and a Christian, in that he is a Christian—and for that cause, if need require, to be ready to spend our blood with them (Matt. 10:42; 1 John 3:16). (6) To call upon God earnestly and with tears. (7) To desire and love Christ's coming and the day of judgment, that an end may be made of the days of sin. (8) To flee all occasions of sin and seriously to endeavor to come to newness of life. (9) To persevere in these things to the last gasp of life. Luther has a good sentence for this purpose: "He that will serve God, must," says he, "believe that which cannot be seen, hope for that which is deferred, and love God when He showeth Himself an enemy, and thus remain to the end."

(6) Now, if so be all the effects of the Spirit are very feeble in the godly, they must know this, that God tries them, yet so as they must not therewith be dismayed, because it is most sure that if they have faith but as much as a grain of mustard seed and be as weak as a young infant is, it is sufficient to engraft them into Christ; and therefore they must not doubt of their election because they see their faith feeble and the effects of the Holy Ghost faint with them.

(7) Neither must he that as yet has not felt in his heart any of those effects presently conclude that he is a reprobate; but let him rather use the Word of God and the sacraments, that he may have an inward sense of the power of Christ drawing him into Him and an assurance of his redemption by Christ's death and passion.

(8) No man may peremptorily set down that himself or any other is a reprobate. For God does oftentimes prefer those which did seem to be most of all estranged from His favor to be in His kingdom above those who in man's judgment were the children of the kingdom. Hence it is that Christ says, "The publicans and harlots go before you" (Matt. 21:31); and, "Many a one is called at the eleventh hour" (10:6), as appears by that notable example of the thief upon the cross.

The uses which may be made of this doctrine of predestination are very many. First, for our instruction, we are taught these things:

(1) That there is neither any justification by works nor any works of ours that are meritorious. For election is by the free grace of God, and therefore in like sort is justification. For as I have said before, the cause of the cause is the cause of the thing caused. And for this reason, in the work of salvation grace does wholly challenge all to itself. "At this time there is a remnant through the election of grace" (Rom. 11:5); "Who has saved us, and called us with an

holy calling, not according to our works, but according to His own purpose and grace, which was given to us, through Christ Jesus before the world was" (2 Tim. 1:9). "To you it is given for Christ, that not only ye should believe Him, but also suffer for His sake" (Phil. 1:29). "We are justified freely by grace" (Rom. 3:24). "Not by the works of righteousness which we had done, but according to His mercy He saved us" (Titus 3:5). "I will cause you to walk in My statutes" (Ezek. 36:27). "The gift of God is eternal life" (Rom. 6:23).

(2) That astrology, teaching by the casting of nativities what men will be, is ridiculous and impious, because it determines that such shall be very like in life and conversation whom God in His predestination has made unlike. Jacob and Esau, born of the same parents and almost in the same moment of time (for Jacob held Esau by the heel as he was born [Gen. 25:26]), were of most unlike dispositions and had divers events. The like may we see in all twins and others which are born at the same time.

(3) That God is most wise, omnipotent, just, and merciful. "O the wonderful riches, both of the wisdom and knowledge of God! how unsearchable are His judgments, and His ways past finding out!" (Rom. 11:33). "Who has predestinated us, to be adopted through Jesus Christ to Himself, according to the good pleasure of His will" (Eph. 1:5).

Secondly, being the servants of Christ, we are admonished:

(1) To fight against all doubting and diffidence of our salvation, because it neither depends upon works nor faith, but upon God's decree, which is immutable (Matt. 24:24). "Rejoice that your names are written in the book of life" (Luke 10:20). "Who shall lay anything to the charge of God's chosen? It is God that justifieth, who shall condemn?" (Rom. 8:33; 2 Tim. 2:19). This teaches that the anchor of hope must be fixed in that truth and stability of the immutable good pleasure of God, so that albeit our faith be so tossed as that in danger of shipwreck, nevertheless it must never sink to the bottom, but even in the midst of danger take hold upon repentance, as on a board, and so recover itself.

(2) To humble our souls under the mighty hand of God, for we are as clay in the hand of the potter. "They through infidelity are broken off, but thou standest through faith. Be not high minded, but fear" (Rom. 11:20).

(3) To give all glory to God. "We ought to give thanks always to God for you brethren, beloved of the Lord, because that God has from the beginning chosen you to salvation" (2 Thess. 2:13).

(4) To bear crosses patiently. "Those which He knew before, He has also predestinate, to be made like to the image of His Son" (Rom. 8:29). This likeness to Christ is in bearing afflictions. "That I may know Him, and the virtue of His resurrection, and the fellowship of His afflictions, to be made conformable to His death" (Phil. 3:10).

(5) To do good works. "We are His workmanship created in Christ Jesus to do good works, which God has ordained, that we should walk in them" (Eph. 2:10).

Thus much concerning theology.

AN EXCELLENT TREATISE
Of comforting such as are troubled
About their predestination:
*Taken out of the second answer of M. [Theodore] Beza, to D. [Jakob] Andreas,[1]
In the act of their colloquy at Mompelgart, etc.*

"Unless," says D. Andreas, "regeneration be always united to baptism and remains in such as are baptized, how should the troubled consciences of those be eased and comforted who because they feel not in themselves any good motions of God's Holy Spirit find none other refuge but the word and sacraments, especially the sacrament of baptism? Now this remedy would be of small force, except it be opposed against those imaginations which the devil casts into a troubled heart; yea, except it taught such that God is greater than our heart, who in baptism has not only offered us the adoption of sons, but has indeed bestowed the same upon us—as it is said by Christ, 'He that believeth, and is baptized, shall be saved' (Mark 16:16); and by Paul, 'Ye which are baptized, have put on Christ' (Gal. 3:27). David, being armed with the like comfort from his circumcision, feared not to join battle with the giant Goliath. And if this were not so, it must needs follow that baptism were nothing else but an idle ceremony, and also the persons of the Trinity would be thought liars. Wherefore, those afflicted men, when Satan assaults them, must resist him with these words: 'Depart from me Satan, thou hast neither part nor portion in the inheritance of my soul, because I am baptized in the name of the holy Trinity, and so am I truly made the son of God by adoption.'" And these are the strong weapons which so many times and in so many words have been objected against me by D. Andreas? And whereby he has gotten the victory? But because this his reason is somewhat intricate, I will explain it after this sort. First, for the place of Scripture which he alledges—namely, that God "is greater than our hearts" (1 John 3:20)—it is so far from comforting an afflicted conscience that it will rather drive him to despair. Neither does 1 John 3:20 make mention of it to ease such as are in despair, showing to them by that sentence the greatness of God's mercies; but rather that He might thereby even bruise in pieces the

1. Jakob Andreae (1528–1590), Lutheran theologian and one of the authors of the Formula of Concord.

hearts of proud persons when they consider the greatness of God's majesty. And for the other place, when as a man doubts of his salvation and feels no testimonies of faith in himself (for such a one we here speak of), what comfort, think you, can he have in these words, "He that believeth, and is baptized, shall be saved" (Mark 16:16)? For he would rather reason contrarily thus: "I indeed am baptized, yet for all that I believe not; and therefore my baptism is not available, I must needs be condemned." For the saying of Augustine in his treatise upon John 6 is very true, who speaking of Simon Magus says, "What good did it to him to be baptized? Brag not therefore," says he, "that you are baptized, as though that were sufficient for you to inherit the kingdom of heaven." As for the place of Paul (Gal. 3:27), I showed plainly before how D. Andreas did violently wrest it to his purpose.

Neither are his reasons taken from the absurdity that would follow of more force than the former, albeit he makes them especial pillars to underprop the truth of his cause. For, I pray you, is God of less truth because His truth is neglected and derided of them that contemn it? Is the ceremony of baptism therefore in vain, because some refuse the grace offered in baptism; others (if we may believe D. Andreas) reject that grace when they have received it. What? Is not the gospel therefore the power of God to salvation, because it is to such as believe not the savor of death to eternal death? May not the Supper of the Lord be a pledge of God's covenant, because so many abuse these holy signs or (as D. Andreas is of opinion) the very body and blood of our Savior Christ? And, that I may reason from that which is true in the experience of every child, can the sun be said to be without light, because they which are blind and asleep have no benefit by the light thereof, neither such as shut their eyes so close that they will not enjoy the comfort of the light? But among all, this one is most childish, that D. Andreas will make this his principal argument—namely, that in vain did men thus tempted flee at all to baptism, unless we conclude with him that all such as are baptized are in baptism adopted the sons of God. For first, if this were a good consequent from baptism, it were in vain for such an afflicted conscience to gather to himself a testimony from the Word of God and the other sacrament of the Lord's Supper, unless we make all those to be in like sort regenerate and adopted to whom the word of God is preached and the Lord's Supper administered, either of which, for D. Andreas to affirm, is a bold untruth.

But to omit this, what if we grant this which D. Andreas requires concerning baptism? May not for all that any that is so tempted by Satan's policy resell this great comforter by his own argument? After this sort, I will grant D. Andreas your question. Suppose I have been baptized and adopted the son of God; yet seeing you teach that the grace of God is not so sure but that I may fall from the same, as indeed I feel that I have grievously fallen, what do you now else but lift me up with one hand to heaven and with the other cast me down into hell? What mean you therefore to teach me those things which are so far from easing me, as that contrarily they do more and more lay out to me mine abominable and ungrateful heart? See now what sure consolation consciences grievously afflicted may reap by this doctrine of their comforter D. Andreas.

Now if any be desirous to know what spiritual comfort is most meet to be ministered to consciences so troubled, I will show them that which is grounded upon a sure foundation and which I myself have often found to be true in my own experience, the which also I purpose to handle more largely for the benefit of the Christian reader. First therefore, we teach contrarily to that which D. Andreas does most falsely object against us that the eternal decree or, as Paul speaks, the purpose of God must not be sought in the bottomless counsel of God, but rather in the manifestation of it—namely, in His vocation by the word and sacraments. This I speak of such as are of years of discretion, as they must needs be whom we seek to comfort in this place.

Now because that external vocation is not proper only to the elect, "for many are called, but few are chosen" (Matt. 22:14), but such a vocation as is effectual—that is, whereby the understanding is not only enlightened with the saving knowledge of God, but in the will also there is created a true though not a perfect hatred of sin, from whence arises an abhorring of sin and love of that which is good, or rather a desire to will and do that which is right. Therefore, when we see one thus dangerously tempted, we apply to his afflicted conscience that true nepenthe[2] and comfortable and restorative medicine which is taken from God's effectual vocation as it were out of an apothecary's box.

If therefore I have to do with such a one who either was never called by the preaching of the gospel, or if he were called yet seems both to himself and others never to have regarded Him that called, and hence concludes that he is not in the number of them whom God has purposed to take pity upon—I forthwith tell him that Satan plays the sophist in teaching him thus to conclude; for this his reason is as untrue as if a man looking at midnight and seeing that the sun is not then risen should therefore affirm that it would never rise. And this is that which when I objected to D. Andreas,[3] he very boldly corrupting my meaning, printed this as my assertion: "Say to a man that is afflicted, the sun is risen, although as yet it be not risen." But I teach not lies, however this depravation of my words came from D. Andreas's printers or himself. And whereas D. Andreas excepted that this consolation were to no purpose because he that

---

2. *Nepenthe*: a drug that brings, or is supposed to bring, forgetfulness of trouble or grief.
3. In-text citation: p. 482.

was afflicted might doubt whether this sun would ever rise or not, I answered to him that which the printers have quite left out and which I will now therefore more fully repeat. I was wont therefore to tell the party thus troubled after he had forsaken his false and devilish position, that although an external vocation were not of force enough to appease an afflicted conscience, yet it was of sufficient force and efficacy against the devil. For I tell him that they which never had external nor internal calling, they (if we regard an ordinary calling) must needs perish; but whoever is once called, he has set as it were his foot in the first entry into the kingdom of heaven; and unless it be by his own default, he shall come afterward into the courts of God and so by degrees into His Majesty's palace. And for the confirmation of this, I use diverse ways. For why, say I, doubt you of His good will toward you, who in mercy has sent me a minister to call you to Him? You have no cause, unless you allege the number of your sins. If this be all, why oppose the infinite greatness of God's mercy against your sins, who has sent me to bring you to Him. The Lord vouchsafes to bring you into the way of the elect. Why are you a stumbling block to yourself? And refuse to follow Him? If you feel not as yet inwardly yourself to be stirred forward, pray that you may know this for a most sure truth, that this desire in you is a pledge of God's fatherly good will toward you. He neither can nor will be wanting to this which He has stirred up in you. After these exhortations, I show him how some are called at the eleventh hour, how the Gentiles after many thousand years were called to be God's people, how the thief was saved upon the cross—these and other remedies I used, whereof I never remember that it repented me.

But if I deal with such as have before obeyed the Lord's calling and either by reason of some grievous sin into which they have fallen or because they have absented themselves from the church of God, or in that they, refusing public and private admonitions, have been oftentimes to the church, or which in my experience has befallen many very good and godly persons, while they satisfy not themselves, they are so altogether busily conversant in reprehending and judging themselves that they for awhile forget the mercy of God. With these, to omit such as for some natural infirmities are if they procure not speedy help of some expert physician, most dangerously tempted—with these, I say, I use this order.

First, I desire that they intimate to me that which especially grieves them, and as I understand both the thing and measure thereof by them, I take especial care of this, that they being already overmuch cast down, that I then by the severe denunciation of the law do not quite overturn them; yet so as that I do not altogether withdraw them, either from condemning their former sins or the meditation of God's judgment. And so, as much as I can, I temper the words of consolation, as that I nothing cloak God's anger against them for their sins.

After I have thus prepared them, I then demand whether they have been ever in this case or no? "Nay," say they, for the most part, "the time was when in great joy and peace of conscience I served the Lord; then was I a happy person, full of faith, full of hope. But now, wretch that I am, I have lost my first love, and there is nothing vexes me more than to remember those times past." But say I, whether consideration is more grievous to you, the apprehension of God's judgments, or the dislike of yourself that you should offend so gracious and loving a father? "Both," say they, "but especially the latter." Therefore, say I, sin also displeases you in that it is sin—namely, because it is evil, and God who is goodness itself is offended with it? "It is even as you told us," say they, "and I am now ashamed that so vile and wicked a wretch as myself should come before so gracious and merciful a father." Then I tell them that no man is offended, but rather is glad when he can injure one whom he hates. This they grant, and withal say, "God forbid, that albeit the Lord hate me, I in like sort should hate Him, to whom, if it were possible, I would be reconciled again." Then I add this: Be of good comfort, my dear brother; you are in good case. For who can love God, especially when he is wounded by Him? Who can bewail the loss of His friendship? Who can desire to come again into His favor, but he whom God still loves, although for a time He be angry with him? Except peradventure you have not learned thus much, that the knowledge of our salvation comes not from flesh and blood, but from God himself, who first vouchsafed to instruct us, and from Christ Jesus, manifesting the Father to us. And that it is God's blessing that we do love God, who loved us first, when we were His enemies. You have therefore, my good brother, just cause why you should be greatly displeased with many things past; but there is no cause why you should despair. Briefly you have inwardly, and, as it were, dwelling with you evident testimonies of your future reconciliation with God—especially if you cease not to pray to Him earnestly, who has laid the foundation of repentance in you, to wit, a dislike of sin and a desire to be reconciled to Him. The sheep which wandered out of the fold ceased not to be a sheep, albeit it went astray for a time; you now are that sheep, to whom that faithful Shepherd of all those sheep, which the Father has committed to Him, leaving those ninety and nine, does not so much by my ministry declare that He seeks you, as having already sought you, though you not seeking Him, has indeed found you. "Knock," says He, "and it shall be opened to you" (Matt. 7:7). And have you now forgotten those promises which were so often made to them that repent? And also, which they had experience of, who in the sight of the world were in a desperate case? "But I," says he, "again feel no sense of faith or hope; but I feel all the contrary." Nay, say I, you deceive yourself, as I told you before. For it is the Comforter alone which teaches you to hate sin not so much for the punishment, as because it is evil and dislikes God, albeit He show not Himself so fully at the first, because you had so many ways grievously offended Him, as that He seems for awhile quite to forsake you. And, that you have not quite lost Him, but that He is yet in some secret corner of your soul, from whence at your instant prayers He will show Himself to you, this will plainly declare to you, which I now admonish you of the second time. But let us grant as much as you can say; yet sure it is that your faith was not dead, but only possessed with a spiritual lethargy. You lived in the womb of your mother, and there were ignorant of your life. A drunken man, although he lose for a time the use of reason and also of his limbs, yet he never loses reason itself. You would think that in winter the trees were dead, but they spring again in the summer season. At night the sun sits, but in the next morning it rises again. And how often see we by experience that he which at one time took the foil in a combat at another did win the prize? And know this, that in a spiritual combat of the flesh with the spirit, the like we may see in many partly through sloth to resist and partly for default to beware. To these he replies, for such temptations are very hardly removed, "I would to God," says he, "I could persuade myself that these promises belonged to me. For my present estate constrains me to doubt whether I am the child of God, or not."

The praise of Christ knows no end.

A Christian and Plain Treatise of the Manner and Order of Predestination, and of the largeness of God's grace.

FIRST WRITTEN IN LATIN
by that Reverend and faithful servant of God,
Master *William Perkins,* late
Preacher of the Word in
Cambridge.

AND CAREFULLY TRANSLATED
into English by FRANCIS CACOT,
and THOMAS TUKE.

Romans 8. Verses 29, 30:
For those which He knew before, He also predestinate to
be made like to the image of His Son, that He might be
the first born among many brethren.
Moreover, whom He predestinate, them also He called,
and whom He called, them also He justified,
and whom He justified, them He also glorified.

LONDON:
Printed for WILLIAM WELBY,
and *Martin Clarke,* 1606.

To the Right Worshipful Sir Peter Buck, Knight; and to the virtuous lady his wife, Grace and peace from God our Father and from our Lord Jesus Christ.

Right Worshipful, among the manifold points of Christian religion, the truth of the doctrine concerning predestination is worthy serious and sober study for the sound understanding thereof. For first, it is something difficult and obscure. Secondly, because it is by some eagerly impugned as a frivolous and forged invention of man's brain. Thirdly, divers opinions have passed from divers men diversely about this one point, whereas notwithstanding there is but one truth and one definite and constant sentence to be found in holy writ concerning it. Fourthly, this one doctrine does give very good evidence and an ample demonstration of God's infinite mercy and exact justice. Fifthly, it affords some taste of His profound and impenetrable counsel. Sixthly, it does notably manifest His admirable wisdom and policy and the incorruptible purity of His nature who wisely disposes all things and uses even evils without injustice and the least receipt of infusion of corruption—and all for the manifestation of the glory of His name and of the splendor of His renowned properties. Seventhly, it confounds the common cavil of many desperate and infatuated atheists who would make God's predestination the pillar of their sensual security and secure sensuality. Lastly, it ministers exceeding comfort to those who renouncing the kingdom of sin do live like saints in the kingdom of grace. First, because it is not possible for any such to sin with full consent of heart. Secondly, because no personal merits are required of them. Thirdly, because the Spirit of God abides in them, who is busy within the hive of their hearts as a bee and works them like wax. Fourthly, because God has eternally predestinated them to eternal joys, and those also incomprehensible and ineffable. Fifthly, because God has in abundance vouchsafed that to them being but a handful, which He has denied to whole heaps besides. Sixthly, for that they being elected can in no wise perish, for the counsel of the Lord shall stand forever (Ps. 33:11). And He loves them with an everlasting love (Jer. 3:4). Though a mother should forget her child, yet He will not forget them, for He has graven them upon the palm of His hand (Isa. 49:15–16) Therefore, He will confirm them to the end (1 Cor. 1:8) and by His power keep them to salvation (1 Peter 1:5). He will love them constantly, though He visit their transgressions with rods (Ps. 89:32–33). He will never turn away from them (Jer. 32:40), though He take them by the neck (as Job speaks, Job 16:12) and beat them, though He cut their reins and break them, and though He pours their gall upon the ground and runs upon them like a giant. Joseph did affect his brethren entirely, though he spake roughly to them. He may also sometimes let them fall as a loving nurse may her child, but He will lift them up again. Therefore, however they may fall,[1] yet they shall not fall away. Indeed, they may leave their first love, as the church of Ephesus did (Rev. 2:4), but they shall never leave to love at all, if ever they loved truly. For (as Paul says) "love does never fall away" (1 Cor. 13:8). It may be lessened, but it cannot be lost. In like manner, their faith may be covered as the sun with a dusky cloud in a gloomy day, or as the trees are with snow sometimes in winter. But yet it continues firmly fixed (though now and then eclipsed) in the sphere of the heart and keeps sap in the root. For the righteous man is as a tree planted by the rivers of waters (Ps. 1:3) and is built by that great builder of heaven and earth upon a rock (Matt. 16:18). These comforts will this one doctrine afford, being thoroughly pondered and understood. And no doubt these and the like considerations moved that holy and learned man of blessed memory to publish this present treatise for the benefit of the church; and the same have also incited us to turn it out of the tongue wherein he wrote it into the English for their profit who are ignorant in the other, and the rather because it is contrived and penned very plainly, soundly, and succinctly, as the subject will permit. The which, Right Worshipful, assuring ourselves of your unfeigned love to the truth, we do present and dedicate to you in token of deserved gratitude for undeserved kindness, not doubting of your courteous and kind acceptance. And thus we humbly take our leave, recommending you and all yours to the protection of Jehovah.

Rochester, this 19th of February, 1605.

Your Worships in all duty,
Francis Cacott and
Thomas Tuke

---

1. In the margin: Piptein. Ecpiptein.

To the Right Worshipful Master John Hayward Major, and the worshipful Jurates, his brethren, and the whole communality of the town and liberty of Fanersham.

Right Worshipful, as many other wholesome and heavenly doctrines grounded upon the Word of God have been and are to this day contradicted and impugned, even so it fares which[1] the divine and deep doctrine of God's predestination, a doctrine not more heavenly than wholesome nor more commodious than comfortable, and yet as heavenly and as commodious as any doctrine whatever which the Scriptures do afford. The Pelagians held that God predestinated men to life or death as He did foresee that they would by their natural free will receive or reject grace offered. They taught that it was in man's power to believe or not to believe. They placed the causes of salvation in men themselves out of God, and held that the elect might fall from grace and perish.

Others hold that albeit the Lord elects some of His mere mercy without respect of anything in them, that yet He rejects those which are rejected because He did foresee that they would reject His grace offered to them in the gospel. Some ubiquitaries[2] hold that Adam's fall came to pass without God's decree or any ordination of His; secondly, that no decree of God depends upon His simple will concerning the salvation of the godly or the rejection of the reprobate; thirdly, that God does utterly nill the reprobation of any; fourthly, that the reprobate may be converted and saved; fifthly, that Christ died for the reprobates, and that it is the purpose and will of God simply that all men without exception should be saved. Some do subject election to God's eternal decree, but not reprobation. Others, putting no difference between reprobation and damnation, do think as God does pass by some men of His mere pleasure, that He does in like sort damn them of His mere will and pleasure, whereas indeed sin is the cause why men are damned. Many of the Romish synagogue do teach that men are elected for their foreseen faith and meritorious works. And it is the common opinion of all papists that the elect cannot be certain and sure of their election unless it be extraordinarily by some special revelation and singular privilege. Many also there are which would not have this doctrine publicly taught by the minister, but without good reason. For

---

1. The original says "which" but probably should say "with."
2. *Ubiquitaries*: a Ubiquitarian; someone, especially a Lutheran, who believes that Christ in His human nature is present everywhere; *specifically* a member of a Protestant sect maintaining this belief.

first, as the minister must not search the secrets of God which are not revealed, so he must not suppress or hide that which is revealed. For things "revealed, belong to us and to our children forever" (Deut. 29:29), as Moses teaches. Therefore, as we may not search into those things which God will have kept secret, so we may in no wise be wholly ignorant of those things which He has revealed to us. But this doctrine of predestination is very plentifully and perspicuously revealed and delivered to us in the Scriptures. Secondly, as the Word of God omits nothing which is needful to be known touching the salvation of our souls, so we must know that it teaches nothing but that which is profitable and worthy to be learned of all. For that speech of Paul to the Romans is true of all the writings of the prophets and apostles also: "Whatsoever things were written, were written for our learning" (Rom. 15:4). But the Word of God does teach this doctrine of election and rejection, as is evident by many places therein. Therefore, it is necessary and fit to be taught of the minister and to be learned of the people. Thirdly, it is the duty of all faithful ministers to teach all the counsel of God, as Paul says he did (Acts 20:37). But predestination is a part of God's counsel. Therefore, it ought to be delivered of us to the people of God, always remembering that we apply ourselves to your capacities and teach it orderly (as occasion serves), keeping ourselves in all sobriety within the limits of the Word. Fourthly, Christ commands the gospel to be preached to every creature (Mark 16:15); but this doctrine belongs to the gospel and therefore is to be preached to the unlearned as to the learned. Lastly, all ministers are bound to keep back nothing which is profitable, but to show it as Paul did (Acts 20:20). But the doctrine of predestination is very profitable. For first, it lets us see the omniscience, the omnipotence, the sovereignty, and immutable nature of God. Secondly, it serves to increase and confirm our faith and hope concerning the eternal felicity of our souls and bodies, seeing it is not founded upon ourselves or upon any sandy foundation, but upon the constant and unchangeable good pleasure of God. Thirdly, it teaches us not to wonder at the small number of believers and at the hardness and blindness of many men's hearts and minds. For it shows that God has elected but a few (Matt. 20:16) and has passed by many, leaving them to themselves and delivering them up into the hands of the devil. Fourthly, it serves to strengthen and comfort us in all afflictions and to arm us against all the fiery darts of the devil and the fury of his limbs. For it shows that nothing can separate us from the love of God and that all things work for the best to them that love God (Rom. 8:28, 39), even to them that are called of His purpose. All storms and waves of woe shall pass over, and in the end we shall rest in the quiet haven of everlasting happiness. Fifthly, this doctrine stays us from taking offence at the apostasy of many professors; for it shows us that all is not gold which glitters, and that some stand for a time and some stand fast forever. "If they had been of us," says John, "they should have continued with us" (1 John 2:19). Sixthly, it teaches us to acknowledge God's singular goodness toward us, who of His mere good will toward us has elected us to eternal life and the fruition of immortal glory in the heavens. Seventhly, it serves to teach us humility and to beat down the pride of our hearts. For it shows that God's grace and not our goodness is the original cause of our welfare and salvation. The cause which moved God to choose us rather than many others was not our foreseen preparations or meritorious works, but His own love and free good will toward us. Lastly (to omit sundry uses which might be made of this one doctrine), it teaches us to ascribe the glory of our salvation to God alone and to walk thankfully before Him, manifesting the gratitude of our hearts by our religious, righteous, and sober lives. To conclude, some are so far out of love with this doctrine that they can scarce with patience endure to hear it spoken of. And many licentious and profane persons do very wickedly abuse it, to take to themselves liberty of licentious and loose living—"for," say they, "if I be ordained to be saved, I cannot be damned; and if damnation be my destiny, I can never be saved. And therefore it skilleth not how I live; for if God have appointed me to be saved, I shall be saved, though I do just nothing. And if He have determined that I shall be damned, I shall never escape it, though I live never so well. For God's decree is constant; His appointment shall stand, whoever says nay to it." But these men forget that God does predestinate men as well to use the means as to attain to the end. As He has appointed a man to live, so He has appointed the same man to use those means which preserve life, as meat, drink, rest, recreation, labor, physic. Even so, as He has appointed a man to be saved, He has appointed him to use the means and to walk in the way of salvation, as to believe. And therefore the Scripture says, "So many as were ordained to everlasting life believed" (Acts 13:48). And Paul shows that those God does call whom He has predestinated and justifies those whom He does effectually call before He glorifies them (Rom. 8:29). And in his epistle to the Ephesians, he teaches that as God has chosen us to life eternal, so He has also chosen us in Christ, "that we should be holy, and without blame before Him in love" (1:4); and that as He has ordained us to salvation, so He has "created us in Christ Jesus to good works, which He has ordained that we should walk in them" (2:10). As the Scripture teaches us that God has elected us to salvation, so it does also teach us that He sent His Son to save us. As God had determined that Christ should not die in His infancy (as the event declared), so He did appoint His father-in-law Joseph to take Him and His mother and to fly into Egypt (Matt. 2:13), when Herod sought to destroy Him. By which we see that as God has predestinated the end, so He has also predestinated the way and means thereto. He therefore that desires to be saved must use the means which God has appointed. His damnation may not without cause be feared, who following the sway of his carnal affections contemns or neglects the means of grace (1 Sam. 2:25) and will not walk in the way which leads to glory. But we (beloved), rejecting all the fancies and fantastic inventions of man, must rectify our judgments by the rule of God's Word; and with discreet diligence and sobriety we ought to labor for the true knowledge and right understanding of this celestial and solacious doctrine of God's eternal predestination, a doctrine not so profound as profitable, and not so abstruse and intricate, as many do imagine. A notable furtherance hereto this treatise following will afford, penned pithily, concisely, and perspicuously by a very learned and judicious divine. Now (my brethren) among many other things which belong to this doctrine, there be two things which I do commend to your Christian consideration. First, the privileges of God's elect and adopted children. Secondly, the notes of election to salvation and the practice of those things whereby a man may come to be in his conscience soundly persuaded that he is a chosen vessel predestinated to eternal life. For the first, many and excellent are the prerogatives and immunities wherewith the elect are privileged and adorned. Therefore, the psalmist says, "Glorious things are spoken of thee, O thou City of God" (Ps. 87:3). And yet as glorious and numerous as they be, they are not easily discerned and acknowledged of the world, first, because their disgrace is common and public by reason of the spiteful and inveterate malice of the serpent and his seed, whereby it comes to pass that the faithful in all ages have acted a part longer or shorter in a doleful tragedy upon the stage of the world, so as that of all men they have always for the most part seemed most miserable and least respected of man and privileged of God. Secondly, because sundry slips and sins have been observed in them. Thirdly, the upright man is such an abomination to the wicked (Prov. 29:27), as that through his cankered spite, his spiteful and rancorous hatred, he cannot behold and fancy his sweet and lovely condition. Fourthly, the principal ornaments of the godly are dark and spiritual, as the psalmist says, "The king's daughter is all glorious within" (Ps. 45:13); and their outward estate is usually obscure, coarse, and ragged, not much unlike to the curtains of the tabernacle, whose outward coverings were of goats' hair, rams' skins, and badgers', but the inward were of fine twined linen, blue silk, purple and scarlet, with the most exquisite embroidering of the cherubim upon them (Exodus 26).

The world, to God's children is as a stepmother, and may be termed God's school house, in which He trains up His children as scholars[3] under the cross, often correcting them with His rod of affliction. Whence it is that the world

---

3. *Scholars*: students.

accounts them unfortunate; and being unable to judge of colors through the dimness of her sight, she considers and commands none but such as are light, though they weary and lose their brightness while she is poring on them. But although the world be bleary eyed and dim-sighted, yet those which are elected out of the world do feel and see and can say much. And the Word of God contains in it many royal and notable privileges and dignities properly belonging to those whom God has elected and adopted, some whereof I will briefly and plainly here set down.

Privilege 1. The first dignity is their glorious and honorable styles and titles. They are called in the Scriptures the people, the redeemed, the sons, the building, the husbandry and household servants of God, the brethren, the spouse, the members, the seed and the sheep of Christ, the temples of the Holy Ghost, the seed, the sons and the daughters of Abraham. They are called lively stones, a spiritual house, heirs of the promise, saints, faithful, kings, priests, yea a holy and princely priesthood, a peculiar people challenged of God, a chosen generation, and a holy nation.

Privilege 2. The faithful and chosen children of God alone have true title to all the outward blessings of God; for they only believe, and they are only God's obedientaries (Isa. 1:19; 1 Tim. 4:3). Reprobates are but indeed usurpers of them in His sight. We lost them in Adam, and we receive right neither in them nor to them, but by Christ. His passions have purchased our possessions.

Privilege 3. The elect only can use God's blessings to a right end and in a right manner. For they only are pure (being purged in the blood of Christ), and they only can pray with a true faith. The wicked make their riches their own ruin and God's benefits their own bane, and either abuse them or use them not as He commands them and causes His own children by His grace to use them.

Privilege 4. God has appointed His holy angels, which for their strength and fortitude are called gods (Ps. 8:5), to guard and protect His people. "The angel of the Lord," says David, "pitcheth round about them that fear Him" (Ps. 34:7). And the apostle says that they "are all ministering spirits, sent forth to minister for their sakes which shall be heirs of salvation" (Heb. 1:14).

Privilege 5. The Lord has honored His elect and no doubt yet does and will (when it pleases Him) by preserving them and providing for them very effectually, and sometimes also very wonderfully (Jer. 36:26). He saved Noah from drowning, Lot from burning, Elijah from famishing, Mordecai from murder, and Paul from those bloody votaries,[4] by providing for them very kindly. He saved Samson miraculously from perishing by thirst, and Daniel from the

---

4. *Votaries*: one who is passionately devoted to a particular pursuit.

teeth of the lions. David says, "The Lord drew him out of many waters, and delivered him from the cruel man, and gave him great deliverances" (Ps. 18:16, 48, 50). He did often and strangely also preserve our late queen of holy and happy memory from the desperate and malicious attempts of popish traitors, set a-work by the devil to murder her. He prolonged her days; He held the crown on her head and kept the scepter in her hand with peace and prosperity, the time and tyranny of nine or ten monsters her mortal enemies,[5] though their slaves continually plotted and practiced against her, and though the prince of the air thundered against her in his lieutenants (as it were from the clouds) with curses and cursed excommunications.[6] Lately also He has vouchsafed an admirable deliverance to His anointed our gracious king, and to us all from a most barbarous and horrible confusion. And of this kind of favor and favorable dealing used of the Lord, we may read plentifully in divine and ecclesiastical stories. And no doubt the wicked have sometimes fared the better for the elect's sake, as Laban did for Jacob (Gen. 30:27) and Potiphar for Joseph (39:5), and those which sailed in that dangerous voyage to Rome for Paul, who was in their company (Acts 27:24). God told Abraham that if there were but ten righteous persons in Sodom, He would not destroy it for their sakes (Gen. 18:32). Eliphaz says that the innocent shall deliver the island (Job 22:30), meaning that God does often deliver a whole country from peril for the just man's sake.

Privilege 6. For His elect God has altered the course of nature. He divided the waters of the Red Sea, that His people might pass dry-shod through it (Ex. 14:22). He caused the sun to stay and the moon to stand still till His people had avenged themselves upon their enemies (Josh. 10:12). For Gideon's sake, He caused the dew to fall only upon a fleece of wool and kept it from falling upon the ground (Judg. 8:38, 40), and afterward at his request He let it fall on the earth and kept the fleece dry. For Hezekiah's sake, He brought the shadow to the dial of Ahaz ten degrees backward (Isa. 38:8) by the which degrees the sun was gone down.

Privilege 7. God does often preserve His chosen children from perils then when He does persecute the wicked. "Many sorrows," says David, "shall befall the wicked, but he that trusteth in the Lord, shall be compassed of mercy" (Ps. 32:10). Noah was delivered when the wicked were drowned. The Israelites passed when the Egyptians perished. When Sodom was burned, Lot was brought forth (Gen. 19:16). When Jericho was sacked, Rahab was saved. When Ahab was slain, Jehoshaphat escaped. When Jerusalem was to be destroyed, the

---

5. In the margin: Paul V, Pius IV, Pius V, Gregory XIII, Sixtus V, Urban VII, Gregory XIV, Innocent IX, Clement VIII.

6. In the margin: Pius V, Gregory XIII, Sixtus V.

Lord commanded the godly to be branded that they might be preserved (Ezek. 9:4). Moreover, when the Lord delivers His own people, then He does sometimes thrust the wicked into their dangers. "The righteous," says Solomon, "escapeth out of trouble, and the wicked shall come in his stead" (Prov. 11:8). And as He does usually cross their cursed counsels, so He does oftentimes curse their malicious and bloody enterprises and cracks them upon their own crowns and breaks them upon their own backs. Haman was hanged on that gallows (Esth. 7:9) which he himself had prepared for Mordecai, whom the king did greatly advance. Daniel was brought from the lions (Dan. 6:23–24), and his accusers being cast into the den among them were devoured of them. God preserved Shadrach, Meshach, and Abednego in the hot fiery furnace (3:22), and slew the men with the flame of the fire that brought them forth to be burned. The Lord delivered good Jehoshaphat and caused his enemies that came against him to help forward their own destruction (2 Chron. 20:23). The Lord has delivered us from these barbarous and blood-thirsty Catholics and has for the honor of His mercy pulled the rotten house of their devilish inventions upon their own heads. His name be praised forever and ever, amen.

Privilege 8. Christ has altered the nature of afflictions to His elect and faithful members. For whereas they are cast upon the wicked as punishments due to them for their sins wherein they live, they are inflicted upon the godly by God as a merciful father that desires the amendment of His children (Ps. 8:31–32; Hab. 12:6). Because our hearts are drowsy, the Lord as our most skillful founder casts us into the furnace of afflictions, that He might refine us. Because we are subject to transgress and go astray, the Lord imparts us within the pales of adversity and hedges us about with the thorny quick-set[7] of the cross, that we might be kept in some compass. David says, "Before I was afflicted, I went astray, but now I keep Thy Word" (Ps. 119:67). Because we are by nature toward that which is good, the Lord uses the cross as a schoolmaster to instruct us. Therefore, David says, "It is good for me that I have been afflicted, that I may learn Thy statutes" (v. 71). Because we are by nature inclined to the love of the world, the Lord as our nurse does wean us from the love thereof by affliction, as the mother or nurse drives her child from the breast by rubbing it with some bitter thing. To be brief, the Lord by afflictions executes our faith and patience, learns us humility, and teaches us how to esteem prosperity. By affliction, He makes us to take experience of His love and of those graces which He has given us. By afflictions, He learns us to be merciful to the miserable, for the sense of sickness and the feeling of poverty through God's blessing is a notable means to make us pity the poor and the sick. The apostle says, "Our light affliction, which

---

7. *Quick-set*: a hedge, dense thicket, or fence.

is but for a moment, worketh to us a far more excellent, and an eternal weight of glory" (2 Cor. 4:17), though not as a cause procuring it (for we are saved by grace, and everlasting life is the free gift of God in Christ) (Eph. 2:8). Yet as a way and means directing and leading us thereto (Rom. 6:23), Christ has two crowns: the one of thorns; the other of glory. He that will be honored with the last must be humbled and tried with the first. Thus, it is evident that God shows Himself a father in afflicting His children. But as for the reprobate, His crosses are curses, and His afflictions are forerunners of further judgments inflicted and sent of God as a severe and dreadful judge.

Privilege 9. God has altered the nature of death to all the elect. For Christ by His death has been the death of death and the death of sin, which is the sting and strength of death. First of all, God by death teaches us to detest sin and to acknowledge the severity and sharpness of His anger against it. Secondly, by death He delivers us utterly from the body of sin. Till death we attain not to perfection, and at death sin is wholly consumed. When we die, sin dies. For sin is something like ivy, which falls down and dies when the tree on which it hanged is cut down. Thirdly, the Lord does sometimes take away His children by death, that they should not see those evils which He has purposed to plague His enemies withal. "Merciful men are taken away," says Isaiah, "and no man understandeth that the righteous is taken away from the evil to come" (57:1). So the Lord took away good Josiah (2 Chron. 34:28), that his eyes might not see all the evil which He purposed to bring upon that place. Yea, such is His love to His saints that He cannot do that to the wicked which He would, so long as they live among them. As the angel told Lot (Gen. 19:32) that He could do nothing till he was gone out of Sodom, even so it may be truly said that God's love is so fervent toward His chosen as that it sometimes keeps Him from scattering His judgments in those places wherein they live. Therefore, He does often remove them by death that He may more freely pour out the vials of His wrath upon the ungodly. Fourthly, by death God learns us to seek a place of rest and to alienate our affections from the world, which being like to bird lime,[8] would otherwise more easily belime our affections, that they could not soar up to the heavens, the place of our home. Fifthly, by death the Lord humbles us and teaches us not to prank and plume up our bodies like peacocks, as if we meant to live forever. Sixthly, the Lord by their deaths occasions their experience and feeling of the virtue of Christ's resurrection. Lastly, as death is the complement of mortification and ends the battle between the flesh and the spirit, so it fully finishes all earthly calamities; and as a ferry it transports us over the tempestuous and broad ocean of tribulations and afflictions into the calm and quiet haven of

---

8. *Bird lime*: a glutinous substance spread upon twigs to catch and ensnare birds.

endless happiness. But as for the reprobate, it is to them as a boat to carry them out of a river of earthly miseries into a restless and bottomless sea of infinite and ineffable torments. And because their felicity (if any) consists in the finite fruition of worldly prosperity, God in His appointed time by death as by a knife cuts asunder the thread of life and so casts them out of their paradise and sends their souls to the place of the damned, where they shall continue terribly tormented till that doleful and dismal day of vengeance.

Privilege 10. God has ordained the writing of His Word, the preaching of it, the administration of the sacraments, and His dispensers of them principally and properly for the benefit of the elect. Saint Paul says, "Whatsoever things are written aforetime, are written for our learning, that we through patience and comfort of the Scriptures, might have hope" (Rom. 15:4). John says he wrote that we might believe in the name of Christ (1 John 5:13). Therefore, his writings properly belong to the children of God. And the apostle, writing to the Ephesians, says that Christ gave some to be apostles, and some prophets, and some evangelists, and some pastors and doctors—but to what end? "For the reparation of the saints, and for the edification of Christ's body" (Eph. 4:12). And this is no small prerogative. For the sacraments are signs and seals of God's grace. The preaching of the gospel is the power of God to salvation to all that do believe. In His Word, He has recorded His will. And His ministers are as it were His trumpeters which do sound in our ears and trumpets of His law and gospel and instruct us when to stand still, when to retire, and when and how to march forward. They are through His assistance our spiritual fathers by whom He does procreate and beget us to Himself for our good and His own glory. Now all these things profit the reprobate nothing at all, but do indeed through the rebellious corruption of their hearts harden and stiffen them, as the sun does clay.

Privilege 11. The Lord has united all His elect and dear children to Christ by His Spirit and by a true and lively faith. And by reason of this union, they are after a sort united to the whole Trinity: Father, Son, and Holy Ghost. Yea, hence it is that we are partakers of Christ's benefits. For as the members of the body have neither sense nor motion unless they be united to the head, and as the giraffe receives no nourishment except it be set in the flock and grow up with it, even so, unless we be united to Christ our stock and spiritual head, we have no spiritual life and motion, neither are we actually partakers of His benefits. But being once united and knit to Him, we receive sense and sap, life and motion.

Privilege 12. All the elect and faithful people of God are partakers of the prayers of all the godly throughout the world. The children of God have fellowship one with another, as with Christ, their head. Whereas on the contrary, they pray for the confusion and final destruction of His and their impenitent, pestilent, and irreconcilable enemies, and cannot but hate and abandon those whom they see to walk perversely in wicked and reprobate courses without remorse of conscience and all show of repentance. For God has put a secret antipathy and mortal enmity between His seed and the seed of the serpent. Therefore, Solomon says, "A wicked man is an abomination to the just, and he that is upright in his way, is an abomination to the wicked" (Prov. 29:27). And as David says, "The wicked practiseth against the just, and gnasheth his teeth against him" (Ps. 37:12). So he also says thus of himself, "I have hated them that give themselves to deceitful vanities" (31:6). And again, "Do not I hate them, O Lord, that hate Thee? I hate them with the perfection of hatred, as if they were mine utter enemies" (139:21). And in the fifteenth psalm, contemning of a vile person—that is, of a wicked wretch—and the honoring of the godly are made an infallible note of a faithful member of the church (v. 4). By which it appears that there is no sincere and solid communion between God's children and the slaves of the devil. And therefore it is one of our privileges and peculiar dignities to enjoy the love and lovely communion of the saints.

Privilege 13. Faith, by which we walk and live, by which we are justified and adopted, without which it is impossible to please God (Heb. 11:6)—this faith, which is a supernatural gift of God above corrupt and created nature, this faith (I say) is peculiar and proper to the elect (Acts 13:48). Therefore, St. Paul calls it "the faith of the elect" (Titus 1:1) and teaches the Thessalonians (2 Thess. 3:2) that it is not common to all men. Secondly, hope is an excellent gift of God (Rom. 5:5), for it makes not ashamed; and by it the apostle says we are saved—that is, by hope we expect and wait for that salvation (8:24) which by faith we apprehend and assure ourselves of for the invaluable merits of Christ. Now, this grace is not given to any besides the elect. For how can the reprobate hope to be saved, seeing they are appointed for the day of evil (Prov. 16:4) and are reserved to the day of destruction (Job 21:30) and shall be brought forth to the day of wrath? Thirdly, love, which springs out of a pure heart (1 Tim. 1:5) and flows from a good conscience and faith unfeigned is given only to God's elect. For it is not possible for the reprobate to love God to that end and in that manner which God requires, seeing He has cast them off from all eternity and purposed not to give them any saving grace, considering also that they are by nature void of purity and do live and die in sin. Now this privilege is the greater, because this grace is very rare and excellent. Love is (as it were) a knife wherewith faith shares and cuts out the duties which we do owe to God and man in some good and acceptable manner. Love is the cock[9] which lets out the water of God's graces out of the cistern of our hearts. Love

---

9. *Cock*: a tap for regulating or stopping the flow of liquids.

is the nurse of humanity, the mother of equity, the maintainer of virtue, the daughter of faith, the preserver of piety, the mistress of modesty, the badge of Christianity, the bane of discord, the staff of concord (Col. 3:14), the keeper of the crown (Job 13:35), the bond of perfection, and the note of a true disciple. Saint Paul in some sort prefers it to faith and hope when he says, "Now abideth faith, hope and love: but the choicest of these is love" (1 Cor. 13:13). By which we see that the Lord has highly honored us in that He confers this glorious grace to none but us. Lastly, that filial fear, which is the beginning of wisdom (Prov. 9:10) and the well spring of life (14:27), to avoid the snares of death, and which makes a man to keep the golden rule of mediocrity, is given only to God's elect. For how can the reprobate, who do love sin and do not love God—how (I say) can they fear to displease Him, because they hate sin and love Him? Or how can the reprobate, who are all ordained to inevitable and eternal perdition, be said to fear God as a son fears his loving father, seeing they be slaves, and considering that the Word of God pronounces him happy and blessed (Ps. 112:4) who stands in awe of God and fears to offend Him? If the reprobate be blessed, then of all men the elect are most accursed. But we shall say that those are blessed whom the Lord has accursed, if we shall say that the reprobate do fear God with that fear whereof I now speak.

Privilege 14. God accounts those injuries as done to Himself which the wicked offer to His faithful servants (2 Chron. 14:11; Nah. 1:9). Saul persecuted the true professors of Christ, yet Christ told him from heaven that he persecuted Him (Acts 9:4). The afflictions of God's children are called in the Scriptures "Christ's afflictions" (Col. 1:24). For such is the union and communion between the head and the members, that if any of them smart, the head is partaker of the grief (Rev. 11:8). If any part be crazed or annoyed, the heart is ready to mourn, the head to consult, the tongue to bewail and utter it, the foot to run to the surgeon, and the hand is ready to do her duty. Even so it is between Christ and His members. If any of them be injuriously vexed and troubled, He takes the wrong as done to Himself. And so Christ may be said to be crucified in that great city which is mystically called Sodom and Babylon—that is, Rome—because He is there put to death in His members and is in them (as it were) slain continually by Romish authority, as He was by it (if we speak properly) crucified and put to death.[10] So in like manner the Lord says, "He which toucheth you, toucheth the apple of Mine eye" (Zech. 1:8). And as Christ esteems of those good deeds which men do to them as done to Himself (Matthew 25), even so He accounts

---

10. In the margin: Romish authority is either heathenish, or popish. Christ died by the former, but in His members He has died by both, and yet does by the latter.

the bare neglecting and the not relieving of them in their wants as if the wicked had been in this kind of duty faulty to Himself.

Privilege 15. God will shorten the world and hasten the coming of His Son for the elect. And so that speech of Christ may be understood, "For the elect's sake those evil days shall be shortened" (24:22). Moreover, such is the patience and good will of God to His elect, as that He stays His coming for a time because He would (as Peter affirms, 2 Peter 3:9) have none of them to perish, but come to repentance, that when He comes they may be welcome to Him, and He to them.

Privilege 16. God does effectually call the elect, and none besides them; and they alone are justified in His sight (Rom. 8:30). For He does pardon them alone, and they only are clothed with the spotless robes of Christ's perfect righteousness. Therefore, the prophet says, "The chastisement of our peace was upon Him. The Lord has laid upon Him the iniquity of us all. For the transgression of My people was He plagued. By His knowledge shall My righteous Servant justify many. He bare the sins of many" (Isa. 53:5–7, 11–12). He does not say "all." For He came to save His own people only from their sins (Matt. 1:21). He did not so much as pray for the reprobate (John 17:9). Now this is a very great and admirable privilege and honor, that God should send His only Son to die for us few despicable wretches, and that Christ should lose His life and shed His heart blood for us only, whereas it was in itself (being the blood of God) sufficient to have redeemed a thousand thousand worlds of sinners (Acts 20:28). If a man had a medicine able to cure all diseases and would not give it any saving some few, they were wonderfully indebted to him. The blood of Christ is able to heal all our soul-sicknesses and to deliver us from all our sins. And it has pleased Him to wash us alone in it and to withhold it from the far greater part of mankind. By which we see how highly He has honored us, and how deep we are in His debt. If three men were in danger of drowning or burning, and a man should come and deliver one of them and leave the other two to the danger, all men might well say that he favored him more than the other. By our sins we were all in danger to be drowned in that sulphury lake and to be consumed with the fire of God's wrath, as well as the reprobates. Our sins deserve it. But Christ has set Himself between His Father and us. He has taken no notice (as it were) of them; and us only, who are elected, He has redeemed. As the Lord drowned the Egyptians only in the sea, so Christ has overwhelmed our sins only in His blood. And as the propitiatory covered the ark and the Decalogue, so Christ covers His elect with His blood and hides them, yea them alone, from the wrath of God. And therefore Paul calls Him the Savior of His body (Eph. 5:23). By which we see His grace and good will is far greater to us than to them.

Privilege 17. It is impossible through the virtue of God's decree and Christ's merits that any of the elect should fall into the sin against the Holy Ghost, into which some reprobates have rushed.

Privilege 18. The elect being once actually redeemed have liberty to serve and worship God without fear of any evil (Luke 1:74). They serve Him chiefly for His love and for conscience of His commandments. The wicked seem to serve Him oftentimes, but it is for some sinister respect, as for fear of damnation (as the slave obeys his master for fear of the whip) or for fear of imprisonment or an ill name, or else for the love of lucre or the desire of glory or credit with men.

Privilege 19. The elect alone do merit at God's hands, for they being alone partakers of Christ's meritorious righteousness do also alone, it being accounted as their own, merit everlasting life of God. Now is not this an exceeding great favor, that we being but worms (Job 25:6) should deserve everlasting happiness of so high a majesty? It does greatly commend the love of God to us, and the rather because He has graced us only with the inestimable merits of His Son, refusing to impart them to many millions of men as noble, as wise, as learned, as beautiful, as mighty, and as wealthy as ourselves.

Privilege 20. The elect being once effectually called do sin thenceforward only of infirmity. Therefore, St. John says that "whosoever is born of God, sinneth not" (1 John 3:9)—that is, with full consent of will. For so far forth as he is regenerate, he does not sin. Wherefore, Paul in the person of all true believers says, "If I do that I would not"—meaning evil—"it is no more I that do it, but the sin that dwelleth in me" (Rom. 7:20). But on the contrary, wickedness (as Job shows, Job 20:12) is sweet in the wicked man's mouth. He hides it under his tongue; he savors it; he will not forsake it, but keeps it close in his mouth. His sin is as his soul. And therefore Solomon says he cannot sleep except he have done evil (Prov. 4:16). And the prophet Isaiah shows that the wicked is so soldered to his sin as that he will not learn righteousness, though mercy be showed to him (Isa. 26:10). In the land of uprightness, where true religion is commanded, countenanced, and professed, he will do wickedly, neither respecting God's merciful dealing nor the good examples of the godly. Whereas the faithful detest and abhor their corruptions and struggle against them, striving and desiring to be delivered of them, as a prisoner of his bolts or as those which are troubled with the disease *incubus*,[11] called the nightmare, desire or struggle to be rid thereof.

Privilege 21. The Scriptures do teach that God has made peace between the creatures and His children. The stones of the field are in league with them

---

11. *Incubus*: a person or thing that oppresses someone during sleep, like a nightmare.

(Job 5:23), and the beasts of the field are at peace with them. The Lord by His prophet Hosea says that He will make a covenant for them with the wild beasts (Hos. 2:18) and with the fowls of the heaven and with that which creeps upon the earth (Ex. 11:7). Do we not read that the sea made way to the Israelites and overwhelmed their enemies which pursued them (14:22, 28)? Do we not read that ravens fed the prophet Elijah (1 Kings 17:6)? Do we not read that the hungry lions favored Daniel, and that the fire spared the three children? Did not a star conduct the wise men to the place where our Lord lay (Matt. 2:9)? Did not the Lord make a covenant for His servant Jonah with the whale, whose teeth (as the Scripture says) are terrible, and by His might He makes the depth to boil like a pot (Job 14:5, 22)? And did He not make a bond of peace for Paul with the venomous viper (Acts 28:5), when he being upon his hand he received no hurt, though the barbarians waited when he should have swollen or fallen down suddenly dead? On the contrary, we read that He drowned the wicked world with water and burned the filthy Sodomites with fire. He met with ambitious Absalom with[12] a tree and slew those wicked children which mocked the prophet Elisha with bears (2 Kings 2:24). He made the dogs to eat the flesh of wicked Jezebel (9:36) and destroyed Herod, that cruel and vain-glorious king, with worms (Acts 12:23). He plagued the Egyptians with frogs, flies, and lice (Exodus 8). Yea, the Lord has all creatures in heaven and earth ready (when it pleases Him) to run upon the wicked and reprobate, as a grey-hound upon his game when the leash is taken off, which He manifests when He says by Jeremiah, "I will," etc. (Jer. 15:3).

Privilege 22. The elect, being once forgiven of God and accepted to ever-lasting life for the merits of Christ, have joy unspeakable and that peace which passes all understanding. "The kingdom of God," says the apostle, "standeth in peace and joy in the Holy Ghost" (Rom. 14:17). If the health of body be such a thing as is rather with comfort enjoyed than in words to be expressed, how great shall we think is the peace of conscience and joy in the Holy Ghost? It may be tasted, but it cannot be expressed. The malefactor has great peace and quietness with himself when the king has granted him his pardon; even so the elect should have great peace and tranquility of mind, when as God, the great King of heaven and earth, has pardoned their sins (Rom. 5:7) and received them to favor. But on the contrary, the reprobate and irreconcilable sinners, that sell themselves to work wickedness and drink iniquity like water, have either no peace at all but are like the raging sea that cannot rest (Isa. 57:20), whose wasters call up mire and dirt, or else are senseless like stocks, laboring

---

12. The original uses "with" twice in the first part of this sentence, despite its awkwardness.

of a spiritual apoplexy and a devilish, dead palsy, being sunk into the gulf of security and having made a league with death and a covenant with hell.

Privilege 23. The elect have an altar whereupon if they lay all their prescribed sacrifices, they shall be accepted of God, as smelling sweetly in His nostrils. But the reprobate and all their sacrifices are odious and abominable in His sight. They want our altar Christ Jesus, who should purge and sanctify their offerings and by whom they should offer them to the Father—and therefore their goodly sacrifices are but goodly sins.

Privilege 24. God gives His Holy Spirit to His elect only, who in God's appointed time makes His habitation in them, who does also sweep the floors of their spirits with the hand of His grace and the beesome[13] of His word and trims up the houses of their hearts with the sweet and pleasant flowers of His Spirit and adorns them with the costly tapestry and precious ornaments of His orient and excellent graces. He perfumed them (as it were) with frankincense and coals of juniper. He builds windows within them, that they may receive the bright and beautiful beams and lovely light, which do shine from the Sun of Righteousness. He constitutes a kingdom within them. He rules them with the strength of His arm and the scepter of His word. He stablishes His throne with justice and mercy. He softens the part regenerate; He bridles and tames the rebel, even the rebellious corruption of the heart, and by little and little consumes it. As for the reprobate, their hearts are the dens of the devil and the cabins of sin, stinking loathsomely like a dead carrion. There is indeed a kingdom within them; but the devil is the king, sin is the queen. His throne is wickedness; his scepter is iniquity; his laws are the liberty of the flesh; his rewards are death; and they are his slaves and vassals.

Privilege 25. As the elect may have grace, so it is possible for them to grow in grace. Therefore, Peter exhortes us "to grow in grace, and in the knowledge of Christ" (2 Peter 3:18) and shows also how we may grow (1 Peter 2:2). But for the reprobate, as they are void of all true saving grace, so they grow not therein; for they cannot increase in that which they want. A man cannot grow in bigness, unless he have a body. A man cannot grow rich, unless he have riches. They may increase in sin and grow in wickedness, as clay does in hardness when the weather is dry, or as the rivers do in depth and breadth when the tide comes. Again, whereas the Lord does very often give the reins to the reprobate and suffers them to rush headlong into horrible enormities, as the Gadarenes' swine did into the sea, He does mercifully preserve His own people and graciously keeps them oftentimes from declining and falling. And whenever they either stumble or fall, they may recover themselves by serious

---

13. *Beesome*: an agent that cleanses, sweeps away, or purifies things material or immaterial.

and sound repentance. But God has not vouchsafed the gift of godly sorrow and true repentance to the reprobate. It belongs only to God's elect. We may read of David's repentance, of Peter's falling and rising, of Paul's conversion; but we never read of any true turning (to turn truly is to return from all sin to God) that ever any reprobate made. If any of them repent, it is but for fashion's sake or for fear of punishment. It is not for love to God, or for the hatred of sin for sin, or for the consideration of God's love to them. As lead being cast into the water cannot but sink, so the reprobate cannot but sin. And as a millstone lying in the bottom of the sea cannot come up, so the reprobate being overwhelmed in the bottomless pit of iniquity cannot repent. Though it were possible to remove a mountain out of his place, yet it were more impossible to remove a reprobate from his corruptions. He may move, but he will not remove. He may turn, but he cannot return. As it is impossible for him to revive who is ordained to perpetual death, so it is impossible for him to revive from sin whom the fountain of all life has righteously forsaken and delivered forever to Satan to hold captive in the grave of sin and in the dark and deadly dungeon of iniquity.

Privilege 26. The children of God have the spirit of prayer and with boldness may approach to the throne of His grace and put up their suits to Him. The king will permit a true subject to come into his presence and speak to him, when a rebel or traitor shall find no such favor. A king's son may speak to his father, when others are not permitted so to do. We are the sons of God and the servants of His Son. Therefore, we may boldly in the name of our elder brother present ourselves before Him and put up our supplications to Him, and the rather because He knows and approves us. For as the apostle says, "The foundation of God remaineth sure, and has this seal, The Lord knoweth who are His" (2 Tim. 2:19). But the reprobate and their prayers are abominable in His sight. They want the spirit of prayer and either cannot pray at all, or not in the right manner. Neither can they approach with boldness to God, seeing they have no part in Christ, nor Christ in them. They cannot pray with confidence to be heard, seeing they are destitute as well of faith as of the favor of God.

Privilege 27. God accepts the sincere will and fervent desires of His faithful and elect children to believe, repent, and obey for faith, repentance, and obedience. For "as a father has compassion on his children, so has the Lord compassion on them that fear Him" (Ps. 103:13). "He will spare them, as a man spareth his own son" (Mal. 3:17). But fathers use to take in good part their children's works, so they do them with care and diligence, though not so perfectly and exactly as indeed were meet. In like manner, if we will and with an honest heart desire to do well, though we do it very weakly, God does notwithstanding take all in good part and regards not the imperfection of the work. A desire of grace is one degree of grace, and a will to do well is with God accounted doing well. Therefore, Paul says, "If there be a willing mind, it is accepted according to that a man has, and not according to that he has not" (2 Cor. 8:12). That which he says of giving alms is true in the performance of all other duties. If there be in a man a ready and willing mind to believe, repent, and obey, though he do not these things perfectly or so well as many of his brethren do, yet God for the merits and intercession of His Son accepts both of him and his imperfect works and in mercy rewards him. David, besides his daily infirmities, did thrice grievously offend God; and yet He told Solomon that if he would walk before Him as David, his father, He would establish the throne of his kingdom (2 Chron. 7:17), so as that he should not want a man to be a ruler in Israel. And albeit in that place He requires that he should do according to all His commandments, whereby He may seem to exact perfect (and therefore impossible) obedience, yet if we consider all things well, it will plainly appear that He means no other thing than that he should labor and seek to please Him in all things—because He sits his father David before his eyes as a pattern to follow, and because elsewhere we read that He makes the same promise to him, only requiring of him "to endeavor himself to do His commandments" (28:7) as he had begun. Now this is a very comfortable doctrine. For when a man considers that God respects his weak obedience and honest heart and accounts the will to do for the deed done, his heart is eased, his conscience is appeased, his mind is settled; and beholding the infinite love of God he is ravished with joy and provoked to magnify His mercy and to struggle against the corruption of his heart to please Him in doing all things which are pleasing in His sight. Now, lest we should beguile ourselves (for man's heart is a mine of subtlety) in thinking we desire and will to believe, repent, and obey, when as we either do not at all or do but as a reprobate may do, I will set down some rules which as the touchstone tries gold and as Solomon's sword found out the right mother, so these may serve to discover the truth of our desires and to desert the goodness of our wills. First of all, if we be grieved that we can desire and will no better than we do. Secondly, if we do desire and will to do these things for the glory of God, and because we are persuaded that both these things and the willing of them are pleasing to God. Thirdly, if we strive to increase in willing and desiring, and if we feed them with the diligent hearing of God's word, with holy meditations, with often prayers, and with setting before us the ensamples of excellent men, as the priests kept the fire upon the altar and fed it continually and suffered it not to go out (Lev. 6:12). Fourthly, if to our wills and desires we join reformation of our lives and in our several callings labor accordingly to serve God. Fifthly, if in our hearts we prefer eternal serving of God in heaven before all momentary profits and pleasures whatever. Sixthly, if we had rather live in a continual cross all our life long, but yet pleasing God and being in His favor, than spend the same in sinful pleasures, continually displeasing His majesty. Seventhly, if we desire and will to serve Him and to return home to Him from all our sins, though we were verily persuaded that there were no hell. Lastly, if we had rather please God, His rod of correction being always exercised upon us, than live without remorse of conscience against our knowledge, in profitable and pleasant sins, continually vexing and displeasing God our gracious Father, though we were certainly (as it were by oracle from heaven) assured that we should at the last gasp repent and be saved, notwithstanding our former rebellion and horrible disloyalty. If we desire and will to believe, repent, and obey, and find these things in us, then our desires will go for currant, God will accept of them and approve them.

Privilege 28. The Lord indeed suffers His children to fall, but it is to let them see that their standing is by His grace and to show them that He is not obliged with any bond of their merits (which are just none) to sustain and uphold them. He does it also to make them cling the closer about Him and to seek more earnestly for His assistance, as the little child screeches out for help when it is fallen and lies flat sprawling upon the ground. He does it to humble them and to abate their natural pride; and as He lets them fall in love, so by their falls He manifests His wisdom and integrity and shows His admirable compassion and humanity in forgiving and in raising them up again. But the falls of the reprobate kindle the coals of God's wrath against them. And further their full and final perdition, they serve to increase their sin and consequently their pains. They serve for punishments sometimes of former offences. And by committing one sin in the neck of another, they put out the light of nature. They harden their hearts and fit themselves for further wickedness, even as the stithy[14] becomes the harder by striking. I grant indeed that oftentimes they are grievously galled and perplexed with their sins. But it is not a sorrow that causes repentance to salvation never to be repented of. And usually it fares with them as it does with young hat makers or such as use to play at stool ball.[15] In the beginning, their fingers may blister, and their hand may ache; but after a while, their hands become hard and brawny and are well armed for such works. And the more they practice, the less pain they feel. So the custom of sinning takes away the sense of the sin. And as the dropsy man, the more he drinks, the drier he is; so the reprobate—the more he falls, the more he fancies falling.

Privilege 29. It is not possible that any of the elect should be damned or that any of them being soundly converted should wholly for a time (much less forever) fall away from God and perish. For God's decree of election (2 Tim.

---

14. *Stithy*: an anvil.

15. *Stool ball*: an old country game somewhat resembling cricket, played chiefly by young women or, sometimes, between young men and women.

2:19) is constant, and His counsel (Isa. 46:10) shall stand. "Him that cometh to Me," says Christ, "I cast not away" (John 6:37)—that is, "I do not cast off or eject him that embraces Me with the hand and arms of a lively faith and testifies the same with the fruits thereof." And whom God has predestined, called, and justified, them He will also glorify (Rom. 8:30). For His covenant with them is an everlasting covenant (Jer. 32:40), and His gifts are without repentance (Rom. 11:29). "Love is strong as death: much water cannot quench love, neither can the floods drown it" (Song 8:6). Piety, which perishes, was never pretty. And true faith (though as small as a grain of mustard seed) cannot altogether vanish and be extinguished, for God will relieve it. He will not break the bruised reed nor quench the smoking flax (Isa. 42:3). Indeed, faith may be shaken, but it cannot be shivered in pieces. It may be moved, but it cannot be removed. It may wither and wax dry, but it cannot wear away quite and die. Satan may sift and towze[16] it, he may lay siege against it; but he cannot sack it. He shall never destroy it. The sun may set and for a time lie hid, but it remains in the heaven. And faith may be covered (as fire with ashes), but yet it continues in the heart. The fish may be in the water, though she float not always aloft. There is sap in the root when the leaves are fallen off and the top naked and in appearance withered. So faith lives though it have lost some signs of life. The sun and the moon may be indeed eclipsed; even so the eye of faith may be dimmed. But as the sun and moon do not perish in their eclipses nor lose their light forever, even so faith does not perish when it is eclipsed. It may indeed receive a buffet, whereby it may (as it were) reel and stagger and fall to the ground and there for a time lie like a man in a swoon or fit of the falling sickness. But it cannot die, because God, the well-spring as well of spiritual life as of natural, will never forsake it. The Thames may suffer an ebb, but it is not stark dry at any time. So faith may come to a very low ebb, but yet it will have water always in the bottom. As a great river may be frozen over with hard ice for a time and so covered with snow, as that it seems rather a rock than a river or like to other ground, even so faith may be (as it were) frozen over with thick ice and so held with the snow of sin, as that it may not be seen at all for a time. But as there is water in the river which is deep, notwithstanding the frost, though it be not seen, even so there is life in faith, though for a time it do not appear. But when the weather is broken, when the Holy Ghost begins to make a thaw with the fresh fire of His grace when the south wind blows hard and when the Sun of Righteousness has melted the ice—then faith will appear and flow again as a river after rain and as the waters do after a thaw. Then grace, which was covered before, will shine bright and clear, as the sun does after a shower, as is evident by the repentance of David

---

16. *Towze*: to push or pull about roughly or out of joint.

and Peter. Moreover, our Savior says that His sheep shall "never perish" (John 10:28). The Lord, says Isaiah, shall feed His flock like a shepherd (Isa. 40:11). He shall gather the lambs with His arms and carry them in His bosom. He makes them to rest in green pastures (Ps. 23:2) and leads them by the still waters. He upholds them in their integrity (41:12) and does set them before His face forever. As Zerubbabel laid the foundation of the temple (Zech. 4:9) and did finish it, so God, that has begun His good work in the temple of our hearts, will finish it to the end (Phil. 1:6). They cannot be taken from Him by strong hand. For He is greater than all (John 10:29–30), and His will to save them is answerable to His power. Therefore, He says He gives to them everlasting life (v. 28), adding also that none shall pluck them out of His hands. Master Tyndale says well, "Christ is thine, and all His deeds are thy deeds; neither canst thou be damned, except He be damned with thee." They cannot perish by seduction, for the elect cannot be seduced (Matt. 24:24). Neither can they of themselves fall away. For God has put His fear in their hearts (Jer. 32:40), that they shall not depart from Him. A man may for a time cease to laugh, but he cannot lose the faculty of laughing. The drunkard loses sometimes the use of reason, but the faculty never. So the graces of God may be crazed, but yet they are not utterly abolished. Finally, God forsakes not them. For His love is everlasting (31:3). Those whom He loves once, He loves to the end (John 13:1). Nothing can separate us from His love (Rom. 8:39). It is like the Israelites' shoes (Deut. 29:5), which waxed not old. It is like the tree of life—he that once truly tastes of it shall not die eternally. As a father does not reject his child when he has broken his face by falling, but rather seeks a plaster—he will (it may be) lash him, but he will not leave to love him.[17] Even so our heavenly Father deals with His children. For He has said that He will never depart from them to do them good (Jer. 32:40). He will not fail them nor forsake them (Heb. 13:6), but will sanctify them throughout (1 Thess. 5:23–24) and keep them safe to the coming of Christ. Indeed, our enemies may wound us, but they shall not win. They may vex us, but they shall not vanquish. They may perhaps press us, but they shall not oppress us. They may cut us, but they cannot kill us. For God, who is greater than all, will not suffer us to be tempted above our power and is very vigilant for us (1 Cor. 13:13). For He that keeps Israel neither slumbers nor sleeps (Ps. 121:4).

Privilege 30. The elect may assuredly be persuaded in this life that they shall be saved in the life to come. For a special and certain persuasion of God's mercy is the very heart and marrow, the life and soul of true faith (Matt. John 1:12; Rom. 4:20). Therefore, Paul says, "We know that if our earthly house of this tabernacle be destroyed, we have a building of God"—that is, "a house not made

---

17. *Leave to love him:* stop loving him.

with hands, eternal in the heavens" (2 Cor. 5:1). Furthermore, if it be not possible for men to know that they shall be saved, how could St. John say, "These things have I written to you that believe in the name of the Son of God, that ye may know that ye have eternal life" (John 20:31). To conclude, if it were impossible for a man to be in his conscience assured that he is the elect and faithful servant of God, effectually called in time and ordained to glory before time, to what end should David inquire who of all professors are the true members of the church militant on earth and shall be of the church triumphant in the heavens (Psalm 15)? And to what end should he set down the marks whereby they may be discerned? And to what purpose should Paul exhort us to prove ourselves whether we are in the faith? Or why should he speak after this manner to us, "Know ye not your own selves, how that Jesus Christ is in you, except ye be reprobates?" (2 Cor. 13:5)? And wherefore should Peter bid us be diligent to make our calling and election sure (2 Peter 1:10)? It remains therefore as an undoubted truth that the elect may be truly assured of their election and may assuredly know (without special revelation) that they shall be saved. Now this is a very great prerogative, and the greater, first, because it may be enjoyed to the end; secondly, because the longer it is enjoyed, the better we are assured; thirdly, it brings with it wonderful joy. For what greater joy can a man here enjoy than to be assured of eternal joy? Fourthly, this assurance makes a man more wary and more unwilling to displease God by sin, whereby nothing is deserved but damnation. Fifthly, this privilege is the more excellent, because they which want this knowledge altogether can have no solid consolation. And as for the reprobate, they have no more to do with this certainty than they have with salvation. As it is impossible for them to be saved, so it is impossible for them to be truly assured of their salvation. He that dreams may think he walks, eats, talks, sees, when he does not; and he may think he is awake, when he is not. So these dreamers may think that they shall be saved and may soothe themselves as if they were cocksure,[18] but they are deceived. He that is in a swoon does sometimes persuade himself that he sees many strange sights, but his persuasion is false. So the reprobates may think all things run round, they may persuade themselves they are in God's favor and shall be saved; but as the things are false whereof they do persuade themselves, so their persuading must needs also be as false. It is but a spiritual swoon or devilish dreaming or dizziness that does to blind their eyes and beguile them.

Privilege 31. The elect only shall be raised up of Christ as a savior and redeemer. And when all people shall be gathered before Him, He will separate His elect from the reprobate (Matthew 25). The elect shall be placed on

---

18. *Cocksure*: absolutely certain.

His right hand, and upon them He will pronounce the white and comfortable sentence of absolution. On the contrary, He will raise up the reprobate as He is a terrible and dreadful judge. He will set them on His left hand like goats and pronounce against them the doleful and black sentence of condemnation. And more also, which may increase their grief, He will use the elect for the approbation of His judgment upon them and upon the wicked angels also. They shall attend upon Him as justices do upon the judge at the assizes and shall approve His sentence. And this St. Paul teaches (1 Cor. 6:2–3), when as he says that the saints shall judge the world and the wicked angels. Now as this is a great honor to the elect to sit as judges upon the wicked, so it must needs minister no small grief to them to be (as it were) judged of those whom they before have derided, condemned, nicknamed, and persecuted. Thus, we have seen many notable privileges of God's elect and faithful children. If Balaam prophesied of the Israelites when he looked upon them dwelling according to their tribes, saying, "How goodly are thy tents, O Jacob, and thy habitations, O Israel" (Num. 24:5), we may well conjecture that God will exceedingly manifest His love to us hereafter in the heavens, seeing He has honored us so highly in this vale of misery and will grace us so much after the resurrection in our entrance into heaven, as that we shall judge the world and the angels.

Privilege 32. The last privilege of the elect whereof I will entreat is that God will give them the kingdom of heaven and everlasting life. "Fear not, little flock," says our Shepherd, "for it is your Father's pleasure to give you the kingdom" (Luke 12:32). And Paul says that God does glorify those whom He has predestinated, called, and justified (Rom. 8:30). Our Savior says that He gives eternal life to all His sheep (John 10:28). As Joshua brought the children of Israel into earthly Canaan, so Christ Jesus, our Joshua, will one day bring all true Israelites into celestial Canaan and will crown them with immortal glory. To describe this blessed estate perfectly surpasses man's capacity, whose knowledge is as yet imperfect. For Paul out of Isaiah says that the eye has not seen and the ear has not heard, neither came it into man's heart to think of those things which God has prepared for them that love Him (1 Cor. 2:9; Isa. 64:4). Nevertheless, it may in part be described according as God has revealed it in His Word to us. In this estate, the elect shall be delivered and set free from all wants and miseries, from sin, and from all the temptations of Satan (Rev. 21:4). They shall have perpetual fellowship with the blessed Trinity and the holy angels. They shall have perfect knowledge, and they shall perfectly love God, who will be all in all to them (1 Cor. 13:12). Their hearts shall be full fraught with endless and unutterable joys. Their tongues shall continually sound out the praises of God. They shall celebrate an everlasting sabbath, serving God most purely forever and ever (Isa. 66:23). Their bodies shall be like to the glorious body of Christ

(Phil. 3:21), bright and beautiful, mobile and full of agility, preserved and sustained by the immediate power of God, without meat, drink, sleep, labor, physic; and therefore Paul calls them spiritual (1 Cor. 15:44). Lastly, to make up their happiness, the place of their abode shall be in the highest heavens, where there are no pains but pleasures (2 Cor. 5:1); no woe but weal; no sin but serving of God; no grief but glory; no want but wealth; no sickness but health; no death but life; no jars but joys; no wars but peace; no treachery but truth; no fighting but triumphing; and no change but everlasting continuance. When a man has lived so many thousand thousand years in all the pleasures of paradise as there are hours in a million millions of years, he shall not attain to the end; for the end is endless, and the time is without time. But on the other side, the reprobate are severed from the solacious sight and comfortable presence of God. Their fellowship is with the devil and his angels in hellfire, where they are unspeakably tormented in soul and body with endless, easeless, and remediless torments. Their life is death, and their death is life—a dying life, and a living death. When they have spent so many years in pains as there be stars in the sky, motes in the sun, sands on the shore, and fishes in the seas, they shall be as far from the end as they were the first day; for the time is infinite, their damnation is everlasting, and their death shall never be put to death. Their worm shall not die, their fire shall never be put out, neither shall they be put out with it (Isa. 66:24). But as the salamander is always in the fire and never wastes, so the wicked shall be continually scorched in hellfire, and yet shall never be consumed. Lo then, beloved, you see the charter of the saints in part. No earthly monarch can grant such a one to his subjects as God has given freely to His elect. All the countries, kingdoms, and cities that have been, are, and shall be cannot show such dignities, such royalties, and such immunities given them by man as I have showed to belong to God's elect and obedient children. The consideration of these benefits and privileges should move us first to acknowledge and laud God's infinite love. Secondly, in [a] way of thankfulness to dedicate our souls and bodies and all that we have to God. Thirdly, to admire the condition of God's children. Fourthly, to be afraid to disgrace them whom the Lord does so grace and countenance. Fifthly, to undergo courageously all adverse blasts and all the crosses of this life. Sixthly, to alienate our hearts from the world. Seventhly, to roll our care upon God and to rely upon His providence. Eighthly, to desire the coming of Christ and not to fear death too much. The sooner we die, the sooner we come to our crowns. Lastly, the consideration of these benefits and privileges should stir us up to seek by all means to be enrolled among them and never to rest till we be in some measure certain and certainly persuaded that we are elected and preordained to salvation. When Ahasuerus had honored Mordecai (Esth. 8:7) and showed favor to the Jews, the Scripture says that much people of the land became Jews. So, seeing the Lord has thus dignified the elect, let us behave ourselves like them and labor to be accounted of their company. Claudius Lysias gave a great sum of money for the freedom of the Romans (Acts 22:28); how much more ought we to seek for these freedoms and royalties which do more surpass the other than the heaven does the earth and the precious pearl does the poorest pebble. They are not indeed to be named or compared together, and yet these may be had without money, though they cannot be had by money. And thus much for the privileges.

I come now briefly to set down the note of election to life and to show how a man may come to be truly persuaded in his conscience that he shall be saved. Let a man that would attain to the knowledge of his election to salvation (1) hear the word of God often and attentively. For faith, whereby we are persuaded of God's special grace to us, is ordinarily wrought by hearing of the word preached (Rom. 10:17). (2) Let him wage war with his infidelity, and let him not listen to Satan tempting him to doubting or desperation. (3) Let him beware of pride and presumption, neither trusting to his own goodness nor oblivious of God's infinite justice. (4) Let him often and earnestly pray for this benefit and desire that God would give him His Spirit, which may witness with him that he is the chosen child of God. (5) Let him reverently receive the sacrament and meditate often of his baptism. For the sacraments are pledges of God's love and serve to increase our faith. He that receives them with an honest and humble heart may assure himself of the remission of his sins and of the salvation of his soul. (6) Consider diligently God's fatherly dealing with you. Lastly, let him expand and dutifully consider the notes of election to eternal life, by the which a man may know that he is ordained to be saved. Note, the jailor demanding of Paul and Silas what he should do to be saved, they made him answer, saying, "Believe in the Lord Jesus Christ, and thou shalt be saved" (Acts 16:31). Secondly, love of our brethren for their piety. "We know," says John, "that we are translated from death to life, because we love the brethren" (1 John 3:14). Thirdly, the fear of God, wherein we are loath to offend Him, chiefly because we love Him and hate sin. "Blessed is the man that feareth the Lord" (Ps. 12:1); is blessed, then elected. [Unreadable] hearty confession, and loathing of our sins. "He that confesseth and forsaketh his sins, shall find mercy" (Prov. 28:13). But God vouchsafes His special mercy only to His own people. Fifthly, confidence and affiance in God. "O Lord of hosts, blessed is the man that trusteth in Thee" (Ps. 84:12). The condition of reprobates is cured. The apostle says our confidence has great recompense of reward (Heb. 10:35). Sixthly, sincere and true calling upon the name of God. For Paul says, "Whosoever shall call upon the name of the Lord, shall be saved" (Rom. 10:13). Seventhly, careful and constant endeavoring to keep all the commandments of God. For "blessed are they that do His commandments, that their right may be in the tree of life, and may enter in through the gates into the city" (Rev. 22:14). As the Lord promised to establish the kingdom of Solomom (1 Chron. 28:7), if he did constantly endeavor to keep His commandments, so the same Lord will establish us forever in the kingdom of heaven, if we will endeavor constantly to serve and obey Him. Eighthly, patient bearing of affliction for the truth's sake. "Blessed are they," says Christ, "which suffer persecution for righteousness' sake: for theirs is the kingdom of heaven" (Matt. 5:10). Ninthly, an earnest and hearty desire to be washed in the blood of Christ and to be invested in the white robes of His righteousness. "Blessed are they which hunger and thirst for righteousness, for they shall be filled" (Matt. 5:6). "To him that is athirst, I will give of the well of the water of life freely" (Rev. 21:6). Tenthly, Christian humility and poverty of spirit, when a man seems naked and base in his own sight and ascribes all to God's grace. "Blessed are the poor in spirit, for theirs is the kingdom of heaven" (Matt. 5:3). Eleventhly, a lusting and longing after the coming of Christ. Paul says that the righteous Judge will give a crown of righteousness to all those that love His appearing (2 Tim. 4:8). Twelfthly, David in the fifteenth Psalm asks the Lord who shall dwell in His tabernacle and rest on His holy mountain, and received answer as it were by oracle from God that he shall who walks uprightly and works righteousness and speaks the truth from his heart. And Peter having commanded us to make our election and calling sure adds saying that if we do "these things, we shall never fall" (2 Peter 1:10), but shall be sure and certain. Now what these things are, he shows—to wit, that we adorn our hearts and lives with virtue, knowledge, temperance, godliness, and love (vv. 5–7). To conclude, he that is sure of his adoption may be also certain of his election; for none are adopted, but such as are elected. Now a man may know his adoption if he find in himself the properties of an obedient and loving son. I will set down some. (1) Property. As a little child, whether in learning good or leaving evil, is either won by a fair word or awed by a check or feared by a frowning look or allured by a trifling gift or stilled by seeing another beaten before him or else quieted by a rod, even so God's children are either affected by His promises or allured by His mercies or awed by His threats or scared by His frowning countenance or humbled by His correcting of others or by His rod which is upon their own backs. (2) A good and wise child is very desirous to know his father's mind or will, that so he may best know how to please and humor him; and such is the disposition of God's child. Job makes it the note of a wicked man to affect the ignorance of God's ways (21:14). (3) A good child, knowing that he has unjustly grieved his father, will not be quiet till they be good friends again. (4) He labors to resemble his father in his rare and excellent virtues. (5) He will bear a blow at his father's hands (though he scorn to put it up at another man's);

and when his father has chided or corrected him, he will not run for comfort to his father's desperate and sworn enemies. (6) He envies not a servant or brother that is more laborious and circumspect in his father's business than himself is. (7) He carries a thankful heart toward his father for his fatherly gifts. (8) He is glad to know his father's prerogatives, his lands and leases (if there be any), specially if he be an heir. (9) He longs to see his father and to hear often of him in his absence. (10) He makes much of those love tokens which his father has given him to keep for a remembrance of him or for a sign of his love. (11) He cannot without grief endure to see his father injured or abused by any. (12) He has a special regard of his father's credit. (13) He rejoices at his father's prosperity. (14) He likes his father's company. He listens to his words and loves to talk to him. (15) He loves his mother entirely; he affects his brethren and sisters, though it be but for his father's sake. (16) He hates the fellowship of his father's injurious and unjust enemies. He is a friend to all his father's faithful friends; he contemns not their companies. (17) He cleaves to his father in the time of trouble and does not cast him off. These are properties of gracious, wise, and godly children; and being applied to the purpose in hand, they are so many infallible notes of God's dutiful and loving child. Those which find them in their hearts and lives may truly and infallibly assure themselves and know that they are the sons and daughters of God, elected before the foundation of the world to everlasting life and happiness. Those which after diligent search find them not to be in them must not despair, though they may justly indeed suspect and bewail their estates. But let them fly to the throne of grace with hungry hearts and incessantly desire favor, remembering also to use all means whereby all these foresaid graces and gracious conditions may be generated, nourished, and augmented in them.

These things (right worshipful and beloved) I have here set down as a preface to the treatise following for your furtherance and encouragement; and being the first fruits of my labors in this kind I do present and give them to you in testimony of my hearty love and earnest desire of your Christian progress in knowledge and in godliness. "The God of peace that brought again from the dead our Lord Jesus Christ, the great Shepherd of the sheep, through the blood of the everlasting covenant make you perfect in all good works to do His will, working in you that which is pleasing in His sight through Jesus Christ, to whom be praise forever and ever. Amen" [Heb. 13:20–21].

Faversham, June 20, 1606.

Your Worship's in Christ Jesus,
Thomas Tuke

Master Perkin's Epistle to the Reader

The doctrine of predestination and God's grace is to be founded upon the written Word of God and not upon the judgments of men. For as Hilary says well, "God cannot be understood, but by God."[1] And again, "We must learn of God what we are to understand of God, because He is the only author of our knowledge of Him." It is also requisite that this doctrine agree with the grounds of common reason and of that knowledge of God which may be obtained by the light of nature. And such are these which follow.

1. God is always just, albeit men do not understand how He is just.

2. God is not governed of, much less does He depend upon second causes, but does justly order them, even then when they work unjustly.

3. God works wisely—to wit, propounding to Himself a certain end. He is ignorant of nothing. He does not will or decree that which He cannot effect. He does not idly behold what shall be or what may be done, but He disposes all things to His glory, and therefore He has decreed to do so.

4. God is not changed. And those things which are changed are not changed without His unchangeable decree, all circumstances being certain and sure.

5. The secret and unsearchable judgments of God are to be honored and acknowledged. Augustine: "It moves me (you say) that he perishes, and another is baptized; it moves me, it moves me as a man. If you will hear the truth, it also moves me, because I am a man. But if you are a man, I am also a man. Let us both hear him that says, O man! Verily, if we be therefore moved because we are men, the apostle speaks to human nature itself being weak and feeble, saying, 'O man! Who art thou which pleadest against God? Shall the thing formed say to him that formed it, Why hast thou made me thus?' (Rom. 9:20). If a beast could speak and did say to God, Why hast Thou made him a man, and me a beast? Might you not justly be angry and say, O beast, who are you? And you are a man, but in comparison of God, you are a beast."[2]

---

1. In the margin: De Trin. Lib. 5 [Hilary (c. 315–67/8), On the Trinity, book 5. Hilary was the Bishop of Poitiers and sometimes called the "Athanasius of the West." He was also known as the "hammer of the Arians," against whom his work on the Trinity was written].

2. In the margin: De verb. Apost. Sec. 11 [Augustine, "On the Words of the Apostles," sermon 11. This is possibly a reference to one of Augustine's sermons with that title].

6. No good thing can be done unless God does absolutely will and work it; and we do that which is good so far forth as God does work in us more or less.

7. No evil can be avoided unless God do hinder it. And we avoid evil so far forth as God does more or less hinder it.

8. The will of God is known not only by the written word or by revelation, but also by the event. For that which comes to pass does therefore come to pass because God has willed that it should come to pass.

9. A man does not that good thing which by grace he is able to do unless God make him do it, as He has made him able to do it if He will.

10. Not a part only, but the whole government of the world and the execution of justice is to be ascribed to God as to the author.

I do not exhibit to you a view and picture of this doctrine composed of these principles and do publish the same, that I might to my power help out[3] those that stick in the difficulties of this doctrine of predestination; and that I might clear the truth that is (as they call it) the Calvinists' doctrine of those reproaches which are cast upon it; and that I might mitigate and appease the minds of some of our brethren which have been more offended at it than was fit. For I do willingly acknowledge and teach universal redemption[4] and grace, so far as it is possible by the Word. My mind is to pursue after peace, which is departing from us; and I would have all men so interpret my fact.

I allege the testimonies of the ancient everywhere, not but that even one evident and perspicuous sentence of sacred Scripture concerning any point of doctrine and faith is of more value and force than all the testimonies of the doctors and schoolmen, but because I hold it necessary that there should be had an example of consent and concord in that doctrine which is expounded in holy books and is propagated to all posterity. And I hope I shall sufficiently persuade an indifferent judge that these things have not been lately hatched at home which we deliver in our congregations and schools, but that we have also defined and fetched them from the fathers themselves.

William Perkins

---

3. In the margin: *theologia studiases*.

4. Perkins is not advocating for universal atonement here, but is stressing that God will redeem His people from all over the earth.

The Order of Predestination As It Is Collected
Out of the Scriptures by the Author

Predestination is the counsel of God touching the last end or estate of man out of this temporal or natural life (1 Cor. 15:46). For as touching natural life, we are all alike; and this kind of life is in the counsel of God only a preparation and step to the spiritual and heavenly life. The supreme end of predestination is the manifestation of God's glory, partly in His mercy and partly in His justice. And this has been the doctrine of the fathers. Saint Augustine says that "one of those two societies of men, which we mystically call two cities, is that which is predestinated to reign eternally with God, and the other to suffer eternal punishment with the devil."[1] Fulgentius says also "that in God's predestination there is prepared either a merciful remission of sins, or a just punishing."[2] And Gregory says "that God being a just creator to all after an admirable manner has fore-elected some and forsaken others in their corruptions."[3] And the more learned schoolmen used to say that God for the more full manifestation of His perfection has predestinated some in manifesting His goodness by the rule of mercy and damned others in representing His perfection by the rule of justice.

The common means of accomplishing this counsel is twofold: the creation and the permission of the fall. Creation is that by which God made the whole man of nothing according to His own image, but yet changeable and endued with a natural life. The permission of the fall is whereby God did justly suffer Adam and his posterity to fall away in that He did not hinder them when He was able, as being indeed bound to none to hinder. And God is said not to hinder evil when He ceases after a sort from His operation, not illuminating the mind and not inclining the will to obey His voice. This permission of the evil of fault is by God's foreknowledge and will, but yet only for the greater good of all, which would be hindered if God did not suffer evil. For if there were not sin, there should be no place for the patience of martyrs and for the sacrifice of Christ offered upon the cross, which does infinitely exceed all the

---

1. In the margin: De Civit. Dei lib. 13 [Augustine, *City of God*, bk. 13].

2. In the margin: Ad Manymum, lib.I. [Fulgentius, *Ad Monymum*, bk. 1. Fulgentius (*c.* 462 or 469–527 or 533) was Bishop of Ruspe].

3. In the margin: Comment. In 1. Reg. Cap.4 [Gregory the Great, *Commentary on Kings*, 1 Kings 4].

sin of the whole world. Augustine says well, "God has judged it better to do good with evils than to permit no evil to be."[4] In like manner, Gregory says, "In His severe judgment He suffers evil to be done, but withal He does in mercy forecast what good things He may bring to pass by these evils which He does ordain by His judgment. For what greater sin is there than that by which we do all die? And what greater goodness than that by which we are delivered from death? And doubtless but that Adam sinned, our Redeemer should not have taken our flesh upon Him. While God was to be born man, the Almighty did foresee that He would make of that evil for which they were to die a good which should be greater than that evil. The greatness of which good what faithful man is there who does not see how wonderfully it does excel? Surely great are the evils which we suffer by the desert of the first fault, but what faithful man would not rather endure worse than to be without so great a Redeemer?"[5] And in this respect elsewhere he calls the fall of Adam *foclicem culpam*, a happy fault.[6] That which I have said of the permission of the fall I do also say of the fall permitted, saving that the permission is a means of the decree by itself, but the fall is a means (of accomplishing the decree) only by the ordination of God, who draws good out of evil.

This fall permitted comes not to pass but God being willing, neither does it come to pass contrariwise or otherwise than God permits, neither can it any further be that He does permit. Yet the will of God is not the cause of the fall, but the will of man left to itself by God and moved by the suggestion of Satan, which will appear by this similitude: I build a house subject to change and falling, which notwithstanding would continue many years if it might be free from the annoyance of winds. Yea, if I would but underprop it, when the storm comes, it would continue stable. But as soon as the winds begin to rage, I do not underprop it; and it is my will not to underprop it because it is my pleasure so to do. Thereupon the house, being weather-beaten, falls down. I see the fall, and in part I will it, because now when I could very easily have hindered the fall, yet I would not. And although thus far I do will the fall, insomuch as it is my will not to hinder it, yet the cause of the fall is not to be imputed to me that did not underprop it, but to the winds which cast it down. So God leaving Adam to himself, that he might be proved by temptation, and that it might appear what the creature is able to do, the Creator ceasing for a time to help and guide is not to be accounted the cause of this fall. For He did not incline the mind to sin. He did not infuse any corruption, neither did He withdraw any gift which He did bestow in the creation. Only it pleased Him to deny or not to confer confirming

---

4. In the margin: Enchir. Cap. 27 [Augustine, Enchiridion, ch. 27].

5. In the margin: Expos. I.Reg.Cap. 4 [Gregory the Great, *Commentary on Kings*, 1 Kings 4].

6. In the margin: Augustine, *In benedict.Cerei Pasc.*

grace. The proper cause of the fall was the devil attempting our overthrow and Adam's will, which when it began to be proved by temptations did not desire God's assistance, but voluntarily bent itself to fall away.

Predestination has two parts: the decree of election and the decree of reprobation. So Isidore says, "There is a double predestination: either of the elect to rest, or of the reprobate to death. And both are done by God that He might make the elect always to follow after heavenly and spiritual things, and that He might suffer the reprobate by forsaking them to be delighted always with earthly and outward things."[7] And Angelome says, "Christ by His secret dispensation has out of an unfaithful people predestinated some to everlasting liberty, quickening them of His free mercy, and damned others in everlasting death in leaving them by His hidden judgment in their wickedness."[8]

The decree of election is that whereby God has ordained certain men to His glorious grace in the obtaining of their salvation and heavenly life by Christ (Eph. 1:5).

In the decree of election according to God's determination, there is (as we conceive) a double act. The former concerns the end; the latter concerns the means tending to the end. (These acts are usually called the decree and the execution of the decree.) This the Holy Ghost seems to me to have taught very evidently, "that the purpose which is according to election might remain" (Rom. 9:11). Here, we see that Paul distinguishes God's eternal purpose and election and places in His decree a certain election in the first place before the purpose of damning or saving. And in Romans 8:29–30, "Those which He knew before, He also predestinated to be made like to the image of His Son. Whom He predestinated, them also He called." In which words, Paul distinguishes between the decree and the execution thereof, which he makes to be in these three: vocation, justification, and glorification. Moreover, He distinguishes the decree into two acts: foreknowledge, whereby He does acknowledge some men for His own before the rest; and predestination, whereby He has determined from eternity to make them like to Christ. In like manner, Peter teaches (1 Peter 1:2), where he says "that the faithful are elected according to the foreknowledge of God the Father to sanctification of the spirit." If any man shall say that by foreknowledge in these places we must understand (as many would) the foreknowledge or foreseeing of future faith, he is manifestly deceived. For whom God foreknew, them He did predestinate that they should be like to

---

7. In the margin: Desummo bo.lib.2.cap.6 [Isidore, *De Summo Bono*, bk. 2, ch. 6. Isidore of Seville (*c.* 560–636) was the Archbishop of Seville for three decades and regarded as the last of the Church Fathers].

8. In the margin: In 2 Reg.c.8 [Angelomus of Luxeuil (died *c* .895), *Commentary on Kings*, 1 King 8. Little is known about this figure].

Christ—that is, that they should be made just and the sons of God. For Paul adds, "That He might be the firstborn among many brethren" (Rom. 8:29). But those which are predestinated to be just and to be the sons of God are also predestinated to believe, because adoption and righteousness are received by faith. Now we cannot rightly say that God does first foreknow that men will believe and afterward predestinate them to believe, because that God has therefore foreknown that those shall believe whom He did foreknow would believe, because He did decree that they should believe. So Justin Martyr calls those elect "who were foreknown that they should believe."[9] And Lombard: "Whom He has foreknown, them He has predestinated"—that is, "by grace conferred He has prepared that they should believe the word preached."[10] Moreover the word "know," when it is given to God speaking of the creature, does very often signify to embrace or approve. "The Lord knoweth the way of the righteous, but the way of the wicked shall perish" (Ps. 1:6). "Depart from Me ye workers of iniquity, I never knew you" (Matt. 7:23). Furthermore, the prescience and purpose of God are by the Holy Ghost put for one and the same thing. "The foundation of God remaineth sure—the Lord knoweth who are His" (2 Tim. 2:19). "Those whom God foreknew are said to be elected according to the election of grace" (Rom. 11:2–3). And therefore, the foreknowledge mentioned by Paul does not signify the foreknowledge of faith or of any other virtue in those which were to be elected. It is also the judgment of Augustine that predestination is sometimes understood by prescience, even in the foresaid place.[11] "Has God cast away His people which He knew before?" (Rom. 11:1–2). And he says that "those are sons in God's foreknowledge, whose names are written in their Father's register, so as they shall never be erased out."[12] Cyril says also that "Christ knows His sheep, electing and foreseeing them to everlasting life."[13] As the apostle says, "God has not cast away His people which He knew before" (Rom. 11:12). For as the Lord is said not to know those whom He does reject, as when He answered the foolish virgins, saying, "Verily I say to you, I know you not" (Matt. 25:12), so He is said to know those whom He does predestinate and fore-appoint to salvation. And Thomas expounds that place in the eighth [chapter] to the Romans after this sort, "Whom He foreknew in His knowledge of approbation, these He has also

---

9. In the margin: Cant. Triph. [Justin Martyr, *Dialogue with Trypho*].

10. In the margin: Comment. In cap. 8.ad Rom:Cognoste.scio. [Peter Lombard (*c.* 1096–1160), *Commentary on Romans*, Romans 8. Peter Lombard was an important medieval figure].

11. In the margin: De persev. sanct. 1.2.c.18 [Augustine, *A Treatise on the Gift of Perseverance*, bk. 2, ch. 18].

12. In the margin: De corrept. & grat.c.9. [Augustine, *On Rebuke and Grace*, ch. 9]

13. In the margin: Expos. In John 7:6 [Cyril of Alexandria, *Commentary on John*, John 7:6].

predestinated. And He will also have an effectual will of conferring grace to be included in the knowledge of approbation."[14]

In the decree of election, the first act is a purpose or rather a part and beginning of the divine purpose whereby God does take certain men which are to be created to His everlasting love and favor, passing by the rest, and by taking makes them vessels of mercy and honor.[15] And this act is of the sole will of God without any respect either of good or evil in the creature. And God does wrong none, although He choose not all, because He is tied to none, and because He has absolute sovereignty and authority over all creatures. We that are but men give leave to men, especially to our friends, to do at their pleasure in many things as they themselves list and to use their own discretions. The rich man is kind to which poor person he pleases, and of beggars he does adopt one and will not adopt another, and that without offering any injury. Now that liberty which we yield to man must much more be granted to God.

The second act is the purpose of saving or conferring glory whereby He does ordain or set apart the very same men which were to fall in Adam to salvation and celestial glory. This act is in no wise to be severed from the former, but to be distinguished in the mind (for orders' sake and for the better unfolding of it); for as by the former men were ordained to grace, so by this latter the means are subordained whereby grace may be conferred and manifested. And therefore this latter makes a way for the execution and accomplishing of the former. Moreover, this act has no impulsive cause over and beside the good pleasure of God, and it is with regard to Christ the Mediator, in whom all are elected to grace and salvation, and to dream of any election out of Him is against all sense, because He is the foundation of election to be executed in regard of the beginning, the means, and the end. Lastly, this act is not of men to be created as was the former, but of men fallen away. Therefore, in this act God respects the corrupted mass of mankind.

Furthermore, in this second act there are five degrees: the ordaining of a mediator, the promising of him being ordained, the exhibiting of him being promised, the applying of him being exhibited or to be exhibited, and the accomplishment of the application. It is not unlike which Bernard says, "The kingdom of God is granted, promised, manifested, perceived. It is granted in

---

14. In the margin: Idem Hugo desanct.Gut. in annot.in Rom. Et Joachim. in Revel. Par.I [Thomas Aquinas, *Commentary on the Letter of Saint Paul to the Romans*; Hugh of Saint Victor (*c.* 1096–1141), *An Exposition of Certain Words of Saint Paul, to the Romans*; Joachim of Fiore (*c.* 1135–1202), *Exposition of the Book of Revelation*, Part 1. Hugh of Saint Victor was a medieval mystic theologian and Joachim of Fiore was a significant monastic theologian].

15. In the margin: 1 Peter 2:9—People which God challengeth to Himself (λαὸς εἰς περιποίησιν).

predestination, promised in vocation, manifested in justification, perceived or received in glorification."[16]

The exhibiting[17] of a mediator is that whereby the second person, being the Son of God, is appointed from all eternity to be a mediator between God Himself and men. And hence it is that Peter says that "Christ was foreknown (προεγνωσμενου) before the foundation of the world" (1 Peter 1:20). And well says Augustine that "Christ was predestinated to be our Head." For howsoever as He is, the substantial Word (λογος) of the Father, or the Son, He does predestinate with the Father and the Holy Ghost; yet as He is the Mediator, He is predestinated Himself.

The promising is that whereby Christ, being from eternity ordained for the salvation and spiritual life of men, is revealed and offered to them together with grace to be obtained by Him. This promise is universal in respect of all and everyone that do believe. "God so loved the world, that He has given His only begotten Son, that every one that believeth in Him should not perish" (John 3:16). "He that believeth in Me has life everlasting" (John 6:47). "Come to Me all ye that are weary and laden, and I will ease you" (Matt. 11:28). "He that shall believe and be baptized, shall be saved: but he that will not believe shall be damned" (Mark 16:16). "That through His name all that believe in Him, shall receive remission of sins" (Acts 10:43). "By Him every one that believeth, is justified" (Acts 13:39). "The Gospel is the power of God to salvation to every one that believeth" (Rom. 1:16). "Christ is the end of the law for righteousness to every one that believeth" (Rom. 10:4). "The Scripture has concluded all under sin, that the promise by the faith of Jesus Christ should be given to them that believe" (Gal. 3:22).

With the promise, there is joined an exhortation or commandment to believe, which is more general than the promise because the promise is made only to believers, but the commandment is given to believers and unbelievers also. For the elect are mingled with the wicked in the same assemblies, and therefore the ministers of the gospel ought indifferently to exhort all and everyone to repent, considering that they are altogether ignorant who and how many be elected and to be converted. Moreover, God by exhortations to repentance means to leave those without excuse whom He does see will never repent. So Abbot Joachim says, "It behooves them to preach for the elects' sake and to declare to men the words of life, that their light may shine before men and that they may fatten the hearts of the elect by anointing them with the oil of spiritual doctrine; but for the reprobate, *ligare aquam coelo*, to tie the water in

---

16. In the margin: De verbis libri sapientiae. [Bernard of Clairvaux, De verbis libri sapientiae].

17. While "exhibiting" is in the original 1606 edition, the *Workes* (1631) has "ordaining" in place of exhibiting.

the clouds."[18] And again, "Lest the reprobate should have excuse and for the elect which are among them, the messenger himself shall be sent who does not only preach this in secret as it were for fear, but cries also with a loud voice, which may be heard far off and of all men also."[19] Some are wont to say that God's commandment by this means does overthwart His decree, because He commands that which He wills not to effect. But I answer, first, that God in His commandments and promises does not utter whatever He has decreed, but does in part only so far forth propound His will as He knows it expedient for the salvation of the elect and the governing of all. By His commandments therefore, He shows what He likes and what He wills that we should do to Him, not what He will do to us or in us. And God who wills not all things alike in all does will conversion in some only in respect of approbation, exhortation, and means. In others, He wills it also as touching the decree of working it. Here is no disagreement in the wills, but sundry degrees of willing in regard of us, according to which God is said both to will and to nill.

Secondly, I answer that the revealed will (εὐδοκία) is never contrary to the will of His good pleasure or to the decree of God (with the which it does always agree both for the beginning as also in the end and scope), but that it is notwithstanding often diverse, and that in show it seems sometimes contrary if we consider the manner wherein it is propounded. God commanded Isaiah to declare to Hezekiah his death (Isaiah 38), and He did also denounce destruction to the Ninevites within forty days (Jonah 3:4)—and yet He had decreed to put neither of them in execution. The human will of Christ did (Matt. 26:3) with a holy dissension in some sort will deliverance from the agony of death, which notwithstanding the divine willed not. Abraham prayed without doubt by divine inspiration (Genesis 28), and therefore with faith that the Sodomites might be spared; and yet he knew that in God's decree they were appointed to destruction. Neither must this seem strange, for one good thing as it is and remains good may be different from another thing that is good. Thirdly, you bid your debtor pay his debt, though in the meantime you do not make him able. Why may not God therefore for just causes command that which He Himself will not do?

The exhibiting of the Mediator is that whereby the Son of God, being born man in the fullness of time, does pay the price of redemption (λύτρον) to God for the sins of men. The virtue and efficacy of this price being paid in respect of merit and operation is infinite; but yet it must be distinguished, for it is either potential or actual. The potential efficacy is whereby the price is in itself

---

18. In the margin: In Revel.p.3.l.2. [Joachim of Fiore, *Exposition of the Book of Revelation*, part 3. l. 2].

19. In the margin: Part.4.l.7 [Joachim of Fiore, *Exposition of the Book of Revelation*, part 4. l. 7].

sufficient to redeem everyone without exception from his sins, albeit there were a thousand worlds of men. But if we consider that actual efficacy, the price is paid in the counsel of God and as touching the event only for those which are elected and predestinated. For the Son does not sacrifice for those for whom He does not pray, because to make intercession and to sacrifice are conjoined. But He prays only for the elect and for believers (John 17:9), and by praying He offers Himself to His Father (v. 19). For (as Illyricus has well observed) this whole prayer in the seventeenth chapter is indeed (as he speaks) an oblatory and expiatory prayer, or (as the papists call that blasphemous form) a canon or rule of sacrifice by which Christ has offered Himself a sacrifice to the Father for the sins of the world. Therefore, the price is appointed and limited to the elect alone by the Father's decree and the Son's intercession and oblation. Secondly, Christ bare their person and stood in their room upon the cross for whom He is a mediator (Eph. 1:6); and consequently, whatever Christ did as a redeemer, the same did all those in Him and with Him which He redeemed (Col. 3:1). Christ dying, rising again, ascending, and sitting at the right hand of the Father, they also die with Him, rise again, ascend and sit at the right hand of God. Now that all these things can be truly said of the elect only, and of such as believe, I prove it thus. To say that anyone of the wicked, which are to perish forever, is raised up in Christ rising again is flat against the truth, because the raising up of Christ is (that I may so speak) His actual absolution from their sins for whom He died. For even as the Father by delivering Christ to death did in very deed condemn their sins imputed to Christ for whom He died, so by raising Him up from death, even *ipso facto* He did absolve Christ from their sins and did withal absolve them in Christ. But being absolved from their sins, they shall not perish, but be saved. Therefore, that wicked man which perishes for his sin cannot be said to have risen again with Christ, and therefore Christ did not bear his person upon the cross. Thirdly, the expiatory sacrifice sanctifies those for whom it is a sacrifice, as the Holy Ghost plainly and absolutely avouches (Heb. 9:13–14). The sacrifice and sanctification appertain to the same persons, and Christ is their perfect Savior whom He saves not only by meriting their salvation, but also by working it effectually. But Christ does sanctify only the elect and such as believe. Therefore, He was a sacrifice only for them.

And this was the judgment of the ancient church in this point. Augustine says, "He which spared not His own Son but gave Him for us all, how has He not also with Him given us all good things? But for what use? For us which are foreknown, predestinated, justified, and glorified."[20] Again, "Those whom He

---

pleased to make His brethren He has released and made fellow heirs."[21] Cyril says, "If God who is most worthy was in the flesh, He was of right sufficient to redeem the whole world."[22] Again, "The Lord Jesus, separating His own from those which were not His, says, I pray only for those which keep My word and carry My yoke. For He does make them alone, and that justly, partakers of the benefit of His meditation, whose Mediator and high priest He is."[23] Gregory says, "The Author of life gave Himself to death for the life of the elect."[24] Again, "The Lord will redeem the souls of His servants, in Psalm 33, to wit, with His precious blood, because He which believes rightly in Him is redeemed from the due thralldom of his sins."[25] Sedulius: "All things are restored which are in the death, seeing (or when) that the men themselves who are predestinated to eternal life are renewed from the corruption of the old man."[26] Bede: "The flesh of the Lord is furnished with spiritual virtue, that it might be a sweet savor sufficient for the salvation of the whole world."[27] Again, "Our Lord and redeemer to the elect—whom He knew to be placed in His flesh; yea and to us also whom He foresaw should believe in the last times, He has procured the remedy of salvation by His death and resurrection."[28] Joachim the Abbot: "The word *all*, which for the most part is universal, does not always signify so much as it seems, as in that place, 'When I shall be lift up I will draw all things to Myself. And by Him He has pleased that all things should be reconciled in Him' (Col. 1:19–20). It seems that in these places 'elect things' only are understood."[29] Angelomus: "What other nation is there in the earth besides the elect people for which God the Son of God vouchsafed to come into this world, as it were into Egypt, that taking upon Him the form of a servant He might with the merchandise of His blood redeem to Himself an acceptable people zealous of good works."[30] Rupertus: "In that hour He washed those only from sin; whom His

---

21. In the margin: tract. 2 [Augustine, *Tractates on the Gospel of John*, tractate 2].

22. In the margin: De Recta fide ad Regin [Cyril of Alexandria, *De Recta fide ad Regin*. Cyril was an important Church Father and significant figure in the Council of Ephesus].

23. In the margin: In Ioan. 1. II. cap. 4 [Cyril of Alexandria, *Commentary on John*, bk. 11, ch. 4].

24. In the margin: 2 Hom. in Ez. lib. 1. [Gregory the Great, *Homilies on the Book of Ezekiel*, bk. 1, homily 2].

25. In the margin: In Psal. 33. [Gregory the Great, *Exposition of the Psalms*, ch.33].

26. In the margin: In Eph. c.1 [Presumably a commentary by Sedulius Scottus (*fl.* 840–60) on Ephesians, ch. 1].

27. In the margin: Homily in sab. post reminise [Bede (*c.* 672/3–735), *Homily in sab. post reminisce*. Bede was an important English Benedictine monk].

28. In the margin: Homily in Vigil Phsc [Bede, *Homily in Vigil Phsc.*].

29. In the margin: In rev.par.I. [Joachim of Fiore, *Exposition of the Book of Revelation*, part 1].

30. In the margin: In 2.Reg.c.7 [Angelomus of Luxeuil, *Commentary on Kings*, on 2 Kings 7].

death finds faithful, whether dead or living."[31] Again, "The passion of Christ is the judgment of the world—that is, salvation severing the whole number of the elect, which were from the beginning of the world to the hour of the same passion, from the reprobate. And the casting out of the prince of this world is the reconciliation of the nations of the elect." Again, "I will draw all things to Myself. What all things? Namely, all elect things, as all the members follow their head."[32] Haimo of Auxerre: "Christ has taken away in the elect not only original but all actual sins also, and has over and besides given them eternal life."[33] Radulphus: "The blood of the High Priest Christ was the purgation of all believers."[34] Innocentius: "Christ's blood was shed effectually for those only who are predestinated, but for all men in regard of sufficiency; for the shedding of the blood of that just one for the unjust was so rich in price, that if everyone had believed in the Redeemer, none at all had been held captive of the devil."[35] Arnoldus Carnotensis: "He redeems none but those whom He calleth and washes by grace; neither does the Spirit sanctify any but those who are cleansed and dead to sin. Redemption, washing away, and sanctification are partakers together."[36]

The application is when as Christ is given to us of God the Father by the Spirit in the lawful use of the word and sacraments, and is received of us by the instrument of a true faith. And Christ being given is made to us of God wisdom, righteousness, sanctification and redemption (1 Cor. 1:30).

The accomplishment of the application is glorification, whereby God shall be all in all by Christ in all the elect.

By this which has been said it is apparent that the decree of election is the cause and foundation of all good gifts and works in men. From hence is true faith: "As many as were ordained to eternal life believed" (Acts 13:48). And calling: "Whom He predestinated, them He called" (Rom. 8:30). And, "who are called of His purpose." Hence adoption: "Predestinated to adoption" (Ephesians 1). And sanctification: "He has chosen us that we should be holy and blameless" (Ephesians 1). Hence good works: "Which He has prepared, that we should walk

---

31. In the margin: In Exod.l.2.cap.6. [Presumably a commentary by Rupertus on Exodus, bk. 2, ch. 6. Exact identity of Rupertus is unknown].

32. In the margin: In Ioan, cap.12 [Presumably a commentary by Rupertus on John, ch. 12].

33. In the margin: In cap 5.ad Rom. Haimo of Auxerre (*d. c.* 865), *Commentary on Romans*, ch. 5. Haimo was a Benedictine monk who wrote a number of theological works and biblical commentaries.

34. In the margin: In Levit.lib.17.cap.2. [Radulphus Flaviacensis, *Commentary on Leviticus*, bk. 17, ch. 2. Radulphus Flaviacensis was a French Benedictine monk].

35. In the margin: Lib.4.de Myst.Missae.cap.4. [Innocent III (1160/1–1216), *On the Mysteries of the Mass*, bk. 4, ch. 4. Innocent was one of the most powerful and influential popes of the medievai period].

36. In the margin: Bone vallis tract.7 de verbis Domini. [Arnoldus Carnotensis (Arnold of Chartres), twelfth century abbot of Bonneval in the diocese of Chartes. The exact title is unknown].

in them" (Ephesians 2). And perseverance: "All that the Father giveth Me, shall come to Me, and him that cometh to Me I cast not away" (John 6:37). Again, "And this is the Father's will, that of all which He has given Me, I should lose nothing" (v. 39). "The foundation of God remaineth sure, and has this seal, the Lord knoweth who are His" (2 Tim. 2:19). Excellent is that saying of Augustine: "He did choose no man worthy, but by choosing He made him worthy."[37] Again, "It is the grace of God whereby He does elect me, not because any worthiness is in me, but because it does vouchsafe to make me worthy." Again, "And did not they also afterward choose him and prefer him before all the good things of this life? But they did choose him because they were chosen; they were not chosen because they chose Him." And thus much of the decree of election.

The decree of reprobation is a work of God's providence whereby He has decreed to pass by certain men in regard of supernatural grace for the manifestation of His justice and wrath in their due destruction; or, it is His will whereby He suffers some men to fall into sin and inflicts the punishment of condemnation for sin.

It has in like manner two acts. The first is the purpose to forsake some men and to make known His justice in them. This act has a small cause, but no impulsive cause out of God. For it arises of God's mere good pleasure, no respect had of good or evil in the creature. For the will of God is the cause of causes. Therefore, we must make our stand in it, and out of or beyond it no reason must be sought for. Yea, indeed there is nothing beyond it. Moreover, [secondly,] every man (as Paul avers, Rom. 9:21) is to God as a lump of clay in the potter's hand. And therefore God according to His supreme authority does make vessels of wrath; He does not find them made. But He should not make them but find them made if we say that God willed in His eternal counsel to pass by men only as they are sinners and not as they are men for cause most just, though unknown to us. Thirdly, if God did reject men because He foresaw that they would reject Him, reprobation should not depend upon God, but upon men themselves. And this is all one as if a man should say that God foresaw that some would choose Him and others refuse Him. And the contempt of the gospel does not befall infants which die out of the covenant of the gospel. Fourthly, Paul, who was a most skillful defender of God's justice, does exclude all works in the first place, out of this wonderful election of one from another made in the counsel of God: "Not by works," says He (v. 11), and therefore excludes all respect of sin. Then afterward being ravished with admiration, he quiets himself in the alone will of God: "Who has resisted His will? But, O man, who art thou which pleadest against God?" (vv. 19–20). Again, "O the deepness

---

37. In the margin: Cont.Jul.Pelag.lilb.5.cap.3. [Augustine, *Against Julian*, bk. 5, ch. 3].

of the riches, both of the wisdom and knowledge of God: how unsearchable are His judgments, and His ways past finding out!" (11:33). To conclude, if it be demanded why God created this world and no more, we must have recourse to the mere will of God. And why must we not do so, if it be demanded why God elects this man and forsakes that man or another? "A part of mankind is redeemed, a part perisheth. But who can tell why God does not pity them, and pities these? The reason of the distinction is unknown, but the distinction or separation itself is not unknown."[38]

The second act is the ordaining of them to punishment or due destruction. This ordination in respect of the diverse consideration thereof may be distinguished, and so it is either simple or comparative. The simple ordination is that whereby this man—suppose Peter or John—is ordained to punishment. And this ordination is of the most just will of God, yet not without respect of original and actual sins. For as men are actually damned for sin, so God has decreed to damn them for the same sin. Yet notwithstanding sin is not the cause of the decree of reprobation, but in regard of order it goes before in God's foreknowledge, not that former, but this latter act. The ordination which stands in comparison is that whereby one man and not another, and this man rather than that being in the like condition, is ordained to punishment. This serves to show the liberty of God's will in the dispensation of supernatural benefits. For in that God chooses this man and not that, it declares the liberty and very great perfection of God. And therefore under the name of a householder, he challenges the same to Himself, when He says: "May I not do with My own what I list?" (Matt. 20:15). And verily though God destroy and condemn all those whom He does forsake, yet should He not be unjust. For we ourselves in the daily killing and slaughtering of beasts will not be counted unjust, neither indeed are we; and yet in comparison of God we are not so much worth as a fly is in respect of us. If it be lawful for you to receive in or to thrust out any out of your house, because you will, it were a point of desperate boldness to take the same right from God in His house.

The cause of this comparative ordination is the sole will of God, yea, even without respect of any sin at all. So Augustine: "God delivers no man but of His free mercy, and condemns no man but most righteously. Now why He delivers this man rather than that, let Him search; who can dive into the great depth of His judgments?"[39] Again, "Why is it thus to this man, and otherwise to this? O man, who are you that you dare dispute with God?" And Gregory: "Let no man desire to search wherefore one should be elected when another is

---

38. In text note: Auther de voc.gent. [The Calling of the Gentiles].
39. In the margin: Lib.I.ad Simpl.q.1 [Augustine, *De Diversis Quaestionibus ad Simplicianum*, bk. 1, q. 1].

rejected—because His judgments are unsearchable, and His ways past finding out."[40] In this second act of reprobation, there be two degrees: a just desertion or forsaking, and damnation for sin. So Fulgentius: "In such," says he, "God begins His judgment by forsaking and ends it in tormenting."[41] Divine desertion is twofold. The first is that whereby God does forsake man only in regard of His assistance and strengthening, by omitting the confirmation of the creature and by not conferring the second grace whereby the first might be made effectual to resist temptations and to persevere in goodness. This is the desertion of trial (*desertion exploraticnis*) and may happen to them who have not themselves as yet forsaken God. For it was in the first man, Adam, who received of God power to do that which he would, but not will to do that which he could. So Augustine: "He received," says he, "power if he willed; but he had not will answerable to his power, for if he had, he should have persevered."[42] Again, "He was able also to persevere, if he would; and in that he would not it proceeded of free will which then was so free that he was able to will well and ill." The cause of this desertion was that Adam and his posterity might know that they could fall by themselves, but that they could not stand much less rise again, and therefore that they should wholly depend on God's mercy. Here also it must be remembered that between this desertion and Adam's sin, there came also Adam's will, whereby he being left to his own strength did by and by perceive the very same, his conscience telling. And yet for all that he willed his own fall by the free motion of his will.

The second desertion is a privation and losing of the gifts, wherewith the mind is adorned, and a delivering into the power of Satan, that he may seduce men and more and more lead them into sin. This is a desertion of punishment (*defatio paenae*), and therefore it follows sin. And of this desertion and not of the former is the rule to be understood: *a Deo desertis Deum priores deservunt*; those which are forsaken of God do themselves first forsake God.

And this is our doctrine of predestination, which favors neither of the errors of the Manicheans, Stoics, Pelagians, nor of Epicurism, but is (as I am persuaded) agreeable to the truth and orthodoxal. But yet it is oppugned by sundry criminations or false accusations, which I will strive with all my strength to overthrow, and that briefly.

[First Objection]

The first crimination is that we teach that certain men, and those but few, are elected. *Answer.* "Certain men," we say. For all the elect are known to God, and

---

40. In the margin: Expos.in John ca.37. [Augustine, *Exposition in John*, ch. 37].
41. In the margin: Lib.ad Mon. [Fulgentius, *Ad Monymum*].
42. In the margin: De correp. Grat.cap.11. [Augustine, *On Rebuke and Grace*, ch. 11].

their number can neither be increased nor diminished. "Few," we do not say, but after a prescript and certain manner. For (to omit the angels) if you consider the elect by themselves, they are many. "I say to you, that many shall come from the East, and West, and shall sit down with Abraham, Isaac, and Jacob in the kingdom of heaven" (Matt. 8:11). "I beheld and lo a great multitude, which no man could number of all nations, kindreds, people and tongues, stood before the throne and before the Lamb, clothed with long white robes, and palms in their hands" (Rev. 7:9). Yea, there is as it were a world of elect. Augustine: "The church which is without spot and wrinkle and gathered together out of all nations and which shall reign with Christ forever, even she is the land of the blessed and the land of the living."[43] Again, the reconciling world "shall be delivered out of the maligning world."[44] Eusebius: "Christ suffered for the salvation of the world, of those which are to be saved."[45] The author of the book *de vocations gentium book 1*: "In those which are elected, foreknown, and severed from the multitude of men, there is a certain special universality counted, that the whole world may seem to be delivered out of the whole world, and that all men may seem to be taken out of all men." Bede calls those "a world to be enlightened and healed who were predestinated to eternal life."[46] Thomas: "The true light enlightens those who come into the world of virtues, not those which come into the world of vices."[47]

Nevertheless, if those same elect be compared with them that are justly damned, we say according to the Scriptures that they are few. "The gate is narrow and the way straight which leadeth to life, and few there be which find it" (Matt. 7:13–14). Again, "Many are called, but few are chosen" (20:16).

[Second Objection]

The second crimination is that we teach that God ordained men to hellfire and created them to the end that He might destroy them. *Answer.* Here the distinction of the double act in reprobation must be repeated and retained. First therefore, I answer that reprobation in regard of the former act is absolute—that is, in regard of the purpose to forsake the creature and to manifest justice in it. So we teach and believe. For we cannot so much as imagine a cause in the creature why it was God's will to pass by it and to suffer some to fall finally from their blessed estate. Yea, sin is itself after the desertion and just

---

43. In the margin: De doctr.chr.lib.3.cap.34. [Augustine, *On Christian Doctrine*, bk. 3, ch. 34].
44. In the margin: Tract.in Joan.111. [Augustine, *Tractates on the Gospel of John*, tractate 111].
45. In the margin: Hist.lib.4.cap.15. [Eusebius, *Ecclesiastical History*, bk. 4, ch. 15].
46. In the margin: In Tobiam. [Bede, *In Tobiam*].
47. In the margin: In Catena in I.Ioan.ex Orig. [presumably Thomas Aquinas, Catena in 1 John of Origen].

permission of God; and therefore it can by no means be the cause of the permission and desertion. Whence it is that Lombard, the master of all the schoolmen, says that "God has rejected whom He would not for any future merits which He did foresee, but yet most righteously, though we cannot conceive the reason thereof."[48] And Jerome long before him does thus expound the place of Paul: "Ere the children were born, and when they had neither done good nor evil" (Rom. 9:11). "If Esau," says he, "and Jacob were not yet born neither had done good or evil whereby they might win to God's favor or offend Him, and if their election and rejection does not show their several deserts, but the will of the elector and rejecter, what shall we say?"[49] Afterward: "If we grant this, that God does whatever He will, and that He either chooses or condemns a man without desert and works, it is not therefore in him that wills nor in him that runs, but in God that shows mercy." Again: "Therefore it is in vain asked, seeing that it is in His power and will either to choose or to refuse a man without good and evil works." Anselm: "It is not ours to know why God denies grace to them which would gladly receive" and consent to grace, "and neglects another that would so well consent to it. This is only known to God."[50] Again: "No creature is able to search out why He is merciful to this man rather than to another."[51] The same do other schoolmen affirm in the midst of papacy. Gregorius Armineus lays down six conclusions concerning predestination. First, that there is nobody predestinated for the willing of free will which God foreknew that he should have. Secondly, that no man is predestinated because he was foreknown to continue to the end without any let of habitual grace. Third, that whomever God predestinated, "him He did predestinate freely, purposely and of His pure mercy." Fourthly, that no man is rejected for the evil using of free will which God foresaw he would be tainted with. Fifthly, that there is not any rejected because he was foreknown to have finally an impediment of divine grace. Sixthly, that whomever God rejected, him He did reject without any cause in him. The very same conclusions has Petrus de Alliaco and Marsilius of Inghen, some of whose words I will set down: "He is predestinated," says he, "to whom God has purposed to give everlasting life. And he is rejected on whom God has

---

48. In the margin: Lib.I.dist.41 [Peter Lombard, *Sentences*, bk. 1, distinction 41. Perkins does not specifically reference the *Sentences*, but this book is mostly likely the reference].

49. In the margin: Ad Hebid.quaest.10 [Jerome (347–420), *The Gospel of the Hebrews*, q. 10. Jerome was an important Church Father and the compiler of the Latin Vulgate. The '*Gospel according to the Hebrews* was an apocryphal gospel used amongst Jewish Christians, as it was regarded at one time was being the original version of Matthew's Gospel].

50. In the margin: Comment.in Matt. C.11. [Anselm of Canterbury (1033/4–1109), *Commentary on Matthew*, ch. 11. Anselm was a significant medieval theologian and the Archbishop of Canterbury].

51. In the margin: In Rom. Cap. 11. [Anselm of Canterbury, *Commentary on Romans*, ch. 11].

determined not to bestow the same, as the apostle teaches (Romans 9)." Again: "No man that is predestinated is predestinated for anything which should be in him in time to come, so also there is no reprobate rejected for any cause which was to be in him in time to come. And everyone that is predestinate is predestinated only by grace and by God's merciful disposition, not for any cause either actual or privative to be found in him while he lives." Again: "To reject is to nill to show mercy, and this is not for the evil works of any creature, for however holy the works were, God would show mercy as He listed."[52] So also Francis of Mayrone[53] says that there are four signs necessary for the understanding of the proceeding of predestination and reprobation. First, in which Peter and Judas are offered to the divine will, as to neither of them both. And then the divine will did preordain Peter to glory, but it had no positive act about Judas, according to Augustine.[54] The second sign is in which He preordained Peter to grace, and then He had no positive act as yet about Judas. The third sign is in which they are left to themselves, and both of them do fall into sin. The fourth sign is that in which Peter rises again, for he cannot continue because he is predestinated by the first sign. But Judas rises not again, because he has not God to raise him up; therefore, he is rejected. "The cause and reason of the whole work of reprobation cannot be said to be in the reprobates, for sin itself cannot be the cause of that permission of sin for which a man is damned, whether it be original or actual, as it appears in infants who die only with original sin. Which verily, however it may be the cause why infants are forsaken in it, yet nevertheless it cannot be the cause and reason why the whole nature of man should be suffered to fall in Adam."[55] And Ferrariensis says that "four things are found in a reprobate—to wit, a sufferance to fall into sin, the sin itself, God's forsaking not raising him from sin, and the punishment or damnation. Now reprobation is not alike but diversely affected to all these. For if we consider sin in itself, reprobation is not caused by it. Although nothing on our parts, to wit, no work of ours be the cause of the whole work of reprobation (for of

---

52. In-text citation: Petrus de Alliaco,lib.I.sent.quest.12.art.2. and Marsilius of Inghen, lib. I.dist.42.q,4 [Petrus of Alliaco (1351–1420), *Quaestiones super libros Sententiarum*, bk. 1, q. 12, art. 2 (As indicated, the book Perkins probably has in mind here is *Quaestiones super libros Sententiarum*); Marsilius of Inghen (c. 1340–1396), bk. 1, distinction 42, q. 4. (the book Perkins may have in mind here is *Quaestiones super quattuor libros Sententiarum*). Petrus of Alliaco was a French theologian and cardinal in the Roman Catholic Church. Marsilius of Inghen was a Dutch Scholastic philosopher].

53. Francis of Mayrone (c. 1280–1328): a French scholastic philosopher and student of John Duns Scotus.

54. In-text citation: Francis.Mar.lib.I.q.31.art.2.3 [Francis of Mayrone, *Commentary on the Sentences*, bk. 1, q. 31, arts. 2 and 3].

55. In text-citation: D. Bannes in I.Thom.qu.23 [D. Bannes in 1 Thomas, q. 23. The author and the title of the work are not known].

all these together—namely, of the permission, forsaking and punishment—the manifestation of God's justice is the alone cause, considering that no work of ours is the cause of the permission), yet notwithstanding our wicked working or sin is the cause why we are damned and punished." Again: "We deny that God is cruel, for we say that God does not punish and torment the reprobate for the fulfilling (as it were) of his own fancy, but for sin eternally foreknown, which He determined so to dispose of by punishing of it, that His justice might be made manifest."[56]

Thomas: "Why He elects these to glory and rejects those, He has no reason but the divine will."[57] Again: "The difference of those which are to be saved from them that are to be damned proceeds from the principal invention of the first Agent." Again: "We must not inquire why He converted these and not those. For this comes of His own mere will." And Augustine upon John: "Why He draws this man and not that, do not desire to judge, if you would not err."[58]

Nevertheless, reprobation in regard of the second act—that is, in respect of the purpose to damn—is not absolute but for sin. For no man perishes but through his own default; and no man is absolutely ordained to hell or destruction but for his sin, having also received before in Adam's power whereby he was able to live holily and happily, if so be that he would. And therefore I say that that which they allege is a very calumny.

Secondly, I answer that God did not simply create man to destroy him, but that he might manifest His judgment by the just destruction of the sinner. Now it is one thing to will the destruction of a man as he is man, and another thing to will the deserved destruction of a man as he is a sinner. Here also the judgment of Cameracesis, a judicial schoolman, is to be heard and observed. "According to the Scripture," says he, "although God should punish or afflict some creature eternally or utterly abolish it without any sin in it, yet He should not deal unjustly or cruelly with it. Whence it is, *Wisdom 12.12*, Who dare accuse Thee, if the nations perish which Thou hast made? God is not bound to laws created, as if anything were just before God did will it, whereas indeed the contrary is true."[59]

---

56. In-text citation: Ferrariensis (in Thom.cont.Gent.pag 603) [Francesco Silvestri (*c.* 1474–1528), *Commentary on Four Books of Thomas Aquinas's Contra Gentiles*, p. 603. Francesco Silvestri was an Italian Dominican theologian most famous for his commentary on Aquinas's *Contra Gentiles*].

57. In the margin: Summ. I.par.quae.23.art.5. [Thomas Aquinas, *Summa Theologicae*, part 1, q. 23, art. 5].

58. In the margin: Contra Gen.l.I.c.44 [Augustine, *Contra Gentiles*, bk. 1, ch. 44].

59. In the margin: In Sent.i.1.qu.2:art.2. [Petrus de Alliaco, *Quaestiones super libros Sententiarum*, bk. 1, q. 22, art. 2. Petrus de Alliaco was also known as Cardinal Cameracesis].

[Third Objection]

The third crimination is that the stoical predestination and fate is brought in by us, because (as they say) we teach that all things come to pass by the necessary and energetical (ἐνέργεματος; powerful in working) decree of God, yea even the fall of Adam, the which (say they) God according to our opinion did decree and will. *Answer.* We say that Adam's fall came to pass [by] God not only foreknowing but also willing and decreeing it—and that without blasphemy, if you will friendly and courteously give leave to show how far forth and in what manner. The will of God is twofold: general and special. The special will (which the Scripture calls *cephets*) is that by which God does both approve and effect a thing; or else it is God's good pleasure, whereby taking delight in something He does will it simply, both as touching the doing of it as also in respect of approbation. The object of this will depends on the will and follows it as the effect follows the cause. And by this will our judgment is according to the word of God that God wills that which is good and nills that which is evil as it is evil. "Thou art a God which willest not iniquity" (Ps. 5:4). And of this kind or rather manner of will are these sentences of Augustine to be understood: "God has foreknown, but He did not foreappoint the works of ungodliness."[60] And, "He does only foreknow and not preordain evils." And, "It is all one to say God is the author and God wills." The general will is that whereby God wills a thing not to be (for that which is not therefore is not because He wills it shall not be); and for certain causes also He wills not to hinder some things and consequently wills that they shall come to pass, which things notwithstanding He does not simply approve. Or, it is the decree of God whereby He wills something not in respect of approbation and effecting of it by Himself, but only in respect of suffering it to be done by others. And here the thing which is to be done does not depend upon God's will, but only upon the will of the creature which falls away. And with this will we say that God willed the fall of Adam, yet not simply but only that it should come to pass. Now it is one thing to will a thing by itself, and another thing to will it as touching the event. Moreover, He wills the event of sin not by effecting it Himself, but by forsaking or not hindering when He might if He would. And if we enquire of the order of willing, it is this: first and properly God does will not to inhibit and not to hinder sin, and by consequent only He wills the event of sin. For that which God does not hinder does therefore come to pass because He does not hinder it; and as no good thing can either be or come to pass unless God make it, so no evil thing can be avoided except God

---

60. In the margin: Hypagnost.lib.6.lib.8.9.9.2. [Augustine, Hypognost., bk. 6, sect. 80, q. 92 (exact title of the work in not known)].

do hinder. And there is not the least thing which may be done without this will, unless we will say that God's providence is idle, which to say were wicked. The reasons of this our judgment are many. The first reason I will draw out of most evident testimonies of Scripture. "Him I say being delivered by the determinate counsel and foreknowledge of God, after you had taken, with wicked hands you have crucified and slain" (Acts 2:23). "They gathered themselves together, to do whatsoever Thine hand and Thy counsel had determined before to be done" (4:27–28). Here it is to be observed that not only Christ's passion but also the works which in respect of the Jews were wicked do come under the decree and will of God—to wit, so far forth as God willed that they should come to pass for just ends. This very thing Augustine signifies when he says, "When the Father delivered the Son, and Christ, His body, and Judas, his master—in this delivering wherefore is God just and man guilty, but because in one thing which they did, there is not one cause for which they did it?"[61] And there is no reason if it should seem harsh to any if speaking of Adam's fall we follow the Holy Scripture on this manner. "When Adam did eat of the forbidden fruit, he did eat that which the hand and counsel of God had determined before to be done." This is that very thing which we say. This is the language of the apostles and of the church, which therefore we may use without the least suspicion of blasphemy. But to the former testimonies I will add one place out of Peter: "It is better (if the will of God be so) that ye suffer for well doing, than for evil dong" (1 Peter 3:17). But to punish men for well doing in respect of men, it is flatly to transgress the law of God. Furthermore, God is said "to bid Shimei to curse David" (2 Sam. 16:10)—that is, to have ordained and decreed, for God bids and commands a thing two ways. First, by His revealed will; and this He does by His word delivered to men. Secondly, by His secret will, which is His providence or hidden decree by which He does so govern all things that nothing can be done without it or against it, as in these places: "I will command and call back the Assyrians against this city" (Jer. 34:22). "Who is he then that saith, and it cometh to pass, and the Lord commandeth it not?" (Lam. 3:37). "He saith to the snow, be thou upon the earth: likewise to the small rain, and to the great rain of His power" (Job 37:6). By which it appears that it may well be said that God decreed that Shimei should curse David, and it is the like kind of speech to say that God did not decree Adam's fall simply, but in some respect (ἁπλῶς κατά τὶ). The second reason follows. It is the common opinion of all men that God does will to suffer sin, but to will to suffer it is to will not to hinder it and to will not to confer grace. Now he which foreknows some future evil and wills not to hinder it when he might and not to confer confirming grace, he does

---

61. In the margin: Epist.ad.Vinc.38. [Augustine, *Letters,* Letter to Vincentius, letter 48].

indeed will that the same should come to pass. Therefore, we do not place that will whereby we say that God does will that sin should come to pass and be in nature either without or beyond the divine permission, but we do enwrap and enfold it in it. And this is that which Calvin says, and no other.[62] The same affirms Beza: "If any man hear that some things come to pass which indeed are done against His will—that is, against His liking—not because He cannot, but because He will not hinder them, I answer that it is all one as if a man should say that they come to pass He being willing they should. For those things which He could surely hinder if He would must needs come to pass, because by not hindering of them He wills that they should come to pass."[63] And whatever God does not hinder, He does therefore not hinder it either because He wills that it should be done or because He does utterly nill that it should be done or because He does not will it should be done or else because He cares not—that is, He neither wills nor nills that it should come to pass. If you grant the first, I have my desire. The second is absurd—namely that God does not hinder evil, because He does utterly nill that it should be done. For this is to make God inconstant. The third, Lombard and the schoolmen affirm. For they say that God in respect of sin has no positive act neither of willing nor of nilling, but only a negative act of not willing to hinder it.

But by this means a great part of those things which are done in the world should come to pass, God being either ignorant or negligent. The very permission also is a certain will and not a pure negation; for not to will to hinder—that is, to suffer—is indeed to will not to hinder. If you will say the fourth, you do wickedly make an idle and Epicurish god. Therefore, we must needs retire to the first—viz., that God does decree that evil should come to pass in such sort as I have declared. Yet the fault must not be for all that translated to Him, because He does justly and holily decree that which men do wickedly.

Thirdly, we know that Adam's revolting is now past and done. Therefore, we must say that God did will that it should be done—unless we shall say that His providence is not in all and every thing. You will say that an evil work is ordained of God—that is, disposed to God's glory, the salvation of the godly, and the destruction of the wicked. I grant it, but not this only. For the providence of God is over the world and every thing therein—both in respect of the end, as also of the beginning of every action. Satan and the wicked do not only

---

62. In the margin: In Genes.cap.3.ver.1. [John Calvin (1509–1564), *Commentary on Genesis*, Genesis 3:1. Calvin was one of the most influential continental Reformers of the Protestant Reformation].

63. In the margin: Ad Acta.colloq.Mampelg.pag.152. [Theodore Beza (1519–1605), *Acta Colloquii Montis Belligartensis*, 152. Theodore Beza was an influential French Reformed theologian, who succeeded Calvin as the leader of the Church in Geneva].

not finish that which they would, but they do not so much as begin it, unless God wills and gives leave. It seems impious to think that anything, though as little as may be, does either exist or come to pass besides that which God being always holy and just has willingly from all eternity decreed.

Fourthly, let us hear the judgment of the ancient church. Augustine: "We must know that all things are either pursued the Lord helping, or permitted the Lord forsaking, that you must know that nothing is at all admitted the Lord being unwilling."[64] Again: "There is nothing done but that which the Almighty wills to be done, either by suffering it to be done or by doing it Himself."[65] Again: "Sometimes a man wills a thing with a holy will which God wills not." Again: "It is possible that a man should will this with an evil will which God wills with a good will. So much difference is there 'tween what is fitting for man to will and what is fitting for God to will, and to what end everyone refers his will, so as that it may be allowed or disapproved." And again, in Psalm 148: "Know that whatever falls out here contrary to our will happens not but by the will of God, His providence, ordinance, appointment and decrees." Tertullian: "God has foreknown all things by disposing them, and disposed them by foreknowing them."[66] Jerome: "Shall I say that anything is done without Thee, and that the wicked can do so much against Thy will? Surely it were blasphemy so to imagine."[67] And again: "Whatever good or evil things are in the world, they happen not by casual chance and without the providence of God, but by His pleasure."[68] Hugo says, "Men may well endure the hearing of this, and it may be said without any scruple or trouble of conscience. God wills that which is good. But if it be said, God wills that which is evil, it is a thing very grievous to be heard, and a religious mind does not easily conceit of that which is goodness itself, that it wills evil; for then it seems to be said that the good loves that which is evil and approves that which is bad, and therefore a godly mind rejects this, not because that which is said is not well said, but because that which is well said is not well understood."[69] But after what sort it ought to be understood, he himself in the selfsame place explains: "This," says he, "is only said, and yet another thing is meant and understood, because God wills that evil be, and yet wills not the evil." And again: "When He does good and suffers evil, His will

---

64. In the margin: De Praed.in grat.c.15. [Augustine, *Of Predestination and Grace*, ch. 15].

65. In the margin: Enchir.c.95.101. [Augustine, *Enchiridion*, chs. 95 and 101].

66. In the margin: Cont.Marcel.lib. [Tertullian, *Contra Marcel*].

67. In the margin: In Abacnc.cap.I. [Jerome, Abacnc, ch. 1 (the exact title of this work is not known)].

68. In the margin: In Jerem.12.cap. [Jerome, Abacnc, ch. 1 (the exact title of this work is not known)].

69. In the margin: Lib.desacra.I.c.13.par.14. [Hugh of Saint Victor, *An Exposition of Certain Words of Saint Paul, to the Romans*, bk. 1, ch. 13, para. 14].

appears in this, because He wills that to be which He does or permits."[70] And again: "The will of God is His good pleasure, and His will is His working, and His will is His permission." Catharinus says, "We need not be afraid to confess that God wills sin, as blessed Augustine says also, not because He wills sin as it is sin and evil, but as it is good—to wit, as it is the punishment of sin and vengeance in the reprobate (for that is God's purpose, and it is good and not evil), or as sin itself is an occasion to good in His beloved and elect."[71]

But they use to object thus: To will that evil be done is proper and belongs to an evil will which is delighted with evils, or would use them to good, contrary to the rule, that no evil should be done that good might come thereof. To this I answer that here are two grounds to be laid. The first is that the object even of man's will is good, and therefore much more of God's will; and the object of the will cannot be evil by itself but by accident. For if the will wills evil, it wills it not as it is evil, but as it is good. The second ground is that there is a certain *summum bonum* or sovereign good with which there is no evil conjoined, because there is a certain thing infinitely good—namely, God—but there is not any absolute evil, because there is nothing so evil but it has some good joined therewith, and therefore it is good that sin should be and come to pass. So says St. Augustine: "Although therefore those things which are evil so far forth as they are evil are not good, nevertheless it is good that there should be not only good things, but also evil. For unless this were good that there should be also evils, they should by no means be suffered by the Almighty, who is goodness itself."[72] Thus therefore I answer that sin in the causes and circumstances thereof fully and exactly weighed is two ways to be considered. First, we consider sin not as it is sin, but so far forth as it has some respect to good with God, which decrees it. And this way taking sin, although God wills it not simply and by itself, yet He decrees it and wills it as touching the event. Moreover, sin has respect to God two manner of ways. First, because it is in that which is good; secondly, because it tends to that which is good. I say it is in that which is good, because every evil is in that which is good as in the subject. Now in respect of the subject—that is, as sin is a motion, an inclination, or an action—God both wills and effects the same. Moreover, sin tends to that which is good because God ordains it to good and from thence draws the good either of trial, chastisement, or punishment. And we say that God is so far forth willing that

---

70. In the margin: Lib.I.cap.part.4,de sur. [Hugh of Saint Victor, *An Exposition of Certain Words of Saint Paul, to the Romans*, bk. 1, ch. 4].

71. In the margin: In ep.Paul, ad Rom. [Catharinus, *Commentary on Romans*. Little is known about this author].

72. In the margin: Enchirid.98. [Augustine, *Enchiridion*, ch. 98].

sin should come to pass as He is able and will by His wonderful wisdom from thence to draw forth that which is good.

Secondly, we consider sin according to the property and natural being thereof—that is, sin as it is sin. And this way also we weigh sin either so far forth as it is sin in itself in regard of men, or as it is sin to God. But God Himself neither wills nor approves nor effects sin as it is sin in itself in regard of the creatures that offend; and yet He wills as touching the event, not simply as those things that are good in themselves, but only by willing to permit that it may be. For there is a threefold action of God's will. The first is that whereby God wills anything by willing it—that is, when He wills it with His whole and absolute will, as Tertullian says; and this way He wills that which is good in itself. The second action is that whereby He wills anything by nilling it, as that which shall never come to pass because God does utterly nill the being thereof. The third and last action is remiss and in the middest between both, whereby He wills some thing by nilling it slackly or remissly—that is, when He partly wills it and partly nills it, or else so far forth wills it as that for just causes He nills it. And after this sort is not absolutely evil, and God draws good out of evil as it is evil in the nature thereof or in itself, as He brought forth light out of darkness even as it was darkness in itself. And if so be that evil were absolutely evil as God is absolutely good, He would in no wise will the event of evil, neither should there be any evil existent at all. For that which God utterly nills has not any being or existence. But sin as it is sin to God (now that is a sin to God which is in itself sin, in His decree whereby all things are ordained as it considers sin), He neither wills it nor approves it nor works it—no in this respect He does not so much as permit it. I do not deny but that God permits and suffers evil as it is evil in itself (otherwise there were not evil properly and naturally), but I deny that He permits it because it is evil. For God never suffers evil for itself, but for the good that is therewith conjoined. And this is the meaning of that saying of Beza: "The Lord never permits sins as they are sins, yea rather He evermore forbids and hinders them." And again: "Sins so far forth as they are permitted by God being thereto willing are not sins but the punishments of sin."[73] And thus using this exposition is the mind and judgment of Master Calvin of blessed memory to be understood, "where as he says that all the sons of Adam did fall away by God's will"; and again, "that it was decreed by God that Adam should perish by his own falling away"; and again, "it was the secret counsel of God in which the fall

---

73. In the margin: Lib.cont.Castel.de praedest [This is probably a reference to Theodore Beza's book against the French theologian Sebastian Castellio (1515–1563), entitled *Responsio ad defensiones et reprehensiones Sebastiani Castellionis* (1563)].

of man was ordained";[74] and again, "Adam did not fall away but according to God's knowledge and ordinance."[75] In these and such like manner of speeches His purpose was to overthrow the opinion of the schoolmen who would have His permission severed from His will. It were good therefore for them better to consider of the matter who without either charity or humanity do with the blasphemies of the Manichees slander and belie this holy man.

Secondly, they use to object that God wills things contrary, if He will that that should come to pass which He forbids in His law. *Answer.* It is true indeed, if He should will one and the same thing to come to pass and not to come to pass in one and the same respect and manner; but God forbids evil as it is evil, and wills it to come to pass as it has respect to good. Hereupon Aquinas says, "That evil be and that evil be not are contradictorily opposed; but that God wills evil to be and that God wills evil not to be are not contradictorily opposed, seeing both are affirmative."[76]

Thirdly, they object thus: that thing which being granted another thing necessarily follows is the cause of that selfsame thing that does follow. But this being granted that God willed the fall of Adam to come to pass, the same came to pass necessarily and infallibly. Therefore, the will of God was in this respect the cause of sin. Whereto I answer that the first proposition of this argument is not general, for in admitting the creation of the world, both the place and the time or continuance thereof are infallibly and without doubt also to be admitted, and yet the creation of the world is not the cause of the continuance thereof and of the place where it now consists. And that this proposition may be true, it is thus to be framed: that thing which being granted another thing infallibly follows (no other cause coming between) is the cause of the very same thing that follows. And the second proposition also fitted to this former is untrue. For this being granted that God wills sin to happen, sin shall not come to pass immediately, but by the means of man's free will. And although it come to pass infallibly on God's part which decrees it, yet it comes to pass freely on man's part; for it had been possible for man not to have sinned when he did sin if he had willed—as may appear by this similitude: God forsakes man by not conferring and bestowing on him necessary and sufficient help for the avoiding of sins. Now man being forsaken by Him sins necessarily, and yet the fault is not to be laid on God because that in this His forsaking him the will of man comes between. For God forsakes man being willing to be forsaken, and not against his will and mind.

---

74. In the margin: Instit,.lib.3e.cap.23.5.4, 5.7. [John Calvin, *Institutes of Christian Religion*, bk. 3, ch. 23.5.4 and ch. 5.7].

75. In the margin: Opust.905.8.616. [Calvin, Opust.905.8.616] .

76. In the margin: Summ.q.9.art.9. [Thomas Aquinas, *Summa Theologicae* [no part given], q. 9, art. 9].

Secondly, I answer to the aforesaid reproach of our doctrine, that we say not that sin is from the decree or of the decree of God, as from the efficient, material, formal, or final cause. But we do teach and aver that sin comes to pass according to the providence or decree of God as the sole consequent thereof. For we assuredly think and judge that the decree of God does so go before the sin of man as that it has no respect to any cause, unless it be of such a one as is a failing and deficient cause. So says Augustine: "Therefore, truly the great works of the Lord are exquisite in all His wills, so that after a wonderful and unspeakable manner that is not done beside His will, which notwithstanding is done contrary to His will."[77]

Again it is objected, he that says that the decree of God is the energetical operative beginning of all things necessarily makes the decree of God the beginning also of sin. Whereto I answer that the Holy Ghost Himself says that the decree of God is the beginning of all things being and existent: "God worketh all things after the counsel of His own will" (Eph. 1:11). And again in the seventeenth [chapter] of Acts, "In Him we live, we move, and have our being." Augustine says, "The will of God is the very cause of all things which are."[78] Hugo de St. Victor says, "There is no cause of the will of God, which is the cause of all things." And this very thing common reason will teach us, because there must first some certain ground be laid from whence everything should have or take the being and existence thereof; and this ground is even the very will of God. For a thing is not first, and then afterward God wills it to come to pass. But, because God has decreed that a thing should come to pass or be done, therefore it is. And yet shall not God therefore be the cause of sin, because sin is not properly a thing, action, or being, but a defect only; and yet nevertheless it is not therefore nothing. For whatever has a being is either really and positively or else in reason only.[79] And under those things which are in reason are contained not only notions and relations, but also privations, because they have not a real matter and form out of the understanding. But sin has not a positive and real being, and yet it has a being in reason (as they term it). For so far forth it is in the nature of things being as it may cause a true composition in the mind, and although it do not exist positively—that is, by matter or form created—yet it is privately[80] because that by the remove or taking away or original righteousness, that does immediately and truly follow and exist. Neither does it follow as

---

77. In the margin: Enchir.cap.101. [Augustine, *Enchiridion*, ch. 101].

78. In the margin: Degene.cont.Manic.lib.1.c.2. [Augustine, *On Genesis: Two Books on Genesis Against the Manichees*].

79. In the margin: Eus Real & Rationale. [Hugh of Saint Victor, Real and Rationale].

80. The Greek in the margin is illegible.

some other natural habit or as a pure negation, but as a certain thing between both—that is, a want and absence of the contrary good.

Some use to object that we to teach that God does incline to sin and that He does positively harden the heart. Whereto I answer that we allow not a bare permission severed utterly from His will, neither do we attribute a positive or natural action to God, as though He did infuse corruption and sin; and yet we say that He does actively harden the heart. The action of God's providence, as says Suidas, in the works of men is threefold. The first is according to His good pleasure (και εὐδοκίαν[81]), whereby God wills any work, allows it, effects it, and is therewith delighted. This action is only in good works, which have their beginning in us from the Holy Ghost. The second action of God's providence is of sustaining (κατὰ οἰκονομίαν[82]), whereby God upholds and maintains the being and all the faculties, motions, actions and passions of nature which offend. "In Him we live, and move, and have our being" (Acts 17:28).

And although God do sustain nature offending and the action of nature, yet is He free from fault, because He upholds the creature only as it is a creature, not as it is evil. For the second cause, as the will of man, can by itself do evily and corruptly; yet it can do nothing by itself unless the effect thereof be reduced to the first cause—as may appear more plainly by this similitude: a man does halt by reason that his leg is out of joint. Now here are two things to be considered: the very walking or motion itself, and his halting. The halting proceeds only from his leg out of joint; the walking, both from his leg and also from the faculty of moving. In like manner, a man sinning, in that he does it is of God; but in that he does evily, it is of himself. We must therefore here know that God does uphold order as it is of nature, but furthers not the will violently breaking out against the order of the moral law. The third action of God's providence is according to concession (κατα συγχωρησιν[83]), whereby God in the evil work of man works some things holily. And this last action is threefold. The first is permission, whereby God forsakes especially the wicked by withdrawing from them His grace and by leaving them according to their deserts to their own wickedness, which He had before restrained, that it might not break forth to so immoderate liberty. And we use commonly to say that he which permits does and effects something—as when the rider gives the reins to his wanton and sporting horse, we say that he does move and encourage him; and we say that the hunter does put his dog on the game when as he lets him slip. The second action (as I may so term it) is occasional, whereby God by proffered occasions, in themselves good or indifferent, outwardly draws forth,

---

81. The Greek in the margin is illegible.
82. The Greek in the margin is illegible.
83. The Greek in the margin is illegible.

stirs up, and brings out sin in those who of themselves openly run into wickedness, to the intent that He may either justly punish their known impiety, or else discover it being closely shrouded. The like have we ordinarily even among ourselves, for the physician by his preservative medicine stirs up, enflames, and draws forth the humors out of the corruption of the body. Admit a house be weakly timbered, which being almost now already fallen will ere long fall, and that I do not with any engines or instruments throw or beat down the same, but only take away the outward hindrances, and on every side as it were open a way for the downfall to the intent that when it falls, it may by the greater fall be broken in pieces. After this sort deals God with the wicked, and hereupon is it that the law is said to stir up and increase sin in Paul (Rom. 7:8). This action is done many manner of ways, as when the hindrances of sin are taken away; when as the way is opened to the committing of one especial sin, and not of another; when as objects are offered, which the ungodly use as instigations to sin. These objects are commandments, threatenings, exhortations, and cogitations either good or indifferent put by God in the minds of ungodly men, from the which the wicked by reason of his wickedness does greedily take an occasion to do ill. And this is the manner and way truly whereby we say that God stirs man to evil without infusing the least drop or jot of evil. For as in the middle region of the air the heat grows stronger by the antiperistalsis[84] or repulsion on every part, from whence proceeds the thunder and lightning; and by the heat round encompassed, the clouds are condensated and made thick, even so the wicked and ungodly when they are stirred up by wholesome precepts do grow more ungodly. And evil does so much the more begin to delight them by how much the more they know that it is little lawful for them— according to the saying of the poet: *netimur in vetitum semper cupimus que negata.* We still endeavor things forbidden, and covet that is denied. The third action is a disposing, whereby God through the evil work of an evil instrument finishes His own work justly and holily. As for example, the sale of Joseph in his brethren was sin. The just action of God in this evil work was the fore-sending of Joseph into Egypt for the common good and benefit of Jacob's family. And from this disposing proceeds it, that God uses the sins of men holily, that He provokes them holily, and orders them as the physician for a medicine orders poison, contrary to the nature thereof; that He orders them holily both according to the causes and beginnings and also according to the ends and issue, as when He disposes the work of the devil infusing corruption, either to the punishment of correction, vengeance, or trial. But concerning these, let us rather give care to ancient writers. Clemens Alexandrinum says, "It belongs to God's

---

84. *Antiperistalsis*: intestine contractions which push the contents in the reverse direction.

wisdom, virtue, and power not only to do good, which is the nature of God, but also especially to bring to some good and profitable end that which has been invented by those which are evil and use profitably those things which do seem evil."[85] Augustine says, "God makes and ordains just men, but He makes not sinners as they are sinners, but orders them only."[86] And again: "As God is the most excellent Creator of good natures, so is He the most just disposer of evil wills." Again: "God verily fulfills certain of His good wills by the evil wills of evil men."[87] Again: "God by those men which do those things which He will not, does Himself those things which He will."[88] And again: "God using well even those that are evil as being Himself absolutely good, so far forth as in them lay they did that which God would not. In this very thing that they did that which was contrary to God's will, even by them His will is done."[89] And again: "Who would not tremble at these judgments of God, whereby God does in the hearts of evil men whatever He will, giving to them according to their deserts?"[90] And again: "It is plain that God works in the hearts of men to incline their wills whithersoever He will, either to those things that are good for mercy or else to evil for their deserts, sometimes verily in His open judgment, sometimes in His secret judgment, but evermore in His just judgment." And again: "God makes not evil wills, but uses them as He list, because He cannot will anything that is unjust."[91] Fulgentius says, "Although God be not the author of evil thoughts, yet He is the disposer of evil wills; and out of the evil work of everyone He does not cease to work that which is good."

In respect of these divers actions concerning sin, it comes to pass that we find it said in the Scripture that God does harden, does make blind, does deceive, does command a work that is evil, yea and does the same, and that He delivers over to beastly affections, etc. (2 Sam. 12:12, 16; 10, 24).

Thirdly, I answer to the aforesaid reproach of this our doctrine that we do utterly abhor and detest the stoical fate because it appoints an inherent necessity in things themselves which should bind even God Himself and all other things and make them subject thereto. For however we do believe that the very decree of God is immutable and therefore necessary, yet in God Himself it was most free (for He could either not have decreed that which He did decree, or else otherwise have decreed it); and He adds to the second causes placed out

---

85. In the margin: Strom.lib.1. [Clement of Alexandria, *Stromata*, bk. 1].

86. In the margin: De gen.ad lit.impers.cap.5. [This is probably a reference to Augustine's essay "A Literal Meaning of Genesis," ch. 5].

87. In the margin: De civit. Dei lib.II.cap.17. [*The City of God*, bk. 2, ch. 17].

88. In the margin: Enchir.ad Laur.c.101. [Augustine, *Enchiridion*, ch. 101].

89. In the margin: De cor. Grat.c.14. [Augustine, *On Rebuke and Grace*, ch. 14].

90. In the margin: De grat. & lib.arb.c.21. [Augustine, *On Grace and Free Will*, ch. 21].

91. In the margin: Cont.Jul.lib.5.cap.3. [Augustine, *Against Julian*, bk. 5, ch. 3].

of God a certain necessity, but yet so free a one as that it is rather to be termed a liberty than a necessity. And this shall easily appear to be as I say if I shall first show what sorts of necessity there be and how far forth it is agreeable to things. First therefore, a thing is necessary two ways: absolutely and conditionally. That is absolutely necessary which cannot be otherwise, or else whose contrary is impossible, as that God is omnipotent and just. And that is conditionally necessary which cannot be otherwise, but yet not simply, but by the granting of one or many things. And this kind of necessity is either by nature or the commandment or decree of God. That is necessary by nature which comes to pass constantly and immutably by reason of that order which God has set in the nature of things. After this sort is it of necessity that fire does burn, that the earth is carried downward, and the heaven moved. That is necessary by commandment which is necessarily to be done because God has commanded it. After this sort it is of necessity that one undergo the office of a magistrate (Rom. 13:5). That is necessary by the decree of God which is so because God has foreknown it and willed either to effect it or at the least to permit it. After this sort everything in respect of God is necessary, and "the will of God," as Augustine says, "is the necessity of things."[92] Secondly, necessity is either of compulsion or infallibility. Necessity of compulsion is that which infers violence to things by some cause working without and forcibly constrains that they do either this or that. And this indeed is the stoical necessity,[93] that a man should do anything against his will being compelled by force and necessity. There is also such a like kind of necessity of the Manicheans, condemned by the fathers, who taught that there was no violence or necessity offered to the will by God, nor that it was forced by necessity to sin. The necessity of infallibility is that whereby a thing according to the event shall certainly and immutably come to pass, yet so as if we consider the cause of a thing by itself, it may either not come to pass or else come otherwise to pass. Of this manner of necessity we must understand that principle: everything that is, when it is, is of necessity. And thus is necessity distinguished. Now will I show how far forth it is agreeable to several things. The events of all things have reference either to the second causes or to God, who is the first cause. Now some things in respect of the second causes are necessary, othersome contingent. From causes which are necessary must needs proceed that which is necessary; from those that are free, that which is free; from those that are natural, that which is natural; and to be brief, such as are the next causes foregoing, such also is the event of things. But

---

92. In the margin: De civit. Dei lib.5.cap.8.9.10.&de genesi ad lit.lib.5.cap.15. [Augustine, *City of God*, bk. 5, chs. 8–10; The second citation is either from Augustine *On Genesis: Two Books on Genesis Against the Manichees* or "A Literal Meaning of Genesis," ch. 5].

93. In the margin: Tull. De Finibus.

in respect of God, all things whatever are partly changeable and partly necessary. In respect of God's liberty, which does that which it does freely, all things are contingent and mutable; however, according to nature and the order of the next causes, they be necessary and immutable. In respect of God's decree, the second causes and the effects of them are all necessary; however, in themselves they be uncertain and contingent. And yet they are not absolutely necessary, but by the supposition of God's decree; neither are they necessary by the necessity of compulsion, but of infallibility only, because God ordained before that those things which should come to pass should be. And this kind of necessity takes not away the contingency and liberty of second causes, but rather establishes and confirms it. For that which is free works freely, and that which is contingent works contingently by the necessary decree of God. Neither do liberty and necessity mutually overthrow each other, but liberty and compulsion. It is manifest therefore that God's decree causes an immutability to all things, of which notwithstanding some in respect of the next cause are necessary, and othersome contingent, but all of them in respect of God's liberty mutable. And as the mutability which things have from God's power takes not away the necessity which they have from the second causes, so the necessity of immutability by God's decree consequently coming to pass takes not away the contingency which they have from the next causes and God's liberty. Moreover, we say that God's decree ordains the second causes and the very liberty itself also of man's will not by compulsion, as if a man should violently throw a stone, but by inclining and gently bending them by objects outwardly offered to the understanding (even as a sheep is said to be drawn when grass is showed her being hungry),[94] that a man may choose by his own free motion or refuse that which God has justly decreed from all eternity.

These things being granted, it is manifest also what we ought to think concerning the fall of Adam, which truly according to the event is necessary by the necessity of infallibility by reason of the foreknowledge and decree of God, yet so as that God is not guilty of any fault, because the decree of God however it was necessary in itself, yet it planted nothing in Adam whereby he should fall into sin, but left him to his own liberty, not hindering his fall when it might. And the same fall in respect of man's will (which does that freely that it does) came to pass contingently and most freely. But you will say that Adam could not withstand God's will—that is, His decree. Wherefore, I answer that even as he could not, so also he would not. But you will say again he could not will otherwise. Which I confess to be true as touching the act and event, but not as

---

94. In the margin: August.de verb.Apost.ser.2. [Augustine, "On the Words of the Apostles," sermon 2 11. This is possibly a reference to one of Augustine's sermons with that title].

touching the very power of his will, which was not compelled but of the own free motion consented to the suggestion of the devil. But to the intent that these things may more plainly be understood, we must make distinction between three times: the time going before his fall, the present time of his fall, and the time after his fall. In the first moment of time, the fall of Adam was necessary in a double respect. First, by reason of the foreknowledge of God, for that which He foreknew would come to pass must needs of necessity come to pass. Secondly, by reason of the permissive decree of God, that fall was according to the event necessary immutably. Honorius Augustodunensis says, "It cannot otherwise be but that all things must come to pass which God has predestinated and foreknown, seeing that He only either does all things or permits them to be done."[95] Hugo de St. Victore says, "Sin follows of necessity by the withdrawing of grace."[96] And the reason hereof is very easy, because evil permitted must come to pass and cannot otherwise come to pass than God permits. For to permit evil is not to stir up the will and not to bestow on him that is tempted the act of resisting, but to leave him as it were to himself; and he whose will is not stirred up by God and to whom the act of resisting is not conferred, however he may have power to withstand, yet can he not actually will to withstand nor persist forever in that uprightness wherein he was created, God denying him strength. I confess truly that this kind of necessity as touching the liberty of man's will was altogether evitable and to be avoided, and yet according to the event of the action it was inevitable. Yet I would not that any man should think that this necessity did any way proceed from the decree of God, which did only follow the decree being granted and admitted; and Adam in his temptation being destitute of the help of God cast himself of his own accord into this same ensuing necessity of sinning. In the second time, his fall being present, there was another necessity thereof, because when it was it was of necessity. In the third time, man drew to himself by his fault, his nature being now corrupted, another necessity of sinning, insomuch that he made himself the servant of sin. Bernard says, "I know not after what evil and strange manner the will itself corrupted or changed to worse makes a necessity to sin; and yet the necessity although it be voluntary is not able to excuse the will, nor the will, although it be enticed, to exclude necessity."

If any man shall say that by this our platform many are tied by an inevitable necessity to be damned, I would have him give care to Augustine, who says, "Hold this most steadfastly and doubt not in any wise that any can perish

---

95. In the margin: Dial.de praed.citat.in catalogo Illyirici. [This is a reference to an unknown title by the twelfth-century theologian Honorius Augustodunensis (1080–c. 1154)].

96. In the margin: Quaest.in Rom.44. [Hugh of Saint Victor (c. 1096–1141), *An Exposition of Certain Words of Saint Paul, to the Romans*, q. 44].

whom God before the creation of the world has of His free goodness made vessels of mercy—or that any of them whom He has not predestinated to eternal life can by any means be saved."[97] And yet I say that the decree of reprobation does not cause a necessity of damnation in any man. For the first act thereof, which is a purpose not to show mercy, causes not this necessity in men, but goes before it as an antecedent. And man himself verily has brought upon himself this necessity with his own most free yet rebelling will. Now the second act of reprobation, which is a purpose of condemning, causes not any necessity of damnation, but by the sin of man coming between. Moreover, the necessity of damnation follows after the same manner by the foreknowledge of God; and yet this never seemed a thing strange to any one. But some will say that the foreknowledge of God does never cause in men any necessity of damnation, although it do assuredly foresee the same. And I say also that reprobation does either not at all cause damnation in man, or that it does not cause it, but for sin. But it may be objected, they that are predestinated to damnation cannot be freed by repentance, although they would. Whereto I answer with Augustine, "As they did fall by their will, so by their will they are content to lie; and he that turns himself away from God has both deprived himself of will to do that which is good and also of power. It does not therefore follow (as they imagine which object such things) that God has taken repentance from those to whom He gave it not, and has thrown down those whom He has not taken up."[98]

Moreover, the selfsame necessity follows of their hypothesis who affirm a bare permission. For that which God permits, the selfsame thing will He not hinder; and evil, if God hinder not, cannot be avoided. And that which cannot be avoided shall come to pass infallibly. And therefore evil, permission being once granted, of necessity comes to pass, although most freely on man's part. Whereupon, it is plain that the decree of God is not more inevitable than is the very permission separated from the decree. I do wish that they would well weigh and consider this who object to us either the stoical fate or the dotages of the Manichees. For we differ from them as much in certain judgments and opinion as whoever do differ most. For first, the Stoics do tie God to the second causes, so that He cannot do otherwise than the nature of them will suffer. We on the other side do hold that all second causes do depend upon and are ordered by God. Secondly, the Stoics say that neither God nor second causes can do otherwise by their nature than they do. We say that some second causes are by God's ordinance mutable, othersome immutable; and that God Himself can either not do that which He does or else do it otherwise. But now to come

---

97. In the margin: De fide ad Peter cap.35. [Augustine, *De fide ad Petrum Diaconum*, ch. 35].
98. In the margin: Art. 15. [Augustine, art. 15 (book not specified].

to the Manichees, who make two coeternal gods; we, but one. They of their two gods make one good and another evil. We say that there is one absolutely good and just God. Thirdly, they will have one of their gods to be the cause and worker of good things, and the other of evil. We make one true God the Creator and ruler of all things and working nothing but that which is most good and most just. Fourthly, they say that they which are created by their good God cannot sin. We say that God does most freely convert whom He will; and when they are converted, they can never in this life perfectly be free from sins, but do sometimes run into such sins as do grievously wound the conscience. Fifthly, they say that they that are created by the evil God simply cannot be converted. We say that unclean spirits and men were created both good and holy, but yet they fell by their own will and fault, and not by any fault but the just permission of the Creator, and brought upon themselves a necessity of sinning. And although it be true that man cannot withhold himself from sinning unless God give him that grace, yet does he not sin of necessity—that is, of compulsion—but willingly. And the will has sufficient liberty if by itself or the nature thereof it be inclinable to the contrary of that which it chooses and does of the own accord choose that which it chooses, although the same liberty be governed and one way limited by God. Wherefore, I am of Anselm's opinion, who says, "Although it be of necessity that those things do come to pass which are foreknown and predestinated, yet some things foreknown and predestinated do not come to pass by that necessity which goes before a thing and causes it, but by the same necessity which follows a thing. For God does not cause, although He does predestinate them, by forcing the will as by resisting it, but by leaving them in the power thereof."[99] And I am also of Gaudentius's opinion, who says, "The Jews were willing to do that evil which they did. And verily, if they had been unwilling to do it they had not done it. And it is a gross sin but to think that God, who is not only good and righteous, but also goodness and righteousness itself, does either command or compel anything to be done which He condemns when it is done."[100] But that I may in a word fully deliver my opinion, if it be demanded how the will of God carries itself to good or evil, I answer that in a good act God carries Himself positively. For first, He determines the event of good by willing effectually to work it; and secondly, He inwardly inclines the will of the creature to do that good which it does. Thirdly, He sometimes lays a necessity of immutability on him that does well, but yet it is joined with an exceeding freedom. After this sort the elect angels do necessarily obey God, yet not by constraint, but greatly coveting and with all

---

99. In the margin: Lib.de concor.grat. & lib.arbitr. [Augustine, *On Rebuke and Grace*].

100. In the margin: Ser. 3.ad Neophy. [This is possibly a reference to the theologian Gaudentius of Brescia (*d.* 410)].

the strength of their will desiring it, not being thereto compelled. In an evil act, I say that God carries Himself privatively, not by a logical, but a natural privation foregoing the habit. For first, He wills that evil come to pass not by doing it Himself, but by willing not to hinder it to be done by others. Secondly, He does not inwardly incline the will to do evil, but He forsakes and outwardly offers objects which are good in themselves. Thirdly, God lays not on us any necessity, but a desertion or want of grace, to which being imposed follows the necessity of sinning, not as the effect does his cause, but as the defect does him that forsakes. And this I am resolved on, that God's decree does altogether order every event partly by inclining and gently bending the will in all things that are good and partly by forsaking it in things that are evil, and yet the will of the creature left to itself is carried headlong of the own accord not of necessity in itself, but contingently that way which the decree of God determined from eternity. We therefore (thanks be given to God) do with all our hearts renounce the doting follies of the Stoics and the Manichees.

[Objection 4]
The fourth crimination is that we do teach, that the greatest part of mankind is deprived of Christ and all saving grace. *Answer 1.* It might happily seem a rigorous course that some should be deprived of Christ, if so be that they had never at any time nor anywhere received saving grace. But all and every one received holiness and happiness in Adam, together with ability to persevere and remain in the same holy and happy estate, if they had willed. But Adam would not, but did of his own accord cast away that grace which was bestowed on him by his Creator; for which being lost, it is a wonder that all without exception are not damned. And therefore it may seem the less strange to any one if grace by Christ be again bestowed upon one and not upon another.

Secondly, I answer that we do acknowledge with glad minds that Christ died for all (the Scripture averring so much); but we utterly deny that He died for all and every one alike in respect of God, or as well for the damned as elect, and that effectually on God's part. For first, let us weigh well the words of Christ: "I never knew you; depart from Me ye workers of iniquity" (Matt. 7:25). Now to know with God is to acknowledge; and therefore, whom Christ never knew, He never acknowledged for His. And those whom He has not sometime acknowledged, He never bought or redeemed with the price of His blood. And therefore, well says Gregory: "Not to know with God is to reject." Again, if all and every one be effectually redeemed, all and every one are reconciled to God, because that the forgiveness of sins and the satisfaction for the same are inseparably joined together. Yea, and Paul places redemption in the remission of sin, where he says: "By whom we have redemption through His blood, even the forgiveness of sins" (Eph. 1:7; Col. 1:14). Very well therefore, says Prosper, "As it is not sufficient for the renewing of men that Christ Jesus was born man, unless they be renewed also in the same Spirit whereof He was born, so it is not sufficient for man's redemption that Christ Jesus was crucified, unless we die together and be buried with Him in baptism."[101] Of these premises therefore I frame this assumption: but all are not reconciled to God, neither do all receive remission of sins; for then all men were blessed (Ps. 32:1). And it were not possible for them to perish, which thing to affirm of all and every one is very gross. Thirdly, Christ gave Himself that He might sanctify to Himself a people peculiar (λαος περιούσιον[102]) (Titus 2:14)—that is, as a precious treasure and His own gotten good selected and chosen from among others. Therefore, it was not Christ's purpose to give Himself for a ransom for all and every one alike. Fourthly, for whom redemption is ordained, to them all is given on God's part the making of them sons by Christ. But the making of sons or adoption is not granted to all and every one, even on God's part (John 1:12). For the power of the adoption whereby a man is made of the child of wrath the child of God is only given to those that believe and apprehend Christ. "They are," says Augustine, "the children of God who are not as yet so to us, and yet they are so to God, because that by believing they should afterward be so through the preaching of the gospel; and yet before this was so, they were engraven the children of God by a steadfast and immutable stability in the register of their Father. And again there are some which in respect even of some present or temporal grace which they have received are said by us to be the children of God, and yet are they not so to God."[103] Fifthly, none are truly redeemed on God's part, but they who are freed from sin, both according to the power that it has to cause damnation and also according to the power that it has to reign in them. In this do the ancient fathers agree. For Augustine says, "By this Mediator God shows that He does make them of evil men eternally good whom He has redeemed with His blood."[104] And again: "Those whom He would make His brethren, He freed and made them fellow heirs."[105] And again: "Christ will have no partaker in that which He has bought, but will possess it wholly to Himself, and to that end gave He so great a price, that He might only possess the same." Tychicus says,

---

101. In the margin: Lib.I.resp.pro Aug.object.9. [Prosper of Aquitane, *Pro Augustino responsiones*, bk. 1, obj. 9. Prosper of Aquitane (*c.* 390–455) was a disciple of Augustine and wrote this series of three defenses of Augustine's writings].

102. Idem Hugo de sanct. Vict. in annot. In Rom and Joachim. in Rev. part I.

103. In the margin: De Correp.& grat.c.9. [Augustine, *On Rebuke and Grace*, ch. 9].

104. In the margin: DeCorreo. & grat.c.11. [Augustine, *On Rebuke and Grace*, ch. 11].

105. In the margin: Tract.in Joh.2.&7. [Augustine, *Tractates on the Gospel of John*, tractates 2 and 7].

"Christ, who suffered for us, has freed us from sin and the bondage thereof."[106] Remigius says, "Thou art the reconciler, Thou art the reconcilement; and blessed shall they be for whom Thou shalt make reconciliation."[107] Out of these I thus conclude: all and every one are not redeemed according to both the aforesaid powers of sin. For let us grant that on God's part they are freed from damnation; yet they are not in such measure endued with grace, as that sin shall no more reign in them. Christ therefore is but only the half redeemer of these, and for that cause not a redeemer. Lastly, let us diligently consider the judgment of ancient writers. Ambrose says, "If you believe not, Christ came not down for you. Neither did He suffer for you."[108] Augustine says, "Everyone that is generated is damned, and no one is freed unless he be regenerated."[109] And again: "It is well said, I will have mercy on whom I will have mercy. For if the whole world being in thralldom and in the power of sin and most justly ordained to punishment be nevertheless in part by God's mercy freed, who can say to God, Why dost Thou condemn the world?"[110] And again: "He that has bought us at so dear a price will not that we whom He has bought should be destroyed. God has given a great price and bought those who He quickens."[111] And again: "Of whose mercy is it but of His who has sent Jesus Christ into the world to save sinners," whom He has both foreknown and predestinated, "and called, and justified, and glorified?"[112] Bernard says, "Christ needed none of those; neither did He any of these things in regard of Himself, but rather in regard of the elect. They were not directly the Jews to whom He was sent, but the elect for whom He was sent."[113] Haimo says, "Even as by one man death and sin came generally to our commendation, so by the one justice of man, which is of Christ, to all men elected and predestinated to eternal life came grace to the justification of life."[114] And again: "He took not away in the elect only original, but also actual

---

106. In the margin: In Levit.lib.1.c.23. [Tychicus, Commentary? on Leviticus, bk. 1, ch. 23. The identity of Tychicus is unknown].

107. In the margin: In Psal. 64. [Remigius of Auxerre, *Commentary on the Psalms*, Psalm 64. Remigius of Auxerre (*c.* 841–908) was a Benedictine monk and commentator].

108. In the margin: De fide ad Gratian. [Ambrose, *On Faith, to Gratian Augustus*].

109. In the margin: Ser.44.de verb. Apost. [Augustine, "On the Words of the Apostles," sermon 44. This is possibly a reference to one of Augustine's sermons with that title].

110. In the margin: Ser.20.de verb.Apost [Augustine, "On the Words of the Apostles," sermon 20. This is possibly a reference to one of Augustine's sermons with that title].

111. In the margin: Serm. 109. [Augustine, "On the Words of the Apostles," sermon 109. This is possibly a reference to one of Augustine's sermons with that title].

112. In the margin: De nat. & grat. Cont. Pel.cap.5. [Augustine, *On Nature and Grace Against the Pelagians*, ch. 5].

113. In the margin: Ser.4.de natali. [Bernard of Clairvaux, Sermon 4, De Natali].

114. In the margin: Comment.in Rom.C.5. [Haimo of Auxerre, *Commentary on Romans*, ch. 5].

sins; and therefore grace and the gift through grace did redound to the elect."[115] Aquinas says, "Christ's merit according to the sufficiency carries itself indifferently to all, but not according to the efficacy. Which happens partly by God's election, through which the effect of Christ's merits is mercifully bestowed on some, and partly by the just judgment of God withdrawn from othersome."[116]

Objection 1. Against this it is thus objected: The Scripture affirms that Christ redeemed the world. Whereto I answer that this word "world" in the writings of the apostles does not signify both all and every man that descended from Adam, but all nations in this last age of the world. "God," says Paul, "was reconciling the world to Him in Christ" (1 Cor. 15:18). What means this word "world" in this place? Surely not all men of all ages, but the Gentiles which were to be called after the ascension of Christ, as Paul plainly explaining his own mind shows. "Wherefore if the fall of them be the riches of the Gentiles, how much more shall their abundance be?" (Rom. 11:12). And again in the fifteenth verse: "If the casting away of them (that is, of the Jews) be the reconciling of the world; what shall the receiving be but life from the dead?" In these very words he plainly shows that the reconciliation of the world is the reconciliation of the Gentiles after the casting away of the Jews. And hereby it is most manifest that all the like places of Scripture which many do think to make for the universal redemption of all and every one are to be understood of some men to be called out of every nation and country after the death of Christ. And hereto also let us join the answer of Augustine, "He calls oftentimes even the church itself by the name of the world according to that, God was reconciling the world to Himself in Christ; and again, the Son of Man came not to judge the world, but that the world might be saved through Him. And John says in his epistle we have an advocate with the Father, Jesus Christ the just, and He is the reconciler of our sins, and not only of ours, but also of the whole world. Therefore, the whole world is the church, and the whole world hates the church. Therefore, the world hates the world, the malignant world the reconciled world, the damned the saved, and the defiled that which is cleansed. But this world which God in Christ reconciles to Himself and which by Christ is saved and to which all sin is through Christ pardoned is elected out of the malignant, damned, and defiled world."[117] Rupertus says, "The world surely which God loved we understand to be mankind—that is, the living and the dead: the dead, which in faith looked for His coming; the living, who should believe in Him, whether they were of the Jews or of the Gentiles. For so He says without any distinction either of Jew or Gentile universally, that everyone that believes in Him shall not perish, but

---

115. In the margin: Ibid. [Haimo, *Commentary on Romans*, ch. 5].
116. In the margin: Summa de verit. Mat.26.q.7. [Aquinas, Summa de verit., Matthew 26, q. 7].
117. In the margin: Tract.87.in John. [Augustine, *Tractates on the Gospel of John*, tractate 87].

have life everlasting."[118] And the common gloss expoundeth the world, "those that be the elect of the world."

Objection 2. Saint Paul says that "God will that all men be saved and come to the knowledge of the truth" (1 Tim. 2:4). I answer, first, that the place is not to be understood of all the posterity of Adam, but properly of those which live in the last age of the world. This I prove by conferring of the like places wherein Paul does plentifully show his meaning. "And the time of this ignorance God regarded not, but[119] now He admonisheth all men everywhere to repent" (Acts 17:30). "By the revelation of the mystery which was kept secret since the world began" (Rom. 16:25). "But now is opened and published—for the obedience of faith among all nations" (Rom. 16:26). "The mystery which was hid since the world began and from all ages is now made manifest to the saints" (Col. 1:26). "To whom God would make known Christ; whom we preach, admonishing every man and teaching every man, that we may present all men perfect in Christ Jesus" (Col. 1:27). And in the second epistle to the Corinthians, the sixth chapter and the second verse, he expounds that place of Isaiah where it is said, "In an acceptable time have I heard thee, and in a day of salvation have I helped thee, and I will preserve thee: and will give thee for a covenant of the people that thou mayest raise up the earth—that thou mayest say to the prisoners, go forth," after this fashion: "Behold, now" says he, "the accepted time"—that is, the time of the New Testament—"behold now the day of salvation." Saint Peter says, "Salvation ordained to be declared in the last times: concerning which the prophets which did prophesy of the grace which should afterward come to you, have searched and inquired" (1 Peter 2:10). And Christ Himself says most plainly of all, "When I shall be lifted up from the earth, I will draw all things to Me" (John 12:32). I therefore grant that God wills that all should be saved, but that God both wills and that He has always willed that all men in all ages should be saved I utterly deny, neither has Paul said so much. And among the ancient writers they which seem to affirm so much do notwithstanding in these kind of speeches doubtfully affirm it: "I do imagine that it may with reason and religion be believed. I do not think it irreligion to believe it. It may properly and religiously be believed."[120]

Secondly, I answer that God will that all men be saved—that is to say, of those that are saved. So says Augustine: "Even as it is said that all shall be

---

118. In the margin: Comment. In John.lib.3.cap.3. in 2 Cor. 8. [Presumably a commentary by Rupertus on John, bk. 3, ch. 3, on 2 Corinthians 5].

119. In the margin: Mark well the form of speech, for it is as much as if he had said, God "now willeth that all men should repent."

120. In the margin: Auth.de vocat.gent. l.2 cap. 8. Bellarm de grat. & lib. Arb.lib.3.cap.5 [Robert Bellarmine, *Of Grace and Liberty*, bk. 3, ch. 5].

quickened in Christ, although very many be punished by eternal death, because all whoever they are that do receive eternal life do not receive it but in Christ. For is it said that God will have all men to be saved, although He will have many not to be saved, because all who are saved are not saved but by Him willing it."[121] And again: "When we read in the holy Scriptures that God will have all men to be saved, although we know assuredly that all men are not saved, yet ought we not therefore so derogate anything from the omnipotent will of God, but thus to understand that which is written: who will have all men to be saved, as if it should be said, that no man was saved but he whom God would have to be saved"[122]—not that there is no man whom He will not have saved. Hayme says, "God will have all men to be saved. Let us then ask what is the reason why all men are not saved. To which answer must be made that that saying in the psalm is true: He spoke the word, and they were made. In like manner, He will save all men who are saved and who by His mercy desire to be saved."[123] For the apostle put the whole for the part, as it is in the gospel where the Lord says, "If I be lifted up from the earth, I will draw all to Me. For He has not drawn neither does He draw all men to Him, but all that are elect, and of all sorts, and nations."

Thirdly, I answer that God will not have everyone of every kind, but the kinds of everyone to be saved—that is to say, of every estate and condition some. Augustine says, "This very saying, Who will have all men to be saved, is so said not because there is no man whom He would have damned, who would not do any powerful miracles among them, who He says would have repented if he had; but that we by all men may understand every sort of men, by whatever differences distinguished, whether they be kings or subjects, noble or ignoble, high or low, learned or unlearned, strong or weak, witty, dull spirited or foolish, rich, poor or mean, men or women, infants or children, youths or young men, middle aged men or old men, in all languages, in all trades, in all conditions, in all professions, in the innumerable variety of wills and consciences, and what other differences soever there is among men."[124] These things says he very truly and rightly, for this word "all" is sometime taken distributively, and then it signifies every several and particular person. And Paul, to the intent that he might signify this (2 Thess. 1:3), joins the word "every one" with the word "all" (ἑκάστου πάντων) It is also often taken collectively, and then it signifies any, and not everyone—as when Christ is said to have healed every disease (Matt. 9:35)—that is, any disease. The double signification of this word Aristotle also

---

121. In the margin: Ep.207.ad vitalem. [Augustine, Epistle 207, *Ad Vitalem*].
122. In the margin: Enchir.ad Lauv.c.103. [Augustine, *Enchiridion*, ch. 103].
123. In the margin: In C.i.cp.I.ad Tine.
124. In the margin: Enchir.ad Laur.c.103. [Augustine, *Enchiridion*, ch. 103].

observed.[125] This word "all," says he, is taken two ways: first for everyone; and secondly, the word "all" is used when it does not signify everyone (ὡς ἑκάστου καί ουκ ὡσ ἑκάστου πάντων).[126] It is plain therefore that the word "all" has a doubtful signification. And of this mind also is St. Jerome: "It is like to that, says he, which is in the psalm, Every man is a liar. If every man be a liar, then is he also a liar which speaketh it, and if he be a liar which speaketh it, then is not that true which he speaketh, namely that every man is a liar. But, if this saying be true, these words every man does lie are (as I said before) to be understood after this sort." A great part of men are liars. And the apostle writeth elsewhere, "teaching every man": and again, "Admonishing every man"; not that he taught all men (for how many are there yet at this day which have neither heard of the apostle's doctrine," nor yet so much as his name?) "but that he should teach and admonish all that are in the church." Sedulus also says, "Many and all in Paul are one."[127]

Fourthly, St. Paul speaks in this place according to the charitable judgment of Christians, and not according to the judgment of secret and infallible certainty. Like to this is that also that he calls the faithful in several churches "men elected," among whom there were many which afterward fell away from the faith. And yet is not the apostle deceived; for it is one thing to speak according to his own affection, and another thing to speak as the matter is according as it is indeed. Augustine says, "We ought so charitably to be affected as to wish that all men be saved, as men that know not who appertain to the number of those that are predestinated and who are not."[128] And again: "We must as much as in us is, being unable to distinguish those that are predestinated from those that are not, desire that all men be saved and use sharp correction to all with an intent to heal them that they perish not."[129]

Hence it appears what we ought to think of Damascene's opinion, who divides the will of God into His precedent and consequent will. He calls that His precedent will whereby God, as He that is absolutely good, wills to bestow all good things, yea blessedness itself upon the creature. And by this will he affirms that God wills that all men should be saved and attain to His kingdom, because He made us not to punish us, but that He might make us partakers of His goodness as being good Himself. But His consequent will is that whereby for some certain circumstances of the creature He absolutely wills this or that. And by this will he says that God wills that man should be damned for sin,

125. In the margin: Pel.lib.2.cap.2. [Augustine, *Against Two Letters of the Pelagians*, ch. 2].
126. Perkins's Greek in the margin here and above is quite illegible.
127. In the margin: In epist.ad Rom. 6:5. [Jerome, *Commentary on Romans*, Romans 6:5].
128. In the margin: De Correp.&grat.6.15. [Augustine, *On Rebuke and Grace*, chs. 6 and 15].
129. In the margin: Cap.10. [Augustine, *On Rebuke and Grace*, ch. 10].

because He is just. And indeed this distinction in itself is to be allowed, but that is not a very fit example which he has set down or alleged concerning His precedent will. For there seems not to be in God such a will or (as they use to term it) such a wishing will,[130] whereby He will indefinitely and upon condition that all and every man of all ages should be saved. For first, it argues a finite power and insufficiency in him that wills. For whatever any one desires and earnestly wills, that will he bring to pass, unless he be hindered. As for example, the merchant desires and earnestly wills to save his ware; but being forced by a tempest, to the intent that himself may escape he does absolutely will to cast them into the sea. Yea indeed, this kind of will seems to argue weakness, because God wills that which shall not come to pass. But you will say that this will is conditional—that is, that God will that they be saved if they shall believe. And I say first that the will of God stands doubtful until the condition be fulfilled, and that the first cause is by this means held in suspense by the second causes. Moreover, there is given to men a free will either to believe or not to believe—that is, flexible and inclinable both ways either by grace or by nature, both which things are false, as I will afterward show. And therefore, this will is rather a human will than a divine. Hear what Anselmus says, "The will of God is taken four manner of ways by the principal doctors: first, for the knowledge of God; then, for the will of the saints, who will in charity that even the unjust should be saved; again, for human reason; and lastly, for God's commandments."[131] Secondly, this conditional will seems idle and unnecessary, especially in him whose power is infinite, because if he earnestly willed he would verily do a thing when he might without hindrance. Thirdly, God's will is not such concerning the angels, whereby He wills that all of them should be saved. Therefore, it may well be demanded whether His will be such concerning man. Fourthly, if God will that all men, as they are men, be saved, in like manner He will that all sinners, as they are sinners, be damned—which is absurd. Fifthly, that will which cannot be resisted is absolute; but God's antecedent or first will cannot be resisted (Rom. 9:19). For there Paul speaks of the will that goes before all causes. Therefore, the precedent will is absolute. And this will I make manifest after another manner. The will of God is that some should believe and persevere, and that othersome should be forsaken either not believing or not persevering. You will ask me haply how I know this. I answer, by the event, for as touching the event some believe and some do not believe. But to believe and to persevere is a certain kind of good action, and on the contrary not to believe or not to persevere is an evil action. And everything

---

130. In the margin: *Enchir. Ca. 98.*
131. In the margin: *Lib.de volunt.Dei.* [Anselm, De Volunt. Dei].

that is good is through the effectual will of God, and so far forth as there is or exists that which is good, so far forth God wills it and makes it to exist by willing it. And that evil, which comes to pass, comes to pass God not hindering it. And because God will not hinder it, therefore consequently it comes to pass. Hereupon it is certain that God wills that some should believe and persevere to the end, and that othersome do not so, yea, even without any condition. And no reason can be rendered wherefore He wills this. Therefore, this will is both absolute and fast; and therefore that universal precedent will concerning the salvation of all and every one in Christ is counterfeit and feigned. Sixthly, the ground of this opinion is that foresaid place of Paul, which I have already showed to be misunderstood. And yet that place lays not down to us any conditional but an absolute will. For there it is first affirmed that "God will have all men to be saved"; afterward, that "he will have all men to come to the knowledge of the truth"—that is, to faith, because by applying faith to the word of God we acknowledge the truth. Where is now then that condition of faith? Lastly, against Damascene I oppose Augustine,[132] who to the Pelagians urging this place of Scripture, God will that all men be saved, makes a double answer. First, he denies that it is not generally to be understood of the universality of men, and that by this argument: that which God wills, He effects. But He does not generally save all men. Therefore, He wills not. Secondly, he says that the place is to be understood of them which are actually saved, because all men which are saved are saved by the will of God. Again, I oppose against him Prosper also, who says, "If the will of God concerning the universal saving of mankind and the calling them to the knowledge of the truth is to be affirmed so indifferently throughout all ages as that it shall be said to overpass no man in whatever place, God's impenetrable and deep judgments receive a great blow."[133] And again: "We cannot say that there is the calling of grace, whereas there is as yet no regeneration of the mother, the church." And again: "He forbad the apostles to preach the gospel to some people; and now as yet He suffers some people to live out of His grace." Also, I oppose Thomas Aquinas against him, who says, "But says some man, God loves all men. Whereto I answer that it is true so far forth as He wills some good to all," and yet He wills not everything that is good to all, that is eternal life. "And therein He is said to hate and reject them."[134] To conclude, I oppose against Hugo de Saint Victor: "Who will," says he, "that all men be saved, according to Ambrose, if they themselves will. But are there not

---

132. In the margin: Hypog.lib.6.cap.8. [Augustine, Hypognost., bk. 6, ch. 8 (exact title of the work in not known)].

133. In the margin: Respon.pro August.lib.I.ob.8. [Prosper of Aquitane, *Pro Augustino responsiones*, bk. 1, obj. 8].

134. In the margin: Quest.13. in Sum.art.3 [Thomas Aquinas, *Summa Theologicae*, q. 13, art. 3].

many who would be saved, and yet are not saved?—or thus, He offers grace to all, by which, if they will, they may be saved. But how is this solution true? Are there not and have there not been many which never heard so much as a word of preaching?"[135]

Objection 3. That which everyone is bound to believe is true. But everyone is bound to believe that he is effectually redeemed by Christ. Therefore, it is manifest that everyone, even the reprobate, is effectually redeemed by the death of Christ. Whereto I answer that the *termini* or parts of the proposition are to be distinguished. That which everyone is bound to believe is true according to the intention of God that binds. But it is not always true according to the event. Jonah preached, and therefore he was bound to believe "yet forty days and Nineveh shall be destroyed." But this was not true according to the event. The assumption also must be distinguished. Everyone in the church who by God's commandment "believes the gospel" is bound to believe that he is redeemed by Christ, yea even the reprobate as well as the elect, but yet notwithstanding in a divers and different respect. The elect is bound to believe that by believing he shall be made partaker of election; the reprobate, that by not believing he may be made inexcusable, even by the intention of God. For God sometimes gives a commandment not that it should be actually done, but that men may be tried, that they perform outward discipline and that they may be convicted of their natural infidelity and be made inexcusable of all their sins before God in the last judgment. For thus I distinguish of God's commandment. There is a certain commandment of obedience, the performance whereof God wills in all. Hither are referred the commandments of the moral law. There is also a certain commandment of trial, as the commandment of sacrificing Isaac (Gen. 22:2), whereas God wills not the act itself, but only the manifestation of obedience. And therefore God must not be said to mock men if by the word preached He do outwardly call those whom He will not have to be saved, for by this means He shows to them the riches of His grace and declares that they perish by their own fault, because they will not receive salvation offered. But you will say they cannot. I confess as much, but that inability whereby they cannot is voluntary and born together with us, not infused into us by God; and therefore it cannot be excused. Very well therefore, says Bernard: "The Master knew well that the weightiness of the commandment exceeded the strength of man. But He thought it expedient even in this, that it put them in remembrance of their own insufficiency. Therefore, by commanding things impossible He makes not men swervers from the truth, but humbles them that every mouth

---

135. In the margin: Annot.in 1.Tim.cap.2 [Hugh of Saint Victor, *Annotations on 1 Timothy*, 1 Timothy 2].

may be stopped,"[136] so says Augustine.[137] Secondly, I answer that that which everyone is bound to believe is true, unless anyone shall by his own unbelief hinder himself. This does the reprobate by his own in-born infidelity. Thirdly, I answer that the argument does follow twice affirmatively in both propositions. For the *termini* or parts of the proposition are thus to be turned: that is true that everyone is bound to believe, but everyone is bound to believe that he is redeemed by Christ. Therefore, that is true.

Objection 4. The fathers which believed aright do affirm that Christ redeemed all and the whole world. *Answer.* Whereas they write that Christ redeemed all men and the world, their meaning is that He did it according to sufficiency and the common cause and common nature of all which Christ did take upon Him, and not effectually on God's part. This very thing does Prosper make plain: "All men," says he, "are rightly said to be redeemed in respect of the one nature of all and the one cause of all which our Lord did truly take upon Him, and yet all are not delivered from captivity."[138] The propriety of redemption "without doubt belongs to them for whom the prince of the world is sent abroad, whose death was not so bestowed for mankind as that it should also pertain to the redemption of them who were not to be regenerated." And again he says, "Our Savior may fitly be said to be crucified for the redemption of all the world both in respect that He truly took upon Him the nature of man and also in respect of the common or general perdition in the first man; and yet He may be said to be crucified only for those to whom His death was available."[139] Moreover, the fathers speak of the universality and of the world of believers. So says he that is the author of the calling of the Gentiles: "The people of God," says he, "have their fullness."[140]

And thus much for the efficacy and greatness of Christ's death. Now as concerning grace, I say, that that is diversity distinguished. For first, it is either restraining or renewing. The restraining grace is that whereby the inbred corruption of the heart is not thereby utterly diminished and taken away, but in some is restrained more, in some less, that it break not violently forth into action. And it is given only for a testimony to man and to preserve order among men in a politic society. And this kind of grace is general—that is, belonging to all and every

---

136. In the margin: Ser.40.in Cant. [Bernard of Clairvaux, *Sermons on the Canticle of Canticles*, sermon 62].

137. In-text citation: *de grat.& lib.arbit.cap.43* [Possibly a reference to Augustine, *On Rebuke and Grace*, ch. 43].

138. In the margin: Resp.ad object.vin.l.2.ob.1. [Prosper of Aquitane, *Pro Augustino Responsiones Ad Capitula Objectionum Vincentianarum*, bk. 1, obj. 9].

139. In the margin: Ad Capit.Gall.cap.9 [Prosper of Aquitane, *Pro Augustino Responsiones Ad Capitula Gallorum*, ch. 9].

140. In the margin: Lib.1.cap.2. [Probably a reference to one of the previous two works].

man, among whom some do exceed othersome in the gifts of civil virtue. And there is no man in whom God does not more or less restrain his natural corruption. Now renewing or Christian grace (as ancient writers do usually call it) is that whereby man has power given him to believe and repent, both in respect of will and power. And it is universal in respect of those that believe, but indefinite in respect of all and every man. Thus we teach, thus we believe.

Secondly, grace is either natural or supernatural, as Augustine himself teaches.[141] Natural grace is that which is bestowed on man together with nature. And this is either of nature perfect or corrupt. Perfect, as the image of God or righteousness bestowed on Adam in his creation. This grace belonged generally to all, because we all were in Adam. And whatever he received that was good, he received it both for himself and his posterity. The grace of nature corrupted is a natural enlightening, whereof John speaks, "He enlighteneth every man that cometh into the world" (John 1:9), yea and every natural gift. And these gifts truly by that order which God has made in nature are due and belonging to nature. But that grace which is supernatural is not due to nature, especially to nature corrupted; but is bestowed by special grace, and therefore is special. This the ancient writers affirm. Augustine says, "Nature is common to all, but not grace."[142] And he only acknowledges a twofold grace—namely, that common grace of nature whereby we are made men, and Christian grace whereby in Christ we are again born new men. And he is of opinion that some that do not believe in Christ do not sin, which is a thing notwithstanding very ungodly and untrue, if grace be as general as nature. Let us well weigh his words: "In that he has," says he, "added, Now they are inexcusable for their sin, it may move men to ask whether those to whom Christ has not come nor spoken may have any excuse for their sin.... To this question according to my understanding I make answer" that "they cannot be inexcusable for every sin which they have committed, but for this sin that they have not believed, to whom Christ did not come, and to whom He did not speak. But they are not in this number to whom He has spoken in His disciples, and by His disciples, which He also now does. For He came to the Gentiles by His church.... It remains for us to demand, whether they can have this excuse, which have been or are prevented by death, before Christ came in His church to the Gentiles, and before they heard His Gospel. I answer that without doubt they may, but they cannot therefore escape damnation: for whosoever have sinned without the law shall also

---

141. In the margin: De praed.sanct.cap.5. [Augustine, *A Treatise on the Gift of Perseverance*, ch. 5].

142. In the margin: De verb.Apost.ser.11. [Augustine, "On the Words of the Apostles," sermon 11].

perish without the law."[143] Again, he says, "Only grace distinguishes those that are saved from those that are damned, who were enwrapped in one lump of corruption by one common cause from the beginning."[144] Chrysostom says, "The grace of God comes to everyone, but it remains with them who do worthily fulfill those things which are in their power, departing quickly from them which do not well behave themselves. Neither does it at all come to those who do not so much as begin to turn to the Lord."[145] Gregory says, "The Gentiles did not any way worship God, neither showed they any sign or token of any good work, for indeed they were forsaken. Among who because there was no lawgiver, nor no one that did according to reason seek after God, there was not as it were a man, but all lived as it were like beasts." And afterward he says, "When our Redeemer came, He so received the calling of grace as that there was not before in it the life of prophecy." And again: "Teachers holding their tongues, the devils go into their place, because none do perish by the silence of the pastors, but they who are not predestinated to eternal life. For they are places for the devils, because in God's foreknowledge they are not preordained to God's tabernacle. Hereupon is it said that when the pastors did preach, as many as were predestinated to eternal life did believe. And hereupon says Paul, whom He has predestinated, those has He called. Hereupon it is that the apostles, desirous to go into Asia, were forbidden by the Holy Ghost. They therefore which are not predestinated, whether they hear the words of the preachers or whether they do not hear them, cannot be called to God's tabernacle." And again: "Sometimes the preachers are silent by God's dispensation, that they holding their peace, they which are not the Lord's may be received of evil spirits."[146] Bede says, "The church in the former state of error being without eyes and blind did neither see from the beginning," neither was it seen at all by God. And again: "All other kinds of faith which are in the world are dead as also the motions of those people and Gentiles which are dead, as they which had not in them Him who said, I am the life. Neither do they regenerate and quicken their people and children by the womb of water and the Spirit, but are fruitless and bereft of the well of life and not enjoying the water which is lively and streams to eternal life. Therefore, that church which is His is only termed

---

143. In the margin: Tract.89.in John. [Augustine, *Tractates on the Gospel of John*, tractate 89].

144. In the margin: Enchir.c.99. [Augustine, *Enchiridion*, ch. 99].

145. In the margin: Lib.de conpunct. cord. [John Chrysostom (*c.* 349–407), de conpunct. cord]. John Chrysostom was the Archbishop of Constantinople and one of the most important Church Fathers. He was particularly known for his preaching ministry, such that his name (Chrysostomos, anglicized as Chrysostom) means "golden-mouthed."

146. In the margin: But if grace be universal, there had always been some church among the Gentiles, although secret and hidden: for it is not likely that all had cast away grace or that they had used it evilly. *Expos. In I.Reg.cap.14*. [Gregory the Great, *Commentary on Kings*, 1 Kings 14].

the life and mother of all the living."[147] Hugo de Saint Victor says, "Some of those who were before the coming of Christ, if they had not had some other sin, they should not have been damned for that they did not believe in Christ, because they have an excuse for that sin."[148] And again: "What if those should enter into consideration how many and how excellent in comparison of you are castaways, which could not attain to this grace which is given to you? Surely you have heard how many generations of men from the beginning even until this day have passed away," who are all without the knowledge of God and the price of His redemption "tumbled down into the gulf of everlasting destruction. Your Redeemer and lover has preferred you before all those, inasmuch as He has given you this grace which none of them was worthy to receive. And what will you say? Wherefore do you think that you are preferred before them all? Have you been more valiant? Have you been more wise? Have you been more noble? Have you been more rich than they all? Because you have obtained this special favor above them all? How many valiant men? How many wise men? How many noble men? How many rich men have there been, and yet they are all forsaken, and have perished like castaways. You only are received before them all, and yet you cannot find out any cause why you should thus be dealt withal, besides the free favor of your Savior."[149]

Hitherto I have opened and defended our opinion of predestination. I will now briefly examine another dissenting with this in many things, having taken it with as much diligence as I could out of the public writings of many men; and to this end, I do this briefly propound it.

First, God created all and every man in Adam to eternal life.

Secondly, He foresaw the fall.

Thirdly, because He is by nature gentle and good, He does seriously will that all men after the fall should be saved and come to the knowledge of the truth and therefore wills to give all the furtherances both of nature and grace that they may be saved, but yet indefinitely, if they themselves shall believe. This will of God (they say) is predestination, and the same with the written gospel. The rule of this will is "whosoever shall believe shall be saved; he that would not believe, shall be damned."

Lastly, election is according to the foreknowledge of future faith (which notwithstanding may be lost utterly for a time, as some say; or finally and forever, as some other will); and reprobation is according to the foreknowledge of infidelity or the contempt of the gospel.

---

147. In the margin: Lib.1.in Isai.cap.1. Bede, Commentary on Isaiah, Isaiah 1].

148. In the margin: In John Elucid.65. [Hugh Saint Victor, In John Elucid.65].

149. In the margin: In Soliloquio dearra animae.

This platform is in very truth (so far as I can judge of it by the Scriptures) a mere invention of man's wit, which will appear by the manifold errors therein contained.

Error 1. First, by this platform or groundwork there follows a certain universal reprobation, and that a very absurd and strange one. For if there be (as they do affirm) a universal election whereby God wills that all men shall be saved indefinitely, if they do believe, He wills also by the like reason that all and each one should be damned if they do not believe. But this reprobation is nowhere to be found in the Scriptures. Yea, hence it follows that God being alike affected to all and seriously willing the conversion and salvation of all does neither choose nor refuse any man.

Error 2. From hence also it follows that God has in vain propounded with Himself the supreme and absolute end of His counsels, which is to communicate His goodness in true felicity even to every man. For if we consider the event, He does not communicate His goodness and eternal life to very many which is otherwise than He purposed—namely, to those that are damned. But we are in no case to say that the supreme end of God's counsels either have an uncertain event or are in vain propounded.

Error 3. Thirdly, this platform attributed to God a certain ordered and fitted will which does wholly depend on man's will. You say that God wills that all men whatever should be saved by Christ. Very well. Tell me therefore why they are not saved. They themselves will not, you say. Yea, but what is this but to set the creature in the throne of almighty God the Creator against the order of nature and of all causes? For the first cause, which indeed is God's will, ought to order and dispose the act of the second cause. And therefore we must not give to God a will that is ordered by the will of the creature, especially considering that all order in heaven and in earth whatever proceeds from Him. That which orders all things is ordered of none. Moreover, men after this sort are elected of themselves by receiving of God's grace being offered by the assistance of common grace and are also rejected of themselves by refusing of grace offered, and men themselves shall be the makers and framers of their own election and reprobation. And God, who chooses, is not so much to be praised as the men that do receive and embrace the blessing offered.

Error 4. Fourthly, this platform lays down a determinate foreknowledge about the evil of fault, without any decree going before concerning the event of the fault, which cannot be. A definite foreknowledge is not the cause of that thing which is to be, but the thing which shall be is the cause of the foreknowledge thereof. For the thing which shall be follows not the foreknowledge of it, but foreknowledge follows the thing which shall be, as Justinus taught.[150] For God does first decree a thing as touching the event. Then afterward He does foreknow by His definite foreknowledge that it shall be. And Anselm: "In that," says he, "a thing is said to be foreknown, it is by that pronounced that it shall be."[151] And Augustine before his time affirmed "that God does foreknow that which shall be." Hence it follows that a thing must exist with God before it can be precisely and definitely known before. And everything exists and is, because God did will and decree to do it if it be good or to suffer it to be done if it be evil, have respect always to the good that is joined with it. Unless we shall hold and grant this, it will follow that something has being of itself—that is, that something is a god. Therefore, the existence or being of things does not go before, but out of all doubt follows the decree of God. For first of all, there is a foreknowledge or (as it pleases others) a knowledge of beholding, whereby God beholds and sees what is possible to be and what not.[152] Then follows the decree either of God's operation or of His voluntary permission, and consequently of the event of the thing. And this decree being once laid down, the definite foreknowledge is conceived whereby it is known what shall come to pass infallibly.

Error 5. The fifth defect in this platform is that it teaches that Christ for His part has redeemed and reconciled all and every man to God, and that very many of them for all that as touching the event are damned, which is very absurd. For if this were so, sin, Satan, death, and hell should be more mighty than Christ the Redeemer, and (as Augustine says), *vitia humano vincitur Deus*—God is overcome by man's sin.[153] If you will say that God is not overcome, yet I say, and that according to this platform, that He is altered; for He has decreed and seriously willed to save all men, and yet notwithstanding another sentence being given He wills to destroy those which will not incline and bend themselves to this counsel.

Error 6. This platform makes saving grace (which indeed is supernatural) to be altogether universal. But this opinion (to speak no harder of it) is a plausible device of man's brain. For first of all, hereby the special covenant made with Abraham and the greatness of God's mercies toward the Gentiles is abolished. And there is no mystery of the vocation of the Gentiles if all and every

---

150. In the margin: Quest.58a. Orthodox. [Probably a reference to the apocryphal writing spuriously attributed to Justin Martyr entitled, "A Christian's Questions to the Greeks," Q. 58a].

151. In the margin: De praed.Sanct.c.14. Augustine, *A Treatise on the Gift of Perseverance*, ch. 14].

152. In the margin: *Scientia intuitiua.*

153. In the margin: De Cor.&grat.cap.7. [Augustine, *On Rebuke and Grace*, ch. 7].

particular man were by certain means called to Christ from the beginning. For those which shall by the help of common grace, which they shall receive, give assent to God calling them, whether it be by extraordinary instinct or by the ministry of the word preached—they shall be accounted among the members of the church and shall belong to the special covenant of the gospel. Moreover, if the first grace be universal, it is either faith actually or in power. For without faith it is impossible to please God and to attain salvation. But actual faith is not common to all. The power of faith is double. The first is that whereby you have received power to be able to believe if you will. But this is not sufficient to salvation, because now after Adam's fall free will in spiritual things is wanting, especially in the conversion of a sinner. And therefore further grace is required whereby a man may be able to will to believe. "No man can come to Christ, but he which is drawn of the Father" (John 6:44). Now, they are not drawn which have received power to believe if they will, but those who oftentimes willing are made actually willing. The second power is that whereby a man has received power to will to believe, but this is not common to all men. "To you," says Christ to His disciples, "it is given to know the mysteries of the Kingdom of heaven, but not so to them, because the Father has hidden them from the wise" (Matt. 11:15). Again: "Therefore could they not believe, because Isaiah foretold this" (John 12:39). Furthermore, if this power were common to all and to each person, faith were common to all. For the will and the deed flows from one and the selfsame grace. "It is God who worketh in you the will and the deed, even of His good pleasure" (Phil. 2:13). "Whosoever has heard and learned of the Father, cometh to Christ" (John 6:45). But whoever has power to will to believe has heard and learned, as being drawn of God. Therefore, whoever has power to will to believe comes to Christ. Well says Augustine, "It follows not that he which can come does come, unless he both will and do it; but everyone that has learned of the Father has not only power to come, but also he does come. Where now there is a *passivilitai, profectalus, & voluntatas affectus, & effectus est.*"[154] So it appears that to will to believe and actually to believe are most nearly conjoined. Yea, seriously to will to believe is in very deed to believe. The publicans and harlots and those which are held captive at the devil's will do repent and are converted; and therefore they do not only receive power if they will, but of nillers[155] and stubborn repugners they are made actually willing.

Thirdly, there are and have been many nations which have had no knowledge of the faith or which have not kept it, and without this knowledge there is not any saving grace. Answer is wont to be made that man receiving natural

---

154. In the margin: Denot.grat.cont.Pelag.c.g. [Augustine, *On Nature and Grace Against the Pelagians*].

155. *Nillers*: those who nill, that is, not will.

light is not to be excused for the want of supernatural knowledge, because if he would do by God's assistance that which lies in him, God would enlighten him with supernatural grace. For thus the schoolmen do usually speak. "Although no man is able by the ministry of men to know the nature of faith if he never heard anything of it, yet he may by God's help if he live morally according to God's law so much as in him lies to do. For then God will succor him either by Himself or by some other—to wit, either man or angel by propounding of faith to him. For as in nature all things, so in supernatural God does minister grace when man is not wanting to himself."[156] I answer that this is false. For if grace be given to him which does that which lies in him to do by the strength of nature, it is given either by merit or promise. Not by merit, because there is no merit before faith; and we do nothing acceptable to God before we have faith. Augustine: "You bring in a kind of men which can please God without the faith of Christ by the law of nature. This is the cause why the Christian church does especially detest you."[157] And it is not given by promise, because there is no promise or divine law to be found in the Scriptures, that grace should by and by be given to him that does that which lies in him to do. It is also false to say that God does minister all things that make for the felicity of nature of this present life. For some are born leprous, blind, foolish, very poor, unmeet for this temporary felicity, neither do they ever attain to it. This opinion also is against experience, because many die in their infancy, and many are foolish and died all their life long, upon whom we cannot say that this universal grace is bestowed. It is also contrary to most plain places of Scripture. "Salvation is not in him that willeth nor in him that runneth, but in God that showeth mercy. And, He has mercy on whom He will, and whom He will He hardeneth. It is given to the disciples to know the secrets of the kingdom of heaven, but to them is not given; the wind bloweth not in all, but where it listeth; the Son does not reveal the Father to all, but to whom He will. All do not believe, but those which are drawn and predestined to life; all do not hear, but those to whom ears are given to hear (Matt. 13:14; John 3:8; John 6; Acts 13:49). Furthermore, it is some impairing of effectual and Christian grace so to place it in man's power, that he may, if he will, receive it; and that he may also, if he will not, refuse and despise it; and to say that God has given to men no other grace than that against which the flesh or perverse will may prevail in all men, and against which it does prevail indeed in the greatest part of mankind, because God will not restrain it. To conclude, let us also hear the testimonies of the fathers. The author of the calling of the Gentiles says thus: "If so be that the grace of the

---

Father do pass by some (as we see it does), it is to be referred to the hidden judgments of divine justice." Augustine: "Nothing deliveres us from this wrath whereby we are all under sin, saving the grace of God by Jesus Christ. Why this grace comes to that infant, and not to this, the cause may be unknown, but not unjust."[158] Again: "It was by divine dispensation that Pharaoh did not tractably consent, but obstinately resist, because that there was not only a just punishment, but a just punishment evidently prepared for such a heart. Whereby those which fear God may be corrected."[159] Again: "The judgments are unsearchable, wherefore of the wicked men being of years aged one should be called so, as that he should follow the caller, and the other should either not be called at all or not called so as that he should follow him that calls him."[160] And again: "He gives to whom He will, because He is merciful, which though He should not give, yet He is just."[161] Again, He does not give to them to whom He will not, "that He might make known the riches of His glory upon the vessels of mercy; for by giving to some who deserve not, He will have it to be His free and by this also His true grace and favor." Again: "Whoever are set apart from original damnation through the bounty of God's grace, it is no doubt but that it shall be procured for them to hear the gospel and to believe when they hear it."[162] Again: "We know that God's grace is not given to all men."[163] And again: "Why one man is so exhorted that he is persuaded, and why it is not so with another; O the depth of the riches!"[164] Thomas: "As He does not open the eyes of all that are blind nor cure all that are crazy, that in those His power might appear and that in the other the order of nature might be preserved, even so He does not by His help prevent all that hinder grace, but some in whom He wills that His mercy should appear, so also that the order of justice should be manifested in others."[165] Isidore: "Spiritual grace is not distributed to all, but is only given to the elect."[166] Again: "It is given to him, because he is evil that would be good; another neither wills, neither is it given him that he might be good." Cameravensis: "Although God be a universal agent over all, so as that He

---

158. In the margin: Lib.depet.merit.c.21. [Augustine, depet.merit, ch. 21].

159. In the margin: In Exod. Quest.18. [Augustine, Question on Exodus, q. 18].

160. In the margin: Lib.de bon.pers.cap.8. [Augustine, *A Treatise on the Gift of Perseverance*, chapter 8. In some editions, the title is, *On the Benefit (de Bono) of Perseverance*].

161. In the margin: Cap.12. [Augustine, *A Treatise on the Gift of Perseverance*, ch. 12].

162. In the margin: Ibid.cap.7. [Augustine, *A Treatise on the Gift of Perseverance*, ch. 7].

163. In the margin: Epist.ad Vital.107. [Augustine, *Ad Vitalem*, Epistle 107].

164. In the margin: Lib.de Spirit.lit.c.34. [Possibily a reference to Thomas Aquinas, *The Gifts of the Holy Spirit*].

165. In the margin: Cont.gent.lib.3.c.161. [Aquinas, *Contra Gentiles*, bk. 3, ch. 161].

166. In the margin: Sent.lib.2.cap.5.&6. [Possibly a reference to Isidore, *Sententiae libri tres*, bk. 2, chs. 5 and 6].

gives to all some gifts of grace, as being, life, knowledge, etc., yet He gives some gifts of special grace to one, which He gives not to another, as namely faith, and the grace which makes us gracious and such like which are the effects of predestination."[167] Finally, Augustine and almost all the schoolmen make two kinds of infidelity: the one negative in those which never heard the gospel; the other privative in those that refuse and contemn the message which they have heard of Christ. And it is to be noted that by this distinction they do confess that God has not vouchsafed so much as an outward calling to every man.

Objection 1. The promise of the seed of the woman is made in Adam to all and to every man. *Answer.* It is made to Adam's posterity, indefinitely, not universal. "When salvation is promised to all men, all men are named for a part of men."[168] The heads of the nations, Cain, Shem, Esau, etc., knew the promised Messiah; but those which came after knew Him not, neither had they the means how to know Him. So says Isaiah: "Me have they not known, of Me have they not heard" (52:15). The nations also next adjoining to the Jews peradventure heard something and had proselytes, but the nations afar off seated in the uttermost parts of the earth had no affairs with the Jews and no proselytes. And therefore it is false which some affirm—to wit, that the choosing of the people of Israel was only a kind of greater courtesy showed to this nation or a more gentle entreating of it, and no peculiar and divers favor whereby He showed Himself to be their Father and Redeemer only. And to make or maintain a hidden and invisible church among the Gentiles before the coming of Christ is altogether to contend against the word: "God is only known in Judah" (Psalm 76). The Israelites only are called "My people" in Hosea (ch. 1); and they only were "Christ's sheepfold" (John 10:16; Eph. 2:14), because Christ when He came made one sheepfold of the Jews and Gentiles.

Objection 2. There is enfolded in God's providence that care of God touching all those things which concern the blessedness of man. But the Gentiles knew this providence of God, and that His goodness was so great that He would pass by nothing which might make for the happiness and salvation of man. Therefore, the Gentiles did after a sort obscurely and by an enfolded knowledge know the doctrine concerning the redemption of mankind. *Answer.* This faith of things unknown is a mere fiction. For faith of the own nature is a certain knowledge. Moreover, although the general do include in itself the species or kinds and the whole his members, yet he which knows the general and the whole does not by and by know all the kinds and parts thereof. The mind may so know the general that yet for all that it may in the meantime be ignorant of

---

167. In the margin: In lib.sent.1.q.12.art.2. [The exact identity of the author is unknown].
168. In the margin: De vocat.gent.statuit.lib.1.cap.3. [Calling of the Gentiles, bk. 1, ch. 3].

the special kinds thereof. We must therefore beware of the schoolmen's opinion who say that salvation was given before Christ's coming for the implicit or enfolded faith concerning the Redeemer in general—namely, when men did believe that there is a God, and that He is a rewarder and the giver of all gifts which concern the good either of soul or body, especially the remedy of sin. But this is nothing else than to imagine a certain saving faith and church which has no word of God at all either written or any other way revealed. Furthermore, this is to accuse Paul of falsehood, who teaches the contrary in these words: "Seeing the world by wisdom knew not God in the wisdom of God, it pleased God by the foolishness of preaching to save them that believe" (1 Cor. 1:21). It is also most certain that we ought to know Christ the Redeemer in special. "This is life eternal that they know Thee to be the only very God and whom Thou hast sent, Jesus Christ" (John 17:3). The same affirm the ancient fathers. Irenaeus: "They being ignorant of that Emmanuel, who is born of the virgin, are deprived of His gift, which is life eternal."[169] Jerome: "We cannot be His sons before, unless we receive the faith and understanding of His Son Jesus Christ."[170] Augustine says "that those which were just in old time, whatever they were, were delivered only by that faith whereby we are delivered—to wit, by the faith of Christ's incarnation."[171] Again: "Whatever truth you say was in those which were just in old time, the faith only of the Mediator saves them, who shed His blood for the forgiveness of sins."

Objection 3. A. (*Propositio*) The power of God is known to the Gentiles (Romans 1). B. (*Assumption*) Christ is the power of God. C. (*Conclusion*) Therefore, Christ is known to the Gentiles. *Answer.* I distinguish of the proposition. The power of God is either the power of creation or of redemption. The power of God in the creation was known to the Gentiles, but not the power of God in the redemption, which is Christ Himself, the preaching of whom is foolishness to the world.

Objection 4. The fathers say that saving grace is universal. First, I answer that the sayings of the fathers are to be understood of the grace of the last time which is common to all men and nations. Irenaeus: "The Lord has reconciled us in the last times by His incarnation, being made a mediator between God and man, reconciling the Father to all…giving to us that conversion which is to our Creator."[172] Origen says: "God has a greater care to save men than the

---

169. In the margin: Lib.de heres.3.c.21. [Irenaeus (*d. c.* 202), *Against Heresies*, bk. 3, ch. 21. Irenaeus was one of the earliest Church Fathers. This was his most important work].

170. In the margin: In Eph. 1. [Jerome, *Commentary on Ephesians*, Ephesians 1].

171. In the margin: Lib.2.cont.2.epist.Pel.cap.21. [Augustine, *Against Two Letters of the Pelagians*, bk. 2, ch. 21].

172. In the margin: De haeres.lib.5.cap.17. [Irenaeus, *Against Heresies*, bk. 5, ch. 17].

devil has to destroy them.... The only begotten, the Son of God Himself (I say), is present with us. He defends, keeps, and draws us to Himself...for He says in another place, When I shall be lifted up I will draw all things to Me."[173] Chrysostom: "Grace is shed abroad over all. It passes by and displays neither Jew or Grecian, nor Barbarian nor Scythian. It is alike affected to all. It shows itself gentle to all. It calls all with equal honor. And let those who neglect the help of grace ascribe this their blindness to themselves. For considering that a way to enter in lies open to all and is forbidden to none, some desperately wicked do refuse to enter through their own corruption." Cyril says, "He is the true light and sends forth His brightness to all. But (as Paul says) the God of this world has blinded the minds of unfaithful men that the light of God's knowledge may not shine in them."[174] Ambrose: "The earth is full of the mercy of God, because pardon of sins is given to all. The mystical Son of Righteousness is risen to all, is come to all, has suffered for all, and has risen again for all. And if any believe not in Christ, he deprives himself of this general benefit.... He shuts out the grace of common light from himself."[175] Gregory says, "The medicine which is from God meets us in every place, because He hath both given unto man commandments not to sin, and has also given remedies to him that sins, lest he should despair."[176] Theodolus Presbyter: "He has said that both Jews and Gentiles should be partakers of grace, yet not all, but those that believe, and because grace is common to all, not without cause."[177]

Answer 2. Secondly, they speak of natural vocation or of the grace of nature consisting in the relics of natural light and understanding in the common gifts of virtues and outward blessings, which are testimonies of God's providence and goodness. The author of *The Calling of the Gentiles*: "For this cause verily the nations may be excused, which being aliens from the commonwealth of Israel, void of hope, and without God in this world have perished under the darkness of ignorance, because this abundance of grace, which does now water the whole world, did not flow so plentifully before. For there is evermore showed to all men a certain measure of doctrine from above, which albeit it proceeds from a more sparing and hidden grace, yet it is sufficient (in the

---

173. In the margin: Hom.20 in Num. [Origen, *Homilies on Numbers*, homily 20].

174. In the margin: Lib.1.in John.cap.11. [John Chrysostom, *Commentary on John*, bk. 1, ch. 11].

175. In the margin: Serm.8.in Psal.118. [This is probably a reference to Cyril of Alexandria, though the exact work is unknown].

176. In the margin: In Job lib:35.cap.14. [Probably a reference to Gregory I (Gregory the Great), *Morals on the Book of Job*, bk. 35, ch. 14].

177. In the margin: Comment.in Rom.cap.3. [Theodolus Presbyter, *Commentary on Romans*, ch. 3. The identity of Theodolus Presbyter is unknown].

Lord's judgment) for a remedy to some, and a witness to all."[178] Again: "Who may not easily perceive that He never denied His divine goodness to the posterity of this brother slayer, if he consider how profitable so long patience of God, such plentiful store of temporal blessings, and such a universal increase of multiplied fruitfulness might have been to them? Which benefits, although they wrought no cure and amendment in those whose hearts were hardened, yet they prove that their apostasy was not caused by God."[179] Again: "In the farthest parts of the world there be some nations to which the light of saving grace has not as yet dawned…to whom that parcel of general assistance is not denied, which is always from above granted to all men. Although the nature of man has received so sharp a wound that it is not possible for any man to come to the knowledge of God by the help of his own voluntary contemplation, unless the true light dispel the darkness of the heart, which the just and good God in His unsearchable judgment has not so shed abroad in times past, as He does in these last days."[180]

Thirdly, the fathers speak of the universal, whereby man's will being by God's ordinary dispensation prevented and helped by the Holy Ghost may believe and be converted, which notwithstanding a stone, stock, or beast cannot. Augustine: "A possibility to have faith is given of nature."[181] Again he says "that man's nature is capable of justification by the grace of the Holy Spirit."[182] Again: "Men may keep God's commandments and believe in God if they will, because that light enlightens every man which comes into this world." Prosper: "To be able to have faith is the nature of men, but to have faith is the grace of the faithful."[183] Augustine: "This difference there is between wicked men and the devils, that men though they be exceedingly wicked may be reconciled, if God will show mercy; but there is no conversion reserved for the devils."[184]

Now as concerning Christian grace whereby a will to be converted and to believe actually in Christ is given to men, the fathers have not so much as dreamed that it is common to all and every one, which notwithstanding some are not[185] now afraid to affirm in their writings.

---

178. In the margin: Lib.2.c.14. [*The Calling of the Gentiles*, bk. 2, ch. 14].

179. In the margin: Chrysostom says that the preserving in the ark is *superna gratia,* grace from above. For the outward reformation of the life. Hom.25.in Gen. Lib.2.c.4. [John Chrysostom, *Homilies on Genesis*, homily 25; *The Calling of the Gentiles*, bk. 2, ch. 4].

180. In the margin: Lib.2.cap.6. [*The Calling of the Gentiles*, bk. 2, ch. 6].

181. In the margin: De praed.cap 5. [Augustine, *Predestination of the Saints*, ch. 5].

182. In the margin: Cont.Iul.lib.2. [Augustine, *Against Julian*, bk. 2].

183. In the margin: De gen.contra Manich.lib.1.cap.3. [Augustine, *On Genesis: Two Books on Genesis Against the Manichees*, bk. 1, ch. 3].

184. In the margin: Ad art.Sibi falso imp.6.

185. In the margin: For they say that God has given every man without exception power to believe if he will himself.

Error 7. This platform teaches that God's foreknowledge of our faith and infidelity is the rule of predestination, which is utterly false. For first of all, the very will is a rule to itself and the divine counsels. "We were predestinated according to His purpose, who worketh all things after the counsel of His own will" (Eph. 1:5, 11). Secondly, God's election is the rule of faith that is to be given or not given (Rom. 11:5). A reformation is made according to the election of grace. Thirdly, the foreknowledge of faith and infidelity does not extend itself so far as predestination, which belongs to all men whatever, many of whom notwithstanding never so much as heard of Christ.[186] Now these cannot have faith nor[187] privative infidelity, but only a negative. The same I say of those which die in their infancy being within the covenant, who we believe are saved by the tenure of the same covenant, who for all that are neither elected for faith nor according to faith, which they as yet had not. But if the foreseeing of faith were the rule or square of election or reprobation, the thing foreseen should belong to all men without exception; for the rule must not be straighter than that which is ruled by it. Fourthly, foreseen faith is the effect of election; therefore, it is not the rule of it. "Who has predestinated us to adoption by Christ" (Eph. 1:5) and therefore also to faith, which receives the benefit of adoption. Augustine: "Let us therefore" says he, "understand[188] that calling whereby they are chosen, who are chosen not because they did believe, but that they should believe; for if they were for that cause chosen because they did believe, they themselves verily had chosen Him before by believing in Him, that they might deserve to be chosen."[189] Again: "Lest any man should say, My faith[190] or some such like thing does distinguish me from other men, the teacher of the Gentiles meeting with such conceits asks, What have you that you have not received, and of whom but of Him who distinguishes you from him, so whom He has not given that which He has given to you." Lombard: "God has elected those whom it pleased Him to elect of His own free mercy, not because they were to be believers, but that they should be believers." Again: "Grace is the effect of predestination."[191] Fifthly, if God did elect according to foreseen faith, tell me

---

186. In the margin: Aug.de cor. & grat. C.10 & 12. [Augustine, *On Rebuke and Grace*, chs. 10 and 12].

187. In the margin: Contempt of the Gospel.

188. In the margin: God's will is the first rule in contingents. [Illegible] loc.com.l.1.5.6. [Possibly a reference to Philipp Melanchthon (1497–1560), *Loci Communes*, bk. 1.5.6. Melanchthon was the leader of the Lutheran Church following Luther's death].

189. In the margin: Lib.de.praed.c.17.c.5. [Augustine, *Predestination of the Saints*, c. 17, ch. 5].

190. In the margin: And Francis Maronis saith, that God's will is the principal in contingents, and that it is ruled and directed of none. Lib.I.dist.42.q.4.lib.l.dist.r42. [Francis of Mayrone, *Commentary on the Sentences*, bk. 1, dist. 42, q. 4].

191. In the margin: In epist.ad Rom.cap.8. [Peter Lombard, *Commentary on Romans*, ch. 8].

why He did foresee faith in one man rather than in another—tell me, I say? For here whether you will or no, you must have recourse to the mere will of God. For God does foresee nothing which is good in any, besides that which He Himself of His pleasure will first make. And what is the cause why He foresees faith in one man rather than in another? But only because it is His will to give one man faith and not another. Lastly, the rule is uncertain; for faith, as appears by this platform, may be utterly lost. And therefore the thing ruled—to wit, predestination—is made uncertain. This a certain author plainly confesses in his exposition of the epistle to the Romans, where he teaches unadvisedly that God's decree may be changed, and that election and reprobation have recourse one to another, because (as he says) they depend upon the conditions of faith and infidelity.

Error 8. Furthermore, this platform teaches that true and saving faith may perish and be lost either wholly or forever, which notwithstanding is not true. *Reason 1.* "Upon this rock will I build My church, and the gates of hell shall not prevail against (κατισχύσουσιν) it" (Matt. 16:18). Here three questions must be asked: what the rock is? What is meant by building on the rock? And what is that which is promised to those which are built upon it? The rock is either faith itself or Christ apprehended by faith. Chrysostom: "Upon this rock—that is," says he, "upon the faith of confession."[192] Again: "He sets our feet upon the rock—that is, upon faith; for faith in Christ may well be said to be that which cannot be broken." Again: "Christ being wise has built His house—that is, His church upon a rock, that is, upon the fortitude of faith, or a strong faith."[193] Now if faith be a rock, it remains constant and immovable. To be built upon the rock is to perceive the doctrine of the gospel, to embrace Christ our Savior with a true faith, and to cleave fast to Him with the heart. For the Corinthians are said to be Paul's building, because he brought them to the faith. And the Ephesians are said to be built upon the foundation of the apostles and prophets, because Paul came and preached to them the gospel of peace. The certainty and firmness of the doctrine of the gospel may also be called a rock. Epiphanius: "They shall not prevail against the rock, that is to say, against the truth."[194] Hillary: "This is your blessed rock of faith, which Peter

---

192. In the margin: Homil. In Matth. 5:5.& Psal. 32. [John Chrysostom, *Homilies on Matthew*, Matthew 5:5; John Chrysostom, *Commentary on the Psalms*, Psalm 32].

193. In the margin: In com. Imperfect. In Mat. Cap. 7. [John Chrysostom, *Commentary on Matthew*, Matthew 7].

194. In the margin: Lib.her.74. [Probably a reference to Epiphanius of Salamis (*c.* 310–403) and his book *Panarion* (also titled, *Against Heresies*). Little is known about this author].

has confessed with his mouth."[195] Augustine: "Upon this rock which you have confessed, I will build My church." Now no man can be built upon the confession and upon the truth, but by faith. Hence I do conclude thus: those that are built upon the rock cannot fall away utterly. But those which truly believe are built upon the rock. Therefore, those which truly believe do not utterly and wholly fall away. Thirdly, the promise made to them that are built upon the rock is that the gates of hell shall not prevail against them (κατισχύσουθαι. κατισχύσουσιν). From hence it follows necessarily that the devils can but make a flourish and show their strength and power against the faith, and that they shall never be able to overcome and conquer. Let us here also weigh the judgments of the fathers. Cyprian: "Lord, to whom shall we go…signifying that the church, which believes in Christ and which keeps that which it has once known, does at no time altogether depart from Him, and that they are the church who do abide in God's house.[196] But that they are not of God the Father's planting, whom we do see to be void of the steadfastness and mass soundness of corn and like to chaff fanned or blown about with the wind of the winnowing enemy—of whom also John speaks in his first epistle, saying, "They went out from us, but they were not of us: for if they had been of us, they had surely remained with us" (1 John 2:19). Augustine: "Love which may be lost was never true."[197] Again: "To believe truly is to believe constantly, steadfastly, valiantly, and firmly, so as that you may not now return to yours and forsake Christ."[198] Again: "Those which are truly saints being predestinated to reign with God by His grace have not only given them now a power to persevere if they will, but perseverance itself." Again: He which makes men good, maketh them to persevere in that which is good."[199] And again: "The church loses none on the earth but those which are wicked and admits none to heaven but those that are good." Again: "As the ark was built of foursquare timber, so the church is built of saints; for that which is foursquare will stand steady on whichever side you set it; and the saints continue steadfast in every temptation."[200] Chrysostom: "This is the property of faith, that however things may fall out contrary to the promises, yet it never falls away utterly and is never wholly confounded."[201] Again: "Let us keep faith, which is a firm and sure rock; for neither the floods, nor the winds can do us any hurt, though they drive hard against us, because we stand

---

195. In the margin: De Trin.lib.3. [Hilary, *On the Trinity*, bk. 3].

196. In the margin: Epist.1.3. [Cyprian (*c.* 200–58), Letters 1 and 3. Cyprian was a Church Father and the bishop of Carthage].

197. In the margin: Decre.de panit.d.2.c.2. [Augustine, Title of work unknown].

198. In the margin: Tract.126.in Joh. [Augustine, *Tractates on the Gospel of John*, tractate 126].

199. In the margin: De cor.& grat.c.12. [Augustine, *On Rebuke and Grace*, ch. 12].

200. In the margin: Epist.16.3. [Augustine, *Letters*, 16 and 3].

201. In the margin: Quest.52.ad Orosium. [John Chrysostom, Title of the work unknown].

steadfast upon a rock. So also if in this life we will choose that true foundation, we shall abide without any detriment or loss (*penitius omnine*)."[202] Again: "You cannot overcome one faithful man. O devil, you know not what the martyrs have done to you—the flesh often faints in the torments, and the strength of faith fails not. Hence it is that in any same place He speaks after this sort. If you make war with man, you shall, it may be, overcome, or perhaps you shall be overcome; but no might can overcome the church."[203] Furthermore: "The church is far stronger than the earth, yea and stronger than heaven." Again: "Faith in God is a certain secure anchor."[204] Gregory: "Because the light of the elect is not extinguished by temptation, we do not say there is a night made but an evening—namely, because temptation does oftentimes hide the light of righteousness in the hearts of the elect, but it does not put it quite out. It makes it as it were twinkle and look wan, but it does not extinguish it."[205] Angelome: "The observation of God's commandments, being established in the hearts of the elect by faith, hope, and love of that heavenly recompense, can by no let of temporal things be dissolved."[206] Again: "The hearts of the elect are compared to a foursquare figure, which have learned so to remain in the strength of faith, that they cannot be removed from the certainty of their estate, by any repugnance of those things they meet with, no not by death itself."[207] Andreas: "Those are found to be abortive or untimely born children who have departed from the true light, which is Christ."[208] Thomas: "If we by the revelation of our heavenly Father shall then confess—namely, when our conversation is in the heavens—that Jesus Christ is the Son of the living God, and if it shall be said to us, You are Peter, for everyone that follows Christ is a rock; but he against whom the gates of hell prevail is neither to be termed the rock whereon Christ does build His church, neither the church, nor a part of the church which Christ builds upon the rock."[209] And again: "Although you must be lifted a little, yet you have the seed of faith hidden in you. Though the leaves be blown down with the tempter's wind, yet the root is fresh."[210]

---

202. In the margin: Hom. I in 2. Tim.1. [John Chrysostom, *Homilies on 2 Timothy*, 2 Timothy 1].

203. In the margin: Hom.de expuls.Chrys. [John Chrysostom, Title of the work unknown].

204. In the margin: Hom.25.in Gen. [John Chrysostom, *Homilies on Genesis*, homily 25].

205. In the margin: In 7 c.Job. [Probably a reference to Gregory the Great, *Morals on the Book of Job*, ch. 7].

206. In the margin: In lib.3.Reg.cap.7. [Gregory the Great, *Commentary on Kings*, bk. 3, ch. 7].

207. In the margin: Ibid.cap.5. [Gregory the Great, *Commentary on Kings*, ch. 5].

208. In the margin: Episc.Capp. in Apoc.com.cap.32. [Jakob Andreae. Title of work unknown].

209. In the margin: Catena in 16.Matt.ex Orig. [Thomas Aquinas, Catena in Matthew 16 of Origen].

210. In the margin: In Luk. 22. Theop. [Thomas Aquinas, Title of work unknown].

Second reason: "Lead us not into temptation," etc. (Matt. 6:13)—that is, "Do not utterly forsake us and deliver us up to Satan." Augustine: "God leads a man into temptation when He suffers him to be tempted, that He may try him and not destroy him. And He delivers from evil when He suffers us not to be tempted beyond our power."[211] Gregory: "The grace of the Holy Ghost qualifies the temptations of the adversary by dispensation, that those which may be may but search with their heat and not burn up with their fire."[212] Hence I thus reason: whatever we ask according to God's will, it shall be given us. But we ask according to God's will that we may not be utterly forsaken in temptation, for our Advocate taught us so to pray. Therefore, that we be not utterly forsaken in temptation shall be given of God. Now whom God does not utterly forsake, he does not utterly fall away. And this Christ takes for granted in the elect: "So as that, if it were possible, they should deceive the very elect" (Matt. 24:24).

Third reason, if there be a total or utter falling away from a true faith, then is there also required a second engrafting into Christ and consequently a seal of the second engrafting, baptizing anew—that is to say, Anabaptism; for so often as we are born again, we are to be baptized. This is Augustine's ground: "As the carnal generation is one, neither can a man enter into the womb again, even so is spiritual regeneration. For we are once born, and we are also once born again. Therefore, also it is requisite that the sacrament of regeneration be once received. If it chance to fall out by sin that some are weakened who are regenerated, they have need of cure by repentance and not by baptism."[213] But those that do utterly or wholly fall away from faith and grace are the second time to be engrafted into Christ; and consequently they are not once regenerated but again, and therefore they are oftener than once to be baptized.

Fourth reason: "whosoever is born of God committeth not sin, because His seed remaineth in him" (1 John 3:9). We must here mark that he says his seed remains in him—that is to say, that it does not depart nor vanish away. And this seed is the very word of God, which remains in us by faith and does not remain faith being utterly lost. This seed also is immortal, because it will never perish if it be truly sown in our hearts.

A fifth reason is taken out of the sixth [chapter] to the Romans. *Propositio*, if Christ having once died cannot die any more, then we which are His members being dead together with Him, shall not die any more in sin. *Assumptio*:

---

211. In the margin: De temp. serm.36. [Augustine, De temp, sermon 36. The title of the work is unknown].

212. In the margin: In Job l:39. [Probably a reference to Gregory the Great, *Morals on the Book of Job*, 1:39].

213. In the margin: Tract.in John II.cap.12. [Augustine, *Tractates on the Gospel of John*, tractate 2, ch. 12].

But Christ having once died cannot die any more. *Conclusion:* Therefore we which are His members shall not die any more in sin. The proposition is in the eighth verse and has a manifest ground. For by the virtue of the mystical communion, which is had with Christ by faith, His spiritual life, which cannot perish, flowing into His members makes them in like manner that they die no more in sin. The assumption is in the ninth and tenth verse; the conclusion, in the eleventh. Moreover, those which are the members of Christ's body shall grow up to a perfect man (Eph. 4:12–13; 1 John 2:29). But all those which have a true faith are members of Christ's body. Therefore, those which have a true saving faith shall grow up to a perfect man, and therefore those which do truly believe shall not perish but obtain salvation.

For the better understanding of this doctrine, two things must be sought for: first, whence it is that faith perishes not? *Answer.* If we consider faith by itself—that is, in the own nature—it may perish and be lost. But if we consider the confirming grace which God has promised to them that believe, saving faith does not perish. It is by reason of the second grace freely promised that the first grace does not perish. "To you it is given for Christ, that ye should not only believe in Him, but also suffer for His sake" (Phil. 1:29). One of these (says Augustine) belongs to the beginning, the other to the end; but both are God's gift, because both are given. A Christian man's beginning is to believe in Christ, and the best end he can make is to suffer for Christ. "I will make an everlasting covenant with them, that I will never depart from them, to do them good"—lo the everlasting forgiveness of sins—"and I will put My fear in their hearts, that they shall not depart from me" (Jer. 32:40). Behold the perseverance of faith, and regeneration that shall never be lost. "He that has begun this good work in you will finish it to the end" (Phil. 1:6).

Secondly, it may be demanded how far forth the faithful lose grace and the Holy Spirit? *Answer.* Distinguish the faithful, and distinguish grace. There be four sorts of believers. The first are they which hear the word and understand it. The second are they which do hear, understand, and for a time approve it. The third are those who do hear, understand, approve, and bring forth some fruits. The fourth are such as do hear, understand, approve, bring forth some fruits, and lay hold upon Christ the Redeemer by the hand of a lively faith to salvation. These are true believers and cannot utterly either fall away from God or perish. However all other besides these, both may and use to fall away and perish. Furthermore, grace is either the first or second. The first is the free favor of God, who embraces those that are His being in Christ to everlasting life. From this grace the faithful are said to fall after this fashion. As soon as they have committed some heinous sin against the law of God, they do grievously offend Him. God being offended changes the effects of grace into the effects of a certain hatred, not against the faithful themselves, but against their sins, and this both within and without. Within, when He makes them to feel an accusing conscience and witnessing that God is displeased and that they are made guilty of death by their sin. Without, when they taste of God's anger against them in the outward chastisements of the body. And thus far they fall from His fatherly love and are become the enemies of God after a sort. I say *after a sort*, because God does not lay down His fatherly affection and does not alter His purpose of adoption and eternal life. Although the faithful do fall away, so much as lies in them, yet God remains a father in Christ; and they also as touching right to eternal life remain sons. "They shall never perish, neither shall any pluck them out of My hand" (John 10:28). Here some do say that the sheep cannot be plucked out, but yet they may of their own accord slink away, but without reason, for the sheep which revolts is plucked away by the devil when it does revolt. And as he which continues in Christ's word is verily His disciple, so he that does not fall away, but abides a sheep, is verily a sheep. "Who shall separate us from the love of Christ?" (Rom. 8:35). "The gifts and calling of God are ἀμεταμέλητα without repentance" (11:29). "The foundation of God remaineth sure, and has this seal, The Lord knoweth who are His" (2 Tim. 2:19).

Second grace is either imputed or inherent. Imputed is justification, a part whereof is remission of sins. And this remains and shall forever remain sure as touching sins passed. That saying of the schoolmen is most true: sins once forgiven continue so always. But when that any faithful man shall fall grievously, the pardon of that fall is granted in God's decree, notwithstanding no pardon is actually given of God or received of man until he do repent. Yea, if he should never repent (which notwithstanding is impossible) he should be damned as being guilty of eternal death by this offence. For there is no pardon of any new sin without a new act of faith and repentance.

Inherent grace is either faith or the gift which follows faith. In saving faith we must consider the act and the habit. The act of faith is the very action of apprehending or an unfeigned apprehension of Christ. Now this faith may be lost according to some act (αυπόκριτος). The very habit also or power of faith may in itself be lost, but by reason of confirming grace faith does not perish as touching the essence thereof, but it is lessened and abated according to some degree. And hence it follows that our communion with Christ may be diminished, but that our union cannot be dissolved. There remained in David after his fall the seed of true faith and regeneration, as appears by his words, "Take not Thy Holy Spirit from me" (Ps. 51:11). It is also the judgment of the ancient fathers that the root of faith in Peter's fall "was not taken away and abolished, but only moved; and that it did as it were wax dry, that it was only shaken and trodden on,"[214] and that it did not utterly vanish. Here also we are to give ear a while to Gratian, who consents with us and to this purpose has gathered many testimonies together out of the fathers. "Has love," says he, "taken root? Be secure; no evil can proceed."[215] Again: "Love does utterly estrange the mind, wherein it has once taken possession from the delights of the world." Again: "Love is joined to God and united inseparably and is always invincible in all." Again: "Love is an invisible unction which stands as it were instead of a root to him in whomever it shall be, which cannot wither though the sun do parch. Whatever is rooted is nourished with the heat of the sun and does not wither." Again: "He looks back after the plow who after that he has begun to do good works returns to evil, which he did forsake. Which in no wise befalls to the elect." Again: "All the elect do so go forward to good things that they do not return to the committing of evil." And again: "The fitting and moving of the Spirit may be thus understood. For as touching some virtues it does always abide in the hearts of the saints, but according to other it comes as that which will return and returns as purposing to come. For as concerning faith, hope, and charity and other graces, without which it is not possible to come to that heavenly country (as namely, humility, chastity, justice, and mercy), it never forsakes their hearts that are upright. But as touching the virtue of prophecy, the eloquence of doctrine, and working of miracles, it is sometimes present with the elect, and sometimes it withdraws itself."

The schoolmen allege Augustine to the contrary opinion, where he says that "doubtless if the man which is renewed and justified do fall back by his own will to an evil life, he cannot say I have not received, because he has by his own free will to evil lost the grace of God which he did receive."[216] And again: "That God does not give the gift of perseverance to some of His children whom He did regenerate in Christ, and to whom He gave faith, hope, and love."[217] But he speaks not these things of those which are indeed the sons of the promise, but of those which are so called of us and which bear the name and profession of sons. Furthermore, he speaks of such as have faith and love in opinion and imagination (κατὰδόκησιν), and truly also as touching outward practice. For Augustine in the same place has so expounded his meaning: "We must believe that some of the sons of perdition do[218] begin to live, and for a time faith-

---

214. In the margin: Greg.lib.25 in Iob. & in Eleb. Omil. 15. Tertull. Lib. De Perset. Chrysost. Hom. 26. In Math.

215. In the margin: De cret.2.pars.c.33.q.e.sine de poenit.d.2.

216. In the margin: De cor.& grat.cap.6.& 8. [Augustine, *On Rebuke and Grace*, chs. 6 and 8].

217. In the margin: Cap.9. [Augustine, *On Rebuke and Grace*, ch. 9].

218. In the margin. Cap.14. He speaketh of the justice of life, and not of the inward righteousness of the heart [Augustine, *On Rebuke and Grace*, ch. 14].

fully and justly in the faith that works by love, and afterward fall."[219] Thirdly, he speaks of faith and love as they are imperfect virtues and as it were lately sprung up, and not as they are found perfect and true—to wit, as touching the truth of their essence. So Augustine: "Love is sprung up with you, but it is not yet perfected. Do not despair, but nourish it, lest it be stifled." And Gratian: "This love which was an herb in Peter before his denial and which springs up in everyone is lost and repaired before it be strengthened and made perfect."[220] And indeed for the manifesting of the truth of faith and love there is required perseverance, by which it might be known that these and such like virtues have taken deep root in the heart and are grounded upon an earnest and constant affection, that they may never be overcome of temptations.

Objection 1. Sin and the grace of the Holy Spirit cannot stand together. *Answer.* This is true of the sin that reigns or which is committed with full consent of will, but the regenerate do not sin with a whole or full will. And I lay this foundation of this our judgment. In temptation, we must consider two things: the beginning or ground and the degrees. The ground is our own concupiscence—that is, our inbred corruption. The subject thereof is the whole man, but especially the faculties of man's soul: the mind, will, and affections. And in these it does immediately exist and reign alone before a sinner be converted. And a man being not regenerated, be he what he will be, he is flesh every lot of him. But after that a man is regenerated, the flesh is no more alone or severed by itself, but mixed with the Spirit, and the Spirit with the flesh, although both these qualities remain as touching nature distinct in one subject—as in the twilight the light does not appear alone, but with darkness, and darkness is not alone but with the light. And the man that is regenerated is not only flesh, nor only spirit, nor flesh in one part, and spirit in another, but the whole man is flesh in every part, and the whole man is spirit in every part. And because those things which are contrary cannot consist together in the highest degrees, therefore albeit the whole man be flesh, yet he is not flesh in the highest degree, nor spirit in the highest degree, but in remiss and lower degrees partly flesh and partly spirit—as lukewarm water is remissly and indifferently cold throughout and remissly also hot throughout. Hence, it follows that concupiscence may exist and be with the grace of the Holy Spirit, so that it bear not rule. The degrees of temptation are, as James teaches (1:14–15), in number five.

---

219. In the margin: Tract.5. in John. Epist. [Augustine, Tractates on the Gospel of John, tractate 5].

220. In the margin: Ibid. cap. 24. [Possibly a reference to Augustine, *On Rebuke and Grace*, ch. 24].

The first, abstraction or drawing away (τὸ εξέλκείν), when the mind receives a thought cast into it about the committing of evil and by this means suffers herself to be drawn away from her duty to other things.

The second is inescation or enticing (τὸ δελεάζσιν), when the mind conceives a morose thought for the committing of sin together with a certain delectation of the affection—as when fishes delight themselves with the bait hanging upon the hook. Thus far all divines think a regenerate man may come, and it is most certain. For hence it is that Paul complains that he was held captive of sin (Rom. 7:23).

The third degree is conception, (τὸ τυλλαμζαίειν) namely, when there is a will, consent, and a purpose to commit evil. And when corruption does come thus far, there be some that say that all repentance and faith is driven out and gone, but not truly. There is indeed in the unregenerate in whom sin reigns a full consent, but in the regenerate, in whom the flesh and the spirit are two contrary foundations of actions, the consent is more remiss and imperfect; for they do so will, as that they will, and so nill as that they will, as Paul has taught by his own example.

The fourth degree (τὸ τίκτειν) is birth of sin, when after consent an evil is actually committed. And in this act the same man being regenerate does at the same instant both sin and not sin. He sins only according to the flesh; and in that part wherein he is renewed he does not sin, but before and after the fact detests his sin. And as when the Spirit prevails, the action is not free from all pollution of the flesh; so when the flesh prevails, the action is not so corrupt in the regenerate as it is in those in whom sin reigns. Nevertheless, I confess that in every grievous fall the flesh does get the mastery, and that the gift of true faith after the receipt of the wound lies flat and in a swoon for a time, but that it is not for all that abolished and quite put out.

The last degree is perfection [τὸ αποτελεῖν]—namely when sin being persisted and ripened by often iteration and custom groweth as it were to a habit. So says Gregory. "Sin always is finished in a work by those same four ways. For first the sin is committed closely; after that it is discovered in the sight of men without blushing at the fault. Then it is brought into a custom. And at the last either it is nourished with the deceit of vain hope or with the obstinacy of wretched despair."[221] And Isidore: "Action brings forth custom; and custom, necessity. And so a man being fettered with these links lies fast bound as it were with a chain of vices." This last degree befalls not the regenerate, and if it did, faith and the Holy Spirit should be shaken out and banished.

---

221. In the margin: Moral lib.4.cap.27. [Probably a reference to Gregory the Great, *Morals on the Book of Job*, bk. 4, ch. 27].

Objection 2. Adam when he was void of corruption fell wholly away. Therefore, much more they who being born and regenerated after Adam shall believe. *Answer.* The reason is unlike. "For we have," says Augustine, "by this grace of God in the receiving of that which is good and in the constant keeping of the same not only power to do that which we will, but also will to do that which we can, which Adam wanted. For one of these was in him, but the other was not. For to receive good he wanted not grace, because as yet he had not lost it. But to continue in it he wanted the help of grace, without which he was not able at all to do it. And he received power if he would, but he had not will answerable to his power; for if it had been in him he should have persevered."[222]

Objection 3. Propositio: The member of a harlot cannot be the member of Christ. *Assumptio:* But he which believes truly, who is actually a member of Christ, may be the member of a harlot. *Conclusion:* Therefore, one that truly believes may come to be no member of Christ. *Answer.* The member of Christ is diversely distinguished, for there is either a true or an apparent member. An apparent member is that which is not a member according to election, nor in itself, but in show only—that is, judged by means of outward profession to be in the visible church. And it is like a wooden leg fastened to the body by art. A true member is either by destination and appointment, or now actually one. Members by appointment are all those who are elected, although they be not as yet regenerated or born. An actual member is either one that is lively or half dead. A lively member is that which is according to election and in very deed engrafted into Christ and ruled by His Spirit. That is a half-dead member which does indeed belong to God's election and is engrafted into Christ, but yet being hurt by some grievous fall has so much as in it is lost the grace of the Holy Spirit. Now I answer to the proposition. First, a member of Christ in show may be the member of a harlot, as a wooden foot which is indeed the member of some image may be an apparent member of a man's body whereto it is fitted by art. Secondly, a member of Christ by appointment (in God's decree) may be the member of a harlot, as Paul, who was separated from the womb, was for a time a member of Satan persecuting the church (Gal. 1:15). Thirdly, he which is a lively and active member of Christ and so continues cannot be the member of a harlot, but a member that is crazy and half dead may be. For however he remains in Christ in respect of incorporation and the mystical union, yet he is out of Him as touching the force and efficacy of the Spirit, which for a time through his own default he does not perceive, until he do repent. A leg that is troubled with the palsy or receives no nourishment is a true leg, because in respect of union it is incorporated into the body, however it has

---

222. In the margin: De cor. & grat. C. 11. [Augustine, *On Rebuke and Grace*, ch. 11].

almost lost all communion and fellowship with the rest of the members (παρά λυσις ἀτροφία). Neither must this which I say seem strange that the members of Christ may in some sort be the member of a harlot, because the conjunction is not of the same kind. The conjunction with Christ is spiritual, but that which is with a harlot is corporal.

Error 9. This platform gives to every man a free will flexible and inclinable to both parts by grace and teaches that it is in man's will to apply himself to grace being given by the help of universal grace or to reject the same through the weakness of corrupt nature. But this is false; for the first, universal grace is not effectual, unless it be confirmed by the second grace following it. As for example, if a man shall receive power to believe if he will, yet he shall never actually and indeed believe, except there be also given the help of the other grace, which brings the former into act. But this second grace is not given to all and every one. Moreover, this opinion is repugnant to very plain places of Scripture. "I will make an everlasting covenant with them, that I will not turn away from them to do them good, and I will put My fear in their hearts that they shall not depart from Me" (Jer. 32:40). Again: "God shall confirm you to the end blameless: God is faithful by whom ye are called to the fellowship of His Son Jesus Christ our Lord" (1 Cor. 1:8–9). It is also contrary to Christ's speech: "Every man that has heard and has learned of the Father cometh to Me" (John 6:45). "This grace," says Augustine, "which is secretly infused into men's hearts by God's liberality is refused of no hard heart."[223] And afterward: "If it had pleased the Father to teach them to come to Christ who accounted the word of the cross foolishness, without all doubt they also would have come. Why does He not teach all? If we shall say, because they will not learn whom He does not teach, it will be answered us; and where is that which is said to Him, Thou O Lord, convertest and quickenest us."[224] Again: "The effect of God's mercy cannot be in man's power so as that He should show mercy to him in vain if man be unwilling, because if He would have mercy on them, He could call them so as they should be fitted to move, understand, and follow."[225] And again: "God shows mercy to none in vain, but to whom He shows mercy, him He calls so, as He knows to be fitting for him, that he may not reject Him who calls him." Neither do I here respect the distinction of sufficient and effectual grace; for I acknowledge no grace sufficient for the conversion of a sinner which is not

---

223. In the margin: Cant.1.3. [Possibly a reference to a commentary or homily of Augustine on Song of Solomon].

224. In the margin: Depraed.Sanct.cap.8. [Augustine, *Predestination of the Saints*, ch. 8].

225. In the margin: Ad Simplic.lib.1.q.2. [Augustine, *De Diversis Quaestionibus ad Simplicianum*, bk. 1, q. 2].

effectual, as I have already said before, because free will is altogether wanting in spiritual things. We are stark dead in sins, and our sufficiency is wholly from God. Therefore, there is in us beside the want of original righteousness a threefold impotency. The first is that whereby we are unable to receive or desire supernatural grace offered by God. The second is that whereby we are unable to use it lawfully. The third is that whereby we are unable to retain and keep it. And therefore there are certain degrees of grace to be bestowed in the true conversion of a sinner, in respect of which Augustine makes a fivefold grace: preventing, preparing, working, coworking, and the gift of perseverance.[226] Preventing grace, *praeveniens*, is that whereby God inspires into the mind of the sinner that is to be converted good thoughts, a good purpose, and a desire of supernatural grace. The means whereby preventing grace is given is the voice and preaching of the gospel, by the which being heard and thought upon the Holy Ghost does show forth His efficacy and power. For hence it is that the gospel is called the "ministry of the Spirit" (2 Cor. 3:6). And that, "faith is said to be by hearing" (Rom. 10:17). Therefore, they which are out of the church do want the preventing grace, unless it be extraordinarily conferred, which yet is very seldom done. Preparing grace, *praeparans*, is that whereby it is given us to consent to God offering grace, or whereby the mind and will are prepared that they may yield assent and obedience to the Holy Spirit. For as all supernatural grace in respect of God's donation is altogether from Him, even so we obtain our consentment and power to receive grace conferred no otherwise than by the gift of God. Working grace, *operans*, is that whereby we are delivered from the dominion of sin and are renewed in mind, will, and affection, having received power to obey God. Coworking grace, *cooperans*, is that whereby God confers and persists the grace of renewing being received. And without this grace following, the first is unprofitable. For when grace is given by God and received of us by the second grace, we do not use it lawfully but by this third grace. Augustine says well: "If in so great weakness of this life the will renewed should be so left to the regenerate that they may remain in God's help if they themselves will, and if God should not make them for to will among so many and so mighty temptations the will would faint by reason of the weakness thereof. Man's weakness therefore is relieved, that through the grace of God there should be will inseparably annexed to the power, and therefore the will though it be but weak, yet should not for all that faint and be overcome by adversity."[227] Again: "Therefore, that we may will He works without us; but when we will, and so will that we do also, He coworks with us. Yet notwithstanding without

---

226. In the margin: De grat.&lib.arb.c.17. [Augustine, *On Grace and Free Will*, ch. 17].
227. In the margin: De cor.&grat.cap.12. [Augustine, *On Rebuke and Grace*, ch. 12].

Him working that we may will, or coworking when we do will, we have no power to perform the good works of godliness."[228] The gift of perseverance is that whereby after that we have received the grace of renovation, we do also receive a will to persevere and continue constantly in that good which we can do. Jerome: "That suffices me not which He has once bestowed. I ask that I may receive, and when I shall receive, I ask again."[229] These five graces spoken of even now, being taken severally and asunder by themselves, are not sufficient to salvation (for the preventing grace is nothing available without the preparing grace, and the working grace without the coworking grace), yet being joined together they are sufficient. And hence it plainly appears that there is not any grace truly sufficient to the salvation of a sinner that is stark dead in sins, the which is not also effectual. If so much strength were given to one that would lift up a mighty burden as were sufficient, that is, so much as did exceed the weight of the thing that is to be lifted up, out of all doubt motion would follow, it would come up—so if God do give so much grace as is sufficient—that is, as would overcome the hardness of the heart—the corruption thereof could not possibly hinder it from being converted. Moreover, if these five graces do concur in the conversion of a sinner, the regenerate person shall not have free will flexible alike either to good or evil, neither shall it be in our choice to obey or resist the motion of the Spirit. Yea, from hence it follows that it multiplies grace and that the will is so effectually ruled by it in those that are truly converted as that they follow faith and godliness with an inflexible and steadfast affection. The Spirit promised us of God does not enable us to walk if we will, but makes us walk indeed (Ezekiel 36–37). Those which are drawn have not only power to run if so be that they themselves will, but they run indeed after Christ (1 John 3:9). He which is born of God sins not; yea, he cannot sin. Furthermore, perseverance in faith does wholly depend upon God's will, as these words of Paul do show: "I have reserved to Myself seven thousand men, which have not bowed the knee to Baal" (Rom. 11:4). And those which do truly believe have received of God both power to persevere in grace if they will and also will to do that which they have power to do. So Augustine: "There is in us by this grace of God (which is by Christ) in receiving of good and in the constant keeping of the same not only power to do that which we will, but will to do that which we have power to do." Therefore, those that do truly believe cannot but persevere.

Objection 1. "O inhabitants of Jerusalem, and ye men of Judah, judge between Me and My vineyard: what could I have done any more to My vineyard that I have not done to it? Why have I looked that it should bring forth

---

228. In the margin: De grat.&lab.arb.c.17. [Augustine, *On Grace and Free Will*, ch. 17].
229. In the margin: Epist. ad. Cresiph. [Jerome, Epist. ad. Cresiph.].

grapes, and it bringeth forth wild grapes?" (Isa. 5:3). These Jews therefore had the help of God, which was thoroughly sufficient to conversion and the leading of a life acceptable to God. *Answer.* God speaks in this place of the sufficiency[230] of outward means—that is, of the preaching of His word, of His benefits, and chastisements whereby they were sufficiently invited and led to salvation, but that they were of such peevish and perverse dispositions. God therefore did that to this wicked vineyard which if He had done in a good vineyard, it would have brought forth the fruit of obedience. And here he speaks not of the sufficiency of inward grace whereby an evil vineyard might be changed into a good vineyard. You will say that God then has no just cause to expostulate with the Jews that they brought not forth fruit, because He gave them not grace to repent and bring forth fruit, which could by no means be had if He do not give it. I answer that God could not justly have expostulated with the Jews if He had owed them grace and being bound to give it had not given it, if they had not cast away the grace which they received in their first parents by which they might have brought forth fruit beseeming repentance, if He had denied them being anew desirous to receive the grace which now is lost. But God is bound to no man; and we have cast away that grace which was bestowed in Adam; and we do not desire or care for it being cast away. Therefore, God does most justly expostulate with us, if we bring not forth fruit.

Objection 2. "How often would I have gathered thy children together, and thou wouldst not" (Matt. 23:37). How did Christ will, and so will that He complains of those who would not, if He had not through His help made them able to will whom He knew could not will? *Answer.* Christ is here said to have willed to gather them together not by the will of His good pleasure, (*Voluntate beneplaciti. Voluil. Signi*), which may never be refitted but by His signifying or revealed will. For He is said to will to gather all unto Himself, because by the preaching of the word He calls all in common unto salvation and prefixes to Himself this end of preaching, that they should commit themselves to His protection and fidelity. By this will therefore He may will to gather the Jews together, though in the meantime He do not help them, that they themselves may be able to will. And He does also justly complain of those that will not, because men's impotency to that which is good and their bondage under sin whereby they are made to nill and unable to will that which is good comes not from the Creator, but from him who of his own accord fell away from the Creator. Secondly, I say that Christ is here said to have willed not as He is God effectually mollifying and converting the hearts of men, but as He was a

---

230. In the margin: So Jerome on this place, Loquitur de sufficientia externorum in edtoruym non interna gratiae.

minister of the circumcision (Rom. 15:8) while He sought the conversion of the Jews by preaching. A place altogether like is in Acts 7:51, where the Jews are said "to have rushed against" or "resisted the Holy Ghost" (ἀντιπίπτετε). But these words are to be understood not in regard of the inward and effectual operation of the spirit, but in respect of the outward ministry of the prophets. It pleased Lombard also to interpret this place, "How often would I have gathered thy children, and thou wouldst not?" thus: "So many as I have gathered together, I did it by My effectual will, you being unwilling."[231]

Objection 3. "I stand at the door and knock, if any shall open it to Me I will come in to him" (Rev. 3:20). Therefore, all at whose door Christ knocks have sufficient grace whereby they are able to open if they will. He is unwise that knocks at the door, if he know assuredly that there is nobody within that is able to open it. *Answer.* This place favors not universal grace, for these at whose door Christ knocks are those which believe and are converted; and He knocks at their hearts partly by His word, partly by afflictions, that He might stir up their languishing faith and increase and confirm His fellowship with them. You may read the like in Song 5:1–2: "Open to me my sister, my love, my dove."

Error 10. Tenthly, this platform disagrees with itself. For it says that God does confer to all men all the helps of nature and grace, and that he is not wanting to any so but that he may obtain salvation. But I say, and that out of this platform, that God is wanting to some offenders, because He gives them only a power to persevere in faith if they will—or (if you had rather) a power to will to persevere (*posse velle perseverare*)—and makes them not to persevere actually and indeed. And unless this grace be given, it is not possible that they should obtain salvation by persevering. For it is a most sure rule: a man does not that good thing which by grace he is able for to do, unless God make him to do it, as He has made him able to do it if he will. Therefore, he to whom the very act of perseverance is not given, being smitten with the violence of some grievous temptation, without delay will fall away from faith and shall be damned.

Error 11. Lastly, this hypothesis or platform is but the varnishing and fresh trimming over of certain opinions which the church in former ages did condemn. The Pelagians taught that all men were redeemed by Christ, but not made free[232] because God distributed His gifts according to the capableness of them which came to receive them. The same did Faustus the Pelagian also affirm: "How has God," says he, "redeemed all the world? Do we not see men

---

231. In the margin: Lib.1.dist.46. [Peter Lombard, *Sentences*, bk. 1, distinction 46].
232. In the margin: Aug.cont.Iul.Pelag.lib.3.cap.3. [Augustine, *Against Julian*, bk. 3, ch. 3].

to live still in their sins? How shall we think that they are ransomed whom we do see still to continue captives? Let us gather that which is here meant by using a similitude—as, for example, if any ambassador or priest purposing to make intercession for a city taken by war shall bestow a very great ransom and set free from his servitude who is the chief commander of all the multitude which is in captivity, insomuch that they are altogether delivered from all constraint or necessity of bondage. And then if happily either their usual delight or some soothing slave shall so instantly urge some of the captives as that everyone turning servant and slave to his own will shall refuse that freely bestowed benefit—shall we say that the contempt of the unthankful captive has lessened the estimation of the ransom? Or that he which refuses liberty does any way diminish the good will of him that ransoms? Surely no. For even as he which returns may be well accepted with him that does ransom him, so is he guilty of contempt who did not return."[233] Thus we see that the Pelagians did forge or frame a redemption through Christ without deliverance. And what else do they who publish in their pamphlets, that all and every one on God's part are redeemed, but not saved, because they will not believe? And now let us hear the confutation of this opinion. Augustine says, "You say they are redeemed, but they are not delivered. They are washed, but they are not cleansed. These be your monstrous opinions. These are the paradoxes of the Pelagian heretics, etc. But I pray you, tell me how can this redemption be understood, if He do not redeem from evil, which redeemed Israel from all their sins? For wherever we make mention of redemption, there also is understood a ransom; and what is that but the precious blood of the immaculate lamb Christ Jesus? And concerning this ransom, why should we ask any other wherefore it was given? Let him that gave the ransom, let him that paid the price make the answer. This is, says He, My blood which is shed for many for the remission of sins. Proceed, I pray proceed, and as you say in the sacrament of our Savior, men are baptized, but they are not saved. They are redeemed, but they are not delivered. So say you also. Christ's blood is shed for them for the remission of sins, but they are cleansed by the remission of no sin. They are wonderful, strange, and untrue things which you affirm.[234] Concerning the redemption of Christ's blood, by reason of the exceeding errors which have grown in respect thereof, insomuch that some, even as their own writings do witness, do hold that it was shed even for those ungodly ones who from the beginning of the world until the passion of our Lord were dead in their ungodliness and punished with eternal damnation, contrary to that saying of the prophet, O death, I will be your death, and

---

233. In the margin: Lib.degrat.&lib.arb.1 cap.16. [Augustine, *On Grace and Free Will*, ch. 16].

234. In the margin: Concil.Valent.Anno 855.cap.4. [Fourth Council of Valence (855 A.D.), ch. 4].

your sting O hell—we do decree that it ought simply and faithfully to be held and taught according to the evangelical and apostolic truth that we judge that this ransom was given for them of whom the Lord Himself says, Even as Moses lifted up the serpent in the wilderness, so must the Son of Man be lifted up, that everyone which believes in Him may not perish but have eternal life. So God loved the world that He gave His only begotten Son, that everyone that believed in Him might not perish, but have everlasting life. And the apostle says, Christ was once offered for the taking away of the sins of many."[235]

Prosper ascribes this platform of general grace to the Pelagians. "This is," says he, "their very opinion and profession, that Adam sinning, every man sinned, and that no man is saved by his own works but by the grace of God in regeneration. And yet that the reconcilement which is in the sacrament of Christ's blood is without exception offered to all men, so that whoever will come to faith and baptism may be saved, and that God did foreknow before the creation of the world who should believe or who should remain in that faith which must afterward be propped and helped by His grace, and that He pre-destinated them to His kingdom who being freely called He foresaw that they would be worthy of election and that they would depart out of this life making a good end. And that therefore every man is provoked to believe and do good by godly institutions, that no man may despair of the attainment of eternal life, seeing that there is a reward prepared for a voluntary devotion."[236] The difference I confess consists in this, that the Pelagians do either wholly ascribe to nature the ability to do well, or else partly to nature and partly to grace. But this platform ascribes all things wholly to grace, which indeed is very right. But while they go about to ordain universal grace, they do not free themselves but are rather more entangled. For most true is that saying of Peter Martyr: "While these men make grace so common to all, they turn grace into nature."[237] And I would willingly be certified whether they who have received this grace be regenerate or no. If they be regenerate, then all men are regenerate. If they be not regenerate, then have all men power to believe and to attain salvation if they will—yea, even while they remain unregenerate. But this power, if it be in man before his conversion, will not differ much from nature. And if so be that grace extend as far as nature, we must not pray more for grace than for nature, neither need we any more pray for the conversion of unbelievers, because it is

---

235. In the margin: Cont.Jul.lib.3.cap.3. [Augustine, *Against Julian*, bk. 3, ch. 3].

236. In the margin: Epist.ad August. [Prosper of Aquitane, *Pro Augustino responsiones*].

237. In the margin: Loc.Com.class.3.c.1. [Peter Martyr Vermigli (1499–1562), *Loci Communes*, class 3, ch. 1. Peter Martyr was an important Italian-born Reformed theologian during the Reformation].

in their own power by reason of general grace to be converted if they will. Prosper also ascribes this platform to the Pelagians in these verses:[238]

> Thus we determine of that grace that makes
> Us God's own people, and to Him full dear:
> But ye affirm that no man it forsakes,
> But that the world from sin it freeth clear,
> And passing none, does proffer mere salvation
> To all without exception; yet they come
> Guided by their own list to this vocation,
> And motions of the mind, directing some,
> To the embracing of that offered light
> Which to all that will, does clear the sight.

> But afterward he condemneth it in this sort:
> Let's see how you can prove, that Christ His grace
> Proffers God's kingdom and true blessedness
> To all men born, letting none overpass,
> To whom it granteth not this happiness.
> When even at this time through the whole world's frame
> And compass of the earth, wherein we live,
> Christ's Gospel is not known, nor yet His name;
> I cannot say but that He could it give
> Even at the first, to all that breathe on earth
> Or ever in this world received birth.

And again, he says:

> If no man be whom He will not redeem,
> No doubt but that His will shall be effected,
> But of a great part He makes no esteem,
> Who in infernal darkness live rejected.
> Now if the divers motions of the mind,
> And a peculiar perfect liberty
> Do make a different cause, to all mankind
> God's will most free from inability
> Either receiveth strength, from human pleasure
> Or wanteth strength, when will attains that treasure.

---

238. In the margin: Lib.car.de ingratis. [Prosper of Aquitaine, Lib.car.de ingratis].

And again, he answers the Pelagians, who say that by willing it we are able to attain God's grace, or else to resist it by nilling it, after this manner:

> How falls it out that this Almighty grace
> Which saveth all, rejects the work it wrought,
> When neither cause, condition, time, nor place,
> Can for a hindrance thereunto be brought?

And again:

> What would you say when you do plainly see
> How Christ His grace in twins a difference makes,
> And those who at one time conceived be,
> And whom the world into her bosom takes
> It does distinguish, granting one heaven's bliss;
> The other hell, where grief and horror is?
> To say the will directs, you speak amiss.

And again:

> No man can hold them justly culpable
> Or guilty of this sin to whom God's might
> Did never show itself so favorable
> As to appear, no not in glimmering light.

Faustus, the semi-Pelagian, accused the Catholics in that they said that our Lord Jesus Christ "did not take upon Him man's flesh for all men, nor died generally for all."[239] And on the other side, the Catholics accuse the Pelagians "in that they say that God repels none from eternal life, but is willing indifferently that all men should be saved and to come to the knowledge of the truth."[240] And again, that "they say that our Lord Jesus Christ died for all mankind, and that no man is utterly exempted from the redemption of His blood, although he lead all this his life estranged from Him, because that the sacrament of God's grace appertains to all men, whereby many are not therefore regenerated because they are foreknown that they have not a will to be regenerated, and that therefore on God's part eternal life is prepared for all men, but in respect of the freedom of the will they say that they only attain everlasting life who do of their own accord believe." And again they say that "they will not admit of that exposition of that saying which is alleged out of Augustine, which is that unless

---

239. In the margin: Lib.1.de lib.arb.cap.19. [Augustine, *On Grace and Free Will*, ch. 19].
240. In the margin: Prosper.ep.ad August. [Prosper of Aquitane, *Pro Augustino responsiones*].

He will have all men to be saved (1 Timothy 2)."[241] And again: "Not only those which appertain to the number of the saints, but all men altogether, without exception of any."

I wish also that thing were marked—namely that the Catholics are accused by the Pelagians that under the name of predestination they did establish a certain fatal necessity, and that they made a kind of violent preordination, which accusation has also been laid against us. And the like crime shows the like cause.[242]

Lastly, this platform does passing well agree with that doctrine concerning predestination which is generally maintained in the schools and synagogues of the papists—yea verily, to speak the truth, it seems to be borrowed even from thence. For if we well consider of the matter, what else has Pighius taught? What else has Catharinus maintained? And else at this day do the gross fat monks maintain who impart God's actions in the case of predestination within these pales. First, say they, God foresaw the natures and sins of all men. Then prepared He Christ the Redeemer. Afterward, He willed for the merit of Christ foreseen to bestow sufficient helps of grace upon all men whereby they might be saved through Christ; and He would it even in this, so much as in Him was, that all men might be saved, His will preceding. Lastly, He did mercifully predestinate those whom He did see would end their lives in God's favor, and He did justly reject othersome either for original or actual sins in which He foresaw they would end their lives.

---

241. In this rather awkward sentence, Perkins seems to be saying that the Roman Catholics are asserting that the Pelagians will not agree with Augustine's exposition of 1 Timothy 2:4 that their view is erroneous unless God actually wills to save everyone.

242. In the margin: Hier.epist.ad August. [Jerome, Letter to Augustine].

A COROLLARY, OR ADDITION.

A most certain theorem or undoubted truth.

GOD HAS NOT REVEALED
Christ to all and every man

The Proofs

This is evident by Scriptures and experience. "That which has not been told them, shall they see, and that which they have not heard, they shall understand" (Isa. 52:14). "Behold Thou shalt call a nation, which Thou hast not known: and nations that knew not Thee shall run to Thee" (55:5). "I have been sought of them, that asked not before, I was found of them, that sought Me not" (65:1). "And in the place where it was said to them, Ye are not My people" (Hos. 1:10). "I will have mercy upon her that was not pitied, and I will say to them which were not My people, thou art My people" (2:23). "God in times past suffered all the Gentiles to walk in their own ways" (Acts 14:16). "And the time of this ignorance God regarded not, but now He admonisheth all men everywhere to repent" (17:30). "To him now that is of power to establish you according to my Gospel and preaching of Jesus Christ, by the revelation of the mystery, which was kept secret since the world began, but now is opened" (Rom. 16:25–26). "Which is the mystery hid since the world began and from all ages, but now is made manifest to His saints, to whom God would make known what is the riches of this glorious mystery among the Gentiles" (Col. 1:26–27). "Ye were at that time without Christ, and had no hope, and were atheists or without God in the world" (Eph. 2:12). "The mystery of Christ in other ages was not opened to the sons of men, as it is now revealed to His holy apostles" (3:5). "He showeth His word to Jacob, His statutes and His judgments to Israel: He has not dealt so with every nation, neither have they known His judgments" (Ps. 147:19–20).

The most wise philosophers among the Gentiles have indeed smattered many things of God; but in the meantime, what say they of Christ? Why should they be so exceeding silent in this point, if Christ were revealed to all? Socrates, being ready to die, said, "I depart out of this life, and they do live with whom I am thoroughly to plead my cause—whether it be good, the immortal gods do know; and indeed I think no man knows. And we owe," says he, "O Crito a cook to Aesculapius to pay the price of the potion."[1] It is reported that Aristotle, being ready to die, cried out, "O you which are the chiefest thing of all things which are, have mercy upon me."[2]

The Gentiles knew not God, that great benefactor, and therefore feigned to themselves certain favors, Castor and Pollux, and Hercules, called Αλεξίκακος, that is, a helper in distress, or repeller of evils, and Aesculapius the physician. Solinus says that there is not as yet any of the Gentiles found who has attained to the height of felicity and may justly be accounted happy.[3] Albinus speaks thus: "When such like questions are propounded why one is judged thus and another after another manner, why this man is blinded, God giving him over, and another enlightened through God's assistance—let not us presume or take upon us to judge of the judgment of so great a judge, but with trembling let us cry out with the apostle, 'O the depth.'"

Consectary 1

The promise concerning the seeds of the woman belongs not to all and to every one. For a promise to whom it is not revealed is not actually a promise.

Consectary 2

However the redemption that is by Christ belongs to all, yet it belongs not to all and to every one. For a benefit to be perceived or received by a supernatural faith, if it be not revealed, is no benefit.

Consectary 3

Vocation and universal saving grace belongs not to all and every particular person, for God calls us by revealing and offering Christ to us.

Consectary 4

The foreknowledge of faith in Christ, and of[4] privative infidelity is not the square and rule according to which God has ordained and disposed His predestination, because there be very many that never so much as heard of Christ, in whom therefore there is neither faith in Christ nor privative infidelity or contempt of the gospel.

Trini-uni Deo Gloria.

FINIS

---

1. In the margin: Lac.lib.7, cap.2. [Probably a reference to Socrates (470–399 B.C.), *Laches*, bk. 7, ch. 2. Socrates was a classical Greek philosopher].
2. In the margin: Ens entium misere mei.
3. In the margin: Collectar.5.cap.7. [Probably a reference to the the third-century Latin grammarian Gaius Julius Solinus and his *Collectanea rerum memorabilium*, bk. 5, ch. 7].
4. In the margin: Contempt of the Gospel.

A Treatise on God's Free Grace
and
Man's Free Will

Printed by John Legate, Printer to the
Universitie of Cambridge.
1608

To the Right Worshipful, Sir Edward Dennie, Knight

Right Worshipful, it is a thing most evident that the present religion of the Church of Rome is an enemy to the grace of God, two ways. First, because it exalts the liberty of man's will and extenuates the grace of God, and this it does in five respects. For first of all, it teaches that natural free will of man has in it not only a passive or potential but also an active power or imperfect strength in duties of godliness, and so much the less power is ascribed to the grace of God. This doctrine of theirs is flat against reason. For the will of man in itself is a natural thing, and therefore it is neither fit nor able to effect any supernatural action (as all actions of godliness are) unless it be first of all (as they say) elevated above his condition by the impressions of a supernatural habit. And the Scripture is utterly against this doctrine when it says, "Ye were once darkness" (Eph. 5:8). We are not sufficient of ourselves, to think anything of ourselves (2 Cor. 3:5). The natural man—that is, he that wants the Spirit of God—cannot perceive of the things of God (1 Cor. 2:14). You were dead in sins and trespasses (Eph. 2:1), without Christ and without God in the world (v. 12). Again, Scripture says further that the heart of man is slow (Luke 24:25) and vain (Ps. 5:9) and hard that cannot repent (Rom. 2:5) and stony (Ezek. 36:26); and that the Jews were obstinate, their neck as an iron sinew, and their brow brass (Isa. 48:4); and that it is God who gives eyes to see and a heart to understand (Deut. 29:4). By these testimonies it is manifest that grace does not only help and assist our weak nature, but altogether change the perverse qualities thereof and bring it from darkness to light (Acts 26:18) and from death to life (Eph. 2:1). Which grace whoever does not so far forth acknowledge never yet knew what the gospel means, neither did he ever consider the words of our Savior Christ: "No man comes to me, unless the Father draw him" (John 6:44). Prosper, the scholar of St. Augustine, has a notable saying, which I marvel the Papists of our time do not consider. "We have, says he, "free will by nature, but for quality and condition it must be changed by our Lord Jesus Christ."

Secondly, some of the Romish religion avouch that the efficacy of God's preventing grace depends upon the cooperation of man's will, and they affirm that the Council of Trent is of this mind. But then to the question of Paul, "Who has separated thee?" (1 Cor. 4:7), the answer may be made, "I myself have done it by my own will." And that shall be false which Paul teaches that beside possible, the power of well-willing, *ipsum velle*—that is, the act of well-willing is of God (Phil. 2:13). Others therefore place the efficacy of grace in the congruity of fit objects and persuasion, as though it were sufficient to stir up the heart and to incline the will in spiritual matters, and our weakness might be cured with so easy a medicine; but God is further said to soften the heart (Ezek. 36:26), to turn the heart (Luke 1:17), to open the heart (Acts 16:14). And because our hearts are over hard, He wounds them (Song 4:9); He circumcises them (Deut. 30:6)—nay, He bruises them (Ezek. 6:9). And when nothing will do good, at length God is said to take away the stony heart (11:19), to quicken them that are contrite (Isa. 57:15; Eph. 2:5), to give a new heart (Ezek. 36:26; Eph. 4:23)—nay, to create a new heart (2:10; 4:28).

Thirdly, they give to God in all contingent actions a depending will whereby God wills and determines nothing but according as before sees that the will of man will determine itself. And thus to maintain the supposed liberty of the will—that is, the indifferency and indetermination thereof—they deprive God of His honor and sovereignty. For by this means, not God but the will itself is the first mover and beginner of her own actions. And there are even of the papists themselves that condemn this doctrine as a conceit.

Fourthly, they teach that the grace which makes us acceptable and grateful to God stands in the inward gifts of the mind, especially in the gifts of charity. But this is most false which they teach, for charity is the fulfilling of the law. And Paul says we are not under the law but under grace (Rom. 6:14). And again, as many as are justified by the law are fallen from grace (Gal. 5:4). Now the grace that does indeed make us grateful to God is the free favor and mercy of God, pardoning our sins in Christ and accepting us to eternal life—and not any quality in us, as Paul signifies when he says we are saved not according to our works, but according to His purpose and grace, which is given to us in Christ before all times (2 Tim. 1:9).

Lastly, they teach that the renewed will of man by the general direction and cooperation of God can perform the duties of godliness without any special help from God by new grace. But the Scripture speaks otherwise. "By the grace of God, I am that I am. I have labored yet not I, but the grace of God which is with me" (1 Cor. 15:10). "No man can say that Jesus is the Lord, but by the Holy Ghost" (12:3). "Without me ye can do nothing" (John 15:5). "After ye believed, ye were sealed with the Spirit" (Eph. 1:13). "He which has begun this good work in you, will finish it until the day of Christ" (Phil. 1:6). "That ye may abound with hope by the virtue of the Spirit" (Rom. 15:13). "It is God that works in you the will and the deed" (Phil. 2:13). "Though the righteous fall, he shall not be cast off, for the Lord puts under his hand" (Ps. 37:24). "Incline my heart to thy testimonies: turn away mine eyes from beholding of vanity, and quicken me in the way" (119:36–37). "Teach me to do thy will, because thou art my God: let thy good spirit lead me in the land of righteousness" (143:10). "Create in me a new heart, renew a right spirit in me—; and establish me by thy free spirit" (51:10, 12). "draw me and I will run after thee." By these and many other places it is evident that God, after He has endued us with His Spirit, does not leave us to be guided by ourselves (for then we should fall again to our former misery); but He directs us, He lifts us up, He leads us, He confirms and sustains us by the same grace and by the same Spirit dwelling in us, that walking in the way of His commandments we may at length attain to everlasting happiness.

The second way whereby the papist shows himself to be an enemy of the grace of God is that he joins the merit of works as a co-cause[1] with the grace of God in that which they call the second justification and in the procurement of eternal life—whereas on the contrary, Paul in the article of justification opposes grace to works, yea to such as are the gifts and fruits of the Spirit. For Abraham did good works not by natural free will, but by faith (Heb. 11:8). And Paul opposes justifying grace to the works of Abraham when he says, "To him that worketh, the wages is not imputed according to grace." And Titus 3:5: "Not of the works of righteousness, which we have done, but of his mercy he saved us." Romans 11:6: "If by grace, then not of works, or else were grace no more grace." Augustine said well that grace is no way grace, unless it be freely given every way.

Thus then, all things considered, it is the best to ascribe all we have or can do that is good wholly to the grace of God. Excellent is the speech of Augustine: "Only hold this as a sure point of godliness, that no good thing can come either to the sense or mind or be any way conceived which is not of God." And Bernard: "The church shows herself to be full of grace when she gives all she has to grace—namely, by ascribing to it both the first and last place. Otherwise, how is she full of grace, if she have anything which is not of grace? Again, I tremble to think anything my own, that I may be my own." This doctrine is the safest and the surest in respect of peace of conscience and the salvation of our souls. So much the papists themselves (betraying their own cause) say and confess. Bellarmine, the Jesuit says, "By reason of the uncertainty of our own justice and for fear of falling into vain glory, it is the safest to put our whole confidence in the alone mercy and goodness of God." Cassander cites a saying of Bonaventure, which is on this manner: "It is the duty of godly minds to ascribe nothing to themselves, but all to the grace of God. Hence it follows, that however much so a man gives to grace, though in giving many things to the grace of God, he takes something from the power of nature and free will, he departs not from godliness; but when anything is taken from the grace of God and given

---

1. "Co-cause" in the original.

to nature, which pertains to grace, there may be some danger."[2] Thus then to hold and maintain justification by faith without works and to ascribe the whole work of our conversion to God without making any division between grace and nature is the safest.

These things I show more at large in this treatise following, which I now present to your Worship as a final testimony of mine humble duty and love, desiring you to accept the mind of the giver and to peruse it at your leisure. And thus I commend your Worship to the protection and grace of God in Christ.

Your Worships in the Lord,
William Perkins

2. In-text citation: in his book called Consultation of Article in question, to Maximilian the Emperor. [Probably a reference to the book by the French theologian Joris Cassander (1513–1566), *Consultatio de Articulis Fidei lute, Catholicos et Protestantes Controversis*].

A Treatise on God's Free Grace and Man's Free Will

"Jerusalem, Jerusalem, which killeth the Prophets, and stoneth them which are sent to thee: how often would I have gathered thy children together, as the hen gathereth her chickens under her wings, and ye would not? Behold, your habitation shall be left to you desolate."

—Matthew 23:37–38

This whole chapter contains a sermon that our Savior Christ made to the Jews at Jerusalem. It has two parts. The first is a reproof of the Jewish doctors— namely, the scribes and Pharisees—for sundry vices, from the beginning of the chapter to the thirty-sixth verse. The second is an invective against Jerusalem in the words I have now read: "Jerusalem, Jerusalem, which killeth the prophets," etc. In the invective, two things are to be considered: the rebellion of Jerusalem in verse 37, and the punishment of this sin in verse 38.

Touching the rebellion itself, three things are set down: the place and persons, in the words, "Jerusalem, Jerusalem"; the degree and practice of rebellion, in these words, "which killeth the Prophets," etc.; the manner and form of their rebellion, in these words, "How oft would I have gathered you, and ye would not."

According to the order of the Holy Ghost, first, I will begin with the place. It is a wonder that Jerusalem, of all the places in the world, should be charged with the height of rebellion against God. For it was the city of God and had prerogatives above all cities in the world. Saint Paul has noted seven of them. The first is that they were Israelites—that is, of the posterity of Jacob. The second is adoption, in that they were reputed and called the children of God. The third is that they had the glory of God—that is, the mercy seat, the pledge of the presence of God. The fourth is the covenants—that is, the two tables of the covenant. The fifth is the giving of the law—namely, of the judicial and ceremonial law. The sixth is the worship of God, the public solemnity whereof was tied to the temple at Jerusalem. The seventh, that to them pertained the promises made to the patriarchs touching the Messiah. To these the prophet Micah adds the eighth privilege, that the first church of the New Testament should be gathered in Jerusalem, and that consequently the preaching of the gospel should pass thence to all nations [Mic. 4:2]. Now, for all these blessings and mercies, Christ our Savior cries out and complains of Jerusalem's rebellion.

And this is not the first time of His complaint. In the days of the prophet Isaiah, He says that when He had done all that He could do for His vineyard, it brought forth nothing but wild grapes [Isa. 5:4]. By the prophet Ezekiel, He sets down a long catalog of His blessings to His people, and withal a catalog of their unthankfulness [Ezekiel 16]. Hence it appears that where God shows the greatest mercy, there oftentimes is the greatest wickedness and unthankfulness. And this is partly verified in this land; for within the compass of this forty years, we have received great blessings from God both for this life and for the life to come—especially, the gospel with peace and protection; and the like have not been seen in former ages. Yet there was never more unthankfulness than now. For now commonly men are weary of the gospel and begin to decline from that which they have been, and the care to please God and do His will is accounted but a curious preciseness of many.

Secondly, hence it may be gathered that God does not tie the infallible assistance of His Spirit to any place or condition of men. If ever any city in the world had this privilege, it was Jerusalem. But Jerusalem, which was the seat and habitation of God, had not this privilege, because it is here charged with rebellion against God. No place therefore nor condition of men has it. It is alleged that God has made a promise to the order of priesthood: "The priest's lips shall preserve knowledge, and thou shalt require the law at his mouth" [Mal. 2:7]. I answer that these words are not a promise, but a commandment. For sometimes words of the future tense are put for words imperative, and therefore the sense is this, "The priest's lips shall keep," that is, "Let them keep knowledge." Again, it is alleged that we are commanded to hear the scribes and Pharisees, because they sit in Moses' chair [Matt. 23:2]. I answer that the chair of Moses is not a place or seat, but the doctrine of Moses, and to this doctrine I grant the Spirit of God is annexed when it is truly taught and believed. Thirdly, it is alleged that God has promised the Spirit of truth to lead men into all truth [John 16:3]. I answer that this promise does not directly and absolutely concern all believers or all ministers, but only the apostles, to whom it was made—and not to them for all times and in all actions, but only while they were in the execution of their apostolic ministry, which stands in the founding of the church of the New Testament partly by publishing the gospel and partly by writing the Scriptures of the New Testament. In a word, no Scripture can be brought to prove that God has, does, or will bind His Spirit to any particular place or persons. Here then falls to the ground three popish conceits. The first, though the members of the Catholic church may severely err, yet they cannot err when they are together in a general council lawfully assembled. The second, that the pope cannot err in his consistory. The third, that personal succession is a mark of the Catholic church, which nevertheless may be severed from the Spirit of God, as we see.

Where our Savior Christ uses a repetition, saying, "O Jerusalem, Jerusalem," He does three things therein. First, He signifies thereby that He takes it for a wonder and for a thing incredible that the Jews after so many blessings should be so exceedingly unthankful. Secondly, He testifies here by His detestation of their unthankfulness. Thirdly, by this repetition He does awake the Jews and stir them up to a serious consideration and loathing of this their sin and does (as it were) proclaim the same to us—and not without cause, for in unthankfulness there be two grievous sins against God: false witness bearing and injustice. False witness bearing, because the unthankful person denies in his heart God to be the fountain and giver of the good things he has, and he ascribes them to his own wisdom, goodness, strength, endeavor. Injustice, because he yields not to God the duties which he owes to Him for His blessings.

The second point to be considered is the degree of the Jewish rebellion. David makes three degrees hereof. The first is to walk in the council of the ungodly. The second is to stand in the way of sinners. The third is to sit down in the scorner's chair [Ps. 1:1]. And this is the very top of desperate rebellion and the sin of Jerusalem. For when Christ says, "Which killest the Prophets, and stonest them which are sent to thee," He notes out three sins in this city: impenitence, whereby they persevered in their wicked ways without hope of amendment; sacrilegious and profane contempt of God and the means of their salvation; cruelty in shedding of blood. And by cruelty, I mean not one or two actions of cruelty, but a habit therein and the custom thereof, for the words are thus to be read: "Jerusalem killing the prophets, and stoning them that are sent to thee," where "stoning" and "killing" signify not one act, but a continuance and multiplication of acts—that is, a custom in shedding of blood.

It may be demanded how the Jews should grow to this height of wickedness. I answer thus: in every actual sin, there be four things distinctly to be considered: the fault, which is the offence of God in any action; the guilt or obligation to punishment for the fault; the punishment itself, which is death; a blot or spot, set in the soul of him that sins, and that by the fault or offence. And this blot is nothing else but a proneness to the sin committed or to any other sin. In the sin of our first parents, beside the fault, guilt, punishment, there followed a blot or deformity in the soul which was the loss of God's image and the disposition of their hearts to all manner of evils. Since the fall of Adam, he that commits an actual offence, beside the fault, guilt, punishment, imprints in his heart a new blot, and that is an increase of his natural proneness to sin—even as the drunkard, the more he drinks, the more he may, and by drinking he increases his thirst. Thus, the Jews by custom in sinning attain to a height in wickedness, because every act of offence has his blot, and the multiplication of offensive acts is the continual increase of the blot or blemish of the soul until the light of nature be extinguished and men come to a reprobate sense. This must be a warning to all men to take heed lest they commit any offence against God in thought, word, or deed, considering every offence imprints a blot in the soul.

Secondly, it may be demanded how Jerusalem, grown to this height of rebellion, can truly be called "the holy City" [Matt. 27:53] or "the City of the great King" [5:35]. I answer, two ways. First, there were many holy men and women in Jewry and Jerusalem that truly feared God and waited for the kingdom of Christ, as Joseph, Mary, Zachariah, Elisabeth, Anna, Simeon, Nicodemus, Joseph of Arimathea, and many others. Now a church is named not of the greater but of the better part—as a heap of corn is so called, though there be more chaff than corn. Secondly, I answer that a people or church that have forsaken God remains still a reputed church till God forsake them, as a wife committing adultery remains still a supposed wife until her husband gives her the bill of divorcement. Jerusalem indeed had forsaken God, but God had not forsaken Jerusalem. For there He preserved still the temple and His worship. Yea, when Jerusalem had condemned and crucified Christ, St. Peter inspired by the Holy Ghost says still, "To you belong the promises, and to your children" [Acts 2:39]. And Jerusalem did not utterly cease to be a city or church of God until they contradicted and blasphemed the apostolical ministry, for then and not before the apostles withdrew themselves from the Jews. Here we see a depth of mercy in God; for though the Jews for their parts had deserved a thousand times to be forsaken, yet God for His part did not forsake them, but sill pursued them with mercy. And we are taught hereby not to give any sentence of the persons of evil men. For though they forsake God, yet know we not whether God have forsaken them or no.

In this example of Jerusalem's rebellion, we learn many things. First, in it we may behold the vileness of man's nature and our violent proneness to sin. For the Jews went to abolish and quench as much as they could the doctrine of salvation—yea, to quench it with blood, and which is more, with the blood of the prophets. And this shows that man drinks iniquity as the fish drinks in water.

Secondly, in Jerusalem we may behold the desperate condition of the Church of Rome at this day. For it follows in rebellion—nay, it goes beyond Jerusalem. If any man will indifferently consider, it will appear that by "the whore of Babylon" is meant the present Church of Rome; and this whore is said to be drunk with the blood of the saints. The locusts out of the bottomless pit go to the kings of the earth to stir them up to war against the church of God. And these locusts are in all likelihood swarms of monks, friars, and Jesuits of the Church of Rome. And we have found it by long and much experience that they of the Roman church have long thirsted for the blood of prince and people in this land.

Thirdly, we are here taught to exercise ourselves in the duties of meekness, goodness, peace to all men. The prophet Isaiah says that men in the kingdom of Christ shall not apply their swords and spears to the hurt of any, as the Jews here do, but shall turn them to instruments of husbandry, as mattocks and fishes [Isa. 2:4]. Whereby is signified that men truly regenerate shall lay aside all purpose and mind of doing any hurt and shall give themselves to do the good they can. Again, he says that "the wolf and the lamb shall dwell together, and that there shall be no hurt in all the holy mount of God" [65:25]. The devil by the sin of our first parents of men made us beasts, lions, wolves, tigers, bears, cockatrices[1]; and Christ again of beasts has made us His lambs and sheep in respect of meekness and patience.

Fourthly, we are here taught not to oppose ourselves against the ministers of God, but without pride and fierceness to yield subjection and obedience to their ministry. Isaiah fortells that in the church of the New Testament a little child—that is, ministers otherwise weak and silly men—shall by their doctrine rule and guide wolves, leopards, lions, that is, fiery and cruel men by nature. "My people," said the Lord, "shall come willingly in the day of assembly," and the sheep of Christ hear His voice and follow Him. The Jews arraign and judge the prophets that are sent to them; but we must suffer them in their ministry to arraign and judge us, that we be not judged of the Lord. Again, the Jews kill their teachers, but we must permit our teachers after a sort to kill us—for their ministry must be as it were a sacrificing knife to kill the old man in us, that we may be an acceptable offering to God.

Lastly, ministers of the word must learn hence not to be troubled if they be hated and persecuted of men. For this befell the holy prophets of God, and that in the city of Jerusalem.

The third point is the manner or form of their rebellion. In it I consider four things. The will of God against which the Jews rebel: "I would." The will of the Jews rebelling: "ye would not." The concord of both: "I would ye would not." The manner of God's will—He wills their salvation in love, "I would have gathered you as an hen gathereth her chickens"; in patience, "How oft would I?" Before I come to handle these points in particular, I will set down a general preamble touching the nature of will.

Will is a power of willing, nilling, choosing, refusing, suspending which depends on reason. By "power" I mean an ability or created faculty; and it is so

---

1. *Cockatrice*: A fable-like animal similar to a basilisk or serpent.

properly in men and angels, but in God only by analogy or proportion, because His will is His essence or Godhead indeed. Secondly, I say it is a "power of will-ing," etc. because to will, nill, choose, refute, suspend, that is neither to will nor to nill are the proper effects of will, whereby it is known and discerned. Lastly, I say it "depends on reason," because it is incident only to natures reasonable—as God, angels, men—and because though it go against good reason, yet is it not without reason altogether. When a man knows and approves that which is good and yet does the contrary, it is because it seems good to him to do the contrary. And in every act of will, there are two things: reason to guide, and election to assent or dissent.

Will has his property, and that is the liberty of the will, which is a freedom from compulsion or constraint, but not from all necessity. From compulsion, because compulsion and will be contrary; and where compulsion takes place, there will gives place. And will constrained is no will. Nevertheless, will and necessity may stand together. God wills many things of absolute necessity, as the eternal generation of the Son, the proceeding of the Holy Ghost, the doing of justice, and such like; and He wills them with most perfect liberty of will. The good angels will their own happiness and the doing of justice, and that of necessity; for they cannot will to sin or to be in misery, and all this they will most freely. Nay, the necessity of not sinning is the glory and ornament of will; for he that does good so as he cannot sin is more at liberty in doing good than he that can do either good or evil. When the creature is in that estate that it willingly serves God and cannot but serve God, then is our perfect liberty. Again, the liberty of will since the fall of man is joined with a necessity of sin-ning, because it stands in bondage under sin. In this respect, it is fitly termed of Augustine "the bond free will." Wherefore, we may not imagine in the will a lib-erty which is a freedom from all necessity. That this may the better appear, let us consider the kinds of necessity. There is a simple or absolute necessity, when a thing cannot possibly be otherwise. Thus we may say there is a God, and He is righteous, etc. This necessity stands not with the will of the creature; yet does it stand with God's will, in whom an absolute necessity of holiness and goodness is joined with absolute freedom of will. Again, there is a necessity by violence or compulsion, and this abolishes freedom and consent of will. Thirdly, there is a necessity of infallibility or of consequence, when something follows necessarily upon a supposed antecedent—as namely upon the determination and decree of God. This necessity and freedom of will may both stand together, for in the doing of a voluntary action it is sufficient that it proceed of judgment and have his beginning from within the will, though otherwise in respect of God's will it be of unchangeable necessity. The certainty of God's decree does not abol-ish the consent of man's will, but rather order it and mildly incline or draw it forth. And the thing that is directly contrary to freedom of will is compulsion, because it abolishes consent.

The liberty of will stands in double power. The first is when it wills anything of its own self to be apt and able to nill the same, and so on the contrary, and it is called in schools "the liberty of contradiction." The second is when it wills anything to be able to will another thing or the contrary, as for example when God willed the creation of the world, He could have nilled the same; and when He willed the creation of one world, He could have willed the creation of more worlds. And this latter is called the liberty of contrariety.

Will by this liberty is distinguished from the inclinations of natural agents, which always show themselves in the same manner. Put matter to the fire, it burns always, and it cannot but burn. Cast up a stone into the air, it falls down always, and cannot but fall down. Secondly, will by this liberty is distinguished from the appetite of beasts, for it follows sense and in choosing or refusing keeps always one order. The sheep flees the wolf; and all sheep do so at all times and in all places. Bees gather honey. They do so always and in all places, and they can do no otherwise. When the beast in the field chooses one herb and refuses another, there is a show of liberty, yet no true liberty. For that which it chooses or refuses once, it chooses or refuses always in the same manner.

Thus much of the general nature of will. Now I come to the points in hand. The first is touching the will of Christ: "I would." According to the two natures of Christ, so be there two wills in Him: the will of His Godhead and the will of His manhood. Some think that these words are meant of the will of His manhood. For they suppose Him here to speak as the minister of circumcision and consequently as a man [Rom. 15:8]. This I think is a truth, but not all the truth, because the thing which He wills—namely, the gathering of Jews by the ministry of the prophets—was begun and practiced long before His incarnation. Wherefore (as I take it) here His divine will is meant, or the will of His Godhead, which is also the will of the Father and the Holy Ghost.

This will is one and the same, as God is one; yet may it be distinguished on this manner: it is either the will of His good pleasure or His signifying will. The truth of this distinction we may see in earthly princes, who bare the image of God. A king determines within himself according to his pleasure what shall be done in his kingdom and what not. This is his will. Again, he signifies some part of his secret pleasure to his subjects as occasion shall be offered, and this is also his will. Even so the pleasure of God within Himself and the significations thereof to His creature either in whole or in part are His will.

The first is mentioned (Eph. 1:5), where Paul says the Ephesians were predestinated according to the good pleasure of His will. That it may rightly be conceived of us, I will set down four things. The first is that this will is God's purpose or decree according to counsel and His decree. His counsel sees all things and all the causes of them. His decree determines what shall be done, and what undone; and He determines according to His own eternal counsel. Yet is not counsel a rule to His will. For there is nothing higher than His will, and His counsel also is according to His will, which is goodness itself. And therefore by Paul "counsel" is called "the counsel of his will" [Eph. 1:11].

Secondly, in God's will there is a sovereignty—that is, an absolute power— whereby He is Lord of all the actions that He wills, willing of Himself without dependence from any, without impediment or controlment what He will and when He will and how He will. Thus much is signified in the parable, "may I not do with mine own as I will?" [Matt. 20:15]. And by Paul, alleging Moses, "I will have mercy on whom I will have mercy" [Rom. 9:15], teaching also that we are at God's pleasure, as clay at the pleasure of the potter. This must teach us when we think or speak of God's works and judgments to think and speak with modesty and sobriety, with admiration and reverence, not daring to search into the reason of them or think hardly of them when they sound not with our reason, contenting ourselves with this, that we know God to have a sovereignty in His will to will at His pleasure, and His will to be good.

The third point is that the will of God is the beginning or first cause of all things without exception, and of all their motions and actions. And it is a beginning two ways: first, in regard of the existence or being of things; secondly, in regard of their goodness. That all things in particular have their being from the will of God as from the first efficient cause, I show it thus. God is of that power that nothing can come to pass which He nills or which is utterly against His will. Therefore, whatever comes to pass, comes to pass because He wills it either simply or in some part. A wise governor of a family or of an army, having all things in his own power, suffers nothing to be done without his will; and he desires in the very simplest matters to have a stroke. And nothing hinders his desire but his own weakness, which is not incident to the majesty of God. God by an unchangeable prescience foresees all things that shall come to pass, and therefore by an unchangeable will He wills the being of them. For God's foreknowledge depends on His will, not because God foresees things to come, therefore they come to pass, but because according to God's will they are to come to pass, therefore He foresees them. Indeed, there is in God a knowledge of things that possibly may be, though they never be; and this knowledge goes before God's decree. Yet the divine knowledge of things that certainly shall be follows the will and determination of God. To proceed further, in that God wills the being of all things, He makes them to be. For His will is operative, not severed from His power, but distinguished. And His willing of anything is His doing of it. And therefore it pleases the Holy Ghost to signify the will of God by an operative word or commandment: "In the beginning God said, let there be this and that, and it was so" [Genesis 1]. Now this commanding word was His will. Again, man lives by every word of God—that is, by anything that God in His pleasure wills to be our food. Things in respect of being must have dependence on the will of God or on themselves, or on some other thing. If they depend on themselves for their being, they are gods. If they depend on any other thing without and beside God, that thing is god also. It remains therefore that all things and acts in the world considered as acts have their being by a dependence on God as on the highest cause or the cause of causes. This doctrine must be remembered. For it is the foundation of true patience when we consider whatever comes to pass befalls us according to the will of God. Upon this ground Job arms himself to patience [Job 1:21], and David says, "I held my tongue and said nothing; because thou Lord didst it" [Ps. 39:9]. Secondly, this doctrine is the means of all true comfort when we consider that all our afflictions are from the good pleasure of God. Thus did the primitive church comfort itself, when it considered that the Jews, Herod, Pontius Pilate, and the rest did nothing against Christ but that which the counsel of God had determined before to be done [Acts 4:28]; and it must be our comfort that we are predestinate to be made conformable to the image of Christ in afflictions [Rom. 8:29; Phil. 3:10].

Furthermore, the will of God is the beginning of the goodness of things. For a thing is not first good and then willed by God; but it is first willed by God, and thus it becomes good. This is a manifest truth; I will not stand upon it. It may here be demanded whence the evil in the creature—namely, sin—has his beginning. I answer, it comes of the will of the declining creature and not from the will of God; yet is it not without the will of God. For though He will not sin properly because He hates it, yet does He will the being of it in the world. For in respect of the counsel of God, it is good that evil should be. And God wills the being of sin not because it is His will to effect, produce, or give a being to it, but because His will is to forsake His creature and not to hinder the being of evil when He may; and thus evil not hindered comes to pass. And whereas God foresaw it in His eternal counsel and yet willed not to hinder it when He might, in effect He willed the being of it in the world, though simply He wills it not.

The last point is that this will of God's good pleasure being hidden from us is not the rule of our actions and of our faith. Moses says, "Secret things belong to the Lord our God, and things revealed to us and to our children" [Deut. 29:29]. Hence it follows that we do and may (with a submission) in our wills dissent from this will of God before it is known to us without sin. Paul would by virtue of his apostolic commission have preached in Asia and Bythinia, and God would not because it is said the Spirit withstood him—yet did not Paul sin herein. One good thing may differ from another, and that which the creature sometime wills without offence God wills otherwise by His most righteous pleasure. Samuel prays for Saul [1 Sam. 16:1] otherwise than the secret pleasure of God was; but when the decree of God was revealed to him, he then stayed his praying. Here sundry men are to be reproved that reason thus: if it be the will of God that I shall be saved, it shall so be, however I live; therefore, I will live as I like. They make the secret will of God the rule of their lives, which should not be, because the revealed will of God is the law or the only rule of things to be done and believed.

Thus we see what the will of God's pleasure is. Now this will is not meant in this text, "how oft would I?" For the pleasure of God cannot be withstood or resisted. "My counsel shall stand, and I will do all my pleasure" [Isa. 46:10]. But the will here mentioned may be resisted and withstood: "I would, you would not."

The signifying will of God is when He reveals some part and portion of His pleasure so far forth as it serves for the good of His creature and the manifestation of His justice or mercy. This signifying will is not indeed the will of God properly, as the will of His good pleasure is; for it is the effect thereof. Yet may it truly be so termed. For as the effects of anger without the passion are called "anger" in God, so the sign and signification of His will may be termed "will."

This will is propounded sometimes more plainly, sometimes more darkly. It is propounded more plainly three ways: by His word, by His permission, by His operation.

His word is His will, for so Paul says, "Prove what is the good will of God" [Rom. 12:2]. And it is not His decree or pleasure, but His signifying will, because it serves to declare and manifest what is pleasing and acceptable to God, what is our duty, and what He requires of us, if we desire to come to life eternal. For this cause, both the law and the gospel and all the commandments, prohibitions, promises, and threatenings thereof are the signifying will of God. For commandments signify what we are to do; prohibitions, what we are to leave undone; promises, what good He will do to us; threatenings, what punishments are due to sin. Furthermore, by reason of the word, the ministry and dispensation thereof is the signifying will of God. For by it God signifies His pleasure touching the salvation of men. Divine permission is likewise the signifying will of God. For by it He signifies that He will not hinder the being of the thing permitted, and consequently that the thing permitted shall come to pass.

Thirdly, every operation or work of God signifies what God will have done, and what must come to pass. For when a thing is done, we know thereby what is and was the pleasure of God, considering nothing comes to pass without His will. When the signifying will is more darkly propounded, it is because some things appertaining to the said will are concealed. And by reason of this concealment, sometimes there seems to be a contrariety between the signifying will and the will of His good pleasure; but indeed there is none. And the end why God does so darkly signify and propound His pleasure is not to hurt or deceive but to procure the good of His creature. Examples of this kind there be in Scriptures three sorts. First of all, God sometimes propounds a commandment to men and conceals the end of the commandment. For the ends of divine precepts are three. One is obedience, when God will have the thing commanded to be done precisely as it is commanded; the other of trial, when He wills not the thing commanded to be done absolutely, but only wills to make trial of the loyalty of His creature. The third is conviction, when by commanding God intends to convince His creature of disobedience. Thus parents sometime give precepts to their children that must be done. Sometime again they give a commandment the doing whereof they intend not, but only intend thereby to make experience of the affection and duty of their children. And sometimes one man commands another only in way of conviction, as when the creditor says to the bankrupt, "Pay your debt," which he never looks for and which peradventure he minds to forgive. Divine precepts therefore be of three sorts: precepts of obedience, as the commandment of the moral law; precepts of trial; and precepts of conviction. Now when the signifying will of God is propounded in a precept, and the end of the precept is concealed, the pleasure of God is darkly signified. God gives a commandment to Abraham, "Offer thine only son Isaac" [Gen. 22:2]. The end was only to try Abraham, and this end was concealed until Abraham was in doing the fact; for then the Angel of the Lord stayed him and said, "Now I see Abraham fears God" [v. 12]. And the very commandment, "Offer Isaac," seems to be flat contrary to the will of God's pleasure or decree; for as it appears by the event Isaac was not to be slain. Therefore, the not slaying of Isaac was decreed by God. Now then it may be said, why should God command anything contrary to His decree? I answer, there is an apparent contrariety by reason the end of the commandment was concealed; but indeed there is none. For as it was the decree of God that Isaac should not be offered, so also was it His decree that Abraham should be tried in offering of Isaac. And with this decree does this commandment accord. For it is a commandment not so much of absolute obedience as of trial, and therefore it is a fit and convenient means to accomplish the decree of God. The Lord by the hand of Moses gave a commandment to Pharaoh, "Let the people go" [Ex. 8:1]; and yet the secret pleasure and purpose of God was that he should not let them go. Here is contrariety in show, but indeed none. For it was also the decree of God to convince Pharaoh of rebellion and hardness of heart; and to this end serves this commandment, because properly according to God's intention it was a commandment of conviction, though Pharaoh for his part was to accept of it as of a commandment to be obeyed and accomplished.

By this doctrine the public ministry of the word received a just defense. Some are of opinion it is a means to delude the world, because in it a commandment is given to all without exception to repent and believe, and yet grace to repent and believe is not. But they are deceived. For the command "repent and believe," though in the intent of the minister it has only one end—namely, the salvation of all—yet in the intention and counsel of God it has diverse ends. In them which be ordained to eternal life, it is a precept of obedience, because God will enable them to do that which He commands. In the rest, it is a commandment of trial or conviction, that to unbelievers their sin might be discovered, and all excuse cut off. Thus when the precept is given to believe and not the grace of faith, God does not delude but reprove and convince men of unbelief, and that in His justice.

The second example of the signifying will of God darkly propounded is when God propounds His promises, concealing the exception or condition thereof. "Ye shall rule over the fowls of the air, the fishes of the sea," etc. [Gen. 1:28]. And of Jerusalem the Lord says, "This is my rest for evermore" [Ps. 132:14]. The promises take no place now, and yet there is no contrariety in God's will, because the said promises must be understood with their exceptions: "Unless ye fall from me, and provoke mine anger by your sins."

The third example is when God propounds His threats, concealing the conditions and exceptions thereof. "I will," said the Lord, "deliver you no more" [Judg. 10:13]; and it was His pleasure afterward to deliver them again and again. "Let me alone, that my wrath may wax hot: for I will consume thee" [Ex. 32:10]; and He spared them at the prayer of Moses. "Yet forty days and Nineveh shall be destroyed"—for all this, Nineveh was spared and not destroyed [Jonah 3:4]. We may not here so much as dream of any change or untruth in God. For all threatenings denounced must be understood with this clause: "except ye repent and turn to me" [Ezekiel 18]. And this exception God conceals, that He may the better terrify the consciences of men and so prepare them to true repentance (Isaiah 38). First, the Lord says by the prophet to Hezekiah, "Set thine house in order, for thou shalt die and not live" [2 Kings 20:1; Isa. 38:1]; and yet he lived fifteen years after. Here God conceals His own pleasure in lengthening the days of Hezekiah and signifies what shall betide him in respect of nature and the helps thereof. In all these examples, we may not surmise any fraud or double dealing in God. For He does not speak one thing and mind another, after the fashion of hypocrites; but He conceals part of His will and reveals part. And this He does not for the hurt of any after the manner of the deceivers, but for the good of men.

Thus much for the signifying will of God. Now I come to the text in hand. The words, "I would have gathered you," are not to be understood of the decree of God, but of His signifying will, and namely of the ministry of the word. For when God sent His word to Jerusalem by His prophets, He thereby signified that it was His pleasure and will to gather and convert them. And He is said to will the conversion of the Jews in and by His word two ways. First, because He approved it as a good thing in itself, being agreeable to His goodness and mercy. Secondly, because He commanded and required it of them as a duty of theirs and as a thing necessary to salvation. Some may haply say it is a point of hard dealing for God to command the Jews to do that which they cannot do and to complain because they are not gathered, and that a master might as well command his servant to carry a mountain upon his back and complain because it is not done. I answer thus: if a master could give to his servant power and ability to carry a mountain, he might then command him to do it; and if he should by his own default lose this ability, the said master might still command him and complain if he did not the thing commanded. And this is the case with God. For He gave all men grace in our first parents to obey any of His commandments. This grace in them we have cast away and do not of ourselves so much as desire it of God, and God for His part is not bound to give us this grace again. He therefore may justly command us to turn to Him, though we now be unable to turn.

If we compare this text with Isaiah 6:10, they may seem to be contrary. For here Christ says, "I would have gathered you"; there, He says, "Harden them that they be not gathered and converted." God therefore seems to will and not to will one and the same thing. *Answer.* There is but one will in God; yet does it not equally will all things, but in divers respects it does will and nill the same thing. He wills the conversion of Jerusalem in that He approves a good thing in itself; in that He commands it and exhorts men to it; in that He gives them outward means of their conversion. He wills it not in that He did not decree effectually to work their conversion. For God does approve and He may require many things which nevertheless for just causes known to Himself He will not do. The confirmation of the angels that fell God approved as a thing good in itself, yet did He not will to confirm them. A judge in compassion approves and wills the life of a malefactor, and yet withal he wills the execution of justice in his death. Even so God sometimes wills that in His signifying will which He wills not in the will of His good pleasure.

By this which has been said, we learn that where God erects the ministry of His word, He signifies thereby that His pleasure is to gather men to salvation. In this regard, the prophet Isaiah says that the preaching of the gospel is "a banner displayed" [Isa. 49:22], that all nations may come to it. All this is verified in this our English nation. For more than forty years has God displayed this banner to us, and more than forty years has He signified in the ministry of His word that His will is to give mercy and salvation to us. First, therefore, we owe to God all thankfulness and praise for this endless mercy. Secondly, we are to reverence the ministry of the word inasmuch as God signifies His good will to us thereby, and we are in all obedience to subject ourselves to it. And for this cause we must suffer ourselves to be converted and gathered by it. Subjects used to reverence the letter of their prince; how much more then must we reverence the letter of the living God sent to us—that is, the ministry of the word—and conform ourselves to it? Thirdly, hence we may learn to foresee our miserable condition in this land. For though God for His part has long signified His will to us touching our everlasting good, yet there is nothing to be found in the most of us but a neglect or contempt of the gospel; and in most places men are weary of it, as the Israelites were of manna. What? Weary of the goodness of God, that offers and proclaims mercy to us? Yea, verily. And the more weary we are of this, the more weary we are of our own happiness and consequently hasten to our own perdition.

Secondly, it is to be observed that the rebellion of Jerusalem is against the signifying will of Christ, when He says, "I would, ye would not." And hence it follows that the signifying will of God is the rule of our obedience, and not the unrevealed will. And therefore, so often as God signifies to us His will and pleasure, we must yield ourselves in obedience to it. Now God signifies His will three ways (as I have said): by His commandments and prohibitions, by His permission, and by His operation. Therefore, when He commands, we must obey. When He forbids we must also obey. When He permits any evil, we must be content. Lastly, when God does anything and brings it to pass, He signifies His pleasure, and we must obey. We are bidden to say, "Thy will be done"; and this is not only the will revealed in His Word, but also His will revealed by any event. For when anything comes to pass, it comes to pass because it was the will of God. Furthermore, this signifying will must be the stay and ground of our patience and comfort. For when a thing is come to pass, the will of God is passed upon it, and He has signified His pleasure—as for example, when a man is slain, the will of God is passed upon his life, and He has revealed His pleasure touching his death. Upon this consideration and in all events, are we to stay our minds.

Thirdly, it appears hence what mind must be in the ministers and teachers of the word. They must put away all blind respects of profit and praise and simply with honest hearts apply themselves and their ministry to this end, that they may gather a people to God; for that which is the mind of the master in any business, the same must also be the mind of the servant. The mind of the master is here set down: "How oft would I have gathered you?"

Thus much of the will of God. Now let us come to the second point, to consider what is the will of man. That this may appear, two things must be handled: the nature of man's will and the strength thereof. Of the nature of will, I spoke something before generally; there is yet somewhat more to be added. The nature of man's will may be gathered by the practice thereof. The practice of will stands in five things. The first is the action of the mind—namely, a consideration of the thing to be done and the end thereof. The second is deliberation of the divers means whereby the aforesaid thing may be done. The third is after deliberation a determination what shall be done. The fourth action is proper to the will, and that is election, whereby the will upon determination of the mind chooses or refuses—that is, wills what shall be done, what not. The fifth is that the will in all her elections keeps and maintains her liberty. Because when it wills or nills anything, it moves itself freely of itself to will or to nill without any external compulsion; and when it wills anything, it so wills as still retaining a natural aptness to nill the same. And when it wills any one particular thing, it remains still apt not to will it, but to will another thing on the contrary.

Again, the will of man must be distinguished from the power of man whereby he does anything. Will and power in God are only distinguished in our conceiving, being indeed one and the same thing—namely, the essence of God. And therefore, what God can will, He can do; what He wills, He does. And His willing of anything is His doing of it. It is not so in man, who can will that which he cannot do—as Paul says, "To will is present with me, but I cannot do that which I would" [Rom. 7:18]. Will therefore is one thing, and power to do the thing willed another.

The second thing to be handled is the strength of will—that is, what will can do, what not; and how far it extends itself. That this may appear, will must be considered according to the four estates of man: the state of innocence before the fall, the state of corruption after the fall, the state of regeneration after conversion, and the state of glory after this life.

In the state of innocence, the will of man is a power of willing either good or evil. For God gave Adam a commandment, in which He forbade him to eat of the tree of knowledge of good and evil. Adam therefore could either keep or break this commandment. This reason holds not in us since the fall, yet does it hold in Adam, because with the commandment he received the power to obey. And that he could not obey, it appeared by the event, because he did not obey. Ecclesiastes says, "God made man righteous" [Eccl. 7:29]. There is the power to will that which is good: "And they found many inventions" [v. 29]. There is also a power to will that which is evil. Moses says to the Israelites, "I set before you this day life or death, blessing and cursing: therefore choose life, that thou and thy seed may live." These words are a sentence of the law telling what we ought to do and not what we can now do, but what we could do by the gift of creation before the fall. Here a difference of powers must be made: the power to will that which is good was a gift put into Adams heart by God; and the power to will that which is evil was in him before his fall, not a gift, but only a possibility to will evil if he should cease to do this duty. And thus had he power to will both good and evil.

In Adam's will, there were two things: liberty and mutability. Liberty was twofold. The first is a liberty simply to will or to nill or to suspend. And this is liberty of nature, because it is founded in the nature of will, from which it cannot possibly be severed. And therefore it still remains in the damned spirits, because, where this liberty is wanting, there is no will.

The second liberty is a liberty of grace, which is a power to will or nill well, or to will that which is good and to nill that which is evil. This liberty is founded not in the nature but in the goodness of the will. By "goodness," I mean the holiness of the will, which is the image of God. And here we must take heed of the opinion of some who think that Adam was created and placed in such a condition in which he was neither righteous nor unrighteous, but in a mean between both. But this is directly contrary to the apostle, who says that man was created in righteousness and holiness [Eph. 4:24; Col. 3:10]. And by this means in the first instance of Adam's creation he wanted liberty of grace. Again, by reason of this second liberty, Adam had a further liberty from sin and a liberty from misery.

The changeableness of Adam's will appears in this, that though it was created in goodness, yet was it made changeably good. For such was the goodness and inclination of his will to obey God as might be altered and changed by force of temptation. The cause of this mutability must be considered, and it is this: that a creature righteous by creation may remain eternal and constantly righteous, two favors or helps of God are required. The first is a power to persevere in goodness. Without this power the creature of itself ceases to be good. The second is an act or deed, and that is the will to persevere or perseverance itself. This also is required with the former, for God gives not only the power but also the will and the deed; and the creature does not the good which it can do unless God cause it to do the said good as He causes it to be able to do good. Both these helps the good angels have, and therefore they stand. And as for Adam, he received of God the first help and not the second. For beside the goodness of his will he received of God a power constantly to persevere in goodness, if he would. Yet the act of perseverance was left to the choice and liberty of his own will. We may behold the like in nature. God creates the eye and puts into it the faculty of seeing, and withal He adds to the eye necessary help by the light of the sun. As for the act of seeing, it is left to man's liberty; for he may see if he will, and again if he will he may shut his eyes. The physician by art procures an appetite. This done, in the next place he provides convenient food. Yet the act of eating is in the pleasure of the patient; for he may eat if he will, and if he will he may abstain. And thus God gave Adam the power to persevere in righteousness, but the will He left to himself.

It may be said, if Adam received power to do good if he would and not the will to will that he could, he then received not sufficient grace. I answer, he received sufficient for the perfection of his nature for the full obedience of the will of God and for the attainment of everlasting happiness, if he would not be wanting to himself. But he received not sufficient grace for the causing of the immutability of his nature, neither was it of necessity to be given to a creature. A goldsmith intends to make a jewel of greatest value and price. He compounds it of gold, pearl, and precious stones. When he has brought it to perfection, he does not put this condition to it, that if it fall, it shall not be bruised or broken. And God created Adam in all perfection and gave him a power and ability to continue in the said perfection, if he would. Yet did not He put to his nature this condition, that he should be unchangeable and unalterable, when it should be assailed by the force of outward temptation.

The use of the former doctrine. In Adam's example, we see the weakness of the most excellent creature in itself without the grace of God. For Adam, having power to persevere, could not for all this act or put in execution the said power without the further help of God. He could fall himself; he could not stand or rise again. He could not avoid the least evil, but as he was helped of God. We therefore being sinful wretches much more are to acknowledge our infirmity and to ascribe all we do or can do that is good to the grace of God. Thus have the godly always done. The Jews in their repentance say, "Convert thou me, and I will convert" [Jer. 31:18]. The spouse of Christ says, "Draw us and we will run after thee" [Song 1:4]. David says, "Incline my heart to thy commandments; turn mine eyes from the beholding of vanity, and quicken me in thy precepts" [Ps. 119:36–37]. Augustine says, "Give that which Thou commandest, and command what Thou wilt." We are to God as the sick man to his keeper, who says, "Take me up, and I will rise; hold me, and I will stand." In regard of this our frailty, it is the best for us to deny ourselves and by faith to depend on the providence and mercy of God.

Again, such as believe in Christ have great cause to be thankful to God. For they have the beginnings of further grace than ever Adam received. He received only the power to persevere in his happy estate, if he himself would. But they that believe beside the power of perseverance receive the will and the deed. Paul says, "Work your salvation with fear and trembling": and then he adds, "It is God that works in us the will and the deed" [Phil 2:13], whereby we run the race to eternal life.

In the estate of corruption, two things are to be considered of man's will: the first, what it can do, and how near it comes to the doing of a good work; the second, what it cannot do. For the declaration of the first, two things must be considered in corrupt will: a liberty and a possibility. The liberty is a certain freedom to will or nill or to suspend. For this liberty is remaining since the fall of Adam and is natural to the will, from which it cannot possibly be severed. This liberty is large and shows itself in three kinds of actions: natural, human, ecclesiastical. Natural actions are such as are common to men and beasts, as to eat, drink, sleep, smell, hear, taste, move. Common experience declares a freedom to will in all these actions. Human actions are such as are common to all men, and I may fitly reduce them to three heads. The first is the study and practice of arts, trades, or occupation, and professions of all kinds. And that man has freedom to will in all these, experience testifies. The second is the government of societies—namely, of families and commonwealths. The Lord said to Cain of Abel, "His appetite shall be subject to thee" [Gen. 4:7]—that is, "In freedom of your will you shall rule over him, and his will shall be subject to yours." Peter said to Ananias that the giving or the not giving of his lands was before he gave them in his own liberty [Acts 5:4]. And Paul says that the father has "power of his own will" [1 Cor. 7:37] to give or not to give his child in marriage, as he shall see occasion. The third is the practice of civil virtue, justice, temperance, liberality, chastity. To this purpose Paul says that the Gentiles "do the things contained in the law" [Rom. 2:14], and that "by nature." For outwardly to be chaste, just, bountiful, and so forth is in the power of natural and corrupt will. It may be said that these things are the gifts of the Holy Ghost. I answer thus: the gifts of the Holy Ghost are twofold—gifts of restraint and gifts of renovation. Gifts of restraint are such as serve only to keep in the corruption of nature and not to mortify or abolish it. And they are common to all men both good and bad and serve only to maintain outward peace and comely order in the societies of men. Of this kind are civil virtues. Gifts of renovation are such graces of the Holy Ghost as serve not only to restrain the corruption of the inward man, but also to mortify it in the root and to make a change of our sinful nature. Now virtues of this kind are only incident to such as are in Christ.

The third kind of actions are ecclesiastical—namely, such as pertain to the outward duties of the worship of God. And there is also a liberty of will in them. For corrupt and sinful man has power and liberty to think of God and to think many things of Him good in themselves [Rom 1:21]; power to read and search the Scriptures [2 Cor. 3:14]; power to speak and talk of the word of God

[Ps. 50:16]; power to come to the congregation and hear a sermon, as the Athenians did [Rom. 9:31]; power to conceive a zeal (I say not a good zeal, but only a zeal I say) for the maintenance of outward duties of religion. Paul says that the obstinate Jews had "a zeal of God, and were followers of the justice of the law," and that himself being a Pharisee unconverted was "unreproveable in respect of the law of God" [James 2:19]. Thus far can man proceed by the freedom of corrupt will. And the devil by natural strength goes somewhat further. For he is said to believe; and he conceives his faith not by illumination of the Spirit of God, as man does, but by the remainders of the light of nature and by the power which yet remains in his corrupted will. For we may not suppose that since his fall he is enlightened by the Spirit of God in anything.

Thus we see what is the liberty of corrupt will. We must yet further conceive it to be full of weakness and imbecilities, which I will express in three rules.

The first, that which the will can will it cannot do, unless God will. Hereupon St. James bids us say, "We will do this or that, if God will." And Paul, wishing that he might have a prosperous journey to Rome, adds this clause, "By the will of God" [Rom. 15:32]. Herod, Pontius Pilate, and the Jews did nothing against Christ but that which the council of God had determined before to be done [Acts 4:28].

The second, that which the will can will, it cannot do without the help of God; for "in him we live, move, and have our being" [Acts 17:28]. This help is twofold: preservation of the will both for power, and act and the direction thereof, whereby it is ordered and applied to the things it wills.

The third, often the will neither wills nor does the things it can will and do, because it is hindered. It is hindered sometimes by the mind, that misleads the will; sometimes again by the work of Satan. Thus Paul says that Satan hindered him from coming [1 Thess. 2:18] to Thessalonica.

The use of this doctrine is twofold. First, the liberty of the will is the condemnation of the world. For in civil and ecclesiastical actions men do not that which they can do—so far be the most from doing that which the gospel requires, that they do not that which nature can do. Some plead that if they be ordained to salvation, they shall certainly be saved, otherwise not. And therefore they say they will leave all to God and live as they like; but this shall be their condemnation, that they have not lived according to civil virtue as they might. They come not to the church; they search not the Scriptures; they hear not sermons. In a word, they use not the good means of salvation so far as they are able to use them by the strength of nature.

Secondly, the weakness of will in his liberty must teach us to abate our pride and to humble ourselves, because we cannot do anything, no not so much as move hand, foot, or finger without the help of God. Jeroboam, when he had stretched out his hand to lay hold on the prophet, could not so much as pull it in again [1 Kings 13:4]. And this consideration must likewise move us to be thankful to God, because the actions we do, we do by Him.

The second thing to be considered in the corrupt will is a possibility of willing that which is good. This possibility is a certain condition of the will whereby it can will that which is good, after that God has prevented us with His grace. A stone is not of this nature, neither is the beast, because they are creatures unreasonable, wanting both will and understanding and therefore no way capable of grace. Whereas man, in that he has will and understanding, has a possibility of doing that which he cannot do. The fathers in this sense say, "To be able to have faith is nature; to have faith indeed is grace."

Hitherto I have showed what will can do in the corrupt estate of man. Now let us see what it cannot do. And because here the main differences come to be considered between us and the Church of Rome, I will first lay down a sure ground and then build upon it. The ground is this: though liberty of nature remain, yet liberty of grace—that is, to will well—is lost, extinguished, abolished by the fall of Adam. I prove it thus. Liberty of grace is founded in the goodness of integrity of the will. Now this goodness of the will is abolished by the fall of Adam, and therefore the liberty itself that founded thereon. That the goodness or integrity of the will is lost, I confirm it thus: that which we put on in our conversion, we want by nature. We put on this goodness in our conversion. For in it we put on the new man created according to the image of God in justice and holiness [Eph. 4:2], as Paul says. Again, if all the motions and inclinations of the heart be evil and only evil and continually evil, there is no goodness in the heart; but the first is true. For the Lord says that He "saw the frame of the thoughts of the heart to be only evil continually" [Gen. 6:5]. Paul makes three parts of man in the estate of innocency: the body, the soul, and the spirit—that is, the image of God wrought by the Spirit, being the ornament and glory of both the former. Now since the fall, the spirit is turned to flesh; for "whatsoever is born of flesh is flesh" [John 3:6], says Christ—that is, wholly flesh, and only flesh. And the natural disposition of the flesh is to lust against the spirit. What goodness then can be in the will? He that must enter into the kingdom of heaven must first be born again. Now look as it is in the first birth, so is it in the second. In the first and imperfect man is not made a perfect man, but that which is no man is made a man; even so in the second birth, he that is a sinner and has nothing in him to please God is made just and righteous. For regeneration is not in respect of substance of body or soul or in respect of the faculties of the soul, but only in respect of the goodness thereof, which is a conformity to the will of God. And if there be any part or portion thereof yet remaining, there cannot be a new birth, but only a repairing of that which decayed with a confirmation and increase of it.

The second reason. There is no power of aptness in the will corrupted to will that which is truly good. Therefore, liberty of grace to will well is lost. The minor I prove thus: "A new heart also will I give you, and a new spirit will I put within you and I will take away the stony heart of your body, and I will give you an heart of flesh" [Ezek. 36:26]. Here two things are set down distinctly. The first, that the new and fleshy heart is the gift of God—that is, a heart ready and apt to give obedience. The second, that there is in us no aptness or ability to receive this gift of God, because our hearts are stony. God therefore gives the fleshy heart and the aptness to receive this gift by taking away the stony heart. Christ says that none can come to Him, unless the Father "draw him." Now if there were in us by nature the least power or aptness to come to Christ, then drawing were needless (for that argues obstinate rebellion); and it were sufficient to succor, help, and confirm the aforesaid power, without any more ado. Saint Paul says that the "wisdom of the flesh"—that is, the best inclinations and motions of the mind of a natural man—are not only enemies, but even "enmity to God" [Rom. 8:7]. Now in enmity, there is nothing but hatred and contempt of God. And in the hatred of God, what inclination or aptness can there be to love and obey Him? Again Paul says the natural man "is not capable of the things of God: for they are foolishness to him: neither can he know them, for they are spiritually discerned" [1 Cor. 2:14]. In the mind of a natural man, there be two things to be considered: the act and the power of knowing and approving that which is truly good. And here Paul gives his sentence of both: of the act, that the mind cannot know the things of God; of the power, that the mind has no capableness or aptness to acknowledge or approve them—as a little vessel has no aptness to receive a great quantity of liquor. Again, we are not "apt or sufficient of ourselves" [2 Cor. 3:5] to think a good thought as of ourselves, but our sufficiency is of God. Therefore, nature corrupted wants ability so much as to think a good thought, much less to will that which is good. Again, Paul tells the Ephesians that they were "dead in sins and trespasses" [Eph. 2:1]. And this deadness is not only in respect of the performance of that which is good, but also in regard of power to perform it. For if the least power to do good remain since the fall, man is not dead as yet, but dying or drawing on, because as yet some portion of spiritual life remains. And if this be so, how are we quickened together with Christ [v. 5]? And how is it a wonder that the "dead hear the voice of Christ" [John 5:25]? Again, Paul says to the Ephesians that they were "once darkness" [Eph. 5:8], but now are light in the Lord. Now in darkness there is no aptness at all either to give or to receive light. But how were they made light? Without any work or cooperation of theirs—even as in the creation light was taken not from some other precedent beginnings of light, but out of darkness [2 Cor. 4:6], which conferred nothing at all to the being of light.

The third reason. There is not only an impotency to good, but such a forcible proneness and disposition to evil as that we can do nothing but sin. Jeremiah says that "the heart of man is wicked above all things" [Jer. 17:9], "who can know it." Paul says that the Romans were once "servants of sin, and free in respect of righteousness" [Rom. 6:20]; and of himself, that the law was spiritual, "he carnal and sold under sin" [7:14]. And of unrepentant sinners, he says that they are in the "snare of the devil, according to his will" [2 Tim. 2:26]. And this disposition of which I speak is not some few sins, but to all sins without exception, because as every man takes of Adam the whole nature of man, even so he takes the whole corruption of man's nature. And where this huge and horrible mass of corruption takes place, there all inclination and power to goodness must needs give place. It may be objected that if the will be in bondage under sin, it has lost his liberty quite. I answer, not so, for both may stand together. The prisoner, though he have lost a great part of his liberty, yet has he not lost all; for within the prison he may (as he will) either sit, stand, lie, or walk. And though he which is captive to sin can do nothing but sin, yet may he in sinning use his liberty and in the divers kinds of evils intended show the freedom of his will.

The fourth reason. All the goodness we have and all we can do that is pleasing to God is wholly in Scripture ascribed to God. He that is the child of God is born of God: "not of blood," that is, not of natural generation; "not of the will of the flesh," that is, not of the power and inclination of natural will; "not of the will of man," that is, the heroic inclination of excellent men [John 1:13]. We are the workmanship of God created in Christ to good works [Eph. 2:10]. Now the creature confers nothing to his creation, which is wholly from the Creator, because to create is not to make something of something, but something of nothing. Christ says, "Without me ye can do nothing." And the reason is there rendered, because Christ is the vine, and they which believe are vine-branches—which branches, that they may bring forth good fruit, must first be set into Christ and then draw their sap, that is, power to do good from Him.

Patrons of nature against the grace of God allege four special reasons for liberty of will in moral acts—that is, in things and actions good according to the moral law. The first is this: God has given sundry commandments to man since his fall, some pertaining to the law, some to the gospel, as commandments to turn to God, to believe, to repent. And all commandments are given in vain unless there be freedom of will to do them or not to do them. I answer first, these commandment set not down what we can do, but what we should do. They signify not our ability but our office and duty whereby we should please God and come to salvation. And if the commandments be impossible, it is not God's fault, but ours; for they are not impossible to created but to corrupt nature. Secondly, though we cannot will to do that which God commands, yet are not His commandments idle. For they are the instruments and means of the Spirit of God whereby He effects in us the good He commands.

The second objection. We are bound to give to God an account of all our doings in the day of judgment, and this were not equal unless we had power to will both good and evil. I answer, it suffices to bind us to a reckoning, that once we had liberty in Adam to will either good or evil. And all men since the fall have some measure of liberty of will: the wicked liberty in sin; the righteous liberty in duties of righteousness.

The third objection from testimonies of Scripture. It is alleged that the Samaritan which lay wounded between Jericho and Jerusalem [Luke 10:30] is a figure of mankind half dead in sin. I answer that in parables nothing may be gathered that is beside the scope thereof; and the scope of this parable is nothing else but to show who is our neighbor. Again, we grant that liberty of will is not abolished, but wounded. Because though liberty of grace to will well be lost, yet liberty of nature to will still remains. Again, the words of Christ to the angel of Laodicea are objected: "Behold I stand at the door and knock: if any man open, I will come in" [Rev. 3:20]. Here, say some, to "knock" is the work of grace, and to "open" the work of free will. I answer that the words "if any man open" are conditional and therefore determine nothing of power of will to or fro. Again, the words set not down what the angel is able to do, but what his office is and what he can do by grace. Furthermore, the place of Deuteronomy is objected, "The word which I command thee, is near thee, that thou mayst do it" [Deut. 30:14]. But in these words Moses set down what the Israelites can do by the grace of a mediator, who fulfilling the law for us and giving grace to obey the same makes the commandments of the law (which otherwise are impossible) to be easy. Thus Paul has expounded this text (Rom. 10:8) where he signifies that sentences of the law must not legally but evangelically be understood of them that are in Christ and fulfill the law by Him.

The fourth objection. When man is converted, he is not converted against his will; for then God should deal with a man after the manner of a stone or a beast. Therefore, he which is converted is converted with the consent of his own will. *Answer*. This consent is not of ourselves, but of God. For as the conversion is of God, so is the will to be converted. Of this point, more afterward.

Upon the ground formerly delivered, sundry questions of great moment are resolved. The first is whether a natural man or an infidel can by the freedom of his will without faith and without the help of God do any work morally good—that is, a work in which there is no sin. They of the Church of Rome for many hundred years have answered, yea; for they confidently teach that a man pressed with no temptation may without faith by the special help of God and without it by his own strength so do that which is morally good that no sin at all be committed therein. We answer, no—and that upon sufficient warrant. For such as the beginning of an action is, such is the action itself. Now the mind and will of man are the beginnings of all their actions; and in them there is no ability to think or to will that which is truly good, but a continual disposition to the contrary. All actions therefore proceeding thence are only and continually evil. Upon this ground Paul says that all is unclean, the use of all things is unclean [Titus 1:15]. And Christ says that an "evil tree cannot bring forth good fruit" [Matt. 7:18]. And, "Whatsoever is not of faith"—without exception—"is sin" [Rom 14:23]. To this doctrine always subscribed the orthodox and ancient church. The Ararsican Council[2] says it is from the gift of God, "that we keep our feet from injustice"; and "that a man does no good things, which God enables him not to do." Cyprian says, "All we can do is God's." Jerome said: "Without Christ every virtue is but a vice." Gregorie: "If faith be not first wrought in our heart, other things cannot be good, though they seem to be so." Augustine says expressly that "all the works of unbelievers are sins, because whatever is not of faith is sin." And he says thus of Pelagius, the heretic: "Sometimes he poised the power of the will with such equal weights in even balance that he might determine how it availed somewhat to cause us not to sin, which if it be so, there is no place reserved for the help of grace, without which we say free will has no force at all in causing us not to sin." In this speech, there are two things worthy of observation. One, that (in Augustine's judgment) free will of itself has no force at all to cause man not to sin. Of the same mind is the master of the Sentences who says that man before he be repaired by grace cannot but sin, though the schools afterward for the most part dissent from him. The second, that it was the heresy of Pelagius to teach that free will *somewhat* avails to cause us not to sin. With this jumps the determination of the Council of Trent, when it says, "Let him be accursed that says all works done anyway before justification are sins indeed." For thus it insinuates closely that will, before the grace of justification, partly helped and partly of itself can do that which is good, at the least morally, as they speak. And this is the resolute sentence almost of all papists. I doubt not therefore to avouch that the present religion of the Church of Rome revives in part the heresy of Pelagius, and in these last days propounds it again to the world with new varnish and fresh colors. To avoid this charge, they answer the place of Augustine before alleged thus: when Pelagius says the will is of force not to sin, his meaning (say they) was that will was of force to

---

2. The precise details of this council are not known.

cause us never to sin throughout the course of our lives. I answer again: Augustine, who knew the meaning of Pelagius, speaks not only of the life of man, but even of particular actions, as appears by these words: "He that prays, 'Lead us not into temptation,' prays that he may not do any evil." Vincentius Lyrinensis took this to be the heresy of Pelagius, that man by his own free will might do some good things. For these are his words: "Who before that profane Pelagius did ever presume that the virtue of free will was so great that he did not think the grace of God was necessary for the helping of it in the doing of good things according to every act?"

It is objected to the contrary that infidels can do things of the law which are good, and that they have been and are indued with many virtues which are the gifts of God. *Answer.* Infidels may do things good in their kind, but they cannot do them well, because they apply them to wrong ends, as honor, profit, pleasure. And a good thing done to a wrong end ceases to be good and is evil in the doer. Again, the virtues of the heathen, as they are of God, are good; yet as they are used or rather abused of men, they are turned to sins.

It is alleged that wicked Pharaoh did a good work, when he said, "I have sinned, the Lord is righteous, I and my people are sinners: pray for me," etc. [Ex. 9:27]. *Answer.* This confession is good in his kind, but not good in Pharaoh, because it proceeded not of love to God but of fear of punishment, and it was made in hypocrisy, because afterward he hardened his heart.

Further, it is alleged that Nebuchadnezzar, a heathen man, was rewarded of God for sacking of Tyrus [Ezek. 29:20], and that God would not have rewarded him if his work had been a sin. *Answer.* The reward was temporal; and he was rewarded for his labor only, and not for the goodness thereof.

Lastly, it may be objected that if we cannot do good works by freedom of corrupt will, then all our actions, our eating, drinking, sleeping, buying, selling, and whatever we can do is sin; and no sin may be done, and therefore nothing must be done. *Answer.* Actions before named incident to the life of man are not sins of themselves, for then they might not be done at all; but they are sins only in respect of the manner of doing, because they are not done in obedience to God and referred to Him as to their right end, but by-ends[3] are propounded. And this is the condition of every man until he be converted, that he can do nothing but sin and displease God, even then when the action is praiseworthy before men.

---

3. *By-end*: An object lying aside from the main one; a subordinate end or aim, especially a secret selfish purpose; a covert purpose of private advantage.

The consideration of this doctrine serves to correct the erroneous opinion of many who think themselves in good case and highly in the favor of God because they are no thieves, murderers, blasphemers, adulterers, etc. But alas, they are deceived. There is matter enough of condemnation within them, though they be no outrageous malefactors. For all they do is sin before God, till they be renewed by grace. In eating, drinking, sleeping, buying, selling, in all they do, they sin. Not that eating, drinking, sleeping, buying, selling are sins in themselves, but because they fail in the right manner of doing these actions.

Secondly, in that we can do nothing but sin till we be regenerate, we are taught to acknowledge our bondage under sin and Satan. Yea, we must labor to feel this bondage and to groan under the burden of it. This being done, we must go further yet and with hungering and thirsting hearts seek to the Mediator Christ, who preaches deliverance to captives and withal gives deliverance from sin, Satan, hell, death, condemnation, to all such as with touched and bruised hearts fly to Him.

The second question is whether a natural man by the power of his will may be able to resist and overcome a temptation. The papist answers that he is able to overcome lesser and easier temptations of himself, yea, and greater too, if he be helped by God; and that sundry temptations do not exceed the strength of man's nature. But we are to hold and we teach the contrary, that the will of man since the fall of Adam cannot overcome so much as the least temptation. Because the power whereby a temptation should be overcome is lost and abolished—that is, the power to nill that that is evil, and to will that that is good. And where is no power to resist, there can be no resistance. When we pray to God and say, "Lead us not into temptation," we acknowledge that there is no temptation at all that we can of ourselves withstand without the help of God. Peter bids us "resist Satan our adversary" [1 Peter 5:9], and he shows the right means when he adds these words: "steadfast in faith."

It is objected that a natural man can either sin or not sin. I answer, 'tis true in regard of actions pertaining to outward government, and in regard of open sins, murder, theft, adultery, etc.; yet not always true, but only at some times. For even the righteous sometime fall into open offences. And though the natural man occasioned to sin, abstain from open offence, yet gets he no victory. For though he avoid the outward act, yet can he not avoid the wicked inclination of his heart. And the abstinence from outward sin is not without sin, because it proceeds from a person unreconciled to God. It has not his beginning from faith. Again, it is for by-respects,[4] for the getting of praise, the avoiding of open shame, and not for the honor of God.

---

4. *By-respect*: regard to something other than the ostensible main object; a side aim or motive.

The third question is whether an unregenerate man by the power of his will can observe the law, though not fully, yet in respect of the substance of the act. The doctrine of long time has been in schools and church, that he can, and that by his own strength he may keep all the moral precepts so as no sin can be committed for some short space of time. But the truth is, he cannot. For if we grant and suppose an action, we must presuppose the ground and beginning thereof. Now the integrity or vanity of will whereby it was able to will that which is good is the ground of a good act and is lost, and therefore there can be no keeping of the law in respect of substance. The substance of the first table is to love God with all the heart, soul, strength; the substance of all negative commandments is, "Thou shalt not lust." And the natural will cannot possibly reach to the doing of these. It is alleged that a natural man may give alms and do justice to others, and such like. I answer, in the substance of any duty commanded there be two things: the act to be done and the manner of doing it. And that is to do it in faith with a mind to obey God, and to intend His honor thereby. And this manner of doing a work is the form of every work that makes it to be good indeed; and without it works commanded in the law are but as a body without life or soul, or as matter without form. Will therefore is unable to observe any one commandment in his own entire substance.

And it must be remembered as a main ground that the law beside external duties requires inward obedience in knowledge of God and His will, in faith, hope, love, patience, and the subjection of our thoughts, wills, and affections to the will of God. In respect of this inward and spiritual obedience, the Holy Ghost says the law is impossible (Rom 8:3), and that the wisdom of the flesh cannot be subject to the law of God (v. 7), that this is the yoke which neither we nor our fathers could bear (Acts 15:10).

Again, it was the heresy of Pelagius that a man by the strength of his own free will may keep all the commandments of God, though (as they say) he does it somewhat hardly. And the papists are not far from this when they say that man by natural strength may keep the whole law for some little time.

The fourth question is whether natural corrupted will can any way prepare and dispose itself to his own conversion and justification—that is, take away the impediments and make himself apt and capable of his justification. The doctrine has been for divers hundreds of years that will can do it; and the doctrine of papists now is that the will, so it be stirred up by God, can do it. But the certain truth is that will cannot. The conversion of a sinner is a creation, and no creature can prepare itself to his own creation. That very thing whereby a man should prepare himself to any good duty is lost by Adam's fall, and therefore the work of preparation is God's and not ours, unless it be possible for a man dead in his sins to prepare himself to his own spiritual justification. By nature we are servants of sin, and our liberty begins in our justification. Therefore, before we are justified, we cannot so much as will that which is good. Indeed, the Israelites "prepared their hearts to seek the Lord" [1 Sam. 7:2], and Ezra "prepared his heart to seek the law of the Lord" [Ezra 7:10]. But this was the work of men regenerate, whereby they renewed in themselves the purpose of obeying God and of persevering in duties of godliness.

The fifth and principal question of all is whether a natural man can will his own conversion or regeneration. The learned among the papists teach on this manner: that will alone by itself cannot; yet that will can, if it be prevented and stirred up by some good cogitation cast into the mind and some good desire stirred up in the heart, and be withal helped and directed by God. They use to open their minds by these comparisons. The eye in darkness sees nothing and is as it were without the faculty of seeing; yet if an object be set before the eye, and light be brought in, then can it see. Again, a man lies asleep in a dungeon, and he does not so much as think of coming forth; yet let a man come and call him and reach down a cord to him, he will then awake, take hold of the cord, and put it under his arm holes, as Jeremiah did, and hang thereupon. And being thus helped he both can and does come forth of the dungeon. The doctrine we teach is the plain contrary, that will before it be turned and converted cannot so much as will his own conversion. This follows upon the former ground, for the power to will that that is truly good is lost. A power to will our conversion is a power to will that which is good. Therefore, the power to will our own conversion is lost. Beside preventing and exciting motions that serve to stir up and help the will, there is further required that the will be regenerate before it can will that which is good; and without this gift of regeneration (which is the true preventing grace), all external motions and excitations to that which is good are of no effect. For the cause must go before the effect. Now that the will may affect and do that which is good, the cause is the regeneration thereof in which is given to the will not only a new action whereby it wills well, but also a new quality whereby it is able and can will well. And this ability of willing well goes before the act of good will, as the cause before the effect. When a man is dead, chafe him and rub him; put *aqua vita*[5] into him to warm him at the heart. When this is done, take him by the hand, pluck him up, and bid him walk. For all this, he will not stir the least joint, neither can he. All chafing and rubbing, all speech and persuasion, and all helps in the world be in vain, unless the soul be restored to the body. Even so, no persuasion offered to the mind nor good desires to the will are of any moment until the image of God standing in holiness, which is a conformity with the will of God, and the very

_____

5. *Aqua vita*: living water.

soul of our souls begin to be restored. Nay, the mind is incapable of any good thought, and the will of a good desire, until God once again create[s] in them a new quality or property of holiness, that the mind in thinking may think well, and the will in willing may will well, or, will that which is good. For though it be the nature of the will to will or nill, yet the power and formal beginning of well-willing is the integrity or goodness of the will. It is objected that the will to accept and receive grace is in us before grace be received. I answer thus: the first act of will whereby the will in his regeneration begins to assent to God and begins to will to be converted is indeed the work of the will (because it is the will that wills), yet does it not arise of the natural strength of the will, but from the grace of God that renews it. For to will to be regenerate is the effect and testimony of regeneration begun. Paul, handling the point of the predestination and justification of a sinner, compares God to a potter and us to clay. Now the clay before it is framed to a vessel of honor and while it is in framing is merely passive and does nothing at all for the framing of itself. When a man is to be regenerate, God takes away the stony heart [Ezek. 36:26] that is by nature disobedient and altogether unapt to obey, and He gives a fleshy heart that is pliable and flexible to obedience. Now to will to be converted is a good thing and one point of true obedience; and therefore it proceeds not from the heart of man until it be mollified and framed by God to that which is good. "What hast thou," says Paul, "that thou hast not received? And if thou hast received it, why dost thou boast?" [1 Cor. 4:7]. Now if to will to be healed were of us, we have matter of boasting in ourselves. Again, he says we are not sufficient or able to think a good thought as of ourselves, but our sufficiency is of God. Much less then can we of ourselves will or desire to be regenerate. The health and life of the soul is of God, who raises us from death to life. Now to will to be healed and to will to live to God is the beginning of health and life. A certain council says, "If any man do avouch that God does expect our will that it may be purged from sin and does not confess that it is the operation of the Spirit of God in us that does make us to will to be purged, he resists the Holy Ghost, saying by Solomon, 'The will is prepared by God.'" Augustine says, "It is not in him that runs, but in God that shows mercy, that all may be given to God, who both prepares the will of man to be helped and helps it being prepared, who prevents him that wills that he may will and follows him with help that wills, that he will not in vain." They which are bodily sick can will to be healed before they begin to be healed, because they be alive; but they which are spiritually sick in sin before their conversion are dead in their sin, and therefore they can neither think nor will nor desire their conversion. When Christ was about to cure a sick man, He moves this question to him, "Wilt thou be healed?" [John 5:6]. And so when God is about the work of regeneration in any man, He inwardly moves the question in the heart whether he will be regenerate or no and by this means stirs up a desire to be regenerate. If any man think that by this doctrine men are regenerate against their wills, I answer, when God begins to regenerate us, He makes us then willing, being otherwise by nature unwilling. And thus He regenerates us not against our will, yet so as the willingness to be regenerate is not of us, but of God. It may be alleged further that the act of the will whereby it wills to be converted goes before the act of God whereby He turns us to Himself, and that otherwise we are converted without our consent and that God works upon us as upon a block of stone. *Answer.* In respect of time, they are both done together; but in respect of order of nature first the will begins to be turned of God before it can will to be turned. For every cause is before his effect, if not in time, yet in priority of nature. The will converted, so soon as God has begun to renew it, wills to be renewed; and it could not will the conversion of itself unless it had formerly tasted the goodness thereof. And though we first feel the desire to be converted before the grace of conversion, it is nothing; for sometimes we perceive the effect before the cause, as we see the light of the sun before the sun, and we see the light of a candle in a house before we see the candle. Therefore, to will to be regenerate may be the effect of regeneration begun, though it first of all appear. For the better clearing of this our doctrine, I will propound two other questions.

The first, whether the will of man by his natural strength be any cause of his own conversion. The answer of the papists is that the will is a cause with the grace of God, and that both together work our conversion—grace as the principal, will as the less principal, and both as causes formally. But we teach and hold (as truth is) that will in the act of working, effecting, producing of our conversion or regeneration is no cause at all, but in itself considered a mere patient or subject to receive the grace of conversion given and wrought by God. It is absurd to think that a creature should be the cause of his creation, or a dead man of his quickening. Therefore (as I think), the doctrine of them that teach that there are three efficient causes of man's conversion—God's Spirit, God's word, man's will—has his defect. The Spirit is the principal cause; the word in his right use is the means or instrument whereby the operation of the Spirit is effectual. And for the will of man, it stands only as a patient or object of divine operation. It is alleged that men which repent are worthy [of] praise therefore, and this cannot well be unless repentance proceeds from freedom of will. I answer, repentance is praised because it is a thing that pleases God and in that respect praiseworthy; and the repentant person is praised not because he is the cause of his own repentance, but because he repents, being thereto enabled by the mercy of God.

The second question is whether the conversion of a sinner be in the power of man's will anyway. The answer of the papist is that our regeneration and conversion is in part in the power of man's will, so as the will stirred up can either apply itself to the grace of God or reject the same. Contrariwise, we teach that regeneration is not within the power of man's will, but that it wholly depends on the will of God; and that when God will convert and renew us, though will for his own nature be apt to resist. Yet in respect of God's unchangeable will and respect of the efficacy of His inward operation, it cannot resist and repel the work of God. For when God Himself works anything, His work cannot be resisted. For His working of a thing is only to will it to be, and His will cannot be resisted. Now in man's conversion, He works the will, and He works the deed, and He causes men to walk in His commandments [Phil. 2:13; Ezek. 36:26]. Resistance therefore cannot be made. Secondly, the Scripture everywhere teaches that our conversion and salvation wholly depends on God's will and not on the will of man. Of the distinction of man and man in the matter of salvation, Paul alleges the testimony of Moses: "It is neither in him that willeth, nor in him that runneth, but in God that sheweth mercy" [Rom. 9:16]. Our Savior Christ teaches that the secrets of the kingdom of God are revealed to some, and to others concealed, "because the pleasure of God is so" [Matt. 11:17], and because this gift of understanding is given to some and not to others [Luke 8:10]. Our conversion is termed a "new generation" and a "new creation." For this cause it cannot depend on the will of man at all, because a creature has not his creation or regeneration in his own will, so as he may either accept or refuse it. And it is a great overshadowing of God's grace to make the having or the not having of it to be in the choice of man's will. But the text in hand is objected. When Christ would have converted Jerusalem, they resisted and would not. I answer, there is a double work of God. One is outwardly in the word and sacraments to offer grace, and this indeed may be resisted. Of this Christ speaks here when He says, "They would not," and Stephen when he says, "they resisted the Holy Ghost" (Acts 7:51). The Lord says in Genesis 6:2, "My spirit shall not always strive with man"; and Peter applies this striving to Noah's ministry, saying that "Christ went in Spirit and preached" (1 Peter 3:19). The second is when God inwardly by His Spirit turns, renews, sanctifies the whole man; and this work cannot be resisted by the will of man, no more than Lazarus could resist the work of Christ when he was raised from the dead. If it be said that this doctrine abolishes liberty because it cannot choose and refuse the grace of God, I answer, the angels of God, which will good and cannot will evil, have nevertheless perfect liberty of will. And it is greater perfection of liberty freely and only to will that which is good than to be able to will both good and evil. He is at more liberty that cannot be a servant than he which may be either a free man or a servant. And a necessity of yielding to the will of God is no hurt to our will, for it is a special liberty to will that which God wills and nothing else. By all this which has been said, it appears what is the difference between us and the Church of Rome in the point of free will. They say liberty of grace to will well is only weakened, diminished, and held captive by sin; we say it is quite lost and abolished by the fall of Adam.

Again, by the former doctrine the common question is easily answered—namely, wherein lies the efficacy of God's grace. Some papists answer that it lies ordinarily in the free consent and cooperation of free will joined with grace. And this seems directly to be the opinion of the Council of Trent. But this is much derogatory to the divine grace of God to place the efficacy thereof in man's will, and it ministers much matter of boasting to men. Others place the efficacy of grace in the congruity of the object—that is, in moral persuasion, which God knows to be apt and fit to move and allure the will according to the condition thereof, even as a beast is moved by the sight of a bale of hay. But there is no efficacy in these persuasions presented to the mind, because the will lies in thralldom and bondage under sin and Satan. And the will must not only be helped but also be delivered from this bondage before any persuasions can move it. Lombard in his time much declined from the purity of the former days, and yet he is far sounder than the Jesuits of our days. For he says thus: "Free will now is hindered by the law of the flesh from doing good and stirred up to evil, so as it cannot will and do good unless it be delivered and helped by grace." We leaving the Papists in their dissentions place the efficacy of grace in the grace itself. For says Christ, "Every man that has heard and learned of the father, comes to me." Again, we place it in this, that God adds the second grace to the first. For having given the power, He stays not there but proceeds further and gives the will, and with the will, the deed. And thus is the grace of God effectual.

The consideration and use of this and the former doctrines is of great consequence. For if liberty of grace be lost, great is the necessity of our redemption by Christ, and great is the excellency thereof. Secondly, this doctrine cuts off the excuse of all sin, for though we sin necessarily because liberty of grace is lost, yet we sin freely because liberty in evil remains. Thirdly, it appears hence that man of himself cannot have or retain any goodness but that which God gives and preserves in us. This thing must move us to pray earnestly for the grace we want and to give hearty thanks for the graces we have. Fourthly, we are taught deeply to humble ourselves for the loss of our liberty, and for the bondage under sin: and to pray instantly for deliverance by Christ. Fifthly, seeing of ourselves we cannot prevail against the least temptation, we must pray to be guided and assisted continually by God. Lastly, seeing our conversion dependeth on God's mercy, and not on our will, we are taught to deny our own wills, wisdom, power and to ascribe our justification and salvation wholly and only to God.

The third estate of man is the estate of regeneration, in which the will has power to will partly that which is good and partly that which is evil, as daily experience declares in the lives of just men. And the reason is because the will of man renewed has in it a threefold liberty. The first is the liberty of nature to will or nill, which is in all men. The second is liberty of sin, whereby the will, when it wills any evil, wills it freely. And this liberty is diminished according to the measure of grace which God bestows. The third is liberty of grace, to will that which pleaseth God, and it is restored in part in regeneration, so far forth as liberty to sin is diminished. And because these three always remain in the will to the death, therefore sometime it wills well, sometime evil, sometime both. And in the best actions we do, there is a mixture, because they are not perfectly good for the time of this life, but partly good and partly evil.

That this power of the will may the better appear, I will propound four questions. The first is whether the will prevented or renewed have any stroke, action, or operation in the first regeneration of a sinner. I answer, in the renovation or conversion of a sinner I consider two things. First, the beginning or ground thereof, and that is the setting or imprinting of the new qualities and inclinations in the mind, will, affections of heart. And this is the entire or mere work of God in us and upon us, and we in it are merely passive, not active. The second is the evidence of the former in new and spiritual actions, as namely in thinking, willing, and defining that that is good. Now these actions are works of God in and by man's will, and man's will is not only a subject of them, but also an instrument: a subject, in that God is the first and principal worker of these works in the will; an instrument, because it pleases God to use the will and to move it by His grace for the acting and effecting of the things which He appoints. And thus the will is not merely passive, but passive and active both— first passive, and then active. For being acted and moved by God, who works the will and the deed, it also acts and moves. And we do not utterly deny the cooperation of man's will with God's grace. It is necessary indeed that God first regenerates us and makes us His children and new creatures. And in this thing we do not cowork with God, but stand as patients, that God may work upon us and reform us, even in the same manner as when He made us in the beginning without any help of ours. Yet after our regeneration, by faith we are brought from death to life, and to will is present with us, though in weak measure by reason of the remainders of corruption; and then we begin to be coworkers with the grace of God, moved to will, and so indeed willing that which is good. In this sense have the learned said that that which is repaired in us is not repaired without us, and that God in them whom He calls prepares the will that it may be a receiver and handmaid of His gifts.

The same answer, in effect, I propound another way. In the work of our regeneration, three graces be required: the preventing grace, the working grace, and the coworking grace. The preventing grace is when God of His mercy sets and imprints in the mind a new light, in the will a new quality or inclination, in the heart new affections. The working grace is when God gives to the will the act of well-willing—namely, the will to believe, the will to repent, the will to obey God in His word. The coworking grace is when God gives the deed to the will—that is, the exercise and practice of faith and repentance. The first gives the power of doing good; the second, the will; the third, the deed. And all three together make the work of regeneration. Now the will of man in respect of operation concurs not with God's preventing grace, but is merely patient as a subject to receive grace. For it is the proper work of God to set or imprint a new faculty or inclination of the will, and that without any action of the said will. Nevertheless, the will being once renewed and prevented concurs by his operation with the working and co-working grace of God. For the will being moved by grace wills and does indeed that whereto it is moved. And the will to obey God or to perform any like duty proceeds jointly from two causes: from grace, in that it moves and causes the will to will to believe; from the will of man, in that being prevented and moved by God it wills to believe or to do any like duty. And therefore the ancient saying has his truth, "He that made you without you does not regenerate or save you without you," because our conversion is not without the motion and consent of will, as our creation was. And that we do not mistake in this point, the order that is between man's will and God's grace must here again be remembered. In respect of time, they are both together and concur in the very first moment of our regeneration; in respect of the order of nature, the will does not first begin that which is good and then after borrow aid from grace, but grace prevents, renews, and moves the will, and then the will moved or changed wills to be converted and to be healed in the first instant of conversion.

This operation of the will to will to believe, to will to repent and to obey is the least grace and sign of God's favor, for nothing can be less than to will to do that which is good, yet is it of great and excellent price, for it has the promise of God annexed to it. The prophet says to the rebellious Israelites, "Wash, and make you clean: cease to do evil, learn to do well" [Isa. 1:16]. Now they might peradventure say, "Alas, we cannot wash ourselves." He therefore adds, "If ye will and obey" [v. 19]—that is, if you do but will to be cleansed and testify this will by your endeavor to obey, "ye shall eat the good things of the land." And Christ says that the heavenly Father gives the Holy Ghost to them that desire Him [Luke 11:13]. And to them that are in Christ God accepts this act of good will for the deed itself. Mark the comfort that flows from this doctrine. The full obedience to the law of God is impossible to all men, except Christ in this life; yea to them which are converted and sanctified, and greatly desire the fulfilling of the law in themselves. And therefore no man can be justified by it before God and obtain salvation thereby. Nevertheless, faith in Christ and repentance is so far forth possible to all that will and have a desire that those who but will in earnest to believe and to be converted do indeed believe and are converted and please God and shall not perish eternally, though the beginning of faith and conversion be weak, so it be in truth and not counterfeit. And yet such is the naughtiness of our nature that faith and conversion is impossible to us unless of the singular mercy of God it be stirred up in the hearts of the elect by His Holy Spirit. In this respect Christ says in Matthew 11:30: "My yoke is easy, and my burden light." And again, "His commandments are not grievous" [1 John 5:3]. It may be objected that the will and desire of renovation and reconciliation with God may [be] where there is a mind and purpose to sin and where is no true hatred and detestation [of] iniquity. *Answer.* The serious and instant will or desire to believe in Christ and to repent includes in it the hatred of sin and the purpose of not sinning. For he that truly desires to believe does so, because he detests his unbelief; and he that desires to repent does so, because he hates his own evil ways and purposes to sin no more.

The second question is whether the will, after it is renewed, be able to cause and bring forth good works of itself, or no? I answer two things. The first, that will cannot unless God further give a double grace. The one is assisting grace, and it stands in three actions: preservation, confirmation, protection. Preservation is whereby God continues the being of the will renewed. For that which is good does not continue good the least moment, unless God make it to continue. Confirmation is when God fixes the mind in that which is good and causes the will constantly to follow the good inclination thereof, it being otherwise mutable and apt to decline. Protection is whereby God defends His grace in us against the violence of temptation. Of this He says to Peter, "Satan has desired to sift you, but I have prayed for thee that thy faith fail not" [Luke 22:31]. And God promises that "he will not suffer the faithful to be tempted above that they are able to bear" [1 Cor. 10:13]. The second grace may be called exacting grace, whereby God moves and stirs up the will that it may indeed will and do the good to be done. And this grace is ordinarily required to the effecting of every good work. David's will was exceedingly renewed by the Holy Ghost, yet he prays still, "Incline mine heart to thy testimonies" [Ps. 119:36]. The Christian soul that is already drawn to Christ prays still, "Draw me, and we will run after thee" [Song 1:3]. Paul says they which are the children of God are guided, moved, or stirred by the Spirit of God [Rom. 8:14]. Again, he says of the Philippians, after they were renewed and wrought their own salvation with fear and trembling, that God did still "work in them" [Phil. 2:13] beside the power the act of willing and of doing that which is good. And He works the will by moving it to will and to do indeed that which it can will and do. And this moving cause is the good will of God. It may not seem strange that I say new grace is required to stir up the will to the doing of every new work. For grace in the will is like a fire of green wood, which hardly burns and continues not to burn, unless it be continually stirred up and blown; even so the good inclination of the will, because it is joined, nay mixed with contrary corruption that presses down, tempts, incites, and draws away the will from God, and all goodness has need continually to be excited, stirred, and moved. The man regenerate is able to pray to God, yet can he not pray sometime by reason of the weight of corruption, unless the Spirit help to bear the infirmities of nature and make request in us by stirring and moving us to make request. The doctrine of the ancient church has been that "new grace is to be given to the doing of every good act," and that we do not that good which we can do unless God makes us do it, as He made us able to do it. This doctrine must the rather be remembered, because the stream of popish doctrine runs another way by teaching that our wills assisted by grace can do good without the concurrence of new grace to excite and stir up the will. Indeed, for the doing of natural actions, the general cooperation of God suffices; but the effecting of actions supernatural, the special help of God is required. A child that can go up and down in an even floor, being stayed by the mother's hand, for all this he cannot go up a pair of stairs unless he be lifted at every step. Like is the case of the children of God in things which concern the kingdom of heaven.

The second part of the answer is that when [the] renewed will does a good work, it does it not perfectly. "To will," says Paul, "is present with me, but I cannot perform the good I would" [Rom. 7:18]—that is, "I cannot perfectly do it as I would." It may be objected thus: the works of God are perfect; good works done by us are works of God; therefore, they are perfect. I answer to the major or first part of the reason, it is true of such works as are works of God alone and of such works are jointly both of God and man, God being the principal agent and man the instrument. For then the work done takes to it the quality and condition of man, considering it proceeds from God through the sinful mind and will of man. The scrivener,[6] when he writes by himself, he writes a perfect hand; but when a learner and he write both together, he taking the learner's hand into his own, then that which is written will carry the imperfection of the learner. Like is the case in all such works as are from God in and by us.

---

6. *Scrivener*: a person authorized to draw up documents.

The third question is whether the relics of corruption be of that force in sinning that they can utterly quench the Spirit of God in the renewed will. The answer is that corruption remaining is of itself apt to do it, and the grace of God's Spirit is apt to be extinguished, because of itself it is mutable. Nevertheless, it wholly and utterly cannot be lost for four causes. The first is the promise of God in the covenant of grace: "I will put my fear into their hearts, that they shall not depart from me" [Jer. 32:40]. And this promise particularly belongs to all them that truly believe, because it is the promise of the evangelical covenant. The second is the intercession of Christ in the behalf of all the elect. Christ says to Peter, "Satan has desired to sift you as wheat, but I have prayed for thee Peter, that thy faith fail not" [Luke 22:31]. And this He did especially in the solemn prayer made (John 17), in which He prayed not only for Peter but for all the apostles and for all that did or should believe in Him. The third cause is the omnipotent power of God in preserving all them that are in Christ. "No man" says Christ, "taketh my sheep forth of my hand" [John 10:28]. And mark the reason: "My Father is greater than all." The last cause is the efficacy of God's Spirit. Saint John says, "That the seed of God remains in him that is born anew," and that this seed "keeps him that he neither does nor can sin in two respects" [Rom. 7:19]. First, if he sin, yet he sins not with full consent of will. For he hates and nills in part the evil which he wills. Secondly, if by human frailty he fall, he makes not a trade of sin, neither does he keep a course in wickedness; but the seed of grace remaining within causes him to return to God and to recover himself by new repentance.

The last question is whether the renewed will can of itself persevere in doing good. I answer that our perseverance depends and proceeds only from the will of God. That we may persevere two things are required: the power to persevere and will of perseverance. And both these being good things are of God. "Because every good giving, and every good gift is from above, and cometh down from the Father of lights" [James 4:17].

This former doctrine is of great use. In that the new birth and regeneration of a sinner is not without the motion of his own will, we are taught that we must, if we desire our own salvation, use the good means and strive against our own corruptions and endeavor earnestly by asking, seeking, knocking. It will be said that faith, repentance, and the rest are all gifts of God. I answer, there is no virtue or gift of God in us without our wills; and in every good act God's grace and man's will concur—God's grace as the principal cause; man's will renewed as the instrument of God. And therefore, in all good things industry and labor and invocation on our part is required.

Secondly, this doctrine ministers true comfort to all true servants of God. For if when they use the good means of salvation, the word, prayer, [and] sacraments, the will [does] lie not dead but [will] begin to oppose itself against unbelief and other corruptions and withal do but so much as will to believe, will to repent, will to be turned to God; they have begun to turn to God, and God has begun to regenerate them—so be it, this will in them to do the good they ought to do, be in good earnest, unfeigned, and they withal be careful to cherish this little grain until it come to a bigger quantity.

Thirdly, seeing to every new act that pleases God new grace is required, we are taught not to presume of our own wisdom, will, and strength, nor to glory in anything we do, but always to acknowledge our own impotency and in every good thing we do to give all the glory to God and to be watchful in prayer continually, because we stand by grace so long as we stand. And having done one work, we do not the second but by a continued supply of new grace.

Lastly, seeing God's preventing and working grace turns our wills and makes them of unwilling most willing wills, all our obedience must be voluntary and come from such freeness of will as if there were no bond in the law of God to force and compel us thereto [Ps. 110:3]. The people of God that are turned and guided by the free Spirit of God must be a voluntary people and with all alacrity and cheerfulness do the duties that pertain to them of a ready mind, even as if there were neither heaven nor hell, judge nor judgment after this life. The Spirit of life that is in Christ must be a law unto them.

The last estate is the estate of glorification after this life. In this estate the liberty of will is a certain freedom only to will that which is good and pleasing to God. For it is the continual voice (as it were) and cry of the glorified will, "I do no evil, and I will not do it. I do that which is good, and I will do it." And this indeed is the perfect liberty in which man's will is conformed to the free will of God and good angels, who will only that which is good and cannot will that which is evil.

By this which has been said it appears that the words of the text in hand— "and ye would not"—are spoke of the will of man according to the estate of corruption. For the voice of the regenerate will is, "I do that which is evil, but I would not do it. I do that which is good, but I cannot do it as I would." And the voice of the corrupted will is, "I do that which is evil, and I will do it. I do not that which is good, and I will not do it." And this last voice is plainly expressed in the words, "And ye would not."

The third point comes now to be considered—namely, the harmony or consent of both wills. For the words are "I would, ye would not." Here it may justly be demanded whether there be a harmony or consent between God's will and man's will, and how it stands with this text. I answer, there is an excellent harmony, and generally it stands in this: that God's will has a sovereign lordship over the will of man, and man's will stands subject to it absolutely and simply depends upon it. And by this means where man has a will, God has an antecedent will; and where man's will has any stroke or action, there God's will formerly had his stroke and action.

Furthermore, man's will depends on God's will in respect of three things—namely, sustentation, determination, ordination or government. It depends on the will of God in respect of sustentation, because man for his nature, strength, and all his motions depends on the will of God and could not have being for the space of one moment, unless it were upheld by God. It may be objected that if God sustain the will which is sinful He sustains not only the will, also the sin thereof. *Answer.* God sustains nature and not the sin of nature; and therefore He only sustains will as will and not as it is corrupt or sinful will. The like we see in nature: when a man halts in walking, the motion of the body is from the soul and is preserved by it; but the halting which goes with the motion and disorders, it is not from the soul neither has it his preservation thence, but from a defect in the leg or foot. By this we are taught to acknowledge the endless longsuffering of God, who sustains the members of our bodies, our souls, the faculties and actions thereof, even in the works in which men offend and dishonor Him. Secondly, we are taught to acknowledge the vile abomination of every sin, for we sin in the very hands of God, sustaining and preserving us, and in the very actions which we could not do, unless we were sustained by Him, we offend Him and provoke Him to anger against us.

Secondly, man's will depends on God's will in respect of determination, because we neither can nor do will anything without the will of God. A sparrow, says Christ, lights not on the ground, "without the heavenly father" [Matt. 10:29]—that is, without His decree or will. The malicious and wicked will of the Jews could not so much as will, much less do anything against Christ, but that "which the hand and council of God had determined to be done" [Acts 4:28]. Moreover, God determines the will two ways. In good things, He inwardly moves and inclines the will to the willing and doing of the good it wills. For in that God's will is the first cause of all good things, man's will depends on it in respect of virtue, in respect of application, and in respect of order of working. In respect of virtue, because the virtues of second places proceed from the first. In respect of application, because God uses the will of man as an instrument of His own will, and He applies it to the doing of things which He intends, even as the carpenter uses, moves, and applies his tools. In respect of order of working, because always the first cause begins the work, and the second moves not without the first. Upon this ground it follows that the good things which man wills, he so wills because God first willed them. And therefore Paul says that good works "are prepared of God" [Eph. 2:10] for us to walk in; and this preparation is made because God decrees and determines with Himself the doing of all works to be done.

In evil things, the determination of God is to will not to hinder them as He may. Upon this will in God follows sin in the will of man as a consequence, not as an effect. As a consequence, because when God suspends or withdraws sustentation and government from the will, it cannot of itself but will amiss—as the staff in my hand presently falls when I do but pull back my hand. To avoid evil is good; and therefore we cannot avoid the least evil, unless God make us able to avoid it. And evil is not the effect of God's will, because God puts nothing into man's will to cause it to will amiss; but He only ceases to confer to it help and direction, which He is not bound to confer.

Here long and tedious disputes are made by many touching the concord of God's decree and the liberty of man's will. And it is alleged that man's will loses his liberty and ceases indeed to be will if it stand subject to the necessary and unchangeable decree of God. I answer, first, that when the will of man determines in itself to one thing, it does not lose his liberty—much more then may the liberty of will stand with the determination of God. Secondly, God's decree does not abolish liberty, but only moderates and orders it by inclining the will in [a] mild and easy manner with fit and convenient objects, and that according to the condition of the will. That Christ should die when He died, it was necessary in respect of God's decree; yet if we respect the constitution of His nature, He might still have prolonged His days. And if we consider the will of Christ, He died most freely and willingly. Otherwise, His death had been no satisfaction for sin. God Himself does some things of an absolute necessity, and yet with perfect freedom of will. Now then if absolute necessity does not abolish freedom of will, much less shall conditional necessity, depending on God's decree, do it. Lastly, the decree of God establishes the liberty of will. For His determination is that the agency of second causes shall be according to their condition, so as natural causes shall work naturally; free causes, freely; necessary causes, necessarily; contingent causes, in contingent and variable sort. And therefore the necessary decree of God is that man shall will this or that, not necessarily in respect of himself, but freely.

Thirdly, man's will depends on God's will in respect of government. This government is of two sorts. First, He governs the wills of the righteous by working His own good work in them and by them. In them, because He moves and inclines them by His Spirit. By them, because they are holy instruments of His will.

Secondly, He governs the wills of the wicked and ungodly by six actions. The first is permission, when God withdraws His grace from the will, not enlightening the mind nor inclining the will but leaving it to itself—as when a man gives the rein to a wild horse. The second is a delivery of the will to Satan [1 Cor. 5:5; 1 Tim. 1:20], and that is when God gives the devil liberty to tempt, assault, and vex the will of man, being left to itself. And this thing is incident to obstinate sinners, and we pray against it these words: "Lead us not into temptation." The third action is a ceasing to refrain corruption of will either in whole or in part—as when He restrains all sins save one, or having refrained for a time for the punishment of former sin He omits restraint, permitting man to the lusts of his own heart. The fourth action is the bending, moving, or inclining of the wicked will. And thus God does not by inward inspiration (for then He should be the cause of sin), but by presenting to the mind and will objects good or at the least indifferent in themselves, upon which objects the will takes occasion to be willful, obstinate, and rebellious, not moved thereto by God, but freely moving itself. The heat of the stomach in the winter season is increased not by the heat of things taken inwardly, but by the cold of the air every way compassing the body. An unbroken horse being spurred, because he goes out of order, he flings out and casts his rider. And thus the sinful will of man, urged by commandments, threatenings, judgments, allured by promises and blessings, grows more sinful and wicked. Paul says that "sin took occasion upon the good commandments of God" [Rom. 7:8, 13] to ruin and to be sinful out of measure. David says that God "moved the hearts" of the Egyptians "to hate his people" [Ps. 105:25]. But how? He blessed the Israelites exceedingly more than the Egyptians. And upon this work of God, they took occasion to envy and to hate the Israelites.

The fifth action is ordination, whereby God uses well the wickedness of the will of man and directs it against the nature thereof to good ends, even as the learned physician sometimes of poison makes a remedy. In this sense Assyria is called the "rod of his indignation" [Isa. 10:5], and the Medes and Persians "his sanctified ones" [13:3]. The Jews in the crucifying of Christ "willed and minded" nothing but His death and destruction; yet God willed and by them wrought the redemption of mankind. He works His own good work by man's will as by an active instrument, and withal He leaves the will to itself to work his own evil work. The last action of God is when a man is going in on his own wickedness He turns him to Himself, of His exceeding mercy; sometimes again He opens a way that that person who of himself runs into wickedness may rush headlong to his own destruction for the further execution of divine justice—as when a house is falling, the owner thereof will not under-prop it, neither will he push it down; but he takes away all impediments and digs away the earth round about it, not touching the foundation, that when it falls, it may fall down right.

Thus we see briefly the harmony of man's will and God's will. Now let us come to the use, which is manifold. First of all, by the former doctrine we are brought to a right understanding of many places of Scripture. The Lord says of Pharaoh, "I will harden his heart" [Ex. 4:21]. And this He is said to do not because He sets and imprints hardness in his heart, but because by sundry actions He orders and governs his wicked will—and they are four. First, He permits Pharaoh to his own ill. Secondly, He leaves him to the malice of the devil and the lusts of his own heart. Thirdly, He urges him with a commandment to let the people go. And Pharaoh, the more he is urged, the stiffer and more stubborn he is, and the more he rebels against God—whereas he ought indeed to have been the more obedient. Lastly, God uses the hardness of Pharaoh's heart to the manifestation of His own justice and judgment. And therefore He opens him a way that he may run headlong to his own destruction. In this manner, and no otherwise, are the places to be understood when the Scripture says that "God put a lying spirit into the mouths of the prophets of Ahab" [Ezek. 14:9; Rom. 1:28; 2 Thess. 2:11]; that, "if a prophet be deceived, the Lord deceived him"; that "he gives up men to reprobate minds"; that "he sends strong illusion to believe lies." In the book of Samuel, it is said, "The Lord commanded Shimei to curse David" [2 Sam. 16:10], because about this cursing there is a twofold action in God. One, that He refrains the wicked heart of Shimei in respect of all other sin and not in respect of this sin of railing, to which God leaves him. The second, He uses him as an instrument to correct and to humble David. And thus likewise must the places be understood when it is said that "God delivered the wives of David to Absalom" [2 Sam. 12:11; 24:1], and "that he stirred up David to number the people" [Gen. 45:5]. Lastly, Joseph says that "the Lord sent him into Egypt," and that for two causes. One, because when his brethren were about to make him away, God by His providence caused merchants to pass by in their sight, whereupon they took occasion to sell him into Egypt. The second, because God disposed this fact of theirs to the good of Jacob and his family in time to come. And thus are all like places of Scripture to be understood.

Again, some school divines, following Damascene, make and ascribe to God an applied or depending will, on this manner. God for His part would have all men without exception to be saved—why then are they not saved? They themselves will not. And because they will not, God therefore chooses some and refuses others. But according to the former doctrine, I take this kind of applied will to be an invention of man's brain. For the contrary is the truth—namely, that man's will wholly depends on the will of God. That vessels be some of honor, some of dishonor. It is not in the power of the clay, but in the will of the potter. The first cause orders the second, and not the second the first. To make God's will depend on man's will is to put God out of His throne of majesty and to set the creature in His room. Others set for the depending will of God in this manner. God, say they, decrees nothing in particular of things that are casual and contingent, but He foresees within Himself what the will of the creature will do or not do when things are thus or thus ordered. And upon this foresight, He consequently determines what shall be done. But this opinion, as it gives to God a common or general providence, so it takes away the certain determination of God touching all particular events. And it is absurd to think that God should foresee the future acts of man's free will, when as yet He has determined nothing; for things that shall be are therefore to come to pass, because God by decree has determined their being. And therefore the foreknowledge of things that shall be follows the decree of God. And if God's decree presupposed man's willing of this or that, and thereupon determine, how shall that speech of the Lord stand, "I will cause them to walk in my statutes" [Ezek. 3:6]? For hereby is signified that God does not attend on the will of man, but brings man's will in subjection to Himself. And therefore this attending will ascribed to God is improved even of the papists themselves.

Thirdly, in that man's will stands subject absolutely to the pleasure of God, our duty is to yield voluntary subjection to Him in all things when His will is manifest to us.

Lastly, this doctrine of the consent and concurrence of man's will and God's will must be the stay and ground of our patience and comfort. For there is no calamity or misery that betides us by and from the will of man without the will of God. The creature can will nothing against us, unless it be first the will of God; and it can do neither more nor less than God wills. The devil could not touch Job without leave, and he could not enter into the herd of swine without leave. Upon this ground David speaks to this effect: "Let Shimei curse, for he curseth because the Lord bid him do so" [2 Sam. 16:10]. Joseph comforts himself and his brethren in this, that not they so much as the Lord sent him into Egypt.

As there is a harmony between God's will and man's will, so there is a dissent between man's will and God's word or His signifying will, as appears by the text in hand. Schoolmen upon this dissent make a distinction of God's grace into sufficient and effectual. Sufficient they call that whereby a man may be saved, if he will not be wanting to himself. Effectual, whereby a man is indeed saved. The first, they say, is given to all men at one time or another; the second is not. And this distinction of grace they gather on this manner. When Christ would have gathered the Jews, they would not. Therefore, they had not effectual grace; and because they would not, they are blamed and rebuked by Christ. Therefore, says the papist, God gave the sufficient grace to be converted, if they would, else could He not have blamed them. I answer, this proves that once God gave them sufficient grace to obey any commandment of His—namely, in the creation. But hence cannot be gathered that when God called the Jews by His word, that then, then I say He gave them sufficient grace. Secondly, it is objected that

God did all that might be done to His vine to make it bring forth good fruit, and yet for all this it brought forth nothing but wild grapes. Therefore, it is said there must needs be a grace sufficient to salvation which is not effectual. I answer, God did that to His vineyard that was sufficient to make a good vine bring forth fruit (and that is the meaning of the place in Isaiah), though not sufficient to change the nature of an evil vine and to make it a good vine. It is urged that the Lord says He waited for grapes, which He would not have done unless there had been hope by reason of sufficient grace given. I answer again that the Lord waited for fruit not because God then gave them sufficient grace when He waited, but because the church of the Jews was in show and pretense a good vine and thereby gave hope of good fruit. Thirdly, it is objected that Adam received sufficient grace, and that he had not effectual grace because he fell. I answer, Adam had sufficient to the perfection of a creature, but not sufficient to unchangeable perseverance, especially if he should be assaulted by temptation. Likewise, he had grace effectual in respect of righteousness and happiness, but not in respect of perseverance in both. Grace in him so far forth as it was sufficient to happiness, it was also effectual. Lastly, it is objected that God forsakes no man until he first forsake God and therefore that God for His part gives grace sufficient to salvation. *Answer.* There is a double kind of forsaking in God: one is for trial; the other, for punishment. The forsaking which is for trial's sake goes before man's sin in which he forsakes God. In this regard, Adam was for order of nature first forsaken of God before he forsook God. The forsaking which is for punishment always follows after sin, and of this must the rule be understood that they which are forsaken of God did first forsake God. Now the truth which we are to hold in this point is thus much. There is a grace which is sufficient to the conviction of a sinner which is not effectual to salvation; and again, there is a grace which is sufficient to the leading of a civil life which is not effectual to salvation. Yet the grace which is indeed sufficient to salvation is also effectual—namely, the gift of regeneration, in which God gives not only the power to be converted, but also the will and the deed.

Thus much of the harmony. Now comes the fourth point to be considered—namely, in what manner Christ willed the conversion of Jerusalem. He willed it first in love; secondly, in patience. His love is set forth by two things. The first, albeit He was God, full of majesty and we vile wretches, His enemies by nature, yet was He content to take upon Him a vile and base condition to be to the Jews as a hen. The second was that He takes to Him the fashions, the disposition, and tender affection of the hen to her young ones.

That all this may the better be conceived, three questions are to be propounded. The first is, whether there be such an affection of love in God as is in man and beast? I answer that affections of the creature are not properly incident to God, because they make many changes, and God is without change. And therefore all affections and the love that is in man and beast is ascribed to God by figure, and that for two causes. First, because there is in God an unchangeable nature that is well pleased with every good thing, and a will that seriously wills the preservation of every good thing; and of this nature and will of God, the best love in the creature is but a light shadow. Secondly, the affection of love is ascribed to God because He does the same things that love makes the creature do, because He bestoweth blessings and benefits upon His creature as the lover does on the person loved. In this sort are all other affections ascribed to God, and no otherwise.

The second question is, whether there be in God a hatred of His creatures, for God is compared to the hen which loves her young ones. *Answer.* If hatred be taken for a passion incident to man, it is not incident to God. If it be taken for a work of God's providence and justice, it is in God—and that in three respects. First of all, in Scripture, hatred sometimes signifies a denial of love and mercy, as when it is said that he which will follow Christ "must hate father and mother" [Luke 14:26]—that is neglect them or not love them in respect of Christ. In this sense, hatred agrees to God. For He is said to love Jacob and to hate Esau [Rom. 9:13]—that is, not to love Easu with that love wherewith He loved Jacob. Again, there is in God a nature that abhors and detests iniquity. Thus says the psalmist that "God loveth righteousness, and hateth iniquity" [Ps. 45:7]. And thus God hates man not simply, because he is the handiwork of God, but because he is a sinner and by reason of the work of the devil in man— namely, sin, which is simply hatred of God. Thirdly, God plagues and punishes offenders, and in this regard He is said to hate them. Thus says David that "God hates the workers of iniquity, and destroys them that speak lies" [Psalm 56]. By this which has been said, it appears that there be two degrees of hatred in God. One is negative, when God as an absolute lord bestows His special love on some and denies it to others because His pleasure is so; the second is positive, when He hates and detests His creature. And this second always follows sin and is ever for sin, but the other goes before sin. And whereas it is said in this text that God is as the hen that loves all her chickens and gathers them all together, it must be understood that our Savior Christ here sets down His dealing not with all His creatures and with all mankind, but only His dealing toward His own church, in which He calls all outwardly by the sound of His word and receives all outwardly into the covenant. By this which has been said, we are taught after the example of God to hate and detest iniquity, and yet always to make difference between the person and the sin.

The third question is, in what thing is Christ as a hen to His church? *Answer.* In temporal blessings and deliverances; in afflictions and manifold corrections; but especially and principally in His word published in the ministry of the prophets. For it is the wing which He spread over His people, and it is the voice whereby He called and (as it were) clucked them to Him.

Thus we see the meaning of the similitude that Christ would have gathered Jerusalem as the hen gathers her chickens. Now follows the use. By this we see the tender love of God to this church and land. For it has pleased Him to propound to us the gospel of salvation, and that now more than forty years. And in so doing He has offered long to embrace us in the arms of His mercy, and in spreading His wing over us to become our God and our Savior. For this tender love our hearts must be filled with love to Christ, and our mouths with praise. Again, we learn hence that the gospel brings all other blessings of God with it. For God in it communicates His own self to us, as the hen to her young ones. The kingdom of God brings all things else with it that may serve for the good of man, and where the gospel is embraced, there is God's kingdom. The peace and protection of this church and land, whereby we have been preserved from being a prey to our enemies, comes by means of the gospel of life. Therefore, foolish and false is the conceit of sundry popish persons that say there was never such plenty in the world as when the old learning (as they say) or old religion was. Secondly, by this we are advertised if we would have all necessary blessings for this life first of all to embrace the gospel of Christ. Thirdly, if Christ take to Him the disposition of the hen, we likewise must take to us the disposition of the chicken in respect of Christ, and that in three things. First, we must suffer ourselves to be gathered to Christ—that is, to be turned to Him from all our sins, to believe in Him, to be of the same mind and disposition with Him, to suffer Him to quicken us with His heavenly and spiritual life, as the hen cherishes her chickens by sitting on them. Secondly, we must attend upon the word and will of Christ as the chicken upon the call of the hen, and suffer Him to rule us both in heart and life for all things. The third thing is that we must depend on the sweet and merciful promises of Christ and shroud ourselves under His wing against hell, Satan, death, damnation. And verily all such among us who are not careful to perform these three things to Christ are no better than monstrous rebels, considering He has in His merciful and tender love sought to win us to Himself for these forty years.

Thus much of the love of Christ. Now I come to His patience, in these words: "How often would I?" The meaning whereof is this: "You have continually from time to time provoked Me by your sins; yet did I not withdraw My love from you, but sent my prophets from time to time to you, to call you and gather you to Me." And this patience of God is here expressed to aggravate the rebellion of Jerusalem; I will therefore speak a little of it. And first it may be demanded whether the virtue of patience that is in men be also in God.

I answer, properly it is not. For where this kind of patience is, there is passion and sufferance. Now God is not subject to any passion or sufferance, because His nature is unchangeable. Again, that which is in God properly is in Him eternally. This patience is not in Him eternally, but for the time of the continuance of this world. Nevertheless, Scripture ascribes this patience to God for two causes. The first is, because there is in God an infinite goodness of will and nature, whereby He never simply wills the perdition or destruction of any creature. Ezekiel says, "God wills not" [Ezek. 18:32]—that is, "takes no delight in the death of a sinner." And whereas it is said that vengeance is God's, and He will repay [Rom. 12:19], it must be thus taken: that God in revenge does not absolutely intend to destroy, but only to execute justice in the punishment of sin. It may be objected that God is said to "make vessels of wrath prepared to destruction" [9:22]. I answer, this place must circumspectly and warily be understood, and I take the meaning of it to be this: that God makes vessels of wrath or vessels for wrath by His will and decree, whereby He decrees to pass by some and to forsake them in respect of His love and mercy. And this act of God in passing by and in forsaking of men, [served] as it were to set them apart to become vessels of wrath. And though God in secret and just judgment does this, yet He never fills any of these vessels with His wrath until they have been tainted with iniquity. And though they be prepared to destruction, yet they are never indeed destroyed but for their sins. Thus then, by reason of this excellent and incomprehensible goodness of God, whereof the virtue of patience is but a shadow, God is said to be patient.

The second cause why God is said to be patient is because He does the same things that patient men do. First, He invites men to repentance; secondly, He promises pardon; thirdly, He defers punishment; fourthly, at the first He only inflicts less punishments—when they do no good, He inflicts greater—and lastly, when there is no hope of amendment, He inflicts everlasting death and destruction.

The end of God's patience is twofold: one, that the elect of God may be gathered and called; the other, that all excuse might be taken from the ungodly [vv. 22–23].

The patience of God is either universal or particular. Universal, which pertains to all men. The decree of divine justice was set down to Adam and in him to all mankind: "When thou shalt eat of the forbidden fruit, in dying thou shalt die" [Gen. 2:17]—that is, presently die the first and second death. Dathan and Abiram, presently upon their rebellion, went down into the earth quick [Num. 16:23]. The captains with their fifties were presently upon their coming to Elias destroyed with fire from heaven. And so oft as any man sins, he deserves present destruction; and so many sins as we have committed, so many damnations have we deserved. Here it may be demanded why God does not execute His decree accordingly. I answer, God in justice remembers mercy; yea His justice gives place to mercy. For there is another decree of mercy which He will have as well to be accomplished as the decree of justice, and that is "the seed of the woman shall bruise the serpent's head." Again, "Ask of me and I will give thee the heathen for thine inheritance, and the ends of the earth for thy possession." That mercy then may be showed upon mankind, justice is executed in great patience by certain degrees. And this patience pertains to all men without exception that come of Adam by generation.

Special patience is that which concerns particular men or countries. Thus God spared the old world 120 years before He sent the flood. He spared the Amorites until their iniquities were full. He spared the Egyptians four hundred years. He deferred the punishment of the idolatry of Israel 390 years, and then He punished it with seventy years' captivity. He winked at the ignorance of the Gentiles four thousand years. Antichrist shall not utterly be destroyed until the coming of Christ. When men blaspheme God and Christ, swearing wounds, blood, heart, sides, nails, life—if they had their defeat they should descend to hell quickly, and that presently. But God forbears them, and sundry such persons are vouchsafed the grace of true repentance. The very least offender upon earth is partaker of the great patience of God. For He sustains the members of our bodies, the powers and motions of the soul in such actions in which we offend Him. And no creature can sufficiently consider the greatness of this longsuffering.

The use to be made of the patience of God follows. First, it serves to teach all men to turn to God by true repentance. Romans 2:4, "Despisest thou the patience and long suffering of God, knowing that the goodness of God leads thee to repentance? God is patient toward us and would have no man to perish, but would have all men to come to repentance." To come more near to ourselves and this English nation, now is the day of our visitation, and has been for the space of the forty years and more in which God in great patience has continually called upon us, knocking at the door of our hearts and stretched out the arms of His mercy to us. Wherefore, the common duty of all English people is to turn to God with all their hearts according to all the law of God, as it is said of Isaiah. And that this duty may indeed be practiced, I will use certain reasons that may serve to stir up our dead minds. First, the time of the continuance of the patience of God is hidden and unknown to us. And hereupon, when men abusing the patience of God shall say, "Peace, peace," then, then shall come sudden destruction, as travail upon a woman. And therefore the time is to be redeemed, and as Peter says, "We must watch and make haste for the coming of the Lord" [1 Thess. 5:5; Eph. 5:15; 2 Peter 3:12]. Secondly, the greater patience of God is and has been, the greater shall His anger be. A blow, the longer it is in coming, the greater it is. Yea, the very wrath of God in itself is most horrible. The wrath of a lion, of a prince [Micah 1], yea, the wrath of all creatures to the wrath of God is but as a drop of water to the whole sea. At His indignation the very mountains melt. The heavens and the elements shall melt at His coming. Much more shall our rocky and stony hearts melt. Thirdly, God has His treasury and storehouses for judgment, and they which go on in their sins from day to day fill this treasury of God with wrath and judgments against the day of wrath [Rom. 2:5]. And when men turn heartily from their evil ways, this treasury is emptied, as appears by the example of the Ninevites. Wherefore, let us all from the highest to the lowest bethink ourselves what evil we have done, and how we have abused the merciful patience of God, and make speed to turn to God and Christ, our merciful Savior. Some will say we abuse not God's patience; we have repented long ago. I answer, the number of them that truly turn to God in their hearts is but small in comparison, even as the gleaning is to the whole harvest. It will be said again, we are not as the Jews that deny Jesus Christ to be the Messiah. I answer, we confess Christ in word, but there is a great multitude among us that deny Him in their deeds and naughty lives. For to omit the sins of the second table, there be five notorious sins that are common among us. Willful ignorance, in that men have little or no care to know God and to know the way of life. The second is the profane contempt of the gospel. For now the obedience to this blessed doctrine of life, yea, the very show of it, is in common reputation "preciseness." And now adages under this name the profession of the gospel comes otherwhiles upon the stage to help to make us the play and to minister matter of mirth. Upon this we may justly fear the gospel is going from us. The third sin is worldliness, which reigns and bears sway in all places as though there were no other world, and as though heaven were upon earth. The fourth sin of our days is lukewarmness. For commonly men are not lost in themselves that they might be found of Christ; they feel not their own poverty; they know not in what need they stand of the blood of Christ; and therefore they make profession of the faith formally, not seriously, only because they are forced to so do by the good laws of a good prince. The last sin is hypocrisy, for all among us come to the Lord's Table and thereby enter into the highest degree of Christianity that can be upon earth. For thereby they make profession that they are united to Christ and have fellowship with Him and grow up therein—and yet the most being departed from this holy sacrament take liberty to live as they like, despising all others that will not say and do as they do. These and many other are the common fruits of all our English vineyard [Song 4:16]. It stands us all in hand to pray to God that He would blow upon His vineyard that we may bring forth better fruit and prevent the judgments that otherwise are like to fall.

Secondly, in that God is so patient toward us, we are taught to exercise ourselves in patience and respect of God when we are afflicted and corrected by Him. For when He lays His hand upon us, we may not be angry, fret, chafe, and rage, but quiet our hearts in His will, though the cross be grievous for measure and long for continuance. This patience to Godward is termed in Scripture by an excellent name, "the silence of the heart," whereby the heart without repining subjects itself to the will of God in all things. Psalm 4:4: "Examine your hearts upon your bed, and be still." And 37:7: "Be silent to Jehovah."

Thirdly, if God be thus patient toward men, we again must be patient one toward another, as Paul says, "Forebear one another, and forgive on another, as God for Christ's sake forgave you" [Eph. 4:31; Col. 3:13]. The faith of the merciful patience of God cannot but breed and bring forth in us patience and longsuffering in regard of anger and revenge.

Lastly, in that God calls us to salvation with great patience, we must suffer ourselves to be called and run the race of our salvation with like patience. We must hear the word and "bring forth fruit with patience" [Luke 8:15]. We must pray without fainting, and without taking repulse, as the woman of Canaan did [Matt. 15:26], and therefore with patience. "Our hope must be by patience and through comfort of the Scriptures" [Rom. 15:4]. In a word, we cannot obtain the "promises without patience" [Heb. 10:36].

The fifth and last point to be considered is what is meant by "the children of Jerusalem." I answer it thus. Children in Scripture are taken four ways. First, some are children by generation—of them read Luke 3, where a long genealogy is set down from Adam to Christ. Secondly, some are called children by adoption without generation. Michal that never bare a child to her death is said to bear five to Adriel, because she did adopt his children and bring them up as her own [2 Sam. 6:13; Num. 21:8]. Thirdly, some are called children in regard of legal succession, in title to this or that thing. Thus Zedechias, who indeed was uncle to Jehoakim, is said to be the son of Jehoakim [2 Kings 24:17; 1 Chron. 3:16], because he did succeed Jehoakim as being the next of the blood in the kingdom. Jeconia or Conias was childless [Jer. 22:30], and yet he is said to beget Salathiel [Matt. 1:12], because Salathiel was to succeed him in the kingdom of Judah in that he was the next of David's house. Lastly, men in that they appertain to anything or place as children do to their parents are called children thereof. Thus men are called children of light, of darkness, of sin, of wrath. Thus Jerusalem is called the "daughter of Sion." And in this text citizens, the inhabitants of Jerusalem, are called the children thereof.

Thus much of the rebellion of Jerusalem. Now follows the punishment in these words: "Behold, your habitation shall be left to you desolate"—or thus, "Your house, that is, both city and temple" (as it is in the next chapter) "shall be left to you as a wilderness."

Here we must first observe that the punishment of Jerusalem's rebellion is a decreed desolation both of city and temple. And the right consideration of it is of great use. For this desolation is as it were a looking glass to this our English nation, in which we may see our future condition, except we repent of our unthankfulness to God for His mercies and show better fruits of the gospel than commonly we do. The old world little regarded the ministry of Noah, the preacher of righteousness, and was destroyed by a universal flood. It is a general decree of God: "The Gentiles and kingdoms that will not serve thee, shall perish, and be utterly destroyed" [Isa. 60:12]. If God spare not the natural branches, He will much less spare us that are but wild branches if we neglect and lightly esteem the Gospel of life, as men everywhere commonly do.

Secondly, the desolation of Jerusalem may be a glass to every one of us who in these days of God's merciful visitation set the ministry of the gospel at naught or lightly respect it; for unless such persons amend, and that betimes, utter desolation will befall both them and their families. God has passed His sentence: "They that withdraw themselves from God shall perish" [Ps. 73:27]. Now they withdraw themselves from God that cannot abide to have fellowship with Him in His word and to bring themselves in subjection thereto. Thirdly, it appears hence by the contrary, that the stability of all kingdoms stands in the obedience of the gospel of Christ; for God's kingdom is most sure and stable, against which nothing can prevail. And when the gospel is obeyed in any kingdom, it is (as it were) founded in the kingdom of God.

Moreover, this desolation is both perpetual and terrible. It is perpetual, that is, to the last judgment. For Jerusalem must be trod under foot, "till the time of the Gentiles be fulfilled" [Luke 21:24]—and this is till there be signs in the sun and moon, and the powers of heaven be shaken, and that is immediately before the last judgment. Hence I gather that there is no city of Jerusalem nor temple now standing. It will be said that since the destruction thereof they might have been redesigned. I answer, by reason of the curse of God, it cannot so be. Three hundred and thirty years after the death of Christ, the Jews by the leave and help of Julian the Emperor went about to build again their temple and city, but their work was overthrown, and they hindered by thunder and lightning and earthquakes, and many of them slain thereby. Again, it may be said that there is a city now standing that is called Jerusalem. I answer, it is either Jerusalem in her ruins or the city Bethara, fenced and walled by Elius Adrianus.[7] Secondly, by this it appears that the wars that were made heretofore for the recovery of the Holy Land and of Jerusalem were in vain. This enterprise was the policy of the pope, that he might the better seat himself in Europe. And there was little good to be looked for in the place that God had accursed with perpetual desolation. Thirdly, by this it appears that pilgrimages made to the Holy Land are superfluous. And lastly, I gather hence that antichrist shall not reign in the temple at Jerusalem. This is but a popish fiction. For how is it possible for him to sit in a temple that is utterly destroyed in such sort that stone does not lie upon stone? It is objected that antichrist shall destroy the two prophets of God "in the city in which Christ was crucified" [Rev. 11:8; Acts 9:5]. I answer, Christ is as well crucified in His members as in His own person; and thus He was and is still crucified in Rome—and in respect of His members more crucified in Rome than in Jerusalem.

Again, this desolation was most terrible and the tribulation thereof so great that the like was never since the beginning of the world [Matt. 24:21]. Histories written thereof declare as much. For the city was the first besieged by the army of Titus Vespasianus, called "the abomination of desolation"; and it was withal compassed with a wall that had thirteen castles on it, to command the whole city. In the time of the siege, the Jews were oppressed with a grievous famine, in which their food was old shoes, old leather, old hay, and the dung of beasts. There died partly of the sword and partly of the famine eleven hundred thousand of the poorer sort; two thousand in one night were emboweled; six thousand were burned in a porch of the temple. The whole city was sacked and burned and laid level to the ground, and ninety-seven thousand taken captives and to be applied to base and miserable service. This horrible desolation must teach us to dread and fear God and to yield unfeigned subjection to Christ, and as the psalmist says, "to kiss the Son lest he be angry" [Ps. 2:12] and we perish in the way, when His wrath shall suddenly burn.

Touching this desolation, there be three things done by Christ. First, He determines it, saying, "Your house shall be left to you desolate." Hence I gather that there is a providence of God touching things that come to pass. That is one point. The second is that the disposition of kingdoms for the beginning, continuance, and end is of God. "The God of heaven," says Cyrus, "has given me all the kingdoms of the world" [Ezra 1:2]. And Daniel to Nebuchadnezzar: "The God of heaven has given thee kingdom, power, and glory" [Dan. 2:37]. And the handwriting upon the wall in the sight of Belshazzar was to this effect: "Thy kingdom is numbered" [Dan. 5:26], for continuance of years; "it is

---

7. *Elius Adrianus*: another name for the Roman Emperor Antonius Pius (86–161 A.D.).

weighed" [vv. 27–28] and found light in respect of the sins of the people; and "it is divided" to the Medes and Persians. This must teach all good subjects in England to lift up their hearts to God for the continuance of peace and protection to this church and land.

Secondly, Christ reveals the desolation of Jerusalem, and that certainly. Yea, He determines the very particular time. "This generation," says He, "shall not pass till all these things be fulfilled" [Matt. 24:34]. And according to this revelation and prediction of Christ, all things came to pass. For within the compass of forty years after it was destroyed. Hence I gather that this Gospel of Matthew and the rest are the very word of God, on this manner: that which foretells particular things to come certainly and truly is of God; but the Gospels foretell particular things to come certainly and truly, as in this place we see; therefore, they are of God.

Thirdly and lastly, Christ labors to bring the Jews to a serious consideration of their punishment, when He says, "Behold." For He does as it were take them by the hand and bring them to a present view of their misery. And thus He has always dealt with His people from the beginning. Yea, thus he dealt with Adam before his fall, when He said, "If thou eat the forbidden fruit, in dying thou shalt die" [Gen. 2:17]. This serious consideration of deserved punishment is of great use. It is an occasion of repentance to man [Amos 4:12]. It is a means, if not of repentance, yet of restraint of open vices. Again, the consideration of everlasting punishments is a means to make us patiently bear lesser crosses that befall us in this life. And therefore it were to be wished that men nowadays would seriously speak and think of hell and of the pains thereof. For then there would be more amendment than there is. But this good is hindered partly by blindness of mind and partly by false imaginations [Isa. 28:18], that the judgments and punishments of God may easily be escaped.

Deo Gloria.

A Fruitful
Dialogue
Concerning
the End of the World

Written many years ago, and then published
by
William Perkins.

Perused and revised

London:
Printed by John Haviland,
1631

TO THE RIGHT HONORABLE
Thomas Lord Sorroys
of the Noble Order of the Garter, and of the Majesties
Honorable Council in the North

Right Honorable, this little treatise is the first fruit of the labor of that great and reverend Master Perkins. Many years ago set out by himself, and now (all his *Works* being to be put together) held fit to be joined with the rest; for though it were written in his young years, yet did these first fruits give assurance of that plentiful harvest of instruction and consolation which the Christian world has since reaped and received from the hand and mouth of that holy man. And in this very beginning did that blessed Spirit begin to show itself which afterward was so mighty and powerful in his tongue and pen. It was first written against covetous hoarding up of corn (among other sins) and was published in a year of dearth, the fitter therefore to be now again reprinted, seeing our sins have brought upon us a dearth, and (which is more lamentable) a dearth without scarcity.

Having perused and revised this treatise, I do humbly present it to your Lordship's reading, and from you to the world's view. The Honorable conceit your Lordship has vouchsafed to hold of me and my poor labors deserve at my hand more service and duty than yet I can perform to your Lordship. Till I can, give me leave thus to rank your Lordship among the religious and honorable patrons of Master Perkins's *Works*. Honor and all true happiness be multiplied upon your Lordship, from God the Father in Jesus Christ. Amen. June 4, 1609.

Your good Lordship's in Christ to be commanded,

W. Crashaw

To the Christian Reader

It is not unknown to you (Christian reader) that Satan is the deadly enemy of mankind, and that he goes about continually like a hunger-bitten lion, seeking whom he may devour. For this cause he uses infinite sleights and conveyances. He lays innumerable sins and snares to entrap men and to bring them into eternal bondage under him. Of this point, you may have a plain view in the people of this land. Some of them neither regarding God's providence nor His judgments which He may send upon them for their sins stand aghast at the signs of heaven, at the conjunctions which ordinarily befall; and at this present, their minds are greatly occupied with foolish dreams of the year next ensuing. Some others (and they peradventure of a better sort) are professors of the gospel, and yet live securely, still weltering in their old corruptions and in very truth not returning to the Lord. For they think they have done their duty and are persuaded they are truly faithful if they do not oppose themselves against the gospel, but give an outward reverence to it and to the ministers of it. As the foolish virgins contented themselves with their lamps, never seeking for oil until it was too late, so these men content themselves with outward show and profession of godliness, never regarding to feel the power of it in themselves. Others there are which no doubt might receive profit by the word which they hear preached, but they cannot abide that the word of God should be applied aright to their consciences. For they themselves never think of anything but of the promises of the gospel, and cannot abide the threatenings of the Law. Yea, they like the ministry of the word when general doctrine is delivered, but if the two-edged sword of God's word pierce into the marrow of their bones and ransack the secret affections and lusts of the flesh, then they are forth of order and storm as furious and madmen. Again, some there are which partly by reason of tenderness of their own consciences, partly by their own ignorance in the word of God are ever anon disquieted and troubled with manifold temptations. In all these sorts of men, you may easily perceive how busy Satan is to deceive and be with men and to keep them still under his dominion, that his kingdom may not be diminished. Now, for the preventing of these evils, I have drawn this little treatise. Read it at your leisure and accept in good part this my endeavor. I trust by God's blessing it shall not be unprofitable to you.

W. P.

A Fruitful Dialogue between the Christian and the Worldling, Concerning the End of the World

Christian. Well overtaken honest man, how far travel you this way?

Worldling. As far as Cambridge, God willing.

Christ. What have you a load, I pray you?

Worldl. As good wheat as ever grew on God's earth. I would I had as good a price as I could wish for it.

Christ. Why would you so?

Worldl. Alas, I have great store of corn in my house at home, and I fear me it will rot upon the floors before I shall be able to sell it, because I cannot get almost anything for it. And they which offered me four marks for a quarter of wheat will not at this present give me four nobles, and scarce twenty shillings.

Christ. Truly I perceive that you are a hard-hearted man, void of any compassion to the poor. You have been one of those that have brought our country into such misery. And to you the prophet Amos speaks after this manner: "Hear this, O ye that swallow up the poor, that ye may make the needy of the land to fail, saying, 'When will the new moon be gone, that we may sell corn? And the Sabbath, that we may set forth wheat, and make the ephah small, and the shekel great, and falsify the weights by deceit? That we may buy the poor for shoes: yea, and sell the refuse for wheat?' The Lord has sworn by the excellency of Jacob, 'Surely I will never forget any of thy works'" (Amos 8:5–7). And even now at this time God has been mindful of His promise, for He has frustrated the desires of all such covetous men as you are; and of His mercy He has heard the cries of the poor and has now given us plenty in this land.

Worldl. I marvel why you should speak against me, and all such as I am; I tell you plainly never any man spoke so much to me as you have done now. In the parish where I dwell I am taken for an honest man; I do no man any hurt. I use not to go to the alehouse and tavern, as many naughty men do; and I have a care to provide for myself and for my family, and I hope you will not condemn me for doing so.

Christ. Did you never hear so much before? Doubtless more is the pity, and now you shall hear more even of me. For all these hoarders up of corn (among which you are one) are as bad as the vilest rascals that be in the land. You say you do no man harm—do you not? And what good ever did you? You stop your ears at the cry of the poor and say to them, "Go your way you stranger; God send you stranger, meat, drink, and clothing," as Sirach says. You play the glutton in the gospel. You do not show so much favor to poor Lazarus crying to you for relief, as the dogs did which licked his sores [Luke 16:21]. The richer sort of you, if a man in any need come to beg or buy something for his sustenance, you cry out, "Away with this beggar. Go whip this slave. To the flocks with this stinking rascal. Stand further off for filling us with your vermin, you lousy wretch." Contrariwise, you which are the poorer sort say, "God help you poor man, I have not for you. I have a great charge and am a poor man myself. You would have corn of me, but you will not go to the price of it. Thus dear it is now; I cannot abate a farthing of it. Therefore, go your ways and trouble me not." And yet forsooth you do no man any harm; you would be sorry to be charged with any dishonesty. But in truth you are murderers, because many are famished by your hoarding up of corn. You are thieves, because you keep back that which belongs to the poor upon a reasonable price. You are cursed idolators, because you set your hearts upon your riches. And in one word, you are very atheists in the world. You distrust God's providence; you love Him not; you fear Him not. You are stark rebels to God, bowing the knees of your hearts before the prince of the world, Satan [Colossians 2; 1 John 2]. You are the rich men of which it is said, "To be an impossible thing for them to enter into the kingdom of heaven: and except with speed you repent, you shall find it to be so" (Matthew 19).

Worldl. What mean you thus to rail on us? What do we but that we may lawfully do? I pray you for all your skill, is it not lawful for us to do with our own what we will? And to make as much of it as we can? You tell us (methinks) that we cannot be saved, but I will always put a good faith in God, say you what you will, and I hope to be saved as well as you.

Christ. It is a pitiful thing to see how the world takes many things for lawful which are flat against the Word of God. As for example, it is thought no fault to raise the market and to take for a man's own whatever he can get and to sell of any price; but this is reproved in the place of the prophet Amos before alleged, where he denounces God's judgments against them that wait for a time in which they make the measure small and the price great and take for their corn according to their covetous desires. You say you have a good faith to Godward, but alas you deceive yourself with a fantasy; for if you had true faith indeed, you would love God with all your heart, and loving God, you would also love your poor brother in whom God's image appears. And if you had a love of your brother, you would be full of pitiful compassion toward him. You would no more sing this song, "May I not take for my own what I can get?" Nay, you would rather do as the faithful did in the primitive church, who sold their possessions and took money and divided it to the poor as they had need. And as the churches of Macedonia did, which being in extreme poverty yet did send plentiful relief to the church at Jerusalem, far distant from them. And you would rather set yourself in misery and poverty than your poor brother, for whom Christ has shed His blood—yea, you would be content to fare hardly and to pinch yourself, that you might relieve your neighbors. For as Paul says, love is bountiful, love seeks not her own, love suffers all things and endures them (2 Cor. 12:4, 5, 7).

Worldl. For mine own part, I could have been content to have sold my corn all the year though for less price, if other would have done so; but other men were so hard that they would stick for a penny. These men indeed were they that did raise the market. I took nothing but that which was offered me; and for my part, I hope God will have me excused.

Christ. The vilest miser and most covetous carle[1] that is among you can say so much. And how can you look for any favor at God's hands, when by your own confession you have done as others have done and given consent to their wickedness? In Sodom and Gomorrah no doubt all were not drunkards and whoremasters. Some were civil and did abstain from this filthiness. Yet because they hated not these sins but approved the doers of them, nothing disliking their filthy behavior, as Lot did, whose righteous heart was vexed at their wickedness, behold God destroys them all alike; and Paul makes him to be a covetous man that favors and gives consent to the doings of a covetous man.

Worldl. How if I should have sold my corn cheap all this year, and nobody else, what good would this have done?

Christ. You should have done great good. For in regard of yourself, you should not have been guilty of the great oppression of this land, and your doings would have condemned the devilish practices of other men, and it might have pleased God by your example to have moved other men to deal more charitably in their bargaining. And the Scripture is plain that the good works and Christian conversation of any man "shining as lights before the eyes of the world, make many men to glorify God's name."

Worldl. You say like an honest man. And I am persuaded, if you will speak your conscience, you that have spoken so much against us cannot but speak something

---

1. *Carle*: a man of the common people; particular a countryman or a husbandman.

in our behalf. You see everywhere what enclosing there is, and you cannot be ignorant that gentlemen and landlords, they have large consciences. They make nothing of it to take great sins and to double and treble their rents. Now if the poor tenants shall not be suffered to sell their corn of a dearer price, how shall they be able to live? How shall they pay their fines and their yearly rents? I tell you plainly, if this may not be suffered, we shall have beggars enough within this land. Yea, even they which are not substantial men will shortly come to vile beggary.

Christ. Indeed I doubt not but these takers of rents and these inclosers, they are unmerciful men. Surely they eat the bread of oppression, and the very stones in the walks and the beams of their fair buildings cry to God for vengeance against them. But what then? They deal unjustly with you; they rob you. Will you deal therefore unjustly and rob others? It is very like that God does use them as means to chastise you, to make you know yourselves, to know God, and to depend upon His providence. You must not therefore in any wise use unlawful means to avoid this cross which God lays upon you by these wealthy oppressors, but rather you are to bear it with patience until such time as God shall deliver you, praying to God (if it be His will) to soften the hearts of these hard-hearted men, who regard nothing but their own pleasure and case.

Worldl. Yea, we should do so indeed. But who are they which do so? I would fain see you do so.

Christ. This is the manner of you all. You think these be dreams which I speak of, and that no man ever did them. But it is a most infallible truth that all they whoever have received the Spirit of God, their minds are so enlightened, their hearts and affections so reformed and brought in order that they cannot but do these things. But you are a worldly, carnal man; you can shift in the world and make a bargain for your own advantage. But as for the will of God in His Word and the performance of it, it seems foolishness to you. You know not the meaning and the reason of it. To let this pass, I marvel why you dare travel abroad from your own house. You seem to be sick and very low brought with sickness, and in my judgment you hazard your life. You do not well; you have small care of yourself.

Worldl. I am brought low indeed, but (I thank God) I have no sickness that I can tell of.

Christ. What is the matter then I pray you, if a man may be so bold as to enquire of you?

Worldl. As I told you, I have great store of corn, and I hoped to have enriched myself by it. Well, on the sudden, the price of corn fell very much. I tell you, it struck me to the heart, and it made me at my wits' end. If I had not been a strong-hearted man and born out my grief, I had not been here now. For when I saw I should have a great loss and almost [be] undone, I had thought to have make away myself;[2] but I hope I shall bear it out now, and because there is no other remedy I am content. Truly, the world is come to that pass; it will not last always.

Christ. You in your talk do verify the saying of St. Paul: "That they that will be rich, do fall into temptations and snares, and into many foolish and noisome lusts, which draw men into perdition and destruction." And he adds, "That the desire of money is the root of all evil, which while some lusted after, they erred from the faith, and pierced themselves through with many sorrows"—all which you have done.

Worldl. But I am in better case now than I have been, and I comfort myself as well as I can. For I see there is no remedy, and I shall not be always in this misery, for the world will last but a while.

Christ. These are silly comforts indeed. You should rather cut off this vice of covetousness, and then you might have found comfort. But how comes this into your mind, that the world cannot last long?

Worldl. How? Why I am sure you know as much as I. They say everywhere that the next year eighty-eight,[3] Doomsday will be.

Christ. They are lying tales.

Worldl. Nay, I promise you. I have some skill, and I have read books of it that are printed; and talk goes that there be old prophecies of this year found in old stone walls.

Christ. I tell you plainly, they are very lies.

Worldl. It seems that you have skill this way. We have yet a good way to go before we come to our journey's end. I pray you let me hear your judgment of it. And what do you say to these verses, which every man has in his mouth:

> *When after Christ's birth there be expired,*
> *Of hundreds fifteen, years eighty-eight,*
> *Then comes the time of dangers to be feared,*
> *And all mankind with dolors it shall fright.*
> *For if the world in that year do not fall,*
> *If sea and land then perish, no decay.*

---

2. *Make away myself*: commit suicide.
3. *Eighty-eight*: 1588.

> *Yet Empires all, and Kingdom alter shall,*
> *And man to ease himself shall have no way.*

Christ. For my part, I make as little account of these verses as of the Merlin's drunken prophecies or the tales of Robin Hood. They import thus much in effect: that either the end of the world shall be the next year; or if the end of the world be not then, yet that there will be great troubles and subversions of kingdoms in the world. And for the satisfying of your desire, I will show you my judgment between you and me: first, of the end of the world; secondly, of the troubles which (as men suppose) shall befall us this next year.

Worldl. I pray you then, what is your judgment of the end of the world? Shall it not be this next year?

Christ. My judgment is this: that it is not possible for any to find out the time of the end of the world; and if it were possible to appoint that time, yet it were not lawful.

Worldl. Everybody thinks that to learned men it is both possible and lawful; for my part I cannot tell, I would be glad to learn, and until I hear what you say, I will say as most do say.

Christ. That we may speak of this point in some order, first, let us consider whether it be possible by any means to set down the end of the world; and for a ground of all that I shall speak hereafter, this I will propound as a principle: that no man can define or truly conjecture, the hour, the day, the week, the month, the year, or the age in which the end of the world shall be.

Worldl. I think not so; how can you prove it by any good reason?

Christ. The Word of God is the ground of this my assertion. In a vision Daniel sees one angel asking another angel clothed in linen when should be the end of the miseries and troubles of the church. The answer was that it would be after a time, two times, and a half a time. Now mark the words of Daniel: "Then I heard it," says he, "but I understood it not: and then I said: O my Lord, what shall be the end of these things? And he said, Go thy way Daniel: for the words are closed up and sealed til the end of the time" (Dan. 12:5, 8, 9). If Daniel could not tell the time, and when an answer was made concerning the end could not understand it, what means can any man living use to conjecture at the day or the year or at the hundred year in which the world shall end? Again, when the disciples of our Savior Christ asked Him whether He would at His ascension restore the kingdom to Israel, this answer was given them: "It is not for you to know the times and seasons, which the Father has put in His own power." Which answer makes very much for me. For it proves also that the special times in which the end of the world shall happen are unknown to man and hidden from him. God keeps them to Himself. And in the apocalypse, the souls of them that were killed for the word of God, longing for a full deliverance, cry with a loud voice, "How long Lord, holy and true?" In the answer which they receive from the Lamb, there is no special time mentioned of their deliverance; but it is told them that after a little season when their fellow servants and brethren shall be killed as they were, that then they shall see the end. In my judgment, these proofs are sufficient to continue that I said before.

Worldl. For my part I have no skill in the Scriptures as you have; you may soon deceive me. But if this be true which you say, then belike all the prophecies which go of the end of the world are false.

Christ. All prophecies are not of God and from His Spirit. Many are from the fantasies of wicked men and from the suggestion of the devil.

Worldl. I pray you therefore show me how I may discern of prophecies whether to be from God or the devil, and so which ought to be regarded as true or despised as false.

Christ. I will to my power do what I can to satisfy your request, and here I will set down certain notes by which you or any man else may discern of any prophecies. First, if the prophet be insufficient, it is a strong suspicion that he is not of God; but it argues that his prophecies come from some other cause. The sufficiency or insufficiency of a prophet may be perceived by these marks:

(1) If he maintain heresies and does not embrace the Christian religion.

(2) If his judgment be rash and inconsistent in other matters.

(3) If he be given to [?][4] as covetousness, or pride, for then he may be suspected, that he speaks by his prophecies to win either some gain or some glory to himself.

(4) If his complexion and the temperature of his body be strange, for then he may be thought to have some disease which hinders the reasonable part. He may have the weakness of the brain, the frenzy, or some such like. And it is certain that in all such Satan has great power and does trouble them with dreams and visions and many strong fantasies and terrors of mind.

(5) If he despise other men's judgments and counsels and sticks to his own opinion. Paul, which was rapt up in the third heaven and saw strange visions, was for all that most humble (2 Cor. 12:2).

(6) Lastly, if the prophet be a young man, not an old; if a woman, and not a man; if babbling and talkative, not silent with wisdom; if unruly and

---

4. The text is illegible.

disordered, not quiet—suspicion may be gathered that the prophecy is an illusion of Satan. For in the weaker sort he most prevails.

Secondly, if it be against the Word of God or any circumstance of it; and if it reveal that particularly which the Word of God foretells in general manner, not laying down the place, the time, the persons, the manner of doing it, it may be taken for a false prophecy.

Thirdly, if the prophecy be uttered in ambiguous words or in speeches which are insolent and strange, not understood of them which hear them and never used in the Scriptures or of the church, it is like to be some sleight. For the Spirit of God speaks plainly; and if it utter things which are not to be known mystically, yet evermore it speaks like itself, as appears in the prophecies of the Old and New Testament.

Fourthly, if the end of the prophecy be God's glory and the profit of God's church, it is to be regarded; but if this be the drift of it, to put some men into a foolish fear, to make disquietness in the church and commonwealth; if it be a platform to bring some to promotion, it is not to be regarded. For example, this is a lying prophecy: "Canterbury was, London is, and York shall be." This prophecy, if men will regard it, tends to strife, contention, and sedition; and it may be a means of wicked attempts, if hereafter time and place do serve: the devil oftentimes sows his seed a long time before he can have it grown up.

Fifthly, if it concerns some private men and some private family. It is to be supposed that the prophecies which come from God's Spirit are commonly general and tend to the profit of the whole church.

If it be false in any one little point or in any circumstance, account it of not value. For those prophecies which are of God are in no jot false; for God is truth itself.

By these notes and many other, we may judge of the prophecies of Merlin, of the prophecies of those that term themselves Elias, of Anabaptistical revelations, of dreams of these lying tales of the second coming of Christ.

Worldl. I know more now than ever I knew in all my life. And I promise you for this I will not believe prophecies which I shall hear, but as well as I can, I will rule them out. But in the meantime, let me hear of your judgment of some special prophecies which concern Doomsday. What say you to Elias's prophecy: *Two thousand vaine, two thousand the Law, two thousand Christ. And for our sins which are many and marvelous, some years which are wanting shall not be expired.*

Christ. Some men there are which make great account of this prophecy, but in truth it is not to be regarded. And if we shall examine it by the former notes, it will appear to be but a foolish prophecy.

First, who is the author of this prophecy? Not Elias the Tishbite, whose history we read in the Old Testament; but a fond Jew of the same name, and the words of the prophecy are found nowhere in the Jewish Talmud.

Secondly, it is against the Word of God. From the beginning of the world to the publishing of the Law were two thousand years, says Elias; 2513, says the Scripture. From the giving of the Law to the passion of our Savior Christ were only 1542 years, says the Scripture. Now seeing two parts of this prophecy are against the chronology which is laid down in the Word of God, why should I believe that Elias says the truth in the third part, which is not yet fulfilled?

Thirdly, this prophecy is a plain viper. It eats out the guts of the Jews' Talmud, and confuses them for saying that Christ is not yet come. For Elias makes but four thousand years from the beginning of the world to the death of Christ; and now almost six thousand years are past since the beginning of the world. So that the Jews, if they will maintain their prophecy, they must grant that Christ is already come, which they deny.

Worldl. You speak too far against this prophecy. Some learned men do say that it is agreeable to the Word of God. For in the fourth [chapter] of Esdras, whereas Esdras demandeth of Vriel the Angel whether the time past be greater than the time to come, the angel does answer by two similitudes and does show to him a burning furnace and afterward a watery cloud, and said, "Mark whether the fire do overcome the smoke, and the shower the drops, or otherwise." To whom Esdras says, "I see, Lord, that a very great smoke does pass away. I see also a very great shower to come pouring down. But afterward I perceive the flame to overcome the smoke, and the drops the shower." Then says the angel, "Now judge of the continuance of the world. Even as the first smoke vanquishes the fire, and the drops the shower, so the years of the time past shall exceed the time which is to come." But now according to the computation of years it is evident that Esdras lived about the third thousand and five hundred years after the world's creation, and awhile after Cyrus's death, from which time about two thousand years are confirmed. Wherefore we do see that this prophecy does marvelously agree with that of Elias, and the end of the world to be nigh at hand.

Christ. I perceive that you have read some books of the matter; but doubtless your reason is of no force. For that book is not canonical, and the place which you allege may be otherwise answered. For the angel by his similitudes does not so much compare the time past with the time to come, as the estate and infidelity of the time to come. For as the smoke vanquishes the fire, and the drops the flower, so shall, says the Angel to Esdras, the wickedness of the time to come be increased more than you have seen now or have heard in times past. And this is that which the Angel principally meaneth in his answer to Esdras.

Worldl. Let us go on further in this point. What say you to the prophecy of the poet Orpheus? I cannot say his words, but the meaning is this: that in the sixth age or sixth thousand year God shall destroy the world.

Christ. You say true; I remember such a thing indeed, alleged by the ancient philosopher Plato. But if the prophecy of Elias is not to be regarded (as in truth it is not), who is so mad as to give any heed to the saying of a fumbling poet? But leave your prophecies; let us hear what can you say else? For it seems that you have read some books of the second coming of Christ.

Worldl. I remember such a reason as this, drawn from the creation. God was six days in making the heaven and the earth, and He rested the seventh day. Now every day is a thousand years, as St. Peter says. Therefore, about six thousand years the end of the world shall be.

Christ. You do abuse the place of Scripture which is in St. Peter. For his meaning is this: that the greatest time and the smallest differ not in respect of God, to whom all times are present. And if your reason were good, I will make another as good sort of the same place against you, after this manner: St. Peter, which says that one day is a thousand years, says also in the same place that a thousand years are but as one day. Out of which words I frame my reason thus: a thousand years are but as one day; the world shall last six thousand years, as you say; therefore, the world shall last but six days. Moreover, your own reason may be retorted against you, thus: you think that the end shall be of all things, this next year [15]88. But as God was six days in creating the world, and He did not rest in the sixth day, but in the seventh, so in like manner (if the six days of the creation resemble the six thousand years of the continuance of the world, as you suppose) the end of the world cannot be before the sixth thousand year be expired—as the rest was not before the sixth day of the creation was expired. And so neither you nor any other have any cause to fear the year next ensuing.

Worldl. You are too subtle for me; I have not been at the university, as you have been, though I travel that way now. But because you are so friendly in talk, I will be bold with you a little more yet. Are not these times in which we live called the last hour and the last times? I know you will grant it; for the Scripture says that our Savior Christ was once offered in the end of the world; and St. Peter says that Christ was made manifest in the last times. And if then were the last times when our Savior did suffer, the end of the world must be looked for every hour.

Christ. You must understand that the whole time of the continuance of the world is divided into the old time, which continues from the beginning of the world to the coming of Christ, and into the latter days or last hour, which is the whole space of time from the coming of Christ to the end of the world—as may appear in the Epistle to the Hebrews. So then your reason proves nothing. For these may be the latter days still and the last hour, and the world may for all that continue on a hundred years or two hundred years longer, for anything we know. Is not the coming of our Savior Christ compared to the coming of a thief, for this cause: that as no man is able truly to conjecture the coming of a thief before he begin to break into the house, so no man can truly conjecture the coming of Christ before he see Him in the clouds; and then he may certainly determine that the end of the world is present.

Worldl. All the signs of the coming of Christ are past. Oh, what earthquakes have there been? What famine? What wars and hurly-burlies[5] among men? What signs in the sun and moon? What flashing the air? What blazing stars? Surely, surely, the world cannot last long. There is some cause that so many men so long ago have spoken of these times, and especially of the next year. I see you do not fear, but I promise you I am afraid.

Christ. Some men these be that think that all the signs of the coming of our Savior Christ are past. And what if they be past, as you say—what then? Must of necessity the end immediately follow them? What should hinder that the coming of Christ should not be two or three hundred years after the signs which signify His coming? You have nothing to show but your own imaginations. But now if the signs of Christ's coming be not all past, what will you say then? Assuredly, very godly and learned men are of this mind.

Worldl. I pray you, show me how all the signs are not yet fulfilled which go before the end of the world.

Christ. According to that measure of knowledge which God has given me, I will do my endeavor to show this point to you. The signs of the coming of Christ are of two sorts; for either they go with the coming of Christ or before it. Of the first sort speaks our Savior Christ in the Gospel of St. Luke, saying: "Then there will be signs in the sun and moon, and in the stars, and upon the earth trouble among the nations, with perplexity: the sea and the waters shall roar"—all these signs shall be fulfilled at the very coming of Christ, "when as the heavens shall pass away with a noise, and the elements shall melt with heat, and the earth with the works that are therein shall be burnt up." The other sort of signs that go before our Savior's coming are very many:

(1) The first sign is the preaching of the gospel, as Christ says. And this gospel of the kingdom shall be preached throughout the whole world for a witness

---

5. *Hurly-burly*: turmoil, uproar, confusion, and strife.

to all nations, and then shall the end come; and this sign is every day more and more accomplished.

(2) The second is the spreading abroad of errors, heresies, and schisms—as St. Paul says, "That in the last days some shall depart from the faith, and give heed to spirits of errors, and doctrines of devils"; and our Savior Christ says, "That many false prophets shall come, and if it were possible, even to deceive the elect." We and our ancestors have seen this sign fulfilled.

(3) The third is a general security of men in every calling and in every place. Which now is evident—when was there ever more atheism? More contempt of God's holy ministry? More shameless hypocrisy, than is in these times in which we now live?

(4) The fourth sign is the apostasy and the revealing of antichrist, which now is known of all men to be the pope, and his church. And they themselves, if they were not past shame, would grant that the second beast coming forth of the earth, having the lamb's horns, but the dragon's mouth—they (I say) would grant that this beast should be the pope, their father.

(5) The fifth sign is the afflictions and miseries of the world by earthquakes, wars, pestilence, famine, and such like.

(6) The sixth sign is the conversion of the Jews to that religion which now they hate, as appears in the eleventh [chapter] to the Romans; and this sign which goes immediately before the coming of Christ to judgment is not yet fulfilled for anything I can tell. These only be the chief signs of which God's Word makes any mention. Of these, some are present, some are to come, so that for anything I can tell there is no cause why we should think that the end of the world should be the next year.

Worldl. I cannot tell whether all the signs of the coming of Christ be past or not; but sure I am that wonderful things are come to pass in these days, and the world is come to that pass of naughtiness, that it cannot last long.

Christ. That is your old song; but if the world be naughty, it is the worse by you that are so covetous. And if you think that the end of the world will be shortly, even the next year, what a mad man are you to be so covetous? Will you heap up riches which you know you shall never enjoy? And will you hoard up treasure for many years, when the world is not to continue one?

Worldl. Well, well, my covetousness is an eyesore to you; you are always harping upon it. Take no care; it shall never hurt you. You shall answer for yourself; you shall not answer for me. If you will not talk quietly with me in good neighborhood, I will hold my tongue.

Christ. I must needs admonish you of this vice which reigns in you. What if you should see a man cast into a water, swimming, and ready to be drowned. Would you not with all speed seek to save his life? And were it not a wicked part in him to be angry with you for your good will?

Worldl. Yes.

Christ. Your case is the very same. You are plunged over head and ears in this sin of covetousness. It presses down your soul to the bottom of hell, and by it you are in fearful danger of eternal death. It pities me to see you in this case. I would with all my heart do anything to bring you forth of danger. Yet for all my good will, thus I am rewarded.

Worldl. It is but your mind that I am in such danger of hellfire. I would be sorry if I had not a good heart to Godward; and I serve Him truly morning and evening, as well as God will give me grace. And if I were so bad a fellow as you would make me, good Lord! What a miserable case is the world in? For I do nothing but that which everybody does. I pray you heartily, let us go on in our former talk.

Christ. Well, go too, I will follow your humor. Say what you can.

Worldl. You reject all prophecies of the end of the world, and all other conjecture you account them as frivolous and not to be regarded. Yet the astronomers are men that are greatly learned and can tell many things which the world knows not. I think you dare say nothing against them.

Christ. Astronomers that take upon them to prognosticate of things to come are babblers, and there is no heed to be given to their sayings. There are many of them in this land that make a living by telling of fortunes and things that are lost and stolen; but in truth they are very thieves, and the good statutes that are made against cozeners[6] might better be urged against them than many others.

Worldl. Methinks you are very rash. Before ever I tell you what they say, you inveigh bitterly against them. They write that about [15]88, the end of the world shall be, or at the least great subversions of kingdoms, wars, confusions, etc.

Christ. In a word, they are all liars and deceivers. They are not able truly to conjecture these things, and I will show it you plainly. The Egyptians and Chaldeans of all other men were most given to the study of the stars, and never any were so skillful in that matter as they. Yet for all that, the Lord by the prophet Isaiah lays this in their teeth: that for all their skill yet they were not able to foretell their own destruction, which was at hand. "Where are now," said the prophet, "thy wise men, that they may tell thee, or may know what the Lord of hosts has determined against Egypt?" And to Babylon he says, "Thou art

---

6. *Cozener*: a deceiver, cheat, or imposter.

wearied in the multitude of thy councils; let now the astrologers, the star-gazers, and prognosticators stand up, and save thee from these things that shall come upon thee: behold, they shall be as stubble: the fire shall burn thee, they shall not deliver their own lives from the power of the flame: there shall be no coals to warm at, nor light to sit by: thus are they with whom thou hast wearied thyself, even thy merchants that have been with thee from thy youth: everyone shall wander in his own quarter: none shall save thee."

Worldl. The prophet in these places speaks against the unskillful, not against the art of astronomy.

Christ. Yea, if you mark and consider the places well, you shall find they are against the art itself and against the most wise and skilful in all Egypt and Chaldea. The Spirit of God here confuses their arrogance and threatens revenge on them, for that they profess to foreshow those things which God has hid in His secret council and cannot be perceived by the stars.

Worldl. Do you think that God would make the heavens and the stars in them for no end? No doubt God has made them for some great use.

Christ. The beautiful frame of the heavens was created for man's use and profit, as to be signs of the ordinary and natural course of all things in the world, as of the time of sowing corn, of reaping, of planting, chopping, etc. Again, they have this use: to distinguish and to make the season of winter, summer, spring, harvest. They make day and night, and the natural course of years is by them. In a word, they are made even as a hen to foster and cherish the creatures here below, and therefore do give heat and cause rain and moisture in the season of the year. As the prophet David says, nothing is hid from the heat of the sun. And the prophet Hosea says, "And in that day, I will hear, saith the Lord, I will hear the heavens, and they shall hear the earth, and the earth shall hear the corn, and the wine, and the oil, and they shall hear Israel." Now God did not make the stars to be means of foretelling things to come, and that men should learn of the them good and evil success: They that reserve the stars to this end abuse the stars and break the third commandment by taking God's name in vain. And therefore God threatens them by His prophet Isaiah that make signs of things to come in the heavens, and says, "I destroy the tokens of the soothsayers, and make them that conjecture, fools, and turn the wise men backward, and make their knowledge foolishness." And to think that by the stars and their course a man may conjecture the end of the world is foolishness, or rather madness. For either the stars must be the cause of the end of the world, or bare signs. Causes they cannot be; for this is a property in nature that everything labours to preserve itself. And therefore it is not like that by the heavens shall be caused the end of the world, for then they should be causes of their own ruin. And again, the course of the stars cannot be a token or sign of the end. Dionysius Areopagite, when he saw the sun to be eclipsed at the full moon, being sore afraid, said, "That either the end of the world was then, or that the God of nature did suffer." And no marvel, for the extraordinary eclipse of the sun was a sign of some strange wonder. But that the natural and ordinary course of the stars in the heavens should signify strange and extraordinary things (such as are subversion of kingdoms and the end of the world), that by no reason can be showed. And yet this is that which astronomers maintain and take as granted. Again, the power and virtue and the operation of the stars is unknown to man; and if it were known, yet by the stars no man could gather what was to come, which I will show you by this similitude. Suppose twenty eggs of twenty divers birds set under one hen. Let her sit on them all and communicate her heat to them all. Can you or any other, by knowing the properties of the hen and by feeling of her heat, tell me of every egg what chickens she will hatch? Whether crows or partridges, or what other fowl? And can you tell by the same means when the hen shall die?

Worldl. I tell you, my wife hatches many chickens in the year, but this passes all my skill and hers too.

Christ. Very well. The heavens are as a hen, fostering and cherishing these earthly things under them; and you cannot by the virtues of the stars, if you knew them never so well, you cannot (I say) conjecture either the event of things upon earth or the dissolution of the world, except you could therewithal know the secret purpose of God and the particular causes of every particular thing.

Worldl. You show me your mind plainly, and methinks it should be true you say. But everywhere there is great talk of conjunctions of planets, and you would wonder to see how simple men (such as I am) listen after such things. And some men have been ready to sell away all their goods for fear of conjunctions. I pray you, is there no such things? And if there be such things, what are they?

Christ. Indeed, astronomers have written of strange conjunctions; and among others, one Cyprianus Leovitius, a Bohemian. And because you are so earnest on me in this point, I will repeat some of his words. In the year of our Lord (says he) 1583, in the month of May, there shall happen a great conjunction of planets in the last end of Pisces, after which straightway in the year '84 shall ensue a wonderful mixture of all the planets in Taurus about the end of March and beginning of April. And which is more, a little after that shall be seen an eclipse of the sun in the twenty degree of Taurus about the head of Algol, a most cruel and hurtful fixed star, governed by Venus, which shall be linked to five planets in Aries, tending toward the twelfth degree. Here we must watch (says he), and I think it meet that all earthly cogitations be cast off, lest we be destroyed being unready. For this great conjunction is of all the last which shall happen in the end of the watery Trigon, and the watery Trigon shall have an end and be turned into the fiery Trigon. Neither shall there be any more in the space of eight hundred years; the end of the watery Trigon shall be nigh. But because about the end of the watery Trigon this Monarchy did begin, it is likely that the same also in the end of the same Trigon shall have an end—[when] sit[s] the Son of God Himself, Jesus Christ our Lord, even in the end of the watery Trigon, [who] took upon Him the nature of man. For six years before His most glorious nativity, the very same conjunction in the end of Pisces and in the beginning of Aries happened. Neither came the like since that time, but when Charles the Great held his empire, which was in the year of our Lord 789; and now the second time such a strange and great conjunction shall come, which undoubtedly does foreshow the other coming of the Son of God and Man in majesty of His glory, at which time we must render an account of life and conversation.

Worldl. I remember that I have read these words in an English book of the second coming of Christ, and I would desire your judgment of them. It seems that the man which wrote these words was deeply learned in astronomy.

Christ. You shall hear as much as I am able to tell you, and I can say somewhat because I have labored in these matters. First therefore, know thus much, that this Leovitius does not truly account the motions of the stars, but is fairly deceived, as by the most exact tables of Erasmus, Reinholdus, and Stadius may appear. And whereas he says that in the year of our Lord 1583 in the month of May there shall happen a great conjunction of the superior planets in the end of Pisces, in truth there is no such thing. For Jupiter and Saturn are almost three degrees asunder, when they are both in the end of Pisces in May; but in April, the month going before, they are in conjunction. And what strange thing can this be which has happened so often since the beginning? To wit, every 140 years, once in the same Trigon (as they say). As for that he says, that in the year 1584 there shall be a mixture of all the planets in Taurus about the end of March, there is no such thing; but in the beginning of April, Saturn and Mars are in conjunction, and then Jupiter is about twelve degrees distant from them. Other mixture of planets to be regarded, I see none. Messahala makes the greatest conjunction of planets to be when the three superior planets are joined all together in Aries, which shall not be either in the year '83 or '84. But be it that there had been then such strange conjunctions of the planets, as Leovitius speaks of—what then? What should follow? Forsooth the end of the world. And why should this be, considering that all these conjunctions are natural and come of the natural and ordinary motions of the heavens? And there have been since the beginning of the world 270 conjunctions of the superior planets Mars, Jupiter, and Saturn. Heretofore they have portended no such dangers, as the effects declare; but there is no remedy, now they must needs signify ruins of kingdoms and the end of the world. Leovitius will have it so, for he speaks very confidently as from an oracle. No doubt (says he) this great and strange conjunction does foreshow the other coming of the Son of God and Man in majesty of His glory. But no doubt God will destroy the signs and confound the fantasies of these men, as hitherto in all ages has been seen. Albumazar, he prophesied that in the year of our Lord 1460 an end shall be made of Christian religion, and yet even then the gospel began most of all to flourish. And a Jew prophesied that in the year 1364 Messiah should come, who should deliver the rest of His own nation out of servitude under the Christians. How true this is, let they themselves judge.

Worldl. You are too sore an enemy to astronomers. You are now near the university; if you were there, you durst not say so much. He is a wise man indeed that is never deceived; and these men though they are deceived sometime, yet they often tell the very truth.

Christ. That is nothing; for it is no marvel, if a man unskillful in shooting, often hit the mark, if he continue in shooting. But I would have these prophetical astronomers show a reason why the great conjunction of planets foreshow the end of the world. Belike they will say that they know it to be so. If they know it, then their knowledge comes either by experience or without any experience. If they say that they know it without experience, then truly they deceive us; for all good knowledge in human learning is builded upon experience. If they know it by experience, then they must needs have observed this, that the destruction of the world has followed such conjunctions. If they have seen this, then they were either in the world or forth of the world. If they were in the world, how did they escape when the world was destroyed? If they were forth of the world, where stood they? But I will here cease to speak of astronomers, leaving to them their vanities until such time as it shall please God to make them acknowledge them and loathe them as the Ephesians did, who being given not to wicked and devilish arts but to such vain and frivolous conceits as these of the astronomers are, after that they were won to the religion of Christ, brought their curious books and openly burned them. And I would have you that are an ignorant man to remember the saying of the prophet Jeremiah: "Be not afraid of the signs of heaven, though the heathen be afraid of such: for the customs of the people are vain."

Worldl. I have heard you hitherto, showing that no man by any probable conjecture can tell the special time of the end of the world. Now show me that it is not lawful for any to search out the end of the world.

Christ. Indeed, I think it is not lawful to be curious to search out the time in which the end shall be. It is a thing in which Christians are not to meddle. For it is the will of God that this should not be known. Therefore, whoever searches this time does against the will of God. To this purpose it is said in the Acts, "It is not for you to know the times and season." Moreover, God has kept the knowledge of this secret to Himself; and neither the angels nor Christ as He is man knows this time. Wherefore, it shall be pride and vanity in man to occupy himself in searching it out. (3) Lastly, the apostles and Daniel the prophet, when they were curious and desired to know the end and asked this question, "When shall these times be?" they had the repulse and never received any answer—which declares that none ought curiously to enquire of that time.

Worldl. But why is it not the will of God that this time should be known?

Christ. The same cause that moved God to conceal from us the hour of death, the same also made Him hide from us the hour and time of His coming—to wit, that we might always watch and pray and have our loins girt round about us and our lamps in our hands burning, as though we every hour did wait for the coming of Christ. And this is the reason which our Savior Christ uses. For after He had showed the uncertainty of the time of His coming, and yet that His coming was most certain and very sudden, He adds an exhortation, saying: "Watch therefore, because you know not when the Son of man will come" (Matt. 14:41). And indeed because the time is unknown, it stirs us up to perpetual watchfulness. The master of a family, if he knew the hour in which the thief would come, he would watch only the same hour; but because he knows that he will come and is uncertain of the hour in which he will come, therefore he watches the whole night throughout.

Worldl. I thank you sir heartily, for that you have showed me your opinion so willingly and so courteously of the end of the world. But yet I would make bold with you a little more in this matter. I often come among my neighbors, and now and then we talk of these matters; and every man will have his own saying, and peradventure we are all deceived. You say it is neither possible nor lawful to search the coming of Christ by any means. How then may a man frame his talk wisely and speak the truth in these matters?

Christ. It is a good question you demand, and I will be careful to make you an answer. Therefore, when you speak with any man of the end of the world, frame your talk after this manner.

(1) That the end of the world is most certain.

(2) That the time of the end of the world is uncertain to man, and that he must not be curious in this matter.

(3) That God would have this time to be unknown that men might live in the fear of His name and not defer their repentance.

(4) That every man must long to see this day in which an end shall be made of sin and wickedness.

(5) That God may come sooner to judgment than we are aware of or the world does imagine, as the parable of the wicked servant shows.

(6) That if God seem to defer His coming, it is that by His longsuffering He might bring us to repentance.

(7) That though God will not end the world, yet He may every moment cut off the life of man. If you shall speak of any of these points, you cannot speak amiss.

Worldl. Surely my memory is naught, and now you do me pleasure in that you tell me your whole mind so briefly and plainly. I pray you, let me make bold to confer with you of the other part of the prophecy, which is that if the end of the world be not this next year, yet there shall be great troubles and subversion of kingdoms. If I knew your opinion of this, I would cease to trouble you.

Christ. Not to make long discourses, my opinion is this: that there must be great troubles in the world, but they are not to be looked for more in the year [15]88 than any other year. And this I will briefly declare to you, and then we will end this matter.

Worldl. Show me first of all that there shall be many troubles in the world, for I would very fain know that.

Christ. Doubtless the reasons of this thing are most evident. First, God's Word threatens plagues and punishments to the disobedient and the transgressors of His commandments. If (says Moses) you will not obey the voice of the Lord your God to keep and do all His commandments which I command you this day, then all these curses shall come upon you and overtake you. Cursed shall you be in the town, and cursed in the field, etc. The Lord shall send upon you cursing, trouble, and shame in all that which you set your hand to do until you be destroyed and perish quickly, etc. And the Lord shall make the pestilence to cleave to you, until He has consumed you forth of the land, whither you go to possess it. The Lord shall smite you with a consumption and with the fever and with a burning ague and with fervent heat, and with the sword and with blasting and mildew. The heaven that is over your head shall be brass, and the earth that is under you, iron. The Lord shall give you for the rain of your land dust and fleas, even from heaven shall it come upon you, till you be destroyed. And the Lord shall cause you to fall before your enemies, etc. Also, Amos the prophet speaks thus: "Behold the eyes of the Lord are upon the sinful nation, and I will destroy it clean out of the earth: nevertheless I will not utterly destroy the bones of Jacob, saith the Lord." And in the third chapter, he speaks of the house of Israel, thus: "They know not to do right (saith the Lord) they stir up violence and robbery in their palaces: therefore thus saith the Lord God, An adversary shall come even round about the country, and shall bring down the strength from thee, and thy palaces shall be spoiled." And the prophet Isaiah pronounces a fearful curse against Israel for her sins: "Behold," says he, "the Lord maketh the earth empty, and he maketh it waste: he turneth it upside down, and scattereth abroad," etc. Well, to the purpose, these are the times in which even through all nations sin and wickedness most abounds. These last times are compared to the days of Noah and of Lot, in which there was nothing but eating and drinking and marrying and building, and a general security possesses all men's hearts. And Paul speaks of these days thus: "This know also, that in the last days there shall come perilous times: for men shall be lovers of their own selves, covetous, boasters, proud, cursed speakers; disobedient to parents, unthankful, unholy, without natural affection, truce-breakers, false accusers, incontinent, fierce, despisers of them that are good, traitors, heady, high minded, lovers of pleasure more than lovers of God, having a show of godliness, but having denied the power thereof." Wherefore, seeing God threatens His curse to the disobedient, and we know that now the whole world is given to disobey God in outrageous manner, and atheism never more abounded—who cannot be a prophet and make this conclusion of these times that there must needs be plagues and punishments in the world and great troubles? For God is not changeable; but as He threateneth plagues to the disobedient, so His immutable justice will require the same.

(2) Secondly, because these are the last times, and Satan sees that he has but a short time to continue, therefore he bestirs himself; his desire is to bring confusions and to make havoc of all. It is a death to him to see God's kingdom to be advanced, the preaching of His word to have free passage, His name to be glorified in the congregation of His saints, the clouds of ignorance be dispelled, and men that have long sat in darkness and in the shadow of death now to walk in the true light and to warm themselves at the comfortable sunshine of His gospel. He does even as tenants do with their farms. When their leaves draw near an end, then they use to rack all things to the uttermost to make money of everything and to scrape to themselves by hook and by crook whatever they can, that afterward they may have wherewith to maintain themselves. Even so fares it with the devil. This is the last hour. Therefore, now he will play reaks everywhere; he ruffles it apace, as though he were wood. He stirs seditions, conspiracies, tumults, wars; and by all means with violence he labors to over-large his own kingdom.

(3) Thirdly, the church of God has always been subject to the cross, and none must marvel if it be. How can the world love them that hate it and have little acquaintance with it and are on the earth as pilgrims, waiting every day for happy passage through the troublesome sea of this life to their own home, even to the heavenly city of Jerusalem? And how can the prince of the world, Satan, love the faithful, that hates God? And how can he show favor to the members, that bitterly detests the head, Christ Jesus? And surely, it is the blessed will of God that His children shall welter and languish under afflictions, that they may learn to despise the world, to know themselves, to love God, to seek to Him, and to set their affections not on things on earth but on the things that are above. He lets the worldlings have their hearts' ease; He lets them feed themselves with the pleasures of this world and set themselves as oxen against the day of slaughter. With His own children He declares after another manner. He takes them as it were by the heels; He flings them into a sea of melting glass. There He lets them for a time to seethe and boil, and in great perplexity to shift for themselves. At length He drags them to the shore and gives them ease of their former miseries. And all this is for this end: to sanctify and purify them and to cleanse them of the filthy dross of sin and to make them with joy of heart to praise and magnify His name, for which end they came into this world. And experience teaches that as there is a perpetual intercourse between day and night, so there is in the church of God not any perpetual quietness, but trouble and quietness, affliction and ease do continually succeed one another. So that it is verified of the church: "Though sorrow come in the evening, yet joy shall be in morning." In the beginning, the church was in Adam's family. And albeit for a time they had prosperity, yet through the malice of Satan, Abel was slain, Adam's only child which feared God.

Before the flood, when giants were upon the earth, what misery was the church in? How was religion profaned? What corruption of manners was there, when the sons of God married with the daughters of them that came of wicked Cain? Though the Lord preserved Noah and his family, yet pitiful is it to see the dangers in which they were after this. Abraham's family, how was it now at rest, now in trouble? He being oppressed with famine was fain to go down into Egypt, and there he was in danger of his life when he deceived the king, saying of Sarah she was his sister. But afterward being very poor, he was made rich, and the land of Canaan was promised him, and he got the victory of five kings. The propagation of God's church was to be preserved in Isaac. And see now to what a straight it is brought. Isaac is bound and laid upon the altar; Abraham stretches forth his hand and takes the knife to kill his only son. Where is now the Messiah? Where is the promised seed? A man would have thought that God would here have made an end of His church, but this was to show what shall be the estate of the church, that though in mysteries to man's judgment it may seem to be destroyed, yet God will preserve it and govern it forever. This intercourse of quietness and afflictions may be seen in Jacob, in the children of Israel being in Egypt, in the wilderness, and in the land of Cannan. But to let pass other times, this thing is apparent: when the Israelites were governed by judges and kings, the Israelites for the space of eight years were in bondage under Chusan, king of Aram. By Othniel afterward they were restored to their liberty for the space of forty years. Again, after this eighteen years together they were in bondage under Eglon, king of Moab, and were given to filthy idolatry. After his decease, Ehud gave them rest for eighty years together. And so to the time of Samuel, they were otherwhiles in peace and otherwhiles in trouble. So it might be showed through all histories, even until this day. And therefore no doubt the churches of God at this time, if they enjoy peace, yet are they continually to look for troubles and afflictions and calamities in this world.

And as all churches must put this in their accounts that they cannot be free from the cross, so above all other must this our church of England. We have had long peace under our gracious Deborah, and no doubt in God's good time we must drink of the cup of afflictions. The prophet Amos says, "Will a lion roar in the forest when he has no prey? Or will a Lion's whelp cry out of his den, if he have taken nothing? And again, will the fowler take up the snare from the earth, and have taken nothing at all? Or shall a trumpet be blown in the city, and the people not be afraid?" Manifold and great are the dangers which our prince has escaped; many assaults have been made against our country. It has been in great peril by enemies at home and enemies abroad; a lingering famine has a long time afflicted us. What are all these things, and many more, but the roaring of the lion forth of the forest? And the sounding of the trumpet? These things are no doubt forerunners of greater judgments, and except we in England with speed repent, the roaring of the lion will not be in vain. Assuredly the lion will have his prey. And thus much shall suffice to declare this point, that in these days we must look for manifold afflictions in every country and kingdom.

Worldl. It is well said of you, I can you thank. I promise you, I think a man cannot speak a truer word than this that you have said; for the world is everywhere so bad, that scarce there can be any quietness or good fellowship among men. Well, I am satisfied for this matter, but one thing I will ask you: do you think that there is no more danger to be feared the next year than any other year?

Christ. As I said, so I now say again: that afflictions, hurly-burlies, subversions of kingdoms are no more to be feared this next year than any other year.

Worldl. What reason moves you to say so?

Christ. This moves me to think so: because I can find no cause of the troubles of this year more than of any other year.

Worldl. Nay, there you are deceived. The strange conjunctions of planets will show their operation this next year. And though you will not grant that they are signs of the end of the world, yet you will confess that they are the causes of plague, pestilence, famine, wars, subversions of kingdoms, and such like; and by this means wise men have prophesied before of this year.

Christ. Your speech is full of impiety. For to divine of things to come belongs to God alone, and none must be so bold as to challenge this to himself—as the prophet Isaiah shows: "Stand to your cause (saith the Lord) bring forth your strong reasons, saith the king of Jacob, let them bring forth, and let them tell us what is to come: let them show the former things what they be, that we may confuse them, and know the latter end of them: either declare us things for to come." Also, it is a wicked part to attribute wars and alterations of kingdoms to the stars, which only belongs to God. And Daniel says, "God, he changeth times and seasons: he taketh away kings, he setteth up kings," etc. And to make wars and peace is not from any conjunctions of the stars, except the ruling of man's heart may come from the stars, which nevertheless is proper to God—as Solomon says, "The heart of the king is in the hands of the Lord, as the rivers of waters, and he turneth it withersoever it pleaseth him." Furthermore, between the heavens and things below there is a great sympathy and consent; and the stars oftentimes make tempests, whirlwinds, drought, continual rain, and so they may be causes of some diseases, of scarcity, and of plenty. But we must account them only as instruments which God uses to bring to pass His council—and this not always, but only at some times. For example, when David was bidden to choose of three diverse things which he would suffer, he chose the plague. Now there is not any man (I think) that will attribute this plague to the stars. And the famine which was in Judea in the days of Elijah and the want of rain was not from any constellations. Nay, rather all these things befall us by reason of our sins, and our wickedness is the chief cause that provokes God to pour these punishments upon us, as that blessed martyr Master Hooper shows, whose words I will recite: The prognostications (says he) of these blind prophets, are good to be borne in a man's bosom, to know the day of the month. The rest of their practices is not worth a haw—as Moses teaches (Leviticus 26; Deuteronomy 28; Malachi 2), whereas you may see all these evils, and many more than the astronomers speak of come to us for sin and the transgression of God's commandments. It is neither sun nor moon, neither Jupiter nor Mars that is the occasion or matter of wealth or woe, plenty or scarcity, war or peace. Neither is pestilence caused by the putrefaction of the air (as Galen writes), but contempt of God's commandments is the cause, as you may read in the places before alleged. The air, the water, nor the earth have any poison in themselves to hurt their Lord and master man. But first man poisons himself with sin, and then God uses these elements ordained for the life of man to be the occasion of his death. Read the places and know that good health is numbered among the blessings of God and appertains to those that fear and keep God's commandments, and not to those that be destined to live long by the favor and aspects of planets. And the evil of whatever kind it be is the malediction of God against sin. The physicians say that the chiefest remedy against the pestilence is to flee from the place where the air is corrupt. God's law says, flee whither you will; the Lord shall make the pestilence cleave and associate you, till it confine you from the world. Again, in the same chapter, the disease or sickness shall be faithful—that is to say, stick fast to you, use what medicines you will. Galen says that the chief remedy to preserve from pestilence is to purge the body from superfluous humors, to have a free and liberal wind, and to avoid the abundance of meat and drink. God says, nothing preserves, but the keeping of His commandments. If we offend, the best remedy is repentance and amendment of life. It makes no force how corrupt the air may be, so the conscience of man be clean from sin. Though there die a thousand on the one side of you, and ten thousand on the other side, you shall be safe, etc. (Psalm 91). And now to make an end, I hope I have satisfied your mind concerning the year next ending [15]88, though I know I am not able to satisfy the learned, neither was it ever my purpose or my thought.

Worldl. Yea, sir, you have indeed. I thank you for it. I hope I shall be the better for your talk as long as I live. I warrant you I shall remember you when you think little on me. And because you are now come to Cambridge, if you will, I will bestow the courtesy of the town on you, even with all my heart.

Christ. I thank you heartily; but the best courtesy you can show to me is this: to relieve the poor, wherein you have been faulty.

Worldl. Alas man! What should we do? The world is hard. But I shall not forget you. Your sayings will make me do more than ever I had thought to have done. Well sir, if it do not please you to take the courtesy of the town at my hands, I will take my leave of you.

Christ. The Lord be with you, and with all them that fear His name. Amen.

F I N I S.

The Antidicson

of a Certain Man of Cambridge, Along with
a Short Treatise that Fully Explains Dickson's
Wicked System of Artificial Memory

Translated by David C. Noe

Printed at London by Henry Middleton, for J. Harison,
1584

To the most eminent London gentleman, Thomas Moufet,
Distinguished Philosopher and Renowned Doctor of Medicine,
G.P. [William Perkins] sends his greetings.

The faculty of memory, my most eminent friend, is both sufficiently well known to you in its own right and such that I cannot render it more renowned by my literary effort. I will make only one remark: that if I should be able to discover something using wisdom and judiciously share and promulgate it, that same thing can scarcely be considered praiseworthy, unless I could hedge it round by the firm grasp of memory.

What then? How much illuminating power of instruction does so great a skill possess? How great and splendid a tool is this for the teaching of precepts? There are two skills: one which relies upon memory places and suggestive images; the other which sets forth individual and combined principles of instruction. This latter skill is called the dialectical arrangement. The contest for the basis of memory is fought with these skills. The first rushed ahead to gain control of that basis and has held it for a long time now—but held something hollow and blind, so to speak. This very skill, when attacked by many assaults and dislodged from its foundation, typically complains in this way: "The ability of polishing the memory is derived from nature. There is no natural intelligence so minuscule and slight which cannot be rendered brilliant when cared for by the effort of this skill. All the power of reason bestowed by nature is kindled and roused by the richness of this skill. Now by the recklessness of a number of men this power of reason has been dislodged from its proper domain, robbed of its wisdom, and all the regard it deserves has been drained away and transferred to another. Therefore, I ask that I might again take possession of my freedom, and that those showy and irresponsible writers on memory be driven back—namely, men like Metrodorus, Rosellius, Nolan, and Dickson. These men are the dangerous cliffs; they are the ravenous whirlpools in which the more refined knowledge of memory would have been completely swallowed unless it had clung to the firm resolve of the Ramean men as to a column."

When I had been roused by such pleas, I decided that I had been given an opportunity both to refute Dickson's foolishness and to bring to light the logical disposition of memory. For no matter where one turns in mind and thought, one will see that there exists no other teaching than this logical disposition by which the ability to call things to mind—which up to this point is still bitter and coarse—can be rendered more sweet and mild.

I have wanted, moreover, for these ruminations of mine on such topics to make their appearance fortified specially by your name. For you are so well known in the esteem of all that you easily beat back the Scepsians's[1] charge and the whole school of Dickson as it boils and breaks out against me. Because when word gets around that Muffet supports my position—a man whom Cambridge polished up with all learning, and Basel emblazoned with the greatest honors, and a man that London has proven to be the chosen flower of doctors—Dickson's men will not be so eager to steal a reputation for glory from their childish stupidities. And so, I especially pray and beseech you to take my Antidicsonus into your safekeeping, though it be really quite amateurish, as though it were some work of Daedalus or one of Livy's fables which does not deserve frequent reading. Still, it belongs in that class of writings that can offer proof both of your love and of my respect.

When Dionysus had arrived at the shrine of Olympian Jupiter, he took off his golden garment and put on a woolen cloak. You, Dickson, in order that your practices might take on the aroma of antiquity, have become a kind of Dionysius. For you have tried to strip bare memory, the mistress and queen of very many virtues who resides in the citadel of the head, of all of her most elegant raiment of logical disposition. And you have tried to clothe her in your own smelly and worn-out undergarments. And I have both shown clearly before this that what I say is true, and your *Defense* can sufficiently demonstrate it. For your *Defense* only a few days ago flew out into the light, raised on typographical wings. There are two things especially which can give evidence of your bad faith in this matter: your silly attempt at refutation, and your excessive license in slandering.

Now your curses, which you were hoping would prove to be a great aid to your *Defense*, seem to be very damaging to you. For a defense which has been established as the truth ought to be gentle and patient and kind. For just as moderate speech and a calm soul typically offer a strong defense of the truth, so also harsh words and a disordered and boorish character take away somewhat from the renown of a true and just cause.

Now as for your *Defense*, what kind was it? It was inflamed, passionate, disturbed, driving, irritable, agitated, and shifting. And where is your pleasant

---

1. Dickson published his work under the pseudonym Heius Scepsius. The former is a Latin rendering of his mother's maiden name, and the latter is a reference to Metrodorus of Scepsis. Throughout the work Perkins refers to Dickson as Scepsius and his followers as Scepsians, since the pseudonym was an open secret. See Frances Yates, *The Art of Memory* (Chicago: University of Chicago Press, 1966), 266ff.

character? Where is your mind inclined toward amazing gentleness? Where is the sweet and moderate speech, graced with the fantastic smoothness of liberal learning? By Hercules, I have not even seen any trace of such praises in you! No, you seem so far from respecting the conventions of liberal learning that it looks like you have completely adopted the guise of hatred and personal vendetta.

But you are by nature meek and mild! And I am the one, no doubt, who has fought you with fire. I have advanced upon you with flaming words! Maybe so. Please, take me for someone who has been stubborn and much too unrestrained in his refutations. Nevertheless, it was your job to break apart my charges by a certain kind of patience, yours to soothe the tides with gentle speech and to urge me, who had such a tendency, toward a recognition of the truth. Finally, it was your job to lead me back toward the path if I were slipping and plunging into errors. But you yourself were never able to aspire to such praise for your learning. For though I desired to warn you in a friendly way and to be kind of an ointment on your sores, you pour out on me such powerful hatred and sharpen your pen for launching unrestrained attacks. Consequently, everyone thinks that your work contains neither a secret and hidden knowledge of memory nor even stylish and erudite words.

But there is something greater which betrays your cause, I mean your pointless attempt and the quite shallow outline of your reply. Those who want to consider something subtler first disprove and dissect the kinds of things that seem to stand opposed to you. Then they carefully seek after all the arguments by which the instruction of those men can be established. As often as your *Defense* has occurred to me, so many times I thought that it ought not to be refuted, but rather greatly pitied. What, good God, is so absolutely ridiculous as your childish ditties and lullabies? Is there anything so full of these kinds of completely invented opinions? What is as meager and threadbare as your cramped arguments? It was indeed quite inappropriate that a logician, stretching forth the light of his own genius and offering it to others, should either make no response or make a bad one in defending his own cause.

You should not have acted like Marc Antony does in Cicero: ignoring what produces trust, twisting your opponent's arguments to a meaning foreign to them, separating arguments that were joined in syllogisms, and finally at one point blatantly telling lies in print, in order to produce a more subtle argument. To be honest, this is why you should really be quite happy, Alexander: either your own nature or some luck gave you a tongue most suited to stirring up contention. Obviously, your poor little *Defense* would have quickly slipped away and fluttered off if you had not held onto it, locking it up and tying it down with strong bands of bad argument. And so, since we all realize that, who would not with good reason say, Dickson, that your memory theory is ridiculous? Has it not often been mocked by many people, when someone remembers how impoverished and meager your *Defense* is?

But that was, so to speak, just a light skirmish with small arms, a kind of first thrust of our main argument. Now I shall sprint toward you in the open arena and make my attack in order to drive back the horns of your disputation.[2] But since your argument was profligate in its trifling repetitions, I thought that their excessive extravagance should be countered by the shortness of my reply. And so I shall pass by that first really dignified element of your *Defense*, i.e. how you scorn and despise me. From me you shall hear no reply about the promises you have made or about my gross faults. I shall also say nothing about the books you wrote praising wisdom. For when it comes to what sort those will be, we can all guess from the outlines you previously released. I shall pass over all those instances in which the prejudice of a disgraceful argument could reside. I will take into account not only what you yourself ought to say, but also what would be proper for me in terms of my refutation. The reader, I hope will make allowance for and accommodate my modesty, so that I can remain silent with regard to your response which dealt with our hostile meeting and my lack of self-restraint. All that rubbish about the Stygian cook, about Stygian absurdities, the snare, the dogs, the hungry little dwarf—realize that I count these as over and done with. Let's have a truce, moreover, with regard to the question of whether the source of your skill is nature. Let there be no mention of the man of Scepsis, whose name you attach as a kind of shadow to the heat of your jealousy as it dissipates. Let's leave out the parade of the likes of Galland, Goveani, Turnèbe, Périon, Charpentier, and Gallonio.[3] Your *Defense* should take its teaching from the school of Cicero and Ramus, and should permit me to make this sizable omission from my refutations. In all these things I think you have thrown your spears very feebly. For you clearly feel that at the outset those men ought not to fight who take into consideration their own strength. Now because your arm has grown hot, and because you can seem to be stronger than

---

2. Although the reader may find this combination of metaphors surprising, Perkins has adapted quite faithfully an expression from Cicero, *Div.* 2.10.26.

3. These men are, respectively: Peter Galland, Regius Professor of Greek (*d.* 1559), said by Pierre Bayle to be an opponent of Peter Ramus; Antonius Goveanus (*c.* 1505–1562), celebrated Italian jurist; Adrien Turnèbe (1512–1565), a French philologist and teacher of Scaliger; Joachim Périon, French humanist and jurist (1499–1559), a Benedictine monk and opponent of Ramus; Jacques Charpentier (1521–1574); and Antonio Gallonio (1556–1605). This last is the only one of the persons Perkins mentions who is alive at the time of the writing of this treatise. This is a response to Dickson from page 6 of his treatise: *Qui cum adversus contumelias, doctorum quamlibet & eruditorum hominum, perpetuum tamen silentium iurarit: nihil Goveano, Gallandio, Perionio, Turnebo, Melanctoni responderit.* The same individuals minus Melanchthon are also given on page 19 of Dickson's *Defensio.* For some reason Perkins leaves out Melanchthon.

the show and pomp of your pitiful effort, bring it on, if you like, so that we can feel the full force of your attacks.

In the meantime, it has occurred to me to ask you why you everywhere marked up and annotated the margin of your book with these elegant phrases: "very gracefully," "with sophistication," "good sport," and "very elegantly." If you wanted somehow to be decked out with sophistication and humor, this sort of thing should not be put in your discourse, but rather ought to be left to the expectation and judgment of others. From this I can quite easily determine how noble you consider yourself, how splendid, how much you look down upon other men as though they were laid out in the dust. For thus your mind seems, when freed from its anxieties, to entertain itself just a little too often.

Do not, Alexander Dickson, stretch your dignity too thin and throw it away lightly. I think you are a brilliant and fabulous man. I think you are the sweetheart and precious delight of the Paris Academy. I think you are the son of a white hen! I say that you are the golden offspring of the Muses. Minerva has polished your genius so exquisitely so that you alone might have an outstanding vein of wit! What are others in comparison with you? Heaven help me! They are all poor losers, rejects, dolts, big empty foreheads, balloon-brains! They have such cramped little minds, so little heart, that they have never really felt your wit unless you first told them, "I'm making a brilliant joke here"; or "This is meant to be sarcastic"; or "I'm trying to be annoying."

Is this really so? Is your genius really so exalted? Does your mind really contain so much arrogance? So much petulance? Perhaps I am seriously mistaken and the things which I am saying never entered your mind. For because we do not perceive your brilliance, all of the fault rests upon you, since you can produce nothing witty, nothing charming, nothing endowed with elegance. Please forgive me if I liken you to some painter who, because he paints rather horribly, when he represents a dog and a rabbit and cannot make a likeness suitable enough to reality, he describes them by particulars: "This is a dog"; "This is a rabbit." In this way your witty comments would have completely turned to lint; and all your power, just like your mind, will completely escape your readers, unless they gather from certain comments placed in the margin some inflection and drift.

But come now, what is the main point of your complaints? What is the basis? You say that I have provoked conflict because I concealed from you my name. Of course as a bashful man I was intending, with a modesty of a young girl, to run away before the conflict. The reason, Dickson, was not as you say. But really in this matter—as I don't want to seem too tender behind the ears (as the saying goes)—it was never my desire to complain with such boundless irritability. But it would have been, in the first place, remarkable and characteristic of a very hardened pattern of speech first to divulge something to the public indiscriminately and then to spread it abroad more widely for the evaluation of the most learned men. And so I kept my identity hidden. I did this not because I wanted to refuse argument, but because I thought that it should not happen among Englishmen and especially men of Cambridge—rather known for their considerable subtlety and piety in forming judgments—that the conversation about my name should somehow trickle out in a very slender stream. But actually, the concealment of my name became for me a cause for deception and reproach. Nevertheless, this problem will never be so great as the fact that while you wear the mask of "Scepsius," under that name you go completely wild and recklessly mimic that boastful Thraso in your commendation.

You will say, "Did I produce that *Defense*? You're wrong, and you speak to me hatefully on a made-up charge. May I die, if my student and associate Scepsius did not work on that *Defense*." Because if I explain that the one who produced the first book on memory was the same as the author of this *Defense*, I will find you to be more mild and more lenient. There are very many reasons why it was the same author. In both there shines forth the same form of talent, albeit unpolished and quite crude. The words in each author display a certain kind of roughness and sort of melancholy. The first work contains expressions that are abrupt, gasping, and truncated. The second one speaks in the style of her choppy and rugged brother. Finally, the same thread of technique is visible everywhere, something quite novel and haughty. What? This very fact[4] has often been relayed to me by trustworthy report of many people in London. You will never succeed in disproving the reliability of their testimony.

But because you have struggled very keenly and with supreme learning over the topic of the concealment of my name, I should want you to gain some profit from this effort of yours, and to produce the kinds of things in which I can acknowledge more generously your talent. What is the consequence? You are trying to cast upon me suspicion of negligence, because when I had proposed that I would speak about the vanity of your craft, I did not completely unfold the inner power and as it were innate distinguishing mark of that vanity in my definition.

"I am amazed," you say, "that, when you treated the issue of Dickson's vanity, you did not first define what vanity was. Among adherents of Ramus, it's true, this does not seem to be a very important quality."

Then,

"But you accomplish nothing. Does Dickson seem vain to you? Don't you hold that there is such a thing as vanity? You don't define it."

---

4. I.e., that Dickson is the real author.

How absurd is this defense? How bullheaded and overwrought? Don't you see that only an exquisite art is refined with glorious definition, set apart by a complete and compact division of subjects, and filled with constant and clear examples? Don't you also see that in a mundane treatment there are no principles that are sharpened to total perfection, nor is any very alluring method of arranging topics scrupulously required? What a man that Julius Caesar was, good gods! In his commentaries, even though nothing happened which was not obvious and plain to see, nevertheless what greater brilliance, what greater sheen of action and expression could you want? But one blemish still marks such distinguished praises: he did not finish his *Civil War*. Our poor little man[5] was really a stranger when it came to dialectics. He was never so much as allowed to taste such fine wisdom. If only, Julius, you could return to your former condition and again enjoy this life. With your help, Dickson would be doing just fine, coming from the schools of the logicians completely elegant and polished. He would be advising others that the sum of your most excellent work should have rested on definition. There is a certain book by Peter Ramus on the customs of the Gauls.[6] But what really are the Gauls' customs? He doesn't say, nor define them. He was quite mistaken, and acted foolishly. Your book, i.e., the *Prosopopeia of Alexander Dicson on an Outline of Reason*,[7] is now in the hands of certain people. Yes, this is quite a nice development. But it is not sufficient. Nobody knows who you are. You should have applied to this setback that illumination of your most glorious definition so that you could cure it. Now if this is the very thing that you think you had to do, then I admit that there is a great fault in my *Admonition*.[8] But if not, you should admit that your *Defense* was packed with the most useless and contemptible arguments.

Come on now, Dickson. Let me speed it up a bit so that I can explain to you quickly the boundless riches of your genius. The next passage of your answer is the one in which you claim that I am inconsistent in my arguments. How is that? I said that your books had not been well regarded, when meanwhile I had said that your name was renowned among the English.[9] Or is this just another one of my dreams? Or am I simply grasping at an enigma? I guess so.

---

5. I.e. Dickson. Perkins is now speaking to Caesar via apostrophe.

6. This is the *Liber De Moribus Veterum Gallorum*, first published 1559 by A. Wechel, Paris. Dickson speaks of the Gauls and Caesar on p. 10 of his *Defensio*. See also p. 12, where Dickson says: *Ut tu iudicatis, Petrum Ramum ab ea re tantum abhorrere, quam in veteribus Gallis tam magnifice laudavit*.

7. Yates, *ibid.*, gives the title only as *De Umbra Rationis*, though Perkins here adds, capitalized, *Prosopopoeia*.

8. This is Perkins's *Friendly Admonition* of 1584.

9. Perkins is facetiously saying that he would be inconsistent if he had said that everyone

But help me out a little, and aim a careful glance at all parts of this argument. You grant, I suppose, that Catiline was renowned[10] in Rome. Surely that is true, but his name was decorated with marvelous trophies of debauchery and prostitution. You acknowledge as well that the name Herostratus is very well known to all nations. Even nowadays it wings its way and is sped along to every location. The name comes and goes as it pleases. But that very man set fire to the Temple of Diana. Likewise, I acknowledge that you are famous and notorious. But you are not so well known for your open and honest wisdom as you are known for your laughable teaching on memory. Now I clearly have the taste of your feelings. Obviously a boundless thirst for recognition grips you. You gasp for and reach fervently after praise. Because I cannot be cajoled into praising you, you try to squeeze from my words some evidence of your inherent value. But why do you feed your soul on foolish hope? Why do you allow yourself to become bound to a blind and vain expectation? Never, good heavens, will I show you so much honor that I would seem to have praised you flippantly. I know you are someone trying to make a name for himself for knowledge out of this petty thing, and to win fame from something inconsequential.[11]

The main point of my admonition was aimed partly at your words and partly at your content. With respect to the words, I said that you showed no gift for style. I also said that your words were harsh and choppy.[12] What did you say? "This is what, you an ignorant fellow,[13] I desire to know, all men of course laugh at this. This was that disrespect which was deadly to one's father. For by no means does it please the Brutuses.[14] Very well then, but it pleases the human race.[15] Do you say it does not? It is suitable here to appeal to the evidence of Johannes Adamus."[16]

In desiring to produce credibility for your case from the testimony of Adamus, you show that your *Defense* has been abandoned and ruined. For

---

loved Dickson's books and that his name was unknown. Dickson treats of this topic on p. 33 and following of his *Defensio*.

10. The word which Perkins uses, *nobilitatum*, bears the same ambiguity as the English word notorious.

11. This unusual phrase, *laureolam in mustaceo quaerere*, "to search for the laurel of praise from a wedding cake," is taken from Cicero (*Ad Atticum* V.20.4).

12. In this quote, Perkins is responding to Dickson's citation of the former's criticism that his essay displayed no blossom of pure style.

13. *Aselle*; p. 34 of *Defensio*.

14. *Defensio*, p. 35.

15. Perkins leaves out of the quote this phrase, *et placuisse sufficiat*, which could be translated "and it should be enough to have pleased them." The marginal note to Dickson's *Defensio* identifies this as "*Dics. oratio qualis*," or an excerpt from one of Dickson's speeches.

16. *iam ignotus*; Perkins also alters slightly the order of quotation. It is not possible to know whether he did this deliberately or simply because he is quoting from memory.

when it comes to philosophy, that which is whole and sound should be entirely proportional to itself. It will be entirely self-supporting; it will not derive any of its power and reliability whatsoever from an individual's acknowledgment. But who is this man Adamus? He is a friend, so I believe, entirely bound to you by every obligation of love. His testimony, therefore, since it was obtained by flattery, has been highly compromised. For he does not seem to be a man as much induced by his own judgment to make rather copious statements like these as he is driven by a unique sort of good will. But to prevent you from saying that I have relied on a feeble slander, I shall sum up the charms of your book in just a few words, and take these as representative of all your writings.

"The Prosopopoeia of Alexander Dickson on the Power of Memory."[17]
What is this *Prosopopoeia*? Do you want to be Sisenna?[18] Do you think that using far-fetched words is the same thing as speaking Latin with eloquence? It is only a *prosopopoeia* when we imagine someone else speaking in the course of our discourse. Because if by chance it was a debate between persons speaking in closely reasoned and separable styles, we typically call that a "dialogue."

"There are two parts of this art: foresight and critical judgment."
I do not scold you here for innovating somewhat in your terminology, but because you have given birth to something new while rejecting the word's twofold sense. You want "providence" to mean that phenomenon whereby we, through force and impulse, fashion places in the mind. Who speaks this way? Will you never give up this pattern of uncultured speech? Do you want the norms of style to be applied like a censor who refutes the arrogance of your phraseology and word choice?

"Therefore, the depravity of ignorance washes over a land that carries the heavy burden of its theme. This is unmitigated wickedness; this fire does not cease to attach a pyramid to the higher circles, transforming it into the shape of a cube."

What are you doing, Dickson? Why are you spilling these extravagant words? What lightning bolts ornament your ideas? I believe that your brain, if its goal were to inspire fear in others, would not have described itself in any other words. But what is the origin of your eloquence? If you say that it comes from yourself, then we embrace your divine sharpness of mind. But if it was acquired through imitating someone else, then we stand in awe of your shrewdness, and all the more so because only one man was found who habitually

---

17. *Alexandri Dicsoni de memoriae virtute Prosopopoeia.*
18. The reference is to a "notorious slanderer in Rome" (Lewis & Short) who is mentioned by the poet Horace, *Satires* I.7.8.

applauded himself eagerly for this type of writing. I mean,[19] St. Jerome wrote against him. And so let us hear Jovinian as he speaks in a beautiful and rhetorical fashion. "I satisfy you as you invite me, not that I might run around with luminous reputation, but that I live free from empty rumor. I plead with the field, the little shoots of our plantations, the shrubs of our tenderness, snatched from the whirlpools of vice, fortified by the columns of those who are listening. We know that the church is rendered unapproachable, impregnable, by hope, faith, and love. There is not in her every teachable immature person; no one can break into her by force or deceive her by skill."[20]

These are the comments of Jovinian, who in a few words has reflected all the praises owed to your style and placed them, so to speak, on the table. But in order to lay bare these praises more precisely and carefully, some individual remarks should be added to these few comments. Those who speak Latin say that the soul bound within the confines of the body lives in the greatest ignorance of its environment. What do you say, you have been rescued from the pits of the Sophists, you fake orator? You say that the "depravity of ignorance washes over a land that carries the heavy burden of its theme." Perhaps for some time now the Greeks' Πειθω and the lifeblood of Suada herself have sat upon your lips.[21] You present yourself as so eloquent that your style seems to eclipse the light of all other speakers. But why, in the end, do you later call ignorance wickedness? If you had named it κακία, I would have granted you that. If you had dubbed it the wickedness of the heart, I would not have objected. But because you think that in Latin ignorance is called "wickedness,"[22] I cannot be led to agree. Finally, those who are accustomed to employ discrete word choice and neatness in their style say that the mind is hindered by ignorance from understanding divine concepts.

Now what about this next point of yours, Dickson, "The fire of ignorance does not cease to attach a pyramid to the higher circles, transforming it into the shape of a cube"? There is nothing, I believe, ever written that is as clumsy and bizarre, which you, the actual, stupendous architect of words have sniffed out. Now let us see whether there is the same dazzling eloquence in the remaining portions.

---

19. Perkins references the fourth century monk who was condemned as a heretic by Pope Siricius and Ambrose of Milan for his anti-ascetic views. He died *c.* 405 A.D.

20. Jerome, *Contra Jovinianum*, I.2. There are many grammatical mistakes and bizarre expressions in the Latin which Jerome records and Perkins cites.

21. These are the two goddesses responsible for persuasion, personifications among the Greeks and Romans respectively.

22. The dispute is over whether the concept *ignorantia* can be described as *malitia*.

"What is in the shade of the light when it rests upon the horizon of it? For if its resting place is on the edge in some way, will the shadow display its inertia and motion in the center? If it passes from the horizon toward this by a kind of system? Let those things that lie beneath be fashioned with respect to the power of the horizon in its view. Finally, no outline is directed toward the horizons of this quality."[23]

Javellus does not compare with you when it comes to the ability to speak poorly, Dickson.[24] He gives you no competition for wretchedness of diction and impurity of sentences. Javellus gladly surrenders to you all skill in speaking confusedly. He confesses that he does not speak Latin, that he does not make his sentences glisten with bright words, that he applies to them no type of culture nor selectivity of expression. But he really ought to confess that in you all these things are far more exalted. For in the same way that your essay is on all counts arrogant, it is especially so when, boiling over with a certain kind of swollenness, it is carried along excitedly toward the horizon and the spheres of heaven away from everyone's sight. No doubt nothing further removed has been sought in writing, but we must search for the ornaments[25] of the most pleasing expressions. You supply this: "Forgetfulness is the lewd behavior of an impotent and dejected mind."

Could the Senate house endure such speech? Could the field of battle? Who could have said such a thing in the Roman forum? Could it have endured so much stylistic affectation? By Hercules, I will never discover how one could say that forgetfulness is lewd behavior. For that is properly understood as a type of lascivious and torpid lust of the heart. From that is derived the term which describes the person who, because of uncontrolled living, is utterly ineffective. If you think that I am saying this as a witty remark, place a wager on your judgment, and I will do the same in return.

"A memory sketch is an imagined species."

Here you call everything which is applied to the task of signifying something else a "sketch," but you do so with excessive filthiness and crudeness. A

---

23. This particular quotation is as opaque in Latin as it is presented here in English. Perkins's point is to demonstrate the poor style and irrationality of Dickson's argument. The larger context is Dickson's advice for image formation for the retention of objects in the memory. In context, the quotation is more reasonable, but when extracted the syntax is indeed entirely insipid.

24. Chrysostomus Javellus (*c.* 1470–1538), was a Dominican monk from the Piedmont region who wrote extensively on Aristotle. Cf. Dennis E. Rhodes, *The First Edition of the Works of Chrysostomus Javellus*, in *The Papers of the Bibliographical Society of America*, Vol. 66, No. 1 (First Quarter, 1972): 13–19.

25. Perkins uses the word *lumina* here with the meaning of ornamentation, but it is also a pun since the whole passage has to do with shadows, light, and Dickson's image-formation system of memory.

cause can be designated the sign of an effect, a contrary can be called the sign of another contrary, and the definition can be called the sign of something that has been defined. But a memory sketch cannot be called the sign of another sketch. What follows next?

"Strict necessity belongs to *prosopopoeia*. To play on the surface. To modify the memory sketch," etc.

You should prove to me that these are Latin expressions, however you wish to do so, and you will make good on what is wished for. I ignore the remaining dung of your words, because I have gone over it before. All this manure stinks without my help and has already been stirred up so dreadfully. I will add this, that almost your entire essay is low class, sleep-inducing with its silly words, split open, badly fractured, promising way too much, shattered and dissipated.

Now, what was my sin in criticizing your words? You laugh at me, because I passed over charging you with lack of clarity and attacked you for the fault of impurity of style. But you have paid little attention to the thread of my argument. For it aims not only at debunking the obscurity of your style, but also its impurity of style. Both of these faults are so vivid in your essay that if one of them is displeasing to somebody, that person cannot find the other fault pleasing either.

Afterword, you decided to try to antagonize me more pointedly for my inexperience. So please focus all the strength of your mind on the following:

"Therefore, when one complains about impure style, does the argument not really concern obscurity? So you will treat obscurity as a fault of grammar, even though everyone else objects."

I think you are not attacking my *Admonition* so much as you are making good on your drunken vows from yesterday's binge match. Obscurity is a fault of grammar. I grant this, but I go further. I think there is also such a thing as both a rhetorical and a dialectical refutation. Words often contain some sort of obscurity and barbarism. Sometimes in figures of speech and tropes there is something cloudy, dark, and less than clear. There is sometimes as well a sort of mist that falls over dialectic. Unless this mist is driven away, there can be nothing obvious, nothing plain.

What follows is your most recent conclusion on the topic of obscurity. This, as I see it, can serve as strong proof that although you want to take your blows,[26] and are ready to confess every category of buffoonery, your *Prosopopoeia*, wounded and weak, can still lift its head and strive for its original glory. I have explained how your expressions have been marshaled using a bloated and somewhat coarse style. As it is, I find that there are two reasons

---

26. *plagam accipere*, i.e. acknowledge your fault with grace.

why there can be something obscure in those expressions. The first is actually a consequence of the esoteric nature of the subject.

"So let's grant this: let's acknowledge that style is obscure. Granted. What now? What is the consequence? What are you angling at? Do you think that obscurity is a fault? It is obvious that people generally think it is and people who are not at all themselves perfidious. But on the other hand you will find some who do not think it is, and who even resolutely argue that it is not." Then in the margin we read, "Maybe being obscure is not a fault."

Why do you kid around like this? Why don't you make up your mind? Why are you feverish with uncertainty? Maybe this is a slippery slope, and you are afraid to fall. Why do you toss in this "almost"? Or is this some kind of a crutch for you to hold onto and by which to pick yourself up when you fall? What then? Obscurity: do you deny that it is a stylistic fault? I should think it is proper to call it a minor sin. In the meantime, admit the mistake to which you have given birth, with the help of mother ignorance, father foolish, and with memory as your midwife. Obviously one's style should be clean and clear, so that it never reaches beyond the understanding of the common person. Your ideas must also be vivid and gleaming, so that the mind can be quickly affected and compelled by grasping these ideas. If something else happens, the craftsman will want to acknowledge freely that he has made a mistake, and to confess that something absurd has slipped in.

Here is another principle derived from the standards of stylistic decency: "Although I draw distinctions between the ancient Egyptians, Thamus, Mercury, Theutates, Socrates, but I credit Thamus with every discussion of memory, as he is clearly the most authoritative and strict ruler. Doesn't everyone recognize that a pithy, compact, highly polished, and almost impenetrable style was appropriate?"

I will grant this: you have dreamed up a dialogue. You introduce these remarkable talking Egyptians as exemplars of antiquity and dignity. That is fine. You concoct for them a style that is compact, highly polished, and sophisticated. So far so good. It would have been inappropriate for someone who boasts in his style that such authoritative characters should be bound by absurd conversations. Meanwhile, it is troubling that the conversation of these men should reek of some obscurity. Romulus spoke one way, Numa another. Crassus favored one type of style, Scaurus a different. One sort of oratory seemed appropriate to Lysander while another suited the Gracchi. But a style that is obscure, shattered, and blinded by chicanery of ideas and words will suit nobody for even one hour.

Next you throw up against me the great fault of impropriety. So I ask, were your praises of your *Defense* carefully measured against the standard of propriety? What if, you child prodigy, I should pour back on your head the suspicion of impropriety which you have sprayed at me? Look for a moment at the letter you have prefaced to your *Defense*. Notice how it speaks in a bumpkiny and boorish manner, as though you had dispatched it to one of your buddies. But then your letter, completely tuckered out from the journey, threw off all modesty. And when its strength was spent, it turned aside to the home of a very famous man where it then demanded lodging. It was not at all proper for you to speak so foolishly, in the first place to Robert Dudley, at that time a patron of letters, and afterward a most noble Count. In the end, and this is the main point, he was the most excellent counselor of her Majesty the Queen. Should academics greet men who are the flower of the nobility by means of letters that are filled with respect? Did Dickson, the inventor of a new discipline, the crowning glory of our kingdom, decline respect for Dudley, the light of Leicester? This is intolerable. But I believe that your habits have not been sufficiently polished by English urbanity,[27] and Dudley thinks you should be forgiven for your Dicsanity.[28] This is the glory of that man, his mild nature.

But leaving aside these matters, you ask why I sent my *Admonition*. Because I thought that someone should write something against you, Dickson, i.e., what your tricks and frauds have contributed to corrupting the youth. Perhaps you will say to me, "I am not opposing you, fool." But it has always been my intention to consider clearly how I might serve my fellow citizens with distinction. You think that I should not have written anything at all. So what reason then led you first to take the risk, then to avoid and refuse it?

"It was Solon whose example you are to follow in such great danger. He should have gotten angry, therefore you should have headed down to the forum naked and pleaded with your fatherland for the resources to crush this threat."

You make these remarks with too much shrewdness, as though people ever followed the insanity of a raging and drunken man. But still, unless I am mistaken, it would have been safer to reject this danger than for you earnestly to flit around throughout London here and there with your mouth so free and ready, to spend your time in attacking me at St. Paul's Cathedral, to attach broadsides on the street corners showing off your memory system, to set up wisdom shops, to entice young men from the most distinguished families as pupils for your delicate ideas, and to insinuate yourself more deeply into their company. I was able to separate every trace of corruption from this account. By that corruption, you yourself only surprisingly strengthened the reputation of your skill while it was still in its infancy.

---

27. Dickson was a Scot by birth and Perkins is marking his rustitude.
28. *Dicsonitatem.*

Now, finally, let us see how you laid bare that part of my *Admonition* which consisted in evaluation.

"G.P. said that Dickson was impure in style, and thus said: therefore, he does not smell of Roman purity."

"G.P. imagined that Dickson was his close friend, and thus imagined: therefore, he does not smell of Roman purity."

"G.P. said that Dickson was obscure, and thus said: therefore, he does not smell of Roman purity."

"G.P. said that Dickson was corrupting the youth and thus said: therefore, he does not smell of Roman purity."

"G.P. said that Dickson was greedy, and thus said: therefore, he does not smell of Roman purity."

Everlasting God! What kind of a dialectician are you, Dickson? Where is your mind? Where is your keen reasoning? You were able to understand that I impeached your essay for its obscurity. Indeed, I said that it had become obscure as a consequence of your desire to make money. I also thought that I should just barely mention your essay, so that you could not rack up a countless supply of money for teaching your trifles. You see how your speech by connecting one thing to another slipped from the charge of obscurity to the more serious crime of corrupting friendship and youth. Dickson, if the Athenians were given the opportunity of reviewing this analysis of yours, and were to place this *Defense* in a chest along with the Minerva of Phidias, they would serve you both nectar and ambrosia in the Prytaneum.[29]

Up to this point, we have seen nothing in your *Defense* except the trifles and absurdities of your unrestrained genius. And so, some hope has overtaken me that you want to drive off the attacks on your craft with subtle answers. Because there are many things which are later disputed, I shall not give each of them my focused attention, but merely pick and choose as seems good, and select as I see fit a few of the many things which seem worth refuting. I maintain that the memory discipline which relies upon image outlines and places is a thorny fabrication of conjecture, because it first emerged from the schools of hallucinating Greeks and did not proceed from the common practice of memory usage. You say that I am sorely mistaken in this, because I have applied a wandering and limping proof to such a keen dispute.

"And because the shrewdness of your judgment is pleasing, please note attention, it may be helpful to repeat it."

"Not all who remember the sermons of theologians are familiar with the art of memory."

---

29. Perkins is being sharply sarcastic in his ridicule of Dickson's supposed accomplishment.

"Therefore A. Dickson has not described well the art of memory."

How poor and stripped of all dialectic are you? Are you going to display a yawning and slumbering wisdom? The topic which concerns us is whether your craft is born from experience. You merely draw another conclusion with great expertise. In place of garlics, you set before us onions. What are you doing this for, little mercenary doctor? Is it so that I might excuse so trivial a fault? Why are you abandoning your good name? Why do you present my writings abridged and torn asunder? I have not put forward that argument, but another that is more inclined to the truth.

"Art is born from experience and from logical deductions to some extent and becomes completely familiar by practice. So at one time in the minds of the Romans nature planted the seeds of grammatical skill. And its practice became fixed in everyone in their letters, syllables, conversation, and public speaking. Thus, although complete ideas of the remaining arts have been worked out for us, nevertheless the particular use and certain remaining features of their applications are only acknowledged. The precepts of artificial memory are not known, nor their application. Not even the precepts are known? Why is this? Is it because we have no innate knowledge of these places and of their memory sketches formed within us? No, rather concerning such matters not even images through our dreams are passed along to our minds. But will its practice stay hidden? No, it is easy to demonstrate the opposite. For men of exceptional intelligence, who apart from instruction remember things merely by the disposition of nature herself, first remember the thesis which is given in a public discourse; then they train their mind to the particulars. Finally, they gather up all the very small portions of the thesis as explanations of the particulars. They never select memory places, nor do they fashion outlines in their mind to remember what they have heard. Therefore, the art of memory has not arisen from practice and experience."

Do you now notice how my little argument, carefully polished by the pumice of your judgment, has lost some of its strength and dignity? Those who study eyesight report that light passed through glass is discolored by that glass.[30] In the same way my reasoning, as represented by your mind, has become somewhat decrepit and has suffered a certain amount of infection of your error. Now, however, since my reasoning has been fully and clearly explained it has bruised those passages, shattered your image copies, broken your moving wheel, scattered your system, and struck a splendid blow to your whole scheme.

Up until now, you were never permitted to see what we were discussing. To be clear, I recognize that you have been specially styled and vigorous in

---

30. The text here is very difficult to read: *lucem per vitrum f..f.m*, fusam (?).

our contest. But now, when a cause presents itself in which the power of your genius can be displayed, and your brilliance can spread itself around more broadly, shake off that excess sloth, and show that you are a man.

"Dickson has not produced a memory system invented according to his ability and judgment, but one he derived, elicited, and drew from nature herself. And so, he would of course strive carefully and precisely so it displays the character of its mother, i.e., nature. You could learn this in chapter 5."

You promise great things, and if you are willing to make good on these promises, I could not say that you are anything but a really distinguished man, and worthy of admiration.

"Just like no one will have oil, figs, or fruit who does not plant a vine, nor guard carefully what he has planted, so no one can prove the worth of my system unless he shall acquire the image copies and places, and cultivate them by the system of motion and its method."

So because he has an analogy drawn from nature, therefore his system is natural and true? Figs? Really? How foolish is this? Could you really be so inexperienced? O you blessed palace of the sun![31] The poet has wronged you because he has placed you in the category of finished works.[32] You certainly were built in a splendid fashion as a true home. What are you doing, Chimeras? Take heart. You have been erased from the Collection of the Mythicals and promoted into the City of Physical Objects. And you, O exalted heavenly signs way up high, by Dickson's particular kindness it happens that you have become things that truly exist in nature. You shall therefore be honored as the light to the one who wanders throughout the world in order to teach his memory craft. And you especially, O heavenly bears, be careful not to gobble up a gilded philosopher! You have won, Dickson, you won. Where is your curile chair?[33] Where are your white horses?[34] Where are the laurel wreaths for your fasces? Where the flowing white robes? The very close-packed assembly of enrolled Senators, to conduct you to the Capitol in glory and triumph? What about me? The only salvation for the conquered lies in hoping for no salvation.[35] What now, I ask, is there left for me to do?

"But at last, when there is no hope of escape, you approach the city and having taken on the disguise of a flatterer or you ingratiate yourself, and as it

---

31. Perkins suddenly apostrophizes the *regia solis* and other mythical creatures since these were part of Dickson's system of image copies.

32. The reference appears to be to Ovid's *Metamorphoses* 2.1ff., where the palace of the sun which Phaethon approaches is described.

33. This chair symbolized the highest official position in Roman civil government.

34. White horses drew the chariot of a Roman *imperator* in triumph.

35. This quotation is from Vergil's *Aeneid*, II.354.

were grasping the knees like a suppliant you announce such things. Even if you should be naturally mild, Dickson, you would not be able to burn with so much anger, nevertheless," etc.

Or did I want to ingratiate myself into your favor by calling upon you more gently? Or maybe to catch you with kindness by a little petty flattery? Come off it! No way! But I would call you gentle and mild. What, I ask, will keep me from being Socrates, I once jokingly mocked you? Never, by Hercules, did I think that you truly could obtain so much praise. But grant that, because you so desire, I would say that you are agreeable and distinguished by an unparalleled reputation for gentleness. As it is, your *Defense* would bring me under suspicion for being irresolute. Are you so mild? Are you gentle? Do you even have that much brilliance, you in whom there are such enormous waves of confusion, such massive tides boil? Now the mind is carried away with happiness, now it is alight with desire, now it melts off with pleasure, now it is swollen and aroused by anger. If only I could really bring you peace and soothe and calm down, as though with some harmony, your overly jubilant mind. Your shrewd remarks are scattered all over this passage. You are, so you claim, a miniature Gorgias. You are an ignorant fellow. O Irony's twin! O lovely sharpness of wit in hurling and releasing ridicule! Tell me please, from your heart: am I an ignorant fellow? So what do you want me to carry? If you want me to carry you, I cannot resist being glad, because like rejoices in like. If you are a salesman of memory, then I'm really unhappy! For I know that it is a nuisance to be led from market to market by forced marches,[36] and that I would be hungry all day long until you yourself made a good profit.

Because I never thought that it was very important to refute someone offering a false opinion, unless that which has the appearance of truth had been fortified by particular arguments, I tried to explain that a logical ordering of words was the only method for equipping memory. For whatever is contained in the subject of dialectic, that is, in the use of reason, this also must be explained in dialectic. But I taught that the faculty of remembering things was contained in the use of reason and cannot be separated from it. I will not say that you have mangled this reason of mine.[37] Rather, I ask how you are attacking its validity and power.

---

36. I.e., as a donkey carrying Dickson.
37. I.e. in his *Defensio*.

"It can seem like a false assumption. For reason and memory are different things. Nor, if some instruction on reason is sought in dialectic, would I also immediately think that it should be sought from memory."[38]

Your mind, Dickson, has been so blinded by error that you cannot perceive anything true and good. Why? You do not see that the faculty of reason and memory are the same thing, and that the actual act of proper recall is nothing other than its own power with reason. The rest of the individual faculties will maintain themselves through you. But proper recall has been fitted and as it were yoked together with the use of reason in such a way that, when it has been separated from that use it can neither continue to exist, nor preserve its own force and value. Therefore, I will chase down your *Defense* as it flees and looks for hiding places.

"Every application of reason must be explained in dialectic."

"Memory is a certain application of reason."

"Therefore, memory must be explained in dialectic."

We may put together same argument in a different order.

"That which pertains to the end of logic must be explained in logic."

"The faculty of recall pertains to the end of logic. It also pertains to arguing properly, and without recall in a person the proper end cannot exist."

"Therefore, the faculty of recall must be explained in logic."

It can also be presented in another manner.

"Art ought not to treat as separate those things which nature has joined together very closely."

"But nature has joined together very closely the faculty of recall in the use of reason."

"Therefore, the faculty of recall and reason should not be treated separately."

If Apelles[39] were painting Alexander, whose likeness would he want to think about carefully? Surely not that of Diogenes? Surely not the image of some centaur? Maybe a Hippocentuar? No way. No, he would instead, after meditating on a true representation, he would adapt his skill and hand to its likeness. So also the art of memory ought to be a kind of picture and type of remembering everyday experiences. But what kind of reason do you think ought to be employed for fashioning this memory? That of images? Or memory places? But for Alexander, that famous general, do you imagine the face of a centaur? Images and places are not used in the typical practice of remembering, and so because they put forward a falsified splendor and effort, they should

---

38. The Latin in this quote from Dickson's *Defensio* is not very good Latin and its meaning is opaque.

39. Apelles was a famous Hellenistic Greek painter from Kos who, according to Pliny the Elder, produced portraits of Alexander the Great, and thus lived until at least 336 B.C.

be rejected. Now, what have you contributed that is suitable for illuminating the true charm of an image? Depict your logical disputation with it. You will possess then a certain form and shape of the natural practice of recall, not indeed the kind suitable to harlotry, or smeared with the cosmetics of counterfeit beauty. But you will have a true one, clear, noteworthy, gleaming, and vigorously complete.

Next you are trying to entangle me in your verbal traps. But as a trivial person you have recourse to your jokes, like some lame person does to a horse, to hide from the sophistication of careful reasoning. You said (and still claim):

"I shall provide you with an art of memory."	– it can be provided
"Disposition is the art of memory."	– it is incomplete
"Disposition is not the art of memory."	– it is complete
"There is no art of memory."	– it is complete
"Logic is the art of memory."	– it is incomplete
"Verner[40] discovered the art of memory."	– it can be discovered
"Doctors supply the precepts of memory."	– not the precepts, but the strategies

You notice how I can extricate myself from these snares that you boast I have been clearly trapped in and caught. I did not say all those things which, had I said them, no blemish of inconsistency would have touched me, because with a certain kind of agreement and harmony they are in full accord with one another. If you were surprised that I say the art of memory is incomplete, consider the fact that no conception of memory can be found derived from bare objects, but only from those things which, with experience as a guide, are bound in place by an understanding of their arrangement.

Next, you try to blame me for unusual dialectic:

"Because you include disposition, intuition, discursive reasoning, syllogism, and method in your precepts and instruction, be careful, please, that you not seem, like your friend Freigius,[41] to have rashly conceived your peculiar dialectic of jurisprudence in the same way that you did your peculiar dialectic of memory."

I have not described dialectical disposition. I have only disclosed the application of particular aspects of disposition in the process of recall. Nor is what you say true, that Freigius developed a unique dialectic for lawyers. Clearly he illustrated a shared art that applied to all aspects of learning, with obvious examples drawn from civil law. So is this what it means to guard your system? Is this

---

40. The text is damaged here.
41. Johann Thomas Freigius (1543–1583), was a Ramist philosopher from Switzerland who wrote on Xenophon and economics.

what it means to teach that sort of life-giving mother of a more perfect memory and, as it were, that parent—which all dub "disposition"—that has not been properly judged? There is only one way to know any given subject. But your method of instruction, if it confers a legitimate method of strengthening the memory, why have you not explained that dialectic is taking complete control of your method,[42] and from it soaking up the greatest praise? You don't try to do that. Your entire system seems to rest upon defending the following: embracing, embellishing, and augmenting your foolish trifles. You linger, dwell, and are fixated on strengthening those trifles. But you so retreat from explaining that disposition is the art of recall that it seems you have abandoned the whole argument, and it all lies buried and forgotten as you seek to fancy up your nonsense. So then, walk away from this mistake; don't go any further into the distaste and distrust which comes from a defense of this thorny and prickly sophism.

Then again, why should I say these things? Is it so that any argument might break you? Is it so that you might root out such an idea that is so deeply planted, so inveterate, and begin to consider a more judicious and reasonable method of instruction? You cannot do so, Dickson, you simply cannot. Such lies neither within your talent nor ability. Indeed, the situation is not so different from the most wretched, fervent opinion, arising from this most vicious position you've taken, that has so attacked the skin of your mind that it can never be washed away, never be burned off.

You claim that I have fallen into the gravest error because I had said that the definition of your art had been overlooked. I did not say that. You deceive yourself and slip because you are confused by my words. No, I actually stated plainly that I did not want to contend with you over a matter which was already thoroughly explained and understood. You define the art of memory as the knowledge of rightly surveying what has gone before. But all that is left is for me to reject this definition so that I might fulfill my desire to refine and illuminate the truth with all good reason. I do not quarrel with you over this, whether careful use of memory is requisite. Our whole dispute rests on the type of recall to be employed, and this is why we are engaged in such a dispute and difference of opinion.

I objected to your division of the art into foresight and discretion, for individual areas of study must be constituted of their own unique properties. Now foresight is derived from logic; it has not arisen from the shoot of this particular craft of memory. So how do you defend yourself on this point? What strategies will you use to beat back the force of my argument? You say: "Really, foresight

---

42. The phrase Perkins uses here, *involare in possessiones*, is taken from Cicero, *De Oratore*, 3.31.

into or discovery of particular subjects has been consigned to an isolated position of irrationality. And this foresight as to logical consequence could also have been consigned to its own precinct. Yet in the meantime we are content with the outline system for memory."

In order for me to diminish the severity implicit in my comment, you reply that discovery is twofold: the one type is that of system; the other that of image copies. It is difficult to say how simple was the reasoning that I used to dislodge and cast you down from that stronghold. For if one kind of discovery consists in common logic, that is, setting forth all manner of arguments, topics, and images, then discovery must not be twofold but rather jointly demarcates argument and image. So then what will prevent this possibility from occurring when the very system of images, taken mutually, can be derived from an argument's most basic effect? You add that foresight is defined as "preparation." So what? This is how logical discovery both is and ought to be defined. You say: "Go on now, as someone who tries to restrain his laughter. All acknowledge that Aristotle is in fact subtle. But nobody indeed before you, that I know of, has said that he is divine."

No doubt you are holding back your laughter that reveals this foolishness, that is a witness to your vanity. Why do you pick at the little particles of words? Why don't you break apart the force of the arguments? This is no different than leaving the citadel of my *Admonition* untouched, but attacking the burnt and poorly equipped strongholds by some fearsome charge. But which of us, in the end, can spar with a more-pointed grammatical thrust? Are you one who denies that Aristotle was a subtle man and that the same one can be called divine? And am I the one who has truly pursued the opinion of Latin authors on this topic? Stop growing nauseous in this way, and please both yourself and everyone else. Stop chasing after deceit in your words and conjuring up these empty, little, snaring syllables.

Next, you hold that the laws governing memory places and images should be placed after their individual definitions and distributions, and you have two arguments for this:

"In the same way that as soon as a city is founded it must first look for a system of government and then the laws, so following this pattern the definition and distribution of any subject first relate its nature, and then follow the laws which explain its particular qualities."

But the logic for establishing a governmental entity is not the same as that for putting together some art. And so you should not have looked to the wisdom involved in managing a commonwealth, but rather the sight the most perfect kind of study should have rested in your mind, and could lock up your artificial system of memory in it. But now we have another argument:

"Ramus attached the conclusion of an adjunct to arguments that were well suited to each other."

You're just fooling yourself with the fallacy of equivocation. Adjunct means either the science of discovering an adjunct, or particular example of an adjunct. The actual science of discovering an adjunct is always naturally posterior to all of its causes, because the logician must understand that any given thing exists before he imagines how something exactly like it exists, whether that is the subject or the adjunct. So if we notice examples of adjuncts in the course of an argument and while practicing a certain skill, often the basic elements are assigned to a distribution of the causes. This is how P. Ramus defines his axioms. After proposing his definition, he gives rules for arriving at truth, falsehood, affirmative and negative arguments, contradictions, and axioms. Finally, he assigns them to particular species, both simple and composite, and explains individual instances of these species again by handling them precisely and very clearly. You are really way too exalted a craftsman of the art of describing logic! The rules for establishing axioms, which P. Ramus has raised up to such a high position of importance, you would have thrown down to the base mob and herd. So then, while the common adjunct must be described by means of a common *locus*, the adjunct particular to a given species must be dealt within a specific *locus*.

I have argued that the mental image is not an imagined species that has been situated in the subject, because there is a certain time when these copies exist only in the mind, nor are they entirely contained by their subjects. You respond:

"What kind of foolishness are you talking about here? What do you mean? Obviously you are mistaken. Can soldiers exist outside the line of battle? What's next? But they cannot exist apart from some specific place. Can painted images exist apart from their canvases? But they cannot exist apart from some specific place. Do you deny that an image copy has been committed to a subject? Do you really not know this? Actually, you understand nothing; you are confused about everything. And it is also not the case that more image copies can exist without the subject than that in dialectic adjuncts can exist without their subjects."

You very skillful sophist! You really accomplish nothing. All you manage to do is attack the truth with your treacherous and petty defense, since a painted picture is not always in a specific place, it is not always on a canvas. Likewise, an image copy cannot fail to exist somewhere, although it is not always stored in a place that is suitable for recall. At the same time, there is also the fact that if some images are in some respect meaningless, why aren't image copies deposited in different places after they have been separated? Next, the image copies have no correspondence to the subjects, but only exist and are called image copies by virtue of those objects which they signify.

But here I have made an error: obviously in such matters I have been oblivious to you and dumbstruck. Terrific! Now because you yourself have been strengthened by such a strong garrison of learning and surrounded by a powerful escort of literature, it would seem entirely fitting your great dignity if you were willing to unburden yourself of some of your knowledge and throw it in my direction.

My position has been that the first division of the image copy into simple and modified is false, because you thereby render the former only a division of sensible things, and the latter that of concepts. But in fact each of the two categories deals with all objects. You respond: "What if I deny this? Then you are utterly lost. But no, even if I should admit it, you will have accomplished nothing. Granted that Alexander holds sway in Macedon. That is his inheritance. But if the same man should also possess the Persian kingdom, what then? Or is jurisdiction so poorly divided into that which is inherited and which is acquired?" But look, if you divide ownership into the hereditary and the acquired, and say that this man is in charge of governing one part, and another man the second part, then you have to be truly deluded. For there is no other definition of the king than a person who possesses absolute jurisdiction, whether over something that is inherited or acquired.

I deny that the simple image copy, as you refer to it, can truly be called a copy. It is the species of that object which produces the image. But your simple image copy is the object itself. What will we make of the image copy of Alladius[43] that is based on Alladius? You should ask Dickson: "The image copy is simple." But if you should ask the truth, it will refute this answer. Why so? Because something cannot be an image of itself.

"You claim that the modified image consists either in objects or in words."

I have said over and over that right here lurks a sin against the law of wisdom which dictates that all things must be explained reciprocally. But what in this precept receives a symmetrical explanation?[44] All the modified images are either of objects or of words. I acknowledge that this is true. All of the objects or the words are modified images—this statement is absolutely false. For the simple images are images of objects. You claim: "Among the precepts of particular arts, not only the first law of truth, but also the second one of justice, and another of wisdom must be observed." I, on the contrary, have rescinded this precept of yours not by a first law [but] by a third one.[45] Therefore, it is

---

43. This king from Roman legend (873–854 B.C.) was a descendent of Aeneas and also known as Romulus Silvius.

44. The phrase which Perkins uses here, *vicissim retro commeat*, is an obvious adaptation of Cicero, *De Natura Deorum* III.12: ...*cumque eadem vicissim retro commeant.*

45. Perkins is here employing a legislative metaphor.

quite absurd to leave as uncertain what is already doubtful, but to conclude that something which no one at all can doubt is in fact uncertain.[46] You add, "The standard division of the argument into what is established and what is assumed is unacceptable. The proper division is between what is consistent and inconsistent, because every argument is either consistent with the object it seeks to establish or is inconsistent." It is not the case, as you claim, that every argument is either consistent or inconsistent, like things that are compared and the evidence for them. And nothing, according to its origins, is either consistent or inconsistent in and of itself, but the entire efficacy of arguing these matters grows and matures completely from the nature of their first principles.

I have demonstrated, Dickson, that your art of memory has been caught in a superb refutation, since it has made from image copies these copies of objects, other copies of words, and still others of numbers. Evidently, your system was ratified by those laws which deal with the perfecting of arts, such that they search out the general principles about everything that exists and does not exist, and never deal more closely with certain species of existence. Consequently, no precept of an image copy should exist if its use does not apply to every class of existence. But, the image copies of numbers are used for numbers, of words for words, and of objects, only for the objects themselves. Now, Alexander, how will you be able to defend yourself? What argument will you use to protect your knowledge against error?

You say, "You're mistaken, because in this instance the image copy is not an underlying material but a part of foresight."

You unhappy man, Dickson, both on the actual topic and because you do not realize in your reply just how unhappy you are! Indeed it was none at all expedient nor proper that a philosopher, wreathed with praise for his memory, should so clumsily brush aside[47] my attacks without every effort of logic and struggle. Your effort, such as it is, is not only ill-suited to the task but it's even false. "Ill-suited?" you say. "How?" My quarrel with you is not that you assigned your image copies to their own categories, but that in the division of image copies you relegate the distinction of existence to the underlying material. Then, this process really seemed to me quite laborious, since you claim that the image copy is not the subject of your art, yet the way you explain it is so tiresome and unusual. And so I will not heed your defense, although it is learned, so immoderately did it burst out with every kind of unrestrained deception!

Regarding your modified image copies, this is the argument I have made against you. You say: "Image copies are drawn from causes, effects, etc. These

---

46. The text here is corrupt, as the reading *id relinquere incertum* does not give the proper meaning. It should read *certum*.

47. *declinere* [sic] for *declinare*.

are exhaustive. Mathematical image copies are drawn from causes, effects, etc. Therefore, they are exhaustive."

Here you fault me for an invalid syllogism. Why? Because my argument was established in the second figure. You misty-minded sophist! You foolish child! Put on your logical thinking cap! Where is that famous genius of yours? You could see that the argument was anticipated in the proposition, and that its proof followed in the assumption. The whole reason for that error, Dickson, must be assigned to your memory. It is guilty of gross arrogance in seeking for itself kingly domination in everything. It forced this fantasy, which had been driven from its position, to leave behind its post and fortify its citadel in the ears. This memory of yours conquered the mind, wore it down, and forced it into submission.

Up to this point the argument has been fairly mild. Now we shall hear, if we are paying close attention, a more subtle reasoning. You define the absolute image copy as something that carries with it no distinction of number. There is general agreement that this has been denied for this reason namely because it arises from the removal or denial of a cause from its effect. You will say, "So what? What if someone denies that? Is there no such thing as a notion that exists by means of a removal? Is there no such description as a detraction?"

No denial explains what something is, but rather makes clear what it is not. You will insist that if something is negated, it will demonstrate anything which does not exist, and from this can be deduced what does exist. That indeed is a tough one! For in the same way that the rule is an accurate measure both of itself and of that which is next to it, so that which is next to it is not an accurate measure both of itself and of the rule. In the meantime, I do not deny that every kind of argument can be closely attached to those tediously long explanations which the poets especially, and also the historians typically employ. But those things that have been negated we must completely separate from the principles of a definitive and subtle science, because nothing should be assigned to it except that which is carefully and uniquely crafted and refined.

You acknowledge that astronomical images still with constellations and stars are not required for establishing the memory, but instead are only offered in your system as examples. You should be scolded for here taking so much joy in how freely you lie. "I am just adding examples," you say. But instead of the mere discovery of image copies for number, it is obvious that you produce from these astronomical examples the following broad principle: "If individual constellations are sequentially allotted 120 individual numbers by tens, and then ten regions of these individual constellations are assigned to ten fingers for demonstration purposes, then you will discover the images for number."

I grant that an example is not a general rule, still, I can bend and accommodate my own thinking to all your obtuse strictures.

"An antecedent skill should not seek an example from a consequent skill, because nothing can be sought from that except what is unknown. Even Aristotle is subject to criticism, because he dealt with the terminology of geometry like point, shape, and simplification under the heading of logic. The art of memory is antecedent, that of astronomy consequent. Therefore, the art of memory cannot use of that of astronomy as a pattern."

And so all can conclude that you, when you had dreamed up these examples, did not think so much about how heaven itself is arranged, but how to arrange for some cold hard cash.[48]

Finally, I have cited against you almost the whole Senate philosophers who—if they weren't weakening the force of your argument by the weight of their reasoning—would still shatter it by the influence of their authority. Chief among these was the renowned Peter Ramus. His genius, as I have explained, burned brightly against the backdrop of your silly arguments. You don't like this, so you go on the offensive. You hope that some breeze of good judgment and concord can blow upon you from Peter Ramus.

"If Peter Ramus should come back to life, he would not allow you to cite him in support of your position."

I take your word for it. He would be too busy reprimanding you with all the keenness of his intellect so you would not dare to utter even a sound. Continue please! Why should I interrupt the rapid flow of your lecture?

"For though he[49] searches for the revered study of memory and recognizes its method, he does not acknowledge image copies. Really these are his words, in case anyone should perhaps deny it. But when he conceives these fantasies in his mind, he connects them to his mind by means of the images of those things that are absent so that it seems like he has them present with him."

Does Peter Ramus really say this? Or have you, rather, auctioned off your sham under his banner? Do you never stop covering and concealing the loathsomeness of your craft with lies? If Ramus said it, come on, where did he say it? Cite the volume, mark the page, point out the chapter. You can't do it. You should open your ears and hear "Veromanduus"[50] arguing against you, and so recognize the broad stream of his genius.

---

48. *coelati argenti*, that is, "engraved silver." There is here a play on words between *coeli ipsius* and *coelati argenti*.

49. Dickson is referring here to Ramus, though not by name.

50. Perkins uses here a demonym for Ramus, as from the Gallic town mentioned in Caesar (*De Bello Gallico* 2.4.16), *Augusta Veromanduorum*. This is identified as the modern town of

If any plan could aid the memory, the following organization will help it. We grant that philosophers and orators who have fashioned a kind of memory craft with places and images will in fact find it quite effective. For they promise nothing that we do not already possess far more completely and readily.[51] There are two gifts of the gods universally bestowed upon human beings, and from these almost all others take their origin, namely reason and speech. The teaching of reason is called dialectic.[52] And whatever is unique to reason that can be practiced apart from speech, this is properly assigned to the art of dialectic. Moreover, there are three divisions of this art: the discovery of arguments, their arrangement according to syllogism and system, and similarly the memorization of them. And all of these are present even in those persons who lack all ability to speak. Yet they reason about objects, and arrange them in patterns, and draw conclusions about them, and remember the same. Therefore, let us hold that there are these three elements of the dialectic skill: discovery, arrangement, and memory.

Anything that properly belongs to some skill is that quality by which the organization of memory and the arrangement of subjects can be improved. By this we can discern what is first, second, and third. Now in the case of memory places and images, as they are commonly called, these are utterly ridiculous, and have deservedly been criticized by certain experts in this field. Indeed, how many images will they need for the speech of Demosthenes against Philip? Really then it is a question of disposition, because instruction in dialectic concerns only the arrangement of material, and from that one can seek support for the memory. Cicero makes the same argument in his treatise, "On the Best Kind of Orators."[53]

So now, what will stop Peter Ramus—as he piles up his logical arrangement to such a height, and diminishes and nullifies your art—from placing not only the true art of memory in this arrangement, but even the only one?

I have now demonstrated, Dickson, that your system has not been well defended, that it is teetering and severely weakened. You are not standing

---

St. Quentin in Aisne. Cf., *inter alia*, the title page of Roger Daniel's 1640 Cambridge reprint of Ramus's *Dialecticae Libri Duo*: *P. Rami Veromandui Regii Professoris*, etc.

51. In-text citation: *Scholae Dialecticae Libri* 20. The full title of this work by Ramus is *Scholae Dialecticae Animadversionum in Organum Aristotelis Libri XX*, published by André Wechel and Sons, Claude de Marne, and John Aubrius at Frankfurt in 1594.

52. In-text citation: *Some Questions of Oratory, Against Cicero Book 1*. Perkins gives the citation *Schol. Ret. contra Cic. lib. I*. By this he means the work of Ramus from 1547, *Brutinae Quaestiones in Oratorem Ciceronis*, published at Paris by Jacob Bogard. A text and translation edited by James Murphy and Carol Newlands was released by Hermagoras Press under the title *Brutinae Quaestiones* in 1992.

53. In-text citation: *Some Questions of Oratory, Against Cicero Book 3*.

guard at your watch post, and you strongly desire to use a sort of illusion in the course of your argument and an empty show, and something very much like an escape from battle. So, there was no good reason for you to keep saying that I was fleeing or in retreat.

"Really (you say), what kind of brazen behavior is this, abject cowardice wrapped up in the shadows of your correspondence? Obviously this is why you acted like that: you thought that I had left for Italy or France. You thought, therefore, that you would send your reply to my previous letter before you could be informed of my departure."

When you write that I waited until you could cross to France—so that this *Admonition* of mine, whatever it is, could be published, and strut around without opposition, and have at least somewhat greater influence as all England suffered misfortune—you reveal that wickedness is deeply ingrained in you and that you are amazingly skilled in the art of lying. So, you claim that I was continually waiting for you to leave? How did you know? Did I myself wait for that,[54] or was it someone else? If you say that it was I, I was not then in London. If you say that it was someone, well who was it? "But I sent a letter," you say. To whom? When? Where? Did you find out who delivered it? Was there any witness? Or maybe it was reported to you, even though nobody really heard it and discussion of it was falsely circulated. No, even that didn't happen. So then, this kind of slander won't get legs without some starting point. But I'm quite worried that you, I mean you, Dickson, are the original source of this rumor, as you seem to snatch at any malicious gossip to try to smear me. But go ahead and accomplish something that can never be given you, and which has never persuaded everybody: explain to me where this tremendous fear of you comes from, which has supposedly overtaken me? Is it because I thought that there would be some danger that you would bury me beneath the rustic refinement of your banter? And that by your immense learning (I see it is thick like a forest) you would blunt the edge of my genius? Modesty prevents you from such a boast; you will not dare to say it. So then, what harm did I fear? Was it that your brow was marked with the tracks of the curling iron? Surely not that your cheeks were painted white and so effeminate? Was I afraid of your blue cloak? Your dainty and close-shaved little beard? That your neck was wrapped round with a nearly endless scarf? Really, was I afraid that your pimping[55] stomach had not been fashioned by nature but fictioned[56] by art? Did I fear

---

54. The discussion seems to concern Perkins's use of the pseudonym G.P., for which Dickson apparently faulted him.

55. *Pimping:* in poor health or condition.

56. I realize this is not an actual English word, but it well preserves both the comic effect at which Perkins is striving, and the play on words in the Latin of "*non factum natura sed fictum arte.*"

none of these things? Therefore, you only let loose your empty slanders, but you can't explain how I have been tarred by gossip and groundless suspicion.

I thought, Dickson, that I should leave you with such remarks, not because I was driven by hatred or eager for a fight, but because I am convinced that I can never see such genuinely contrived and contemptible skills as yours.

A Short Treatise That Fully Explains Dickson's Wicked System
of Artificial Memory

G.P.[1] sends his greetings to the reader.

Although there are many people, reader, who fawn all over that system of memory which depends on places and images, as though over their own little daughter, I have made it my obsession to bring its mysteries to the broader public and allow them to slither forward. Therefore, in this treatise I shall very clearly and in a few words explain the precepts of memory. When these ideas have been properly handled and shaken, then all can see how they are utterly devoid of truth and completely packed with stupidity. So it happened that Dickson tried to stir up envy against me, because I dared to argue against his system which I found absolutely opposed (as he says) to my own sentiments. I did that for this reason, so that a charge like this would not be going to me, nor that man's stated position continue to linger. And yet, reader, may your zeal in pursuit of the art of memory neither be shattered nor grow weak. The whole subject is so simple, that spending just one hour can make anyone a sufficiently competent practitioner of the art of memory.

The Parts of the System of Memory[2]
I. Discovery in
  A. Places
    a. Places without additional reference
    b. Auxiliary places
  B. Images
    a. Simple images
    b. Images derived
      i. from objects
        1. Without additional reference
        2. Numbers
      ii. from words
II. The Assignment of its Parts
  A. Method
  B. Movement

---

1. G.P. is *Guilelmus* (William) *Perkinsus* (Perkins).

2. This is rendered on the page with the use of brackets and in both vertical and horizontal orientation. It has been simplified by placing it in an outline, while strictly retaining all relationships of hierarchy.

Book 1, Discovery
Chapter 1
The craft of memory is the art of successful reflection or recall. For since these three activities are distinct—looking ahead, looking through, and looking back—the first two will be pointless without the third. The brain is a sphere, and sensation, vision, and deliberation are the orbs of this sphere, and the limitation of the senses is found in the instruments of which it makes use. Therefore, just as nothing can arrive at the center without moving through the intervening orbs, likewise the memory possesses nothing except what it has received through the senses, vision, and deliberation.

G.P.'s Critique
It is proper to exercise good memory together with Adam, Abraham, Noah, Thales, Plato, Cicero, and all the most wise men, and to employ their practice. This practice moreover did not consist in using images and places, but in applying a particular arrangement of material according to axioms, syllogism, and orderly method.

Chapter 2
The craft of memory consists in two parts: discovery and assignment of objects. Discovery is the first part, which involves acquiring memory places and images.

G.P.'s Critique
Logical discovery furnishes as much instruction in discovering the image copy and the image itself as it does in the drawing out of an argument. For both the arguments of subjects and their image copies are sought by the same design. And so here an error is committed against the rule of justice and wisdom.

Chapter 3
A memory location is the receptacle for the image. Here, by memory location or subject we must not understand the subject as in a proposition—whether it be the initial material, something natural, or something artificial—but as partly natural and partly artificial, whatever is suited to the recovering of the image copies. These could be, for example, a house, a window, a corner, etc.

The memory location is either principal or auxiliary.

A principal location is always constructed either by skill or by nature.

A principal location is either very familiar, like the sphere of the world, or less familiar, like a particular land, the city, a home and its parts, but typically image locales are sought from the last three classes.

An auxiliary locale is one which is joined to a principal one to strengthen the understanding of the images.

An auxiliary image arises from the deliberation of the one exercising recall and moves according to his desire. For example, if I want to represent the suppression of revolution, I imagine a man standing in a corner were next to a column, and brandishing and extending a sword. In this instance, moreover, the principal locale is the corner, and the auxiliary one is the man with the sword.

G.P.'s Critique

The comments discussed here on subject and memory locale are errors against the law of wisdom. For the image locale should be defined in a logic system once, and the use of that definition should be applied to all particular image locales whether they are imagined or even real, inasmuch as referents, genus, species, and causes are only explained once in logic. Next, a memory locale should not be defined more from the image it adopts than a species is from the particular adjunct which it generally contains.

Chapter 4

Rules Governing Image Locations

Image locations should be visible.

Image locations should not be either too bright or excessively dark.

Image locations must be of average size. For when they are large, the images tend to escape the mind. When small, they do not properly receive the images.

The spaces between the images must be of moderate distance.

The spaces between the images should be empty.

Make sure the images are imagined as different in shape and form.

Careful order must be observed in the memory positions so that one can affix a number to each of them, and repeat them either by advancing from the first one to the last, as well as in the opposite direction.

The memory locale should accept and receive something from the image, in the same way that paper is affected by written letters.

Memory positions must preserve their images until something new is committed to memory, and at that point the images must be wiped clean.

G.P.'s Critique

These rules should have been placed after the definition of the memory locale, because they properly belong to its individual species.

Chapter 5

An image is the fashioned species of an object interested to a subject and adopted for the reliable perception of that object. Here, however by species is not meant Plato's archetype, that is, not an incorporeal essence, not the natural form of the object, but whatever effect which can point to something else through thought, such as when we paint a blind woman to represent fortune, and one who is standing upon a spinning wheel.

An image copy is either simple or derived.

It is a simple copy when any object is used for representing itself. Thus Socrates is a kind of copy of Socrates, and Plato of Plato, as well as the actual image.

A derived copy is when anything external to the object is used to represent. For example, daylight is derived for shadow, timepiece for hour, death for life, and the circling of vultures indicates a cadaver.

Likewise, a derived copy is both of objects as well as of words.

G.P.'s Critique

No principle should be taught in any general art except one that accords with everything that exists and does not exist. Consequently, this distribution, whether it is material, corporeal, or incorporeal, has no place in a logical treatment. Likewise, this distribution of the syllogism into apodictic, dialectic, and sophistic has been rejected. So principles that deal with the images of words, objects, and numbers are not general precepts applying to everything that is and is not, but are only posited for words, objects, and numbers. Thus, according to the rules of logic an image is inappropriately divided up into segments.

Chapter 6

Images of objects are either absolute, or they are numbers. Absolute image copies are those that are not copies of number. Absolute image copies are derived from the places of arguments.

1. A cause is sometimes the image of an effect, as Archimedes is the image of geometry, Romulus stands for Rome, and cement and wood for a home.

2. Sometimes the effect is the image of the cause. Thus the creation and conservation of the world is the image of God, and words, writings, deeds, and intentions, indicate agents.

3. A subject is sometimes the image of an adjunct, as for the adjunct's strong, long, or weak body there are the images strength, length, and weakness. The subject color is the image of the adjunct vision, flavor for that of tasting, and number for arithmetic.

4. An adjunct is sometimes the image of a subject, as the swallow for spring, weapons and missiles for war, and clothing for a clothed body.

5. A contrary is the image of the contrary, as the emblems of victory stand for the victory itself, peace stands for war, man stands for beast, blindness for vision, father for son, servant for master.

6. One compared item represents the image of another, as fire's flame for pyropus[3] and Mercury for Asclepius. Therefore, the greater stands in for the copy of the lesser. In this way like is indicated by like, and unlike by unlike.

8. Part stands for whole, and species for genus, as rough for home, one squadron for the entire cavalry, home for city, Mercury or Prometheus for wisdom, some lion or another for animal, etc.

Chapter 7

Image copies for numbers, because they cannot be simple nor derived from the places of arguments, must be gotten as follows. Take the number 120. Generally speaking, this is the largest number found in everyday use when referring to books, chapters, and verses. If someone wants to indicate by an image a number no larger than this one, he should do the following. First, divide this number into ten (i.e. twelve groups), then assign each of these in order to a particular marker. Thus, let Aries signify the first tenth, starting from the ones column and extending to the tenth number. Taurus marks the second group of ten from the tenth number to twenty, and so on. Then, because there are many ones in each group of ten, these also should be noted through several divisions of the individual numbers. And thus the full image of number will be completed. The following visual diagram illustrates my thinking more fully.

	Aries	Taurus	Gemini	Cancer	Leo	Virgo	Libra	Scorpius	Sagittarius	Capricorn	Aquarius	Pisces
Head	1	11	21	31	41	51	61	71	81	91	101	111
Neck	2	12	22	32	42	52	62	72	82	92	102	112
Shoulders	3	13	23	33	43	53	63	73	83	93	103	113
Heart	4	14	24	34	44	54	64	74	84	94	104	114
Stomach	5	15	25	35	45	55	65	75	85	95	105	115
Liver	6	16	26	36	46	56	66	76	86	96	106	116
Intestines	7	17	27	37	47	57	67	77	87	97	107	117
Genitalia	8	18	28	38	48	58	68	78	88	98	108	118
Knee	9	19	29	39	49	59	69	79	89	99	109	119
Foot	10	20	30	40	50	60	70	80	90	100	110	120

The application of this table for committing something to memory is simple. If you want to have an image of the number two, do this: find the number two in the table, and next to it "Aries" will refer to it at the very top, and "neck"

---

3. *Pyropus*: an alloy of copper and gold.

will be on its left. So place "Aries" in one of the acquired positions and imagine that there is some sort of marker on its neck, and thus you will have the image of the number two. If you want an image copy of the number 30, you should think of twins struggling with gout, and continue on like that for the remaining instances.

Because Cancer, Libra, and Pisces do not have these ten divisions, other images whether of men or of animals can take their places in turn. The preceding table can be expanded using the images of the seven planets, and an image of the dragon of the moon. Here, each individual image should also be different, so that there are many Arieses, many Tauruses, many Leos, so that the similarity does not slow down the memory in retrieving the particular markers.

G.P.'s Critique

This instruction on the image copies for numbers is ridiculous. For arts must be learned and taught with an order. First the general arts should be taught, i.e. grammar, rhetoric and dialectic. Afterword the particular ones that are derived from these, namely arithmetic first and then geometry. Afterward come optics, then astronomy, next physics, and finally ethics and politics. A consequent art can provide no use of its own nor any example for illuminating an antecedent art. For in that instance something which is unknown is explained by means of another thing that is even more unfamiliar. When the former arts[4] have been precisely explained, it is obvious that it is pointless and foolish to look for a precept or example from astronomy. Furthermore, is there anyone so congenitally sluggish and dense as not to be able to imagine quite easily rules of that kind? So then, let me propose another system of discovering the images for number using the following table:

1000 Dog	100 Standing	10 Shin guards	1 Painter
2000 Horse	200 Sitting	20 Cloak	2 Butcher
3000 Lion	300 Sleeping	30 Crown	3 Astronomer
4000 Monkey	400 Kneeling	40 Boots	4 Musician
5000 Snake	500 Leaning	50 Fur Cap	5 Geometer
6000 Basilisk[5]	600 Lying	60 Undershirt	6 Sorcerer
7000 Magpie	700 Walking	70 Gold Chain	7 Doctor
8000 Bear	800 Hanging	80 Bracelet	8 Merchant
9000 Parrot	900 Stretching	90 Gloves	9 Beggar

---

4. *Former arts*: the general ones.

5. *Basilisk*: a legendary crested serpent, perhaps a cobra.

There are four columns in this table, and the first column of items indicates the value of the number. They have this value when taken individually. The second column indicates tenths, the third indicates hundredths, while the fourth shows the thousandths. So then, the table should be used for numbers as follows.

For the number eight I set down "merchant," and I imagine him—so that the thought does not dissipate—carrying in his hand a very large, golden number. For the number 24, I think of some musician dressed in a golden cloak. For 435, I imagine a geometer like Archimedes kneeling, and investigating the trick of Hiero's crown. For the number 4,161, I place a certain painter standing and in his undershirt painting a monkey. This is because monkey signifies 4,000, standing 100, undershirt 60, and painter the one's place. When these individual images are combined they equal 4,161.

Chapter 8

The images for very many words can be derived from notation. For example the word "a human being" is indicated by the word "humus."[6] "Agriculture" is marked from the cultivating of the field, and so forth. But the following may serve as a general theorem for the discovery of image copies for all words.

When 30 letters have been set out in order—a, b, c, d, e, f, g, h, i, k, l, m, n, o, p, q, r, s, t, u, x, y, z, ψ, φ, ς, θ, ζ, 𝔶, 𝔴—then let thirty individual persons be found with their effects and adjuncts to indicate those letters.[7] According to the manifold composition of those persons with their effects and adjuncts, the image copies for words will arise. Here is an example:

	People	Effects	Adjuncts And Particular Subjects
A	Archimedes[8]	Contemplation	Sphere
B	Bootes[9]	Guarding	Bear
C	Catiline	Arson	Eagle
D	Diogenes	Laughing	Jar
E	Europa	Living Chastely	Bull
F	Adam	Digging	Tree
G	Ganymede	Serving At Table	Cup

---

6. *Humus*: of the earth.

7. Each of these letters in the table is majuscule, while here in the text they are minuscule. In addition the order of the last three is different, and after the φ in this list there is a ς, while in the table it is followed by Ω. In other words, the list and the table are not the same.

8. *Archimedes*: Greek mathematician, (*fl.* 287 B.C.).

9. *Boote*: the legendary hunter.

H	Hercules	Raging	Club
I	Juno	Bringing Help	Childbirth
K	Agrippa	Bewitching	Wool Cap
L	Caesar	Triumphing	Spear
M	Mercury	Deceiving	Caduceus[10]
N	Neptune	Swimming	Trident
O	Orion	Hunting	Dog
P	Pythagoras	Singing	Lyre
Q	Munster	Measuring	Radius
R	Rhadamanthus	Judging	Something Frightening
S	Cyrus	Planting	Purple
T	Tullius[11]	Public Speaking	Toga
V	Verres	Overturning[12]	Portrait
X	Xerxes	Competing	Gold
Y	Epicurus	Eating	Bed
Z	Zeuxis	Painting	Paintbrush
Ψ	Romulus	Ruling	Crown
Θ	Saturn	Sowing	Black Garment
Φ	Daedalus	Inventing	Calipers
Ω	Asclepius	Healing	Urine
ע	Milo	Carrying	Ox
ζ	Endymion	Sleeping	Chain
שׁ	Vitellio	Seeing	Mirror

The proper use of the table

Take "amo"[13] as the word for wish I am seeking an image copy. Because "A" is the first letter, I look for the image's letter "A" in the first column, and it is "Archimedes." "M" is the second letter and I found its image in the second column, as "deceiving." The third letter, "O," has its image in the third column, namely dog. Now in order to combine the image for the entire verb, Archimedes, "deceiving," and "dog" must be combined like this: "Archimedes deceives a dog by throwing it a stone instead of a piece of bread."

Another word may serve as an example of a bisyllabic, namely "Taurus."[14] The image for the first syllable is "Tullis surveying models of heaven." For the second syllable I imagine Rhadamanthus overturning something purple.

---

10. *Caduceus*: Mercury's famous divining rod, by which he conducted souls to the underworld.
11. *Tullius*: Cicero.
12. Perhaps there is a pun here on Verres's name, i.e. -*ver* for *evertere*.
13. *Amo*: I love.
14. *Taurus*: bull.

But because every syllabic composition is not composed of only three letters, one must look for another method for producing an image of that syllable which is made up of four or five letters. Now because only a few letters constitute the fourth or fifth position in the syllable, additional columns did not have to be constructed. These five letters are, l, n, r, s, and t. A table can be designed for these as follows:[15]

T	Standing	East
N	Sitting	West
R	Lying	North
L	Bending	South
S	Hanging	The Pole

These letters occur either at the end of a syllable or in the middle of it. If they occur in the middle, then the first column of this table will stand for them. But if they occur at the end, then the second column. This way, the image should be constructed for a syllable made up of four or five letters. Take the word "stans."[16] For "S" I put Cyrus, for "T" I imagine him standing. For "A," he is gazing, for "N" I place "Trident," and for "S" I put the "pole," because it is at the end. Consequently it is just like if I were placing Cyrus standing in the position and gazing upon a trident painted on the pole of heaven.

The first syllable of "flagrans" is *fla-*. and this is represented by Adam winning a victory, or rejoicing with the sphere in his hand. The second syllable *-grans* is indicated by Ganymede lying down and gazing upon a trident painted on the pole of heaven.

Such people as these should be used everywhere in various ways, as there are many Adams, many Caesars, etc. Each person can fashion according to his own convenience tables like this. By these methods image copies of words are discovered, and we can use these same images to write letters or really anything secretly.

The critique of Peter Ramus from Scholae Dialecticae Libri *20*
Words derive no help from art, except perhaps that when subjects have been set out in order they carry with themselves the actual words. Consequently, "Even words will follow, though unwilling, an unforeseen event."[17]

---

15. The order given here for the letters, i.e. alphabetical, does not correspond to their order in the table.

16. *Stans*: A participle that can be translated as "standing."

17. This is a line of hexameter from the Roman poet Horace (65–68 B.C.), *Ars Poetica,* 311.

Orators completely disorder the memory of words by an endless number of forms, while, because of individual words, they must have recourse to individual images.

Chapter 9
Rules for images.

1. An image must be visible.

2. An image should be both vivid and well-defined. It must be distinguished by its unusual and absurd traits.

3. Images must be placed exactly in their positions so that they don't wander off and get lost, so to speak, in the air.

4. Images must always be active in their places or with respect to them.

5. Images should be of average size for this reason: if they are too small, or much larger than it is fitting, then the second group should be diminished, and the first enlarged. So, for the sake of example, the ant should not be used as an image, but either many ants together, or something else. The sky cannot be an image, but a sphere can be set down to represent the sky.

Book 2, Arrangement of Parts

Chapter 1

Up to this point we have dealt with the preparation of memory places and images. There now follows their arrangement. Arrangement is the second part of artificial memory, and deals with properly organizing image copies and places.

There are two parts of arrangement: method and movement. Method consists partly in the ordering of places, and partly in the placement of image copies. There should be a general understanding and archetype of all image places, but the latter must be further divided into its less common parts. And these individual parts should again be assigned to specific and unique locations. The image of a general object must, to repeat, be attached to a general location, and the image of an object subordinate to it must be placed in a less common location. The image of an individual object goes in a particular location. For example, let us imagine a person that has acquired for himself one hundred image locations from some town, and has gotten these from individual buildings. In this instance, the town itself will be a very common image location, and is, so to speak, the archetype of all image places. Individual houses are less common image locations, and their parts—like doorways, windows, beds, etc.—are specific and unique image locations. Now if, during a lecture or some other occasion, one wanted to commit something to memory, he should place the general topic under debate in general location, and the points of the individual arguments in unique image places. Moreover, one can construct as many image locations for himself as one wishes, and then connect them to yet smaller distributions at his discretion.

G.P.'s Critique
So that no one thinks Dickson has proposed here a genuine method, we must understand that a logical method possesses genuine memory places that are distinct according to the nature of the subject. In this art of his, on the contrary, we see that there are only imagined and hallucinatory memory places. Next, note that a logical method makes use of living and natural images. In this class are definitions, distinctions, and examples. We note as well that Dickson's system includes absurd and idiotic images, and ones aimed only at provoking laughter.

Chapter 2
Movement is nothing other than a kind of design for producing living and highly active images. This will occur, moreover, if we assign to an image transient qualities and highly unique attributes. If this movement is not natural or intuitive, it must be at least discrete and authentic. This happens when we cause an image to provoke certain emotions, like anger, hatred, fear, desire, envy, expectation, pity, etc. Consequently, an image can also be contained in the soul, and can be very tightly joined with the actual object which it denotes. For example, let us commit to memory the word "fire." Because fire is something visible, its image copy will be simple. So then, I will place fire in some image location. But I will not imagine a roof covered in ash, for then it would have been able to slip from my memory. But instead I think about the burning place, and I imagine a group of men present trying to put the fire out. I think of women's shouts going up at the sight of the inferno. This whole event stirs up emotions; this produces a focused reflection of the mind; this produces movement.

G.P.'s Critique
The whole of movement that depends on image copies and places was vitiated and spontaneously burnt to a crisp by the glaring stain of impiety. For this kind of movement cannot exist without arousing perverse emotions in the mind of the one who is causing these images to move. I mean emotions like anger, hatred, fear, and lust.[18] Ravenna[19] writes in his work *On Artificial Memory* that

---

18. In Dickson's list—*iram, odium, timorem, cupiditatem,* etc.—Perkins substitutes *metus* and *libido* for the last two. These are both, by general consent, more derogatory terms.

19. Peter of Ravenna (*c.* 1448–1508), who was famous for writing a memory treatise called *Phoenix*, which served as inspiration for Bruno.

he suggested young men make use of a certain mystery that had been taboo for a long time. Why exactly was that? Obviously because those images were very memorable and stuck in their minds for a very long time, that is, images derived from those subjects which can provoke lust. These would be images dealing with women and girls. We also find this in Dickson's method of instruction, because he does not forbid the arousal of any emotions. But it is just not right to summon forth evil emotions latent within us. No, such things must be tamed and repressed through genuine self-control. I often ponder the fact that such an art has never been practiced, tested, nor cherished by people who are righteous, but only by wicked scoundrels. These men have shaken off themselves all zeal for divine law. So, dear reader, I want you to stay on your guard against the habit of producing moving images, for this is how your soul becomes calloused. And in the end, you will feel that there is nothing that stirs up any emotion.

Chapter 3
Application
For the purpose of entrusting something to memory, multiple image places should be acquired in sequence that are mutually coherent, and fashioned according to the methods we described in Chapter 4. In addition, these must always be close at hand, like a piece of paper, or wax tablets which we use for writing. And to begin with, there should be twenty or thirty of them. Afterward, more should be developed proportional to the system of usage. As an example, the following image places are found at the Castle in Cambridge.[20]

1. the gate of the castle
2. the men's prison
3. the chamber room of the prison guard
4. the steps of the bedroom
5. a little garden
6. a well from which water is drawn
7. a putrid well
8. a doorway facing East
9. a judge's tribunal
10. the secretaries' table
11. the cloister for the jailers
12. the gallows
13. the hogs' pen
14. the corner of the wall
15. the women's prison

---

20. Cambridge Castle was built in the eleventh century and also goes by the name Castle Mound.

Now that these image places have been acquired, we must first consider how to recall words and simple objects. For remembering sentences takes concentrated effort; in this memory must be later exercised. So then, I will set out some objects and words to remember as an example.

1. Lght	7. Cold
2. Moving	8. Old man
3. Cal.[21]	9. A tree
4. Arrogance	10. If
5. 9.8.9	11. Then
6. Honey	12. I deny

The following method must be used to remember these items. "Light" is the first of these, so the image copy of "light" will be the light of the sun, the species, quite obviously, of the genus. The light of the sun, because it is the image copy of the very first object according to this method, must be placed in the first position, namely at the "gate." Now, so that I can keep in my memory the fact that the light is in the gate, I need to get a moving element for the light of the sun. And so I imagine that the light of the sun, by a violent flare, catches the gate on fire and destroys it.

"Moving" is second, so then it is in the second memory position, in the men's prison. I imagine someone imprisoned and that he is a notorious criminal. In his sleep he is being harassed and almost dragged away by lice, for this is how the soul is bothered by petty concerns.

"Calendar" is third. The image copy of this should be sought from the table of terms, by the plan explained in chapter 8. And so according to this table, I imagine in the third position, namely the chamber room of the prison guard "Catiline contemplating," I imagine a "spear" in the sky, and that this is made up of "comets."

"Arrogance" is fourth. Here the image copy can be taken from the subject, and therefore on the steps of the chamber room I place Tarquin the Proud strutting around. But it will be better if I could put there someone familiar. "9.8.9" is fifth. According to our table in chapter 7, I imagine a doctor with a number of bracelets, stretching in a little garden. And the same method applies for the remainder of the objects

It is really not surprising, moreover, that many people can either repeat multiple objects in the same order in which they are set forth, or in reverse order. For they know the order of the image basis so well that they can determine based on those places which is first, which one is tenth, and which

---

21. *Cal.*: calendar.

one-hundredth. But in terms of the order of the image copies, the order will not be obscure because they are situated in those locations. And the objects themselves, because they follow the image copies, will display the same order together with the copies.

Up to this point we have dealt with simple objects and words. Now we must look at the application of this artificial memory system in the case of compound objects and words. We use the same system for remembering sentences as we did with individual objects and words. The only difference is that we must drop a broader number of image copies, and a more careful application of motion. As an example, let us say that the following lines of poetry needed to be memorized:

If you point your nose South with your mouth hung slack,
Then your teeth tell the time from the front to the back.[22]

In some image locations of those which I have secured for strengthening my memory, I imagine a person with a prominent nose and open mouth, looking at the sun. And on his teeth there are clearly painted lines for the hours of the day, and the shadow of his nose points at the hour. This is how the verses will stick in the mind.

Let's take another sentence as an example: "Greed does not remain in the realm of virtue."[23] Now to fix these words in memory, I imagine a little house in some memory location, and a greedy man driving a good man away from this house. The good man represents "virtue," the little house means "realm," and "driving away" stands for "does not remain." The greedy man indicates "greed."

[Perkins's reply and summary][24]
Someone will say that if Dickson's artificial memory system has any value then it ought not to have been completely rejected. Instead, I should have to improve it in every way possible. I really wish that somehow I could be convinced this does justice to the truth. For Socrates desired that all instruction given on any topic would be not only useful, but also true. Everybody agrees that the

---

22. This is translated from an elegiac couplet: *Si tuus ad solem statuatur nasus, hianti; Ore, bene ostendas dentibus hora quota est.* The couplet is attributed to the Emperor Trajan (53–117 A.D.) and survives in its Greek original, while the translation into Latin was done by the Roman Catholic humanist Thomas More (1478–1535). Cf. *Florilegium Epigrammatum Graecorum, Eorumque Latino Versu a variis redditorum* (London: Felix Kingston, 1629), 36.

23. *in virtutis regno non consistit avaritia.* This expression is original to Dickson and not a quotation, though the phrase "in regno non consistit" is axiomatic.

24. After the previous two chapters, Perkins has included the heading *Censura G.P.* before he begins adding his own comments. He does not follow that approach here, but clearly he is now speaking *in propria persona*. Brackets have been inserted for clarity.

study of astronomy[25] is useful and worthy of a noble mind. I don't doubt it, but that is not enough. I also hold that precepts which arise from utility must be aimed at acquiring general truth. Now the hypotheses of astronomy are altogether gross fictions, and pretty much just the nighttime dreams of silly old women. Likewise, I have shown that Dickson's memory system is a mere figment, and is not drawn from deep down inside nature. On the other hand, the system of logical arrangement is both broadly useful and sparkles with the truth. And of course it is what nature herself abounds in and has produced. But even if we should ask which of these two systems of memory device provided has greater advantages, then there is no doubt that logical arrangement should be given priority. This is because it not only helps the memory, it also greatly sharpens the intelligence, and vigorously molds and fashions a person's natural genius. But when the mind is engulfed in remembering all manner of subjects and image copies, as well as the objects themselves which the former represent, then it is so bent on these things that meanwhile the very concept of truth inevitably breaks free and flies away. This follows that famous dictum: "A mind all bent on countless needs, is thereby weak for lesser deeds."[26]

To conclude: let us use logical disposition which strengthens both the memory and our intelligence. But as for those image copies that indeed do aid the memory but utterly destroy intelligence, we must reject them.

To God alone be the glory.

---

25. Given the context, and Perkins's antipathy to Bruno's methods, "astrology" is likely a better translation.

26. This is the hexameter line *pluribus intentus minor est ad singula sensus*. It is of unknown origin.

A Handbook on Memory
and the Most Reliable Method of Accurate Recall

by William Perkins of Cambridge,

Translated by David C. Noe

combined with a Friendly Admonition to
Alexander Dickson on the vanity of that Art of Memory
which he publicly maintains.

Published at London by Robert Waldegrave, 1584.

**To his most distinguished colleague John Verner,
William Perkins sends his greetings.**

I have requested for some time now, or rather demanded, that you, dear Verner, should share your reliable mnemonic method. For I am really quite hopeful that as you address this topic, the truth, which has lain crushed under so many wrongs, may be able to emerge and be summoned back to the light of day, so to speak, after a long hiatus. And so I believe that you must do this all the more, first because it is your obligation, and then because you have the ability. Indeed, you owe this obligation even to literature itself, so that those writings which first made you distinguished, should through you, that same man, become distinguished themselves. In addition, you absolutely have the ability, if anyone does, of meeting many people's expectations on this topic, especially since you have become marvelously endowed with an expansive knowledge of the most important subjects. Therefore, I ask you to attempt to enrich this quite resourceless and impoverished craft with your specific set of gifts, as though with a dowry, since the philosophers have left it bereft of any dowry and disheveled. For the art of memory first came forth from Simonides, and later Metrodorus smoothed it over with a little more polish. But the writings of these men became so worn over time that they no longer survive. Many years later the Romans became inflamed with a desire for this same skill. And since for a long time it was held in great esteem, the skill began gradually to be written down. But, good Lord,[1] how meager are the instructions for this skill found in Cicero! Nor are there many even in Quintilian, while in Seneca and other Romans there are almost none.

Our own age has also produced many who have attained a prominent position due to a particular reputation for exceptional memory. These include Petrarch,[2] Ravennas,[3] Buschius,[4] and Rosselius.[5] So why is it now so unpopular? Why is it so decayed, why so obscure? What did all these men do to the craft of memory? Oh may heaven help me! They smack of nothing completely

---

1. *Deus bone.*
2. Francesco Petrarca (1304–1374): an Italian poet and humanist.
3. Peter of Ravenna (1448–1508): an Italian jurist, best known for his writing on memorization techniques.
4. Hermann von dem Busche (1468–1534): a German humanist.
5. Cosmas Rosselius (*d.* 1578): a member of the Franciscan order and creator of three different one-handed alphabets.

sound and erudite, but rather reek of some kind of barbarian "Dunsicality."[6] Consequently, take your ease from all your affairs—or release yourself from them—and bring forth from that innermost skill of yours something that will help me, and make you shine with the highest praises. Meanwhile, as you work on that I am sending you the brief essay I wrote on this very topic. It is, to be sure, perhaps somewhat slender. But it fits my purpose, namely to illuminate more fully the goodwill I feel toward you. Farewell.

------

6. Perkins uses the adjective *Dunsicum*, which originally meant relating to Duns Scotus but became proverbial for "stupid." The word "Dunsicality" is from Yates, p. 275.

A Handbook on Memory

Chapter 1: The Faculty of Memory

Memory is that faculty of the will which safeguards the conceptions received from the senses. For it serves absolutely no purpose for someone to possess an innate power of perceiving something unless he also has the ability to retain that same perception. The philosophers have placed the seat of memory in the occipital portion of the head. Almost all of them hold that position. "The brain is endowed with three ventricles. The first or anterior one which faces the forehead is dubbed the ventricle of common perception, because from it the nerves of the five senses depart. Then by their aid smells, tastes, sounds, colors and tactile experiences are carried back to this ventricle. The second ventricle in the middle of the brain is the seat of imagery, while the third is that of memory. All representations of objects are stored in it."[1] Such fabricated opinions, by Hercules, are scarcely worthy of old ladies' nighttime musing. For what reasoning compelled writers to situate three interior senses in every living being? Surely not because the same senses possess certain individual actions of their own? But such persons are keenly deceived who try to fashion the representations of objects according to the variety of the effects to which they give rise. The light of the sun, for example, has many uses and advantages: warming, burning, drying, cleansing, and illuminating. But to fashion representations distinct from one another proportional to these manifold effects of light would be an utter, raving foolishness. What then is the reason why the ability to perceive the objects of the senses, to evaluate them more completely and to remember them should be the same in the brain?[2] It is established with absolute certainty that in the human being the intellect embraces in itself the power of common perception and imagery formation. For this reason the memory must not be located in the narrows of the occipital region, when it actually spreads itself to all the regions of the brain.

The Peripatetics strenuously deny this whole argument, and assert two reasons for their conclusion. The first is that the occipital region is quite hard, and

---

1. Perkins does not give the citation for this opinion of almost all philosophers, and means it to be a summary of received opinion.
2. Perkins is asking why, if the common philosophical account of memory is true, everyone does not have the same ability to recall representations of objects.

thus more rigid for retaining memories. The second is that when the memory is wounded, doctors apply their cures only to the occipital part. These are rather slight grounds and not only unworthy of philosophy, but not even worthy of average intelligence. For in the first place, there is not one individual preeminent in anatomy who would say that the occipital portion of the brain is quite hard. What else? Is it really probable that Galen, chiefly famous for the quality of his dissections, was such a dull and stupid observer as not to notice the brain's innate structure? Or that Vesalius[3] also had such bleary and distorted eyes? Or, finally, that Columbus[4] and Fallopius,[5] men of outstanding diligence, were never able in their investigations to root out what the drowsy Peripatetics had found in their speculations? It is not plausible, by Hercules, still less should we expect it. But let us grant them something which cannot even be proven, namely that the occipital portion of the brain is very hard. What second argument then follows? Surely that is not sufficient to weaken our position, as they desperately desire? Absolutely not. For almost all doctors have contradicted this point, men who by applying remedy not so much to the occipital portion as to the rest of the brain have restored a weakened and feeble memory.

An old idea has for a long time now held complete sway in the schools of the philosophers, namely that the memory is obliterated after this life. I know what occurs to them as to why they should speak like this and hold such a wretched opinion. They want, I believe, for the human mind to be drawn and plucked from heaven; moreover, for the sense of feeling and the memory to have emerged from almost the lowest dregs of the body. And so they think that the mind when the body has dissipated travels back to heaven as though to its natural abode, and then the sense of feeling and the memory immediately vanish. Yet even if they conclude that someone's soul after death flits off to those dwelling places—where there is nothing that is not blessed and filled with gladness—why do they withdraw from the soul sensation, feelings, and memory? Why do they strip it of its adornments and splendor? If they remove memory, who indeed would want to remember the deeds done nobly in this present life? If sensation and all the affections fall away, what pure-flowing and honest pleasures could ever pour into the soul? Such an action, indeed, is not only not to bestow happiness upon souls, but it even counts as seriously afflicting them with all miseries.

---

3. Andries van Wesel (1514–1564): the Dutch author of *De Humani Corporis Fabrica*.

4. Realdo Colombo (1515–1559): an Italian anatomist and surgeon at the University of Padua and author of *De Re Anatomica*.

5. Gabriello Fallopio (1523–1562): an Italian anatomist and author of *Observationes Antomicae*.

Chapter 2: The Art and Representation of Memory

Up to this point our discussion has concerned the faculty of memory. Now we must shed some light on and point out the paths which lead to its execution. Because the faculties of the soul which God has planted within us are weak and feeble for the task of careful investigation, we must make use of a certain instruction and proper pattern of learning. For this reason, just as certain rules of learning govern other subjects, so also there is a particular art that must be related which can both increase and sort of nourish in us faculty of remembering. This entire art, moreover, is contained in the second part of logic, I mean of course disposition.[6] For the rules of disposition drawn up in Peter Ramus's quite beautiful treatment seem very effective not only for making determinations but also for stimulating the memory. In short, the logical disposition is twofold, i.e. both noetic and dianoetic. The noetic type of disposition is that which artificially combines a proposition from arguments. But although the disposition of a proposition may be very straightforward and thin, nevertheless memory acquires from it a quite unique support. For suppose there is someone who wants to store the following ideas for recall:

> *man*
> > *the dust of the ground*
> > *the rational soul*
> > *the glory of God*

If he deposits these in his memory in an unconnected way, they immediately flee the soul. Nor will such things reside in the memory until they are bound in place by a precise disposition of a proposition. This can happen as follows:

> *God, into man created from the dust of the ground, breathed a rational soul, so that in him His greatest glory might shine.*[7]

The use of the proposition appears most often to be especially marked in the writings of the ancients. For if a somewhat longer speech needed to be gotten by memory, it would be compressed into a brief and clear proposition (if that could be done manageably). Provided this is done properly and carefully, however, the whole speech will remain impressed and emblazoned on the mind. And so that I not seem perhaps to be arguing these points rather dispiritedly, I thought that I should offer some examples.

---

6. Perkins uses here a form of the term *dispositio*, which has a long history in the study and practice of rhetoric.

7. The word order as translated makes for quite awkward English. This is necessary, however, to demonstrate the disposition of the five terms individually as represented in the proposition.

Example 1:
Cicero, *De Republica* 6: *You see that the same earth is as it were wreathed and surrounded by certain bands, two of which are by far the most different from each, and on both sides rest upon the highest points of the sky. Moreover, there is one placed between that is also very large, scorched by the heat of the sun. Two can suffer human habitation, one of which is the southern part. Here dwell those who place their footsteps opposite of ours,*[8] *a race not at all similar to ours. But the other one is positioned to the north, which you all inhabit. Note how slender a part of it lies adjacent to us.*[9]

A recapitulation of this example in the form of a proposition:
Of the different regions, two are intemperate, one is scorched, two are temperate.

Example 2:
Ovid (*Metamorphoses*, II.1–6):
On pillars high the palace lofty sat,
the sun's, in shining gold and purple bright,
like flame; its utmost peaks the ivory
sleek covered round while glistened silver doors:
This costly stuff the craftsmanship excelled,
Since Vulcan there the lands had etched in place
Midst all-encircling seas.

A recapitulation of this example in the form of a proposition:[10]
The sun's palace was made from gold, purple, ivory, silver,[11] and was engraved by Vulcan.

Chapter 3: The Syllogism
There are two kinds of dianoetic arrangement, namely the syllogism and its method. That the syllogism has some value in strengthening the memory can be proved to us by the following, namely that its elements are joined together one after another in an orderly arrangement, and all of them are fitted and bound together mutually. The syllogisms in the notable works of the ancients are either compact and unadorned, or sometimes more extensive and extended.

---

8. A reference to the famous "antipodes," dwellers on the other side of the spherical earth who "walk" in our footsteps.

9. Cf. Cicero, *De Republica*, VI.21.

10. Although Perkins seems to have put this proposition in the form of an elegiac couplet (i.e. one line of hexameter followed by a pentameter or double hemi-epes), it does not scan well.

11. It would be better English to include a conjunction here, but this translation is an attempt to reflect the compression of Perkins's example.

If they are unadorned, it is not at all difficult to commit them to memory. Thus, in some way or another the natural consequence is that these syllogisms glide into the mind with a certain kind of pleasantness, as is evident from the examples included below.

Example 1:
Cicero, *Tusculan Disputations* 3: *The mind's task is to use reason, and the mind of the wise man is always so disposed that it makes use of reason in the best way. Therefore, his mind is never troubled.*[12]

Example 2:
Cicero, *De Officiis* II: *For they hold that whatever is just, that is also personally advantageous. And likewise, that which is morally upright, the same is also just. From this it follows that whatever is morally upright, that same things is personally advantageous.*[13]

Example 3:
When Paris shall endure to breathe
while Oenone has been let go,
The Xanthus then back to its source
shall with its waters run astray.
Now back you go, O Xanthus, and
your waters hurry, backward flow:
Paris manages to live e'en
though he jettisoned Oenone.[14]

The sorites here has some use, for the very reason that it is composed of several syllogisms.

Example[15]
Cicero, *De Officiis* 3: *And so, even if nature dictates this—that one person should desire to look after the interests of any other person whatsoever just for this reason, because he is a person—it is necessary that, in accordance with nature, the benefit of all things be held in common. Now if this is the case, then we are all held*

---

12. Cicero, Tusculan Disputations, III.15.

13. This syllogism runs as follows: All A's are B's; all C's are A's; ergo all C's are B's.

14. Ovid's *Heroides* V.32–35, in which the nymph Oenone asks the river Xanthus to flow backward, as her husband Paris has broken his oath in order to marry stolen Helen. The meter is elegiac couplet, which I have rendered in lines of 8 feet each, rhyming the second and fourth lines of the first quatrain to those in the second.

15. Perkins does not number this *exemplum*, though the reason why is not clear.

together by the same law of nature. And if that is so, obviously we are forbidden by the law of nature from despoiling another person. But the first point is true, therefore the last one is as well.[16]

Because if by chance in the course of a quite long oration a syllogism contains elements both more dispersed and extended, they ought to be compressed into a small space, and all their pre-syllogisms should be described rather precisely. For otherwise one's memory, weighed down by the diversity and excessive abundance of subjects, must be enfeebled.

Example[17]

Cicero, *De Legibus. Atticus: Indeed that is the grove of trees, and that is the memorable oak of the people of Arpinum, as I have often read in* Marius.[18] *If that oak still stands, this is no doubt it. For it was quite old. Quintus: Indeed, my Atticus, it is standing, and it always will. For it was planted under a good star. No stock could be sown by the effort of a farmer as long-lasting as by the poet's verse. Atticus: So how does that happen, Quintus? Or how do the poets produce that effect? For you seem to me by praising your brother to cast a vote for yourself. Quintus: That doesn't bother me. But still, so long as Latin literature has a voice, the oak which is called "Marius"' will not leave this spot. And as Scaevola said about my brother's* Marius: *"White with age it grows in endless years." Unless perhaps your Athens was able to retain its everlasting olive on the citadel. Or maybe what Homeric Ulysses said he had seen at Delos, that tall and slender palm. Today they parade out the same one. And there are many other such things in many other places more lasting in memory, than could still stand by nature. Therefore, this oak bearing acorns, from which once fell:* "The golden messenger of Jupiter, marvelous in its shapely appearance." *Let's say this is the one. But when a storm or long age shall chew it up, then still will stand in these places*[19] *the oak which they call "Marius."*

A Syllogistic Analysis of the Example

If that oak remains, this indeed is the one. *This proposition is illustrated by joining to it the following:*

---

16. Cicero, *De Officiis* III.27.

17. Perkins does not number this *exemplum*, though the reason why is not clear.

18. *Arpinum*: a small town southeast of Rome in the province Latium, was the birthplace of Cicero and his famous countryman Marius. About the latter, Cicero wrote a poem of the same name, celebrating Marius's many accomplishments, including be elected to the consulate seven times. A mere thirteen lines of this poem survive, quoted in one of Cicero's other works, namely *On Divination*.

19. I.e. in memory.

I. Its age

But that oak remains. *This assumption is proved. 1. from its efficient cause, the reputation of the oak remains, not its nature. 2. the assumption is illustrated by things that are equal to it. So long as Latin literature will remain, the oak will not be missing from this place. When Scaevola's testimony is added, 3. how the olive tree at Athens and the palm at Delphi survive in memory not in nature, so also the oak.*

Therefore, we have the following: this combination contains a description of the oak from things associated with one another, that it bears acorns, that an eagle flies down from it.

Chapter 4: The Method

Although these arrangements of proposition and syllogism provide the memory with a particular illumination, nevertheless if we ask what one element strengthens the memory most of all, then clearly the winner is method. For this is the golden one, and by grasping it an infinite series of items can be so bound together that one item easily follows upon another. Let us imagine that a rustic and simple man is gripped by a zeal for acquiring a discipline. It would be difficult, I believe, for his mind to become softened up so as to receive useful sowings of learning.[20] But if there is any hope introduced that he could become someone equipped with learning, it is method that will, by itself, produce almost that entire result. And lest anyone suppose that perhaps I am bestowing on method mere hollow praises, let him test my entire claim by the following example.

The Type of Ethics[21]

Ethics is the instruction of how to live well: living well means living according to virtue. In virtue we find:

I. The species: Virtues are either
    A. Of the will, such as either
        i. those virtues that relate to the one who possesses them
           1. gentleness in controlling anger
           2. moderation in restraining pleasures
               a. chastity
               b. sobriety in food and drink

---

20. Perkins is developing a metaphor of the countryman, *agrestem*, who wants to plant knowledge in his own mind.

21. Perkins and his publisher employ here an elaborate tree diagram in which the text partly reads horizontally, partly on the vertical. The editors have opted for a much simpler, and easier to format, outline, while carefully preserving each of the hierarchical relationships. The editors have used the same method for subsequent diagrams.

        ii.   those virtues that are directed toward other persons
           1. the disposition of money, as generosity; if this generosity becomes too extensive, it is deemed ostentation
           2. as regards the law, such as
               a. that which justice determines
               b. that which courage defends and guards
    B. Of the mind, like foresight

II. Virtue as an affection, as when the following are joined with it:
    A. Modesty[22]
    B. Friendship

Chapter 5: The Memory

There are many people who, although this logical arrangement pleases them a good deal, nevertheless they have found other means of aiding the memory. For if some item should present itself, and they want to remember several things about it, they immediately take it through all the memory places of arguments. Thus, for example, if they must say something about "a human being," argue a case, or give a speech, they would handle this topic as follows:

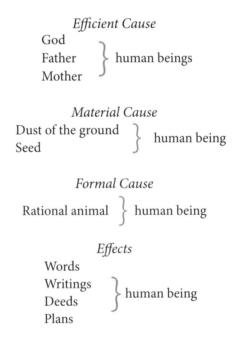

Efficient Cause

God
Father   } human beings
Mother

Material Cause

Dust of the ground }
Seed   human being

Formal Cause

Rational animal } human being

Effects

Words
Writings }
Deeds   human being
Plans

---

22. Perkins uses *pudor*, the breadth of whose meaning, from "shame" and "embarrassment" to "chastity" and "decency," seems a cause for ambiguity in this context.

Final Cause

The glory of God } human being

Subjects

The place
The proposed matters } human being
   which he treats

Adjuncts

Possessions
Virtues
Skills } human being
Clothing

Things that Differ

The learned man } { But not rich
The brave man } { But very small

Disparate matters

Sky   earth
Tree   stone } human being

Things that are Mutually Referent

Human being   master } { human being   servant
Human being   father } { human being   son

Contrariety

Beast } human being

Contradiction

Human being } non-human being

Privatives

Intoxication } { Sobriety } human being
Poverty } { Riches }

Things that are Equal

The human being has as much free will as the Angels.
The brave human being is } as he is just.
   as successful

Arguments from Greaters

The excellence of the human being } the excellence of a beast

Arguments from Lessers

Things of this earth are inferior to } the human being

Things that are Similar

The human being } { a trifle
The human being is to God } { as clay is to potter

Things that are Dissimilar

Breath
Air } the human being

Things that are Conjoined

Human
Humanly } the human being

Notation

The earth[23] } the human being

Distribution

the human being { Socrates
Plato
Aristides

Definition

the human being } rational animal

Now indeed as I acknowledge that this is a useful approach to the memorization of these items, I likewise deny that it contains any skill of the memory. For such a separation of a topic into different places is foreign to the natural practice of those who must remember it. Nothing, moreover, should be prescribed in any art which is contrary to habit and practice. Nor, in fact, does this method of memorizing help all people, but only those who are both expert in dialectics, and very comfortable in the works of many authors.[24]

---

23. The comparison here is *humus > homo*. Perkins suggests an etymological connection which is lost in English translation.

24. Perkins's phrase, *in plurimorum libris studiose volutati*, is reminiscent of Cicero, *De Oratore* 3.10.39.

Chapter 6: Practicing

There is general agreement throughout the whole record of antiquity that more distinguished men have arisen in pursuits other than the practice of memorizing. Of course the reason is not that the knowledge of memorizing is drawn from hidden sources (for what could be considered easier?), but because training is very definitely needed for strengthening that memory. For sure the chief point (which nobody, to speak plainly, does because of its particular difficulty) is to concentrate very carefully. The method of concentration, moreover, was laid out wisely by Quintilian. For he wrote, "The strategy is to learn it one piece at a time, and with a quiet voice and a sort of whisper, that the memory might be helped by the twofold action of reciting and hearing. It is really remarkable to note—nor is the reason evident—how much support an intervening night provides the memory, whether the work rests quietly or hastens on and is completed."[25] This strategy of Quintilian is really divine and should be inscribed in small golden letters. For it produces the effect that, not only are the objects comprehended, but we also hold them fortified and hedged about by the memory as by a kind of entrenchment, so to speak.

It will not seem strange to those who are devoted to literature to follow Pythagoras's practice. It was his fixed habit to review quite carefully at night before going to sleep—by repeating them—those things which he had meditated upon the whole day. He realized, I suppose, being a wise man, that whatever had been lightly impressed upon his mind by daytime ruminations, that same thing was emblazoned more deeply on his permanent memory by nighttime reflection. In the end, we take it to be a sufficient argument that the memory must be perfected especially by practice, that all its strength and abilities atrophy through interruption of effort.

Chapter 7

The surviving advice of medical doctors on the topic of preserving memory should not be neglected, especially since the tremendous benefits derived from their suggestions contribute to the pursuit of literature. The story goes that a man of Eleus named Hippias restored a memory that had been completely ruined by the help of certain medicines. And Carneades made the focus of his mind keen and sharp by using Hellebore,[26] as the most ancient histories state.

---

25. Perkins here combines and excerpts two different portions of *De Institutione Oratoria* from the Roman orator Quintilian (35–100 A.D.) The first is from Book XI.2.33, and the second from XI.2.43.

26. *Hellebore*: This ancient medicine, derived from the flower of the same name, came in two varieties, black and white. Hippocrates administered it as a purgative though its effects were unpredictable and sometimes lethal.

So while doctors have argued about these remedies in virtually all their works, I will compress these cures into one space, as though into a tight circle.

I. The Following Destroy the Memory:
    A. Diverse anxieties
    B. The indiscriminate reading of books
    C. Excessive modesty
    D. Sluggishness
    E. Excessive sleep
    F. Sleeping while lying down
    G. Inebriation
    H. Excessive sex[27]
    I. Studying too late into the night
    J. Onions
    K. Walnuts
    L. Large meals
    M. Washing of the head
    N. Putting the head underwater
    O. Hair that is too long

II. The Following Preserve the Memory:
    A. Eating the brain of rooster, sparrow, and partridge
    B. Coriander seed boiled in vinegar and coated in sugar
    C. Quince apple preserves taken at supper or lunch
    D. Aromas of
        i.   Aloe wood
        ii.   crowned Betony
        iii. Rosemary flowers
        iv.   Nigella[28]
        v.   thorny rose
        vi.   Basil
        vii. Spikenard
        viii. Honeysuckle flowers
        ix.   Lavender
        x.   Secera
    E. Benedict's Thistle taken with food
    F. Oil of
        i. Castor
        ii. Nigella

---

27. Venus.
28. *Nigella*: during Perkins's lifetime Englishmen called this Love-in-a-Mist.

iii. Euphorbia

iv. Costus

G. Lily of the Valley distilled with strong wine, and sipped in very small quantities.

H. The dust of Euphorbia

I. Rubbing

III. The Following Preserve the Memory if the Brain is moist and cold:

A. Marjoram

B. Peony

C. Mistletoe

D. Hyssop

E. Betony

F. Iris roots

G. Elecampane[29]

H. Radish

I. Turmeric

J. Cassia

K. Cinnamon

L. Nutmeg

M. Mace

N. Ginger

O. Bastard Balm

P. Primrose

IV. The Following Preserve the Memory if the Brain is cold and dry:

A. Borage[30]

B. Sweet almonds

C. Pistachio

D. Hazelnut

E. Sugar

F. Honey

G. Pine nuts

H. Waterlily

I. Licorice

J. Sweet wine

K. Chestnut

---

29. *Elecampan*: This is also called helenium and elfwort.

30. *Borage*: This is also called starflower.

L. Pomegranate[31]
M. Newly-laid eggs
N. Fresh butter
O. Raisins

The End

---

31. *Pomegranate*: Punic apple.

A Friendly Admonition to Alexander Dickson
on the worthlessness of that *Art of Memory*
which he publicly proclaims.

They say, Dickson, that long ago the image of Minerva was both seen and approved at the same time. In the case of your little book, things turned out so very poorly that I hear many saw the book, hardly anyone approved of it. If you want to know why, there are two obvious reasons, and these are readily apparent to everyone: first, its words, and second, its content. Let me summarize what many thought about the language. What generally happens when one sits down to a meal, the same typically occurs in men's writings. We do not want just the food; no, we also desire things palatable and juicy, foods that have not been seasoned too coyly. And the writings of a learned man are scarcely pleasing if they do not strike an illuminated and magnificent tone.

But your little book, did it have any blossom of pure style, any gleam of clear and luminous speech? It surely did not, by Hercules, give off any aroma of Roman purity. No, it stank of something I couldn't identify and also of barbarism. You would say that eloquence in philosophical topics is not appropriate, and that it should be clothed in a mild style and one marvelously intelligible. There is no reason, Dickson, as you say, why you should want to pour forth a kind of darkness and, as it were, night in your writings other than this: that you were building for yourself a path for earning money. For as a wise man you have foreseen the future, namely that many men who are burning with a desire to perfect their memory will fly to you very quickly, so that the ideas of your pamphlet could fish for them with gold or at least silver hooks.

Your slogan has been for a long time now that you accept no one into your program before he has showered you with twenty coins. Good Lord![1] Exactly how large a ravenous abyss are you? How large a cash-chasm? It is not proper for you to invite carefully chosen young men into your school by promising them the very heights, and by explaining your childish trifles, only to take from them as much money as you can. If you had done such a thing in those parts of the world where people were not already well disposed toward learning, nor distinguished for literature, it would perhaps have been more acceptable. But to stain with your utterly absurd opinions those upright youth[2] who were raised

---

1. *Deus bone.*
2. The text here has the false form *inventutem* for the proper *iuventutem*.

for every distinction, in England—which has nurtured many men most refined in all knowledge, and at its head, London—this is absolutely intolerable. And so your greed and avarice should take a breather for a while. Stop, finally, making so great and rich a profit from your trifles—unless you truly wish to win for yourself the kind of ignominy that the life to come will never wash away.

You understand the reason why I do not at all approve of your style. Now, in a few words, I will try to weaken and destroy that art of memory which you vehemently recommend. You maintain that this art consists first in finding subjects and images. Then one must carefully place those same images in their locales using the power of motion and a system. But I deny this whole approach, and argue against you that this whole art was imagined and dreamed up by the ancients.

1. A true account of the art should derive from practice and experience.
2. The account of artificial memory given in locales, images, motion, and a method is not derived from practice and experience.
3. Therefore, the account of the true art of memory does not reside in these elements.

I am not using here a twisted and thorny false syllogism, but one that is sound, robust, and based on sure judgment. So now what is there, Dickson, which you suppose must be disproven? What hiding place will you employ to conceal your mistake? Or will you first deny that every skill flows forth from practice as though from its own fountain? But be careful that I do not show[3] that you are a stranger and foreigner to the principles of memory strengthening! For from all such studies nothing is found that can depict and illustrate these arts with its own precepts except that which falls under the rubric of human usage and custom. Thus, rhetoric describes only that eloquence which once flowed from the tongues of Romans more sweetly and fluidly than honey; while dialectic does not reveal the discolored subtleties of dispute, but rather teases out the explicit and prominent image of natural human reason.

But since those topics which apply to common experience are unique, they certainly will never be able to be reduced to the narrow compass of any skill unless, by some rationale, they become universal. And so certain principles that bring together diverse concepts and connect them by a shared aspect of their nature ought to be employed. There are, in fact, four of these especially: perception, observation, induction, and practice. First, perception recognizes individual instances. Then observation repeatedly marks off those things that

---

3. Perkins uses here the future indicative *demonstrabo*, which seems to be unprecedented and solecistic with the negative conjunction *ne* that introduces a prohibitive.

have been perceived, after induction gathers together the marked off instances. Finally, practice strengthens those individual instances that were established by induction and mutually gathered together. Thus a logical arrangement assembles from these same deliverances a correct and generic theorem of the art.

What I have described is the means, the sole methodology by which wise men have desired to discover the practical principles of various arts. For if, by chance, something arises that was not born from experience, this in no way should be considered the determination of a sober and reasonable man, but rather the absurd fancy of a disordered mind. At one time in the schools of the philosophers the notion was entertained that there was a scorched region, yet everyday experience taught that this was just a made-up old wives' tale. For when the Portuguese had set forth from Spain to survey all the coasts of the New World, they learned that a region free from all the harmful effects of heat was missing. No, instead (and this is quite surprising), the temperature in America is just as tolerable and mild when the sun stands at the peak of its position in the sky.[4] Legend has it that Scythia[5] gave rise to the Pygmies, and that Africa produced people famous for every sort of deformity. These are mere tales, since we have experience to refute them.

Now let us grant that all such examples are far removed from the notion of art, and let us discuss the principles of the arts themselves. Teachers of grammar have divided the verb into six moods: indicative, imperative, optative, potential, subjunctive, and infinitive. Yet usage has now shown that this was poorly conceived, since any writers who spoke with polish and precision routinely combine these moods. In the discipline of logic, the demonstrative syllogism is thought to be the discovery of no man in particular, but rather a divine oracle, instilled in us from heaven. But really this is a total sophism: devoid of truth, and completely filled with stupidity. For the demonstrative syllogism never just arises in the common usage of reasoning. Thus, absolutely every precept that was not derived from usage was either stumbled upon accidentally in the liberal arts, or was painstakingly wrought by logicians.[6] Therefore the conclusion stands, Dickson, that the discoverer and corrector of the arts is experience.[7]

Now let us proceed next to the minor premise, and let us fortify it with all its supports. I posit that the art of memory as I have described it did not arise

4. This whole discussion may be taken from Cicero's *De Republica* VI and its account of the habitable regions, as Perkins discusses that passage previously in his *Libellus de Memoria*.

5. *Scythia*: Roughly the area of present-day Ukraine, famous in antiquity for its "noble savages." Cf. Herodotus's *Histories* IV.

6. It is unclear whether Perkins is using the term *sophistis* here derogatorily. It is probable that he is not, though he does so later.

7. Perkins uses the terms *usus* and *experientia* sometimes as synonyms, sometimes distinctly.

from the experience of people who were by nature successfully recalling things they had learned. No, it was devised in the schools of the Greeks by Sophists who had too much time on their hands and overly fertile intelligences. That this is the case you can easily recognize from what follows.

First, consider if you will those who have spent time at the lectures of theologians, as to what means they use to recall what they have heard. As I well know, they will answer that first they note the actual thesis. Then they apply their mind to its individual aspects, and finally to assembling the most discrete explanations of those aspects. They will maintain this order of memorization with the most wondrous accolades, and will say that it is the one which has brought to men's memories so many helps. So look closely at these men, as to whether they ever adopt memory places or fashion images in their minds in order to hold very firmly in their grasp those things they have heard. For sure they are willing to admit that they have never known your memory art, and that it is entirely foreign to the common understanding of men.

Now perhaps you will say that I am talking nonsense like a Sophist.[8] What? Am I a trifler? Is it not the case that your mind is so densely packed with errors that it does not realize how I am refuting you as you dream up these senile, old-womanish[9] theatrics? It is my contention that the artificial memory system should be derived not from the clever design and conjecture of any philosopher, nor from any school in particular, but from the natural practice of memory that shines forth in everyone.

Why is it then, Dickson, that these trivial and ephemeral inanities please you so much? What benefit does your memory system possess? What do those made up memory locales have? What about those pointless images? That leaden methodology? What about your bizarre system of movement? What does this entire show, like some empty parade, accomplish? Trust me, these are pointless exercises, i.e. discovering the dreams and images of wine-bibbers, then setting in order and animating the images once discovered.

I now see why your analogies were enshrouded in so many wordy coverings. You were afraid, I believe, that if the mysteries of your art flowed down onto the mob, then by necessity, when these mysteries were published, all your hope of earning money would vanish. Although, Dickson, you are by nature a mild man, nor overly prone to burn with rage, still I am quite afraid that even you will begin to get ornery. You can hardly bear with a calm and peaceful mind the fact that we have so utterly weakened the very system by which your name has come to be wonderfully famous and celebrated among Englishmen.

---

8. *Sophistice.*
9. *aniles.*

For you will say that I have never once hit upon the truth, that the system of artificial memory you have described is difficult and sophisticated, that those who have been trained to understand it even a little bit can hope for great distinction by the excellence of their memory. I think that is what you will say.

But it is not necessary that we immediately test and retain every instance of instruction that offers us any help in human life. Astronomy, for example, is indeed useful for explaining the movements of all the stars. Yet nothing is more inane, nothing more worthy of disregarding. For almost the whole of it is assembled, not from true precepts, but from the emptiest hypotheses. Certainly there is nowhere an old woman so ignorant that she thinks there are epicycles, eccentrics, or equal circles in the heavens. In arithmetic, what is more profound, if we should consider practical use, than the rule of falsification? But if we have regard for the rule itself, is there anything more insignificant? Has a philosopher ever discovered something duller? For all disciplines, although they are very useful, nevertheless forfeit their own luster, and immediately lose their value unless they have been discovered and regularized by the method I previously discussed.

To this point I have sought to invalidate Dickson's false memory art. Now I will try, if it is indeed possible, to present something known to be more precise and accurate. Therefore, I think that a logical disposition is the best discipline for strengthening and refining the memory. Yet someone will object that we can in no way remember simple notions by a logical disposition, but only those that have been logically distributed. Thus, they would say, we should not at all search for the art of memory in logical disposition. For just as the abilities of the memory—or rather, its uses—correspond completely to the whole sum of items to be remembered, so the use of that art which describes those items ought to extend and apply itself to all of them.

Indeed, along with Peter Ramus I maintain that the perfect art of memory either has not yet been discovered, or if any such thing can exist by nature, logical disposition itself is it. And lest perhaps you think that my opinion on this subject is vacillating and fickle, it is worth the effort for me to add here one or two supporting arguments.

Major premise: *There are as many things in need of description in any particular area of skill as there are items in their proper and natural content. For if you should withdraw anything from that skill, it will become mutilated. If, on the other hand, you add anything, it will seem quite unnatural.*

Minor premise: *The major premise holds when it comes to the content of the dialectical art. The natural use of reason comprises not only the ability of discovering and analyzing things, but also that of remembering them.*

Conclusion: *Therefore, these three faculties must be described in logic. Invention, moreover, is wholly removed from the process of shaping the memory. Therefore, as logical disposition is the knowledge of proper analysis, so it is also that of proper recall. For just as by the power of that natural logical disposition we come to remember those things that have escaped us, so the artificial disposition causes us to remember well those same items.*

Do you notice, Discon, how I have found the true art of aiding the memory? And how I have shattered the entire basis of your method of instruction? For if logical disposition is the inborn and genuine system of good memory, how foolishly you behave in wanting young people to arrive at that same distinction by some other, so to speak, unblazed and savage path? So then, if there should be any who—driven by an excessive desire for what you have contrived—are caught, they are free to learn this art from me, if only they maintain the moderation in learning and practicing it. Because my art when compared to yours is like when one merely sips a delicate and finds it more pleasing than to drink the whole thing. But if the choice were actually up to me, I would want those who are intent on literature to have been very carefully trained in the use of logical disposition. That is how much weight I put on it for the proper adornment of the literary man.

These are our comments concerning the art of memory as a whole. Now let us proceed to explaining the individual elements in closer detail. In order, moreover, to demonstrate the topic more suitably, let us apply to it Aristotle's laws on matter and form. These can be used to discover truth and error, to cut off and pull out every last straw of information. The laws of matter are 1.) with respect to the whole, 2.) with respect to the subject itself, and of the universal.[10] The law of truth with respect to the whole requires that no principle of art be false, but that all of them be completely and necessarily true. The law of justice with respect to the subject itself will compel all the topics—which flow forth and indeed overflow toward other arts—to run in its own particular banks and channels. That of the universal requires that every precept whatsoever be reciprocal, i.e., that items of a genus be grouped with those of its genus, and of a species with those of its species. Because if we should by chance assign something that belongs to a genus to its species, then we will be acting like those

---

10. Perkins uses the Greek phrases κατὰ παντός, καθ' αὐτό, and καθόλου πρώτου respectively. Cf. Aristotle's *Prior Analytics* I.xxxi.

who tried to fit a boot on Hercules's infant foot.[11] And, on the other hand, to attribute something which belongs to the species to its genus is like one who, though in the dress of a dwarf, desires to clothe himself like a giant. The law which governs the form of some skill dictates that everything be arranged with a view to the perspicuity of the subject's own nature: that which by nature is more important is placed first, and that which is secondary is placed second. So then, let us weigh the precepts of your art by these laws as though upon the exact scale of a goldsmith.

Now, setting aside the definition, how do you organize your artificial memory? You say that the two parts of your art are: foresight and careful judgment.[12] Yet foresight is not a natural and genuine element of memory but was derived and acquired from another source. For it clearly does not come from that logical discovery[13] by the principles of which all subjects of study and their contours are found out. So I congratulate, Dickson, the supreme good fortune of your genius: you have on your own surpassed all philosophers by the abundance and precision of your arguing! You deserve to be the first to gain the crown from the Olympians. Among the wisest of mere mortals, I think it is agreed that Aristotle is so remarkably subtle a writer that nothing more divine than he can be imagined. Still, when the same critics read your *Prosopopoeia*[14] they will easily conclude that though Aristotle has always surpassed all other philosophers, Alexander Dickson has beaten Aristotle himself! Aristotle in his *Organum* described only sixteen types of discovery: the first, the *categoremata*; the second, the *categories*; the third, the middle argument; the fourth, the apodictic middle. In the *Topics* he speaks of four instruments: the fifth, propositions; the sixth, distinguishing between equivocals; the seventh, *differentiae*; the eighth, similitudes; the ninth, *accidens simplex*; the tenth, *accidens comparatum*; the eleventh, *genus*; the twelfth, the *proprium*; the thirteenth, definitions; the fourteenth, identity and diversity; the fifteenth, stating of a question; and the sixteenth, the answering of a question. To all of these, then, you alone have added another invention—discovered all by yourself!—indeed, the useful discovery of subjects and copies for remembering. May the Lord

---

11. *Tried to fit a boot on Hercules's infant foot*: attempting to put together things that are unsuitable one to another. The anecdote is mentioned in Quintilian, *Institutiones Rhetoricae* VI.36, and repeated by Erasmus, *Adages* III.vi.67.

12. These are *providentia* and *criterium* (the Latinized κριτήριον) respectively.

13. *Inventio*, a term prominently used in the study and practice of classical rhetoric, is the skill of deriving topics for discussion and debate from any given material. Cicero devoted an entire essay to the topic in two books, entitled *De Inventione*.

14. Perkins's point in using this Greek rhetorical term seems to be that Dickson's *Art of Memory* is a kind of obvious mockery, as *prosopopoeia* requires suspension of belief on the part of the audience or reader.

help us, you would be a man with a very stingy and miserly soul if you were unwilling to boast with complete abandon over such an astounding discovery. No, you should like this go on to shout with Archimedes, "I've found it! I've found it!" For his discovery concerned the counterfeiting of a crown, while your lovely trick exposed a method of discovery.

Nevertheless, let us look at your discovery more closely, so that everyone may understand how cleverly it was contrived. You want, I think, for your discovery to deal with acquiring memory places, and the searching for copies (i.e. arguments that have been provided for indicating a different topic). Very well. But what is the purpose of such things, and what is their value? Obviously so that these copies might be stored in their memory places for strengthening the memory. What nonsense! What lies! What Dicksonian shadows,[15] more insubstantial than the shade[16] of any tree trunk and stalk! Indeed, your discovery puts forth and suggests these arguments in a bare sense. But they are employed only *as an axiom* for teaching, proclaiming, providing examples, explaining, etc. They are used *in syllogism* for proving a thesis, strenghtening it, refuting another one, etc. Such are the standard and proper uses of arguments, nor by common consent do any other uses, in human experience, exist. Consequently, you seem to misuse arguments horribly, in my estimation, when you want them to be stored in these memory places just to remember something else.

Because my treatise has now veered off course due to these rocky shoals, let us hurry back to the remaining elements of our personification. You define "subjects" as the holding places for the copies. Then you divide these subjects into two classes: absolute and auxiliary, and last, you pile up a large number of guidelines for these subjects. You seem to me, by Hercules, to have only a strong memory—you are quite weak in judgment. Who ever built and joined together the precepts of their art so inexpertly? You are certainly quite unusual, since you are both artless in discovering topics and completely inept at constructing these same topics into a proper system. For it is well established that the rules governing subjects, because they are more famous than nature's innate worth,[17] must come before the partitioning of those same subjects. But because you seem to me only slightly experienced in the proper way to lay out the form of any skill, I will give you some few words of advice. Using my comments, you can very easily finish off your art with the right kind of system. Therefore, in the correct establishment of any kind of knowledge, its precepts follow mutually upon one another like this:

---

15. Perkins here equivocates on the meanings of *umbra* as "outline" or sketch, an extended or metaphorical meaning, and that of a shadow cast by an object.

16. Cf. the previous note.

17. *naturae dignitate.*

1. Definitions, because these contain the whole nature of the topic

2. Divisions into primary categories.

3. Explanations of their innate properties, e.g. causes, effects, and adjuncts. These are called commonplaces, axioms, and the most important rules.

4. Divisions into species.

5. Illustrations by examples, because these both illustrate the truth of all the precepts and explain their usefulness.

This is the path, and this the approach of those who have ever applied to the fashioning of their systems any kind of more precise and more focused type of arrangement. So then, what consideration provoked you to depart from this set course that the most learned men have left behind, trod and marked by their own footsteps?

Still, let us forget that and listen in for a little bit while you expound on your most sophisticated rules. From all your rules, let us focus on this one: that objects ought not to be excessively unusual. Why is this, you very fine constructor of laws? Because, you say, they are offensive in their radiant brightness. Offensive? How? Do you mean they offend the eye or the mind? If they offend the eye, how in fact will that happen when vision seldom perceives the memory passages and objects? If you mean the soul, just look at how many traps into which you have led yourself. For why shall we say that the mind's understanding is darkened by the brightness of light? Which of the old writers ever published or passed such a law? Plato said many things about light, Aristotle made certain comments as well. Vitellius made even more, and Alazen[18] by no means much less than he. But good Lord,[19] did none of them see what that master craftsman of the memory, I mean Dickson, saw here? By Hercules, that is really amazing! They were, I guess, quite inexperienced in such matters, nor did they try to attain such a refined knowledge of literature. But come now, shake the slumber off your mind for a moment, and that excessive somnolence. Turn all the strength of your genius to the topic before us in order that you might notice your slip and mistake. So then, mark this: even if the eyes should be affected by a very bright light and become sluggish, nevertheless one can manage pretty well with the understanding which neither any brilliance nor the very radiance of the sun can blot out. As for the fact that later on you demand that parallel intervals of passages and the intervening portions of the

---

18. *Alazen* (date unknown): A medical authority on the eye and vision, he is mentioned by a number of seventeenth and eighteenth century authors. Specifically, Scipio Claramontius Caesans references Alazenus in his 1654 work *On the Iris against Aristotle*, 50 (Cesena).

19. *At deus bone.*

area be removed,[20] these points are more trivial than to bear refutation. And in such matters that man Rosselius[21] has refuted your garbage.[22]

We have sufficiently demolished your teaching on the topic of objects. Now I will cause all your shadowy copies[23] to scatter and vanish by the brilliance of my arguments. Therefore, how do you in your definition unroll the highly involved nature of this copy?[24] The copy, you say, is also the rendered, trustworthy representation of the object that has been adopted indeed according to the sure perception. But it is not acceptable that the whole outline be entrusted to any object. For just as there can be soldiers even though they have not yet been formed up into a line, and as there are pictures of objects, although they are not tied to canvases, so there is nothing to prevent copies from existing even though they are not situated in their backgrounds and condensed when fashioned. For first they must be discovered unadorned, next they must be arranged in their subjects. At this point I could poke you with your own needles, since you have wonderfully larded your entire little treatise with unadorned examples of copies.

You divide your copies into two types, simple and modified. The one who possesses Dickson's volume, possesses the practical knowledge that is in you, so that he is not really all that far from being actually wise. What a marvelous distinction you have proposed. No, in fact it is one that has been steeped in all kinds of foolishness. Obviously perceptual objects possess not only simple copies but also modified ones. Just as also do those objects which are called universal. Add to this that your simple copies yield no appearance of an outline. The actual object is one thing, the imprinting and sealing of the appearance of that object in the mind is another. It is not the case, as you yourself suppose, that man exists as the outline of a man, that Alladius has the outline of Alladius, or a brute has that of a brute.

Nor, to be sure, should we work to make perceptual objects themselves possess their own copies, especially since these are stored spontaneously in their memory places and they're always so present and as it were at our beck and call that they come into our minds even when not summoned. Go ahead then, my

---

20. These expressions have reference to those portions of Dickson's memory construction that gave strict instructions for the proper placement of images and their relation to one another within a measured system. The exact references are obscure without direct access to Dickson's works.

21. The text here has *Rosseluis*, since the letters "u" and "i" have been transposed. It is being taken as nominative, i.e. *Rosselius*, as this is not the standard way that an adjective is formed on a proper name. It is taken to be the subject of the deponent verb *refragatur*.

22. *tuae fecis.*

23. There is again a play on words here: *umbrae* means both the shadows cast by a light, and the copies or memory sketches advocated by Dickson among others.

24. I.e., *umbra.*

good Alexander, and babble like Sophists do about your modified copies. You claim the copies both of the objects and also of the words have been modified. You should prove to me that this division is proper, and then the victory palm festooned with ribbons shall be yours. This division seems to me really quite fallacious and embroiled in sophistry. For in fact every kind of outline whatsoever is either of the objects or even of words, and not only those ones which are called modified. If you had listened to Marcus Cicero, you never would have fallen so foolishly into this art which you profess. This is what that renowned man says: "Because images ought to be like their objects, we ought to choose from all available words[25] likenesses that are familiar to us. So likenesses ought to be of two kinds: one of objects, the other of words." Consequently, you have disregarded the first law of predication,[26] because you have ignorantly assigned to one part that which should have been ascribed more wisely to the whole. But let us grant that this division is not sophistic, let us grant also that it is proper. Nevertheless, it is wholly foreign to this art of memory, because it supplies a distinction to a material object.

This is because [of the],

Major Premise
A general and shared art does not introduce a division in the material with which it deals. In the dialectical art of discovery and in the careful presentation of sound judgment there is not one material that applies to objects, and another that applies to words. Instead the whole corresponds to all those objects that are both to be discovered and judged. In the grammatical and rhetorical arts there must not be any distinction between the objects which are expounded in them. Why not? Because there must be a complete description with respect to all the objects with which they deal, and because these arts are jointly exercised. Nor is the kind of instruction for this shared art[27] unique to it, and foreign to the other.[28] As Aristotle said, those things that belong to a genus must be explained by that genus.[29] And as there is one Thames River in London, adapted for different purposes: for drinking, washing, irrigating, cleaning, putting out fires, and transporting goods. And thus its individual currents are not dedicated to these particular uses but to all the same ones in common. Likewise, not only all general arts but even their most specific subdivisions concern all these topics.

---

25. Cicero here uses *rebus* whereas Perkins's text has *verbis*. The quotation is from *Rhetorica Ad Herennium*, 3.33.
26. *legem* καθολουπρῶτον
27. *shared art*: the rhetorical art.
28. *the other*: the grammatical art.
29. γενικὰ γενικῶς

Minor Premise
The art of memory is wholly a common art. It is not hedged off by any railings to keep it from being able to roam freely and deal with all topics. For even the natural faculty of memory must have an equally broad application, and this is one particular description of it.

Conclusion
Therefore, the art of memory must not divide up the material presented to it, but relay its one common instruction as that of recalling objects as well as words. This, Dickson, you do not at all do since you fabricate one set of copies for objects, another for words. And you teach a twofold instruction of them.

Look then, you Memory Doctor, at my weapons. Look at the wounds inflicted on your method. Now you lie there. Now you are despairing. You lower your spears, nor can you savor any hope that your method, altogether enfeebled and weakened by this fresh wound, can at some point recover. May I be favored that you are enveloped with joy and at the same time stripped of all the outer garments of your pretense. As it is, what lay hidden in obscurity can now be made clear to all: you are not instructing the youth of England in the sincere course of study of some subject. No, by your open hustling in London you are collecting very wealthy advocates for your foolishness and empty, trivial genius.

You also prepare copies for the most general topics as well as mathematical ones. You are quite off the mark, you venal doctor, and you separate those things which are mutually held together by the closest relationship.

This is because,

Major Premise
Copies—which are derived from causes—are completely distinguished from effects, subjects, adjunjcts, contraries, comparisons, terms, distribution, definition and testimony.

Minor Premise
Mathematical copies are derived from causes, effects, subjects, adjuncts, etc. The regions of the Zodiac and the ten districts when they are employed for representing numbers, we make use of them as subjects for remembering things that are conjoined to them. Thus also thirty elements together with their effects and adjuncts are the adjuncts of words.

Conclusion
Therefore, mathematical copies are completely distinct.

Come now, you Silver-grubber. Deflect this carefully aimed spear if you can. If you cannot, then you must grant that by this same spear thrust all your copies have been shattered. If I had divided up the man into soul, body, head, and stomach, you would have split your sides quite arrogantly in laughter. Why is that? Because, you will say, the stomach and the head are not separate parts of the man himself, but they are sort of like limbs which are attached to the body for completing its constitution. Clearly, in a similar way, when I weigh the categorization of the memory outline which you have provided, I could barely restrain myself even a little from laughter, even if I were asked to do so. You fashion one example of your memory outline so enormous and of such broad application that it encompasses in its circuit the rest of the mutual relationships. Such a thing as this the very poets themselves, even granting their typical freedom for fabrication, would never have dreamed up. But what is your purpose? Do you just mean to play with us, Dickson? Why? Will you bewitch our eyes with the magic potion of your really trivial handiwork? Surely you don't think Englishmen are so devoid of judgment that they do not notice the barrenness and aridity of your mind? If so, you really must disabuse yourself of that expectation. And when it comes to our countrymen, you must form a somewhat more flattering appraisal.

Now you will say that I dislike you because I am scrutinizing your system with a more excessive precision than is fair. And you will add that it is your intention to fashion and shape it according to the variable interests of different people, people to whom vices are often pleasing. For example, a wart on the knuckle of a boy, even if it is a blemish to the body still Alcaeus found it pleasing.[30] Likewise the utter foolishness and arrogance of your systems of classification may prove pleasing to your readers. But in fact the reader who is endowed with the most refined sorts of skills will never choke down these foolishnesses and follies of yours.

You define as absolute those memory copies which admit no internal distinction of number. My good Doctor, my quite distinguished Professor—actually just an ape of your teacher Aristotle. "He defined *genus* in the same way in his *Topics*: *genus* is that which is neither how it differs from something else, nor the particular quality that makes it unique, nor some accident." Both of you have given birth to a method of refutation, because the negative definition of something does not teach knowledge of a subject, but rather only disabuses someone of their ignorance.

---

30. The reference is to the archaic Greek poet from Lesbos.

Our discussion should now hasten on to your mathematical memory copies. For a great hope dawns upon me that I may be able to draw out from these
something divine and previously hidden.

Mathematical objects, you claim, *are extended neither to simple copies nor*
absolute ones, that is, to things that have been modified by logical arguments.

Numbers are mathematical objects. – (This premise is absent).

Therefore, numbers are extended neither to simple nor absolute copies.

I keenly regret, Dickson, that you are such a little child in mathematics, nor
have you even touched that learned arena. Come on now, please [pull] yourself up from this sluggishness and your ignorance, so that you might be able
to recognize along with me the actual truth. The proposition of your syllogism
has been polluted by an incredible lie. First, tell me plainly why mathematical
topics do not admit of simple memory copies? Or is it because they do not seem
to be sensible objects? But in fact, at first glance they do fall under the category
of the senses. For to the extent that each subject is one that is held in common,
to the same extent it is not only quite evident to the mind but also to the senses
of themselves. And yet even when it comes to general matters of knowledge in
the case of individual items that are to be understood, these two are especially
subject to the senses. Something that moves at a distance, first to be sure we say
that it is a body, then that it is a living creature, and then afterward that it is a
human being. For this reason, in treatises on optics, there is the theorem that
general classes of visible objects appear to the eyes before those that are specific.
Nor am I persuaded one wit just because you say that mathematical subjects are
abstract, and removed from all agglutination with matter. No doubt, although
these things are withdrawn from the mind nevertheless they are really joined
with and connected to individual objects in such a way that you can in no way
force them apart. Note the very learned opinion of Peter Ramus, so that you
can finally see how the principles of your art are unreliably lame. "Although,"
he says, "lengths, shapes, surfaces, lines, and points are abstracted by the mind
from physical qualities—as are sensible qualities like thin, thick, hot, cold, light,
heavy, moist, and dry—nevertheless these things truly exist in the actual physical
bodies, as Aristotle often and carefully establishes in his *Physics.* There he word
for word says that there are rational accounts and logical proofs for quantitative
perceptions available through our senses. These are not however insofar as they
are available through our senses, but merely as they are in and of themselves.
And Vitellius, likewise, quite essentially agrees in his comments on *Physics,*
book 3 chapter 2: 'every line by which light reaches an opposing body from a
light giving body is a natural, sensible line possessing a certain breadth. In this
breadth there ought to be accounted a mathematical line as a representation

of the imagining faculty. Finally, the comprehension of geometrical size is a quality of the mind, but size itself—like a line, a surface, a physical object, actually resides in a sensible and physical object."' This is the clear teaching of Peter Ramus, as well as of Aristotle, and of the *Optics*.[31] Since, therefore, mathematical subjects possess simple memory copies, what will prevent them from having absolute ones as well?[32] Or will you dare to deny that there are causes of these memory copies, and effects, and adjuncts, contraries, similarities, *species*, and an entire *genus* of argument? I would like you to decide in your own mind that your method of reasoning is like a river which cannot keep within any banks but bursts forth, and is spilled out far and wide over everything in its path.

But in order that I can prove to you your mistake in matters of mathematics, please show me why you are trafficking in the signs of the zodiac, and with the head and the tail of the dragon[33] of the moon? You see, I think, that your art is a mere trifle and quite childish. And in that it is like this: you are plucking and gathering little flowers from every source of opinion. You do this so that your art might be unique, and sprinkled over with these petals. But if you meant that from signs and the orbits of the zodiac we are furnished with a sort of boundless supply of memory copies, you should be suspected of error and foolishness. For:

> Arts[34] *that are consequent are not required for their antecedents, because without the consequent arts these prior ones have explanatory power, and the opposite is not true.*

> *The art of memory is antecedent, learning which concerns itself with signs and the orbits of the moon follow after. The arts of a genus are by nature prior, while those which deal with a species are naturally posterior.*

> *The art of memory belongs to that of a genus while the learning which concerns signs, I mean astronomy, belongs to the species because the former concerns every class of thing while the latter only the heavens. Therefore, neither astronomy nor any element of that discipline is required for the art of memory.*[35]

Do you see how I am arguing? Do you notice how I refute you? How I snuff out the strength of your skill? How I dash to pieces your trifles, ridiculous

---

31. *The Optics*: of Vitellius.

32. The contrast that Perkins is developing here is between *umbrae simplices* and *umbrae absolutae*.

33. The constellation Draco was the basis of Dickson's imagery system for memorization.

34. *Arts*: those belonging to that of images and the zodiac.

35. Perkins is not quoting from anyone. Rather he is seeking to present his argument in a formal syllogism.

as they are and scorned by everyone? But what would do this? Why am I so fervent to refute you? Why do I despise and forswear the use of signs? Their use can be at the same time both very famous and completely unfamiliar to me. Therefore, memory doctor, make clear to us the riches and fine adornments of your genius. Indeed, reveal that new and fine use of figures. You say:

> Now because we are dealing with the concept of number, let its first division be into segments according to the signs of the zodiac. Next let individual signs of this circle be apportioned by lot, and let them each contain ten equally proportioned sections. Then, so that the fingers might be inserted into these groups of ten, let all the signs be divided and separated into ten parts. There will therefore be 120 separate signs. If these do not seem to be enough, the same procedure must be followed also with the various movements of the Dragon and its image. Thus, there will be 200 separate signs, the use of which in reviewing the chapters of books and other similar things—as well as in the reliable comprehension of the same—seems almost unbelievable.

This is a kind of pain which tortures me somewhat—that no empty space is left in the heavens. For you are really a deserving man, you who fashion a thirteenth sign, something that you have engendered as a very useful application of the signs. But if I were able to arrange to have some god lop off the horns of Taurus, I would hope that at some time you could be exhibited in the heavens.

There is no need for me to provide a lengthier discussion concerning your method and how you mentally animate the images. For because these are very closely bound together with the copies and their objects, if these prove worthless then there can be no way that your method and system of animation will not also collapse, dragged down by the very same descent.

Now, finally, let us compare the method of the dialecticians with this art of yours, and its application with the respectability of theirs. In this way one can easily see to which of the two in the end we ought to grant priority. Their method has been derived from the sources of nature, and to that nature all persons have recourse when something has to be entrusted to memory. So what about that artificial memory system of yours, Dickson? Does it trace itself back to nature's root? Does it possess any stamp of approval from actual practice and trial? No, it first sprung from the addled brain of some little Greek or another. It is entirely opposed to the normally accepted practice of sound memorization. The method of the dialecticians contains true memory *loci*, separated from one another according to the differences in their subjects. The broadest *genera* (as they are called) are relegated to the most important position, while certain of the intermediate and intervening places are reserved for various subordinate *species*. And the subjects that are most specific in their nature are lumped together in the lowest positions.

What are the memory *loci* like in your art? Will you tell us what they truly are or just give us things that have been made up? If you tell us what they truly are, you are a liar. If you tell us things that are made up, I will not object because you are spreading reproach over your art. In the dialecticians' method, the images for objects are not opaque and dark but gleaming; well-delineated and luminous images are offered. Of course the whole method is marked out by and replete with the most notable definitions and divisions as though by stars. Your art, on the other hand, merely describes the fleeing shadows and puffs of smoke, as it were, that immediately disappear by their very insignificance. And thus your broken and disabled study of memory should yield the palm of victory to the method of the dialecticians.

The following is my brief synopsis of your art: everyone will agree that a puerile and thorny subtleness comes from it, such that it is despised by the most learned men and utterly rejected. Or first, if that art were respectable, and if it had one speck of truth to it or of correctness, would Peter Ramus have despised it? Obviously he did not understand this most lucid art, and a tide of who knows what kind of genius overwhelmed him, the sort that pulled him away from exposing the truth.

So really what you have to say? Is your diligence more profound than Peter Ramus's ever was? Or your wisdom, your judgment? Is your intellectual precision greater? Your diligence and devotion to learning? If these had existed in Ramus in even the tiniest degree, they would have been thought extremely great in comparison to your abilities. Now since he holds among cultured humanists a noble position, is it really any wonder if he has wrenched the crown from you, a man who has barely made his way from the starting blocks? But Ramus would sooner be burned a thousand times by all the remarks of those who slander him than surrender a single letter for augmenting the praise of this art of yours. Moreover, what reason is there that those philosophers—men so praiseworthy for the sharpness of their intellect as well as their skill in memory, I mean Quintilian, Talaeus, Frigius, Berhusius, Patricius, and Valerius—why, I ask, would such philosophers not have received as their rightful inheritance this art, rejected and so abandoned? Why have they not as good guardians of that inheritance, so to speak, seen to the nourishment of this orphaned and impoverished art? In no way whatsoever, by Hercules, should we accept that such philosophers could lose their footing and get lost on such an easy path, when they ride along, as it were, on four-horse chariots right through the midst of praise for their wisdom. But then who could be so blind as to think that? On the other hand, who is so sharp-sighted?[36] Who would not at some time run into it head on?

So now, what ought you to do, Dickson? You cannot without danger persist in your error unless you genuinely want the blemish of disgrace—the shame that you yourself have long since earned—to settle down forever on your name and become fixed there. And so now change your mind. Trust me. Forget your so-called art and your stated position. Hold fast no longer to that position you have adopted in the fleeting of this your judgment as though you are carried to it by a wind. Don't stick to it any longer as though to a rock.

---

36. The implication of these two questions and their unexpected juxtaposition seems to be that whether one is blind or blessed with exceptional vision they ought to be able to see clearly the truth of Perkins's position on the art of memory, as well as the gross error of Dickson's position.

Scripture Index

Subject Index